Arbitration of Labor–Management Disputes

Arbitration of Labor–Management Disputes

MAURICE S. TROTTA

amacom

A Division of American Management Associations

INTERNATIONAL STANDARD BOOK NUMBER: 0-8144-5332-5
LIBRARY OF CONGRESS CATALOG CARD NUMBER: 73-77956

SECOND PRINTING

PREFACE

Since the publication of the first edition of this book in 1961, the use of arbitration as a means of resolving disputes between management and labor has been greatly expanded. The number of cases administered by the American Arbitration Association has increased 367 percent, and the case load of the Federal Mediation and Conciliation Service has increased 283 percent. The use of arbitration to resolve grievances will increase still further with the continued growth of collective bargaining in the public sector. In addition, a growing number of disputes over contract provisions are being resolved through the arbitration process.

It is interesting to note that the fact-finding process, which is closely related to arbitration, is being used with increasing frequency, and a very high percentage of the recommendations of fact-finding panels have been accepted by the parties. This development is evidenced by the municipal ordinance signed by the Mayor of the City of New York on January 12, 1972, which is discussed in Chapter 12.

Non-unionized companies are now beginning to provide grievance procedures that terminate in arbitration. Another interesting development is the adoption by the Roman Catholic Church of arbitration procedures to resolve disputes involving bishops, priests, and lay persons. Colleges and universities are also beginning to recognize the value of the arbitral process as a means of resolving personnel problems and insuring due process to faculty and staff. It is difficult to determine the numbers of cases submitted to arbitrators each year because large numbers of cases are not processed through the appointing agencies. A rough estimate is that between 30,000 and 50,000 cases are decided each year, but only a small percentage of these cases are published. The universal acceptance and the continued growth of arbitration is a clear indication that it meets a social need.

Since arbitrators are selected by the parties involved, and most of the active arbitrators have been serving for about 25 years, it is evident that their awards are acceptable to both management and labor.

The foundation of the entire arbitral process has been built tier by tier on the opinions and awards written over the past 25 years. After reading hundreds of these published cases, one cannot but be impressed by the clarity and logic of the opinions and awards rendered. It is evident that the arbitral process rests upon a solid foundation. The fact that arbitrators give reasons for their awards is, in my opinion, one of the main reasons for the universal acceptance of the process. I am indebted to my fellow arbitrators for the insights these opinions have given me. I am also indebted to the lawyers who have attended my course in Labor Arbitration offered by the Graduate Division, New York University School of Law. Their observations and arguments helped to sharpen and refine the issues discussed.

This book is not intended to be an exhaustive treatise but rather a source of basic information for those connected with the arbitral process. It was written to serve the needs of industrial relations and personnel executives and other managerial personnel; graduate and undergraduate students studying labor law and industrial relations; and union officers and grievance committee men. This book should also be helpful to lawyers who represent either management or unions in arbitration proceedings.

It is not possible to write a book of this nature without the assistance of many persons. Those who have made significant contributions include Arvid Anderson, Director of the New York City Office of Collective Bargaining; Robert Coulson, President of the American Arbitration Association; Gerald Aksen, General Counsel for the American Arbitration Association; and Daniel Collins, Professor of Labor Law, New York University School of Law. I wish to acknowledge the diligent research work, particularly in the public sector, done by Steven Glickman during the spring of 1971 after he graduated from the School of Industrial and Labor Relations at Cornell University. Deborah A. Heskes, a graduate student at the School of Industrial and Labor Relations, was very helpful, particularly in researching new case materials. Harry A. Gudenberg, Manager of Industrial Relations at ITT, collaborated in analyzing the data regarding the use of arbitration in non-union plants. Vincent Finan, who has had many years of experience as a director of industrial relations and as a consultant, reviewed and edited the digests of the arbitration cases in Part II. Chapter 1, "Historical Development," is an abridged version of Chapter 1 of the 1961 edition, which was contributed by Professor O. William Ross.

Many of the concepts expressed in this book have been sharpened by my discussions over many years with Walter Eisenberg, Dean of Graduate Studies at Hunter College, City University of New York, and also a public member of the Office of Collective Bargaining of the City of New York; and with Matthew Kelly, Professor of Industrial Relations at the Cornell University School of Industrial and Labor Relations and also a well-known arbitrator. Finally, I am particularly indebted to Walter Bishop, a friend and a valued collaborator, who edited the manuscript.

MAURICE S. TROTTA

CONTENTS

Part III   Appendixes

PART ONE

Principles and Procedures

INTRODUCTION

A judicial system is one of the essentials of civilized society. It is needed to resolve the disputes that inevitably arise among men. The wisdom of Solomon in settling disputes among the early Israelites is proverbial. Even in primitive societies the head of the tribe usually serves as the chief judicial officer.

With the growth of industrial society and the introduction of the concept of collective bargaining, a need has arisen for a procedure to resolve labor-management disputes. This need has been met by a new type of judicial system, private in nature. It has been voluntarily established by labor and management to resolve disputes arising primarily over the interpretation of collective bargaining agreements.

In this private judicial system, the disputants select the judges and agree in advance to be bound by the award rendered. These judges are called arbitrators.

Conflict

Conflict between management and labor is inevitable. Not to recognize this fact is to ignore the history of the human race. Throughout history groups of people with different goals, drives, aspirations, and economic, social, and psychological needs have been in conflict.

Conflict can be resolved through military strength, through economic power, or through a judicial system based on law, reason, and justice. The *Pax* Romana, a period when conflict was at a low point, was a result of military domination by Rome. Economic domination can often be as effective as military domination in reducing the incidence of open conflict. But history proves that domination inevitably gives rise to opposing forces that erupt into open conflict at the first opportunity.

It is not surprising, then, that divergent interests of management and labor should cause conflict. One hundred years ago management dominated labor by virtue of its economic power. Management's decisions concerning wages, hours, and working conditions were made unilaterally on the basis of its own self-interest, with little concern for how these decisions would affect labor. Like all other forms of domination, this sowed seeds of unrest and often resulted in open conflict.

As a result of the legal recognition given to the process of collective bargaining, and the economic power gained by labor organizations, labor has acquired means for avoiding domination by management. But the legal and economic power it has acquired can at the same time be used to dominate weak management.

Just as the domination of labor by management led to legal remedies, so the domination of management by labor has resulted in corrective legislation.

Concomitant with the development of labor laws has been the growth of a judicial system to resolve disputes. Conflicts regarding the interpretation of labor laws are resolved by the courts and by administrative agencies such as the National Labor Relations Board. Conflicts regarding the meaning of the provisions of collective bargaining agreements are resolved by the arbitral process.

Conflict Analysis

The first step toward conflict resolution is to study the nature and causes of conflict. In its simplest terms, a conflict occurs when individiuals or groups of people come to different decisions. When a foreman decides that Tom Jones is to be fired, and Tom Jones comes to a decision that he should not be fired, we have a typical conflict. When a union negotiating committee decides that it will strike unless it gets two more paid holidays and 20 cents more an hour than management has offered, and management decides that it will *not* give two more paid holidays or raise its wage offer by 20 cents an hour, conflict results. The first step toward resolving these conflicts is to analyze the factors that led to the differing decisions.

The Nature of Man

The first factor to consider is the nature of man himself. Man is essentially egocentric. His assumptions, opinions, value judgments, interpretations, and decisions are molded by how the result will affect him. An owner of a business may make a decision based on protection of his management prerogatives. A union leader may make a decision based on how it will affect his own political future.

Man also finds it difficult to admit error, even when the error is obvious. Having made a decision, he will find innumerable reasons to justify that decision, even though his reasons may be illogical or unsubstantiated by fact.

Man's emotional characteristics are an important element in explaining his behavior. When his logic is in conflict with his emotions, the latter often wins. When his ego is involved, even a person who is highly educated or has considerable managerial experience will make decisions based on his emotions. For example, it is generally assumed that a person who is well trained in an academic discipline which utilizes the scientific method will make objective administrative decisions affecting other persons. That this assumption is fallacious is well known to anyone connected with educational institutions. It explains why schools, colleges, universities, and even the Roman Catholic Church are adopting grievance procedures terminating in arbitration.

Similarly, industry frequently promotes brilliant scientists into managerial positions only to find out that their scientific knowledge does not qualify them to handle personnel problems or even their purely managerial functions. A manager needs different kinds of skills and knowledge than does a scientist.

Communications

The inability of man to communicate effectively is a frequent cause of conflict. Communication is effective only when the written or spoken word generates in the mind of the receiver the exact concept held by the sender. The barriers to effective communications are many. In the first place, the same word, particularly an abstract one, has various meanings to different people. The parties to a labor contract may agree that no person should be disciplined or discharged except for just cause, but their definitions of "just cause" may differ greatly.

Selective blocking is another impediment to communications. We generally hear and remember only those facts and incidents that are favorable to our own position. If a foreman dislikes a subordinate, he will remember only the bad things he has heard about him. If an employee dislikes a foreman, he will remember only the unpleasant jobs assigned by him.

In conflict situations the disputants may hear each other's words, but they seldom listen with the intent of trying to understand the other's position. This is particularly prevalent during contract negotiations.

Professor Matthew Kelly of the School of Industrial and Labor Relations at Cornell University, a well-known mediator and arbitrator, recommends that initial negotiation meetings should be devoted to a thorough understanding of each other's position. This requires that each side disclose how it interprets the other's statement of its position and ask whether it is accurate. Such a discussion will invariably disclose misinterpretations, which could seriously impede or prolong negotiations if not cleared up.

During heated arguments while one person is talking, the other person seldom hears what is being said because his mind is occupied in developing an argument to defend his position. The two arguments may have no relevancy to each other. Intelligent dialogue requires that each side listen with the intent of understanding. Each must refute the other's argument with facts, figures, and reason.

During one unsuccessful negotiation the issue of increased productivity raised by management was rejected by the union with the argument that the company was trying to create slave-labor conditions. The company responded by charging that all employees were loafing on the job and that the union was protecting them. The result of these cross-accusations was a strike. The issue was ultimately resolved by a joint technical committee that worked for a year to uncover the facts and work out solutions.

Spoken and written words in themselves are not the only means of communication. Words spoken in an angry, authoritative, or arrogant tone convey a different meaning than the same words spoken in a friendly, conversational tone. Even facial expressions or body movements are a means of communicating.

Unfortunately, too many persons are not aware of the importance of good communications or of the deleterious effect of bad communications, which can lead to strikes and grievances. One of the functions of the arbitral process is to uncover the communication factors that led to the grievance. Many disputes could be settled by the parties themselves if they focused their attention on the misunderstandings that were created by faulty communications.

Changing Cultural Patterns

With the passage of time, cultural patterns change. We have seen radical changes in our concepts of government, the rights of individuals, and even religious tenets. The concept of the divine right of kings, which was defended by intellectuals for over 1,000 years, has been discarded. The Bill of Rights in the U.S. Constitution represented a radical change in the relations between a citizen and his government. More recently in the churches of the Western world, especially in the Catholic Church, new ideas have replaced long established traditions. The legal relationship between employer and employee was determined not too many years ago by the law of master and servant. Today, employees in the public as well as the private sectors have the right to bargain collectively.

Culture and the Decisional Process

Man is a captive of his own culture. His assumptions, opinions, and concepts of right and wrong, all of which enter into his decisional process, are a reflection of his own culture. Most persons are not aware of how their cultural biases affect their decisions. Cultural differences exist not only between ethnic groups but also between different segments of the same ethnic group. Management has a body of concepts that differ materially from those held by labor. Supervisors' concepts often differ from the concepts of those they supervise.

Different cultural concepts result in different decisions. This point was eloquently brought home in a speech in defense of cannibalism made by a cannibal chief and recorded by a missionary. The chief was disturbed by what he considered propaganda disseminated by the missionary, which urged his tribesmen not to eat their enemies. In the chief's frame of reference, the missionary was undermining his authority, weakening one of the cohesive forces that kept his tribe together, and destroying a long tradition. He argued that if they failed to eat their enemies, a population explosion would result and not enough food could be grown to feed the increased population. He also linked cannibalism with the love and affection members of the tribe show for each other, and claimed it was the mainspring of human progress. The chief was very convincing to his tribesmen, because they had the same cultural heritage and frame of reference.

The changes that have taken place in the past hundred years are illustrated by a notice that was posted by John Wanamaker in his New York department store in 1861. He advised his employees that they would be given one night off each week for courting purposes and a second night if they went to prayer meeting regularly. He also cautioned that if they were seen smoking Spanish cigars or getting shaved in a barbershop, their honesty and integrity would be questioned. He told his employees that they were expected to contribute $5.00 a year to the church, and that after 14 hours per day of work in his store, they were expected to read good literature. Certainly John Wanamaker, one of the country's leading merchants whose department store is still in existence, would have been highly indignant if his advice to his employees had been questioned. He could have found innumerable reasons why his decisions were reasonable, highly moral, and most generous.

Today, because we have an entirely different frame of reference, these ideas are considered ridiculous. We should pause to reflect on the policies and attitudes we defend with righteous indignation today and consider how ridiculous they may seem a hundred years from now. The following true stories illustrate the inevitability of change and the conflict that results from different cultural patterns.

Recently a young college student of the Mohammedan faith obtained a part-time job in a Roman Catholic hospital administered by a nun wearing the traditional habit. On her second day at the hospital, her supervisor asked her to remove the black silk handkerchief she had on her head. The student explained that, according to her religious faith, she was required to wear a head covering and dress very modestly. The supervisor again asked her to remove it and told her that if she did not follow her instructions she would have to see the administrator of the hospital. The nun-administrator took the same attitude as the supervisor. It was decided that the student would not be discharged, but the nun told her that they did not approve of her wearing the head covering, just as they did not condone the wearing of saris by employees from India. The nun-administrator could not see the inconsistency in her position. She wore a head covering and a long dress because her religion decreed it, but she could not see that it was inconsistent to deny the same privilege to another.

A hospital administrator in a nonsectarian hospital sought advice from a consultant on how to solve a similar personnel problem: A young man of the Hebrew faith insisted on wearing his yarmulke. The consultant asked whether the yarmulke interfered with his work duties. When the response was in the negative, the consultant pointed out that the Pope in Rome wears one all the time and that it was nothing to get upset about.

This type of inflexible thinking is very common, because we are all captives of our culture. Conflict, particularly in a multicultural society, is thus inevitable.

The Decisional Process

In order to make a sound judgment, a decision maker not only must be aware of the nature of man, communications, and cultural patterns, but also must analyze the process by which decisions are made. Much labor—management conflict which is ultimatetly submitted to arbitration could have been avoided or settled by the parties themselves if they had taken the time to distinguish between facts and allegations, to recognize their assumptions, to analyze the basis for their opinions, and to try to understand how each decision maker's personality influenced his decisions.

FACTS. A fact is something that cannot be disputed, such as a man's age, date of hire, or seniority. If such data are disputable, they are not facts.

ALLEGATIONS. An allegation is a statement that a disputant claims to be a fact. Whether an allegation is to be considered as a fact depends upon supporting evidence.

For example, an allegation that an employee is a poor worker can be treated as a fact only if production, scrap, and quality control records support this allegation. The allegation that a man has been excessively absent depends on his attendance records and also on how the word "excessive" is interpreted.

ASSUMPTIONS. An assumption is a concept that is taken for granted and assumed to be true without proof. Decision makers are frequently not conscious of the assumptions that have influenced their decisions; or, if they are aware of these assumptions, they have not taken time to determine their validity.

In one instance a rather important local businessman serving as a juror quickly came to the conclusion that the defendant in an accident case was right. When the evidence of two witnesses for the plaintiff was brought to his attention, he responded that they could not be believed because they did not even speak English correctly. His decision was based upon the assumption that foreign born who speak with an accent cannot be believed. But if he himself had been a witness in France and spoke with an American accent, he would be highly indignant if he were assumed to be a liar because he spoke broken French.

In one arbitration case a highly intelligent industrial relations director testified that he turned down the recommended promotion of the grievant because the man was unreliable. He explained that on one occasion when he was walking through the plant with some home office executives, he saw the grievant on a ladder with his arms folded, doing nothing. On a subsequent occasion he saw him chatting with the shop steward. The grievant admitted sitting with his arms folded, but explained that when he realized that the group of management executives would be walking under his ladder, he stopped moving lead pipes from one bin to another, crossed his arms, and waited until they were out of danger. He also explained that when seen with the shop steward, he was filing his grievance, not chatting. On cross-examination the industrial relations director admitted he was too far away to actually hear what they were saying. His conclusions were obviously based upon assumptions.

Too frequently we make erroneous assumptions based on cultural attitudes toward races, nationalities, religion, mode of dress, and political affiliation, or lack of full information. In one case a school teacher who reported she was sick was seen later the same day going into a taxicab. When this was reported to the principal, he assumed she was not sick. The principal did not know that she had called a doctor, who requested, in spite of her 102-degree fever, that she take a taxi to his office.

A faculty member in a Midwestern college complained that he had not received a salary increase in many years; the dean responded by saying that the department chairman must have had good reasons for not recommending salary increases. If the dean had investigated, he would have discovered that the chairman readily admitted his error because he had discovered that his decision was based on the false assumption that certain information communicated to him was true.

A man working on the night shift was summarily discharged for sleeping on the job. The testimony indicated that the foreman looked for this employee at the work station assigned to him at the beginning of the shift but could not find him. He then looked around the work area for him briefly, without success. About one hour later, at about 3:10 A.M., during the half-hour lunch break, the foreman found the employee asleep in the foreman's office. He awakened him at 3:32 A.M. and summarily fired him for sleeping on the job. At the hearing the employee explained that he was not at his work station because the foreman had given him another assignment; he described the work he performed and named the place where he was working. The foreman had forgotten this assignment, and when he found the employee asleep at 3:10 A.M., he assumed that he had been sleeping since about 2 A.M. The evidence indicated that this assumption was false.

OPINIONS. In the sense that the word is used here, an "opinion" is a deduction made by a person capable of evaluating the evidence upon which the opinion is based.

To be valid, the opinion must be based upon sufficient representative evidence. An industrial engineer cannot make a valid judgment of work load if his data are too limited. A foreman cannot normally decide whether an employee is a good or bad worker on the basis of one day's work. Merely because an employee is absent twice during the first week of his assignment to a new foreman does not warrant the conclusion that he is an unrealiable employee. His absentee record for the previous six months or year must be taken into consideration.

Even when adequate evidence is available, the person evaluating it must be competent. In one case a foreman assigned a mechanic to repair a machine in another department. At the end of 6 hours, the foreman needed the man on another job and went to investigate why he had been away so long. When he saw him still working, he accused him of loafing on the job. The employee was offended and a heated argument resulted. The employee was then given a disciplinary suspension for using abusive language. On cross-examination it became evident that the foreman did not know anything about the problems involved in fixing that particular machine, and therefore he was not in a position to give an opinion as to how long it should take to repair it.

PERSONALITY. Each person has a unique combination of human qualities and characteristics, which may be referred to as his personality. Although each person is unique, certain characteristics commonly predominate, permitting generalized classifications of people. These classifications include: aggressive, optimistic, arrogant, domineering, suspicious, submissive, pessimistic, subservient, and naive, with varying degrees of each trait.

Most people are not aware of how their personality traits influence their decisions. Two persons given the same facts will come to different decisions because of differing personalities. An arrogant supervisor may decide to discharge an employee as a result of an angry exchange of words, but another, more easygoing supervisor might give an oral reprimand for the same incident.

An aggressive shop steward may decide to file a grievance, whereas a less aggressive one would try to settle the problem informally.

An autocratically minded person demands compliance with orders and gives little, if any, consideration to the point of view of the subordinate. If the employee raises any question with regard to the decision, he will be charged with insubordination. The democratic approach is more flexible, requires consideration of how the decision will affect the subordinate, and welcomes his participation in the decisional process. This approach involves the evaluation of many more factors and may well result in a different decision.

If the decision of the autocratic decision maker is questioned, his immediate reaction is to prove that he is right. He does this by listing all the arguments in his favor and ignoring all the arguments indicating that he is wrong. Having justified his decision to himself, he closes his mind to any opposing arguments because he cannot question his own judgment or admit he is wrong. This would be a sign of weakness and would destroy his confidence in his infallibility. It is interesting to observe that people who resent autocratic behavior when they are subordinates frequently acquire autocratic characteristics when they become supervisors because they assume that acting autocratically is part of the supervisory role.

Obviously, decisions are not based on facts alone.

Weighting

Weighting may be defined as the degree of importance given to a fact or an opinion. If an employee uses vile language, one supervisor may consider it a very serious matter and give it considerable weight in deciding his course of action. Another person may merely consider it normal shop language and give it no weight at all. Each person assumes that his weighting is correct. He is usually surprised when his colleagues give the same fact a different weight. In the final analysis the arbitator must decide the appropriate weight of the fact or opinion.

VALUE JUDGMENTS. The weight we give to human events depends upon our value system. Value judgments vary considerably from person to person and group to group. Since value judgments affect decisions, interpersonal conflict is inevitable. If the matter is submitted to arbitration, the arbitrator's value judgment will prevail. However, it should be pointed out that the arbitrator—both as an interpretator and as a contributor to standards of human behavior in industrial society—applies to a given situation not his own personal value judgments, but those he believes are representative of society at large. For instance, the concept of progressive or corrective discipline has been accepted in industrial society. When an employee with many years of service has been summarily discharged for his first offense, the arbitrator will apply this concept and (except for serious offenses) reduce the penalty.

The limits of an employee's obligation to work overtime are dependent on the value judgment of the decision maker. They vary from an absolute obligation to work overtime, irrespective of personal considerations, to an obligation (limited by due notice) to work a reasonable amount of overtime. The trend is to minimize the obligation. Some people believe that there is no obligation to work overtime, that such work should be purely voluntary, and that refusal to work overtime for any reason should not subject the employee to disciplinary action.

Our value judgments as well as our personalities are the result of a great many factors, including broad cultural concepts, the amount of money earned, where we live, the role we play. For instance, the value judgments of a shop steward or union president often change when he is given management responsibilities.

Conflict Resolution

To reduce the incidence and severity of conflict and to increase the frequency of amicable settlements. it is essential that managers at all levels be given training in decision making. It cannot be assumed that because a man is a good machinist, engineer, marketing expert, dean of a college, or president of a university, he has the ability to resolve interpersonal problems. This is a field that requires special knowledge, aptitudes, and attitudes that are complex and by no means acquired automatically.

The arbitral process provides a review in depth of the decisional process utilized by both labor and management. When decision makers know that their decisions will be judicially reviewed by an arbitrator, they tend to think out problems with greater care before coming to a decision. The arbitral process thus results in better decisions.

1

HISTORICAL DEVELOPMENT

Arbitration as a method of settling disputes outside the regular courts of law is as old as civilization itself. There is evidence that it was used over 3,500 years ago in Egypt and in Homer's Greece in the ninth century B.C. Around 400 B.C. it was used in Athens to relieve the badly congested courts, although parties dissatisfied with an arbitration award could appeal to a court of law.*

Arbitration agreements in seventeenth-century England were not uncommon. In 1609 Lord Coke held that an arbitration agreement was revokable by either party.[1]

The Society of Friends resorted to arbitration because they did not wish to disclose their quarrels in courts of law. In colonial America the Quakers resolved commercial transactions and marital disagreements at their meetings.

Early Concepts of Labor Arbitration

In 1786 the Chamber of Commerce of New York City organized an arbitration tribunal to hear a dispute involving the wages of seamen.[2]

However, it is believed that in the late eighteenth and early nineteenth centuries the word "arbitration," when applied to labor disputes, did not mean adjudication by an impartial outsider. It is probable that an arbitration tribunal consisted of representatives of the parties who met to negotiate a settlement of the dispute.[3] This was evidently the nature of the arbitration process in the *Pittsburgh Boilers* (Puddlers) case in 1865, reported by the Bureau of Labor Statistics in 1929 as being the first instance of labor arbitration in the United States.[4]

This same concept of arbitration prevailed when the National Labor Union (1866) passed a resolution at its first congress held in Baltimore, Maryland, stating that each trades assembly should appoint "an Arbitration Committee, to whom should be referred all matters of dispute arising between employers and employees."

The Noble Order of the Knights of Labor (1869) declared in its Decla-

---

* Over two thousand years later we again find the arbitral process being utilized to relieve congested court calendars in the United States.

ration of Principles that one of its major objectives was "to persuade all employers to agree to arbitrate all differences which may arise between them and their employees, in order that bonds of sympathy between them may be strengthened, and that strikes may be rendered unnecessary" (quoted in Witte,[3] p. 6).

The modern concept of arbitration appeared in an article by Terrance V. Powderly, Grand Master Workman of the Knights of Labor, in the September 1892 issue of the *North American Review*. Commenting on the Homestead strike, Powderly wrote: "It should be the law in every state that in disputed cases the employer should be obliged to select two arbitrators and the employees two, these four to select a fifth, this arbitration commission to have access to all books, papers and facts bearing on the question at issue from both sides" (quoted in Mote[5]).

He also suggested that there should be no resort to strikes or lockouts before the decision of the arbitration board was handed down and that provision should be made for an appeal from the decision. Whether the appeal should be made to the courts or some other tribunal is not made clear. He did not view the arbitration award as final and binding.

Late Nineteenth Century

In the late 1800s the new concept of arbitration as a means of settling labor disputes was supported by labor organizations and the general public because of the many serious strikes that occurred during this period.

The State of Maryland in 1878 passed the first law in the United States providing for arbitration of labor disputes, but no permanent agency was established. In 1880 New Jersey passed a law permitting a majority of employees in any manufacturing establishment to propose submitting a dispute to arbitration and naming an arbitrator. A second arbitrator could be designated by the employer. These two would then select a third. This arbitration panel could render a binding award.

Similar laws were enacted in Pennsylvania (1883), Ohio (1885), Kansas (1886), and Iowa (1886). According to Edwin Witte, an arbitration tribunal for the coal industry operated for two years in Pennsylvania; this is the only known instance where these laws were utilized.[6]

PERMANENT STATE BOARDS. The first permanent, full-time state boards of arbitration were established by the states of Massachusetts and New York in 1886. Before 1900, 15 additional states passed arbitration laws. Some state boards coupled arbitration with mediation and conciliation activities. In New York the original name was State Board of Arbitration, but one year after its formation (1887), the word "Mediation" was added to the title.

However, with the exception of the Massachusetts Board, state boards rendered primarily mediation services. The New York Board acted on 409 disputes in the period 1886 to 1900, but only 21 disputes were settled by arbitration.[7]

JOINT BOARDS. Joint boards comprising representatives of labor and management were established in certain industries to settle disputes in the late 1800s. However, the Chicago Carpenters' agreement of 1890 provided a joint arbitration board, complete with an umpire.

Two significant developments occurred in the 1870s. A committee of the Anthracite Board of Trade and a committee of the Workingmen's Benevolent Association selected Judge Elwell to arbitrate two issues in 1871.[8]

In 1874 a committee of operators' and miners' representatives in Ohio met to discuss a wage dispute. The committee passed the following resolution: "Resolved, that the present differences in prices between the operators and miners in the Tuscarawas Valley be submitted to a committee of three operators and three miners, who shall elect an umpire, whose decision shall be final and binding on both parties." Judge S. J. Andrews of Cleveland was chosen as the Umpire.[9]

FEDERAL POLICY. As early as 1888, Congress encouraged the voluntary arbitration of labor disputes in the railroad industry. President Cleveland, in a special message to Congress in 1886, proposed a permanent board for voluntary arbitration. However, the Arbitration Act of 1888 provided for the establishment of ad hoc arbitration boards on the agreement of both parties.[10] This Act was repealed by the Erdman Act of 1898, which set up procedures for mediation and voluntary arbitration of disputes. The Act provided that if mediation did not succeed, the parties "shall at once endeavor to bring about arbitration of said controversy."

PUBLIC INTEREST IN LABOR ARBITRATION. Public interest in arbitration as a means of settling disputes manifested itself in the formation of the Congress on Industrial Conciliation and Arbitration held in Chicago in 1894. Sponsored by the Civic Federation of Chicago, it attracted leaders from industry, labor, and government.

The American Federation of Labor (AFL), in its 1900 convention, approved of voluntary arbitration but opposed compulsory arbitration, a position it takes today. It is significant to note that arbitration was viewed at this period as a means of settling contract disputes that could lead to strikes.

Early Twentieth Century

The National Civic Federation sponsored two National Conferences on Industrial Conciliation and Arbitration in New York City in 1900 and 1901. The industrial, labor, religious, and civic leaders who attended these conferences supported conciliation and arbitration as substitutes for economic warfare.

The Anthracite Coal Strike in 1902, which lasted more than five months and involved 140,000 miners, was settled by arbitration at the suggestion of President Theodore Roosevelt. The President appointed the members of the Anthracite Coal Strike Commission, which submitted its report[11] in 1902. Its award included the establishment of a Board of Conciliation (consisting of six members, three from the miners and three from the operators) to resolve disputes arising under the award and provided for appointment of an umpire to decide cases in the event of a Board disagreement.

According to Edwin Witte, this Board was "the first permanent machinery ever established in this country for the interpretation and application of what amounted to a trade agreement, and the Umpire's decisions in its functioning [were] the real beginnings of this type of arbitration." [12]

Louis D. Brandeis, a lawyer who later was a distingushed member of the U.S. Supreme Court, was responsible for what became known as the "Protocol of Peace," which settled the serious strike in the women's clothing industry in New York City in 1910. Among other things, this agreement provided machinery for the settlement of disputes consisting of a joint Board of Grievances and a Board of Arbitration.

The Board of Arbitration consisted of a representative of labor and management. The third member "represented nobody—that is the public." All served without pay. Although these Boards were not very effective, they laid the foundation for the effective arbitration machinery that now exists in all the needle trades.

Labor trouble in the railroads in the early 1900s brought about a demand for compulsory arbitration, but this was opposed by both unions and management. Under the Erdman Act (1898) there was some success in settling disputes in the railroad industry. Until the passage by Congress of the Newlands Act in 1913, 12 of 48 cases were resolved by arbitration, the remaining 36 through mediation. Under the Newlands Act a Board of Mediation and Conciliation was established, which arranged 21 arbitrations. The Board of Mediation functioned until Congress passed the Transportation Act of 1920, which created the Railroad Labor Board. The Railway Labor Act passed in 1926, as did its predecessors, encouraged voluntary arbitration. The Act set up a National Railroad Adjustment Board to hear and resolve grievances arising from interpretation and application of the collective bargaining agreement. The Board consists of representatives of management and labor. If they cannot agree, a "neutral" person is selected to arbitrate the issue. The Act also established the National Mediation Board to handle contract disputes.

It is significant that Congress for the first time resorted to compulsory arbitration in 1963 to avert a nationwide railroad strike over the issue of firemen on diesel locomotives. The legislation was upheld by the courts and the award of the arbitration panel enforced.

World War I

There was no clear-cut federal labor policy at this time. Labor was clamoring for more recognition, and the principle of labor representation on government committees was recognized. This period was characterized by a multitude of strikes and a plethora of boards to handle them, such as the

Shipbuilding Labor Adjustment Board, the Fuel Administration's Bureau of Labor to handle mine disputes, and a Harness and Saddlery Commission.

In January 1918, President Wilson appointed a War Labor Conference Board of 12 persons, 5 members each from industry and labor and 2 public members who served as co-chairmen. The Board recommended the abandonment of strikes and lockouts for the duration of the war and the creation of a National War Labor Board to handle "controversies arising between employers and employees with a view to guaranteeing the uninterrupted operation of industry and maximum production of war materials." The Board heard disputes and made awards. By the end of World War I, labor had made significant gains, but much antagonism existed between industry and labor. Compulsory arbitration was frequently suggested as a means of preventing strikes.

President Wilson called an industrial conference, which met late in 1919 and recommended settling labor disputes through regional and national boards of inquiry, adjustment, and voluntary arbitration.

New York State passed a modern arbitration law in 1920. Although it did not apply to labor disputes it established the framework for modern labor arbitration. This law revoked the common law rule, enunciated by Lord Coke in *Vynior's case* (1609), that an agreement to arbitrate was not enforceable; that it could be revoked at the will of either party at any time before an award was rendered. The law also closed the courts to the parties until they had fully complied with their agreements to arbitrate. Courts were empowered to enforce such agreements and appoint arbitrators when necessary.

As a result of the enactment of this law, the Arbitration Society of America was formed in 1922. It carried on a vast educational program to make arbitration better known throughout the country. In 1926 it changed its name to the American Arbitration Association (AAA). In 1937 the Association established a Voluntary Labor Arbitration Tribunal. Although initially most of its cases were commercial, today the reverse is true. In 1973 the AAA handled 18,380 labor arbitration cases.

Mid-Twentieth Century

World War II

NATIONAL DEFENSE MEDIATION BOARD. In December 1940 President Roosevelt proposed that the United States become the "arsenal of democracy." War production rose and strikes increased. To cope with a situation that many felt threatened the national safety, the President created the National Defense Mediation Board in March 1941 with jurisdiction over those labor disputes certified by the Secretary of Labor as threatening to burden or obstruct the production or transportation of equipment or materials essential to national defense. The Executive Order suggested voluntary arbitration if mediation of the labor dispute failed.

The Mediation Board was tripartite in character; labor, employers, and the public had equal representation on the board. Unfortunately, the board members served only part time. As a result it was difficult for them to participate actively in disputes brought before them. A case was normally considered by a panel of three members, but in one case four successive labor members sat on a panel dealing with a dispute.[13]

According to a study by the Brookings Institution,[14] the Mediation Board was ineffective "because it combined mediation and arbitration functions without having authority to enforce its arbitral awards."

The Board ceased to function late in 1941 when the CIO members withdrew because, by a vote of nine to two (CIO members dissenting), the Board recommended against granting the union demand for a union shop in a dispute involving captive bituminous coal mines and the United Mine Workers of America, then affiliated with the CIO.

It is significant to note that before the Board acted, it endeavored to get the parties to submit the dispute to voluntary arbitration, but the union was unwilling.

The experience of the Mediation Board pointed to the need for arbitration machinery to be added to mediation, which was finally realized in the National War Labor Board (NWLB).

NATIONAL WAR LABOR BOARD. Public concern over the growing number of strikes was reflected in the passage by the House of Representatives of the Smith Bill, which provided for drastic controls of unions and labor relations. Before the Senate acted on this bill, the White House called a labor–management conference in December 1941 to head off this type of legislation.

The conference led to the establishment of the National War Labor Board. Its primary responsibility was to act as an arbitration agency for the settlement of all labor disputes affecting the war effort. The almost universal use of labor arbitration today is the direct result of the work of the NWLB. Most of the presently active arbitrators in the United States served in either the regional offices or the Washington office of the Board.

The Board was comprised of twelve members—four public (one of whom was chairman), four labor, and four management—all of whom were appointed by the President.

There has been some difference of opinion as to whether the system of arbitration provided by the NWLB was compulsory or voluntary.[15] In practice the parties to a dispute were obligated not to resort to strikes but to submit controversies to the Board for adjudication. With some important exceptions, labor and management cooperated and abided by the orders of the Board.

In 1942 the Board was given the additional function of stabilizing wages. To carry out this function and to cope with the growing volume of dispute cases, regional offices with tripartite boards were opened in the fall of 1942.

When a dispute was certified to the Board by the U.S. Conciliation

Service, it was assigned to a Hearing Officer or a tripartite panel at the appropriate regional office. The public member, called "Public Panel Chairman," served as the chairman and wrote the report.

At the hearing the parties presented their respective positions. These were presented to the Board together with a recommendation. The Board could adopt or modify the recommendation and issue an order to the parties.

Appeals from the regional boards could be taken to the National Board. About 21,000 labor disputes[16] were thus adjudicated by the arbitral process. The parties found that this process was effective in resolving disputes, and a growing number of collective bargaining contracts included grievance procedures terminating in final and binding arbitration.

Immediately after World War II, the acceptance of labor arbitration as a means of settling grievances was indicated by the fact that the Labor–Management Conference of 1945 unanimously recommended the use of arbitration to settle disputes involving an interpretation of labor contracts. It also recommended: "If direct negotiations and conciliation have not been successful, voluntary arbitration may be considered by the parties." [17] Unfortunately, it could agree on little else and was considered a failure.

Post–World War II Developments

NATIONAL ACADEMY OF ARBITRATORS. With the founding of the National Academy of Arbitrators (NAA) in 1947, arbitration as a distinct profession became a reality. Most of the founders were associated with the National War Labor Board. They felt that a professional society was needed "to establish and foster high standards and competence among those engaged in the arbitration of industrial disputes on a professional basis, to adopt canons of ethics to govern the conduct of arbitration, to promote the study and understanding of the arbitration of industrial disputes."

The annual meeting of the NAA is attended not only by arbitrators but also by representatives of management and labor, attorneys, and government officials. Since 1955 the Bureau of National Affairs (BNA) has published the proceedings, which have become an important source of information about labor arbitration. In 1966 the NAA Annual Meeting was held in Puerto Rico. Montreal, Canada, was the site of the 1970 meeting. All other meetings have been held in various parts of the country, ranging from Boston and Washington, D.C., to Los Angeles.

The Academy, in cooperation with the American Arbitration Association and the Federal Mediation and Conciliation Service (FMCS), developed a Code of Ethics and Procedural Standards for Labor–Management Arbitration. The adopted code is reproduced as Appendix I,1.

SOCIETY OF PROFESSIONALS IN DISPUTE RESOLUTION. The latest professional organization to be created, which includes in its membership not only arbitrators but also mediators and fact-finders, is called the Society of

Professionals in Dispute Resolution (SPIDR). The inaugural convention of this association was held in Washington, D.C., on October 17–19, 1973. Robert D. Helsby, chairman of the New York State Public Employment Relations Board, was officially elected its first president in September 1973. Membership at the time of the convention approximated 600. The speakers at the first convention included Secretary of Labor Peter J. Brennan and David L. Cole, chairman of the National Commission on Industrial Peace.

ADVISORY ARBITRATION. Although the procedures followed in advisory arbitration are the same as in final and binding arbitration, the award is merely advisory. The parties are not legally obligated to follow the award, but the analysis of the issues and the suggested solution frequently persuade the parties to settle their dispute on the terms suggested by the arbitrator.

In the past, advisory arbitration was used in disputes involving public employees because the courts held that city officials were not permitted to bargain away or delegate to others the authority given to them by law. Moreover, the discharge of employees was governed by civil service rules and regulations.[18]

One of the early cases that held a contrary view is *Norwalk Teachers Association v. Board of Education* (1951).[19] The court considered the question, "Is arbitration a permissible method under Connecticut law to settle or adjust disputes between the plaintiff and the defendant"? It held:

The power of a town to enter into an agreement of arbitration was originally denied on the ground that it was an unlawful delegation of authority. . . . If it is borne in mind that arbitration is the result of mutual agreement, there is no reason to deny the power of the defendant (the city) to enter voluntarily into a contract to arbitrate a specific dispute. . . . Arbitration as a method of settling disputes is growing in importance and, in a proper case, "deserves the enthusiastic support of the courts". . . . The best answer we can give is "yes, arbitration may be a permissible method as to certain specific, arbitrable issues." [20]

The action in the 1950s taken by the City of Detroit is further evidence of the trend away from advisory arbitration. In 1951 the Charter of the City of Detroit was amended to permit final and binding arbitration of almost all disputes between Fire Department employees and the Board of Fire Commissioners, upon request by a petition signed by not less than half of the employees in the Department.

The Charter also empowered the Board of Street Railway Commissioners to bargain collectively with representatives of its employees and "in case of dispute over wages or conditions of employment, said Board is authorized and directed to arbitrate any question or questions, provided each party shall agree in advance to pay half the expense of such arbitration." [21]

Some collective bargaining agreements between boards of education and teachers' associations provide that the board of education may act as the final arbiter. The theory is that they represent the public and can impartially review disputes between the teachers and the superintendents of schools or other administrative officers. Teachers' associations, however, do not view the board of education as impartial. Boards are reluctant to accept final and binding arbitration because it is a limitation on their decision-making power. As a compromise, the parties often agree to advisory arbitration. If boards of education consistently refuse to abide by advisory awards, grievance machinery will have little meaning for the teachers.

There is a definite trend toward final and binding arbitration of teachers' disputes. This is inevitable for several reasons. As both board members and teachers become familiar with the arbitral process, they will have more confidence in it. Moreover, board members are not paid and serve only part time. They soon find out that to conduct a proper hearing and write an analytical opinion and award is very time-consuming and requires some degree of professional competence.

Where the board has ordered its school administrators to follow a certain interpretation of the contract, the board cannot logically claim to be impartial if a teacher objects to the administrator's interpretation of the contract.

ARBITRATION FOR FEDERAL EMPLOYEES. As early as 1940 the Tennessee Valley Authority (TVA) had binding arbitration of grievances for its blue-collar employees; in 1950 it was extended to white-collar employees. The recently promulgated executive order 11491 provides for the arbitration of grievances. This order is discussed in Chapter 15 and reproduced in Appendix III,2.

ARBITRATION IN NON-UNION PLANTS. There is a definite trend toward the acceptance of final and binding arbitration, even in plants that do not have collective bargaining agreements. V. Clayton Sherman, a personnel manager, stated: "Gripes, complaints and grievances are a natural outgrowth and result of people working together. While much can be done to remove specific causes of grievances, it isn't possible to remove all the underlying causes. It therefore becomes imperative that some procedure or system be devised to effectively resolve human frictions once they've arisen." [22]

Other recent developments in non-union arbitration are discussed in Chapter 16.

REFERENCES

1. Vynior's Case, 4 Co. Rep. 302, 305 (K.B. 1609).
2. Francis Keller, *American Arbitration—Its History, Functions, and Achievements.* New York: Harper & Row, 1948, p. 3.
3. Edwin F. Witte, *Historical Survey of Labor Arbitration.* Philadelphia: University of Pennsylvania Press, 1952, pp. 5–6.
4. *Monthly Labor Review*, 16. U.S. Dept. of Labor, Bureau of Labor Statistics, November 1929.

5. Carl H. Mote, *Industrial Arbitration*. Indianapolis: Bobbs-Merrill Co., 1916, p. 145.
6. Edwin F. Witte, *op. cit.*, p.7.
7. Leonard W. Hatch, "Government Industrial Arbitration." *U.S. Bureau of Labor Statistics Bulletin 60*, 1905.
8. Carroll D. Wright, "Industrial Conciliation and Arbitration." *Massachusetts Bureau of Labor Statistics*, 1881, pp. 134–136.
9. Carroll D. Wright, *op. cit.*, p. 157.
10. "Use of Federal Power in Settlement of Railway Labor Disputes." *U.S. Bureau of Labor Statistics Bulletin 303*, 1922.
11. "Report on the Anthracite Coal Strike Commission." *U.S. Department of Labor Bulletin 42*, 1903.
12. Edwin F. Witte, *op. cit.*, p. 23.
13. "Report on the Work of the National Defense Mediation Board." *U.S. Bureau of Labor Statistics Bulletin 714*, 1942, p. 7.
14. Harold W. Mitz and Meyer Jacobstein, *A National Labor Policy*. Washington, D.C.: The Brookings Institution, 1947, p. 17.
15. Maurice S. Trotta, *Labor Arbitration*. New York: Simmons-Boardman, 1961, p. 23.
16. *The Termination Reports of the National War Labor Board*. Washington, D.C.: U.S. Government Printing Office, 1947.
17. "The President's National Labor–Management Conference." *U.S. Department of Labor, Division of Standards, Bulletin 77*, 1946, p. 37.
18. Charles S. Rhyne, *Labor Union and Municipal Employee Law*. Washington, D.C.: National Institute of Municipal Law, 1946 (with 1949 supplement), p. 43.
19. Norwalk Teachers Assoc. v. Board of Education, 83 A. 2d. 482.
20. Charles S. Rhyne, *op cit.*, p. 486.
21. Charter of the City of Detroit, Sec. XIX, Title IV, Chapter VIII.
22. V. Clayton Sherman, "What the Non-Union Company Can Learn from the Unionized Company." In *Industrial Relations Guide*. Englewood Cliffs, N.J.: Prentice-Hall, 1970, pp. 42, 117.

2

THE ARBITRATION PROCESS

Voluntary labor arbitration is a judicial proceeding presided over by an arbitrator who is empowered by the parties to render a final and binding decision in a labor dispute. An arbitrator is selected by the parties to hear and determine specific disputes. He is virtually a judge; he hears the evidence and renders a decision that the parties obligate themselves to carry out.

According to Shulman, an arbitrator "is not a public tribunal imposed upon the parties by a superior authority which the parties are obliged to accept. He has no general character to administer justice for a community which transcends the parties. He is rather part of a system of self-government created by and confined to the parties." [1]

Arbitration: A Private Judicial System

The arbitration system has other unique characteristics. Unlike judges in our courts of law, arbitrators have no tenure of office and are not politically appointed or elected. An arbitrator's continued selection depends upon how satisfactorily and effectively he serves the needs of the parties in settling industrial disputes. In effect, management and labor have established a private judicial system whereby they select their own judges and fix their own rules of procedure. The system is recognized by law. When the parties have agreed to final and binding arbitration, the courts will enforce the agreement and the arbitrator's award.

Distinguished from a Court of Law

In arbitration, the parties have no right to a jury trial. The arbitrator serves as both jury and trial judge, as in a court of equity. He ascertains the essential facts and interprets the law, which in grievance arbitration is the collective bargaining agreement between the parties. The procedures followed in an arbitration case are quite different from those in a court of law. The latter are formal, whereas arbitration proceedings are informal. A judge under the doctrine of *stare decisis* is obliged to follow precedents set by other judges. Arbitrators are not obligated to follow precedents set by other arbitrators in similar cases.

The rules of evidence established in courts of law are not followed in arbitration proceedings. What might be admissible in an arbitration case would not necessarily be admissible in a court of law. The arbitrator determines what is admissible evidence.

In courts of law, decisions may be appealed to a higher court, but in arbitration there is no comparable appeal recourse.

With the exception of certain specialized courts, judges hear a great variety of cases and are not usually experts in the particular subject matter brought before them. Most labor arbitrators, on the other hand, have extensive background and knowledge of the manifold problems in industrial relations, and they hear only industrial disputes. This specialized experience enables them to become eminently qualified as experts in this field.

In courts of law it is not uncommon for two years or more to elapse before a case is brought to trial. This may be due to a heavy backlog of cases or the technical maneuvering of lawyers. Such a time lapse is nonexistent in arbitration proceedings. A case is seldom delayed more than a month or two after the demand for arbitration is filed.

The complexity of public court procedures (except in small claims court) makes it almost impossible for a person to pursue a claim without the aid of an attorney. In arbitration hearings the procedures are simple and, where the issues are not complicated and technical, the services of an attorney are not essential.

Fees paid to an arbitrator are shared equally by the parties. The total cost of an arbitration proceeding is far less than costs of a lawsuit.

Arbitration, in sum, is a nontechnical and relatively inexpensive procedure for obtaining a quick solution to industrial disputes by persons who have specialized knowledge of labor–management relations.

Distinguished from Mediation

A *mediator* is a disinterested third party, usually a government employee, who helps to settle disputes involving the terms and conditions of a collective bargaining agreement. He is assigned and paid by the state or federal agency by which he is employed. He is not selected by the parties. The mediator renders no final and binding decision. He merely suggests solutions. As a means of avoiding a strike, mediators frequently suggest to the parties that they agree to submit the issue in dispute to an arbitrator. Although the parties are generally reluctant to submit *contract disputes* to arbitration, many accept arbitration to avoid strikes.

Distinguished from Fact-Finding Boards

As stated earlier in this chapter, an arbitrator renders a final and binding award. A *fact-finding board*, however, does not make a final and binding determination of the matters in dispute. The primary responsibility of such a board is to determine the precise issues in dispute and the position of the parties with regard to each issue. Usually, a board is asked to recommend a solution to the matters in dispute, but these recommendations are not binding on the parties.

Members of fact-finding boards are generally selected by a government official. Sometimes the selection accords with the recommendation of the parties. The procedure followed in the conduct of hearings is similar to that in arbitration proceedings. It is not uncommon for members of a board to serve as informal mediators during and immediately after a hearing. Arbitrators, of course, seldom try to mediate a dispute.

Rights and Interest Disputes

There are two categories of labor disputes: rights and interest. When the issue to be arbitrated requires an interpretation of a collective bargaining agreement, it is known as a "rights" dispute. Over 95 percent of all issues arbitrated fall into this category. When the issue requires the arbitrator to determine the terms and conditions of a collective bargaining agreement, it is known as an "interest" dispute.

The usual arbitration clauses in collective bargaining agreements empower the arbitrator to interpret *only* the contract. Few contracts provide for the arbitration of "interest" disputes. When the terms and conditions of an agreement are in dispute, they are usually submitted to arbitration by means of a special contract, called a submission agreement, which is signed by the disputants.

Distinguished from Commercial Arbitration

The broad field of arbitration may be subdivided into two areas: (1) *labor arbitration*, which is concerned with disputes between management and labor; and (2) *commercial arbitration*, which is concerned with disputes involving commercial transactions.

To save time and expense, businessmen tend with increasing frequency to settle disputes through arbitration so that they can bypass the courts. Commercial arbitrators are selected on the basis of their specialized knowledge in the area of the dispute. Commercial arbitration provides a method for prompt adjudication of disputes by experts, frequently at no cost.

Commercial arbitration hearings follow the same informal pattern as that in the arbitration of labor issues. Labor arbitrators generally write detailed and analytical opinions, but commercial arbitrators usually render awards without opinions.

Functions of Voluntary Labor Arbitration

The primary function of voluntary labor arbitration is to provide (1) a process for the orderly disposition of disputes and (2) a foundation for stable labor-management relations. Thus, a medium is provided for the elimination of the sources of friction that cause industrial unrest. It also serves as a safety valve for emotional flare-ups, which are so easily stirred up in intimate human relationships. Arbitration awards set standards of conduct and behavior, and encourage a more careful consideration of the facts before a decision is made.

Highly regarded and effective arbitrators can establish standards of conduct which will be accepted and followed readily by both parties. For example, if arbitrators consistently follow the rule (called progressive or corrective discipline) that, except for major offenses such as stealing and fighting, an employee should be warned or suspended before he is discharged, the parties will soon adopt the practice. A body of sound labor law has been developed by arbitrators who have served over the past 25 years. Their decisions have established standards to guide management and labor.

The arbitrator serves as a symbol of justice. He represents the forum where reason replaces force, where logic supplants emotion, and where a sincere and honest effort is made to determine the facts and fairly resolve grievances.

The Decisional Process

Every grievance submitted to arbitration represents a series of decisions made by the individual grievant, his supervisor, the shop steward, union officials, and representatives of management. It is important for arbitrators to understand the process by which these decisions are made.

Unfortunately, even intelligent and well-meaning persons can make serious errors in judgment. Arbitrators see these errors frequently. It is one of the important reasons why unions insist that grievance procedures terminate in final and binding arbitration. It may also explain in part the growth of teachers' unions, for even the possession of several academic degrees or an important title does not guarantee an objective and a judicial approach to the solution of every personnel problem.

The mere existence of a procedure for fully exploring the reasons for a decision will in itself serve to insure better decisions. Knowing that his decisions may be subject to judicial review, a supervisor will be more careful and more objective when making a decision; thus, he can avoid hasty and ill-advised decisions that might later have to be defended.

After an arbitrator hears the testimony and evaluates the evidence and arguments of both sides, he writes his opinion, giving the reasons why he has arrived at a particular conclusion. His written opinion states why he believes that certain arguments have more value than others. When the parties receive a decision, they first read the award to determine whether they have won or lost. Although this is understandable, it is important that they also read the opinion to discover the reasons why they won or lost.

The arbitrator is aware that he is an integral part of a relatively new process that, on a case-by-case basis, is formulating a new common law of labor relations. He realizes that he is a judge in a private court system and that he will serve in this capacity only as long as he is selected by the parties because of their confidence in his intelligence and integrity.

He knows that he is at the center of a vortex of fluid social concepts, and changing assumptions, and that in such a climate reasonable men can have different opinions. Both the parties and the arbitrator have the common obligation of examining objectively every issue with a judicial frame of mind.

The need for and the function of arbitration are more clearly seen if there is an understanding of the nature of labor–management relations. When a group of people work together, disputes are unavoidable. Each individual is unique in that he is endowed with distinctive personality traits, attitudes, and skills. Moreover, he has certain emotions, fears, drives, hates, loves, and hopes that result in definite behavior patterns. Thus, any organization that has rules and regulations administered by someone in a supervisory capacity is bound to experience unavoidable disputes. Close daily contact is likely to develop some friction, which is not easily adjusted if a supervisor or shop steward lacks tact or understanding, is belligerent, or exceeds his authority.

Unless a means is provided for the settlement of these day-to-day disputes, industrial unrest inevitably results and manifests itself in strikes, slowdowns, high turnover of personnel, uncooperative employees, poor workmanship, and other conditions detrimental to production. Where emotions replace logic and reason, it is difficult and frequently impossible for a meeting of minds between labor and management.

In recent years both management and labor have taken steps to correct the basic causes of disputes. Supervisors and shop stewards are being trained to handle interpersonal realtionships. For example, The Amalgamated Meat Cutters and Butcher Workmen of North America have sponsored a booklet entitled "The Steward and His Job," which advises that in dealing with any individual workman or foreman, a shop steward should be considerate and understanding, investigate each complaint or incident carefully and thoroughly, be accurate and honest in reporting the facts, and be prompt, businesslike, and diplomatic in handling all situations. Many companies are training their supervisors in human relations, in a similar manner, for the express purpose of reducing grievances.

Grievance Procedure

Practically all collective bargaining agreements provide for the orderly handling of industrial disputes, a process known as the grievance procedure. A study made by the U.S. Dept. of Labor in 1964 found that of 1,717 major agreements studied, 99 percent included grievance procedures and 94 percent terminated in arbitration.[2]

The grievance procedure requires that the parties follow certain definite steps before any dispute can be submitted to arbitration. The following quote is taken from the collective bargaining agreement between Royal McBee Corporation and Royal Industrial Union, United Automobile, Aircraft and Agriculture Workers of America. It clearly sets forth in detail the respective rights of the parties and the power of the arbitrator:

Section 1. In the event of any difference between the Company and any employee or group of employees as to hours, wages or working conditions, an earnest effort will be made to settle such difference as soon as possible according to the following sequence and procedure.

Section 2. The grievance of any employee or group of employees shall be presented in writing to the department foreman by the employee or the steward of the department. The foreman shall make a decision thereon within one working day if reasonably possible.

Section 3. If the grievance is not adjusted by the foreman or by the foreman and the department steward it shall then be referred to the Personnel Manager who shall cause the same to be investigated and who shall, upon request, meet with the steward and the chief steward. A decision thereon shall be rendered not later than ten (10) working days of the presentation of the grievance to the Personnel Manager unless the time therefor is extended by mutual agreement.

Section 4. In the event that the decision on the grievance is not then acceptable to the Union, or in the event that no decision has been rendered thereon within the time limits required under Section 3, it may be referred to the Business Agent of the Union who may request in writing a meeting between the Committee of the Union and the executive representatives of the Company for discussion or determination. The executive representatives of the Company shall meet with the Committee of the Union not later than ten (10) working days after receipt of said written notice unless otherwise mutually agreed upon. A decision thereon shall be rendered not later than ten (10) working days after the holding of such meeting or within such time as may be mutually agreed upon in writing. At such meeting the Committee of the Union shall consist of not more than five employees of the Company, one from each floor, who may be accompanied by the Business Agent and the President with or without an International Representative of the Union.

Section 5. In the event that a decision by the Company representatives under Section 4 is not made within ten (10) working days after the conclusion of the meeting the Committee of the Union may elect, within five (5) working days thereafter, to notify the Company that the grievance shall be referred to arbitration, which notice shall be in writing.

Section 6. There shall be meetings between the Committee of the Union and executive representatives of the Company to be held whenever necessary but not more frequently than once every two weeks. Before the holding of such a meeting the Committee of the Union must have presented to the Personnel Manager an agenda in writing at least forty-eight hours previous thereto stating fully the specific grievances to be dealt with at that meeting.

Section 7. Should any appeal from the decision of the Company on a grievance under Sections 2 and 3 not be taken within five (5) working days after such decision is given by the Company representatives then the decision on such grievance shall be final and conclusive and shall not thereafter be reopened for discussion. Should there be no referral to arbitration, as provided for in Sections 5 and 9 hereof, of the decision of the Company under Sections 3 and 4 then the decision on such grievance shall be final and conclusive and shall not thereafter be reopened for discussion.

Any disposition of a grievance accepted by the Union or from which no appeal has been taken or referral to arbitration been made shall be final and conclusive and binding on all employees, the Company and the Union.

Section 8. Any grievance not presented for disposition through the grievance procedure described under Section 2 above within ten (10) working days of the grievance shall not thereafter be considered a grievance under this agreement unless previously presented orally to the foreman and the steward for investigation.

Section 9. All differences, disputes and grievances between the Company and any employee or group of employees, except any matter involving wages and bonuses, that shall not have been satisfactorily settled shall, after following the above grievance procedure and at the request of either party, be submitted to arbitration in accordance with the following precedure only if such submission is made within twenty (20) working days after a decision has been rendered thereon or notice of intent to submit to arbitration has been given by the Union under Section 5 above.

(a) By an arbitrator mutually acceptable to the Union and the Company, or by the American Arbitration Association which shall be requested to furnish an arbitrator under its rules and procedure, the decision of the arbitrator to be final and binding upon both parties.

(b) Expenses of the arbitration shall be equally divided between the Company and the Union.

(c) There shall be no power to add to, subtract from or modify this agreement or to establish or change any rates of pay or wages. (The change of job from one classification to another classification shall be considered in arbitration under Section 9 of Article IV a change of rate.)

(d) Grievances that are completely unrelated as to individuals or departments concerned or as to procedural, contractual or substantive problems involved shall not be heard by the same arbitrator at one hearing except by mutual agreement.

ELEMENTS OF A GOOD GRIEVANCE PROCEDURE. The President's National Labor–Management Conference of 1945 recommended the following elements as essential for a sound and effective grievance procedure[3]:

The procedure should be designed to facilitate the settlement of grievances and disputes as soon as possible after they arise. To this end:

(1) The agreement should provide adequate stated time limits for the presentation of grievances and disputes, the rendering of decisions, and the taking of appeals.

(2) Issues should be clearly formulated at the earliest possible moment. In all cases which cannot be settled in the first informal discussions, the positions of both sides should be reduced to writing.

(3) Management and Union should encourage their representatives to settle

at the lower steps grievances which do not involve broad questions of policy or of contract interpretation and should delegate sufficient authority to them to accomplish this end.

(4) The agreement should provide adequate opportunity for both parties to investigate grievances under discussion.

(5) Provision should be made for priority handling of grievances involving discharge, suspension, or other disciplinary action.

THE LABOR-MANAGEMENT RELATIONS ACT, 1947. Under this amendment to the National Labor Relations Act (Section 9a), an employee may present and adjust a grievance with a representative of the management, without the intervention or assistance of the union. However, a union representative must have the opportunity to be present, and whatever adjustment is made must be consistent with the provisions of the collective bargaining agreement.

MANAGEMENT–LABOR ATTITUDES. The success of a grievance procedure depends not only on its procedural aspects but also upon the attitudes of the representatives of unions and management who have the responsibility for the handling of grievances. If shop stewards, for example, fail to make a distinction between a minor or vague complaint and a real grievance, the procedure will never be effective, nor will it serve its proper and intended function. The facts must be ascertained after an unbiased and honest investigation, and union politics must not be permitted to color the inquiry. The effectiveness of the grievance procedure will also be impaired if management's representatives oppose every grievance as a matter of principle and policy rather than obtain the facts honestly and impartially.

Responsibilities of the Arbitrator

The focal point in the arbitral process is the arbitrator. An understanding of his responsibilities, and his acumen in handling each problem he faces, gives a clearer picture of the nature and function of arbitration.

SOCIAL STANDARDS. The arbitrator functions in effect as an instrumentality of industrial society. He must therefore apply accepted standards of social justice to the settlement of each industrial dispute. This requires a sound and broad social viewpoint coupled with a sensitivity for changing social concepts and industrial practices. Personal standards of justice cannot be applied; his personal philosophy and predilections must be set aside. However, as the arbitral process becomes completely integrated into the fabric of industrial society, the arbitrator will, no doubt, play an important role in molding standards of social justice.

INTERPRETING THE CONTRACT. The major function of the arbitrator is the interpretation of the provisions of the collective bargaining agreement. The intent of the contracting parties is of the utmost importance. The words used in the contract must be closely and carefully analyzed with respect to accepted industrial practices. There must be an understanding of the language as well as the practice of industrial relations.

DETERMINING PAST PRACTICE. Collective bargaining agreements do not cover every phase of the relationship between management and labor. Practices frequently develop which are not specifically stated in a contract, but which both parties consider as contractual obligations. For example, management may unilaterally initiate a particular practice and follow it for a considerable period of time. Subsequently, the union may claim that the practice is an integral part of the collective bargaining agreement. Thus, the arbitrator must determine whether a practice is in fact a part of the contract.

DETERMINING JURISDICTION. In many disputes the question may arise as to whether the dispute is arbitrable under the terms of the collective bargaining agreement. The arbitrator may be required to determine the scope of his jurisdiction under the arbitration clause or the submission agreement. If he exceeds his jurisdiction, his award will be set aside by a court of law.

DETERMINING THE FACTS. The arbitrator must be able to determine the facts despite both conflicting testimony and inadequate evidence. The successful and effective arbitrator must develop the ability to evaluate correctly the credibility of witnesses, which requires an understanding of human nature and the acuity to recognize plausible but false evidence. He must search for the whole truth, since it is only natural for a witness to color his evidence and remember only that which is favorable to his position. An arbitrator must therefore be able to appraise testimony quickly and critically, always remembering that individuals with different frames of reference may view the same incident differently.[4]

WEIGHING THE FACTS. Having determined the facts, the arbitrator must evaluate all the evidence before he can come to a decision. An illustration, based on a type of issue that arises frequently in labor–management relations, will highlight the problem facing the arbitrator. Assume the following facts: (1) The employee used abusive language when answering a foreman; (2) the foreman provoked the incident by also using abusive language; (3) the employee had been in the employ of the company for ten years; (4) eight years previously the employee had been given a written warning for having used abusive language to a fellow worker; (5) the employee was discharged immediately after the offense; and (6) the union requested reinstatement with full back pay.

In this case the arbitrator was faced with the problem of deciding whether discharge, a lesser penalty, or reinstatement with full back pay was the proper remedy. Each fact had to be given an appropriate value, and its relative importance had to be weighed before the arbitrator could determine a fair and proper remedy.

The Arbitrator's View of the Arbitration Process

The arbitrator's view of the arbitration process is different from that of the parties. For both parties, there is one object—to win the case. In some instances, a disputant may have some doubts as to the justice of his position, but he may be nevertheless obligated to pursue the case through many hours of fruitless discussion, through each step of the grievance procedure, in order to back up a supervisor or to support an active union member (who would otherwise charge that the union is not properly protecting his rights). Whatever a disputant's private thoughts may be. his goal at the hearing is to convince the arbitrator by facts, figures, documents, and argument that the award should be in his favor. Winning the case is all-important.

The arbitrator views the case quite differently. He is interested in facts, not assumptions. He wants proof of allegations in the form of documents and records, and prefers not to have hearsay testimony. He is looking for well-reasoned and -documented arguments. He is constantly evaluating the credibility of the witnesses and weighing the evidence as it is being presented. Of utmost importance to him is not the number of the arguments but their relevance and weight.

He will listen to attempts to frame the issue so as to give one side an advantage. He will hear testimony by witnesses who remember only incidents or facts that are favorable and have no recollection of unfavorable facts, even on cross-examination. He will hear testimony that is irrelevant as well as relevant and which is often hearsay. He will see witnesses become angry because their unsupported opinions are challenged. Such witnesses are not able to understand why their word (for example, that the employee is a poor worker or a good worker) has to be supported by evidence.

SIFTING THE EVIDENCE. The arbitrator may hear two witnesses tell diametrically opposite stories. He must then determine whether false testimony is being consciously given or whether both witnesses, having different views and different frames of reference, have honestly come to different conclusions. The arbitrator is conscious of the fact that the parties, not knowing what facts or arguments will convince the arbitrator, will tend to place before him everything even remotely connected with the issue.

Even though an experienced arbitrator may prefer to hear only logical arguments and pertinent reliable evidence, he recognizes the necessity of listening to *irrelevant* matter when it serves to release pent-up emotions. Having his day in court and being able to tell the other side exactly what is on his mind may be as important to a disputant as winning a case. This does not mean that the arbitrator should tolerate successive rounds of disputants' personal cross-attacks. Instead of directing arguments against the *position* of his opponent, one party may attack the other's integrity and honesty. This naturally evokes emotional reaction that further impedes logical discussion of the issues. The arbitrator should prevent such a development by curtailing this type of presentation.

IDENTIFYING THE ISSUES. During the initial stages of the hearing, particularly if there is a difference of opinion as to what the issue is, the arbitrator may observe that no real attempt has been previously made to resolve the dispute. Discussions relating to the issue may have taken place without a thorough and honest exchange of views. Each side may have repeated its own position at each step of the grievance, without really trying to understand the opposing position.

Frequently, after the arbitrator has succeeded in obtaining agreement on the issues and an opening statement from each side outlining the main arguments, the parties themselves settle the matter because the solution becomes obvious.

Whatever the arguments advanced, it is important for the arbitrator to understand them, even though he may disagree. He must listen to and comprehend all arguments in order to evaluate their weight. His evaluation of the evidence is of prime importance. Both sides will advance arguments that have at least a surface validity, and the decision will depend upon the value of these arguments. Since the arbitrator has no previous knowledge of the facts in the case, he needs this opening statement in order to be informed of the position of each side, what each intends to prove, and a brief summary of the nature of the supporting evidence. Such a statement enables the arbitrator to follow the testimony with more comprehension.

CLARIFYING BACKGROUND DATA. During the opening statements and the initial stages of the hearing, the parties often fail to recognize that the arbitrator is the only one in the room who has not been previously involved in the grievance. They overlook the fact that he has no knowledge of the names, titles, and relationships of the various people involved. He may not have any information on the product produced, the names of machines involved, the layout of the plant, and other information that may be pertinent to the issue. Because everyone in the room other than the arbitrator has this information, it is unconsciously assumed that the arbitrator has it also. Even when this background information is presented to the arbitrator it is often done in a perfunctory manner. In one case, the author, while acting as arbitrator, could not understand the evidence because the parties failed to indicate that the work station of the grievant was a metal cage suspended from a ceiling about 20 feet high.

Almost every plant has its own shop language, which is obvious and clear to those who know it but unintelligible to an arbitrator unless he happens to be familiar with the industry. For instance, in the printing industry, reference is made to "dark jobs." In certain types of restaurants people called "cashiers" do not do the work normally considered as cashiers' work; this is done by other individuals who are called "checkers." If the word "cashier" is used, the arbitrator will naturally assume that the work performed is that normally done by cashiers, and this erroneous conclusion may affect his decision. The arbitrator has the right to expect the parties to define their terms when they use shop language. Moreover, since it is frequently difficult and sometimes almost impossible to give an accurate word picture, the parties should arrange to have the arbitrator visit the plant and view the operation.

RECORDING OF EVIDENCE. After the opening statements are made, each side presents witnesses who give testimony. If the parties do not provide the arbitrator with a stenographic transcript, they must allow sufficient time for the arbitrator to make detailed notes. Even though most arbitrators can recall from memory much of the essential evidence, they cannot register miscellaneous details in tape-recorder fashion. Moreover, it is not easy, even for experienced arbitrators, to visualize and absorb immediately a complicated situation.

WEIGHING THE EVIDENCE. When a witness is testifying, the arbitrator looks for those facts that are directly known by the witness. He considers hearsay evidence to be weak evidence. Moreover, the arbitrator is not particularly interested in the witness's opinion unless he is qualified as an expert to give an opinion. From an arbitrator's point of view, a conclusion expressed by a witness should, whenever possible, be supported by documentary proof. For instance, a foreman may testify that the grievant is a poor worker or is always late or absent. The arbitrator is interested in production records, reject or scrap records, or lateness and attendance records to support the conclusions expressed by the foreman. Some foremen and supervisors are insulted by what appears to them to be a questioning of their honesty and integrity when documentary proof is sought by the arbitrator. They do not know that the judicial process requires this procedure.

INTERPRETATION OF EVIDENCE. Witnesses are not aware that their generalizations about a worker may be based upon some isolated recent incident. For instance, if three weeks previously an employee was late on two consecutive days and his lateness held up production, his foreman may testify that he is always late, when in fact the records may show that he is very seldom late. The arbitrator will recognize this not necessarily as an attempt to maliciously distort the facts but as a natural emotional reaction. Experienced arbitrators are aware that a witness tends to remember only those events that are favorable to him and that he seldom reveals the whole truth. When such a witness is testifying, the arbitrator may be called upon to evaluate his credibility. This is frequently a difficult task, but the manner in which a man testifies and the consistency of his evidence (particularly the details) are important factors in determining credibility.

Witnesses frequently express conclusions based upon unspoken and unconscious assumptions. For instance, a foreman may come to the conclusion that an employee was insubordinate. This conclusion may be based upon a subconscious assumption that an employee must show proper respect for his superior. Whether an act is considered by a person to be insubordinate may well depend upon his patterns of thought regarding what he considers the proper relationship between an employee and his foreman. An act may be considered insubordinate by one person and not by another. Some foremen are unaware of different and changing concepts, and assume that their patterns of thinking are correct and universally held.

On the other hand, an antagonistic employee will interpret a casual remark by a supervisor as having special meaning, detrimental to him, when in fact none was intended. He will then relate some act to this remark and testify with conviction that the act was directed toward him. Unfortunately, most persons are unaware of their subconscious assumptions and emotional reactions, and this lack of perception leads them to erroneous conclusions.

The arbitrator must examine all assumptions, particularly as they relate to labor–management relations. He must be alert to the fluid nature of industrial relations concepts. What are commonly accepted principles today may be modified in the future.

REFERENCES

1. Harry Shulman, "Reason, Contract and Law in Labor Relations." *Harv. L. Rev.*, 68 (1955), p. 999. Quoted with approval by the United States Supreme Court in United Steelworkers of America v. Warrior and Gulf Navigation Co., 46 LRRM 2416 (1960).
2. "Grievance Procedures," *United States Department of Labor, Bulletin No. 1425*, November 1964, p. 1.
3. "The President's National Labor-Management Conference, November 5–30, 1945." *Division of Labor Standards Bulletin 77*. Washington, D.C.: U.S. Department of Labor, 1946, pp. 45, 46.
4. Willard Lewis, "Arbitrating a Wildcat Strike." *Harv. Bus. Rev.* (July 1949).

3

ARBITRATION TRIBUNALS

Several different forms of arbitration tribunals have been developed. The major types are the ad hoc (for this case alone) arbitrator, the permanent arbitrator, and the tripartite board of arbitration. In addition, special mention should be made of the arbitration tribunals established under the Railway Labor Act.

The Ad Hoc Arbitrator

The most common form of arbitration tribunal is the single ad hoc arbitrator selected by the parties after a dispute has arisen to hear one case or a group of cases. He may be selected frequently by the same parties, but he has no prearranged relationship with them. Generally speaking, the largest number of arbitration awards are made by ad hoc arbitrators; they are most often used by parties who have relatively few issues to arbitrate.

ADVANTAGES. The temporary arbitrator offers certain advantages. For one thing, if a dispute about technical problems arises, an arbitrator with special training and knowledge may be selected. A good example is a case dealing with wage incentives. In such a matter it is not unusual for the parties to choose an industrial engineer. Or, because of legal issues, they may prefer to have a lawyer as an arbitrator. Furthermore, it is less expensive to engage a temporary arbitrator if disputes requiring arbitration are few and far between.

DISADVANTAGES. The fact that the ad hoc arbitrator serves in a temporary capacity* may also present a number of disadvantages. Since his time is limited, he cannot go very deeply into important background considerations. At best, his knowledge of the company, its management–union relations, and the industry and its customs and practices will be limited. This may have an important bearing on the ability of the arbitrator to write an award that the parties can live with.

Reasonable men may differ in their interpretation of the same set of facts or contract clauses. Therefore the danger of conflicting decisions is ever present if ad hoc arbitrators are used. As one writer put it, "An award

---

* His job is done when he renders the award. From that moment on, he has discharged all his responsibility and has no further connection with the case.

36

by one temporary arbitrator may have so little precedential force as viewed by a subsequent arbitrator that the latter will decide contra." [1]

It is a rare human being who can see the wisdom and sterling virtues of an arbitrator who has decided a case against him. Losing parties are known to maneuver the same issue (or a slightly disguised version) before another arbitrator in the hope of winning a favorable award.

SELECTING THE ARBITRATOR. Ad hoc arbitrators may be selected by the parties or appointed by a third person. In many instances they are selected by the parties themselves, who may agree on a particular person and communicate directly with him. More often, the parties, in accordance with the arbitration clause in the contract, request the American Arbitration Association (AAA), the Federal Mediation and Conciliation Service (FMCS), or a state Board of Mediation to provide them with a panel (usually with 5 to 11 names) of arbitrators from which a selection can be made.

There are three basic methods of selecting an arbitrator from a list of names. The first is by simple agreement; the second is by a system of rating or ranking; and the third is by a process of direct elimination.

The method of simple agreement is self-explanatory. The parties agree on one person, he is notified, and (if he accepts) that ends the problem of selection.

Under the rating or ranking method, each side independently rates every man on the list by placing a number alongside his name. Thus, if there were 11 names, the arbitrator most preferred would be rated number 1. The number 11 would be put next to the name of the man least desired. The agency handling this matter for the parties would then add the number assigned by the union to the number indicated by the company. The name with the lowest score would then be selected as arbitrator.

The direct elimination process has several variations. Each party alternately crosses off one name from a list of five (or other odd number) until one name remains. That person is selected as the arbitrator. By another method, each party to the arbitration proceeding independently strikes out the names of those who are unacceptable. The agency (AAA, FMCS, or state board) then selects an arbitrator from the names remaining. A third method combines the first two by ranking the names not eliminated; and choosing an arbitrator from those ranked highest. If all the names on the panel are unacceptable, a second or even a third list may be sent to the parties. If these, too, do not include acceptable names, the agency itself will designate the arbitrator without further circulation of lists, but the person chosen would be one whose name was not previously submitted.

Sometimes the parties do not select the arbitrator but rely on a third person or an arbitration agency to designate one. Occasionally, a judge or a prominent public official such as the U.S. Secretary of Labor may be selected by the parties to designate the arbitrator. A number of collective bargaining agreements name the person authorized to make such a selection.

The Permanent Arbitrator

The permanent arbitrator is usually appointed for the life of the contract on a full-time or part-time (as needed) basis to deal continuously with such disputes as may arise requiring arbitral decision. The ad hoc arbitrator completes his responsibility when he renders an award in the case assigned, usually within 30 days after the close of the hearing.

When the permanent arbitrator sits alone, he is frequently called an *impartial umpire*. When he is the single impartial member of a board of arbitration (the others being the partisan representatives of labor and management, respectively), he is generally referred to as an *impartial chairman*. However, there is no uniform nomenclature.

The title "permanent arbitrator" should not mislead the unsophisticated into believing that such an arbitrator cannot be removed under any circumstances. To the contrary, his tenure of office is limited by contract or depends on the will of the parties.

While it is true that the so-called permanent arbitrator is selected to serve for a period of time, unlike the ad hoc arbitrator who is limited to one case or a group of cases, his "term of office" can end abruptly even before the period of time has run out. For example, the Ford agreement provides that "the services of the . . . Impartial Umpire may be terminated at any time by either party. . . ." The General Motors umpire holds his office only as long as "he continues to be acceptable to both parties." [2] Although no actual survey has been made, it is unlikely that many permanent arbitrators have been dismissed before their allotted time has expired. The point is made here to emphasize the fact that the possibility of removal is always present.

THE MEN WHO SERVE. Many arbitrators, whether ad hoc or permanent, are associated with colleges and universities as teachers of industrial relations, labor economics, or law. Some are lawyers by profession who spend most of their time practicing law and only occasionally sit as arbitrator in an arbitration case. Many have served on government boards such as the National War Labor Board and state and federal mediation boards. Most arbitrators are on the panels of the American Arbitration Association, the Federal Mediation and Conciliation Service, and various state boards of mediation. A number of experienced arbitrators handle labor–management disputes exclusively.

Advantages

One of the most important considerations in favor of the permanent arbitrator is that he has the time to become thoroughly familiar with the company and the union, their personalities, problems, practices, and general relationship. He is also in a position to learn a great deal about the industry for which he is permanent arbitrator. This background knowledge often has an important bearing on a labor dispute and on any decision rendered to settle it.

Because of his continuous dealings with the parties, an important function that a permanent arbitrator can perform is that of providing a coherent body of principles to guide them in their day-to-day relations. In this connection, the late Dr. George W. Taylor, who served for many years as an impartial chairman, once observed that a permanent arbitrator is a prime requisite for stability in industrial relations. "Out of the continuing relationship," he said, "consistent policy and mutually acceptable procedures can gradually be evolved." [3]

The author's experience as impartial chairman in the restaurant industry in New York City since 1943, supports the conclusions of Dr. Taylor. During the period 1943 to 1949, two to four cases were submitted to me for arbitration almost every week. Practically every clause in the master agreement between the Affiliated Restaurateurs, Inc., and the Cafeteria Employees Union, Local 302, was subject to dispute and had to be interpreted. Practically all discharges were hotly contested. The arbitrations were held on neutral ground in a hotel room, even though the employers' association had adequate facilities for hearings. The relations between the parties could hardly have been described as harmonious.

But gradually the number of issues submitted to arbitration declined, and many of the discharge and discipline cases, as well as other disputes, were settled between the parties themselves. Relations between the parties improved and they agreed to hold arbitration hearings in the association offices. The reasons for the improvement were the high caliber of the representatives of both the employers' association and the union, and the fact that the hundreds of cases decided in arbitration constituted a body of precedent and principles to which the parties could refer. The interpretation of controversial clauses in the contract and the awards rendered in discipline and discharge cases served as a guide for the settlement (prior to arbitration) of subsequent cases. As a result, the arbitration case load has been considerably reduced.

One of the chief advantages of having a permanent arbitrator is the speed with which a case can be heard and decided. In the first place, no time is lost in selecting the arbitrator and setting a hearing date agreeable to the parties. Secondly, since he is already familiar with the parties and the industry, the arbitrator requires less time to grasp the various aspects of the case. Hearings need not be quite so long as they sometimes are when conducted by the ad hoc arbitrator. Thirdly, if the guiding principles have already been developed in previous cases, a long opinion is not necessary, and an award may be sufficient. These items add up to the saving of valuable time. Obviously, then, it is less costly to have a permanent arbitrator when the parties have a large number of disputes.

Prevalence of Permanent Arbitrators

Because so little has been written about the work of permanent arbitrators, the extent to which their services are used is not generally known. In the New York metropolitan area alone, about 30 impartial chairmanships have been established. There are more than 300 permanent arbitrator arrangements throughout the country, according to a rough estimate. Some of the largest corporations, such as General Motors, Bethlehem Steel, U.S. Steel, International Harvester, Swift and Co., Goodyear Tire & Rubber, and North American Aviation have established the office of impartial chairman in agreements with unions representing their employees.

Many collective bargaining agreements between employers' associations and unions contain impartial chairman arrangements. A master agreement exists in the garment industry, for example, between the Clothing Manufacturers Association and the Amalgamated Clothing Workers; this agreement sets up conventional grievance machinery and provides that "any and all matters in dispute which have not been adjusted . . . shall be referred for arbitration and final determination to the Impartial Chairman."

The hotel industry in New York City has also established permanent arbitration machinery. The master agreement between the Hotel Association of New York City, Inc., and the New York Hotel Trade Council, AFL–CIO, provides that all disputes shall be submitted to a "labor manager," appointed and employed by the association, and "a duly accredited representative" of the union. Acting jointly, the two appointees consider the grievance and make an adjustment. Their decision is binding on both parties. In the event that they do not agree, the contract provides that:

> The question in dispute shall be referred to a permanent umpire to be known as the Impartial Chairman, and his decision shall be final and binding upon the parties hereto. . . . The decision rendered by the Impartial Chairman shall have the effect of a judgment entered upon an award made, as provided by the Arbitration Laws of the State of New York, entitling the entry of judgment in a court of competent jurisdiction against the defaulting party who fails to carry out or abide by such a decision.

A number of employers' associations have been organized by businesses employing relatively few workers, their object being to equalize bargaining strength because of the necessity of negotiating with a large union. A good example is the Affiliated Restaurateurs, Inc., whose membership consists of more than 100 large cafeterias in the City of New York. A committee representing the Association negotiates a master agreement with the Cafeteria Employees Union, Local 302. This agreement covers about 3,000 employees who work in the cafeterias of the members; it also sets patterns of wages for all other unionized cafeterias in the City.

In 1938 a contract was negotiated by the Affiliated Restaurateurs and Local 302, which provided for an impartial chairman to hear and settle disputes. Prior to this time, if an employer wished to discharge an employee he had to appear before the executive board of the union and plead his case. The union rendered the decision. The first impartial chairman served from 1938 to 1943, when the second permanent arbitrator was selected and still continues to serve.

Before a case is presented to the impartial chairman, the manager of the Affiliated Restaurateurs (or his representative) meets with a representative of the union. They confer with the particular employer and employee involved, the latter being accompanied by his shop steward. A serious attempt to settle the dispute is made, but if this fails the case goes to arbitration. Often the attorneys for the employer and the union make another effort to settle when they meet with the parties at the arbitration hearing. It is not unusual for a case to be settled after the hearing has been held and the essential facts in the case have been fully disclosed. Obviously, this eliminates the necessity for a decision by the arbitrator.

The current contract between the Affiliated Restaurateurs and the Cafeteria Employees Union is quoted below at some length because it provides important detail on the workings of the office of impartial chairman:

It is . . . agreed . . . that . . . all disputes which may arise under this contract between the contracting parties hereto, between the Union and any of the employers who are members of the Association . . . shall be submitted to arbitration to [name], who shall be the Impartial Chairman . . . and his decision on all matters shall be final and binding on both parties.

Any matter in dispute . . . may be submitted by either party to said [name] by serving notice in writing upon the other party setting forth the matter in dispute and asking that arbitration be held as soon as possible, the date to be set by the Impartial Chairman.

It is the intention of the parties hereto that the Impartial Chairman shall set aside one afternoon each week for the purpose of hearing all disputes between the parties, and both parties agree that all disputes which may have arisen between the last date of arbitration and the following date shall be submitted upon such day. The Impartial Chairman shall have the right to establish the rules of procedure, shall have the right to hear witnesses, subpoena witnesses, and at his discretion, shall have the right to keep or not to keep stenographic records of the meetings. All decisions shall be in writing and copies thereof shall be served upon the Association and the Union. Both parties hereto waive any oath by the Impartial Chairman, and all future submissions need not be signed by either party. Mere service of written notice of the desire to submit shall be sufficient to bring the matter on for arbitration.

•　　•　　•

In the event, for any reason whatsoever, the Impartial Chairman is incapacitated and cannot act as Impartial Chairman under this agreement, both parties shall meet within five (5) days after such incapacity, and shall attempt to agree upon an Impartial Chairman. If they cannot agree within three (3) days thereafter, the New York State Mediation Board shall be called upon to name an arbitrator who shall thereupon become the Impartial Chairman for the balance of the time during which the Impartial Chairman named herein shall remain incapacitated.

The Union agrees to take proper steps to see to it that any obligation on its part under the decision of the Impartial Chairman as hereinabove provided, shall be carried out, and the Association agrees that should any member of the Association fail to comply with the decision of such Impartial Chairman, such member will then, upon the request of the Union, be expelled from the Association; and it is further agreed by the Association and the employer that the Union may terminate this agreement as to any employer who fails to abide by the decision of the Impartial Chairman above referred to, or who fails to observe the terms and conditions of this contract.

•   •   •

. . . There shall be no strike or stoppage during the life of this agreement, except for the refusal of the employer to obey the decision of the Impartial Chairman, and there shall be no lockout except for the refusal of the Union to obey the decision of the Impartial Chairman.

Powers and Functions of Permanent Arbitrators*

Basically, the arbitrator's authority derives from the collective bargaining agreement or submission agreement executed by the parties and from existing arbitration law. The important point to remember is that the agreement of the parties creates the power of the arbitrator. In the words "and his decision shall be final and binding upon the parties" lies the source of the arbitrator's authority.

The arbitrator's power is not comparable to that of a judge in a court of law. The latter is a public officer vested with authority that stems from the sovereignty of a state. Among other things, he can impose penalties for contempt and for violations of law; he can issue subpoenas and enforce compliance with them. The arbitrator's power is simply the authority to settle a dispute and determine the disputants' course of action by the "final and binding" nature of his decision.

What has been said above about the powers of an arbitrator applies equally to both ad hoc and permanent arbitrators. An important difference between them may arise with respect to their functions. The ad hoc arbitrator acts essentially in a judicial capacity; that is, he hears the evidence presented by each side and renders an award. Often the permanent arbitrator will be called upon to mediate a dispute; he tries to effect a reconciliation between the disputing parties, acting as an unbiased friend of each. If mediation fails, the parties proceed to arbitration as the last resort. It is not unusual for the parties who created the office to seek the advice of an impartial chairman in a wide variety of industry problems. Obviously, when a permanent arbitrator wins the full confidence of labor and management, he is in a position to be extremely helpful to both. This is regarded by many

---

* This subject is explored at length in Chapter 6, "Powers of the Arbitrator." Sometimes the parties agree to confer upon the arbitrator (see above section quoted from Affiliated Restaurateurs–Cafeteria Employees Contract) power to subpoena witnesses. In any case, the labor laws of most states empower arbitrators to subpoena witnesses.

as one of the chief advantages of the permanent arbitrator over the ad hoc type.

There is, however, no unanimity of opinion as to the desirability of mediation by an individual selected to serve as an arbitrator. Some believe that the arbitrator impairs his usefulness when he attempts to settle the dispute by mediation. Dr. George W. Taylor, an ardent advocate of mediation by an impartial chairman, agreed that this technique cannot be used in all cases but only "when both parties see eye-to-eye on the point." Certainly, the disputing parties who have set up permanent arbitration machinery should spell out clearly what they expect from the arbitrator. If they want his help as a mediator first, they should say so; if they do not, they should state this clearly.

In many instances the parties set forth in detail the powers and limitations of the arbitrator. A good example is the following clause from a Production Maintenance Contract between the International Harvester Company and the United Farm Equipment and Metal Workers (UE):

> The function of the arbitrator shall be of a judicial rather than a legislative nature. He shall not have power to add to, ignore or to modify any of the terms and conditions of this agreement. His decisions shall not go beyond what is necessary to interpret and as interpreted, apply the provisions of this contract to the settlement of the grievance before him.

In short, the powers and functions of the permanent arbitrator vary from industry to industry. The powers that he exercises are determined by the parties that appoint him. What the parties expect from him depends, in the final analysis, upon three factors: the conditions that created the need for a neutral "outsider" to act as permanent arbitrator, the attitudes of the key representatives of labor and management, and the personality of the arbitrator himself.

Time Spent and Fees

The pattern of time spent by permanent arbitrators in the actual work of arbitration varies, and their remuneration also varies. In a few industries, the impartial chairman spends his entire time arbitrating for one industry. In most instances he devotes only a portion of his time to his duties as impartial chairman for one company and union or in a particular industry. Sometimes he acts as permanent arbitrator for several industries and also as an ad hoc arbitrator as cases arise requiring his services. Some arbitrators who are on the teaching staffs at universities set aside one day a week for the hearing of disputes. The needs of the parties constitute the chief determinant of the amount of time a permanent arbitrator devotes to his duties as impartial chairman or umpire. Because of the variation in the amount of time demanded, the financial arrangements also vary considerably. In all instances, however, payment of the arbitrator's fee is shared equally between the company or association and the union.

Permanent Arbitration Systems

Permanent arbitration systems have grown steadily in recent years and have become a significant factor in stabilizing labor relations. Papers that describe the origin, development, and operation of these systems have been written by permanent arbitrators and presented at the annual meetings of the National Academy of Arbitrators. At the Eleventh Annual Meeting of the Academy, David A. Wolff, the permanent arbitrator, presented a paper describing the umpire system of Chrysler–United Automobile, Aircraft and Implement Workers of America (UAW).[4] A discussion of the Chrysler–UAW system follows.

The Chrysler–UAW System

The umpire system for Chrysler–UAW production and maintenance employees came into being with the parties' agreement reached in 1943. Earlier agreements had established several grievance steps that were similar to those contained in most collective bargaining contracts. In a 1939 agreement an appeals board had been created, composed of two executives of the corporation and two representatives of the International Union, but having no impartial fifth member. This early appeals board, meeting in closed sessions, settled a substantial number of grievances. A degree of objectivity was provided by ruling that board members were to be managers of plants not involved in the particular grievances before the board, and were to include also the International representatives who had been with the local unions other than those directly concerned in the proceedings. Although it was a step forward, it was not an ideal one because board members found it difficult to act in a capacity other than advocate for their respective interests.

Immediately after the start of World War II, representatives of organized labor and industry met in the Labor–Management Conference called by the President in 1941. It was agreed to refrain from strikes and lockouts for the duration of the war emergency and to refer disputed issues to the National War Labor Board for final decision. The Board encouraged the use of private arbitration as a terminal point in the application of agreements.

In 1942 the UAW submitted proposals to the Chrysler Corporation, including demands for maintenance of membership and dues check-off, and for "a standing impartial umpire . . . whose jurisdiction and duties shall be to decide all grievances and disputes arising under the provisions of the collective bargaining agreement." When these demands were rejected, the resulting dispute was certified to the National War Labor Board (NWLB).

In a 1943 directive order, the NWLB referred specified "minor" issues back to the parties and denied the union's request for maintenance of membership and check-off. The order specified that:

The present grievance procedure shall be supplemented by the appointment of an *impartial chairman to the appeal board.* The union and company representatives of the appeal board shall attempt to settle all grievances properly referred to the board. In the event that they are unable to settle the matters, the chairman shall make decisions which shall be final and binding.

In its accompanying opinion the Board noted the large number of strikes at the Corporation's plants after 1941 as evidence that "the grievance procedure at Chrysler is not functioning properly." It also referred to its policy statement issued in 1943, "calling upon parties in collective bargaining agreements to work out a terminal point for the handling of grievances over the interpretation and application of agreements." [4]

The Board said that the impartial chairman should be employed on a continuing basis, that cases "shall be determined by decision of the impartial chairman and not by a majority vote of the [appeal] board," [4] and that "the impartial chairman shall have the right, however, to participate in all discussions and meetings of the appeal board and shall also have the duty of assisting the parties in resolving particular questions." [4]

In their efforts to work out a satisfactory and practical implementation of the directive order, the parties held meetings with the NWLB representative, who later became the impartial chairman. It was agreed that much of the old system should be retained and that the majority of grievances could be worked out by the parties through collective bargaining. Accordingly, some basic understandings were arrived at: definite restrictions were to be placed on the types of cases subject to arbitration; the impartial chairman was to serve on a continuing but part-time basis, was to be called upon to determine only a limited number of cases, and was not to function as part of the normal collective bargaining process; the facts, issues, and arguments in all cases were first to be fully investigated, disclosed, and discussed by the parties' appeal board representatives, meeting without the chairman; the parties themselves were to attempt to dispose of cases without calling upon the chairman. Cases requiring determination by the chairman were to be presented to him in appellate proceedings, without the presence of witnesses or others. Decisions by the impartial chairman were to be in strict accordance with the provisions of the parties' agreements, and were to serve as guides to the parties in their bargaining in other situations.

LIMITED POWER AND AUTHORITY. Like most parties to a collective bargaining agreement, neither the corporation nor the union has wanted to make certain types of issues arbitrable. Thus, during the entire period of the system, the authority delegated to the appeal board and the chairman was limited generally to correct classification of employees and the application and interpretation of the provisions of the agreement. This limitation has been reinforced by a further prohibition that the appeal board chairman "shall not have authority to add to or subtract from or to modify any of the terms of the agreement or to establish or change any wage or rate of pay," and by additional restrictions in certain specific areas.

Although the NWLB chairman favored the right of arbitrators to modify penalties in disciplinary cases, the parties to the agreement had not given him such authority. Therefore, in his opinion, he could not substitute his judgment as to penalty. As a result, most of the penalties imposed in early disciplinary cases were either wholly sustained or wholly rescinded, but not reduced.

In 1945 the Chairman was expressly empowered "in proper cases" to modify "penalties assessed by the management in disciplinary discharges and layoffs." [4] This authority was continued thereafter in all agreements. However, the parties retained a contractual clause prohibiting the Chairman from approving back pay to employees who violated the strikes and lockouts section of the agreement.

A 1955 agreement changed the Chairman's power and authority over production standards. Even though he could no longer concern himself with the matter of production rates, he could determine whether the rate of production on a job was too fast. The 1955 agreement rescinded this authority and provided that "the Chairman must refer back to the parties, without decision, any case on which he has no power to rule." [4]

CASE VOLUME. While the umpire system existed, the number of covered employees ranged approximately from 80,000 to 140,000. The number of decisions issued annually decreased from 23 to 15 in the next ten years and was as few as 12 in 1957. This low case volume was a result of the basic view that parties should work out their own problems without resort to arbitration. The participants in the Chrysler–UAW system believed that a few well-chosen key cases would serve as models for settling unresolved issues without appealing to the umpire. This viewpoint was expressed as:

Many of the concrete factors which have tended to restrict the number of cases requiring arbitration, are treated in some detail (in other connections) elsewhere in this study. Some of the more important of these have been the presence of an Agreement-provided "declaratory judgment" procedure for securing determinations of basic issues in advance of actual grievance situations, the efficient functioning of the appeal board in its pre-arbitration sessions, and the parties' intelligent use of the chairman's (umpire's) decisions. Other measures and methods have been devised to help avoid an excessive use of the arbitration process.[4]

THE USE OF PRECEDENT. In every case the Chairman made a careful review of all previous decisions relevant to the one being heard. His findings were based on earlier cases. Frequently, patterns and standards evolved gradually on a case-by-case basis, with determinations being made on unprecedented aspects of a particular problem. Contract provisions were uniformly applied until the parties themselves negotiated changes. Consistent application was sought as a matter of fairness and to promote predictability and workability in the parties' collective bargaining relationships. In this way a body of case law was built up.

The parties applied the principles of the decisions in other arbitration cases and in their day-to-day relationships. At the local levels, the parties attempted to make plant practices conform to principles announced in umpire decisions. They referred to decided cases when working out problems. These practices had a noticeable impact on screening or settlement of subsequent cases and were often considered and discussed during succeeding contract negotiations.

PROBLEM AREAS COVERED. Decisions issued by the Chairman covered most of the problem areas normally involved in the administration of a labor-management contract. Most of the cases concerned disciplinary action and matters involving the classification of employees. These cases dealt primarily with factual questions and applications of basic principles to particular situations. The majority of cases occurred during the first five years of the system.

THE IMPARTIAL CHAIRMAN AND HIS ROLE. The impartial chairman served on a part-time basis only, and his compensation depended on the cases decided by him. He paid his own expenses and maintained his own office and staff.

The chairman participated only in those cases referred to him for decision, and acted only as an arbitrator and not as a mediator or labor relations advisor. Matters submitted to him for decision were not referred back to the parties for compromise or further bargaining unless the appeal board lacked power to make a substantive ruling (in which case, of course, referral was mandatory). His findings and order were grounded upon the facts of the particular case and the provisions of the Agreement.

Pending issues were never discussed when only one party was present. However, the chairman could advise on procedural problems and discuss cases in which decisions had been issued.

CONCLUSIONS. In most areas of labor–management relations, the aims and interests of the parties in an umpire system are seldom precisely co-extensive. but they do have two objectives in common: (1) retention and strengthening of the collective bargaining processes through which they are able to work out their own problems; and (2) an expeditious procedure for final, orderly, and impartial settlement of disputes.

Methods and procedures of the umpire system were calculated to emphasize the parties' own collective bargaining responsibilities. The system's success in this respect was demonstrated by the low case volume and avoidance of arbitration in cases that did not need determination by a third person. During the operation of the system, many basic issues were settled. A number of the guides and principles established then have been applied to new problems, which are the inevitable product of each era and phase of development. A real sense of stability was due to the knowledge that the

system offered a readily accessible terminal point for disputes not disposed
of at the bargaining table. This achievement was noted in the study of the
umpire system:

> The extent to which the objectives of the parties are capable of being met, and
> have been met, by their umpire system, may be indicated through a study of the
> foregoing description of the system itself, and, in some measure at least, by its
> having endured in substantially the same form and principle through a relatively
> long and eventful period. Of course, longevity in an umpire system is not an
> automatic sign of perfection. However, it should serve as some evidence of the
> system's workability and acceptance.

> It seems fair to conclude that the Chrysler-U.A.W. umpire system has worked,
> and worked well, for both the Union and the Company. It contains much which
> should merit thoughtful consideration by others. Nevertheless, to say that any
> identical, or even substantially similar, system would be right for any other parties,
> would be both presumptuous and unwise. Each system of arbitration must reflect
> the concepts of the parties which it serves. Each must be adapted to the desires of
> the particular company and union in the context of their relationship." [4]

The Chrysler–UAW and Ford–UAW Systems: A Comparison

The Chrysler–UAW permanent arbitration system is not typical of all
umpire systems. A number of other large and well-known companies have
had somewhat different types of permanent arbitration agreements.

The policies and procedures developed by each system have been the
result of the history of the relationships between the parties, their particular
needs, and the personalities of the representatives of management and labor
and the impartial umpire.

A comparison of the Chrysler and Ford umpire systems discloses many
fundamental differences, the most noteworthy of which is the number of
cases heard and decided under the two respective systems. In one year, for
example, only 12 decisions were made under the Chrysler–UAW system,
whereas 435 cases were handled under the Ford–UAW system. This vast
difference cannot be explained in terms of the number of employees covered
by the contract or the stability of labor relations. After hearing David A.
Wolff[4] describe the Chrysler–UAW permanent arbitration system at the
Eleventh Annual Meeting of the National Academy of Arbitrators, Harry
H. Platt, the umpire under the Ford–UAW agreement, discussed, analyzed,
and compared in detail the two systems. A study of his remarks shows the
basic differences in the operation of these systems.

> There has been a good deal of speculation as to the reasons for the vast dif-
> ference in the volume of umpire cases in the Big Three automobile companies.
> Some people have suggested that this may be due, in part at last, to the rigid pre-
> arbitration union screening procedures that exist in the other companies but not
> at Ford; others attribute it to the manner in which the parties investigate and
> prepare their cases before they come to arbitration; and still others believe it
> may be due to differences of philosophy and content of umpire decisions.[5]

THE UMPIRE CASE LOAD. Chrysler and General Motors *always* had a relatively small umpire case load, whereas Ford *always* had a relatively large umpire case load. Traditionally, Chrysler employees were accustomed to having their grievances judged in the light of pertinent precedents, whereas Ford employees were accustomed to having their grievances judged by the umpire on the merits of individual cases. Chrysler employees had their grievance appeals screened by a committee of local union presidents, but Ford employees looked to their own union locals to decide if their grievances merited review by the umpire. Patterns of conduct thus developed in grievance administration and became embedded in the parties' relationship. The significant fact is that traditional practice greatly influenced the umpire's case load.

FORMALITY AT HEARINGS. Comparing experiences at Ford and Chrysler demonstrates the relationship between case load and other characteristics of the umpire and board systems. The Appeal Board hearings at Chrysler were more formal and excluded supervisors and workers. The impartial chairman did not inspect affected plant areas or operations. Thus, the lower echelons were not familiar with the arbitration processes, and did not pursue them.

SETTLEMENT OF GRIEVANCES. A grievance was seldom, if ever, settled at Chrysler after arbitration had begun. Matters submitted for decision were not referred back to the parties for compromise or further bargaining unless the appeal board lacked power to rule on them. At Ford, cases were settled by the parties after the arbitration hearing had begun, some at the suggestion of the umpire and others because the presentation developed new facts that led the parties to reconsider their earlier positions and adjust the grievance amicably. This might seem to reflect upon the adequacy of case presentation so that a larger number of unsubstantiated grievances would be appealed to the Ford umpire and thus increase case load. Actually, grievances presented before the umpire de novo often disclosed an underlying misunderstanding that might have blocked an earlier settlement, or the hearing uncovered new thoughts, new facts, and occasionally new areas of agreement that provided real opportunities for constructive settlements.

CONDUCT OF HEARINGS. Aside from considerations of case load, other features of the Chrysler–UAW system inhibited disposition of grievances. Hearings were attended only by the chairman and two appeal board members who acted as advocates for their principals; all witnesses, including the aggrieved employee, were excluded from the hearing; and the chairman never saw the principals involved in the grievances. This was unlike other arbitration systems in which the grievant is permitted to participate in the hearing, with his witnesses and the company's witnesses allowed to testify orally and be cross-examined. Where conflicting versions of a particular event are testified to, the opportunity to examine and cross-examine a witness is most important.

RELATIVE FLEXIBILITY OF THE SYSTEMS. The Chrysler–UAW system was a "strict arbitration" system in which the chairman acted as a "final impartial court of appeal." According to Harry Platt:

> It is not altogether clear . . . what is meant by a "strict arbitration" system. Is it a system in which the chairman acts wholly outside the union–management relationship and only to redress past wrongs, as a court does? . . . Grievance arbitration, as George Taylor once said, is very handy. Yet it is a flexible process. And if a strict appeal procedure best suits the needs and tastes of some parties, then by all means they should adopt a strict procedure. . . . Many parties conceive their permanent umpire systems as mechanisms suitable not merely for resolving a particular stalemate but suitable for continuation of the parties' efforts at mutual understanding of their problems and suitable for developing the collective bargaining process. With this concept of arbitration, a strict appeal and hearing procedure such as that under the Chrysler–UAW system would be an anomaly.[5]

The Deere & Company–UAW System

While permanent arbitration systems generally follow a basic pattern, some systems have unusual deviations, which have been most effective and satisfactory in their operation. A noteworthy example is the system in effect between Deere & Company and the United Automobile, Aircraft and Implement Workers of America.

The first collective bargaining agreement was negotiated in 1943, but it did not provide for arbitration. In the 1945 agreement, grievance arbitration was introduced for the first time on an ad hoc basis. The contract was amended in 1946 to provide for permanent arbitration.

JURISDICTION OF ARBITRATOR LIMITED. At the Tenth Annual Meeting of the National Academy of Arbitrators, Harold W. Davey, who has served as permanent arbitrator, discussed the significant and unusual features of the system. Following are some of his remarks.

> The permanent arbitrator's authority and jurisdiction have always been carefully defined. No contract has ever provided for unlimited arbitration. However, there has been some variation in the scope of the arbitrator's jurisdiction. In early contracts, the arbitrator had authority to rule on issues over the propriety of piece rates and rates on new hourly or incentive jobs. The permanent arbitrator's authority was made congruent with a comprehensive no strike–no lockout clause in these contracts.
> In the 1950–55 contracts, however, the arbitrator was specifically precluded from ruling on piece rates and rates on new jobs. In the 1955–1958 contracts, the arbitrator's authority is expanded to cover certain incentive grievances alleging improper standards. However, his new authority is strictly circumscribed as follows:
> "The jurisdiction of the Arbitrator is specifically limited and restricted to the sole determination of the following questions:
> (1) Was there a clerical error in the computation of the Incentive Standard, or

(2) Was there a change in design, equipment, material specifications or manufacturing methods, and/or (3) If there was a change in design, equipment, material specifications or manufacturing methods, what elements were changed?

In addition to the foregoing narrow questions, the arbitrator can also hear grievances on incentive standards which question whether the standard was established in conformance with the Standard Hour Incentive Plan or which raise the question "of the adequacy or inadequacy of the standard."

In the first year under the 1955–1958 contracts, no disputes reached arbitration under these headings.

The 1955–1958 contracts specifically exclude four categories of grievances from the arbitrator's jurisdiction. These same categories are not covered by the contracts' no strike–no lockout clauses. The four excluded categories are: (1) changes in existing incentive standards, except for disputes of the type just described, (2) establishment of new incentive standards, (3) rate ranges for new hourly paid job classifications, and (4) occupational rates for new incentive work job classifications.[6]

JUDICIAL ARBITRATION. In addition to a careful definition of the arbitrator's jurisdiction, the parties had a clear and detailed grievance procedure. It provided for regular weekly meetings and time limitations at each step in the grievance procedure. The arbitrator was not expected to act as a mediator; the parties requested "judicial" arbitration. When a case was presented to the arbitrator and all attempts at settlement had failed, the parties assumed that it was the arbitrator's function to render a clear-cut decision based on an interpretation and application of the provisions of the collective bargaining agreement. The effectiveness of the system was attested by the fact that relatively few cases went to arbitration. In 1956, a typical year, only 24 cases were arbitrated.

Tripartite Board of Arbitration

The tripartite board usually consists of three members: representatives of the company and the union, and an impartial member, who acts as the chairman. Some collective bargaining agreements provide for a five-man board, which consists of an impartial arbitrator, the chairman, two representatives from the company, and two from the union. Occasionally the five-man board may consist of three neutral arbitrators and one company representative and one union official.

When the board meets to discuss a case after the hearing, the arbitrators representing the company and the union advance their respective positions with regard to the particular issue in dispute. It is almost a certainty that each party is likely to be biased in presenting its side of the case. The net effect is that the impartial chairman must make the decision, write the opinion, and render the award. The other two members either concur or dissent, but to validate the decision, the majority of the board must concur.

Frequently, when contracts provide for a tripartite board, the parties waive the requirement and submit the dispute to a single impartial arbitrator.

The value of tripartite boards is often questioned because, in practically all cases, the decision is made finally by the impartial chairman. Yet the process does afford the parties opportunities that are not otherwise present. It is not unusual for both labor and management to look upon the tripartite board as providing opportunity to take a "second crack" at the issues in dispute. In post-hearing deliberations the arbitrators, reperesenting the company and the union, endeavor to amplify their views and positions on the issues in dispute, and emphasize certain points that may not have been fully developed during the hearing itself. In this manner, they strive to influence the impartial chairman. Although, strictly speaking, new evidence may not be introduced or transmitted after the hearing is closed, yet the tripartite board offers a means by which one party or the other, or both, may attempt to accomplish this objective.

Relative Values of a Tripartite Board

The most common objections to a tripartite board of arbitration are: (1) The decisions are usually made by the impartial chairman rather than the entire board; (2) too much time is required for the hearing and board conferences, which not only delays decisions unnecessarily but also raises the costs of the arbitration proceedings; and (3) the board is of little value when cases are relatively simple and do not require any special knowledge of the industry or a technical process.

On the other hand, a tripartite panel does serve a real purpose where the issue in dispute requires a knowledge of industry practice and custom and an understanding of a technical process or delicate political problems. Moreover, the impartial chairman can call upon the party representatives on the board for information that may be vital to the decision.

In such cases, discussion by the full board will assist the impartial chairman in arriving at a just and workable solution to the problem at issue. This is particularly true when the terms of a collective bargaining agreement are in dispute. The chairman is better informed on the real positions of the parties as distinguished from their official positions.

National Railroad Adjustment Board

This Board was established by the Railway Labor Act. It is a rather unique governmental agency because it is strictly bipartisan. It consists of 36 members, 18 of whom are selected and compensated by the carriers and 18 by the railroad labor organizations. The Board is organized into four independent divisions and each one is an arbitration tribunal with jurisdiction over specified classes of railroad employees.

The Adjustment Board is empowered to hear "disputes between an employee or group of employees and a carrier or carriers growing out of grievances or out of the interpretation or application of agreements concerning rates of pay, rules, or working conditions." [7]

Before a dispute is referred to the Board, it must be cleared through the chief operating officer of the carrier designated to handle such disputes. Upon referral, a hearing is held unless waived. After a hearing, the division decides the case.

A unanimous vote is necessary, but when this is not possible a referee may be selected to sit with the division as a temporary member. He is usually appointed to hear and determine a group of cases. The referee's knowledge of the case usually comes from the parties through written submissions, briefs, and arguments presented by members of the division. If requested, a division may at its own discretion permit oral arguments by the parties before the referee.

If this award is in favor of the employees, the division is directed by the Railway Labor Act to order the carrier to make the award effective. If not complied with, the party in whose favor it stands may start suit in a U.S. District Court. The party against whom the award is directed has no right to take the award to the courts.

National Mediation Board

This Board, which was also established by the Railway Labor Act, has jurisdiction over any "disputes concerning changes in rates of pay, rules, or working conditions not adjusted by the parties in conference or any other disputes not referable to the National Railway Adjustment Board and not adjusted in conference between the parties or where conferences are refused." [8] The Board is empowered to help the parties to reach agreement through mediation. If unsuccessful, the Board seeks to induce the parties to submit the controversy to voluntary arbitration. The parties, however, are not compelled to arbitrate the dispute.

Section 7 of the Railway Labor Act provides for the organization of this arbitration tribunal. When a controversy is not settled, it may, by agreement of the parties, be submitted "to the arbitration of a board of three (or if the parties to the controversy so stipulate, of six) persons. . . ." If the Board consists of three persons, then each party selects one member and the two so selected choose the neutral member. If a Board of six is desired, each side selects two members and those four persons choose two neutral members. If a neutral member cannot be agreed upon by the members, the Mediation Board selects the neutral member or members.

The board of arbitration selects one of its members to serve as chairman. Each party compensates its appointees and the Mediation Board compensates neutral members.

An award, signed by the majority of the board, may be filed with the clerk of the U.S. District Court in which the controversy arose or the arbitration was entered into. The award, when filed, is conclusive as to the facts and merits of the controversy; unless within 10 days a petition to impeach it, on grounds specifically set forth in the Act, is filed with the court, judgment will be entered on the award.[9]

REFERENCES

1. Frank Elkouri, *How Arbitration Works*. Washington, D.C.: The Bureau of National Affairs, 1952, p. 40.
2. U.S. Dept. of Labor, Bureau of Labor Statistics, *Arbitration Provisions in Union Agreements, Bulletin 780*. Washington, D.C.: GPO, 1944, p. 4.
3. George W. Taylor, "Effectuating the Labor Contract Through Arbitration." In *The Profession of Labor Arbitration* (selected papers from the first seven annual meetings of the National Academy of Arbitrators, 1948–1954). Washington, D.C.: The Bureau of National Affairs, 1952, p. 20.
4. David A. Wolff, Louis A. Crane, and Howard A. Cole, "The Chrysler–U.A.W. Umpire System." In *The Arbitrator and the Parties* (Proceedings of the Eleventh Annual Meeting of the National Academy of Arbitrators). Washington. D.C.: The Bureau of National Affairs. 1958, pp. 111–148.
5. Harry H. Platt. Discussion of paper titled "The Chrysler–UAW Umpire System," by David A. Wolff, Louis A. Crane, and Howard A. Cole. In *The Arbitrator and the Parties, op. cit.,* pp. 141–145.
6. Harold W. Davey, "The John Deere Company-U.A.W. Permanent Arbitration System." In *Critical Issues in Labor Arbitration* (Proceedings of the Tenth Annual Meeting of the National Academy of Arbitrators). Washington, D.C.: The Bureau of National Affairs, 1957, pp. 161–192.
7. Railway Labor Act, Sec. 3 (i).
8. Railway Labor Act, Sec. 5.
9. Railway Labor Act, Sec. 9.

4

ARBITRATION AGENCIES

The voluntary arbitration of labor disputes has been facilitated by both private and public agencies. The American Arbitration Association, a non-profit private organization, has been doing an outstanding job in providing facilities for the arbitration of labor disputes.

The United States Government, through the Federal Mediation and Conciliation Service, maintains panels of experienced arbitrators and as a matter of policy encourages voluntary arbitration of labor disputes (see Appendix III,4).

Many states have passed legislation (see Appendix I,2) which provides facilities for the mediation of disputes and encourages arbitration.[1,2] There is considerable variety, however, in the organization, functions, and powers of these agencies. Many states have set up tripartite mediation boards. In a few instances the board itself does not have the power to mediate and, more frequently, it does not have the power to arbitrate.

In New York State the mediators also arbitrate disputes, whereas in New Jersey they are not permitted to act in the dual capacity of mediator and arbitrator. In North Carolina, an arbitration service established in the Department of Labor maintains a list of qualified arbitrators. The State Board of Mediation and Arbitration in Connecticut does not maintain lists of qualified arbitrators, but the Board itself frequently arbitrates disputes. The State of Delaware makes no provision for the mediation or arbitration of industrial disputes. The Department of Industrial Relations in California is authorized not only to mediate disputes but also to arbitrate or arrange for the selection of boards of arbitration. Boards of conciliation and arbitration have been established in Maine, Massachusetts, Montana, New Hampshire, and Oklahoma. The Nevada Court of Industrial Relations will accept for voluntary arbitration all disputes that are submitted to it.[3]

According to Braun, "a substantial number of municipalities . . . maintain small claims branches in their courts which, upon consent of the parties concerned, have the power to settle controversies about rights, including disputes between employers and employees, not only through conciliation but also through arbitration."[4] Thus, a great variation exists in the organization, functions, and powers of the various agencies engaged in the arbitration of labor disputes. To give the reader a clearer concept of how these agencies function, the work of six agencies will be briefly described.

Federal Mediation and Conciliation Service

The Federal Mediation and Conciliation Service (FMCS) was established in 1947 by the Labor Management Relations Act. The Act abolished its predecessor, the United States Conciliation Service, which was set up under the terms of the 1913 Act that established the Department of Labor. The FMCS, unlike its predecessor, is an independent agency, not a branch of the Department of Labor.

ORGANIZATION. The FMCS is headed by a full time, salaried director who is appointed by the President, with the advice and consent of the Senate. The director's immediate staff of eight administrators includes the general counsel, who is in charge of the arbitration division. The service maintains a national office in Washington, D.C., and seven regional offices located in New York, Philadelphia, Atlanta, Cleveland, Chicago, St. Louis, and San Francisco.

The national office staff is concerned with the following matters: basic policies and procedures, coordination of regional activity, supervision of nationally significant dispute cases, liaison with other governmental agencies and representatives of industry and labor, administration of the arbitration program, conduct of operations audits, direction of the training and related activities programs, mediator selection and placement, and administrative management and fiscal control.

The regional directors have full authority and responsibility in the following areas: to determine jurisdiction in given dispute situations; assign and supervise mediators; maintain liaison with representatves of labor, management, elected officials, and civil leaders in their communities; represent the service at meetings and conferences related to labor-management relations; and supervise the varied administrative functions essential to effective regional operations. Offices and conference rooms are provided at the regional offices.

FUNCTIONS. Providing experienced mediators free of charge to assist in settling labor disputes is the prime function of the Federal Mediation and Conciliation Service. The parties to a dispute may request the services of a mediator, or his services may be offered. If he is unable to bring the parties to agreement by mediation, he often recommends voluntary arbitration to prevent strikes and lockouts.

Under the provisions of the Labor–Management Relations Act, labor and management are charged with the responsibility of peacefully settling grievance disputes growing out of the application or interpretation of their agreements. The secondary function of the Service is to assist the parties by maintaining a panel of experienced arbitrators qualified to handle grievance and contract disputes. (Before 1947 several members of the regular staff served as arbitrators without compensation.)

PROCEDURES. The FMCS receives a request from the parties, usually accompanied by a brief statement of the issues in dispute, and copies of the pertinent contract clauses. The Service then submits to the parties the names of three, five, seven, or more arbitrators as desired by the parties. A short statement of the background, qualifications, and experience of each of the arbitrators is also furnished.

On receiving the panels, the parties may strike out unacceptable names, number the names in order of preference, or make the selection in any mutually agreed manner. If the parties cannot choose an arbitrator from the first list, the Service will provide a second. On rare occasions, the director may name an arbitrator, but only with approval of the parties.

The arbitrator selected is employed by and responsible to the parties. His award is mailed directly to the parties. A copy is sent to the Service. Thus, awards are absolutely free of any possible governmental influence. The Service does, however, recommend certain fees and procedures.

During the year 1972 the Service submitted 13,842 panels of arbitrators in response to 13,005 requests, and 6,263 appointments were made. Awards totaled 2,840. The number of requests has risen steadily over the years. For example, in 1963 the corresponding figures were 4,497, 4,279, 2,757, and 1,618.

JURISDICTION. The jurisdiction of the Service is limited to disputes having a substantial effect on interstate commerce, excluding railroads and airlines. The latter are covered by the Railway Labor Act.

In practice, however, there is an overlapping of jurisdiction between the FMCS and the State Boards of Mediation. Frequently federal and state mediators cooperate and work on the same dispute.

American Arbitration Association

The American Arbitration Association (AAA) is a private, nonprofit organization founded in 1926 to foster arbitration. Its two sources of income are modest administrative fees charged for tribunal services, annual memberships, and contributions. In commercial cases, fees are based upon a percentage of the amount involved. An administrative fee of $50 is charged each party for the initial hearing in a labor case. The fee for each subsequent hearing is $25 payable by each party on cases which are clerked by the AAA or held in a hearing room provided by AAA. A fee of $25 is payable by any party who causes a postponement of a scheduled hearing. Fees are sometimes waived in whole or in part, depending upon the ability of the parties to pay.

Members of AAA include companies, labor unions, trade associations, civic groups, foundations, and organizations of all kinds, as well as interested individuals. They receive AAA publications and have access to the agency's research and educational facilities, but receive no preferential treatment when they have occasion to use its arbitration services. The Association also cooperates closely with members of the bar and trade associations.

ORGANIZATION. The AAA is supervised by a board of directors, made up of leading representatives of management, labor unions, and the public, which is responsible to the membership. The board acts through an executive committee, which meets monthly. It is assisted by three major committees—arbitration law, budget, and arbitration practice—made up of representatives from all fields of arbitration activity. A professional staff at central headquarters in New York City and branch offices carries on the day-to-day work of the organization.

The AAA has five major tribunals: commercial, labor, accident claims, construction, and textile. Each tribunal is administered by rules and standards of procedure that govern the conduct of the parties, arbitrators, and the administrative agency. The Association's 21 branch offices are located in various parts of the United States. The central office in New York City has well-appointed hearing rooms, a library, and a research center.

FUNCTIONS. The Association maintains a national panel of more than 40,000 persons, each of whom is an expert in his chosen field and qualified to render impartial decisions. Included are about 1,500 specialists in labor–management relations. Arbitrators pay no fee for membership on the panel. Upon request, the AAA submits names of qualified arbitrators to disputants, schedules hearings, assigns a tribunal administrator to perform administrative duties, delivers awards, and submits bills for the arbitrator. During the year 1973 the AAA received more than 8,000 requests for labor arbitration panels.

In addition, the AAA is an important center of information, education, and research on arbitration. It conducts educational programs at universities, law schools, bar associations, labor unions, trade associations, and civic groups. Special research projects undertaken at the request of member organizations help adapt arbitration procedures to the needs of particular industries. The association has microfilmed its labor arbitration awards and this information is made available to all interested parties, including students.

Among AAA's publications are a quarterly magazine, three quarterly arbitration law–reporting services, a labor arbitration award–reporting service, a monthly news bulletin for members, specialized pamphlets on arbitration practice, and procedure and outlines for teaching labor–management arbitration and arbitration law courses.

New York State Board of Mediation

In 1886 the first state arbitration agency, known as the State Board of Arbitration, was established in New York to provide "for the amicable adjustment of grievances and disputes that may arise between employers and employees." In the following year, the word "Mediation" was added to the title, and in the ensuing years other transactions occurred in name and structure. The current Board, in its present form, was established in 1937 by an act of the state legislature. Although the problems the Board now handles are more complex, its basic objectives are unchanged.

ORGANIZATION. The Board is an independent agency within the State Department of Labor, and was established as a successor to earlier boards. The Governor, with the approval of the State Senate, appoints seven members to the Board. They are drawn from the fields of public service, education, and labor relations, and are compensated only on a per diem basis. The administrative functions of the Board are performed by an executive director, assistant director, and district directors with offices in Albany, Buffalo, New York City, and Syracuse.

FUNCTIONS. The primary function of the Board is to mediate labor disputes. The mediators often serve, however, as arbitrators and handle a rather large volume of cases free of charge. This is a unique public service for a mediation board to render. To reduce the rather heavy case load, the Board encourages the parties to select arbitrators from its panel of experienced persons who have been approved by a vote of the full Board. A list of arbitrators who have specialized experience in such matters as wage determination and job evaluation is also maintained.

PROCEDURE. An arbitration may be initiated by a simple request from either party, accompanied by a copy of the arbitration clause in the contract or by a submission agreement.

If the parties wish free arbitration, a staff mediator is designated to hear the case, depending on the nature of the case, the parties involved, the extent of the case load, and the demands of mediation, which is the primary function. If the parties prefer to select the arbitrator from the panel, a list of five names is submitted. Each party may delete two names and number the remainder in order of preference. A second list of five names is furnished if one or both parties strike out all names. If the list is not returned within five days, the Board will assume that all persons are acceptable and will designate an arbitrator.

The person selected to arbitrate has no legal relationship with the Board. He deals directly with the parties. The award is sent directly to the parties and a copy is sent to the Board for its files. Contested awards (see Appendix IV,1) are settled in the courts.

New Jersey State Board of Mediation

In 1941 the New Jersey State Legislature declared, as a matter of public policy, that "the best interests of the people of the State are served by the prevention or prompt settlement of labor disputes." To carry out this policy, the legislature passed the New Jersey Mediation Act, which created the State Board of Mediation.

ORGANIZATION. The Board is composed of seven part-time members appointed by the Governor with the advice and consent of the State Senate. Two members are representatives of labor, two of management, and three of the public. One member is designated by the Governor as chairman. A staff of five mediators is headed by a full-time executive secretary, who is the operating head of the agency. The Board maintains a main office with conference room facilities in Newark and a branch office in Camden.

Unlike the Connecticut Board of Mediation and Arbitration, the New Jersey Board does not itself arbitrate labor disputes.

FUNCTIONS. Although the primary function of the Board is to provide mediators to assist in the settlement of labor disputes, it also maintains a panel of accredited arbitrators from which parties may select a qualified person. One member of the staff is assigned the full-time duty of meeting requests for lists of arbitrators. The arbitrator selected thereafter deals directly with the parties. He mails a copy of his award to the Board (see Appendix IV,2).

PROCEDURES. In the State of New Jersey, many collective bargaining agreements specifically name the State Board of Mediation as the agency through which arbitrators are selected. Arbitration proceedings may be instituted by either party, which submits a demand for arbitration together with a copy of the arbitration provision of the contract. In the absence of an arbitration clause the parties may jointly submit an issue to arbitration.

The Board, under its rules promulgated in May 1973, provides the parties with identical lists of names and biographical sketches of seven arbitrators chosen from the panel. The parties strike out names of those unacceptable and the Board then selects the person most acceptable to both sides. If either party objects to the first list of seven names, it may request the Board to submit a new list. If either party objects to the second complete list of seven names as submitted, or if an appointment cannot be made from the second list, the Board submits a new list of three names to the parties. The parties have five working days from the date of mailing the third list to strike only one name and return the list to the Board. The parties are not required to strike one name; however, any name not stricken is deemed acceptable to the parties for designation as arbitrator by the Board. When either party or both parties fail to return the third list within the specified five days, any person whose name has not been stricken is deemed acceptable and the Board is empowered to designate any arbitrator named on that list.

If the parties in writing make a joint request to waive the third list and authorize the Board to appoint an arbitrator, the Board will honor such joint request.

The number of requests for arbitrators has increased from year to year. During the fiscal year ending June 30, 1973, the Board processed 1,453 arbitration requests.

JURISDICTION. Disputes arising in the State of New Jersey are within the jurisdiction of the Board. An overlapping of jurisdiction with the Federal

Mediation and Conciliation Service occurs, however, in disputes affecting interstate commerce.

Connecticut Board of Mediation and Arbitration

The Connecticut Board is a division within the State Labor Department. The services of the Board are available to employers and unions without cost. The Board functions as a relatively independent agency within the labor department and establishes its own policies and procedures.

ORGANIZATION. The Board is composed of six members who serve on a part-time basis. Two members represent the public; two, management; and two, labor. Members are appointed by the Governor for terms of six years, with two appointments expiring every second year. Of the two Board members representing the public, one acts as chairman and the other as deputy chairman. Members of the Board may be reappointed and, in fact, several have served successive terms.

When needed, the Chairman of the Board or the State Labor Commissioner may request the Governor to appoint alternate members for short periods of time, not to exceed six months. In the event of a vacancy on the Board, the Governor fills the vacancy for the unexpired portion of the term. These provisions are designed to help the Board render more efficient service and to encourage Connecticut employers and employees to use its services and facilities.

The appointment of either a labor or industry member is generally made from lists submitted by the labor commissioner to the Governor. The Manufacturers Association of Connecticut makes recommendations for the industry representative. In choosing representatives of labor, the statute's only stipulation is that they not be from the same national labor organization. In practice, state labor organizations make recommendations to the labor commissioner. The public members are selected by the Governor from recommendations by both interests and come from the ranks of college professors and the clergy.

In actual operation the Board is represented by a panel of three of its members—one each from the public, labor, and management. The permanent administrative staff are employees of the State Labor Department, their work being integrated with the overall operations of the department.

FUNCTIONS. The Connecticut Board, unlike the New Jersey Board, often arbitrates labor disputes. A high percentage of the awards issued by its tripartite panels have been unanimous. This is somewhat unusual, but may be explained in part by the relatively permanent nature of the Board.

The Board also maintains a panel of qualified arbitrators. The scope of this service is limited, however, and once names on the panel have been submitted, the parties are requested to deal directly with the person chosen.

The Board is often designated as arbitrator in collective bargaining agreements. In the absence of such a designation, the Board requires the parties to sign a submission agreement, which sets forth the issues to be determined.

By statute the Board is directed to mediate labor disputes. In addition to mediators, tripartite panels of Board members also mediate disputes.

State of California Conciliation Service

ORGANIZATION. The California State Conciliation Service, organized in 1947, is a division of the Department of Industrial Relations. It is headed by a Supervisor of Conciliation, who supervises the work of nine conciliators working out of three offices located in San Francisco, Los Angeles, and Fresno.

FUNCTION. Under Section 65 of the California Labor Code, the Conciliation Service is authorized to "investigate and mediate labor disputes." It may also "arbitrate or arrange for the selection of boards of arbitration on such terms as all the bona fide parties to such dispute may agree upon."

The Service maintains a panel of qualified arbitrators. It aids the parties in the designation of a mutually accepted neutral arbitrator, or in the creation of a tripartite arbitration board.

Unlike the practice in New York State, members of the conciliation staff do not serve as arbitrators. However, under special circumstances the Supervisor of Conciliation may serve as an arbitrator. When requested by the parties, he may directly designate an arbitrator.

Public-Sector Agencies

Other agencies in the public sector, such as the New York State Public Employment Relations Board, the New Jersey Public Employment Relations Commission, and the New York City Office of Collective Bargaining, select fact finders, mediators, and sometimes arbitrators.

REFERENCES

1. Commerce Clearing House, *Labor Law Reporter State Laws*, Vol. 1, pp. 40, 355.
2. Clarence M. Updegraff and Whitely P. McCoy, *Arbitration of Labor Disputes*, 2d ed. Washington, D.C.: The Bureau of National Affairs, 1961, pp. 289–292.
3. Kurt Braun, *Labor Disputes and Their Settlement*. Baltimore: Johns Hopkins University Press, 1955, pp. 274–294.
4. *Ibid.*, p. 289.

5

THE ARBITRATOR

An arbitrator is essentially a judge. He must therefore possess those judicial qualities of mind and temperament which will enable him to make dispassionate and objective decisions.

In the discharge of his responsibilities he must be able to evaluate evidence critically, determine the credibility of witnesses, and distinguish between relevant and irrelevant testimony. His decisions should be made only after a careful and thorough study of all evidence presented in the particular case. Any judgment rendered must be based on sufficient and reliable evidence.

In addition to these qualities and capabilities of a jurist, an arbitrator must have an intimate knowledge of industrial society and its manifold problems of human relationships. He will be concerned with men in a working environment, with unions and management, and with social concepts. He must understand the social and psychological forces that motivate or are motivated by self-interest, political considerations, loyalties, individual rights, management prerogatives, and industrial practices.

Distinction between Arbitrators and Judges

A well-qualified arbitrator must have a working knowledge of federal, state, and local laws as they relate to management and labor. This entails a knowledge of how these various laws have been interpreted by the courts and the administrative agencies that have been established to administer and enforce the statutes affecting labor–management relations. This specialized knowledge is essential to decision making in labor–management cases. It is not often possessed by judges in general courts of law or courts of equity. For this reason many students of industrial relations believe that public courts are not the proper tribunals for the adjudication of industrial disputes.

Arbitrators, of course, are not infallible. Unfortunately no mathematical formula is applicable to the human problems involved in labor disputes. It is doubtful, however, that errors made by arbitrators exceed the errors made by the courts, as evidenced by the substantial number of lower court decisions that are reversed.

The number of decisions reversed is not the only measure of judicial errors made in the lower courts. The huge backlog of cases in urban areas often does not permit a judge to devote the time required for proper evaluation of an issue. It is almost impossible for even the best judge to read, analyze, and evaluate the affidavits and hear arguments in the time he can afford to devote to any one matter, particularly motions. Under these conditions, errors in judgment are inevitable.

Even when obvious errors are made, the party adversely affected may have inadequate financial resources to appeal, or the cost of the appeal may exceed the monetary losses caused by judicial error. The time and trouble involved and the long delays due to overcrowded court calendars also discourage appeals to correct errors.

Some judges hand down faulty or improper decisions because they examine cases superficially, knowing that the cases may not be appealed. In a rush to dispose of as many cases as possible, they tend toward making decisions rather than rendering justice. Since they do not have adequate time to probe into all aspects of cases, they rely too frequently on general impressions and assumptions that may be false.

It is significant that parties in commercial disputes are increasingly utilizing the arbitral process for those cases that would normally go before a court of law. Moreover, the judicial system has recognized the effectiveness of the arbitral process and frequently recommends its use. In the City of New York, suits for less than $3,000 may be arbitrated.

Although most active arbitrators have been rendering awards for over 25 years, they do not have the privilege of tenure in office, as do judges. If an arbitrator makes too many errors, he soon ceases to be an arbitrator. He is simply not selected by the parties. Obviously, the quality of an opinion and award is more important in arbitration than the quantity of cases decided. The ability of the arbitrator to render logical, well-reasoned, impartial awards is judged by the parties who must abide by the award, and by their attorneys. Lawyers who participate in his selection base their opinion on prior experience, an analysis of his published awards, and his reputation in the legal profession. If a person can survive 25 years as an active arbitrator, he must be rendering a public service.

Although arbitrators' awards cannot be appealed on their merits,* the expendability of arbitrators may be a greater safeguard against error than the right to appeal. Two arbitrators hearing the same set of facts may come to different conclusions. This is often viewed as a weakness of the arbitral process. It is cited as a proof of error and evidence that an appeal procedure is warranted. Differences of opinion among those who serve in a judicial capacity have been characteristic of our judicial system for centuries. The U.S. Supreme Court is a good example of how nine learned men, hearing the same case, can disagree. Moreover, as years pass and

---

* For the grounds upon which an award may be attacked, see Updegraff and McCoy.[1]

social concepts change, many majority decisions of previous courts have been reversed. Differences of opinion are inevitable in any society that is dynamic and whose social concepts are fluid.

Characteristics of Active Arbitrators

The National Academy of Arbitrators (NAA) sponsored a survey of the arbitration profession in 1970.[2] This survey was preceded by others made in 1952, 1957, and 1962. Of all the members queried, 222 responded, which was 60.5 percent of the Academy's membership at that time.

AGE. The average age of the respondents as of December 31, 1969, was 57 years, whereas in 1962 it was 52.7 years. This increase of four years in average age in the seven-year period probably indicates that very few young men are entering the profession, since only 1.8 percent had not reached their forties, and 72.5 percent were in their fifties and sixties.

EDUCATION. The average arbitrator is very well educated. Only three members of the NAA do not hold a college degree. Bachelor degrees are held by 189 persons. Of these, many also hold an advanced degree. The most widely held advanced degrees, and the number held, are LL.B. or J.D. (81), M.A. (75), and Ph.D. (65). The leading fields of concentration in college are economics (70), political science (46), history (21), and law and prelaw (14). Arbitrators did their professional or graduate study primarily in the fields of law (122) and economics (75).

EXPERIENCE. The great majority of active arbitrators entered the field between 1940 and 1950, many as a result of their experience at the National War Labor Board (1941–1945). It is significant that 19.4 percent received their first case in the period 1940–1944, and 24 percent in 1945–1949, a total of 33.4 percent before 1950. In the period 1950–1954, 20.7 percent received their first case. Only 14.3 percent got their first case in 1960–1964 and 2.3 percent in 1965. This indicates that over one-third have been arbitrating for almost 20 years.

TIME SPENT IN ARBITRATION. About three-quarters of the respondents arbitrate on a part-time basis. Of the 160 part-time arbitrators, 97 said they were teachers; 36, lawyers; 10, consultants; 6, educational administrators; and 6, members of governmental labor relations agencies.

SHORTAGE OF ARBITRATORS. Because of the average age of active arbitrators, the National Academy has been concerned about the problem of training new arbitrators. Several members of the Academy have served as trainers and sponsors of new arbitrators.

Since age and maturity are assets for those who serve in a judicial capacity, the current group of active arbitrators will be serving for many years to come. In addition, many experienced but under-utilized arbitrators can absorb the increased case load. However, concern about the continued supply of well-qualified and experienced arbitrators to serve the needs of society is justified.

Sources of New Arbitrators

New arbitrators will come from four main sources: (1) colleges and universities, particularly schools of business and law schools; (2) governmental agencies, especially those dealing with labor problems; (3) attorneys; and (4) mediators and fact finders.

People who teach labor law, economics, and industrial relations are an important source of new arbitrators. Many arbitrators have worked as mediators for the Federal Mediation and Conciliation Service or for a State Board of Mediation. Attorneys who have handled labor-relations problems are sometimes asked to serve as arbitrators. Anyone who has acquired a good reputation as a mediator has no difficulty in becoming an arbitrator. The new people who are serving as mediators and fact finders in the public sector are a more recent and important source of arbitrators.

It is frequently said among those engaged in industrial relations work that there are few new arbitrators because it is rather difficult for a newcomer to participate actively, even though he is well qualified. The reason for this is that when the appointing agencies add new names to the lists sent to the parties, the new persons are seldom selected because parties look for familiar names and known records of capability. The need for developing a larger body of experienced and acceptable arbitrators has been the subject of much discussion by the Committee on Research and Education of the National Academy of Arbitrators. The Committee suggested a training program for new arbitrators, which would include (1) attendance at arbitration hearings and mediation conferences; (2) the study of reported cases and literature; (3) the handling of less involved cases at lower rates by special referrals from designating organizations; and (4) service as full-time apprentice or intern under the leadership of an established arbitrator.

An evaluation of arbitration apprenticeships was made by Arnold M. Zack, who believes that adoption of the plan can increase the supply of trained arbitrators.[3]

EXPENDABILITY OF ARBITRATORS. An arbitrator has no assurance or guarantee that he will continue to serve indefinitely in this capacity. This lack of tenure is perhaps the best guarantee that the most capable people will be in the greatest demand in handling industrial disputes. While the parties are not always objective in the selection of arbitrators, it is believed that the present system is better than one in which tenure would be granted to the arbitrator.

Ethical Standards of Arbitrators

An arbitrator has the obligation of maintaining a high level of professional ethics in his relationships with the parties and the appointing agencies. He also has a responsibility to society. His conduct should be above reproach.

In effect, he is a judge, and his ethics must be on the same high level as the code that governs the conduct of judicial tribunals.

The absence of judicial rituals does not minimize the judicial functions of the arbitrator. Decisions made by the arbitrator vitally affect the rights and responsibilities of the parties. When a judge makes a decision, it can be appealed to a higher tribunal. The absence of a similar appeal procedure in arbitration places a much heavier responsibility upon the arbitrator. The parties also have ethical responsibilities. Their words and actions should not place the arbitrator in a position where a question of ethics can be raised.

The American Arbitration Association (AAA), recognizing the importance of high ethical standards, submitted in 1948 its proposed Code of Ethics for examination and criticism to more than one hundred arbitrators and representatives of labor and management. The National Academy of Arbitrators coincidentally instructed its Committee on Ethics to consider this same problem. A joint meeting was held with a committee from the AAA and representatives of the Federal Mediation and Conciliation Service (FMCS). The end result of these cooperative efforts in 1950 was a "Code of Ethics and Procedural Standards for Labor–Management Arbitration." It was finally prepared jointly by the AAA and the NAA and approved by the FMCS. After publication of the Code, it was endorsed by the industrial relations division or boards of mediation of many states.

The provisions of the Code of Ethics are reproduced in Appendix I,1, Part 1.

Strict adherence to the standards set forth in the Code of Ethics assures the parties of fair and impartial decisions. Obviously, an arbitrator can have no personal, financial, or family relationship with the parties, nor can he have any pecuniary interest in the outcome of a dispute. The Code has undoubtedly had a salutary effect on arbitration proceedings, and the whole process for settling industrial dispute has grown in stature because of it.

Opinions of the Committee on Ethics

The Committee on Ethics of the NAA, which was given the responsibility of interpreting the Code of Ethics, made its first report on May 1, 1953. The report contained a statement of the functions of the Committee, the procedures followed, and the first two opinions on ethics promulgated by the Committee.

As an example of how the Committee on Ethics functions, the first two opinions are summarized because of their historical significance.

ETHICS OPINION NO. 1. The Committee was asked to give its opinion on the ethics of an arbitrator's conduct. The arbitrator had agreed to serve at a rate of $50 for a one-day hearing and $50 for the preparation of his award. At the hearing he stated that he believed the fee arranged was too low and, in view of fees paid to other arbitrators, he should be allowed

$100 a day with a minimum of $300. The parties agreed to an increase of $200.

The Committee was without knowledge of the accuracy of the statement of facts, since it had not heard evidence. It did not know the nature of the discussions prior to the hearing, the nature of the original agreement as to fees, or how the question of a revision of fees came to be raised. Therefore, its consensus had to be based solely on the statement of facts as submitted.

It was the members' opinion that the conduct of the arbitrator was not proper or consistent with the Code of Ethics of the Academy as provided in Part II, Section 1(b), of the Code, which states that: "A fee previously fixed by the parties or by schedule should not be altered during the proceeding or after the award is delivered."

The Committee reasoned that the parties had a technical right to reject a proposed increase in fees, even though the exercise of that right might cause embarrassment. Selection of an arbitrator involves a grant of power to him by the parties, neither of whom would wish to displease the arbitrator for fear of prejudicing the case he has been called upon to decide. Any attempt by an arbitrator to use his power as a lever to raise his fees would be unethical, the Committee held.

ETHICS OPINION NO. 2. In this case the Committee was asked to give its opinion on the ethical obligations of an arbitrator under the following circumstances:

An arbitrator served in a dispute between a company and a local union in one of its plants; to his knowledge, the award had not been published. Subsequently, he was asked to serve in another dispute between the same company and another local union affiliated with another international in a different plant. After accepting the appointment, he learned that the issues in both cases were identical, but in the second case the union did not know of his participation in the earlier case.

The questions involved were: (1) Was the arbitrator under ethical obligation to disclose to the union the facts in the first case, and (2) would a different ethical standard apply if the award in the first case had been published, or if the local union involved in the second dispute was affiliated with the same international as the local involved in the first dispute?

A principle set forth in the Code of Ethics makes it "incumbent upon the arbitrator at the time of his selection to disclose to the parties any circumstances, associations or relationships that might reasonably raise any doubt as to his impartiality." The question presented was whether the circumstances "might reasonably raise" a doubt as to the arbitrator's impartiality. In the judgment of the Committee they did not.

In this case the Committee reasoned that it is virtually impossible for an arbitrator to know until actual submission whether an issue is identical with one he has previously decided. Although it may appear to be fundamentally the same, each new case may have some unique, distinguishing feature that requires special consideration. The decisive ethical question is not whether he has considered a similar or identical issue before, but whether he is open to persuasion either way. If he feels free to reverse his prior decision, no disclosure is necessary; but if he feels bound by a prior decision, then he should disclose that fact.

The Committee concluded in its opinion that the parties are entitled to an honest, rather than an uninformed, decision. A contrary conclusion would lead to the disqualification of arbitrators solely on the basis of their experience.

The Duty to Disclose

Rule 3 of the Code of Ethics and Procedural Standards provides: "Any person whom the parties or the appointing agency choose to regard as qualified to determine their dispute is entitled to act as their arbitrator. It is, however, incumbent upon the arbitrator at the time of his selection to disclose to the parties any circumstances, associations or relationships that might reasonably raise any doubt as to his impartiality or his technical qualifications for the particular case."

A study of the duty of disclosure has been made by Herbert L. Sherman, Jr., Professor of Law and Industrial Relations, University of Pittsburgh. His findings and conclusions were presented to the AAA and published in its journal, as follows[4]:

1. An arbitrator has a duty to disclose to the parties that ten years previously he received a consulting fee of $500 from one of the parties for a matter not related to labor relations. But he has no duty to disclose that he received a similar fee from another company in the same industry for a matter not related to labor relations.

2. There is no duty to disclose that the arbitrator served as a lecturer or conference participant on labor relations and [that] the conference included a representative of the parties and he received a free lunch.

3. An arbitrator has no duty to disclose that a representative of one of the parties is a former degree-seeking student of the arbitrator. However, where the student was a research assistant for the arbitrator or he wrote his graduate thesis for the arbitrator these facts should be disclosed.

4. The arbitrator has no duty to disclose that the company or union representative has given a talk to the arbitrator's class at the request of the arbitrator.

5. Any amount of stock ownership by the arbitrator or his wife in the company should be disclosed.

6. There is no need to disclose the arbitrator's status as a taxpayer or as a customer of a utility in disputes involving public employees or utilities.

7. An arbitrator has no duty to disclose that he found himself sitting beside a representative of one of the parties on the plane trip to the hearing.

8. There is no need to disclose that a representative of one of the parties, see-

ing the arbitrator in the hotel lobby the night before the hearing, offered him a drink, or that one of the parties reserved for the arbitrator a hotel room customarily reserved on a continuing basis for that party.

9. Disclosure is not necessary where the arbitrator and the company or union representative belong to the same neighborhood civic association.

10. There is no duty to disclose that a representative of one of the parties took him out to dinner at the last annual meeting of the National Academy of Arbitrators.

11. There is no majority view among arbitrators on whether an arbitrator has a duty to disclose [that] he has played golf or poker with a representative of the parties on prior occasions. However, most company and union representatives believe that there is no duty to disclose this information.

12. Where the arbitrator is a member of an organization which is working against the interest of one of the parties (an organization working against an increase in milk prices or to force construction unions to admit more blacks) [he] has a duty to disclose.

13. The arbitrator has no duty to disclose that only one of the two parties has presented a prior case to the arbitrator.

14. Most arbitrators and representatives of companies and unions believe that the arbitrator has no duty to disclose that for a short period of time, many years ago, the arbitrator was an inactive member of a local union affiliated with the International Union seeking his services.

15. If the arbitrator, however, was a former officer of the Union he would have the duty to disclose.

16. A remark by one of the parties after the hearing that "this is a very important case which we cannot afford to lose" is viewed as general propaganda and does not need to be disclosed.

17. An arbitrator has no duty to disclose that he recognizes one of the representatives of the parties as a fellow member of the National Academy of Arbitrators.

18. Most arbitrators believe that an arbitrator has a duty to disclose that the Union representative has advised the arbitrator that a hearing must be held for "political" reasons, and that he has asked the arbitrator to agree in advance of the hearing to adopt the company position. However, company representatives tend to say that there is no duty of disclosure, whereas union representatives tend to say there is a duty of disclosure.

Where the union representative does not ask the arbitrator to agree, but merely indicates that the hearing must be held for "political" reasons, the prevailing view among arbitrators is that there is no duty to disclose.

A New Code of Professional Responsibility

In a paper delivered at the Annual Meeting of the National Academy of Arbitrators in January 1971,[5] Alex Elson recommended that a new "Code of Professional Responsibility for Labor Arbitrators" be drafted. He borrowed the title from the American Bar Association's recent revision of its canons of ethics.

Elson assumed that most of the present code would be incorporated into the new code, but nevertheless he suggested reaffirmation of and greater emphasis on "positive obligations of arbitrators to achieve the high objectives of the arbitration process—that of an impartial, competent, expeditious and relatively inexpensive method of dispute resolution."

Although the author has been actively engaged in the arbitration profession for over 25 years, he has never found other than an extremely high level of integrity, not only among his fellow arbitrators but also among the parties.

Since the parties select the arbitrator, unethical or incompetent arbitrators can be eliminated simply by not selecting them. This simple solution is not, of course, applicable to unethical or unprofessional judges in the courts. Whereas an arbitrator with a questionable reputation can be eliminated within a few months, the tenure accorded a judge makes the procedure complicated and of long duration.

The Arbitrator's Role

A question frequently raised is whether an arbitrator should serve strictly in a judicial capacity. The late Dr. George Taylor, a nationally known arbitrator who served on the faculty of the University of Pennsylvania, often advanced the view that arbitrators should not hesitate to mediate when in their judgment this is desirable. A permanent arbitrator is not infrequently expected by the parties to mediate disputes. Often it is the most effective method of settling a dispute. However, in ad hoc cases, arbitrators are expected to adjudicate, not to mediate.

In an address before the NAA, Robert M. Segal, Counsel for the Massachusetts Federation of Labor, stated:

> Unions have problems with an arbitrator who tries to mediate a case that is presented for arbitration. With few limited exceptions mostly confined to permanent arbitrators or tripartite setups, unions want the arbitrator to hand down a written decision rather than a mediation settlement. When the case has gone to arbitration and an arbitrator has been called in, I find that the unions want a decision rather than any mediation attempts they could have tried to obtain by other means if they so desired." [6]

A somewhat different view was expressed in a paper prepared by C. W. Ahner of Ahner Associates, management consultants, and presented at the same meeting of the NAA.

> Whether an arbitrator should attempt mediation depends, it seems to me, upon the parties, the kind of issues, the arbitrator and the relationship he enjoys with the parties, his perceptivity and deftness. Where the parties, having thoroughly exhausted possibilities of settlement and being obviously aware of the risk of an unfavorable award come prepared to present evidence and try a case on its merits, an arbitrator would be unwise to attempt mediation. And the arbitrator who is unable to recognize such a situation could not successfully mediate anyway. But when an arbitrator finds the issue before him to be one that is quite obviously

a matter for negotiations, when he finds that attitudes have not completely crystallized, it is my feeling that he has a responsibility to explore the possibilities of settlement. The guiding rule should not be what taboos have been erected around arbitration proceedings, but rather what will improve the relationship between the parties. The important question, it seems to me, is not whether the arbitrator should attempt mediation, but how to go about it.[7]

The ad hoc arbitrator should not, except under very unusual circumstances, take it upon himself to change his role to that of mediator. This is a matter that should be decided by the parties. The ad hoc arbitrator usually knows little about the background of the issue and less about the history of the relationship between the parties involved in the dispute.[8]

Arbitrator Benjamin Roberts, formerly a mediator of the New York State Board of Mediation, proposed that the parties might seek the assistance of a mediator preliminary to grievance arbitration. Persons who serve as arbitrators could also serve as mediators, but not in the same case.

Arbitrators as Judges in a New Judicial System

Under our system of voluntary arbitration a new private judicial system has been established. Traditionally, judges have been designated by the Crown, the government, or elected by the people. In order to insure the independence of the judge, he was given assurance of tenure in office and could not be removed except for cause. To enhance his prestige and to engender in the general public a respect for his office, the judge was required to sit on a high bench, wear a wig, and flowing robes. His presence was announced, and people stood in respect when he entered the court. Lawyers addressed him subserviently and sought his indulgence at every turn. If this code of conduct was breached, the judge had the power to hold the offender in contempt of court and order his imprisonment.

A system of appellate courts was adopted to correct errors and establish principles of law. Rules of evidence were developed which strictly controlled the admissibility of evidence. It is not to be implied, however, that these rules did not serve a real need when a case was submitted to a jury. In order to insure the stability and continuity of legal concepts, the principle of stare decisis was developed, which meant, simply, that precedent controlled decisions.* When changes in economic and social institutions required a change in legal concepts, the principle of stare decisis impeded the change.

Under the system of voluntary arbitration in effect in the United States, the tradition described above has been set aside. The arbitrator—the judge of industrial disputes—is created by the parties. His tenure is dependent upon his acceptability to the parties. As already noted, an arbitrator is expendable. He is selected because of his reputation for impartiality. Political considerations play no part in his selection.

---

* For a discussion of the doctrine of stare decisis, see Moore.[9]

The arbitrator's "courtroom" may be his office, a room in a hotel, a conference room at an industrial plant, or a hearing room at the AAA or at a state mediation agency. On occasion he may conduct a portion of the hearings in the shop, standing at a machine together with union and company representatives. No robes of office are required, and he is simply addressed as "Mister." He has no power to hold the parties in contempt, and the respect given him is the result of his own personal dignity and integrity.

There is no appeal procedure whereby the decision of the arbitrator can be affirmed or revised. His decisions are not controlled by the principle of stare decisis. This permits judicial concepts to be molded by social needs. Neither are his decisions influenced by appointing agencies, since they are the last to receive a copy of the decision.

Rules of evidence as developed by the courts are not controlling. The arbitrator hears all the evidence he considers to be material and relevant. He tries to uncover the underlying causes of the dispute and to consider the contractual, social, industrial, and human elements involved.

He takes ample time to hear all aspects of the case and knows that time, patience, and attention to details are the essential requirements of a just and sound decision. He also knows that his continuance as an arbitrator depends on the fairness of his decision, which rests on his comprehension of the case and his understanding of industrial practices.

The National Academy of Arbitrators

Shortly after World War II, when voluntary arbitration was becoming accepted and used as a method of settling industrial disputes, the feeling grew among active arbitrators that they had need for a professional society. A group of arbitrators met in Chicago and on September 13, 1947, founded the National Academy of Arbitrators. The first annual meeting was held in that city in January of the following year.

The purpose of the Academy, as stated in its constitution, is

To establish and foster the highest standards of integrity, competence, honor and character among those engaged in the arbitration of industrial disputes on a professional basis; to adopt and encourage the acceptance of and adherence to canons of ethics to govern the conduct of arbitrators; to promote the study and understanding of the arbitration of industrial disputes; to encourage friendly association among the members of the profession; to cooperate with other organizations, institutions and learned societies interested in industrial relations; and to do any and all things which shall be appropriate in the furtherance of these purposes.

Experience as an arbitrator is a prerequisite for membership in the Academy, and all new members must be recommended to and approved by the membership committee. Annual meetings are held in different parts of the country, and are attended not only by arbitrators but also by representatives of management, labor, and government. The informal exchange of views that takes place is as important as the papers that are presented at the meetings. Proceedings of the Annual Meetings is published by the Bureau of National Affairs, Washington, D.C., and the papers in this symposium contain valuable source material for students of arbitration.

Sources of Information about Arbitrators

Those who are actually engaged in arbitration work and who participate in the selection of arbitrators require sources of information concerning prospective arbitrators. Qualifications of those selected must be ascertained in terms of education, experience, general reputation, and competence in handling technical cases.

The sources of this information are the appointing agencies (American Arbitration Association, the Federal Mediation and Conciliation Service, the State Boards of Mediation), chambers of commerce, employers' associations, Labor Arbitration Reports (published by the Bureau of National Affairs and by Commerce Clearing House), lawyers, industrial relations and personnel executives, and the international offices of the various unions.

When a party to a dispute requests a list of arbitrators from one of the appointing agencies, he also receives a short biographical sketch of each person named. This sketch contains complete data on the education, experience, and professional affiliations of the arbitrators listed.

Some of the sources listed above endeavor to maintain very complete and comprehensive data about each individual. For example, some chambers of commerce and employers' associations try to serve as central clearing houses of information on arbitrators. A chamber of commerce or association may obtain a copy of each award in which a member is involved and may request from that member an appraisal of the arbitrator. The Bureau of National Affairs and the Commerce Clearing House publish arbitration awards as well as biographical sketches of arbitrators. The cases are indexed so that opinions written by a particular arbitrator are readily accessible.

These latter sources have some disadvantages. An arbitrator may have relatively few reported cases, and those reported may not be representative of his work as an arbitrator. Also, the decisions by a particular arbitrator presented in the published cases may be predominantly for either management or labor, which may give the erroneous impression that he is biased.

Lawyers representing either union or management, as well as management and union officers, who actively participate in arbitration proceedings, frequently exchange information concerning arbitrators. Again, these sources present dangers of prejudice because of their respective positions and interests. Such information should be accepted with caution.

It must be recognized, however, that in the final analysis no amount of information about an arbitrator will indicate how he will decide a particular case. Furthermore, in seeking appraisals of an arbitrator, an industrial relations director or a union business agent is likely to choose an arbitrator who has decided a case in his favor. The best recommendation is, "He decided against us but he's a good man, a fair man, anyway."

Since it is the parties who "create" an arbitrator, they have the responsibility of selecting those who are competent and have high ethical standards. Labor and management should not judge arbitrators solely by the number of cases each has won, but rather on their ability to comprehend the issue, to arrive at a conclusion through sound logic and reason, to be impartial in judgment, and to write a clear and fair decision. If this approach is followed consistently, the services of outstanding arbitrators will always be available to the parties for the adjudication of their industrial disputes.

Arbitration Fees

Prior to World War II, relatively few arbitrators received fees. With the exception of permanent arbitrators, they were called upon infrequently to adjudicate disputes, and were considered public servants rendering a public service.

This attitude was reflected in a letter dated July 20, 1942, which was sent by the New Jersey State Board of Mediation to a number of individuals who engaged in arbitration work. It provides an interesting insight into the early development of arbitration, particularly as it relates to fees.

The letter stated that when the Board was formed, it expected to obtain public-spirited citizens who would serve without remuneration but whose expenses would be compensated. It quickly became apparent that this procedure was not fair and equitable because the assignments required many days of hard work and frequently involved great personal inconvenience. It was accordingly decided to pay arbitrators on a fee basis. Initially, fees were inadequate and in many instances did not even cover expenses. However, the decision did establish a fee for services and arbitrators were relieved of the necessity for itemizing their expenses.

It is of historic interest to note that the 1942 letter specified the fee for an arbitration as $10 per case when the hearing lasted one day or fraction thereof, and $25 if more than one day. In September 1959, the New Jersey State Board of Mediation changed its scale of recommended fees and adopted the following rules:

Rule VII–1. Regular Arbitrator's Fees: The Board recommends that an arbitrator be paid up to $100 per diem, such fee to be divided equally between the parties to the arbitration unless the Labor agreement specified otherwise.* The arbitrator's fee will be due no later than 30 days following receipt of the award.

* A few collective bargaining agreements provide that the party losing the case shall pay the entire fee. [M. T.]

Rule VII–2. Technical Arbitrator's Fees: Where a technical arbitrator is selected from a special list maintained by the Board for determination of technical wage, job classifications, and time and motion study cases, complete arrangements regarding fees, time, and place of hearings will be made between the parties and selected arbitrator, subject to the concurrence of the Board.[10]

When arbitrators who served on the panels of the American Arbitration Association commenced receiving fees from the parties, fees ranged from $25 to $75 per diem. A study made by this Association in 1954 showed that of 1195 cases processed, 23.6 percent of the arbitrators received a fee of $75 per diem, and 57.7 percent received a fee of $100 per diem.[11] The 1959 Twelfth Annual Report of the Federal Mediation and Conciliation Service states that in 1949 the average per diem fee was approximately $75, whereas in 1959 it was $100.

Arbitrators' fees, like all other professional fees, wages, and salaries, have increased. In 1973 the fees of most active ad hoc arbitrators were about $200 per diem.

The arbitrator's total fee is based upon the number of days spent in hearings, studying the issues, and writing the opinion and the award. The average case requires two days—one day spent on the hearings and one day on the opinion and the award. Of course, if a stenographic record is made of the proceedings and briefs are submitted, or if the issue is complicated and technical, more than two days may be required.

In some industries a permanent arbitrator may devote full time to arbitrating disputes, and he is then paid an annual fee. If a permanent arbitrator is named in the contract, but spends only a portion of his time arbitrating, he may receive an annual retainer that is proportionate to the average monthly case load, or he may receive a small annual retainer plus a per diem rate for each case heard.

Costs other than the arbitrator's fees can be considerable. The making of a transcript of the testimony (although it is not customary to do so) and preliminary hearing and post-hearing briefs are all expensive. Attorneys' fees are also substantial. If the parties have not agreed on the issue and considerable time is spent at the hearing to frame it, the case may require additional time and expense.

The AAA has published a very helpful pamphlet[12] that lists the following ways to control and cut arbitration costs: (1) Know your arbitrator and be sure he has the technical qualifications; (2) reduce the cost of reporting; (3) agree on the arbitrator's per diem fees in advance; (4) stipulate as many facts as possible before the hearing; (5) if practical, dispense with a written opinion; (6) reduce citations for arbitrators to read and consider; (7) avoid futile arguments about procedural matters; (8) adhere to the schedule and do not indiscriminately postpone hearings; and (9), in general, avoid delays as much as possible which may increase liability for back pay.

REFERENCES

1. Clarence M. Updegraff and Whitley P. McCoy, *Arbitration of Labor Disputes*, 2d. ed. Washington, D.C.: The Bureau of National Affairs, 1961.
2. National Academy of Arbitrators: (a) "Survey of the Arbitration Profession in 1952," Appendix E in *The Profession of Labor Arbitration* (1957), Report of the Committee on Research and Education, pp. 176–182. (b) "Research and Education Committee Report and Recommendations," Appendix D, and "Statistical Tables Based on the Survey of Arbitration Work of Members of the Academy in 1957," Appendix E in *Arbitration and the Law* (1959), Proceedings of the Twelfth Annual Meeting, National Academy of Arbitrators, pp. 179–184 and 185–190. (c) "Survey of Arbitration in 1962," in *Labor Arbitration: Perspectives and Problems* (1964), Proceedings of the Seventeenth Annual Meeting of the National Academy of Arbitrators, pp. 292–316. Washington, D.C.: The Bureau of National Affairs.
3. Arnold M. Zack, "An Evaluation of Arbitration Apprenticeships," in *Challenges to Arbitration* (Proceedings of the Thirteenth Annual Meeting of the National Academy of Arbitrators). Washington, D.C.: The Bureau of National Affairs, 1960, pp. 169–176.
4. Herbert L. Sherman, Jr., "The Duty of Disclosure in Labor Arbitration," *The Arbitration Journal*, Vol. 25, No. 2 (1970), p. 73; also *University of Pittsburgh Law Review*, Vol. 31, No. 3 (Spring 1970), p. 377.
5. Alex Elson, "Code of Professional Responsibility for Labor Arbitrators" (Proceedings of the Twenty-fourth Annual Meeting of the National Academy of Arbitrators). Washington, D.C.: The Bureau of National Affairs, 1971, pp. 194–203.
6. Robert M. Segal, "Arbitration: A Union Viewpoint," in *The Arbitrator and the Parties* (Proceedings of the Eleventh Annual Meeting of the National Academy of Arbitrators). Washington, D.C.: The Bureau of National Affairs, 1958, p. 55.
7. C. W. Ahner, "Arbitration: A Management Viewpoint," in *The Arbitrator and the Parties* (Proceedings of the Eleventh Annual Meeting of the National Academy of Arbitrators). Washington, D.C.: The Bureau of National Affairs, 1958, pp. 83, 87.
8. Maurice S. Trotta, "Discussion," in *The Arbitrator and the Parties* (Proceedings of the Eleventh Annual Meeting of the National Academy of Arbitrators). Washington, D.C.: The Bureau of National Affairs, 1958, pp. 87, 92.
9. Russell F. Moore, *Stare Decisis — Some Trends in British and American Application of the Doctrine*. New York: Simmons–Boardman Publishing Corporation, 1958.
10. New Jersey State Board of Mediation, "Rules and Regulations for Arbitration," March 15, 1948 (amended Sept. 9, 1959).
11. American Arbitration Association, "Procedural Aspects of Labor–Management Arbitration," 28 LA 933.
12. American Arbitration Association, "Nine Ways to Cut Arbitration Costs," February 1972.

6

POWERS OF THE ARBITRATOR

Except in the rare instances of compulsory arbitration, the arbitrator's powers to hear and determine an issue are derived from the parties to an industrial dispute. The power is usually expressed in the collective bargaining agreement or the submission agreement. The court's function is to enforce the contractual obligation to arbitrate.

Express Powers

The scope and limitations of the arbitrator's power are determined solely by the parties. He has no right to exceed the powers expressly granted to him. If he exceeds them, his award can be set aside by the courts. A study of collective bargaining agreements discloses different types of arbitration clauses with varying degrees of power granted to the arbitrator. This power may be very limited or unusually broad in scope.

POWER TO ARBITRATE ANY DISPUTE. The contract clause that gives the arbitrator the broadest scope of power is commonly known as the "disputes" clause. The following excerpt from a contract is illustrative: "Any difference or dispute arising between the company and the union or its members shall be settled in the following manner. . . ."

This type of clause grants the arbitrator jurisdiction to hear and determine practically any matter in dispute between the parties. Moreover, he is not necessarily limited to matters specifically stated in the contract. It is common, however, for some relationship to be shown between the matter in dispute and the provisions of the contract. On the basis of this type of clause, the courts have held that since no limit was placed upon the arbitrator, he was empowered to decide the method to be followed for resolving the issues arising when parties in a deadlocked conference endeavored to effect modifications in a contract.[1]

In another dispute[2] the union sought arbitration of a discharge case, although the collective bargaining agreement did not contain a "for cause" limitation on the employer's right to discharge. The employer moved to stay arbitration by the plea of nonarbitrability. The New York Court of Appeals, which at that time was not inclined to favor the jurisdiction of arbitrators, nevertheless upheld arbitrability in this case on the grounds that the "disputes" clause placed the issue in the hands of the arbitrator.

POWER OF INTERPRETATION AND APPLICATION OF THE CONTRACT. The most common arbitration clause restricts the arbitrator's power to hear and determine disputes arising out of an interpretation of the collective bargaining agreement. The following examples of such clauses are typical.

In the 1960 collective bargaining agreement between Freuhauf Trailer Company and Allied Industrial Workers of America Local 259, the following clause appears: [Article VI. Grievances] "The Board of Arbitrators shall be empowered to rule on all disputes pertaining to the interpretation or application of this agreement. . . ."

The 1956 contract between Kroger Company (Charleston, W. Va.) and Food Store Employees Union Local 347 contains the following provision: "Should any differences, disputes or complaints arise over the interpretation of the contents of this agreement, there shall be an earnest effort on the part of both parties to settle such promptly . . . In the event that the difference cannot be adjusted it will be referred within ten (10) days to a Board of Arbitration. . . ."

Again a literal reading of these clauses suggests the intent to confine the arbitrator to matters covered by the contract and not to have him decide any dispute that happens to arise. But the conclusiveness of this intent is not at all clear. The problem still remains whether the dispute does in fact concern the contract and whether it involves the interpretation or application of one of its terms. A few examples will serve to illustrate the problem.

In *Kroger Company v. Food Stores Employees Union Local 347* (1956)[3] the company opened one of its stores for six nights per week. The union refused to perform night work unless the company agreed to pay a premium. The union protested the unilateral action of the management. No clause in the contract bore directly on the point. But the union rested its plea on the following clause: "The hours for each employee shall be scheduled by the employer. The Employer will post a satisfactory schedule of hours to govern working hours and time off for regular full-time employees." Based on this clause, the arbitrator took jurisdiction of the dispute.

In *Minneapolis-Honeywell Regulator Co. v. Utility Workers Union of America* (1957)[4] the union protested the removal of a swing-shift nurse, under a contract having this type of arbitration clause. No provision of the contract required the hiring of such a nurse. But the union alleged, and the arbitrator agreed, that a contractual provision for making "reasonable provisions" for safety and health encompassed this issue.

In *John Deere Manufacturing Co. v. International Association of Machinists* (1954)[5] the contract contained the type of arbitration clause under discussion. The union presented a grievance in which it claimed that the company had added a requirement to grievant's duties, which was in effect a unilateral change in the requirements of grievant's job classification.

The arbitrator decided the issue was arbitrable. The contract made no provision concerning change of job classifications. The arbitrator said: "Exhibits A and B are integral parts of the contract. The classifications mentioned therein had job descriptions established for them at the time of the contract's negotiation. If it could be shown that the company had unilaterally altered the functions of a particular job classification, it seems to me that a question would be properly raised as to whether such action is consonant with or in conflict with the contract."

It can be seen that even where the arbitration clause narrows the scope of arbitrability to matters contractual, what is a matter of contract is not always clear. According to some arbitrators, if it is a matter affected by the contract, it is enough to render it arbitrable.

NO POWER TO ADD TO OR SUBTRACT FROM THE CONTRACT. Some arbitration clauses limit the arbitrator's power to an interpretation and application of the contract and further specifically provide that he "shall have no power to add to or subtract from the contract." Such a clause might read: "The arbitrator shall have no power to add to or subtract from or modify any of the terms of the agreement. . . ."

Such clauses clearly state the parties' intention that the arbitrator will be empowered only to interpret the contract but not add to or modify it. The distinction between an award that merely interprets and one that adds to or modifies the contract is not always easy to make. What an arbitrator may consider as merely an interpretation of a contractual provision may be viewed by one of the parties as an addition to or a modification of the contract.

On the other hand, a refusal by an arbitrator to rule because in his opinion he would be adding to or modifying the contract may be interpreted by one of the parties as a rationalization for refusing to make a decision. A far more effective way to narrow the range of arbitral power is to state exactly what matter he is *not* to handle.

The following clause represents a type of limitation that is fairly representative:

> The Umpire shall have no power to add to or subtract from or modify any of the terms of this agreement or any agreements made supplementary hereto; nor to establish or change any wage; nor to rule on any dispute arising . . . regarding Production Standards.
>
> The Umpire shall have no power to rule on any issue or dispute arising under the Pension Plan, Insurance Program and Supplemental Unemployment Benefit Plan or the Waiver Section.
>
> Any case appealed to the Umpire on which he has no power to rule shall be referred back to the Parties without decision.[6]

In general, it can be said that the setting of wage rates is not arbitrable. Some recent contracts have made an exception when the wage rate to be established was for a new job. Setting standards of production is also usually not arbitrable. Where the contract provides for the use of discretion, management will usually object to an arbitrator's substituting his discretion for that of the company. Some contracts, however, expressly confer upon the arbitrator the power to set wages and production standards, or even to decide what the terms of the new contract should be.*

POWER TO ARBITRATE SPECIFIC ISSUES. Arbitration clauses in collective bargaining agreements may expressly provide what the arbitrator can do. Some contracts go even further in delineating the arbitrator's power. For example, the contract may set forth the precise question to be decided or limit his decision to certain specific questions of fact, as in the following clause, which refers to the arbitration of disputes that might arise under a guaranteed annual wage plan:

If any arbitration . . . shall be required, the impartial umpire shall answer only the following questions:
Shortage of Raw Sugar
  (i) Is there a shortage of raw sugar due to reasons beyond the Company's control?
 (ii) Does such shortage adversely affect the Company's operations?
(iii) As a result of such adverse effect on operations, is or was it impracticable for the Company to provide the particular employee . . . with work?
 (iv) If questions (i) (ii) and (iii) are answered affirmatively, to what extent should the figure of 2,000 hours be or have been reduced?
. . .
Major Breakdown
  (i) Did a major breakdown occur?
 (ii) Did the major breakdown make it impracticable for the Company to provide the employee . . . with work?
(iii) If questions (i) and (ii) are answered affirmatively, to what extent should the figure of 2,000 hours be or have been reduced?[7]

In a case reported in *The New York Times*[8], an arbitrator issued an award directing an employer to reopen his closed factory and pay the union over $200,000 in damages for having moved his factory to another state in violation of the collective bargaining agreement. The powers exercised by the arbitrator in this case represent an extension of the powers usually exercised by arbitrators. The New York Appellate Division denied the employer's application to stay arbitration pending an appeal from a decision of the New York Supreme Court, which held that the employer was subject to the collective bargaining agreement with the union and bound by its arbitration provisions.

There are many interesting aspects to this case. In the first place, the

---

* The contract effective May 1, 1960, between Trafalgar Hospital in New York City and Local 1199, Drug and Employees Hospital Union, AFL–CIO, provides for the arbitration of wage rates [Article XVI—Reopening. Section 1]: . . . "Should the parties fail or be unable to arrive at a mutually satisfactory agreement with respect to such a wage revision, the matter shall be submitted to an arbitrator whose award shall be final and binding upon the parties. The award made by the arbitrator shall be deemed incorporated in and a part of this agreement."

contract gives the impartial chairman broad powers. Article XIX of the 1957–1960 and 1960–1963 agreements provides:

In addition to the powers which the Impartial Chairman may possess pursuant to this agreement or by operation of law, it is expressly agreed that in the Agreement, the Impartial Chairman may issue an award providing for a mandatory direction, prohibition, order, or money damages.[8]

The arbitrator's authority to order the reopening of the plant and to award damages to the union depended not only on the clause cited above but also upon what he considered to be the law of the state of New York. In his award he stated:

It is the established law of our State that an arbitrator possesses the powers of an equity judge in fashioning such relief as he believes to be called for by the circumstances. (*In Re* Feuer Transportation, Inc., 295 N.Y. 87, 92.) It has been stated that an arbitrator may act to remedy a situation in a manner which may even be beyond the powers of an equity court. (Staklinski v. Pyramid Electric Company, 6 A.D. 2d 565; affd. 6 N.Y. 2d 159.)

The collective bargaining agreement contained several other provisions which are pertinent and somewhat unique. Article XV of the Market Agreement of 1957–1960 provided:

A. During the term of this agreement the Employer agrees that he shall not, without the consent of the New York Joint Board, remove or cause to be removed his present plant or plants from the City or cities in which such plant or plants are located.

B. During the term of this Agreement the Employer shall not, without the consent of the New York Joint Board, manufacture garments or cause them to be manufactured in a factory other than his present factory or factories.

Article XXIII of the agreement provided that unless the written consent of the New York Joint Board had first been obtained:

No employer and no person who is now or becomes an officer, substantial stockholder, director or partner of any Employer during the term of this Agreement shall become, directly or indirectly, interested in any clothing establishment or a subsidiary or affiliate thereof operating as a manufacturing jobber, manufacturing wholesaler, manufacturing retailer, or contractor which is not in contractual relationship with the New York Joint Board.

This article also provided that such consent is not to be withheld unreasonably and, if withheld, the person seeking the consent can present the matter to the impartial chairman of the industry for his determination.

The arbitrator held in this case that the employer violated these contractual obligations, and he directed the employer to reopen its New York factory and pay damages totaling $204,681 to the union.

POWER TO DECIDE ARBITRABILITY. It should be noted at this point that some collective bargaining agreements specifically confer on the arbitrator the power to decide the arbitrability of a dispute. By such an express conferral of power, the question of arbitrability is taken out of the jurisdiction of the courts.

POWER TO MEDIATE. Occasionally an arbitration clause expressly confers upon the arbitrator the power to mediate prior to arbitration. The following clause is typical: "The Arbitrator shall be free, if in his discretion he deems it desirable so to do, to attempt to adjust any difference or dispute by mediation before or during the course of any arbitration." [9]

POWER TO RENDER A FINAL AND BINDING AWARD. In almost all arbitration clauses in the private sector the arbitrator is granted the express power to render an award that is final and binding on both parties. This is one of the salient features of arbitration.

There is no formal procedure whereby an arbitrator's award can be appealed on its merits. The absence of an appeal procedure prevents long, drawn-out litigation, which is often so characteristic of our courts. The nature of industrial disputes is such that a prompt final determination is essential to industrial peace.

THE SUBMISSION AGREEMENT. Although the contract may establish the breadth of the arbitrator's power and the limits of his authority, his power may be more sharply defined in the submission agreement. Frequently, the parties jointly formulate in writing the specific issues to be decided by the arbitrator. Sometimes the arbitrator is asked by the parties to frame the issue on the basis of the written grievance or the case as presented.

The parties sometimes find framing the issues a difficult task. Each side may feel it can gain an advantage by narrowing or broadening the disputed issue. The issue argued in the grievance procedure may be quite different from what finally emerges in the submission agreement. Arbitrators and courts scrutinize these submissions with great care and endeavor to avoid too liberal a construction of their content.

In general, the arbitrator is expected to decide those questions expressly stated and limited in the submission agreement. However, since arbitration is the final resort for the adjudication of disputes, the arbitrator will assume that he has the power to make a final settlement. To illustrate: Assume that the submission empowers the arbitrator to decide whether Mr. X was discharged for "just cause." The arbitrator in this instance would assume that his powers extended beyond giving a yes-or-no answer and included the power to reinstate Mr. X with or without back pay.

While some leeway is implied from the circumstances and the contract, the arbitrator will normally not prescribe proper procedures for the future relations of the parties unless expressly authorized to do so.[10] Nor may he resolve other grievances that are not precipitated by the same facts.[11] It is important to note that even if the particular issue is noncontractual or is not arbitrable under the contract, the parties may stipulate to arbitrate such issue in the submission agreement. The arbitrator then has full authority to handle the matter.[12]

LIMITATION OF POWER. An arbitrator may delegate certain duties of a routine character to assist in handling a case, but he may not delegate the power to decide the issues and render a decision.[13] The parties, of course, may consent to such delegation, but this would be tantamount to an agreement to appoint another arbitrator. Failure to object to the designation of a delegate may be considered a waiver.[14]

Implied and Derived Powers

One of the most troublesome issues in labor arbitration is whether the arbitrator has the power to hear and determine the particular matter in dispute. When the contract contains a standard "interpretation and application" clause and the dispute clearly falls within some express provision of the contract, the parties are not likely to raise the issue of arbitrability. If, however, one of the parties feels that the matter in dispute does not fall within an express provision of the contract, he may question the arbitrator's right to hear and determine the matter.

DETERMINING ARBITRABILITY. When the issue of arbitrability is raised, the question arises whether the arbitrator has the power to determine his own jurisdiction or whether the issue of arbitrability should be decided by the courts.

There is no problem where the contract expressly gives the arbitrator authority to determine arbitrability. For example, the following clause in a contract makes clear the intent of the parties to relegate this issue to the arbitrator: "If a question arises as to whether or not a defined grievance or stated issue is arbitrable under the provisions of this Article, the question may be submitted to arbitration hereunder; if need be, at the request of either party." [15]

This is not the case in most contracts. In the majority of cases, as Elkouri pointed out: "The parties acquiesce in the arbitrator's determination of arbitrability even though under prevailing law there might be a basis for challenging the finality of his ruling." [16]

The National Academy of Arbitrators (NAA) proposed a federal labor arbitration act[17] that recommended that questions of arbitrability should be submitted to the arbitrator in the first instance unless the contract expressly provided otherwise.* United States Supreme Court Decisions have made it clear that although arbitrability is a court question, the parties may properly present this issue in the forum of arbitration.[18]

Criteria Used in Specific Issues

In many cases the question of arbitrability is raised before the arbitrator.[19] The most common clause in the arbitration agreement is one that restricts

---

* Former Academy President Leo Brown, S.J., explained the proposal as consonant with the intention of the parties to settle disputes by arbitration, an intention that is thwarted if either side can run to a different forum. "Private collective bargaining," he said, "assumes the original determination of this question by the parties' own agency of arbitration, with the right of resort to the courts kept in reserve as a function . . . only of review." (See Ref. 17.)

the jurisdiction of the arbitrator to matters affecting interpretation and application. Generally the body of the agreement gives little guidance in a specific case. The fact is that most agreements do not purport to cover every specific instance of possible future disagreement.[20]

This would appear to be the essence of the dictum in Mr. Justice Douglas' characterization of arbitration as part of the collective bargaining process, viewing the agreement as but one stage in a continuum.[21] In this open-end process the arbitrator is eminently qualified to determine the arbitrability of a submitted dispute. However, no clear or definite standards of arbitrability exist which can be applied in any specific case, and a study of the decisions of arbitrators reveals no unifying thread or any reliable consistency. What does emerge is the tendency of arbitrators to find matters arbitrable when they feel a contract right has been affected, directly or indirectly, although the limits are not easily defined. The discussion that follows shows how arbitrators have met the problem of arbitrability in specific issues.[22]

SENIORITY. Issues involving seniority are normally found to be arbitrable. Seniority is a featured clause in virtually all collective bargaining agreements. The following two cases illustrate how the handling of this issue works out in actual practice.

In one case, involving an educational standard set up by the company to select employees for promotion, the arbitrator denied the company's claim that the matter was not arbitrable.[23]

In another case, involving a memorandum of agreement regulating return from military service, the company's contention that the matter was not arbitrable was rejected by the arbitrator.[24]

The arbitrators found, since the educational standard and the memorandum of agreement regulating return from military service directly affected the seniority provisions of contracts, that these issues were arbitrable. But in another case an arbitrator found a seniority matter arbitrable, even though the arbitrable matters defined in the contract did not include the seniority clause. He held that if the parties had wanted to exclude that article it should have been expressly stated.[25]

DISCHARGE. Arbitrators are hesitant to dismiss a discharge case on jurisdictional grounds. Jurisdiction is clear when an employee has been fired for "just cause" and management's disciplinary power is restricted in the contract.[26] This is also true when management has an express right to discharge or discipline.[27] Unless these two rights are clearly and expressly removed from arbitral jurisdiction, it is unlikely that arbitrators will find difficulty in rejecting a claim of nonarbitrability.

WAGES, HOURS, AND WORKING CONDITIONS. Disputes on these matters are not always easily decided. There is a trend toward arbitrability,* but

* A wage dispute was found to be arbitrable even though one clause implied that the matter was negotiable.

the movement is slow.[28] When an issue has some rational and tangible connection to hours or working conditions, arbitrators are not hesitant to take jurisdiction.[29] Safety measures are also found to be within the scope of working conditions.[30]

RETIREMENT. Retirement matters, especially when there is a mandatory requirement, have fallen into the arbitrator's jurisdiction on the grounds of an indirect link to numerous contract clauses,[31] particularly seniority[32] provisions.

FORMULATION OF THE ISSUE. The precise wording of the issue should be agreed upon by the parties, to avoid a dispute about arbitrability. In one case where this had not been done, the company alleged that the matter was not arbitrable. It was held, however, to be arbitrable on the grounds that the intent and purpose of the arbitration clause could be frustrated by an unreasonable refusal to agree on the exact wording of the issue. It was held further that where the nature of the controversy is clear from the statement of the grievance and the company's answer, the precise language of the issue could be supplied by the arbitrator.

RIGHTS OF MANAGEMENT. A "management rights' clause" is not always sufficient support for an argument against arbitration. A situation in point is where management is alleged to have encroached on some implied contractual provision or on simply an implied covenant of good faith. A dispute will always be arbitrable when there is an express contractual limitation on a management prerogative. It has been suggested that two factors will tend to limit this prerogative: (1) when rights have been bargained away in prior years, and (2) when past practices have become fixed and are not subject to unilateral change.[33]

The mere presence of a management "rights' clause" will not necessarily impose an absolute restriction on what an arbitrator may do. He will always weigh the opposing interest. It has been suggested that the trend in subcontracting cases has progressed to the point where the arbitrator is likely to find an implied covenant of good faith to be a sound basis for rendering the dispute arbitrable.[34]

The union's argument for arbitration rests on two theses: (1) It is the exclusive bargaining agent under the "recognition clause" of the agreement; (2) the "benefit" provisions impose an obligation on the company not to reduce either the scope of the bargaining unit or the rights and benefits specified in the agreement.[35]

Similarly, decisions affecting the qualifications of women to perform a new job,[36] the nature of a ten-day shutdown,[37] and the unilateral assignment of employees to a job[38] illustrate the tendency of arbitrators to find that there are some benefits under the agreement and that the management's "rights' clause" is not enough to outweigh the claim of arbitrability. The scope of arbitrable matters is increasing.

PAST PRACTICE. To what extent past practice is incorporated in a contract is not always clear. No agreement today is likely to be considered as the exclusive and complete statement of all rights and obligations of the parties. To what extent past practice will be inherent in the agreement is never absolutely certain. Some decisions limit the arbitrability of a past-practice question to what can be implied from some express contractual provision.[39] If past practice can be specifically defined, arbitration is even more certain.[40] When past practice appears to be based on mutual under-standing, it is likely to be interpreted as a collateral agreement and arbitrability will be found.

NATIONAL LABOR RELATIONS BOARD MATTERS. Sometimes disputes involve conduct that may be an unfair labor practice. Arbitrators have assumed jurisdiction of these disputes[41] even though the NLRB is not bound by their determination (see Chapter 10).

GRIEVANCE PROCEDURE. Some arbitrators have hestitated to hold a dispute to be nonarbitrable for failure to observe the proper time limits,[42] but some case decisions have held the reverse.[43] Before arbitrators will accept jurisdiction, however, they insist that the grievance procedure be observed.[44] Because arbitration is a final step, it should not become a substitute for voluntary settlement between the parties. A procedural objec-tion may be waived by a party and, where a waiver is found, the arbitrator will assume jurisdiction.[45]

INJUNCTIONS. In some labor arbitration awards, management is re-quired to take some specific action. If management refuses to comply, the union may obtain a court order to enforce the arbitrator's award. Manage-ment, however, also has certain rights. The courts have handed down deci-sions in which the union is required to take some action.

The New York Court of Appeals, in a ground-breaking opinion, held in *Matter of Ruppert* (1958)[46] that an arbitrator's injunction against the union would be enforceable in the courts. It is significant to note that the ruling was sustained, notwithstanding the fact that provisions of the New York law relating to injunctions issued in labor disputes,[47] like the federal Norris–LaGuardia Act, might have prevented the courts from granting relief had they heard the complaint initially.

This case should not be interpreted too broadly. The particular circum-stances clearly warranted this injunctive relief. The union had engaged in a slowdown, which was forbidden in the contract. A provision in the agree-ment for handling this kind of a situation also specified arbitration within 24 hours of the request by either party. The court, in sustaining the arbi-trator's order that the union eliminate the slowdown, felt that the contrac-tual provision for speedy arbitration would have been abrogated unless the remedy contemplated (quick resolution of the dispute) was such as to satisfy the clause. An injunction therefore was implied, said the court, from the expressed desire of the parties to settle such disputes quickly. The court also found no bar to a private agreement to permit an injunction, notwithstanding the statutory bar to labor injunctions, since the statute was designed to protect unions.

While the circumstances of the *Ruppert* case seemed to require that the court must find some intent to obtain quick relief for the parties, there is no doubt that the logic of the case is rooted in the concept that what is applicable to management is also applicable to unions.

It is evident from this survey that arbitrators are likely to find a dispute arbitrable whenever the dispute involves (1) an express clause of the contract, (2) an implied provision, or (3) violations of working relationships that can be tied to an express or implied provision of the agreement. But it cannot be assumed that because a dispute is arbitrable, a claim will necessarily be sustained on the merits. While a decision against arbitrability is in effect a denial of the claim, the converse is not true. Recent awards reveal a sensitivity to the emergent needs of the parties and to the function of the arbitral process.

REFERENCES

1. Northland v. Amalagamated Assn., U.S. District Court, District of Minnesota, 18 LRRM 2205.
2. Matter of Bohlenger, 305 N.Y. 539 (1933).
3. Kroger Company v. Food Store Employees Union Local 347, 27 LA 236.
4. Minneapolis-Honeywell Regulator Company v. Utility Workers Union of America, 28 LA 150.
5. John Deere Manufacturing Company v. International Association of Machinists, 23 LA 206.
6. General Motors and Auto Workers, 51 CBNC 265.
7. National Sugar Refining Co. and Packinghouse Workers, 53 CBNC 447.
8. *The New York Times*, "Union Forcing Plant to Return to City" (in the matter of arbitration between the Amalgamated Clothing Workers of America and the New York Joint Board of the Amalgamated Clothing Workers Union and Jack Meilman Employer), July 14, 1960, p. 1.
9. Trinity Bag and Paper Co. and Truck Drivers and Chauffeurs Union, Local 478, Ind., 1960 Collective Bargaining Agreement.
10. (a) North American Cement Corp., 28 LA 414; (b) Southwestern Bell Telephone Co., 30 LA 262.
11. Compare American Airlines, Inc., 27 LA 448; with Sylvania Electric Products, Inc., 24 LA 199.
12. Corn Products Refining Co., 21 LA 852.
13. Twin Lakes Reservoir & Canal Co. v. Platt Rogers, Inc., 94 P 2d 1090.
14. Building Services Employees International Union v. Filene Holding Corp., 43 N.Y.S. 2d 309.
15. Consolidated Edison Co. of N.Y. Inc. and Bro. of Consolidated Edison Employees Ind. Cited at par. 64,067, P-H Labor Arbitration.
16. Frank Elkouri, *How Arbitration Works*. Washington, D.C.: The Bureau of National Affairs, 1952, p. 36.
17. L.A. II (May 4, 1960).
18. United States Steelworkers of America v. Warrior and Gulf Navigation Co. 46 LRRM 2416.

19. "Substantive Aspects of Labor–Management Arbitration." American Arbitration Association report, 28 LA 943.
20. Archibald Cox, "Reflections Upon Labor Arbitration." *Harv. L. Rev.*, Vol. 72 (1959), p. 1482.
21. United States Steelworkers of America v. Warrior and Gulf Navigation Co. 8 Sup. Ct. 1347, 46 LRRM 2416.
22. Wilbur L. Collins, *Arbitrability and Arbitration.* Albany, N.Y.: Matthew Bender & Co., Inc., 1960, p. 449.
23. Philip Carey Manufacturing Co., 30 LA 659.
24. Southwestern Bell Telephone Co., 33 LA 132.
25. Plymouth Cordage Co., 27 LA 816.
26. (a) Wertheimer Bag Co., 33 LA 694; (b) Davison Chemical Co., 31 LA 920; (c) Ring's End Fuel Co., 25 LA 608; (d) American Bakeries Co., 34 LA 360.
27. (a) The Kellogg Co., 28 LA 303; (b) Campbell Soup Co., 26 LA 910.
28. McCord Corp., 30 LA 290.
29. (a) The Kroger Co., 27 LA 236; (b) Borden Mfg. Co., 25 LA 629; (c) Olin Mathieson Chemical Corp., 34 LA 190.
30. (a) Linde Co., 34 LA 1; (b) Minneapolis–Honeywell Co., 28 LA 150.
31. (a) Trans World Airlines, Inc., 31 LA 45; (b) Hale Bros. Stores, 32 LA 713; (c) Western Airlines, Inc., 33 LA 84.
32. Sandia Corp., 27 LA 669.
33. Jules Justin. "How to Preserve Management's Rights Under the Labor Contract." *Lab. L. J.*, 11 (1960), p. 189.
34. Wilbur L. Collins, *op. cit.*
35. Lukens Steel Co., 33 LA 228.
36. Morton Salt Co., 29 LA 59.
37. Cone Mills Corp., 29 LA 346.
38. Continental Emsco Co., 34 LA 278.
39. (a) U.S. Industrial Chemical Co., 28 LA 401; (b) Cone Mills Corp., 30 LA 100.
40. (a) Crompton and Knowles Corp., 34 LA 59 (use of cashier's window a condition of employment); (b) New Jersey Brewers Association, 33 LA 320 (Sunday overtime work part of wage rate).
41. (a) Jesco Lubricants, Inc., 33 LA 488; (b) Conover–Cable Piano Co., 31 LA 589; (c) Bendix–Westinghouse Corp., 30 LA 620.
42. (a) Standard–Thompson Corp., 26 LA 633; (b) United States Pipe & Foundry Co., 28 LA 775; (c) Roco Manser Precision Engineering Corp., 33 LA 199.
43. (a) West Penn. Power Co., 31 LA 297; (b) Rockwell Mfg. Co., 25 LA 534.
44. (a) Borg–Warner Corp., 27 LA 58D; (b) American Airlines, Inc., 27 LA 448; (c) Bridgeport Brass Co., 30 LA 622.
45. (a) Bird and Son, Inc., 33 LA 777· (b) Ironrite, Inc., 28 LA 398.
46. Ruppert v. Egelhofer, 3 N.Y. 2d 576; 148 N.E. 2d 129 (1958).
47. (a) "Lawyer's Arbitration Letter," No. 4 (Nov. 15, 1960), pp. 1–3. (b) Russell F. Moore, note, "In the Matter of the Arbitration between Jacob Ruppert *et al.*, Respondents, and Int'l. Brotherhood of Toastmasters. Chauffeurs, Warehousemen and Helpers of America, A. F. of L.–CIO," *N.Y. Law Forum*, Vol. 4 (1958), p. 437.

7

ARBITRATION PROCEDURES

Arbitration procedures are determined by the arbitrator. His power to regulate the proceedings is circumscribed, however, by statute and the rules of the administrative agency. The American Arbitration Association (AAA) has formulated procedural standards for arbitrators, which have been published as part of the Code of Ethics (see Appendix I,1).

Although arbitration proceedings are informal, each party is given full opportunity to present his case in an orderly manner. The arbitrator first obtains the names and addresses of all persons appearing on behalf of the union and the company. He then requests a statement of the issue before him. If the parties have not already agreed to the exact wording of the issue, the arbitrator may assist in its formulation.

Each side will then be requested to present an opening statement. This is a statement of each party's position and an outline of the evidence to support that position. The opening statement enables the arbitrator to comprehend the nature of the problem and to more intelligently follow the evidence.

The collective bargaining agreement is usually the first joint exhibit. It contains the arbitration clause that defines the arbitrator's power. At this time the parties usually point out those clauses in the contract that are pertinent to the issue.

In discipline and discharge cases, management presents its case first; in other cases the claimant proceeds first. The next step is direct and cross-examination of the witnesses for each side.

A summation by each party closes the hearing and the case. If, however, the parties exchange briefs, the case will be closed upon the receipt of the briefs. Usually the award is handed down within 30 days after the close of the case, except when the time is extended by the parties. (See later section, "New Documents," and also Appendixes II,1, Rule 29,1, and III,4, sec. 10(e).)

Where the parties have developed procedures to meet their special needs, the arbitrator should, when possible, endeavor to follow such procedures. Where an industry has a permanent arbitrator, hearings are frequently more informal. The degree of informality is often determined by the personality of the arbitrator and the nature of the issue. Hotly contested and complicated legal issues are usually arbitrated in a more formal manner.

The Arbitrator's Oath of Office

Many states require that the arbitrator take an oath of office. The New York statute states that "before hearing any testimony, an arbitrator shall be sworn to hear and decide the controversy faithfully and fairly by an officer authorized to administer an oath." (See Appendix III, sec. 7506(a).) The statute also provides that this requirement may be waived by the written consent of the parties or their attorneys, or by continued arbitration without objection. (See Appendix III, sec. 7506(f).)

Some people question the utility of the oath and consider it as no more than a holdover from formal court procedures. A survey made by the AAA suggests that parties are aware of this fact.[1] It appeared that in 62.5 percent of the sampled cases, the oath was waived. The survey pointed out, however, that in all AAA cases, the arbitrator's oath to faithfully and fairly hear and examine the matters in controversy and make a just award is included in the "Notice of Appointment" form (see Appendix V, Form 8), which all arbitrators sign on accepting a case. It is doubtful that the percentage shown in the survey would be altered if such a form were not required. The fact is that, in the minds of the parties, the oath is merely a formality.

Swearing Witnesses

The requirement for the swearing of witnesses is also one of questionable value, although there are considerations here that are absent in the case of the arbitrator's oath. The arbitrator's authority to swear witnesses is derived from statute. Many state statutes give the arbitrator authority to swear witnesses; others do not. Few require that the oath be administered. The chief argument in favor of swearing witnesses is that it serves to impress upon them the solemnity and legitimacy of the proceedings, which they might otherwise ignore. Arbitrators have no power to penalize witnesses who commit perjury.

Representation of Parties by Counsel

Although the proceedings are relatively informal, the matters dealt with are often complicated and of crucial importance to the parties. The impact of an adverse award may be very great. Additionally, the presentation of testimony, documentary evidence, and argument requires a great deal of skill and study. Therefore, attorneys are utilized by both sides in a great many arbitration proceedings. A sample study indicates that of the cases surveyed, over 63 percent had one or both parties represented by counsel.

Of this group, 48.4 percent of the cases had both parties represented by counsel; in 38.7 percent, only the company had counsel; and in 12.9 percent only the union had counsel.[2]

The question frequently arises whether the parties to an arbitration should be represented by counsel. Where the issue is complex and involves legal questions, counsel is indispensable. In other matters, attorneys may be helpful but not essential. Many industrial relations executives and union officials have developed skills that enable them to present cases effectively.

One advantage of being represented by counsel is the preparation of the case for the hearing; unfortunately, too many cases that are not properly prepared are presented to arbitrators. The effectiveness of an attorney is in large measure determined by his familiarity with industrial relations problems, practices, and procedures.

Most issues that are arbitrated are quite different from the usual matters adjudicated by courts of law. The attorney must understand the many psychological and political factors that cause grievances. He cannot view a collective bargaining agreement as an abstract document, but must see it in the framework of accepted industrial practice. Nevertheless, he must always bear in mind that a collective bargaining agreement is a legal contract binding on both parties. An attorney who has no knowledge of industrial practice and whose experience is limited to business contracts and courts of law can unnecessarily complicate a simple arbitrable issue.

It should be noted that Section 7506(d) of the New York Arbitration Law (Appendix IV,1) grants the privilege of counsel to a party and declares that it is irrevocable.

Use of Transcripts

The parties are not obliged to have a transcript made of the proceedings. It is a requirement, however, in some arbitration clauses,[3] but this is an exception to general practice. The AAA survey showed that a stenographic record was taken in only 22.7 percent of the cases sampled.[4] The principal reasons why transcripts are not taken are the simple nature of many cases, the expense involved, and the time required to have transcripts reproduced.

In cases that involve complicated issues, the testimony of many witnesses, and technical evidence, a stenographic record of the proceedings is important and valuable. It is not always possible for an arbitrator to take copious and exact notes and at the same time observe the witnesses and evaluate the credibility of their testimony, particularly in involved technical cases.

Typing several hundred pages of testimony will, of course, take time and delay the rendition of the award. Statistics show that in cases where transcripts were taken, the average time from submission to award was from four to five months, compared with one to two months where no transcript was made. It should be noted, however, that delays may also be due to such factors as the complexity and technical nature of the issues and the filing of post-hearing briefs.

Use of Subpoena

Over 25 state statutes empower the arbitrator to issue a subpoena to compel the appearance of persons or the production of relevant records.* Thus, pertinent evidence can be obtained when a person is reluctant to produce it. Similarly, one who is not a party to the proceeding, but whose participation would be helpful, may also be compelled to appear. A subpoena is particularly effective when a witness whose testimony is important works for another employer, and is reluctant to ask for a day off.

Arbitrators, however, are cautious in issuing a subpoena. Normally the parties are eager to cooperate with the arbitrator. Failure to produce relevant evidence on request may be construed as hostility, and therefore the party (unless he is planning to contest the award) is likely to cooperate. Also, the known power of the arbitrator is sufficient to persuade a reluctant witness to comply with an informal request. Considering the continuing nature of labor–management relations, it may be unwise to use a subpoena to force a reluctant witness to testify against a fellow employee.

Admissibility of Evidence

Rules of evidence applicable in courts of law have been developed over many years for the purposes of avoiding fraud and confusion and of confining evidence to relevant testimony. These rules of evidence should be known by the arbitrator as well as by the parties because they can serve as a guide for the admissibility and the weight of the evidence. Nevertheless, for reasons that will be explained below, these rules of evidence are not strictly adhered to in arbitration hearings.

APPLICABILITY OF RULES OF EVIDENCE. Some testimony presented in arbitration hearings has little probative value, but it may give a witness an opportunity to vent pent-up feelings that may reveal the underlying reasons why a grievance was filed or could not be settled. Sometimes the opportunity to express a point of view to an impartial person is more important than the ultimate decision.

Where an impartial chairman of an industry has a continuing relationship with the parties, the nonjudicial phases of an arbitration proceeding become very important in settling many issues without an award. The arbitrator also acquires a greater understanding of the underlying causes for the dispute. Industrial strife may be reduced or avoided if its basic causes are discovered.

* The proposed Uniform Arbitration Act (see Appendix IV,3) for all states would endow arbitrators with this power.

ADMISSIBILITY DETERMINED BY ARBITRATOR. The arbitrator determines the admissibility of evidence. Where the issue is a legal one or involves an interpretation of a provision in the contract, arbitrators are more careful about the nature of the evidence introduced. In these cases the rules of evidence as developed in our courts of law serve as a guide for arbitrators. The parties may specify that certain types of evidence will not be admissible, but this restriction is rarely imposed.

In most cases, as previously stated, the arbitrator determines the conduct of proceedings, from the order of presentation of evidence to the types of evidence that will be heard. He also has the power to adjust and change the rules, provided the revisions have no prejudicial effects on any party. This broad approach to the admissibility of evidence is epitomized in the AAA rules. Rule 28 (see Appendix II,1) permits parties to present whatever evidence they wish, but also enjoins them to provide all evidence requested by the arbitrator, who is the sole judge of its relevancy and materiality.

THE HEARSAY RULE. Hearsay evidence is information that is based not on the witness's personal knowledge but on matters told him by another. Under the hearsay rule such evidence cannot be used in courts of law for the purpose of establishing the truth of the matters related to the witness.

The hearsay rule is practically never strictly enforced by arbitrators. This rule and other exclusionary rules that are followed by the courts have often been considered impediments. According to Wigmore, the hearsay rule may be "a needless obstruction to investigation of truth." [5] While heresay rules serve a purpose in jury trials, such rules are often not invoked in nonjury trials. Whatever the rationale for their continued existence in the courts—and this is persuasive—there is no concomitant reason for using them in arbitration proceedings.

The principal basis for many rules of exclusion is to protect the jury, on the assumption that its members are not competent enough to evaluate some evidence. This is not applicable in arbitration proceedings, for much the same reasons that such rules are often not applied in cases heard by a judge alone or in administrative tribunals. The arbitrator is often a lawyer or, if not, a person capable of evaluating evidence.

In general, everything said or done by everyone connected with the incident should be heard, and the parties should trust in the arbitrator's ability to separate truth from falsehood or distortion of the facts and give proper weight to the evidence.

RELEVANCE AND MATERIALITY. It would appear proper to exclude evidence that is not relevant or material to the issue. Although this rule may be desirable in courts of law, it is generally agreed that in arbitration proceedings it is unwise to always exclude evidence on the grounds of irrelevance and immateriality. Frequently the admission of this type of evidence, particularly in discharge cases, provides a catharsis for the parties.

The late Harry Shulman felt that "the more serious danger is not that the arbitrator will hear too much irrelevancy, but rather that he will not hear enough of the relevant." [6]

An additional legal reason for admitting evidence of doubtful relevance and materiality is that the courts may refuse to enforce an award on the grounds that the arbitrator failed to admit material or relevant evidence.

PAROLE EVIDENCE. When the contract provision is clear and unambiguous, the general rule is that "parole evidence" is not admissible. If an ambiguity exists, proof of oral statements made during negotiations by the contracting parties is admissible. However, a problem arises when one party to the dispute is a successor company to the one originally at the bargaining table. In this situation, the acquiring company may not have first-hand evidence to substantiate the claims involved in the grievance.

Thus, oral statements are admissible to assist the arbitrator to interpret an ambiguous clause. Parole evidence is also admissible to establish past practice and establish how the parties have by their conduct interpreted or applied the clauses in question. However, it is generally agreed that arbitrators can require that past practices must have met certain standards.[7, 8]

Parole evidence should be excluded if it is intended to prove how a particular contract provision is interpreted by a company not party to the contract. However, parole evidence of how other members of the industry interpret a clause in an industry-wide master contract should not be excluded.

It is generally agreed that parole evidence is admissible to establish a collateral agreement, even when the contract between the parties expressly states that all prior agreements are incorporated in the agreement and that all collateral agreements must be in writing. The weight given to such evidence, however, must be determined in the light of such limitations.

THE BEST-EVIDENCE RULE. Although better evidence may be available (original letter), its existence does not exclude admission of relevant evidence (copy of the letter). Original documents may be lost or may be in the possession of a third party, or may be physically or legally impossible to remove, or may be business records in constant use whose removal could cause great inconvenience. If a person can recollect the contents of a document that is not available, such testimony should be permitted.

OPINION EVIDENCE. An opinion is an inference from data observed or made available to the witness. Many courts follow the rule that if the data from which opinion is derived can be made available to the jury, then the opinions of witnesses will be excluded. This rule has been criticized.

The opinion of an expert is, of course, admissible. However, although strict court rules for establishing the qualifications of an expert need not be insisted upon, the parties should agree on minimum requirements that qualify the witness as an expert. However, if the expert depends upon hearsay data for his testimony, his opinion will carry little or no weight.

UTILIZING EXPERT TESTIMONY. An arbitrator should not seek expert advice without informing the parties of his intention. However, under certain circumstances, such as when the experts selected by the parties give conflicting testimony, the arbitrator may suggest the use of an impartial expert, selected by him. If the parties agree, the opinion of this person should be made known to all parties, who should submit their comments before the arbitrator writes his opinion and award. This problem usually applies in cases involving job evaluations and incentives. In discharge cases involving medical evidence, the conflict is usually between the employee's physician, who finds the employee able to work, and the company physician, who diagnoses the physical state of the employee as unfit for employment.

Basically, the arbitrator weighs medical evidence in the same way as any other evidence. He evaluates the quantity and quality of the testimony and the documentary proof offered by both parties, finding for the party whose evidence seems most persuasive. In a study of arbitrators' awards reported in the *Arbitration Journal*, it was found that "the arbitrator was most influenced in his decision by the party who had the most comprehensive grasp of all the pertinent facts, regardless of who analyzed them—generalist, specialist, or impartial consultant." [9] The arbitrator is usually hesitant to use an impartial expert of his own selection without the consent of the parties because of increased costs and the possibility of political repercussions and/or increased tensions.

CIRCUMSTANTIAL EVIDENCE. A distinction must be made between circumstantial evidence and testimonial or direct evidence. The latter refers to what the witness saw or heard. His testimony that he saw the employee strike the foreman is factual, or direct, evidence. If he testifies that on the previous day he heard the same employee and foreman having a heated argument, or heard the accused employee tell another employee that someday he would "beat up" the foreman, this would be circumstantial evidence. Since circumstantial evidence has corroborative value, it should be admissible. The weight to be given to circumstantial evidence, however, is less than the weight given to direct evidence.

The weight of direct evidence is dependent on the credibility of the witness. The weight of circumstantial evidence is dependent upon the reasonableness of the inference drawn from it as well as on the credibility of the witness. Even so, plausible inference offered by the aggrieved may tend to modify direct evidence and negate its apparent import.

ADMISSIONS. An admission is a statement made prior to the arbitration hearing and which is not consistent with the claim or defense in the matter before the arbitrator. Admissions by the grievant during grievance procedures are admissible testimony. However, care must be exercised in accepting certain admissions, such as one made by the union representative when the grievant was not present. As a safeguard, the arbitrator must make rulings to qualify such admissions so that the effectiveness of the grievance procedures is not jeopardized.

COMPROMISE OFFERS. To avoid arbitrating a particular grievance the company may offer to compromise by reinstating a discharged employee without back pay. If the union rejects the compromise offer, it would be improper to permit it to use the company's offer as an admission that the grievant was wrongfully discharged. For this reason, offers of compromise made prior to arbitration are normally inadmissible. Arbitrators are aware of the negotiations that may precede arbitration and of the merits of encouraging attempts by the parties to compromise and bargain at pre-arbitration stages. However, if such offers of settlement were introduced as evidence in subsequent arbitration hearings, fewer settlements would be made. As a consequence, the decisions show an almost uniform refusal to admit this type of evidence.

INDEPENDENT INQUIRIES. An arbitrator may not make independent inquiries to develop facts beyond those brought out in the hearing, unless this action is expressly approved by the parties or stipulated in the contract. Occasionally a permanent arbitrator will have this authority, but it is rarely given in ad hoc arbitration proceedings.

NEW EVIDENCE. Sometimes evidence is offered at arbitration proceedings that was not introduced previously in the processing of the grievance. There seems to be no reason for refusing to admit such evidence if it was not previously available, provided full opportunity is given for rebuttal. If the opposing party claims surprise and is not prepared to rebut, an adjournment may be appropriate.

However, the problem is more troublesome when evidence has been deliberately suppressed. If the attitude of the parties is rigid and antagonistic, one party may seek to gain an advantage by withholding evidence until it can "surprise" the other side at arbitration. When the parties use the grievance procedure as a battleground rather than a process for the settlement of disputes, the antagonistic attitude of the withholding party is understandable. Under these circumstances the evidence should be heard.[10] Where the relationships are more reasonable. the issue is unlikely to arise.

The contract may require that all evidence available to one party will be accessible if requested by the other party; otherwise, it will be barred later. This is more likely to be found in those sections of the contract that relate to discipline and discharge.[11] Where this is the case, the arbitrator is bound by the will of the parties.

NEW ARGUMENTS. A somewhat different problem is created when a party introduces before the arbitrator an argument that has not been raised earlier in the grievance procedure. This problem should be handled in a way similar to that for suppression of evidence. The arbitrator should judge each case on its merits, but should subject it to certain qualifications. For example, an employee who is charged with committing acts X and Y should not be confronted with charge Z at the arbitration hearing when only charges X and Y were advanced against him at an earlier hearing. Generally, the rule is that addenda to original charges are not acceptable.[12]

New Documents. After a hearing is closed, AAA Rule 29 provides that documents may be submitted after the hearing when arrangements for the submission of such documents were made "at the hearing or subsequently by agreement of the parties." (See Appendix II,1.) This rule also provides that documents "shall be filed with the AAA for transmission to the Arbitrator." It further stipulates that "all parties shall be afforded opportunity to examine such documents."

This rule provides a sound procedure that avoids prejudice or unfairness to either party. If the evidence is significant enough, it may be necessary to reconvene a hearing. It is advisable to persuade the parties to agree to a rehearing and an extension on the time limit for the award. The AAA Rule 32 provides that when no time limit has been set for the award, the arbitrator is free to reconvene the hearing.

The principal points to bear in mind in connection with the submission of evidence after the close of the hearing are that (1) the offended party must have an opportunity to examine and rebut it, and (2) any unilateral communication with the arbitrator may lead to invalidating his award. Where the evidence is discovered after the hearing, both parties should agree to its submission. If this is impossible, a rehearing should be sought.

Use of Polygraph. There appears to be a tendency on the part of arbitrators to exclude evidence obtained from a polygraph, commonly referred to as a lie detector. When such evidence is offered, it is given little weight,[13] and courts of law typically do not admit it, thus granting the rights of protection against self-incrimination, invasion of privacy, and circumstantial implications of actions or statements accompanying the examination.[14]

Collateral Criminal Proceedings. If criminal proceedings are directly related to the original cause of discipline or discharge, they may be properly submitted in evidence. However, if the purpose is to support a new or different charge not brought to the attention of the grievant or the union during the grievance procedure, these proceedings should be excluded by the arbitrator.

Affidavits. The arbitrator may receive and consider evidence of witnesses by affidavit, but shall give it only such weight as he deems proper after considering any objections that are made to its admission.

Affidavits by physicians are frequently offered in evidence. If the statement is challenged and is critical to the issue, the physician should be requested to testify in person, and opposing counsel should have the opportunity of cross-examination. If a doctor's certificate is admitted into evidence, it is not entitled to the same weight as evidence given in person.

Sources of Evidence

Company records which are not normally available to the union but which are relevant to the issue should be subject to examination and admitted as evidence. The admissibility of evidence obtained by breaking into an employee's locker is a controversial subject. It is argued that, since the locker is company property, it is subject to inspection by the company and its contents are admissible in evidence. The opposing argument is that an employee outside the plant is protected by the Constitution against violation of privacy and against unlawful search and seizure, even by police officers. Nothing in the Constitution states that these rights can be abrogated by or limited to a citizen's location. Moreover, violation of these constitutional rights is not conducive to good labor relations.

PRIVILEGED COMMUNICATIONS.[15] The circumstances in which privileged communications can be claimed are as follows:

1. *Physician-patient.*[16] A patient may claim privileged communications with his physician in any situation where such claim could be made in a court of law. Although the content of a communication is privileged, the fact that the employee has communicated with his physician is not privileged.

However, if by contract, past practice, or company rule, his continued employment is dependent on his physical condition, the employee may not claim this privilege. It should be noted that if, for reasonable cause, the employee objects to general disclosure, the arbitrator may limit such disclosure to selected representatives of the parties.

2. *Husband–wife.* A confidential communication between husband and wife is privileged.

3. *Witness–attorney.* Communications between a witness and either the union's or company's attorney are privileged.

4. *Union–employer communications.* Intraunion and intracompany communications are not privileged.

5. *Grievance discussions.*[17] Unless the parties have agreed otherwise, evidence relating to discussions during grievance proceedings is not privileged. However, this does not apply to offers of settlement or compromise, which are inadmissible as evidence.

6. *Grand jury.* A witness may refuse to disclose information given to a grand jury unless the findings of the grand jury have been filed in court or publicized otherwise.

7. *Classified information.* A witness who has acquired, in the course of his employment, official or classified information relating to the internal affairs of government may refuse to disclose such information to the arbitrator. However, the privilege may not be claimed if the arbitrator has government clearance for access to such information.

8. *Constitutional privilege.*[18] A witness may invoke his constitutional privilege to refuse to disclose any information on matters that would tend to subject him to incrimination in a statutory criminal action.

PRESUMPTIONS. In the normal course of an arbitration hearing, the arbitrator will make certain common presumptions such as (1) a letter deposited in a United States Mail Box shall be presumed to have been received; (2) a letter or any other writing prepared, published, or delivered by an official representative of the company, union, or a third party shall be presumed to have been authorized. It should be noted, however, that all presumptions are rebuttable.

JUDICIAL NOTICE. Arbitrators are expected to take judicial notice of any facts or laws that courts of law generally cite. These would include (1) specific facts so widely promulgated that they are not subjects for reasonable dispute, and (2) specific facts and generalized knowledge capable of immediate and accurate verification in easily accessible sources of undisputable accuracy.

The parties should make known to each other and the arbitrator those undisputed facts that are pertinent to the case.

OPINIONS AND TRANSCRIPTS OF GOVERNMENT AGENCIES. Generally the decisions, opinions, and transcripts from the Workmen's Compensation Board, Unemployment Compensation Commission, Labor Relations Board, and similar government agencies should be admitted into evidence. Transcripts may be used to impeach testimony or to establish admissions against interest.

The weight to be given to decisions and opinions depends upon whether the hearing was adversary in character or based upon an investigator's report. The latter type is entitled to little weight.

Direct and Cross-Examination

STANDARDS FOR DIRECT EXAMINATION. On direct examination it is permissible to ask leading questions only when the information sought is noncontroversial, such as job title and date of hire. A leading question usually asks the witness to affirm a statement of facts presented by the attorney. The purpose of such questions is to expedite the hearing.

Leading questions on controversial matters should not be permitted if objected to by opposing counsel. The problem with leading questions is that they attempt to elicit from the witness answers that do not conform to his knowledge.

STANDARDS FOR CROSS-EXAMINATION. Leading questions are permissible in cross-examination. Cross-examination enables the opposition to question the credibility of the witness (see discussion below) and the accuracy of his testimony. Cross-examination should not be curtailed unless (1) the questions have no bearing on the issue, (2) the witness is not competent to respond, (3) the witness is intimidated or abused, (4) the questions are so involved that they cannot be answered intelligently, or (5) the questions are repetitious.

CALLING WITNESSES FROM THE OTHER SIDE. Calling wittnesses from the other side should not be encouraged. Except under unusual circumstances, such as where the grievant knows best what occurred and under what circumstances, an arbitrator should rule that a grievant may not be called as a witness by the company at the outset of a case involving his discharge or discipline.

CREDIBILITY OF THE WITNESS. In many cases the decision may hinge on the arbitrator's conviction that one party is not telling the truth. Edgar A. Jones, in a paper delivered before the National Academy of Arbitrators, cautioned that "anyone driven by necessity of decision to fret about credibility, who has listened over a number of years to sworn testimony, knows that as much truth must have been uttered by shifty-eyed, perspiring, lip-licking, nail-biting, guilty-looking, ill at ease, fidgety witnesses as have lies issued from calm, collected, imperturbable, urbane, straight-in-the-eye perjurers." [19]

Jones also enumerated eleven factors listed in the California Evidence Code which should be considered when a witness testifies.

1. His demeanor while testifying and the manner in which he testifies
2. The character of his testimony
3. The extent of his capacity to perceive, to recollect, or to communicate any matter about which he testifies
4. The extent of his opportunity to perceive any matter about which he testifies
5. His character for honesty or veracity or their opposites
6. The existence or non-existence of a bias, interest or other motive
7. A statement previously made by him that is consistent with his statement at the hearing
8. A statement made by him that is inconsistent with any part of his testimony at the hearing
9. The existence or non-existence of any fact testified to by him
10. His attitude toward the action in which he testifies or toward the giving of testimony
11. His admission of untruthfulness

DEGREES OF PROOF. Proof must be distinguished from evidence. Evidence is the medium, proof is the result. A conclusion drawn from the evidence is proof. Proof is a judgment based upon the evidence.

There are three degrees of proof which a party may be required to sustain: (1) preponderance of the evidence, (2) clear and convincing proof, (3) proof beyond a reasonable doubt. The degree of proof required by the arbitrator will vary according to the seriousness of the charges against the grievant. When an employee is charged with acts of moral turpitude, proof beyond a reasonable doubt is required.

ORDER OF PROOF. Rule 26 of the AAA (see Appendix II,1) specifies how proceedings should be opened. It also states that "the Arbitrator may, in his discretion, vary the normal procedure . . . but . . . shall afford full and equal opportunity to all parties for presentation of relevant proofs." Again we find that conventional court rules governing the order in which evidence is presented are not uniformly applicable. The facts of the case determine whether fairness requires one or the other party to proceed first. For example, it has become customary in discharge cases for the company to present its case first and then for the union to dispute the reasons for the discharge.

Briefs

PRE-HEARING BRIEFS. The purpose of a pre-hearing brief is to give the arbitrator a statement of the issue and the position of the parties prior to the hearing. Although pre-hearing briefs are infrequently submitted, they can be of real value to the arbitrator in complicated cases. Advance knowledge of the positions of the parties will enable the arbitrator to comprehend the nature of the issue, the relevance of the testimony, and the arguments advanced by each side before the hearing begins. Having this preliminary statement enables him to suggest possible areas for stipulations of fact and other procedures that might expedite the hearings.

POST-HEARING BRIEFS. The use of post-hearing briefs is a technique often employed by the parties to supplement their presentations. Rules for the handling of this phase of the proceedings should be stipulated in advance unless agency regulations are applicable. The AAA Rule 29 (Appendix II,1) provides that such briefs must be filed with the tribunal clerk for submission to the arbitrator. In the study conducted by the AAA (see Ref. 1), it was found that briefs were filed in less than 42 percent of the sampled cases.[20] Briefs are usually filed in the more complicated and hotly contested cases, and in those for which transcripts are made. A well-prepared and concise brief may facilitate the arbitrator's decision by providing him with a clear picture of the positions of the parties.[21]

The Award

When all the evidence is in and the hearing is closed, the arbitrator must render his award. It has been pointed out that the award must be confined to the issues submitted for adjudication and must not go beyond the authority that the parties have conferred on the arbitrator. Many statutes require that the award be in writing[17] and fulfill certain other formal requirements. Section 7507 of the New York Arbitration Law (Appendix IV,1) provides that "the award shall be in writing, signed and acknowledged by the arbitrator making it within the time fixed by the agreement, or, if the time is not fixed, within such time as the court orders." It also provides for extending the time, and states the conditions under which a party waives his objection to delays in handing down the award.

The rules of the AAA (Appendix II,1, Rule 38) also require that the award be in writing, signed and acknowledged by the arbitrator (see also Appendix III, Sec. 7507). The AAA rules state that the award "shall be made promptly" and must not be made more than 30 days from the date the hearing closes or the date on which final proofs and statements are transmitted, unless the parties agree otherwise (Appendix II,1, Rule 37). If the parties settle their dispute during the course of the hearing, they may request the arbitrator to incorporate the terms of the settlement in the award (Appendix II,1, Rule 39).

The award need not set forth an opinion (Appendix II,1, Rule 38), although one usually accompanies it. An opinion is of great value to the parties because it reveals the reasons for the award and gives the arbitrator's logic and analysis of the issue. In short, the opinion serves the salutary purpose of clarifying the respective viewpoints of all parties with respect to the controversy and explains the logical basis for the award.

The award must be final and complete in order to be enforced, and must settle all issues submitted for arbitration.[18] Its provisions must be definitive so that the parties can carry it out. After making the award, the arbitrator has no authority to issue interpretations or refinements of his opinion unless the parties mutually agree that this is necessary.[22] Some state statutes permit modification of the award by a court, provided it is not defective in any material respect. (See Appendix IV,1, Sec. 7511(c).)

COMPROMISE AWARDS. In some cases, awards may be characterized by the recipient as "split down the middle." This implies that the arbitrator has tried to compromise and thus please both parties. Whether in fact a particular award is simply a compromise is difficult to determine. Every experienced arbitrator has at some time been faced with issues that are practically impossible to resolve equitably by rendering a decision wholly in favor of one side. Moreover, arbitrators are aware that because the parties have daily contact, the decision rendered must be one that they "can live with." It is unfair to characterize these awards simply as an attempt not to antagonize either party.

In general, it can be said that parties do not want a decision that is purely a compromise, but prefer a clear-cut award. With few exceptions the arbitrator is expected to adjudicate, not mediate, the dispute. Arbitrators who attempt to please both sides actually please no one and render a disservice to the arbitral process. The arbitrator must be willing to stand by his award and take the risks involved, no matter who dislikes his decision. One of the advantages of our system of voluntary arbitration, in which the arbitrators are selected by the parties, is that arbitrators who frequently make compromise awards eventually damage their reputations and professional standing seriously enough to make their future selection questionable.

AGREED AWARDS. An "agreed award" is one made by an arbitrator in conformance with the joint wishes of the parties. This type has been criticized because of the danger of collusion between the parties, to the detriment of the grievant. Situations sometimes develop where the settlement of a particular issue is obvious, equitable, and acceptable to the officials of the union and the company, but which could not have been made prior to the arbitration hearing because of political or psychological considerations. In this type of situation, where the arbitrator is satisfied that the proposed solution is fair and equitable and the grievant's rights are fully protected, he may incorporate in his award the solution offered by the parties.

Ad hoc arbitrators are not usually familiar with the manifold facets of a particular union–management relationship. In complicated and delicate situations, an ad hoc arbitrator may unknowingly create more problems than he solves if he fails to consider the wishes of the parties. At times, the parties can more readily work out solutions that they can live with than can the arbitrator. Thus, under special circumstances, there is a place for the "agreed award," provided it is eminently fair and equitable to both the parties and the grievant.

CONFIRMATION OF AN AWARD. Under the New York Arbitration Law (Appendix IV,1, Sec. 7510) awards will be confirmed by the court if the party makes application within one year after he receives it. This confirmation enables him to secure a judgment against his opponent. This provision is typical of the law in most states.

VACATING OR MODIFYING AN AWARD. Most state laws are similar to New York law (Appendix IV,1, Sec. 7511), which provides that a party may, within 90 days after delivery of the award, make an application to a court to vacate or modify it if he believes that fraud, partiality, and similar influences have prejudiced his rights.

REFERENCES

1. American Arbitration Association, (a) "Procedural Aspects of Labor–Management Arbitration," 28 LA 933 (1957); (b) "Substantive Aspects of Labor–Management," 28 LA 943 (1957).
2. *Ibid.*, 28 LA 936, Table 6 ("Representation by Counsel").
3. P–H Lab. Arb. Serv., par. 64, 163 (1960).
4. American Arbitration Association, *op. cit.*, 28 LA 938.
5. *Wigmore on Evidence*, 3rd. ed. Boston: Little, Brown, 1940. Vol. 5, p. 209, par. 1429.
6. Harry Shulman, "Reason, Contract, and Law in Labor Relations." *Harv. L. Rev.*, Vol. 68, No. 6 (April 1955), p. 1017.
7. Benjamin Aaron, "The Uses of the Past in Arbitration" (Proceedings of the Eighth Annual Meeting of the National Academy of Arbitrators). Washington, D.C.: The Bureau of National Affairs, 1955, p. 11.
8. Richard Mittenthal, "Past Practice and the Administration of Collective Bargaining Agreements" (Proceedings of the Thirteenth Annual Meeting of the National Academy of Arbitrators). Washington, D.C.: The Bureau of National Affairs, p. 30 (with comments).
9. Linda E. Rafferty, "Conflict of Medical Evidence in Labor Arbitration," *Arbitration Journal*, Vol. 23, No. 3 (1968), p. 180.
10. Bethlehem Steel Co., 6 LA 617.

11. American Steel and Wire Co., 5 LA 193.
12. Bethlehem Steel Co., 29 LA 635.
13. Louis Zahn Drug Co., 63-1 CCH Lab. Arb., par. 8344 (Sembower, 1963).
14. Owens–Corning Fiberglas Corp., 67-1 CCH Lab. Arb. 8278 (Doyle, 1967).
15. (a) "Problems of Proof in Arbitration—Workshop" (Proceedings of the Nineteenth Annual Meeting of the National Academy of Arbitrators). Washington, D.C.: The Bureau of National Affairs, 1966, pp. 298, 299. (b) "Lawyers Arbitration Letter." *Evidence in Arbitration*, Vol. 1. No. 1 (1973), p. 3.
16. Dick v. Supreme Body of International Congress, 138 Mich. 372; 101 NW 564 (1904).
17. Frank Elkouri and Edna Asper Elkouri, "Evidence Offers of Compromise and Admissions." Chapter 8 in *How Arbitration Works*, rev. ed. Washington, D.C.: The Bureau of National Affairs, 1960, pp. 195–196. See also Price-Pfister Brass Mfg. Co. and United Steelworkers of America, Local 2018, 25 LA 398 (1965).
18. (a) Bamberger's New Jersey and Department Store Drivers, Warehouse Men and Helpers of Northern New Jersey, Local 177 IBT, 60 LA 960 (1973). (b) R. W. Fleming, "Some Problems of Evidence: The Privilege Against Self Incrimination." Chapter 7 in *The Arbitration Process*. Urbana: University of Illinois Press, 1965, pp. 181–186. See also Langemyr v. Campbell, 21 NY 2d 796 (1968); 288 N.Y.S. 2d 629 (1968); and 235 NE 2d 770 (1968).
19. Edgar A. Jones, Jr., "Problems of Proof in the Arbitration Process" (Proceedings of the Nineteenth Annual Meeting of the National Academy of Arbitrators). Washington, D.C.: The Bureau of National Affairs, 1966, p. 208.
20. American Arbitration Association, *op. cit.* (a).
21. *Ibid.*
22. (a) Matter of McMahon, 63 N.Y.S. 2d 657. (b) Associated Corset and Brassiere Mfg. v. Corset and Brassiere Workers Union 172, Misc. 1029, 16 N.Y.S. 2d 736.

8

ARBITRATION AND THE LAW

Historically the courts looked upon arbitration agreements as contracts and applied strict rules of contract law to such agreements. The reluctance of the courts to relinquish jurisdiction had a plausible explanation. According to Gregory and Orlikoff, "The income received by seventeenth and eighteenth-century English judges consisted mainly of fees received from the cases they heard. Perhaps for that reason judges naturally looked upon arbitrations as devices which 'ousted their jurisdiction.' " [1]

Common Law

As early as 1609 Lord Coke ruled that an agreement to submit a dispute to arbitration was revocable at the will of either party.[2] This rule has persisted as common law and, where no statute applies, continues to be the rule.[3] The theory appears to be that consent of both parties must persist until an award is made, and either party may withdraw consent before that occurs.[4] At common law the submission agreement could be declared orally as well as in writing,[5] and the same rule applied to the arbitrator's award.

A concomitant of these rules is the general common law rule on agreements to arbitrate future disputes, as distinguished from agreements to arbitrate an existing controversy. The former type of agreement, while treated as valid at common law,* is not specifically enforceable and either party may withdraw at will. However, the aggrieved party is permitted to seek damages for the breach of contract.[6]

POWER OF ARBITRATORS. Common law does not give arbitrators power to subpoena witnesses or records, or to administer oaths, since they do not have the power of a court.[7] Such powers are granted only by statute.

If more than one arbitrator sits on a case, the rule evolved at common law is that the parties have a right to be heard by *all* the arbitrators; therefore, if one is absent, there may be a valid ground for setting aside any

---

* For a more comprehensive discussion of the rules of common law, see Gregory and Orlikoff.[1]

106

subsequent award.[8] Similarly, where the parties had not expressly provided otherwise, many early cases held that the award must be unanimous.[9] As with most of the common law requirements, this is generally no longer the rule. (See Appendix IV,1, Sec. 7506(e)).

AWARDS. The enforcement of the arbitrator's award at common law was a tenuous process because it had no legal status. The winning party was compelled to go to court and sue to enforce the original contract, using the award only as evidence of the justice of his claim. In essence, the matter had to be argued twice, once before the arbitrator and again in court.[10]

Federal Laws

United States Arbitration Act

On February 12, 1925, Congress enacted the U.S. Arbitration Act, which was amended in 1947 and 1954 with Chapter 2 added in 1970 (see Appendix III,1). The Act substantially modified the common law as it related to agreements to arbitrate.[11]

Section 1 of the Act provides ". . . nothing herein contained shall apply to contracts of employment of seamen, railroad employees, or any other class of workers engaged in foreign or interstate commerce." This section has been interpreted to mean that agreements to arbitrate labor disputes are not covered by the Act.[12] However, recent decisions from the U.S. Court of Appeals in the Second, Third, and Seventh Circuits have applied procedures of the Act to cases qualified by Section 301 of the National Labor Relations Act (NLRA). Gerald Aksen, General Counsel of the American Arbitration Association, reviewed these cases in a paper delivered before the Twenty-Second Annual Conference sponsored by New York University.[13] Several illustrative actions are discussed here.

In *International Ass'n. of Machine & Automotive Workers v. General Electric Co.* (1969),[14] the company sought reversal of a district court decision compelling arbitration of the union's grievance against the company. As grounds for reversal, the company urged that the union committed procedural error by commencing its action under Section 4 of the U.S. Arbitration Act (instead of proceeding by complaint under Section 301 of the Labor–Management Relations Act), and by thereafter using the summary procedures of the Arbitration Act. The company's position was based upon the "silence" of the majority opinion in *Lincoln Mills* (cited at the end of this section), alluded to by Justice Frankfurter in his dissent. The Court of Appeals rejected the company's position, and held that the summary procedures of the U.S. Arbitration Act were available in Section 301 actions.

In *Scalzitti v. International Union of Operating Engineers Local 150* (1965)[15] the company was suing the union under Section 301, claiming damages for breach of a no-strike clause. The union then moved to stay the court proceedings pending arbitration. The company opposed the motion, claiming that the collective bargaining agreement was a "contract of employment" within the meaning of Section 1 of the U.S. Arbitration Act (Appendix III,1) and that therefore the procedures of the Act were not applicable, since Section 1 provides that "nothing herein contained shall apply to contracts of employment of seamen, railroad employees, or any other class of workers engaged in foreign or interstate commerce." The district court granted the union's motion to stay pending arbitration, and the Court of Appeals affirmed, stating: "the terms 'foreign or interstate commerce,' as used in the exemption, were not intended to apply to collective bargaining agreements similar to the one before us in the instant case." [16]

Newark Stereotypers' Union v. Newark Morning Ledger Co. (1968)[17] involved the union's motion to vacate an arbitral award under Section 10 of the U.S. Arbitration Act, and the company's cross-motion to confirm. The district court confirmed the award, and the court of appeals affirmed. The appellate court, noting that an earlier stage of the same case had involved a motion to compel arbitration and a motion to appoint a neutral arbitrator under Section 5, found the applicable law in the U.S. Arbitration Act.[18]

As Gerald Aksen pointed out, even in cases where the parties do not in their pleadings attempt to cite the provisions of the U.S. Arbitration Act as a basis for relief, the grounds that dissatisfied parties in fact have specified as justification for vacatur are usually found to be identical to those contained in the Arbitration Act. The case of *Torrington Co. v. Local 1645 Metal Prods. Workers* (1966)[19] from the Second Circuit Court of Appeals is illustrative of this point. There, the company moved to vacate an arbitrator's award on the ground that he "exceeded his authority under the collective bargaining agreement." The Arbitration Act [Sec. 10(d)] specifically lists as one of the grounds under which a district court may vacate the award: "where the arbitrators exceeded their powers." The court first went through the exercise of determining whether or not a court may subject a labor arbitrator's award to any type of judicial review. On this point they found that a labor arbitrator's authority to determine the issue in dispute is subject to court scrutiny. The district court can overrule an arbitrator's decision that he has authority under the collective bargaining agreement when the reviewing court "can clearly perceive that [the arbitrator] has derived that authority from sources outside the collective bargaining agreement." [20] In one sense, the court must be viewed as holding that it has the authority conferred by Section 10 of the Arbitration Act, without deciding whether the act applies to labor arbitrators. According to Gerald Aksen, it would be much simpler and much more helpful to the labor–management community if we know once and for all whether or not all sections of the U.S. Arbitration Act could be utilized in the practice of labor arbitration.

Labor–Management Relations Act[21]

It is clear from the provisions of the Labor–Management Relations Act (LMRA) that it was the intent of the Congress to encourage private settlement of disputes through arbitration. Section 201(b) of LMRA provides that "the settlement of issues between employers and employees through collective bargaining may be advanced by making available full and adequate governmental facilities for conciliation, mediation and voluntary arbitration."

Section 201(c) encourages the inclusion in labor contracts of clauses providing "for the final adjustment of grievances or questions regarding the application or interpretation of such agreement, and other provisions designed to prevent the subsequent arising of such controversies."

Again, in Section 203(d) of LMRA, the parties are encouraged to provide for the final adjustment of labor disputes. It was not, however, until a decade after the passage of the Act that the courts sanctioned the widespread use of arbitration, and the sanction derived from the interpretation of a section of the statute, which might at first seem surprising. Section 301(a) of the Act reads as follows: "Suits for violation of contracts between an employer and a labor organization representing employees in an industry affecting commerce as defined in this Act may be brought in any district court of the United States having jurisdiction of the parties, without respect to the amount in controversy or without regard to the citizenship of the parties."

In *Textile Workers v. Lincoln Mills* (1957),[22] the U.S. Supreme Court held that agreements to arbitrate future disputes are specifically enforceable under this section of the Act. Moreover, it held that federal substantive law would govern the determination of such suits. The Court said: "We conclude that the substantive law to apply in suits under Sec. 301(a) is federal law, which the courts must fashion from the policy of our national labor laws." [23] State law is an appropriate source provided it is not incompatible with the policies reflected in federal legislation. The Court also disposed of the alleged bar posed by the Norris-LaGuardia Act ban on injunctions in labor disputes as being inconsistent with the apparent "congressional policy in favor of the enforcement of agreements to arbitrate grievance disputes." The *Lincoln Mills* decision generated considerable comment, both favorable and otherwise, but taken together with the opinions of the high court in the Warrior & Gulf, American Manufacturing, and Enterprise Corp. cases,[24] the pattern of an evolving judicial approval and encouragement of the arbitration process is clear. The reader is referred to the articles highlighting the legal problems raised by the *Lincoln Mills* case.[25, 26]

State Laws

In Chapter 4, mention was made of several states that have provided for arbitration procedures and have legislated into statute the standards and processes required in arbitrative proceedings. One of the states mentioned was New York.

NEW YORK. Article 75—the New York State Arbitration Law—is reproduced in Appendix IV,1. Of particular interest are the following sections:

1. *Compelling Arbitration* [Section 7503(a)]. A party who refuses to arbitrate under a valid arbitration clause may be ordered by the court to arbitrate, provided his opposing party acts within the statute of limitations.

2. *Stay of Arbitration* [Section 7503(c)]. A disputant cannot apply for a stay of arbitration unless he acts within ten days after receiving notice that the complainant intends to arbitrate.

3. *Confirming an Award* [Section 7510]. An award will be confirmed by the court within one year of its issuance, provided it is not vacated or modified for reasons given in Section 7511. (See item 6 below.)

4. *Judgment on an Award* [Section 7514(a)]. After the court confirms an award, a judgment may be entered.

5. *Powers of the Arbitrator* [Section 7505; Section 7506(b,c,e), Hearing]. These sections empower the arbitrator to issue subpoenas and administer oaths, to appoint the time and place for a hearing, to notify parties in advance (8 days) of the hearing, to adjourn or postpone, to hear and determine the controversy in the absence of a notified party. If more than one arbitrator conducts the hearing, all must be present, but only a majority is needed to rule on questions and determine the award.

6. *Vacating or Modifying Award* (Section 7511). This section specifies when an application must be made, and gives grounds for vacating and for modifying an award.

PROPOSED UNIFORM ARBITRATION ACT. The National Conference of Commissioners on Uniform State Laws and the House of Delegates of the American Bar Association have collaborated in drawing up a model for arbitration legislation in those states that at present do not have modernized statutes governing arbitration. This proposed federal act is abstracted in Appendix IV,3. The *Introduction* to the version provided by AAA explains why this Uniform Arbitration Act is supported by labor–management interests.

Many agreements to arbitrate are specifically enforceable under the Federal Arbitration Act and under arbitration laws similar in content to this [proposed] Act. In thirty states, the general advantages of such modern laws are that they make possible the use of future dispute arbitration clauses in a wide variety of contracts. . . . They include minimum standards of procedure and rules for confirming awards in court and invalidating awards for procedural defects. They establish procedures by which court actions in violation of agreements to arbitrate may be stayed. The effect of modern arbitration statutes is to endow agreements to arbitrate with the same legal protections that other legitimate private agreements have. This makes it possible for the lawyer to use arbitration as one of the effective tools of his profession.

Judicial Interpretation

The rulings of the courts have had a more profound effect upon the entire arbitral process than have statutory enactments. Final determinations lie with the courts, which must interpret and apply the laws to specific situations. How the courts have ruled in specific cases, therefore, becomes an important area of study for the student of arbitration.

The courts usually acquire jurisdiction in several ways: when a party seeks an order of the court to stay arbitration proceedings on the ground of nonarbitrability; when a party makes a motion to compel arbitration; and when the court is asked to enforce, vacate, or modify an arbitrator's award.

The New York statute gives the courts authority to review and decide questions relating to the existence of an agreement to arbitrate and the breach thereof. The courts have held that where there is proof of an agreement to arbitrate and a breach thereof, the matter must be referred to an arbitrator.[27] The courts will, however, scrutinize the claim proffered for arbitration and make certain that it does not approach frivolity or unconscionableness.[28]

In the *Cutler-Hammer* case,[29] the contract provided that the "Company agrees to meet with the union early in July 1946 to discuss payment of a bonus for the first six months of 1946." The collective bargaining agreement also provided for the arbitration of disputes relating to the meaning and application of the contract.

After discussion with the union, the company refused to pay the bonus. The union claimed that the clause in the agreement should be interpreted to mean that the only purpose of the meeting was to decide the *amount of the bonus* and not whether the *bonus itself was to be paid*. The company refused to arbitrate and the union subsequently applied to the courts for an order compelling arbitration.

The New York Appellate Division reversed a Special Term order compelling arbitration, and the New York Court of Appeals affirmed the reversal on the ground that the language of the contract was beyond dispute and therefore there was in fact nothing to arbitrate. The court said:

> While the contract provides for arbitration of disputes as to the "meaning, performance, non-performance or application" of its provisions, the mere assertion by a party of a meaning of a provision which is clearly contrary to the plain meaning of the words cannot make an arbitrable issue. It is for the courts to determine whether the contract contains a provision for arbitration of the dispute tendered and in the exercise of that jurisdiction the court must determine

whether there is such a dispute. If the meaning of the provision of the contract sought to be arbitrated is beyond dispute, there cannot be anything to arbitrate and the contract cannot be said to provide for arbitration.[29]

In its decision the court in fact interpreted the provisions of the contract that the parties had agreed to arbitrate. The court thus arrogated to itself the interpretation of the contract.

The rulings of the U.S. Supreme Court (see next section) are contrary to the rulings in the *Cutler-Hammer* case. In the *Enterprise* case,[30] the court said: "It is for the arbitrator's construction which was bargained for; and so far as the arbitrator's decision concerns construction of the contract the courts have no business overruling him because their interpretation of the contract is different from his."

Scoles, writing in the *University of Chicago Law Review*,[31] said that "judicial review of labor arbitration awards on jurisdictional grounds is necessary and proper," but that the review should determine only the scope of the submission agreement. The arbitrator should consider submission of questions of arbitrability to be as effective as other submissions; thus, the award would be binding on both parties. Scoles said further that the court should not employ jurisdictional review as a guise to retry the merits of arbitrability. In his view, this would deprecate the valuable service available to industry, labor, and the public, which the courts had not extended and probably could not extend.

Federal Court Decisions

On June 20, 1960, the U.S. Supreme Court handed down three decisions,[32] commonly referred to as the "Trilogy," which have had an important bearing on the arbitral process. These three cases support the concept that when the parties have agreed to set up grievance–arbitration procedures to resolve a disputed interpretation of the collective bargaining agreement, the courts should not inject themselves into the merits of the dispute nor deny an order to arbitrate unless it is absolutely clear that the dispute is not covered by the arbitration clause. Any doubts should be resolved in favor of arbitrability.

The Court went even further in support of the arbitration process. In the Warrior case, the Court stated:

The present federal policy is to promote industrial stabilization through the collective bargaining agreement. . . . A major factor in achieving industrial peace is the inclusion of a provision for arbitration of grievances in the collective bargaining agreement.

But the grievance machinery under a collective bargaining agreement is at the very heart of the system of industrial self-government. Arbitration is the means of solving the unforseeable by molding a system of private law for all the problems which may arise and to provide for their solution in a way which will generally accord with the variant needs and desires of the parties. The processing of disputes through the grievance machinery is actually a vehicle by which meaning and content is given to the collective bargaining agreement.

Apart from matters that the parties specifically exclude, all of the questions on which the parties disagree must, therefore, come within the scope of the grievance and arbitration provisions of the collective agreement. The grievance procedure is, in other words, a part of the continuous collective bargaining process. It, rather than the strike, is the terminal point of a disagreement.

A proper conception of the arbitrator's function is basic. He is not a public tribunal imposed upon the parties by superior authority which the parties are obliged to accept. He has no general character to administer justice for a community which transcends the parties. He is rather part of a system of self-government created by and confined to the parties. (Shulman, *Reason, Contract and Law in Labor Relations*, 68 HARVARD LAW REVIEW 999, at 1016.)

The Labor arbitrator performs functions which are not normal to the courts; the considerations which help him fashion judgments may indeed be foreign to the competence of courts. The labor arbitrator's source of law is not confined to the express provisions of the contract, as the industrial common law—the practices of the industry and the shop—is equally a part of the collective bargaining agreement although not expressed in it.

The labor arbitrator is usually chosen because of the parties' confidence in his knowledge of the common law of the shop and their trust in his personal judgment to bring to bear considerations which are not expressed in the contract as criteria for judgment.

The parties expect that his judgment of a particular grievance will reflect not only what the contract says but, insofar as the collective bargaining agreement permits, such factors as the effect upon productivity of a particular result, its consequence to the morale of the shop, his judgment whether tensions will be heightened or diminished.

For the parties' objective in using the arbitration process is primarily to further their common goal of uninterrupted production under the agreement, to make the agreement serve their specialized needs. The ablest Judge cannot be expected to bring the same experience and competence to bear upon the determination of a grievance because he cannot be similarly informed.

In the absence of any express provision excluding a particular grievance from arbitration, we think only the most forceful evidence of a purpose to exclude the claim from arbitration can prevail, particularly where, as here, the exclusion clause is vague and the arbitration clause quite broad. Since any attempt by a court to infer such a purpose necessarily comprehends the merits, the court should view with suspicion an attempt to persuade it to become entangled in the construction of the substantive provisions of a labor agreement, even through the back door of interpreting the arbitration clause, when the alternative is to utilize the services of an arbitrator.[32b]

The Court recognized that the arbitrator is a judge in a private judicial system set up by the parties in their collective bargaining agreement to govern their relationships. If the parties have agreed to be bound by the award of an arbitrator, who has been mutually selected because of his specialized knowledge of industrial relations, then the court should not substitute its judgment for that of the arbitrator. The Court specifically stated that the *Cutler-Hammer* doctrine should not be followed. If the arbitrator bases his award on the contract, the courts are obliged to enforce his award, even if they disagree with it.

In *United Steelworkers of America v. American Manufacturing Co.* (1960),[32a] the Court held:

The function of the court is very limited when the parties have agreed to submit all questions of contract interpretation to the arbitrator. It is confined to ascertaining whether the party seeking arbitration is making a claim which on its face is governed by the contract. Whether the moving party is right or wrong is for the arbitrator to decide.

In the *Warrior* case the opinion was that the courts cannot weigh the merits of a claim.[32b] An opinion in the *American Manufacturing* case supplemented this:

The judicial inquiry under 301 of the Labor Management Relations Act must be strictly confined to the question of whether the reluctant party did agree to arbitrate the grievance or did agree to give the arbitrator power to make the award he made. An order to arbitrate should not be denied unless it can be said with positive assurance that the arbitration clause is not susceptible to an interpretation that covers the asserted dispute. Doubts should be resolved in favor of coverage.[33a]

Again, in the *Warrior* case, the Court ruled:

In the absence of any express provision excluding a particular grievance from arbitration, only the most forceful evidence of a purpose to exclude the claim from arbitration can prevail, particularly where the exclusion clause is vague and the arbitration clause is broad.[33b]

In the *Enterprise* case,[33c] the Court found:

The refusal of courts to review the merits of an arbitration award is the proper approach under collective bargaining agreements. . . .[34a]

• • •

Nevertheless, an arbitrator is confined to interpretation and application of the collective bargaining agreement. . . . He may of course look for guidance from many sources, yet his award is legitimate only so long as it draws its essence from the collective bargaining agreement. When arbitrators' words manifest an infidelity to this obligation courts have no choice but to refuse enforcement of the award.[34b]

The doctrines laid down by the Trilogy were elaborated in *Atkinson v. Sinclair Refining Co.* (1962).[35] The company docked three employees a total of $2.19. In response, 999 of its 1,700 employees participated in a strike or work stoppage. The company filed a suit for damages and an injunction.

The company said that a collective bargaining agreement between themselves and the union contained a promise by the union not to strike over any cause that could be the subject of a grievance under the provisions of the contract. It said that the union had violated the contract by calling a strike over pay claims, which were properly the subject of grievance procedures under the contract.

The union filed a motion to dismiss the complaint, which sought damages and an injunction, because all issues in the suit were referable to arbitration under the collective bargaining contract.

The court decided that an employer may sue for damages if a union violates a no-strike clause when (as in the collective bargaining agreement in this case) the right to invoke arbitration is reserved exclusively to the union. The Court referred to Article XXVI—Grievance and Arbitration Procedure of the collective bargaining agreement, which reads: "If such a decision [management's decision in the last step of the grievance procedure] is not satisfactory, then upon request of the President or any District Director of the Oil, Chemical and Atomic Workers International Union, AFL–CIO . . . there shall be set up a local Arbitration Board."

The court based its decisions on the opinion in *Warrior* which says that "arbitration is a matter of contract and a party cannot be required to submit to arbitration any dispute which he has not agreed so to submit." [36]

The Court then said that: "the contract here involved is not susceptible to a construction that the Company was bound to arbitrate its claim for damages against the union for breach of the undertaking not to strike." [37]

Another case in which a company was allowed to bring a damage action against a union was *Old Dutch Farms, Inc. v. Milk Drivers Union Local 584* (1966). [38]

The National Labor Relations Board (NLRB) held that the union had violated the Labor–Management Relations Act by engaging in unlawful secondary activity. The company began an action for damages (which was the subject of the case) based on Section 303(b) of LMRA, which authorizes such action when a labor organization injures a company's business.

The union made a motion to stay the suit pending arbitration, claiming that the dispute came within the purview of the general arbitration clause in their collective bargaining agreement. The court decided:

This action bears no meaningful connection with the terms, conditions or subject matter of the parties collective bargaining agreement. The fact that the union activity which forms the basis for the section 303 damage suit was provoked by an alleged breach of contract by the employer is no reason to conclude that this suit arises under or is connected with the interpretation of the collective bargaining agreement within the meaning of the arbitration clause. This is so, not only because this suit rests solely on sec. 303 and cannot be considered as a contract claim but, more significantly, because whether or not the employer violated . . . the collective agreement has no bearing on the validity of the section 303 suit and the issues it presents, viz., whether the union violated section 8(b) (4) of NLRA and whether and to what extent the employer sustained actual damages as a result of this union activity.[39]

The court went on to say that the dispute was unrelated to the collective bargaining agreement because it concerned tort damages, which were not covered by the agreement.

The court recognized that our national labor policy favors arbitration, but said that this principle was formulated in connection with actions arising under LMRA, Section 301(a), which authorized suits for the violation of collective bargaining agreements and pertained to the desirability of contract arbitration as a means of insuring industrial peace. Moreover, the court said:

> Such reasoning ... does not apply with equal force to suits ... which arise under section 303 since the issues raised in such a proceeding are the kind which have traditionally been determined by courts and concern matters to which the expertise of labor arbitrators does not necessarily extend. . . .[40]

In the case of *Drake Bakeries v. American Bakery and Confectionery Workers* (1962),[41] the facts are as follows: The company notified the union that because Christmas and New Year would both fall on a Friday and because it was desirable to have fresh bakery products to sell on Mondays following the holidays, employees would not work on the Thursdays before Christmas and New Year, but would work on Saturdays following those holidays. The union objected and a compromise was worked out. However, insufficient employees reported on January 2, and the company could not produce its goods. It filed suit for damages under the Labor Management Relations Act, alleging that the union had violated the no-strike clause in the contract. The union denied that there had been a strike.

The district court and the Court of Appeals held that the employer's claim was an arbitrable matter under the contract, and that the suit had to be stayed pending arbitration. The court interpreted the contract to mean that arbitration was the proper means of settling the dispute. However, the company asserted that even if it had agreed in the contract to arbitrate union violations of the no-strike clause, it was excused from arbitrating by the union's violation of the contract. It argued that the strike automatically was such a breach or repudiation of the arbitration clause by the union that the company was excused from arbitrating. In answer to this the court said:

> Arbitration provisions which themselves have not been repudiated are meant to survive breaches of contract in many contexts, even total breach; and in determining whether one party has so repudiated his promise to arbitrate that the other party is excused the circumstances of the claimed repudiation are critically important. In this case the Union denies having repudiated in any respect its promise to arbitrate (and) denies this was a strike . . ." [42]

•   •   •

We do not decide in this case that in no circumstances would a strike in violation of the no-strike clause contained in this or other contracts entitle the employer to rescind or abandon the entire contract or to declare its promise to arbitrate forever discharged or to refuse to arbitrate its damage claim against the Union. We do decide . . . that [the arbitration clause] of the contract obligates the Company to arbitrate its claims for damages from forbidden strikes by the Union . . . intertwined as it is with the Union's denials that there was any strike or any breach of contract at all.[43]

Here the court is holding that the duty to arbitrate is not conditional on the absolute observance by the union of its no-strike pledge. This is supported by the opinion handed down in *United Packinghouse Workers v. Needham Packing Co.* (1964),[44] in which the Court held that the employer's allegations that the union had breached the no-strike clause did not release the employer from its duty to arbitrate.

Court Review of Arbitration Awards

Most courts have interpreted the *Warrior* case to mean that, under a standard arbitration clause, even farfetched claims of contract violations must be submitted to arbitration. Express language to exclude is needed before courts can hear a question.[45] The courts have sometimes evaded the Trilogy by reviewing arbitration awards on the basis of the opinion in the *Enterprise* case, which states that the courts have no choice but to refuse enforcement of an award that does not draw its essence from the collective bargaining agreement.

Although the Trilogy forbids the courts to review the merits of a case, it is almost impossible for a court not to consider merit when it must determine whether an award has no basis in the contract.

Courts have refused to enforce an award if they are sufficiently shocked by it. In *Truck Drivers Union v. Ulry-Talbert Co.* (1946),[46] the court refused to enforce an award that clearly violated the provisions of the collective bargaining agreement. Two of the major cases involving review of arbitration awards are *Torrington* and *H. K. Porter*, both of which are summarized below.

Torrington Co. v. Metal Products Workers (1966)[47] involved·a 20-year-old policy, unilaterally instituted by the company and not included in the collective bargaining agreement, of granting employees paid time for voting. The company unilaterally discontinued this policy in December 1962. When negotiations began in August 1963 for a new agreement, the company announced that it would not reinstate its old policy, and the union presented a written demand that this decision be rescinded. When the old agreement expired in September 1963, the union called a strike. In January 1964, a new agreement was executed, but it contained no provision for paid time to vote. Nonstrikers were not paid for time off during the November 1963 elections and no one was paid in November 1964. The union went to arbitration over the company's refusal to reinstate the policy, and the arbitrator ruled that the company could not abandon it unilaterally.

The district court ruled that the arbitrator had exceeded and abused his authority by reading an implied contractual relationship into the contract, and the Court of Appeals affirmed. The union had argued that the district court, in deciding that the arbitrator had exceeded his authority in making the award, had also exceeded the scope of its own authority by improperly examining the merits of the arbitrator's award, relying on the *Enterprise* case[48] for precedent.

In its decision, the court stated that every grievance is arbitrable unless the arbitration clause can in no way be interpreted to cover the asserted dispute. The court felt, however, that the appropriate scope of judicial review of awards made after arbitration was not conclusively delineated. It said:

Although the arbitrator's decision on the merits is final as to questions of law and fact, his authority is contractual in nature and is limited to powers confined in the collective bargaining agreement.

The arbitrators held that [the voting pay] provision was implied by the prior practice of the parties. In some cases, it may be appropriate exercise of an arbitrator's authority to resolve ambiguities in the scope of the collective bargaining agreement on the basis of prior practice, since no agreement can reduce all aspects of the labor–management relationship to writing. However, while courts should be wary of rejecting the arbitrator's interpretation of the implications of the parties' prior practices, the mandate that the arbitrator stay within the confines of the collective bargaining agreement requires a reviewing court to pass upon whether the agreement authorizes the arbitrator to expand its express terms on the basis of the parties' prior practice. Therefore we hold that the question of an arbitrator's decision that he has authority should not be accepted where the reviewing court can clearly perceive that he has derived that authority from sources outside the collective bargaining agreement at issue.[49]

In *Porter v. United Saw Workers* (1964),[50] the contract provided that pensions would be paid only to retiring employees who reached age 65 with at least 25 years of continuous service. In actual practice, pensions were often paid to individuals with records of long service who did not meet the age requirement. Relying on this custom, an arbitrator awarded full pensions to employees who had not reached age 65, but had served at least 25 years, and to employees who had reached age 65, but had not had 25 years of service. The court recognized that the arbitrator may use past practice to supplement the words of the contract. But, since only the first part of the award was supportable on these grounds, the part based solely on age was vacated.

In commenting on the two cases cited above, Clarke W. Brinckerhoff said:

Although the opinions in both cases are couched in terms of the arbitrator's lack of authority under the contract to find as he did, both cases in fact run contrary to the basic ruling of the Trilogy that the court must not review the "merits" of the case. In each case the actual rationale for the result seems to have been that the arbitrator clearly misapplied the evidence and came to the wrong conclusion. . . . Although the result in each case seems reasonable, the courts clearly indulged in a full review of the merits.[51]

Brinckerhoff commented that "limited review is necessary to avoid subjecting the parties, against their intentions, to clearly unsupportable awards. . . . When the arbitrator bases his judgment on the past practices of the parties, the only method for ascertaining whether the award has its 'essence' in the contract is to (1) review those practices and (2) vacate the award if it is not supported by them."

He went on to say that the Supreme Court had stated in *Warrior and Gulf* that a collective bargaining agreement "is more than a contract, it is a generalized code to govern myriad of cases which the draftsmen cannot wholly anticipate." [52] This incorporated by inference a "common law of the shop which implements and furnishes the context of the agreement." [53] And so the arbitrator had to look to the past practices of the parties as well as to the words of the contract in reaching a decision. The author concludes that "since the 'common law of the shop' is part of the contract, it seems equally reasonable for the court to vacate an award which is not supported by the parties' established customs."

(See also the discussion of the *Torrington* case.[54])

State Court Decisions

In *Matter of Fitzgerald v. General Electric Co.* (1965),[55] the New York Supreme Court, First Department, quoted relevant parts of the Trilogy, stating that "Federal and New York laws are alike in respect to arbitration pursuant to collective bargaining agreements." [56]

In *Posner v. Grunwald–Marx, Inc.* (1961)[57], a case not covered by federal jurisdiction, the California Supreme Court ruled that California would follow the federal law of the Trilogy.

In *Todd Shipyards Corp. v. Marine and Shipbuilding Workers* (1965),[58] an employee, who was a member of the defendant union, was terminated by the plaintiff company because of a hearing loss. The defendant union filed a grievance, which was arbitrated. The arbitrator ruled that the company was correct in relying on its physician's opinion and he upheld the discharge.

When the employee asked for further employment doing any kind of work he was capable of performing and his application was denied, the defendant filed a second grievance. This was rejected and the defendant requested arbitration.

The plaintiff contended that the grievance presented no arbitral issue because the subject matter of the grievance had been determined by the first arbitrator. The defendant denied that the court had jurisdiction to determine the issue of arbitrability, since the grievance at issue was not the same one that had been arbitrated previously.

The court held:

> Ordinarily, where there is a broad arbitration clause as here, a grievance which arguably comes within the clause should be submitted to arbitration [citing Warrior]. There is no dispute that, absent the first award, arbitration would clearly be required. Instead the court is faced with the problem of determining the effect of a previous award on the arbitrability of a subsequent grievance. Counterbalancing the liberal policy favoring arbitration is the policy favoring finality of arbitration awards. . . .[59]

The court then decided that the first award was res judicata. The basic question of fact here was whether or not the physical disability that made the employee unfit for his first job would make him unfit for the new position he sought to fill. The question of procedure is dependent on the choice of the party who should determine the similarity of the two positions. This choice in effect determines whether the first arbitration is res judicata relative to the claim.

The dispute here over job content is arbitrable. Even if the union's claim that the employee's disability would not affect his performance in a new job is frivolous, the sense of the Trilogy would seem to require the courts to defer to the arbitrator.

It would seem in this case that the court's decision to reexamine the res judicata implications of the first award with respect to the second claim was incorrect. To do that, it had to go into the merits of the case and decide a fact question concerning job content.

"Successor Employer" and "Procedural Arbitrability"

In *John Wiley & Sons v. Livingston* (1964),[60] Interscience Publishers merged with John Wiley & Sons, Inc., and ceased to do business as a separate entity. Interscience had a collective bargaining agreement with a union, but it did not contain a successor clause that would assure continuity of the agreement. The union's position was that, despite the merger, it continued to represent union members of Interscience who were retained by Wiley. It argued that Wiley was obligated to recognize certain rights of these employees in accordance with the Interscience bargaining agreement.

To accommodate its own pension plan, Wiley recognized the seniority of the Interscience employees transferred, but said that terms of the merger made no provision for assumption of the bargaining agreement. It refused to recognize the union as a bargaining agent, and therefore the union sought to compel arbitration after the expiration of the Interscience bargaining agreement.

The issues before the Court were: (1) whether a corporate employer must arbitrate with a union under a bargaining agreement between the union and another corporation that has merged with the employer; and (2), if so, whether the courts or the arbitrator is the appropriate body to decide whether procedural prerequisites that condition the duty to arbitrate (under the original bargaining agreement) have been met.

The Court decided that its preliminary duty was to ascertain whether the arbitration provision of the collective bargaining agreement survived the Wiley–Interscience merger, and was therefore operative against Wiley, since this was a question of contract interpretation.

The Court felt that "the disappearance by merger of a corporate employer which has entered into a collective bargaining agreement with a union does not automatically terminate all the rights of the employees covered by the agreement, and that in appropriate circumstances, present here, the successor employer may be required to arbitrate with the union under the agreement." [61]

Recognizing "the central role of arbitration" as a "substitute for industrial strife," the Court said that it "would derogate from the federal policy of settling labor disputes by arbitration if a change in the corporate structure or ownership of a business enterprise had the automatic consequence of removing a duty to arbitrate previously established; this is so as much in cases like the present . . . as in those in which one owner replaces another but the business entity remains the same." [62]

The Court felt that because employees ordinarily do not take part in negotiations leading to a change in corporate leadership, they must be afforded some protection from a sudden change in the employment relationship. The court ruled that arbitration was indeed warranted:

Although the duty to arbitrate . . . must be founded on contract, the impressive policy considerations favoring arbitration are not wholly overborne by the fact that Wiley did not sign the contract being construed. . . . There was a contract, and Interscience, Wiley's predecessor, was party to it. We thus find Wiley's obligation to arbitrate the dispute in the Interscience contract construed in the context of a national labor policy." [63]

The court cited in a footnote:

Compare the principle that when a contract is scrutinized for evidence of an intention to arbitrate a particular kind of dispute, *national labor policy* requires, within reason, that "an interpretation that covers the asserted dispute" [64] be favored.

We do not hold that in every case in which the ownership or corporate structure of an enterprise is changed, the duty to arbitrate survive . . . there may be cases in which the lack of any substantial continuity of identity in the business enterprise before and after a change would make a duty to arbitrate something imposed from without, not reasonably to be found in the particular bargaining agreement and the acts of the parties involved. So too, we do not rule out the possibility that a union might abandon its right to arbitration by failing to make its claim known.

The court also said that the procedural and substantive aspects of labor disputes, like those involved in the case, were intertwined. Therefore it decided that "once it is determined . . . that the parties are obligated to submit the subject matter of a dispute to arbitration, 'procedural' questions which grow out of the dispute and bear on its final disposition should be left to the arbitrator."

In *Wackenhut Corp. v. United Plant Guard Workers* (1964),[65] the court said: "The specific rule which we derive from Wiley is that where there is substantial similarity of operation and continuity of identity of the business enterprise before and after a change in ownership, a collective bargaining agreement containing an arbitration provision, entered into by the predecessor employer is binding upon the successor employer."

A similar ruling* was handed down in the case of *United Steelworkers v. Reliance Universal* (1964).[66] However, in *McGuire v. Humble Oil* (1966),[67] a purchase was made of part of the business of another concern where a different union represented the employees of the purchasing corporation. Only 13 of the former employees of Weber and Quinn were integrated into the group of 260 truck drivers and 95 mechanics employed by Humble. The National Labor Relations Board (NLRB) had ruled that the former employees of Weber could not be considered a separate appropriate unit, after Humble petitioned for clarification of the appropriate bargaining unit.

The Court felt that the presence of another union at Humble covering the same employees (a problem that did not occur in *Wiley*†) and the decision of the NLRB would make enforcement of the arbitration clause against Humble, as requested by the old local from Weber, impractical and inequitable.

In *Carey v. Westinghouse Corp.* (1964),[69] a union representing production and maintenance workers filed a grievance, asserting that certain employees represented by another union, which did not represent production and maintenance employees, were performing production and maintenance work. Westinghouse refused to arbitrate on the grounds that the controversy represented a representation matter for the NLRB. The union relied on a collective bargaining agreement, which contained a grievance arbitration procedure to resolve disputes, including those involving the "interpretation, application or claimed violation" of the agreement.

The Court first decided that the National Labor Relations Act (NLRA) and its remedies for jurisdictional controversies concerning work-assignment disputes are not applicable unless a strike or a threat of a strike has occurred. While recognizing that only one of the two unions involved had moved for arbitration and that arbitration therefore might not put an end to the dispute, the Court still felt that arbitration might, as a practical matter, put an end to the dispute or motivate forces that would resolve it.

---

* This involved the sale of the company rather than a merger with another. Here, too, the collective bargaining agreement was held binding.
† The broadness of the *Wiley* ruling has been discussed by Smith and Jones.[68]

Citing Section 10(K) of the NLRA as actively encouraging voluntary settlements of work-assignment disputes, the Court concluded that grievance procedures pursued to arbitration would strengthen the policies of the Act. If the dispute was considered not to be one concerning work assignments, but instead one that involved a representational problem concerning the duty of an employer to bargain collectively with the representative of the employees, the Court concluded that the charge would constitute an unfair labor practice. The union or employer might petition the NLRB for clarification, but in the opinion of the Court, the existence of these remedies did not bar arbitration and thus the arbitration procedure was the correct course to follow in either case.

REFERENCES

1. Charles O. Gregory and Richard M. Orlikoff, "The Enforcement of Labor Arbitration agreements," *Chi. L. Rev.*, Vol. 17 (1950), pp. 233, 235.
2. Vynior's case, 4 Co. Rep. 302,305 (K.B. 1609).
3. Insurance Company of North America v. Kempner, 132 Ark. 215, 200 S.W. 986 (1918).
4. People ex rel. Union Insurance Co. v. Nash, 111 N.Y. 310, 18 N.E. 630 (1888).
5. Davy v. Faw, 7 Cranch (11 U.S.) 171 (1812). (Decision written by Chief Justice Marshall.)
6. Red Cross Line v. Atlantic Fruit Co., 264 U.S. 109 (1924).
7. Renaud v. State Court of Med. & Arb., 124 Mich. 648, 83 N.W. 620 (1900).
8. Brush v. Fisher, 70 Mich. 469, 38 N.W. 446 (1888).
9. City of Omaha v. Omaha Water Co., 218 U.S. 180 (1910).
10. Black v. Woodruff, 193 Ala. 327, 69 So. 97 (1915).
11. Title 9: U.S. Code, pars. 1–14, first enacted February 12, 1925 (43 Stat. 883); codified July 30, 1947 (61 Stat. 669); amended September 3, 1954 (68 Stat. 1233).
12. (a) Amalgamated Assn. v. Pennsylvania Greyhound Lines, 192 F. 2d. 310 (1951); (b) Pennsylvania Greyhound Lines v. Amalgamated Assn., 193 F. 2d. 327 (1952).
13. Gerald Aksen, "Some Legal and Practical Problems of Labor Legislation," in *Proceedings of New York University Twenty-Second Annual Conference on Labor*, Thomas G. S. Christensen (ed.), 1972, p. 121.
14. International Ass'n. of Marine & Automotive Workers v. General Electric Co., 406 F. 2d. 1046 (2d. Cir.).
15. Scalzitti v. International Union of Operating Engineers Local 150, 351 F. 2d. 576 (7th Cir.).
16. *Ibid.*, at 580.
17. Newark Stereotypers' Union v. Newark Morning Ledger Co., 397 F. 2d. 594 (3d. Cir.); cert. denied, 89 S.Ct. 378.
18. *Ibid.*, at 596.
19. Torrington Co. v. Local 1645 Metal Prods. Workers, 362 F. 2d. 677.
20. (a) *Ibid.*, at 677, n. 26; (b) Textile Workers v. American Thread Co., 291 F. 2d. 894 (4th Cir.), 1961.

21. 61 Stat. 136 (1947).
22. Textile Workers' Union v. Lincoln Mills, 353 U.S. 448 (1957).
23. *Ibid.*, at 456.
24. (a) United Steelworkers of America v. American Manufacturing Co., 363 U.S. 564; 80 S.Ct. 1343, 4 Led. 2d. 1403 (1960). (b) United Steelworkers of America v. Warrior and Gulf Navigation Co., 363 U.S. 574; 80 S.Ct. 1347, 4 Led. 2d. 1409 (1960). (c) United Steelworkers of America v. Enterprise Wheel and Car Co., 363 U.S. 592 (1960).
25. Benjamin Aaron, "On First Looking into the Lincoln Mills Decision," in *Arbitration and the Law* (Proceedings of the Twelfth Annual Meeting of the National Academy of Arbitrators). Washington, D.C.: The Bureau of National Affairs, 1959.
26. Archibald Cox, "Reflections Upon Labor Arbitration in the Light of the Lincoln Mills Case," in *Arbitration and the Law* (Proceedings of the Twelfth Annual Meeting of the National Academy of Arbitrators). Washington, D.C.: The Bureau of National Affairs, 1959.
27. (a) Freydberg Bros., Inc. v. Corey, 177 Misc. 560, 31 N.Y.S. 2d. 10 (1941); (b) Mencher v. B. & S. Abeles & Kahn, 27 App. Div., 585; 84 N.Y.S. 2d. 718 (1948).
28. S. A. Wenger & Co. v. Propper Silk Hosiery Mills, Inc., 239 N.Y. 199 (1924).
29. Cutler-Hammer Inc. v. International Association of Machinists District 15 Local 402, 297 N.Y. 519 (1947); 20 LRRM 2445; 19 LRRM 2232.
30. Steelworkers v. Enterprise Wheel and Car, *op. cit.*
31. Eugene F. Scoles, "Review of Labor Arbitration Awards on Jurisdictional Grounds," *U. Chi. L. Rev.*, Vol. 17 (1950), pp. 616, 633.
32. (a) Steelworkers v. American Mfg., *op. cit.* (b) Steelworkers v. Warrior and Gulf, *op. cit.* (c) Steelworkers v. Enterprise Wheel and Car, *op. cit.*
33. (a) *Ibid.*, at 363 U.S. 582–83; 80 S.Ct. 1353. (b) *Ibid.*, 363 U.S. 584–85; 80 S.Ct. 1354. (c) *Ibid.*, 363 U.S. 593, 80 S.Ct. 1358.
34. (a) *Ibid.*, 363 U.S. 596; 80 S.Ct. 1360. (b) *Ibid.*, 363 U.S. 597; 80 S.Ct. 1361.
35. Atkinson v. Sinclair Refining Co., 370 U.S. 238; 826 S.Ct. 1318, 8 Led. 2d. 462.
36. Steelworkers v. Warrior and Gulf, *op. cit.*, 582.
37. Atkinson v. Sinclair, *op. cit.*, 370 U.S. 241; 826 S.Ct. 1321.
38. Old Dutch Farms, Inc. v. Milk Drivers Union Local 584, 359 F. 2d. 598 (2d. Cir.).
39. *Ibid.*, at 601.
40. *Ibid.*, at 602–03.
41. Drake Bakeries, Inc. v. American Bakery and Confectionery Workers Union Local 50, 370 U.S. 254; 82 S.Ct. 1346, 8 Led. 2d. 747.
42. *Ibid.*, 370 U.S. 262–63; 82 S.Ct. 1351–52.
43. *Ibid.*, 370 U.S. 265–66; 82 S.Ct. 1353.
44. United Packinghouse Workers Union Local 721 v. Needham Packing Co., 376 U.S. II Led. 2d. 680; 84 S.Ct. 773.
45. (a) Belk v. Allied Aviation Service Co. of New Jersey, Inc., 315 F. 2d. 513, 517, 2d. Cir. (1963). (b) International Union of Elec., Radio & Mach. Workers Local 787 v. Collins Radio Co., 317 F. 2d. 214 (5th Cir. 1963).
46. Truck Drivers Union v. Ulry-Talbert Co., 330 F. 2d. 562 (8th Cir.).

47. Torrington Co. v. Metal Products Workers Union, U.A.W. AFL-CIO, Local 1645, 362 F. 2d. 677 (2d. Cir.).
48. Steelworkers v. Enterprise Wheel and Car, *op. cit.*
49. *Ibid.*, 363.
50. H. K. Porter v. United Saw Workers, 333 F. 2d. 596 (3d. Cir.).
51. Clarke W. Brinckerhoff, law note, *Cornell L. Rev.*, vol. 53 (1967), pp. 136, 140–41.
52. Steelworkers v. Warrior and Gulf, *op. cit.*, 574, 578.
53. *Ibid.*, at 580.
54. "The Torrington Case," *Stanford L. Rev.*, vol. 20 (1966), pp. 41, 48.
55. Fitzgerald v. General Electric Co., 23 A.D. 2d. 288; 260 N.Y.S. 2d. 470.
56. *Ibid.*, 23 A.D. 290; 260 N.Y.S. 169.
57. Posner v. Grunwald-Marx, Inc., 56 Calif. 2d. 169; 363 P. 2d. 313.
58. Todd Shipyards Corp. v. Marine and Shipbuilding Workers Union Local 15, 242 F. suppl. 606.
59. *Ibid.*, 610–11.
60. John Wiley & Sons, Inc., v. Livingston, 376 U.S. 543; 84 S.Ct. 909.
61. *Ibid.*, 376 U.S. 548; 84 S.Ct. at 914.
62. *Ibid.*, 376 U.S. 549; 84 S.Ct. at 914.
63. *Ibid.*, 376 U.S. 550–51; 84 S.Ct. at 915.
64. Steelworkers v. Warrior and Gull, *op. cit.*, 582–83.
65. Wackenhut Corp. v. United Plant Guard Workers Union Local 151, 332 F. 2d. 954 (9th Cir.).
66. United Steelworkers of America v. Reliance Universal Inc., 335 F. 2d. 891 (3d. Cir.).
67. McGuire v. Humble Oil and Refining Co., 355 F. 2d. 352 (2d. Cir.).
68. Russell A. Smith and Dallas L. Jones, "The Impact of the Emerging Federal Law of Grievance Arbitration on Judges, Arbitrators, and Parties." *Va. L. Rev.*, vol. 52 (1966), pp. 831, 860–62.
69. Carey v. Westinghouse Corp., 375 U.S. 261; 84 S.Ct. 401, II Led. 2d. 320.

9

RIGHTS OF THE
INDIVIDUAL IN ARBITRATION

A collective bargaining agreement sets forth the rights and obligations of the contracting parties. By this document, the union as an entity and its members as individuals acquire certain rights. If it is alleged that these rights are breached by the company, the union, or the individual, grievant may invoke the grievance-arbitration provision, which is found in almost every collective bargaining agreement.

The purpose of grievance procedures is to provide for preliminary discussions by management and labor in an attempt to settle the alleged violation of contract. If no settlement is possible and the grievance procedure terminates in arbitration, an arbitrator is then selected to adjudicate the dispute and render a final and binding award.

If the union representatives agree with management that the grievant's contractual rights have not been violated and refuse to file a grievance, or if the union settles the grievance in the company's favor and refuses to permit the issue to go before an arbitrator, then many serious questions arise as to the individual grievant's rights.

Individual Rights vs. Union Rights

It has been argued that when an individual joins a union, he agrees to relinquish some of his rights and subordinate them to the collective interests of all members.

Clyde W. Summers[1] expounded a different view and pointed out that although agreements are negotiated by the union and the company:

The freedom to agree, however, is not absolute, for there is a competing concern for the rights of individual employees who are governed by the collective agreement. Union and management cannot, for example, establish rules which create invidious or arbitrary distinctions, nor agree that the law of the plant shall be applied to achieve that end. Regardless of their mutual interests, under Taft-Hartley they cannot agree that only union members shall be hired, or that employment shall be conditioned on obedience to union rules. Indeed, the collective parties cannot ever agree to establish a system of industrial government without first obtaining the approval of a majority of the employees. Thus the freedom of collective agreement is limited by individual rights. Drawing the boundaries to accommodate these competing values poses some of the most difficult problems within the statutory structure.

R. W. Fleming[2] is "concerned that the very collective process which offers them (individuals) protection may well subjugate individual rights. Critics have long struggled with the problem without finding a completely satisfactory solution. One aspect of the problem . . . is the question of how accessible the arbitration machinery should be to the individual for purposes of determining his contractual rights."

The problem presented, therefore, is one of determining and protecting the rights of the individual and the accommodation of these rights to the collective rights of the union.

Judicial Review

Early decisions concerning individual rights are illustrated in the New York case of *Parker v. Borock* (1959),[3] where the court found that "a reading of the existing agreements indicates that plaintiff has entrusted his rights to his union representative. It may be that the Union failed to preserve them. . . . The only conclusion which logically follows is that the employee is without any remedy, except as against his own union. . . ."

A concurring judge in the same case held that the individual loses his rights. He stated: ". . . absent specific language giving the employee the right to act on his own behalf . . . the union alone has a right to control the prosecution of discharge cases." [3]

This line of reasoning was followed by the New York courts in the *Matter of Soto* (1960).[4] Workers represented by the National Jewelry Workers Union became dissatisfied, joined a rival union, and went on strike. When the strike was enjoined, the workers returned to work. The Company charged seven workers with a slowdown and notified the union of its intent to discharge these workers. After going through the grievance procedures, the matter was submitted to arbitration. The grievants appeared at the hearing with their own counsel, claiming that the union's counsel had previously represented the employer in enjoining the wildcat strike. The court found against the right of the individual to be represented by independent counsel.

A different line of reasoning was followed by the Wisconsin courts. In *Pattenge v. Wagner* (1957)[5] the court decided:

We do not construe the contract or the law as requiring an individual employee to invoke this grievance procedure to assert an accrued pecuniary claim in circumstances where it is reasonably apparent that the union is hostile to him and will not give him adequate representation. To do so would place the employee's accrued rights against his employer more or less at the mercy of an unfriendly union.[5]

With reference to the question of the duty of fair representation, the Wisconsin court in *Clark v. Heiss-Werner Corp.* (1959)[6] stated:

So long as the Union is fighting the battle of the employees through arbitration proceedings the employees' interests are being represented and there is no need for courts to provide protection to the employees. However, where the interests of two groups of employees are diametrically opposed to each other and the union espouses the cause of one in the arbitration it follows as a matter of law that there has been no fair representation of the other group.[6]

These cases are illustrative of the divergent views held by courts in the various states.

The Preemption Issue

The federal courts entered the controversy over individual rights on the issue of preemption. The question was whether jurisdiction in this area had been preempted by the National Labor Relations Board (NLRB). The "right" of exclusive jurisdiction of the NLRB was discussed in *Smith v. Evening News Association* (1962).[7] The court held that "the authority of the Board to deal with an unfair labor practice which also violates a collective bargaining contract is not displaced by sec. 301, but it is not exclusive and does not destroy the jurisdiction of the courts in suits under sec. 301."

In *Vaca v. Sipes* (1967),[8] a landmark case in this area, the U.S. Supreme Court explained the reasons for the preemption rule, its nature, and its inapplicability to cases concerning duty of fair representation. It said:

The decision to pre-empt federal and state court jurisdiction over a given class of cases must depend upon the nature of the particular interests being asserted and the effect upon the administration of national labor policies of concurrent judicial and administrative remedies.

A primary justification for the pre-emption doctrine—the need to avoid conflicting rules of substantive law in the labor relations area and the desirability of leaving the development of such rules to the administrative agency created by Congress for that purpose—is not applicable to cases involving alleged breaches of the union's duty of fair representation. . . . It can be doubted whether the Board brings substantially greater expertise to bear on these problems than do the courts, which have been engaged in this type of review since the Steele decision. . . .

We cannot assume from the NLRB's tardy assumption of jurisdiction in these cases that Congress, when it enacted N.L.R.A. sec 8(b) in 1947, intended to oust the courts of their traditional jurisdiction to curb arbitrary conduct by the individual employee's statutory representation.[8]

With reference to federal–state court relationships, the U.S. Supreme Court in *Textile Workers Union v. Lincoln Mills* (1957)[9] held:

We conclude that the substantive law to apply in suits under sec. 301(a) is federal law which the courts must fashion from the policy of our national labor laws.

Federal interpretation of the federal law will govern, not state law. Any state law applied, however, will be absorbed as federal law and will not be an independent source of private rights.

It is not uncommon for federal courts to fashion federal law where federal rights are concerned.[9]

Individual Responsibilities

Before pursuing his remedy in the courts the individual has the responsibility of utilizing the grievance procedures set forth in the contract. In *Republic Steel Corp. v. Maddox* (1965),[10] it was found that "as a general rule in cases to which federal law applies, federal labor policy requires that individual employees wishing to assert contract grievances must attempt use of the contract grievance procedure agreed upon by employer and union as the mode of redress."

This concept was further clarified in *Vaca v. Sipes* which held that "it is settled that the employee must at least attempt to exhaust exclusive grievance and arbitration procedures established by the bargaining agreement." [11]

Duty of Fair Representation

The first case to define the union's duty of fair representation was *Steele v. Louisville and Nashville R.R.* (1944).[12] Even though it involved the Railway Labor Act, it set a precedent for subsequent fair representation cases. The Court held:

So long as a labor union assumes to act as the statutory representative of a craft, it cannot rightly refuse to perform the duty, which is inseperable from the power of representation conferred upon it, to represent the entire membership of the craft. While the statute [Railway Labor Act] does not deny to such a bargaining labor organization the right to determine eligibility to it membership, it does require the union, in collective bargaining and in making contracts with the waiver, to represent nonunion or minority union members of the craft without hostile discrimination, fairly, impartially, and in good faith. Wherever necessary to that end, the union is required to consider requests of non-union members of the craft and expressions of their views with respect to collective bargaining with the employer and to give to them notice of and opportunity for hearing upon its proposed action.

This line of reasoning was followed in *Vaca v. Sipes* when the Court stated that "we think the wrongfully discharged employee may bring an action against his employer in the face of a defense based upon the failure to exhaust remedies, provided the employee can prove that the union as bargaining agent breached its duty of fair representation in its handling of the employee's grievance." [13]

In *Vaca* the Court clarified breach of duty of fair representation when it stated that "we conclude that a union does not breach its duty of fair representation, and thereby open up a suit by the employee for breach of contract, merely because it settled the grievance short of arbitration." [13]

With reference to the right of the union to settle grievances, the Court held in *Vaca* that "in administering the grievance and arbitration machinery as statutory agent of the employees, a union must, in good faith and in a nonarbitrary manner, make decisions as to the merits of particular grievances." [13]

A more serious issue arises when the union stops short of arbitration, deciding that the grievance did not merit going to arbitration. and the individual brings the grievance to the courts, which decide that the grievance is meritorious. Can the individual sue the union for breach of its duty of fair representation because the grievance was meritorious?

In *Vaca* the Court reasoned that if a union could be sued by an individual when a grievance has been determined meritorious, the incentive to resolve a grievance short of arbitration will be greatly reduced. This would not only cause a breakdown in the efficiency and effectiveness of the grievance procedure, but could also retard the relationship between labor and management. The Court's opinion was that "since the union's statutory duty of fair representation protects the individual employee from arbitrary abuses of the settlement device by providing him with recourse against both employer (in a sec. 301 suit) and union, this severe limitation on the power to settle grievances is neither necessary nor desirable." In further clarification of this issue, the Court held that "a breach of the statutory duty of fair representation occurs only when a union's conduct toward a member of the collective bargaining unit is arbitrary, discriminatory, or in bad faith."

Limits on Individual Rights

The *Vaca* decision also set limits to individual rights when it stated that "though we accept the proposition that a union may not arbitrarily ignore a meritorious grievance or process it in perfunctory fashion, we do not agree that the individual employee has an absolute right to have his grievance taken to arbitration regardless of the provisions of the applicable collective bargaining agreement." [13]

This ruling is an attempt to avoid undermining the ability of the union to settle grievances before arbitration.

Conclusion

The object of the arbitral process is the protection of rights, individual as well as collective rights. Union representatives have a positive responsibility to represent the individual fairly and effectively in the protection of contractual rights. This does not mean, however, that union representatives have no power to settle the grievance or find that the merits of the case do not warrant submitting it to arbitration. The criterion of fair representation is not whether in fact their judgment regarding the merits of the case is correct but whether the union's conduct is arbitrary, discriminatory, or in bad faith.

Moreover, the individual has the obligation to attempt to exhaust his remedy under the contract before seeking the aid of the courts.

The passage of Title VII (Equal Employment Opportunity) of the Civil Rights Act of 1964[14] has affected concepts concerning individual rights. This subject is discussed by Sherman[15] and also by Sovern.[16]

REFERENCES

1. Clyde W. Summers, *"Individual Rights in Collective Agreements and Arbitration." New York Univ. L. Rev.*, Vol. 37 (May 1962), p. 362.
2. R. W. Fleming, *The Arbitration Process.* Urbana: University of Illinois Press, 1965, pp. 130, 131.
3. Parker v. Borock, 5 N.Y. 2d. 156; 156 N.E. 2d. 297.
4. Soto v. National Jewelry Workers Union, 165 N.E. 2d. 855.
5. Pattenge v. Wagner, 82 N.W. 2d. 172.
6. Clark v. Heiss-Werner Corp., 93 N.W. 2d. 132.
7. Smith v. Evening News Assoc., 371 U.S. 195.
8. Vaca v. Sipes, 386 U.S. 171.
9. Textile Workers Union v. Lincoln Mills, 353 U.S. 448.
10. Republic Steel Corp. v. Maddox, 379 U.S. 650.
11. Vaca v. Sipes, *op. cit.*
12. Steele v. Louisville and Nashville R.R., 323 U.S. 192.
13. Vaca v. Sipes, *op. cit.*
14. 78 Stat 253, 42 U.S.C., par. 2000(e); F.C.A. 42, par. 2000(e).
15. Herbert L. Sherman, Jr., "Union's Duty of Fair Representation and the Civil Rights Act of 1964." *Minn. L. Rev.*, Vol. 49 (1965), p. 771.
16. Michael I. Sovern, "Race Discrimination and the National Labor Relations Act; The Brave New World of Miranda." *Proceedings of N.Y.U. Sixteenth Conference on Labor* (1963).

10

ARBITRATION AND THE NATIONAL LABOR RELATIONS BOARD

The relationship between arbitration and the National Labor Relations Board (NLRB) is a very close one. According to Arnold Ordman,* "regardless of how people feel about the Board's work in relation to arbitration, there is no question that the Board and the arbitration processes are, in effect, married to one another. Like any marriage, there is give and take and there are occasional unpleasant moments, but the foundation of a lasting and blissful relationship is based on a harmonious and cooperative spirit." [1]

The basis for this relationship is found in the National Labor Relations Act (NLRA), which specifies in Section 203(d) the functions of the Federal Mediation and Conciliation Service (FMCS) and states that "final adjustment by a method agreed upon by the parties is hereby declared to be the desirable method for settlement of grievance disputes arising over the application or interpretation of an existing collective bargaining agreement."

Section 10(a) of the Act provides that "the Board is empowered, as hereinafter provided, to prevent any person from engaging in any unfair practice (listed in Section 8) affecting commerce. This power shall not be affected by any other means of adjustment or prevention that has been or may be established by agreement, law or otherwise."

Implicit in these two sections are both the legality of the marriage and the seeds of discord. Frank W. McCulloch† expressed the view that "in dealing with two possibly conflicting systems of resolving industrial disputes the initial question must be: What working formula should one system adopt in regard to the other? Although there are those who have continued to espouse the doctrine of Board preemption in this area, the Board itself has consistently taken the position that concurrent jurisdiction is possible,

---

* General Counsel, National Labor Relations Board, Washington, D.C.
† Chairman, National Labor Relations Board, Washington, D.C.

The Supreme Court has clearly been of this view." [2] McCulloch was speaking in reference to *Carey v. Westinghouse Electric Corp.* (1964).[3] The court said: "By allowing the dispute to go to arbitration its fragmentation is avoided to a substantial extent; and those conciliatory measures which Congress deemed vital to 'industrial peace' . . . and which may be dispositive of the entire dispute are encouraged. The superior authority of the Board may be invoked at any time. Meanwhile the therapy of arbitration is brought to bear in a complicated and troubled area." [3]

A brief prepared by the NLRB for the U.S. Supreme Court in *Carey v. Westinghouse* stated: "As a general rule the existence of the NLRB remedies do not preclude seeking a judicial or arbitral remedy for the same or an overlapping controversy under the terms of a collective bargaining agreement. The point was squarely decided . . . in *Smith v. Evening News Association.* The bare fact that IUE might have sought similar relief under Section 8(a)(5) would not oust the court of jurisdiction to enforce the agreement to arbitrate." [4]

Dual Jurisdiction

Arbitral issues frequently involve matters within the jurisdiction of the NLRB. Under Section 10 of the NRLA, the Board may ignore an arbitration award if it has jurisdiction over the subject matter of the dispute out of which the award arose.[5] Although it has the power, the NRLB does not ignore arbitration awards covering subject matter over which it has jurisdiction. In practice, it often withholds its jurisdiction pending the outcome of arbitration.[6] In 1955 the Board decided *Spielberg Manufacturing Company* (1955),[7] which contained the Spielberg doctrine. In that case, the Board honored an arbitration award that denied reinstatement to certain individuals allegedly guilty of strike misconduct. The Board stated that it would honor an arbitration award where "the proceedings appear to have been fair and regular, all parties had agreed to be bound, and the decision of the arbitration panel is not clearly repugnant to the purposes and policies of the Act." [8]

The Spielberg doctrine does not declare a policy of automatic acceptance of all arbitration awards. The proceedings must be fair and regular,[9] there must be adequate notice and representation,[10] the arbitrator must pass on the issue of the alleged unfair labor practice,[11] and all parties must agree to be bound by the arbitration award.[12] An ambiguous award will not be recognized[13] and the Board will not enforce an award which is repugnant to the policies of the Act.[14] The Board will disregard the arbitrator's award when its investigations disclose new evidence not presented to the arbitrator.[15]

In *International Harvester Company* (1962)[16] the Board evinced a strong belief in the arbitral process by accepting an arbitrator's award as "not palpably wrong" even though the employee, who had charged various breaches of the Act by his employer and his union, had not agreed to be bound by the award, had no notice of the hearing, and did not participate in the hearing. The Board decided that there had been no denial of due process, because the employer had had an interest in the outcome of the arbitration and had vigorously defended the employee's position. The Board concluded by stating that to require more of the Board would mean substituting the Board's judgment for that of the arbitrator, thereby defeating the purposes of the Act and the common goal of national labor policy concerning the final adjustment of disputes as part and parcel of the collective bargaining process.[17]

Although the *International Harvester* and *Spielberg* cases suggest a deference toward arbitrators' awards, there are indications that in actual practice the Board is not committed to it. Alan Kanzer commented that:

Although the Board rivalled the Supreme Court in praising arbitration the rhetoric of *International Harvester* was never thoroughly implemented in practice even in the heyday of the deference doctrine between 1960 and 1964; the Board in fact deferred in only about 2390 of the cases in which the issue of arbitration was discussed. By the time the Supreme Court decided *Carey v. Westinghouse*, 375 U.S. 261 (1964), moreover, even the Board's rhetorical infatuation had begun to subside. . . . The Board has since withdrawn from its most extreme phrasing of the "clearly repugnant" and "palpably wrong" test. . . . Under the critical test of what the Board has done in practice, the proposition of cases in which the Board has deferred to arbitration has fallen from 2390 to 1290 of the cases in which the deference issue was discussed during the period 1965–67.[18]

An example of the direction in which the Board is moving can be seen in the area of representation cases. In *Raley's, Inc.* (1963)[19] the NLRB stated: "We believe that the same considerations which moved the Board to honor arbitration awards in unfair labor practice cases are equally persuasive to a similar acceptance of the arbitral process in a representation proceeding."

The application, however, of the rule in *Raley's* has been limited in several cases,[20] the most important being *Westinghouse Electric Corp.* (1967).[21] This case was the aftermath of *Carey v. Westinghouse Corp.*,[22] the details of which were given in Chapter 8. The Board cited *Raley's*[23] but went on to state that *Hotel Employers' Association of San Francisco*[24] had limited its scope, noting that in *Raley's* the contested question— namely, whether the contract included a specified group of employees— was the sole issue presented to the Board. In *Hotel Employers' Association*, the Board found, the arbitrator's award had not resolved the ultimate issue of representation, since the arbitrator did not consider the demand of a rival union, which claimed that it represented the employees in question.

Here, as in the *Hotel Employers' Association* case, the ultimate issue of representation could not be decided by the arbitrator on the basis of his interpreting the contract under which he was authorized to act, but could only be resolved by utilization of Board criteria for making unit determinations. In such cases the arbitrators award must clearly reflect the use of and be consonant with Board standards.

In this case, apparently not all the evidence concerning all these standards was available to the arbitrator for his consideration. . . . Consequently, while we give some consideration to the award, we do not think it will effectuate statutory policy to defer to it entirely.[25]

The Board has followed the Spielberg doctrine in refusal-to-bargain cases. Some of these cases have involved refusals to furnish information,[26] to accept a unilateral change in jobs,[27] and to approve plant removal or the establishment of new plants.[28] The Board has also recognized the Spielberg doctrine in jurisdictional disputes involving two or more unions claiming the same work.[29]

In several cases the Board has not recognized an award if either the employer or one or both unions refused to submit to the arbitral jurisdiction.[30]

The construction industry has tried to resolve the numerous jurisdictional disputes that plague it by resorting to tripartite arbitration. In April 1965 the National Joint Board for the Settlement of Jurisdictional Disputes was established. The Joint Board established new standards and new appeals procedures for the settlement of disputes in the construction industry. In *Carpenters & Joiners v. Don Cartage Co.* (1965),[31] the NLRB expressed an opinion that it should defer to the new Joint Board in order to give it a chance to arrange voluntary settlements. However, the Court of Appeals for the District of Columbia reversed and remanded the case to the Board, saying that "it was the duty of the Board, in the circumstances here shown, to decide the jurisdictional issue presented and fully developed in a hearing before it." [32]

One factor of importance in the *Don Cartage* case is the refusal of the employers to be bound by the procedures of the Joint Board. In an NLRA Section 301 case where the parties had agreed to be bound, the court recognized the settlement.[33]

Interpreting the Collective Bargaining Agreement

In two cases, the Supreme Court passed on the power of the NLRB to construe collective bargaining agreements, where necessary to determine if an unfair labor practice has been committed. In *NLRB v. C & C Plywood* (1967),[34] the Court of Appeals refused to enforce an NLRB order to an employer to cease and desist from giving premium payments during the life of a collective bargaining agreement. The order had been issued despite the employer's argument that his action was authorized by a provision of the agreement. The Court of Appeals said that the question for settlement was one of contract interpretation and therefore a state or federal court, under Section 301 of the NLRA, was the proper body to hear the case because the NLRB lacked jurisdiction. Since the collective bargaining agreement contained no arbitration provision, there was no possible conflict with the doctrine expressed by the U.S. Supreme Court in the Trilogy cases (discussed in Chapter 8).

The Supreme Court reversed the Court of Appeals, holding that the NLRB is not without jurisdiction to adjudicate an unfair labor practice charge merely because its decision requires the interpretation of a provision of a collective bargaining agreement on which the employer's argument relied.

In a second case, *NLRB v. Acme Industrial Co.* (1967),[35] the collective bargaining agreement provided for arbitration but stated that it was the employer's policy not to "sub-contract work which [was] normally performed by employees in the bargaining unit." It also stated that if, except as provided in the agreement, "equipment of the plant . . . [was] hereafter moved to another location of the company, employees . . . who [were] subjected to reduction in classification or layoff as a result thereof [might] transfer to the new location with full rights and seniority." When certain machinery was moved, the union asked about the circumstances and were told that there was no violation of the agreement and therefore no obligation to answer questions about the machinery. Unfair labor practice charges were filed with the NLRB, which issued a cease-and-desist order to the company after finding that (1) the information was necessary to enable the union to evaluate the grievances filed and (2) the agreement contained no waiver of the union's statutory rights to such information.

The Court of Appeals refused to enforce the NLRB order, holding that the provision for binding arbitration foreclosed the NLRB exercise of power, as the construction and application of the contract provisions are solely for the arbitrator.

The Supreme Court reversed, saying that the Board's decision did not consider the merits of the decision, but merely affirmed that the information requested was relevant to the arbitration process: "Far from intruding upon the preserve of the arbitrator, the Board's action was an aid in the arbitral process. . . ."[36]

The two cases, taken together, suggest that the NLRB may engage in contract interpretation when an unfair labor practice dispute is involved. Neither NLRA Section 301 nor the Trilogy's deference to arbitration will bar the NLRB from exercising jurisdiction.

Robert G. Howlett concluded:

C & C Plywood and Acme Industrial vest in the NLRB a contract interpretation power that the trial courts are directed by the Supreme Court [in the Trilogy] to avoid. And this seems essential in the labor relations area. If a court interprets a contract, it substitutes itself for the arbitrator, the decision-making official selected by many parties to interpret their agreement. The NLRB, on the other hand, has a statutory function to perform. Interpretation of a contract may be essential in the exercise of this duty.[37]

Arnold Ordman pointed out that the duty to bargain [Section 8(a)(5)] and the Board's power [Section 10(a)] to prevent unfair labor practices unaffected by any other means of adjustment or prevention preclude a view of the Trilogy as requiring automatic deferral by the Board to the primary determination of an arbitrator.[38]

Arbitral Issues Involving Violation of Law

How much consideration should an arbitrator give to statutory material that may have relevance in a dispute? Some arbitrators take the position that they should consider only the question of whether or not the contract has been violated. In *Rowland Tompkins & Son* (1960)[39] the arbitrator said:

> I am limited . . . to the four corners of the Collective Bargaining Agreement. I may interpret any of its provisions . . . but beyond that I may not go.
> I have interpreted section 25 of the agreement . . . and have determined that the Company is in violation of (it). . . . It may well be that the Union may be engaged in an unfair labor practice under Section 8 (b) (4) (B) of the Taft–Hartley Act . . . ; however . . . I may not decide [that issue]. . . . In exercising my authority to construe the Collective Bargaining Agreement, I may not stray beyond the Agreement in order to determine whether or not any clause therein is illegal by virtue of that law.[39]

Milton Friedman has stated that the function of the arbitrator is simply to determine contract rights: "I think that Spielberg and the Board's overall respect for the Arbitrator's role assume that the Arbitrator will decide the contract issue under the contract. If the award then meets Spielberg's standard it will not be disturbed by the Board." [40] Friedman does not feel that it is within the arbitrator's province to interpret the NLRA. "The frequency with which the courts overturn the Board . . . further highlights the danger of Arbitrators applying the Act in preference to the Contract. If the Board's application of the Act is held at times to be improper, it is safe to assume that [an] Arbitrator's would fare even worse." [41]

Many arbitrators take an entirely different view. They feel that the requirements of the NLRA and other statutes must be considered by the arbitrator if they appear relevant to a dispute.[42]

Robert G. Howlett stated that the arbitrator's consideration of a statute is consistent with the Spielberg doctrine, because an arbitrator who has not passed upon the statutory issues involved in a dispute will not have his award honored by the NLRB.[43, 44]

> If he is to be useful in reducing the NLRB case load [an Arbitrator should probe to determine whether a statutory issue is involved]; particularly in discharge cases, [when he should] inquire as to the possibility of section 8 (a) and 8 (b) violations. . . . Unless he does so neither the General Counsel nor the Board will "defer" to the Arbitrator's decision. . . .

The Arbitrator who does not follow the practice . . . will never reach Spielberg, for the Board will be required to assume jurisdiction and decide the case. . . .[45]

Arnold Ordman said "that where a statute such as the Civil Rights Act or the National Labor Relations Act sticks out like a sore thumb and makes it obvious that it is very heavily involved, [the Arbitrator should] also pay some attention to that. The law of the Contract is controlling, but the public law is relevant." [46]

In evaluating contractual provisions urged as a defense to unfair labor practice charges involving unilateral action, many arbitrators differ from the Board in their approach. The Board's evaluation of the circumstances in which the claim of privileged unilateral action is made usually involves considerations other than the interpretation of a single, specific contract provision. The Board has developed statutory principles for evaluating these general circumstances.[47]

Many arbitrators, since they are concerned solely with whether there has been a breach of contract, consider it improper for arbitrators to apply the statutory principles developed by the Board or to apply them differently than the Board does. Some arbitrators apply the so-called residual rights theory, which permits management to take unilateral action, holding that management is free to act unless the collective bargaining agreement expressly prohibits the challenged conduct.[48, 49]

Ordman said:

The view that the Contract is the exclusive statement of the bargaining agent's rights and privileges is inconsistent with *Fibreboard Paper Products Corp. v. NLRB*, 379 U.S. 203 (1964), which held that the Act in certain circumstances requires bargaining about sub-contracting apart from any contractual requirement. In addition, a doctrine which is bottomed upon the theory that management has all residual rights is also in conflict with the Board-developed and court-approved principle that a statutory waiver must be express and clear.[50]

The Collyer Doctrine

In the case of *Collyer v. Electrical Workers* (1971),[51] the National Labor Relations Board further developed its policies regarding arbitration awards. The decision issued in August 1971 reviewed prior Board decisions. Because of its significance, selected portions of the decision are quoted or digested.

During contract negotiations, the employer several times proposed wage raises for maintenance employees over and above those being negotiated for the production and maintenance unit generally. The union rejected those proposals, and the contract did not include any provision for such raises.

It is clear, nevertheless, that the matter of a "skill factor" increase was left open, in some measure, for further negotiations after the execution of the agreement. The parties sharply disputed, however, the extent to which the matter remained open and the conditions that were to surround further discussions. The union asserted, and the trial examiner found, that the union was willing, and made known its willingness, to negotiate further wage adjustments only on a plantwide basis, consistent with the job evaluation system. The company insisted that it understood the union's position to be that wage increases for maintenance employees only might still be agreed to by the union after the signing of the contract, if such increases could be justified under the job evaluation system.

After the contract negotiations were completed, the employer and the union continued to discuss the employer's desire to raise the wages of maintenance employees. Finally, the employer unilaterally instituted an upward adjustment of 20 cents per hour. The union protested and restated its desire for a reevaluation of all jobs in the plant. The company's representative agreed to consider such an evaluation on a plantwide basis, upon union agreement to the increases for the skilled tradesmen. The trial examiner found that the union did not agree to this. However, the rate increase became effective November 17, 1969.

Contract Provisions

The contract in effect between the parties provides for the employer's adjustment of its employees' wages during the contract term. The contract provisions appear to consider changes in rates for both incentive and non-incentive jobs. Article IX, Section 2, states:

The Corporation agrees to establish rates and differentials of pay for all employees according to their skill, experience and hazards of employment, and to review rates and differentials from time to time. The Corporation agrees to pay all operators their average earnings for samples and unusual processes; untimed portions of already rated jobs will be paid for at an allowed pay hour of 8.8 and adjustment in pay will be made after the rate is fully established. It is agreed that untimed portions of already rated jobs will be studied within a maximum of one work week. In the event that this time limit is not met, the worker will receive his average hourly rate starting as of the first day. However, no change in the general scale of pay now in existence shall be made during the term of this Agreement. This Article IX is applicable to the general wage scale, but shall not be deemed to prevent adjustments in individual rates from time to time to remove inequalities or for other proper reasons.

Further evidence of the contractual intent to permit the employer to modify job rates subject to review through the grievance and arbitration procedures is found in Article XIII, Section 3, paragraph b, covering new or changed jobs. That paragraph provides that the union shall have seven days to consider any new rating established by the company and to submit objections. Thereafter, even absent union agreement, this provision vests in the company authority to institute a new pay rate. The union, if dissatisfied, may then challenge the propriety of the rate by invoking the grievance procedure, which culminates in arbitration.

Finally, the breadth of the arbitration provision makes clear that the parties intended to make the grievance and arbitration machinery the exclusive forum for resolving contract disputes. In Article IV of the contract, the parties agree that the grievance machinery "shall be adopted for any complaint or dispute . . . which may arise between any employee or group of employees and the Corporation." That intent is further evidenced by the no-strike, no-lockout provision (Article XI), which declares, in part: "All questions, disputes or controversies under this Agreement shall be settled and determined solely and exclusively by the conciliation and arbitration procedures provided in this Agreement." A grievance is defined as any controversy between an employee and his supervisor or any controversy between the union and the employer involving "the interpretation, application or violation of any provision of this agreement or supplement thereto." The arbitration clause (Article V) provides that "any grievance" may be submitted to an impartial arbitrator for decision and that the decision of the arbitrator "shall be final and binding upon the parties" if not contrary to law.

Trial Examiner's Decision

The trial examiner's decision reviewed in careful detail the employer's actions which gave rise to this proceeding. The trial examiner found that the subject of the skill-factor increase for maintenance tradesmen was discussed at September and October meetings and that the employer's decision to grant such an increase was announced on November 12. He also found that despite these discussions, the union did not accede to the proposed change. He further found that the contract did not authorize the employer to act unilaterally in the matter, and that by so acting the employer had sought to escape from the basic wage framework established in the contract. This, the trial examined concluded, had been in violation of Section 8(a)(5).

In considering the reassignment of duties, the trial examiner found that the employer's actions were not sanctioned by the contract and had not been made the subject of bargaining between the union and the employer. Accordingly, he found that, in this respect also, Section 8(a)(5) had been violated. He said:

Board's Discussion

We find merit in respondent's [employer's] exceptions that because this dispute in its entirety arises from the contract between the parties, and from the parties' relationship under the contract, it ought to be resolved in the manner which that contract prescribes. We conclude that the Board is vested with authority to withhold its processes in this case, and that the contract here made available a quick and fair means for the resolution of this dispute including, if appropriate, a fully effective remedy for any breach of contract which occurred. We conclude, in sum, that our obligation to advance the purposes of the Act is best discharged by the dismissal of this complaint.

In our view, disputes such as these can better be resolved by arbitrators with special skill and experience in deciding matters arising under established bargaining relationships than by the application by this Board of a particular provision of our statute. The necessity for such special skill and expertise is apparent upon examination of the issues arising from Respondent's actions with respect to the operators' rates, the skill factor increase, and the reassignment of duties relating to the worm gear removal. Those issues include, specifically: (a) the extent to which these actions were intended to be reserved to the management, subject to later adjustment by grievance and arbitration; (b) the extent to which the skill factor increase should properly be construed, under article IX of the agreement, as a "change in the general scale of pay" or, conversely, as "adjustments in individual rates . . . to remove inequalities or for other proper reason"; (c) the extent, if any, to which the procedures of article XIII governing new or changed jobs and job rates should have been made applicable to the skill factor increase here; and (d) the extent to which any of these issues may be affected by the long course of dealing between the parties. The determination of these issues, we think, is best left to discussions in the grievance procedure by the parties who negotiated the applicable provisions or, if such discussions do not resolve them, then to an arbitrator chosen under the agreement and authorized by it to resolve such issues.

The Board's authority, in its discretion, to defer to the arbitration process has never been questioned by the courts of appeals, or by the Supreme Court. Although Section 10(a) of the Act clearly vests the Board with jurisdiction over conduct which constitutes a violation of the provisions of Section 8, notwithstanding the existence of methods of "adjustment or prevention that might be established by agreement," nothing in the Act intimates that the Board must exercise jurisdiction where such methods exist. On the contrary in *Carey v. Westinghouse Electric Corporation*, 375 U.S. 261, 271 (1964), the Court indicated that it favors our deference to such agreed methods by quoting at length with obvious approval the following language from the Board's decision in *International Harvester Co.*

"There is no question that the Board is not precluded from adjudicating unfair labor practice charges even though they might have been the subject of an arbitration proceeding and award. Section 10(a) of the Act expressly makes this plain, and the courts have uniformly so held. However, it is equally well established that *the Board has considerable discretion to respect an arbitration award and decline to exercise its authority over alleged unfair labor practices if to do so will serve the fundamental aims of the Act.*

"The Act, as has repeatedly been stated, is primarily designed to promote industrial peace and stability by encouraging the practice and procedure of collective bargaining. Experience has demonstrated that collective-bargaining agreements that provide for final and binding arbitration of grievance and disputes arising thereunder, 'as a substitute for industrial strife,' contribute significantly to the attainment of this statutory objective." (Emphasis supplied.)

In an earlier case, *Smith v. Evening News Assn.*, the Supreme Court had likewise observed that "the Board has, on prior occasions, declined to exercise its jurisdiction to deal with unfair labor practices in circumstances where, in its judgment, federal labor policy would best be served by leaving the parties to other processes of law." As in *Carey v. Westinghouse*, the decision carries a clear implication that the Court approved the informed use of such discretion.

The policy favoring voluntary settlement of labor disputes through arbitral processes finds specific expression in Section 203(d) of the LMRA [Labor Management Relations Act], in which Congress declared: "Final adjustment by a method agreed upon by the parties is hereby declared to be the desirable method for settlement of grievance disputes arising over the application or interpretation of an existing collective-bargaining agreement." And, of course, disputes under Section 301 of the LMRA called forth from the Supreme Court the celebrated affirmation of that national policy in the *Steelworkers* trilogy.

Admittedly, neither Section 203 nor Section 301 applies specifically to the Board. However, labor law as administered by the Board does not operate in a vacuum isolated from other parts of the Act, or, indeed, from other acts of Congress. In fact, the legislative history suggests that at the time the Taft–Hartley amendments were being considered, Congress anticipated that the Board would "develop by rules and regulations, a policy of entertaining under these provisions only such cases . . . as cannot be settled by resort to the machinery established by the contract itself, voluntary arbitration. . . ."

The question whether the Board should withhold its process arises, of course, only when a set of facts may present not only an alleged violation of the Act but also an alleged breach of the collective-bargaining agreement subject to arbitration. Thus, this case like each such case compels an accommodation between, on the one hand, the statutory policy favoring the fullest use of collective bargaining and the arbitral process and, on the other, the statutory policy reflected by Congress' grant to the Board of exclusive jurisdiction to prevent unfair labor practices.

We address the accommodation required here with the benefit of the Board's full history of such accommodations in similar cases. From the start the Board has, case by case, both asserted jurisdiction and declined, as the balance was struck on particular facts and at various stages in the long ascent of collective bargaining to its present state of wide acceptance. Those cases reveal that the Board has honored the distinction between two broad but distinct classes of cases, those in which there has been an arbitral award, and those in which there has not.

In the former class of cases the Board has long given hospitable acceptance to the arbitral process. In *Timken Roller Bearing Company*, the Board refrained from exercising jurisdiction, in deference to an arbitrator's decision, despite the fact that the Board would otherwise have found that an unfair labor practice had been committed. The Board explained it "would not comport with the sound exercise of our administrative discretion to permit the Union to seek redress under the Act after having initiated arbitration proceedings which, at the Union's request, resulted in a determination upon the merits." *Id.* at 501. The Board's policy was refined in *Spielberg Manufacturing Company*, where the Board established the now settled rule that it would limit its inquiry, in the presence of an arbitrator's award, to whether the procedures were fair and the results not repugnant to the Act.

In those cases in which no award had issued, the Board's guidelines have been less clear. At times the Board has dealt with the unfair labor practice, and at other times it has left the parties to their contract remedies. In an early case, *Consolidated Aircraft Corporation*, the Board, after pointing out that the charging party had failed to utilize the grievance procedures, stated:

"It will not effectuate the statutory policy of encouraging the practice and procedure of collective bargaining for the Board to assume the role of policing collective contracts between employers and labor organizations by attempting to decide whether disputes as to the meaning and administration of such contracts constitute unfair labor practices under the Act. On the contrary, we believe that parties to collective contracts would thereby be encouraged to abandon their efforts to dispose of disputes under the contracts through collective bargaining or through the settlement procedures mutually agreed upon by them, and to remit the interpretation and administration of their contracts to the Board. We therefore do not deem it wise to exercise our jurisdiction in such a case, where the parties have not exhausted their rights and remedies under the contract as to which this dispute has arisen."

The Board has continued to apply the doctrine enunciated in *Consolidated Aircraft*, although not consistently.

Jos. Schlitz Brewing Company is the most significant recent case in which the Board has exercised its discretion to defer. The underlying dispute in *Schlitz* was strikingly similar to the one now before us. In *Schlitz* the respondent employer decided to halt its production line during employee breaks. That decision was a departure from an established practice of maintaining extra employees, relief men, to fill in for regular employees during breaktime. The change resulted in, among other things, elimination of the relief man job classification. The change elicited a union protest leading to an unfair labor practice proceeding in which the Board ruled that the case should be "left for resolution within the framework of the agreed upon settlement procedures." The majority there explained its decision in these words:

"Thus, we believe that where, as here, the contract clearly provides for grievance and arbitration machinery, where the unilateral action taken is not designed to undermine the Union and is not patently erroneous but rather is based on a substantial claim of contractual privilege, and it appears that the arbitral interpretation of the contract will resolve both the unfair labor practice issue and the contract interpretation issue in a manner compatible with the purposes of the Act, then the Board should defer to the arbitration clause conceived by the parties. This particular case is indeed an appropriate one for just such deferral. The parties have an unusually long established and successful bargaining relationship; they have a dispute involving substantive contract interpretation almost classical in its form, each party asserting a reasonable claim in good faith in a situation wholly devoid of unlawful conduct or aggravated circumstances of any kind; they have a clearly defined grievance-arbitration procedure which Respondent has urged the Union to use for resolving their dispute; and, significantly, the Respondent, the party which in fact desires to abide by the terms of its contract, is the same party which, although it firmly believed in good faith in its right under the contract to take the action it did take, offered to discuss the entire matter with the Union prior to taking such action. Accordingly, under the principles above stated, and the persuasive facts in this case, we believe that the policy of promoting industrial peace and stability through collective bargaining obliges us to defer the parties to the grievance-arbitration procedures they themselves have voluntarily established." [175 NLRB No. 23, sl. op. at 5–6. Footnotes omitted.]

The circumstances of this case, no less than those in *Schlitz*, weigh heavily in favor of deferral. Here, as in *Schlitz*, this dispute arises within the confines of a long and productive collective-bargaining relationship. The parties before us have, for 35 years, mutually and voluntarily resolved the conflicts which inhere in collective bargaining. Here, as there, no claim is made of enmity by Respondent to empolyees' exercise of protected rights. Respondent here has credibly asserted its willingness to resort to arbitration under a clause providing for arbitration in a very broad range of disputes and unquestionably broad enough to embrace this dispute.

Finally, here as in *Schlitz*, the dispute is one eminently well suited to resolution by arbitration. The contract and its meaning in present circumstances lie at the center of this dispute. In contrast, the Act and its policies become involved only if it is determined that the agreement between the parties, examined in the light of its negotiating history and the practices of the parties thereunder, did not sanction Respondent's right to make the disputed changes, subject to review if sought by the Union, under the contractually prescribed procedure. That threshold determination is clearly within the expertise of a mutually agreed-upon arbitrator. In this regard we note especially that here, as in *Schlitz*, the dispute between these parties is the very stuff of labor contract arbitration. The competence of a mutually selected arbitrator to decide the issue and fashion an appropriate remedy, if needed, can no longer be gainsaid.

We find no basis for the assertion of our dissenting colleagues that our decision here modifies the standards established in *Spielberg* for judging the acceptability of an arbitrator's award. *Spielberg, supra* at 1082, established that such awards would not be contravened by this Board where:

"The proceedings appear to have been fair and regular, all parties had agreed to be bound, and the decision of the arbitration panel is not clearly repugnant to the purposes and policies of the Act."

As already noted, the contract between Respondent and the Union unquestionably obligates each party to submit to arbitration any dispute arising under the contract and binds both parties to the result thereof. It is true, manifestly, that we cannot judge the regularity or statutory acceptability of the result in an arbitration proceeding which has not occurred. However, we are unwilling to adopt the presumption that such a proceeding will be invalid under *Spielberg* and to exercise our decisional authority at this juncture on the basis of a mere possibility that such a proceeding might be unacceptable under *Spielberg* standards. That risk is far better accommodated, we believe, by the result reached here of retaining jurisdiction against an event which years of experience with labor arbitration have now made clear is a remote hazard.

Member Fanning's dissenting opinion incorrectly characterizes this decision as instituting "compulsory arbitration" and as creating an opportunity for employers and unions to "strip parties of statutory rights."

We are not compelling any party to agree to arbitrate disputes arising during a contract term, but are merely giving full effect to their own voluntary agreements to submit all such disputes to arbitration, rather than permitting such agreements to be sidestepped and permitting the substitution of our processes, a forum not contemplated by their own agreement.

Nor are we "stripping" any party of "statutory rights." The courts have long recognized that an industrial relations dispute may involve conduct which, at least arguably, may contravene both the collective agreement and our statute. When the parties have contractually committed themselves to mutually agreeable procedures for resolving their disputes during the period of the contract, we are of the view that those procedures should be afforded full opportunity to function. The long and successful functioning of grievance and arbitration procedures suggests to us that in the overwhelming majority of cases, the utilization of such means will resolve the underlying dispute and make it unnecessary for either party to follow the more formal, and sometimes lengthy, combination of administrative and judicial litigation provided for under our statute. At the same time, by our reservation of jurisdiction, *infra,* we guarantee that there will be no sacrifice of statutory rights if the parties' own processes fail to function in a manner consistent with the dictates of our law. This approach, we believe, effectuates the salutary policy announced in *Spielberg,* which the dissenting opinion correctly summarizes as one of not requiring the "serious machinery of the Board where the record indicates that the parties are in the process of resolving their dispute in a manner sufficient to effectuate the policies of the Act."

We are especially mindful, finally, that the policy of this Nation to avoid industrial strife through voluntary resolution of industrial disputes is not static, but is dynamic. The years since enactment of Section 203(d) have been vital ones, and the policy then expressed has helped to shape an industrial system in which the institution of contract arbitration has grown not only pervasive but, literally, indispensable. The Board has both witnessed and participated in the growth, a complex interaction where the growth of arbitration in response to Congress' will has called forth and nurtured gradually broader conceptions of the basic policy. The Supreme Court which in *Lincoln Mills* first upheld the enforceability of agreements to arbitrate disputes has recently, in *Boys Markets, Inc. v. Retail Clerks,* suggested that arbitration has become "the central institution in the administration of collective bargaining contracts." After *Boys Market* it may truly be said that where a contract provides for arbitration, either party has at hand legal and effective means to ensure that the arbitration will occur. We believe it to be consistent with the fundamental objectives of Federal law to require the parties here to honor their contractual obligations rather than, by casting this dispute in statutory terms, to ignore their agreed-upon procedures.

REMEDY

Without prejudice to any party and without deciding the merits of the controversy, we shall order that the complaint herein be dismissed, but we shall retain jurisdiction for a limited purpose. Our decision represents a developmental step in the Board's treatment of these problems and the controversy here arose at a time when the Board decisions may have led the parties to conclude that the Board approved dual litigation of this controversy before the Board and before an arbitrator. We are also aware that the parties herein have not resolved their dispute by the contractual grievance and arbitration procedure and that, therefore, we cannot now inquire whether resolution of the dispute will comport with the standards set forth in *Spielberg, supra.* In order to eliminate the risk of prejudice to any party we shall retain jurisdiction over this dispute solely for the purpose of entertaining an appropriate and timely motion for further consideration upon a proper showing that either (a) the dispute has not, with reasonable promptness after the issuance of this decision, either been resolved by amicable settlement in the grievance procedure or submitted promptly to arbitration, or (b) the grievance or arbitration procedures have not been fair and regular or have reached a result which is repugnant to the Act.

ORDER

Pursuant to Section 10(c) of the National Labor Relations Act, as amended, the National Labor Relations Board orders that the complaint herein be, and it hereby is, dismissed; provided, however, that:

Jurisdiction of this proceeding is hereby retained for the limited purposes indicated in that portion of our Decision and Order herein entitled "Remedy."

Modified Collyer Doctrine

The General Counsel of the National Labor Relations Board has issued two memoranda (February 28, 1972, and May 10, 1973) regarding the Board's arbitration deferral policy under *Collyer*. The guidelines set forth in the first memorandum are modified in the second to accord with Board policy developed in cases heard after the first memorandum was issued.

The stated objective of the Board's policy is still to encourage "the expeditious and private settlement of industrial disputes through deferral on the part of the Board to the arbitral process."

The May 10, 1973 memorandum states that the *Collyer* policy has been expanded by the Board to apply to charges alleging violations of Sections 8(a)(1), (2), and (3) and 8(b)(1) A and B and 8(b)(2) and (3), in addition to Section 8(a)5.

It also sets forth the following significant changes in the earlier guidelines:

1. Broadening the application of the Board's *Collyer* doctrine to all cases in which (a) the issues are susceptible to resolution under the contract grievance–arbitration procedures, and (b) there is no reason to believe that this machinery will not resolve the issues in a manner compatible with *Spielberg* standards.

2. (a) Providing the respondent an opportunity to express a willingness to arbitrate the dispute, and thus to secure deferral of the charge under *Collyer* (where all other requirements for deferral are met), prior to a final determination of the regional office as to the merits of the unfair labor practice charge.

(b) Requiring as a condition of deferral that, at the latest, respondent express its willingness to arbitrate no more than seven days after a regional office communicates to the respondent its final determination that the charge is meritorious.

3. (a) Refusing to defer under the *Collyer* policy in a dispute over a request for information relevant to grievance processing even though the underlying grievance is already before an arbitrator.

(b) Refusing to defer charges pertaining to the basic, underlying grievance if deferral is inappropriate as to a dispute over a request for information which is relevant to that grievance.

4. Adopting special criteria for the deferral of charges filed by individual employees.

5. Providing the charging party the right, under Board Rule 102.19, to appeal

a decision of the regional office to defer action on a charge under the *Collyer* policy.

REFERENCES

1. Arnold Ordman, "The Arbitrator and the NRLB." Paper presented to Midwest Seminar on Advanced Arbitration, University of Chicago Center for Continuing Education, Chicago, June 5, 1964.
2. Frank W. McCulloch, "Recent Developments Affecting Arbitration and the NLRB." Address delivered to Labor Arbitration Institute, Boston University School of Law, Boston, April 25, 1964.
3. Carey v. Westinghouse Electric Corp., 375 U.S. 261.
4. *Ibid.*
5. (a) NLRB v. Walt Disney Productions, 146 F. 2d. 44, 47–49, 15 LRRM 691 (9th Cir., 1944); cert. denied 324 U.S. 877 (1945), 16 LRRM 918. (b) Machinists Union Lodge 743 v. United Aircraft Corp., 337 F. 2d. 5, 57 LRRM 2245 (2d. Cir., 1964); cert. denied 380 U.S. 908 (1965), 58 LRRM 2496.
6. (a) Bernard D. Meltzer, "Ruminations About Ideology, Law and Arbitration," in *The Arbitrator, the NLRB and the Courts* (Proceedings of the Twentieth Annual Meeting of the National Academy of Arbitrators). Washington, D.C.: The Bureau of Public Affairs, 1967, p. 6. (b) Arnold Ordman, *loc. cit.* at 56. (c) Dubo Mfg. Co., 142 NLRB 431, 53 LRRM 1070 (1963).
7. Spielberg Manufacturing Co., 112 NLRB 1080, 36 LRRM 1152.
8. *Ibid.* at 1082.
9. Denver–Chicago Trucking Co., 132 NLRB 1416, 48 LRRM 1524 (1961).
10. Gateway Transportation Co., 137 NLRB 1763, 50 LRRM 1495 (1962).
11. (a) I. Oscherwitz & Sons, 130 NLRB 1078, 47 LRRM 1415 (1961). (b) Monsanto Chemical Co., 130 NLRB 1097, 47 LRRM 1451 (1961).
12. Operating Engineers Union Local 18 v. Building Trades Employers' Association, 145 NLRB 1492, 55 LRRM 1188 (1964).
13. Dubo Mfg. Co., 148 LLRB 1114, 57 LRRM 1111 (1964).
14. (a) International Union, United Automobile, Aircraft and Agricultural Implement Workers of America (CIO) Local 291 v. Wisconsin Axle Division The Timken Detroit Axle Co., 92 NLRB 968, 27 LRRM 1188 (1950). (b) Virginia–Carolina Freight Lines, Inc., 155 NLRB 52, 60 LRRM 1331 (1965).
15. Precision Fittings Inc., 1414 NLRB 1034, 52 LRRM 1443 (1963). aff'd. sub. (b) Ramsey v. NLRB, 327 F. 2d. 784, 55 LRRM 2441 (7th Cir., 1964); cert. denied 377 U.S. 1003 (1964), 56 LRRM 2544.
16. (a) International Harvester Company, 138 NLRB 923; 51 LRRM 1155,
17. *Ibid.* at 929.
18. Alan Kanzer, "The NLRB and Deference to Arbitration," *Yale L. J.*, Vol. 77 (1968), pp. 1191, 1193.
19. Raley's, Inc., 143 NLRB 256, 258–59, 53 LRRM 1347.
20. (a) Pullman Industries, 159 NLRB 44, 62 LRRM 1273 (1966). (b) Hotel Employers' Association of San Francisco, 159 NLRB 143, 62 LRRM 1215 (1966).
21. Westinghouse Electric Corp., 162 NLRB 768, 64 LRRM (1967).

22. Carey v. Westinghouse, *op. cit.*
23. Raley's, Inc., *op. cit.*
24. Hotel Employers' Association, *op. cit.*
25. Westinghouse Electric Corp., *op. cit.* at 771.
26. Puerto Rico Telephone Co., 149 NLRB 950, 57 LRRM (1964).
27. McDonnell Aircraft Corp., 109 NLRB 930, 94 LRRM 1472 (1954).
28. Montgomery Ward & Co., Inc., 137 NLRB 418, 50 LRRM 1162 (1962).
29. International Brotherhood of Electrical Workers AFL–CIO v. McClosky & Co., 147 NLRB 1498, 56 LRRM 1402 (1964).
30. (a) Sheet Metal Workers Union Local 162 v. Lusterlite Corp., 151 NLRB 195, 58 LRRM 1385 (1965). (b) Plumber & Pipe Fitters Union Local 7 v. James N. Maloy, Inc., 150 NLRB 50, 58 LRRM 1125 (1964).
31. United Brotherhood of Carpenters & Joiners, Millwrights Union Local 1102 v. Don Cartage Co., 154 NLRB 45, 59 LRRM 1772 (1965).
32. Quinn v. National Labor Relations Board, 61 LRRM 2690, 2691 (D.C. Cir. 1966).
33. Sheet Metal Workers Union, AFL–CIO, Union Local 17 v. Aetna Steel Products Corp., 246 F. Supp. 236, 60 LRRM 2273 (U.S.D.C., Mass., 1965).
34. NLRB v. C & C Plywood, 385 U.S. 421, 87 S.Ct. 559 (1967).
35. NLRB v. Acme Industrial Co., 385 U.S. 432, 87 S.Ct. 565 (1967).
36. *Ibid.*, at 438.
37. Robert G. Howlett, "The Arbitrator and the NLRB," in *The Arbitrator, the NLRB and the Courts* (Proceedings of the Twentieth Annual Meeting of the National Academy of Arbitrators). Washington, D.C.: The Bureau of Public Affairs, 1967, p. 76.
38. Arnold Ordman, *loc. cit.*, at 62.
39. Rowland Tompkins & Son, 35 LA 154, 156.
40. Milton Friedman, "The Arbitrator and the NLRB: Workshop Session," in *The Arbitrator, the NLRB and the Courts, op. cit.* at 118.
41. *Ibid.* at 117.
42. (a) Pennsylvania Electric Co., 47 LA 526 (1967). (b) General American Transportation Corp., 42 LA 1308 (1964).
43. Robert G. Howlett, *loc. cit.* at 87.
44. (a) Raytheon Co., 140 NLRB 883, 52 LRRM 1129 (1963). (b) Monsanto Chemical Co., 130 NLRB 1097, 47 LRRM 1451 (1961).
45. Robert G. Howlett, *loc. cit.* at 92.
46. Arnold Ordman, *loc. cit.* at 130.
47. (a) NLRB v. Perkins Machine Co., 326 F. 2d. 488 (1st Cir., 1964). (b) Timken Roller Bearing Co. v. NLRB, 325 F. 2d. 746, 751 (6th Cir., 1963); cert. denied 376 U.S. 971 (1964). (c) Fafnir Bearing Co. v. NLRB, 362 F. 2d. 716 (2d. Cir., 1966).
48. Arnold Ordman, *loc. cit.* at 64–65.
49. (a) C. Finbeiner, Inc., 44 LA 1109 (1965). (b) Bethlehem Steel Co., 30 LA 678 (1958).
50. Arnold Ordman, *loc, cit.* at 66.
51. Collyer Insulated Wire Co. (a Gulf and Western Systems Co.) v. International Brotherhood of Electrical Workers Union Local 1098, AFL–CIO, 192 NLRB 150, 77 LRRM, 1971.

11

COMPULSORY ARBITRATION

When the parties to a labor dispute are compelled by law to submit the dispute to an arbitrator or an arbitration panel and are obligated to abide by the award, the process is called *compulsory arbitration*.

National War Labor Board

The National War Labor Board was established under Executive Order 9017 in January 1942.[1] It was the first time that the federal government had adopted such a strong measure as compulsory arbitration for the settlement of industrial disputes. In the war emergency it was imperative that there be no interruption in production for the war effort. The order prohibited strikes and compelled disputants to submit all disputes to the National War Labor Board (NWLB), which was empowered to issue a final and binding decision. Although the Board had compulsive powers, it encouraged collective bargaining, mediation, and voluntary arbitration.

The Executive Order, Section 3, provided:

The Procedure for adjusting and settling labor disputes which might interrupt work which contributes to the effective prosecution of the war shall be as follows:

(a) The parties shall first resort to direct negotiations or to the procedures provided in a collective bargaining agreement.

(b) If not settled in this manner, the Commissioners of Conciliation of the Department of Labor shall be notified if they have not already intervened in the dispute.

(c) If not promptly settled by conciliation, the Secretary of Labor shall certify the dispute to the Board, provided, however, that the Board in its discretion after consultation with the Secretary may take jurisdiction of the dispute on its own motion. After it takes jurisdiction, the Board shall *finally* determine the dispute and for this purpose may use mediation, voluntary arbitration or arbitration under the rules established by the Board.

The Board consisted of 12 members, of whom the public, industry, and labor had four representatives each. It was deliberately intended to be tripartite in character and represent all points of view.

For administrative purposes the country was divided into 12 regions.

The regional board was also tripartite in character, and all labor disputes within a particular region were submitted to the regional board for decision.

Because of the large number of disputes, it was not possible for the regional board to hear each case. Disputes, therefore, were assigned either to a single hearing officer or a three-man panel consisting of representatives of labor, management, and the public. The public representative was called the "public panel chairman" and was responsible for the conduct of the hearing and the preparation of the panel report. He also had the responsibility of notifying the parties to appear at a specific time for the hearing and present their respective positions.

At the conclusion of the hearing, the chairman prepared a statement for the board, setting forth the issues, the company and union positions, and a recommended decision. The board would study the report, adopt, modify, or reject the recommendations made, and issue its decision by which both parties were obligated to abide.

Public Utility Disputes—State Laws

After World War II a number of states (New Jersey, Florida, Massachusetts, Pennsylvania, Indiana, and Wisconsin) passed compulsory arbitration statutes,[2] which were limited to labor disputes involving public utilities. Since the welfare of the public was considered paramount to the interests of management or labor, state legislatures sought to prevent the interruption of essential services to the public by strikes and to compel both parties to submit their labor disputes to arbitration. An insight into the manifold problems of the compulsory arbitration of public utility disputes can be gained by a study of the statutes enacted in such states as New Jersey and Wisconsin and the court decisions based on these laws.

New Jersey Statute

The New Jersey statute, enacted in 1946,[3] declared that such basic and all-inclusive utilities as heat, light, power, sanitation, transportation, communication, and water were so essential to the life of the people that the possibility of labor strife in such enterprises, or even threatened interruption of these vital services, was a threat to public health and welfare. The statute authorized the Governor to take possession of any public utility plant for use and operation by the state if he deemed it was necessary to insure continuous service. The law also provided for the appointment of members of a panel by the parties or by the State Board of Mediation with power to conduct public hearings and report to the Governor its findings of fact and recommendations.

In 1947 the Act was amended[4] to forbid strikes and lockouts after seizure, and also to provide for the appointment by the Governor of a board of arbitration within ten days after seizure. The board was empowered to hear disputes, make written findings of fact, and promulgate a decision subject to review by the Appellate Division of the New Jersey Superior Court. Violations were to be punished by fine or imprisonment, or both, and a civil penalty of $10,000 for each day of violation, recoverable by the state.

Shortly after the Act was amended, the Traffic-Telephone Workers Federation of New Jersey called a strike against the New Jersey Bell Telephone Company in April 1947. The Governor promptly seized the company, and three telephone operators who had participated in the strike were arrested. The union obtained a temporary restraining order in the United States District Court in Newark, enjoining the state to hold in status quo all further action until the constitutionality of the statute could be determined. The state then commenced a proceeding in the state courts to test the constitutionality of the statute. The court held that the provisions for compulsory arbitration were unconstitutional because "they delegate legislative power to an administrative agency, without setting up adequate standards to guide the administrative agency in the exercise of the powers delegated to it." [5]

To correct the defect in the law with regard to adequate standards, the legislature met in special session and added a new section with enumerated specific factors that were to be followed by the boards of arbitration in rendering decisions in cases involving the terms and conditions of new contracts.[6] In 1950 the legislature repealed the provisions for fact-finding panels on the grounds that public hearings before these panels had become unnecessary.[7] In 1951 the U.S. Supreme Court held unconstitutional a similar statute in the State of Wisconsin.[8] Since that time the Governor has failed to appoint arbitration boards, presumably because of doubt concerning its constitutionality.

Wisconsin Statute

The Wisconsin statute was enacted as a result of strikes that affected the supply of gas and telephone service. It provided that when an impasse was reached in negotiation between a union and the management of a public utility, which might cause an interruption of essential service, the Wisconsin Employment Relations Board was empowered to name a conciliator to settle the dispute. If no settlement had been reached at the end of a 15-day period allowed for conciliation, the Board was authorized to designate a board of arbitration. Hearings were required and awards were rendered on the basis of the evidence presented. Certain standards were set up to guide the board of arbitration in its deliberations. Awards were binding and effective for one year from the date of filing. The statute forbade the calling of a strike or a lockout. The Employment Relations Board was given power to obtain compliance by filing an action for an injunction in the state courts. An injunction was sought against the Amalgamated Association of Street Electric Railway and Motor Coach Employees of America. The Wisconsin Supreme Court affirmed a judgment granting a perpetual injunction, and the defendants appealed to the U.S. Supreme Court.[8]

The Board also obtained an injunction against the Milwaukee Gas Light Company and the United Gas Coke and Chemical Workers of America, CIO, because of a strike. The Wisconsin Supreme Court affirmed a judgment holding the union and others in contempt.[9] This order was appealed to the U.S. Supreme Court. Both cases were considered at the same time, and in an opinion handed down by Chief Justice Vinson, the court held: "The National Labor Relations Act of 1935 and the Labor Management Relations Act of 1947 passed by Congress pursuant to its powers under the Commerce Clause, are the supreme law of the land under Article IV of the Constitution. Having found that the Wisconsin Public Utility Anti-Strike Law conflicts with that federal legislation, the judgments enforcing the Wisconsin Act cannot stand." [10]

It is of some significance to note that the Florida Public Utility Arbitration Law was held unconstitutional by the Florida Supreme Court on the basis of the Wisconsin decision.[11] The Missouri statute, which is almost identical with the New Jersey statute, was also considered unconstitutional in the opinion of the State Attorney General.[12]

The problem of compulsory arbitration as it applies to public utility disputes has been the subject of much discussion. In January 1954 the President of the United States recommended an amendment to the Labor–Management Relations Act that was designed to eliminate any possible conflict between federal law and state statutes enacted to cope with emergencies endangering the health and safety of citizens. Such a bill was introduced by Senator Smith of New Jersey but was not passed by Congress.

Compulsory Arbitration of Public Utility Disputes

In January 1954 the Governor of New Jersey created a tripartite committee* to study the problem of legislation relating to public utility labor disputes. The committee consisted of representatives of labor, industry, and the public. As part of the study, members analyzed the responses received to a questionnaire sent to representatives of labor and management, government officials, and arbitrators who had had experience with legislation concerning public utility disputes. The findings and recommendations of this committee are set forth below in some detail because they represent

* The committee was headed by David Cole, a former director of the Federal Mediation and Conciliation Service and currently chairman of the National Commission for Industrial Peace.

an excellent analysis of this very difficult problem. The committee made the following recommendations:

a. That the Public Utility Labor Disputes Law and its several amendments be repealed.

b. That Chapter 100, Laws of 1941, under which the New Jersey State Board of Mediation was created, be amended to require both the union and the company in all cases in which a strike in a public utility is scheduled to start at a definite time, to inform the New Jersey State Board of Mediation thereof at least 72 hours before said scheduled time, and if a strike occurs, to report to said Board every 48 hours while the strike is in effect indicating the status, the progress, and the efforts then being made to terminate the strike.

c. That the Legislature adopt a joint resolution expressing:

(1) Its confidence in collective bargaining as the proper and most efficient means of resolving differences between public utility management and labor, under our declared industrial policy.

(2) Its confidence that in reposing reliance on the parties to work out their differences through negotiations at the bargaining table, the parties will conduct themselves in a manner consistent with the public interest in the maintenance of essential services.

(3) Its desire and hope that before a public utility strike is called, the parties, in the public interest, will in good faith utilize the services of the State Board of Mediation, and respond to reasonable suggestions made by that agency or by the Governor of means that may be employed to resolve their differences.

(4) Its desire and hope that before a public utility strike is called the parties will in good faith give full consideration to the possible use of voluntary arbitration or voluntary fact-finding with recommendations as a means for settling their differences and thereby avoiding harm to the public.

(5) Its expectation and desire that if a public utility strike should occur which critically affects the health, safety or welfare of the people of the State or of any community, the Governor will exercise his authority as chief executive immediately to alleviate the condition and, if necessary, promptly convene the Legislature for the purpose of determining what additional steps should then be taken for the protection of the public.

These recommendations were based upon the following findings made by the committee:

a. State laws designed to outlaw strikes in the public utility or other essential industries are now of doubtful constitutionality because of conflict with federal law on the subject, under recent decisions of the United States Supreme Court.

(1) The failure of the Congress to act on the President's recommendation to delegate such authority to the states has added further doubt.

b. Collective bargaining and the promotion of equality in bargaining power constitute the essential part of the industrial policy of both the United States and the State of New Jersey, and it is imperative that the course followed by the State be consistent with this policy.

c. The most successful restraints on the use of the strike seem to have been those which the parties have voluntarily imposed on themselves.

(1) In contrast with compulsive types of legislation which have tended to arouse resentment and antagonism and thereby to have made their voluntary efforts at settlement less productive.

d. Upon review, it appears that laws which aim to prohibit strikes have been detrimental to the process of collective bargaining, not only in this country but in Great Britain, Australia and New Zealand as well.

(1) The existence of such laws has acted as a restraint on the bargaining parties; they are disinclined to make concessions, expecting their differences to be settled ultimately by the techniques provided in the law rather than through their own efforts.

e. Such laws have not diminished the frequency or threats of strikes; states without such laws have fared at least as well as those which have such laws.

(1) In New Jersey the instances in which public utility strikes have occurred or have been threatened have increased since the law was enacted in 1946.

f. Public utility industry and labor representatives have demonstrated over the years a serious concern for the public welfare and it is a mistake to relieve them of this sense of duty.

(1) The industry has submitted to voluntary arbitration to spare the public the hazards of a strike.

(2) It is the policy of major labor organizations not to strike without first offering to submit their differences to voluntary arbitration.

(3) In time of strike, other than in transit, company supervisors man the work stations for long hours to provide as much service as possible.

(4) During strikes, the unions have not seriously tried to prevent supervisors from continuing such operations and have in some instances volunteered to render assistance in case of serious breakdowns due to accident or adverse weather conditions.

(5) Considering the tensions inherent in a strike situation there is a reasonably good record of observance of our existing laws set up to protect public utility facilities and to prevent interference with their functions.

g. Despite fears to the contrary, we have never suffered a paralyzing emergency because of a strike of the kind contemplated by our Public Utility Labor Disputes Law, and there is no reason to expect that we shall in the foreseeable future.

(1) On the contrary, since the validity of the law became questionable in 1951, the law has never been fully employed in accordance with its terms, and the parties seem to have been able to make progress in their negotiations without unduly inconveniencing or harming the public.

(2) It is not the threat or even the commencement of a strike that creates the hazard which is feared but rather its undue prolongation, except at times of unusual stress.

h. If we should nevertheless be faced with a shutdown of public utility operations which causes a genuine threat to the health, safety, or welfare of the people, we would not be helpless or impotent to protect ourselves.

(1) The Governor's inherent powers as chief executive would then be exercised, in the same sense in which he could act to meet other types of disaster or emergency.

(2) The Governor could very quickly convene our Legislature in special session to work out the course to be followed or to ratify and approve the steps which he has already taken.

i. It is unwise and unwarranted to give the public a false sense of security by having a law of doubtful effectiveness on the books.

(1) In most instances when such laws have included severe penalties, it has been found that they could not be enforced, and promptly after efforts were made to enforce them, they have been modified or repealed. This happened, for example, in New Jersey in 1947, and in Great Britain in 1951.

j. It is incompatible with our tradition and with our basic philosophy to undertake to regulate wages and working conditions by government directive rather than by agreement of the parties.

(1) Moreover, the most effective means of minimizing strikes have been those which have been developed by the parties themselves.

k. If circumstances change because of unfavorable attitudes or irresponsible behavior on the part of these industries or their employee groups, or because we enter into a period of war or other stress, we can then review the problem and do what may then seen appropriate and necessary in the light of all the facts and developments.

Contract Disputes in the Private Sector

Compulsory arbitration of contract disputes as a method of resolving impasses in collective bargaining has been both condemned and supported. Whenever a serious strike affects the national economy or inconveniences the public, compulsory arbitration is suggested. Although management and labor continue to voice strong objections to compulsory arbitration, there appears to be a reluctant but definite trend toward accepting it under limited conditions.

Moreover, although only about 1 to 2 percent of contract disputes are voluntarily submitted to arbitration,[13] there is evidence that management and labor are gradually accepting voluntary arbitration as a method of avoiding strikes and settling disputes over the terms and conditions of a collective bargaining agreement.

The March 1973 agreement between labor and management in the steel industry to submit disputes over their next contract to binding arbitration is an important development. According to *The New York Times* (April 22, 1973), the maritime industry is also considering voluntary arbitration to resolve impasses; and David Cole, chairman of the National Commission for Industrial Peace, stated in an interview that the commission would seek to persuade labor and management in the trucking, maritime, construction, food retailing, auto, and defense industries, as well as in public service, to agree to no-strike, no-lockout experiments and to submit their disputes to arbitration. It is interesting to note that the New York Employees' Fair Employment Act[14] (usually called the Taylor act or Taylor law) authorizes voluntary arbitration of impasses and that the Postal Reorganization Act[15] provides for both fact finding and voluntary arbitration procedures for the resolution of contract disputes.

Opposition to Compulsory Arbitration

Those who oppose compulsory arbitration argue that any system which involves compulsion is repugnant to our principles of voluntarism and the right of individuals to handle their private affairs without government domination or intervention. These opponents also warn that it would undermine our system of free collective bargaining, which is the keystone of our national labor policy, because parties compelled to arbitrate by law would not make a bona fide attempt to negotiate. The employer might consider it inadvisable to make a final offer of settlement, since the union would not accept this offer but would use it as a springboard in arbitration to try to obtain more. Toward this end, the union might reason that the arbitrator would not award less than the last offer and might award more. Moreover, compulsory arbitration involves judicial enforcement of the arbitrator's award, and experience has shown that legal sanctions are difficult to apply among large groups of employees.

Opponents have also raised the question of who would appoint the arbitrator. If he is appointed by a politically elected official or a government agency, political considerations might influence the selection. There is also the danger that the person selected may be unqualified and not have the confidence of the parties.

A wide spectrum of knowledgeable people and associations have expressed opposition to compulsory arbitration. G. Allan Dash, Jr.[16] supported the view that the National Academy of Arbitrators should state its "complete and certain disapproval of compulsory arbitration." Disapproval has also been expressed by John T. Dunlop,[17] Thomas Kennedy,[18] and George W. Taylor.[19, 20] Recently, Thomas Kennedy reiterated his opposition to compulsory arbitration. The following quotation from his article is an excellent summary of the arguments against compulsory arbitration:

It has often been proposed that strikes in the private sector be made illegal. The managements of the railroads and the maritime industry openly advocate compulsory arbitration as a desirable alternative to free collective bargaining. There is reason to believe, as indicated earlier, that unions in industries where automation has reduced the strike power will also move to that position. Suppliers and customers hurt by a strike are likely to mutter, "It should be outlawed."

Unfortunately, it is not a matter of eliminating strikes by devices which have no costs. The various compulsory settlement methods also are expensive, and it may be that managements, unions, and the public would find such costs more onerous than the costs of strikes. We should be fully aware of these costs before abandoning the present free collective bargaining system in the private sector.

As stated earlier, the costliness of a strike to management and labor is in itself a strong incentive for them to reach agreement. What happens if that incentive is removed? There is reason to believe that the number of failures to reach agreement would increase greatly. This was our experience during World War II, when the strike was replaced with compulsory settlement by a government agency. It was also our experience in the late 1940's, when a number of states replaced free collective bargaining in public utilities with compulsory arbitration.

There are two reasons that the companies and unions find it more difficult to reach agreement when the possibility of the strike has been removed:

1. The parties are not under so much pressure to work out a contract because, while the compulsory settlement may be less desirable than the contract that could have been negotiated, it does not carry a threat of immediate loss of production and wages.

2. If the compulsory settlement authority . . . has the right to decide on what it thinks is a fair settlement, then the company and the union may well hesitate to make a move toward a settlement, fearing that the other party will hold at its old position and that the . . . arbitrator will split the difference. If, for example, the company is offering a $10-per-hour increase, and the union is asking for $16 per hour, why should the company move to $12 when there can be no strike anyhow and when the authority might then decide between $12 and $16 instead of between $10 and $16? For like reasons, the union hesitates to move down from $16 to $14. Thus, compulsory settlement interferes with the process of voluntary settlement.

In order to avoid the effect just described, the Nixon Administration now proposes that when strikes are threatened in the transportation industries, the President be permitted to order arbitration proceedings in which the arbitrator is required to decide only which of the two final offers of the parties is the more reasonable. It is believed that this method would remove one of the undesirable effects of the usual type of arbitration—that is, the hesitancy of the parties to improve their offers for fear that the arbitrator will split the difference. However, the new proposal has the disadvantage of forcing the arbitrator to choose between two proposals, both of which may seem unfair to him.

While the type of arbitration now proposed by the Administration would probably be less harmful than ordinary compulsory arbitration in terms of hampering efforts to reach a voluntary settlement, it would still have some such effect, for management and labor would not be prodded by fears of strike costs. I believe it is erroneous to expect that the number of disputes which would go to an arbitrator would be the same as the number of strikes which would occur without compulsory settlement. The removal of the strong incentive to settle would result in a great many more failures to reach agreement voluntarily. It would therefore be necessary to establish a sizable government bureaucracy to handle the increased volume of unsettled contract disputes.

The size of the bureaucracy could be lessened by using private arbitrators (with the parties given an opportunity to choose the men they like) instead of a labor board or a labor court. However, the government would have to become involved when the parties were unable to agree on an arbitrator. Moreover, while the Federal Mediation and Conciliation Service has been free from political bias in placing arbitrators' names on its lists for selection by the parties in grievance arbitrations, there can be no guarantee that politics would not play a role in the selection process if the stakes were high enough—as they would be in the compulsory arbitration of new contract terms in the steel, coal, automobile, and other major industries.

If a board or labor court were used to settle disputes, it would have the possible advantage of being able to establish continuing policies. Nevertheless, appointment of at least some of the members would be made by the Administration. (A board could be tripartite, in which case some members would be appointed by labor and some by management.) One of the costs of compulsory settlement, therefore, would be to move management–labor disputes—to some degree at least—from the economic to the political arena.

Under the free collective bargaining system, the government has no problem of enforcement. For instance, while both the company and the employees suffered serious losses during the 14-week GE strike, once it was over both the management and the workers returned to their jobs voluntarily. This illustrates an important advantage of the present system which is often overlooked—that no use of force by the government is required. Moreover, since the agreement is one which the parties themselves have negotiated, the day-to-day operations under it are likely to be more cooperative. The company representatives sell it to management, and the union representatives sell it to the employees. Since the contract is the negotiators' own handiwork, they make a real effort to get it to work—a greater effort, I believe, than they would make if the agreement were the work of some authority appointed by the government.

This country's experience with legislation that has prohibited strikes on the part of public employees indicates that such legislation does not automatically put an end to the strikes. The Condon-Wadlin Act, which prohibited strikes by state and local government employees in New York State from 1947 to 1967, was violated often, but on only a few occasions were its penalties actually enforced. Since 1967 the Taylor Act, which also prohibits strikes by public employees in New York State, has been subject to numerous violations. Likewise, the illegality of strikes by federal employees has not prevented them from leaving the job.

What would happen, under compulsory settlement, if workers in the coal, steel, automobile, trucking, or some other major industry decided that they did not wish to accept the terms prescribed by the arbitrator or labor court and refused to work? How does a democratic government force 100,000 coal miners, 400,000 steel workers, 700,000 automobile workers, or 450,000 truckers to perform their tasks effectively when they elect not to do so? Perhaps it can be done—but I suggest that this is a question which it is well not to have to answer. It is unwise to run the risk of placing government in a position where the government may reveal its impotence unless it is absolutely necessary to do so.[21]

According to Theodore Kheel,* free collective bargaining is at the heart of labor–management relations, and we should focus our attention on how to make it work better rather than to find substitutes. The strike, he believes, is an integral part of the collective bargaining process, and the danger of a strike is one of the compelling forces toward a settlement.

Kheel recognized, however, that a strike may be so damaging that the right of the public to be protected outweighs the right of the public to have collective bargaining by workers and employers. Under these limited circumstances, according to Kheel, the strike has to be banned and the

* Kheel's opinion was expressed in a WNBC-TV interview conducted by Edwin Newman, December 5, 1970.

alternative to collective bargaining (that is, compulsory arbitration) must be utilized.

When Senator Smathers (D.-Fla.) sponsored a bill to set up a labor court with power to settle national emergency disputes, the National Association of Manufacturers opposed the bill because of its compulsory arbitration features.[22]

As the 1970 expiration date of contracts with the New York City policemen, firemen, and sanitation men drew near, Mayor Lindsay urged the City Council to authorize compulsory arbitration by the Office of Collective Bargaining, with the right to appeal a decision within 30 days to the Appellate Division of the State Supreme Court.[23] The New York City Central Labor Council issued a statement which said, "We oppose passage of any type of compulsory arbitration and strongly urge defeat of this proposal." [24]

Toward Compulsory Arbitration

On January 10, 1971, a *New York Times* article, "Arbitration: Fear Slowly Gives Way," began by saying, "Not too long ago, compulsory arbitration was viewed with considerable distrust by both management and labor in both the public and private sector. Now, all that is changing."

Since World War II the U.S. Congress has twice reluctantly enacted compulsory arbitration legislation to prevent or halt nationwide railroad strikes.

In 1963 the New York State Legislature passed the New York Labor Law,[25] which compels arbitration of all disputes involving private voluntary or nonprofitmaking hospitals and residential day-care centers.

In 1970 President Nixon asked Congress[26] to modify the provisions of the Taft–Hartley Act relating to emergency disputes to enable him (1) to extend the cooling-off period for up to 30 days if he believes a settlement is near, (2) to authorize partial operation to minimize danger to the national health and safety, and (3) to invoke the "final offer selection procedure." This procedure, which is a relatively new approach, would give the deadlocked union and management three days to submit one or two "final" offers to the Secretary of Labor, and five more days to bargain over these offers. Failing agreement, a neutral panel of three persons chosen by the disputants—or by the President if the disputants could not agree—would select one of the final offers, in the exact form in which it was presented, and impose it as the final settlement. The panel could not rewrite the terms of any offer or attempt mediation, but could choose only the offer it considered to be most reasonable and fair to both sides.

According to *The New York Times*, when George Meany, president of the American Federation of Labor, heard of this proposal, he opposed it because it amounted to compulsory arbitration. However, administration officials distinguished this plan from compulsory arbitration by pointing out that the terms would have to be fixed by the disputants instead of an outside party, as in compulsory arbitration. It is significant, however, that in the report, "Labor Looks at the 91st Congress," issued by the AFL–CIO in January 1971, George Meany is said to have recommended to the Federal Labor Relations Council, set up under Executive Order 11491 [see Appendix III(2)], "impartial arbitration of unresolved issues after 90 days of bargaining on motion of either party."

C. W. Cook, chairman of the General Foods Corporation, is quoted in *The New York Times* (January 17, 1971) as saying: "I have reluctantly come to the conclusion that we must have machinery which will provide mandatory arbitration and make decisions within established bounds."

Arvid Anderson, Chairman of the Office of Collective Bargaining, stated:

The traditional private employment attitude toward arbitration as a means of contract settlement is that it is bad because it won't work and because it will destroy free collective bargaining. . . . Arbitration, it is charged, won't work because it will not prevent strikes or bring about settlements. . . . It is argued that compulsory arbitration will result in the piling up of all kinds of disputes to be submitted to third parties for solution who do not understand the problems and who have no continuing responsibility for the results.[27]

Events, according to Anderson, require us to reexamine "the arbitration process as a means of contract settlement and as an alternative to the strike."

In the New York strike of sanitation workers in 1968, arbitration was used to settle the dispute, without expressed statutory authority. The Corporation Counsel in an informal opinion upheld the right of the City to enter into a voluntary arbitration agreement in an emergency situation. Compulsory arbitration has been used as a procedure for dispute settlement in many states, including Rhode Island, Pennsylvania, and Michigan, for police and fire disputes.

The 1969 Taylor act amendments in New York authorize voluntary arbitration of contract terms (Sec. 209.3d). This law also requires a legislative body to conduct an order-to-show-cause hearing in the event the recommendations of the fact finder have been rejected. It gives to the legislative body the authority to determine whether it will modify the fact-finder's recommendations, which in effect makes it the final arbiter of the contract dispute.

The Canadian statutes provide for the compulsory arbitration of disputes involving federal employees.

Arvid Anderson, who considers the fact-finding process as a first cousin to compulsory arbitration, found that "fact finding with public recommendations in ten or more jurisdictions where it has been adopted is compulsory or at least a non-option procedure if requested by one of the parties." [27] According to Anderson, the fact that the vast majority of recommendations have been accepted, or have induced settlements short of the issuance of recommendations, indicates that this procedure works.

Legal Status of Compulsory Arbitration Statutes

It has been argued and frequently held in the past by the courts that these statutes result in an unconstitutional delegation of authority by elected officials to arbitrators who in effect enact budgets and establish tax rates when settling public disputes. Recent court decisions do not concur with this reasoning. The constitutionality of the Rhode Island, Pennsylvania, and Wyoming statutes has been upheld. In Wyoming the court found[28] that the statute conferred on arbitrators the power to execute the law and not the power to make the law. It argued that the state had the authority to fix the minimum salaries to be paid firemen and thus had equal authority to establish a "formula through the medium of arbitration for fixing a specific amount above the minimum. . . ."

The Pennsylvania Supreme Court[29] upheld the constitutionality of a compulsory arbitration statute for police and firemen even in the absence of expressed guides for arbitrators. The court relied on an amendment to the State Constitution which expressly authorized compulsory arbitration of police and fire disputes.

The Rhode Island Supreme Court[30] upheld the constitutionality of the compulsory arbitration statute. It rejected the arguments that it was invalid because it failed to provide sufficient standards to guide the arbitrators and that it delegated legislative power to private persons. With reference to the delegation of powers to third persons, the court held that arbitrators were public officers or agents of the legislature when they were carrying out their arbitration duties under the statute. The court concluded that each member of a board of arbitration is a public officer, and that collectively these officers constitute an administrative government agency.

The Court of Appeals of the State of New York in *Mount St. Mary's Hospital v. Catherwood* et al.[31] upheld the constitutionality of compulsory arbitration of disputes involving hospitals. The court said:

At issue is the constitutionality of section 716 of the Labor Law, providing among other things for the compulsory arbitration of disputes in labor contract negotiations with private voluntary or non-profitmaking hospitals. Mount St. Mary's Hospital, such a hospital in dispute with a labor union, brought this action for a declaratory judgment to invalidate the compulsory arbitration features of the statute. It appeals as of right on constitutional grounds from adverse decisions sustaining the statute (CPLR 5601, subd. (b)).

Section 716 (L. 1963, ch. 515, sec. 5, as amd. by L. 1969, ch. 526, SS 1–3) provides that every collective bargaining contract between employees and non-profitmaking hospitals or residential care centers shall be deemed to include provisions for mediation and final binding arbitration, at the request of both parties, or by motion of the State Industrial Commissioner, of disputes arising in the course of negotiating terms of a new collective bargaining contract [subds. 1, 3, par (b)]. Even if there is no existing collective bargaining agreement there is a similar procedure for compulsory arbitration provided to mandate the terms of a collective bargaining contract between the parties (subd. 4). Grievances, as defined, arising out of an existing collective bargaining contract are also subject to arbitration, at the request of either party (subds. 1, 2). It is interesting to observe that in the last instance either party may invoke compulsory arbitration, in contrast to the situation where the making of a contract is in dispute, in which case only the Industrial Commissioner may order arbitration if both parties have not agreed to such arbitration. Application to confirm, modify, correct or vacate an arbitration award shall be made in accordance with CPLR article 75, the article governing arbitration generally [subd. 6, par. (b)].

After protracted negotiations, initiated in 1965, the hospital failed to reach a collective bargaining agreement with the employees' bargaining respresentative (Buffalo and Western New York Hospital and Nursing Home Council, AFL-CIO). Following unsuccessful mediation, the Industrial Commissioner directed that the dispute be submitted to compulsory arbitration pursuant to section 716.

In summary, on this issue, since the non-profitmaking hospital is so affected with a profound public interest directly related to the health and lives in the community, and is so dependent on governmental subsidies, reimbursements, and exemptions, there is no doubt that the extraordinary provision for compulsory arbitration is constitutionally justified. On the same reasoning, however, the limited review of awards indicated, but no less than such review, is both warranted and sufficient.[31]

Criteria for Arbitration Awards

Several of the statutes that provide for compulsory arbitration set forth the criteria to be followed by arbitrators when rendering awards. These guidelines include the factors normally considered by experienced arbitrators. Illustrative of these guidelines are the directives found in the Michigan, Rhode Island, and New York statutes, which are digested below.[32]

MICHIGAN. The Michigan statute instructs the arbitration panel to base its opinions, findings, and decisions on eight factors:

1. The lawful authority of management (the employer).

2. The stipulations of the parties.

3. The interests and welfare of the public and the financial capability of the governmental unit that will have to meet the costs.

4. The wages, hours, and conditions of the arbitrating employees as compared with those of employees in other public and private sectors of similar communities.

5. The average cost-of-living prices for goods and services.

6. All direct and indirect benefits and compensation received by the employees.

7. All changes in items 1–6 while arbitration is proceeding.

8. All other public or private employment services (other than items 1–7) that would be ordinarily considered in determining wages, hours, and

conditions agreed upon by labor and management through the various procedures (collective bargaining, arbitration, etc.).

RHODE ISLAND. The Rhode Island statute has a similar clause, but applies specifically to firefighters. It, too, compares wage rates and hourly conditions with those of similar services performed locally or with those of cities or towns of comparable size. It also calls for comparison of fire-fighting requirements with those of other trades or professions, such as physical, educational, and mental qualifications. It requires the arbitrator(s) to consider the hazards of employment and the job training and skills needed in contrast to other kinds of employment.

NEW YORK. The section in the New York statute that is comparable to the Michigan and Rhode Island statutes particularly refers to disputes involving nonprofit hospitals, but they are relevant to other kinds of employment as well. The standards affecting final arbitration decisions cover the interest and welfare of the public; changes in cost of living; comparison of wages, hours, and conditions of arbitrating employees with those in other sectors, such as private enterprises of like nature, nonprofitmaking hospitals, and residential care centers. This statute includes a unique directive to consider the security and tenure of employment, the effect of technological changes and the training needed for continued qualification, and particularly the economic factors pertaining to the respective parties involved in the arbitration proceedings.

Application of Guidelines

Guidelines serve a useful purpose, but they are of limited value in specific situations. The guidelines (Michigan, item 3 above) require the arbitrator to consider the "financial ability of the unit of government to meet these costs." In determining the ability of a community to pay, what are the determining factors: the opinion of the town officials, the amount of money actually in the budget, the value of ratables, the tax rate? The ability of the community to raise the salaries of their teachers may depend on how much they are paying policemen, the total interest and amortization on the new town hall, the budget for the highway department, etc. The ability to pay for certain services involves the decision to establish priorities of services, which is a value judgment. Whose value judgment is to prevail, that of the elected town officials or of the arbitrator?

The Michigan statute (also true of Rhode Island and New York) requires that the arbitrators base their findings on a comparison of the wages, hours, and conditions of employment of the employees with those of other employees performing similar services. Unfortunately, accurate comparative wage and salary data are not often available. If they are not, must the arbitrator make his own survey (as the author was obligated to do in one instance) or must he rely on the often conflicting data submitted by the parties? The comparative wage and salary data submitted by the parties usually indicates only job titles. Since job descriptions do not usually accompany the titles, how does the arbitrator know that the jobs are in fact comparable or similar? The arbitrator is expected to consider wages and salaries paid "in public employment in comparable communities" and "in private employment in comparable communities." But what is a comparable community? Communities vary according to population, ratables, area covered, proportion of taxes paid by industry or home owners, amount of tax-free land used as parks or for educational purposes, etc. Tax rates cannot be compared because they are related to assessed valuations, the bases for which vary according to location, use, type of structure, etc.

Complicating these problems is the relative amount of the community's resources to be utilized for various public services, which is frequently the result of chance. What is spent for law and order or for education will be dependent on who is in office and how long he has participated in the decision-making process. The pet project of an influential town official for a new town hall may well affect the salaries paid to persons who perform services to the community.

Under these circumstances what is paid for similar work in another otherwise "comparable" town may not be relevant. Moreover, previous across-the-board percentage increases may have aggravated salary inequities.

Arbitrators and Tangible Evidence

It must be obvious from the foregoing discussion that it is impossible for an arbitrator or a judge in a labor court, however well-informed or intelligent he may be, to determine with precision the wages, hours, and working conditions that are fair and proper in the infinite variety of situations he is called upon to adjudicate. Neither are there any standards for determining fringe benefits such as vacation or sick leave.

The arbitrator has no crystal ball that will give him the answers to the questions he is asked to resolve. No matter what he decides, he can be criticized by either party, or both, because the absence of accurate economic data and the absence of reliable standards for evaluating jobs and services make it impossible in the usual case to render an award that is more than an intelligent and impartial evaluation of the mass of data presented to him.

Merely advancing reasons to show that the award might have been different is no basis for concluding that the arbitration process did not function properly and that the award is erroneous. As every lawyer, judge, and arbitrator knows, reasons can be found to support almost any position. Witness the changes in the reasoning used by the courts in cases involving the legality of arbitration.

The assumption is made that the parties to a dispute, being better informed in the manifold aspects of the issue, will always arrive at a solution to their problems which is better than any found by an outside arbitrator. This may be true in some cases, but it is also true that a settlement by the parties may be less than fair to either the employee or the employer. Economic power of the employer or of the union is often the determinant of a particular settlement.

If contract disputes are submitted to arbitration, it is doubtful that the arbitrator will be less rational in coming to a conclusion than will the parties. The chances are that his award will be based more on economic data and less on economic power and emotion than a settlement by the parties. The parties, it seems, may come to a settlement whose basis in economics and logic is hard to discern, but an arbitrator's award is somehow expected to follow a mathematical formula. The widespread acceptance of fact-finders' recommendations in contract disputes is a clear indication that decisions made by outside third parties are not unreasonable and are acceptable to the parties.

The same fears that now exist concerning the arbitration of contract disputes existed 30 years ago about grievance arbitration. Arbitrators are frequently presented grievances that are highly complicated and potentially very costly. The fact that over 95 percent of all contracts provide for final and binding arbitration is a clear indication that it works. Experienced arbitrators should be able to cope as successfully with contract issues as they have with grievances. Under limited conditions, and as a last resort, compulsory arbitration should not be excluded as a method of resolving disputes, particularly where the alternative would put an undue burden on the economy or disrupt essential services to the public.

However, it is essential that compulsory arbitration statutes include a provision, as in grievance arbitration, for the parties to select the arbitrator. This will avoid political problems and insure competency.

Objections to Labor Courts

Many people feel that labor courts should be established to hear and determine contract disputes. It is reasoned that labor courts could handle these problems much as our system of courts for juvenile, matrimonial, and criminal matters handle specialized cases. Recently the general public has come to realize that our entire judicial system is in need of urgent reforms. Only recently has it been revealed that our juvenile courts, which were established to protect children, are not functioning properly and that children's rights and welfare are often neglected. Investigations of prison riots show that our criminal courts, particularly in big cities, are totally inadequate to cope with the huge case loads and the human problems involved in criminal cases.

Unless a person has had experience with our lower courts, his image of a court is the U.S. Supreme Court, whose judges hand down well-reasoned, written opinions. Our lower courts make judgments that are not always supported by written decisions, so that it is impossible to determine the rationale of the conclusion reached.

It is assumed that all judges are qualified to hear and determine the issues that come before them and are not politically or financially influenced. Unfortunately, newspaper reports of resignations and removal of judges do not substantiate this assumption.

From the questions and comments directed to this author during speeches on arbitration given over the past 20 years, the average person's concept of courts can be deduced. In his view a tribunal called a court of law, presided over by a judge in a black robe in a courthouse, will produce better results than a tribunal called an arbitration hearing, conducted by an arbitrator in a business suit in a plant conference room.

Lawyers who are familiar with both procedures often comment that arbitrators are frequently more qualified than judges and that their written opinions are usually of high caliber. Perhaps this is so because they are not rushed by long court calendars and can devote the time necessary to understand the issues. Hearings are not delayed for years, as in some courts.

Improving Collective Bargaining

If parties want to avoid compulsory arbitration, they should seek to improve the bargaining process by setting up joint specialized subcommittees to analyze detailed technical and other problems long before the termination of the contract. It might even be desirable to make these joint subcommittees function on an year-round basis.

A serious attempt should be made by each side to understand thoroughly the position of the other side before active negotiations commence. All too frequently arguments are advanced against a proposal before it is understood. Once a position is taken, there is a tendency to justify it, to save face. This does not make for intelligent negotiations. It would be desirable, after the demands are made, for each side to sit, listen, and ask questions and make no comments while the other side explains its position. Both sides should present only economic data that are accurate, representative, and undistorted. Where conflicting economic data are presented, there should be a joint effort to determine the reason for the conflict.

Recognition by management of the responsibilities of a union representative and the political nature of unions will help explain certain behavior patterns and decisions, and thus eliminate a source of friction. Union recognition of the functions and problems of management will also tend to prevent the taking of positions that inevitably lead to an impasse. All negotiators should be students of the nature of conflict and the techniques of conflict resolution.

Voluntary Arbitration of Contract Disputes

If an impasse is reached in spite of the best efforts of both sides to agree on all terms of a contract, the parties should try voluntary arbitration on a limited basis. It is likely that they will find arbitration awards in interest disputes to be just as useful as in rights disputes. There is no basic reason why contract arbitration should not be as successful as grievance arbitration. The evidence shows that both management and labor are slowly coming to this conclusion.

In contract arbitration, provision might be made for a one-step appeal to a second arbitration panel of three arbitrators, to prevent gross errors. The party objecting to an award may be ordered to show cause why he should not abide by the award. If the second arbitration panel finds no cause for vacating or modifying the award, it should be forthwith entered in a court of law as a judgment and enforced.

By utilizing the system of voluntary arbitration now in existence, the parties can select their own arbitrators and thus insure quality decisions. The alternative to compulsory arbitration is voluntary arbitration of contract disputes.

Arbitration of Contract Terms—A Survey

Jack Steibe, director of the School of Labor and Industrial Relations at Michigan State University, made a very informative survey on voluntary arbitration of contract terms. He concluded:

> We do not expect and indeed would deplore the widespread use of contract arbitration to resolve labor–management disputes. Nor is it desirable that arbitration be invoked to avoid strikes in all cases where negotiations have failed to produce a settlement. Collective bargaining must continue to be the primary method for reaching agreements between unions and companies. However, voluntary contract arbitration has proved itself as a useful and constructive method for settling disputes in the past, and there is reason to believe that circumstances will prevail which will be particularly adaptable to its use in the future.[33]

The survey itself sought to determine how much respondents' attitudes toward grievance arbitration and contract arbitration had changed since 1955. The responses indicated that grievance arbitration was so widespread and the experience with it so satisfactory that attitudes toward contract arbitration could not be explained as a carryover from attitudes toward grievance arbitration.

Responses were received from 237 management representatives, of whom 60 (or 25.3 percent) had had some experience with contract arbitration since 1955. Very few of those who had experience with contract arbitration were not satisfied. Of the 138 union representatives who responded, 61 (or 44.2 percent) had had experience with contract arbitration. More union than management representatives were dissatisfied, but in common with the responses from management, a large majority were satisfied.[34] In terms of the possible growth of contract arbitration, the survey revealed that responses from 41.5 percent of management representatives and from 63.8 percent of union representatives indicated that they would be willing to consider contract arbitration.

However, Steibe pointed out that "the interest in contract arbitration is not nearly as strong as the bare statistics appear to indicate. Two out of every three respondents indicated willingness to consider contract arbitration, [but they would] do so only conditionally, and many specifically rule out certain issues from arbitration." Despite these limitations, Steibe felt that "both management and unions are more open-minded toward the use of contract arbitration than is generally supposed." Some confirmation of this has been provided by Ezra K. Bryan[35] in a recent paper that reports the successful use of advisory arbitration by the United Press and Associated Press with the United Telegraph Workers, AFL–CIO.

Selection of Best Final Offer

In 1971, the City of Eugene, Oregon, passed Ordinance 16298, which confines the Board of Arbitrators to a selection of the most reasonable final offer submitted by either party and expressly prohibits the Board from compromising or altering the final offer that it selects. It also provides [in Section 2(7)(j)] that "the Board shall give written and/or oral explanation of its selection to the parties in dispute."

Pursuant to this ordinance a three-member arbitration panel was established to review the final offers made by the City and the Fire Fighters Association Local 851.[36] The Board selected the last offer made by the City. However, Paul R. Hanlon, chairman of the Board, made the following significant comment:

This case presents an interesting study of the difference in final result which may occur in "last offer" arbitration as contrasted with conventional arbitration. If this case had been submitted under conventional arbitration procedures, it seems fairly clear that a majority of the Board of Arbitrators would have adopted the alternative proposal of the Association after eliminating therefrom the clauses dealing with Civil Service Commission rules and manning requirements. Under the strict limitations imposed by the last offer concept, however, such amendments were prohibited, and the entire Association proposal with its many meritorious and acceptable provisions foundered on the single issue of contract manning requirements which a majority of the Board found so unacceptable and objectionable as a matter of principle that a contract including such a provision could not be accepted.[36]

Arbitration of Public Sector Disputes in Canada

The Public Service Staff Relations Act[37] adopted by the Canadian Parliament in 1967 established a system of collective bargaining for federal public "servants."

Grievance Arbitration

Under this Act, grievance disputes that are not settled by discussion between the parties must be referred to final and binding determination by an arbitrator or a board of arbitration selected by the parties. An arbitrator or an arbitration board may be selected for one grievance or to adjudicate all grievances arising under the contract over a period of time.

A rather unique feature of the Act gives to all public employees, even though they are not covered by a collective bargaining agreement, the right to adjudicate any grievance relating to a disciplinary action by the employer which results in discharge, suspension, or imposition of a financial penalty. The decision of the adjudicator (arbitrator) is final and binding.

According to J. Finkelman, Q.C., chairman of the Public Service Staff Relations Board, grievances are heard by a "permanent corps of adjudicators (grievance arbitrators) . . . established under the supervision of a chief adjudicator, all adjudicators having tenure for a fixed term of years. The independence of the adjudicators is assured through a two-tier system of appointment. The appointment of adjudicators rests with the Government, but appointments can only be made on the recommendation of the Public Service Staff Relations Board." [38] This is a tripartite board with independent status.

Contract Disputes

The Canadian statute approaches in a rather unique fashion the difficult problem of the right of public employees to strike. It provides that the employee organization, certified by the Public Service Staff Relations Board, has the right to choose one of two procedures for the resolution of contract disputes, either arbitration or conciliation. If it picks arbitration, it gives up the right to strike. If it selects the conciliation board process, it may go on strike if no agreement is reached.

However, the choice must be made before the bargaining agent gives notice to the employer of its desire to bargain. The option is a prerogative of the bargaining agent and cannot be vetoed by the employer, although the employer can influence indirectly the decision of the bargaining agent.

If arbitration is selected, the matter is heard by the Public Service Arbitration Tribunal. This is a permanent tripartite tribunal. The chairman of the Tribunal has maximum tenure of five years. In the hearing of a particular case, one member represents the interests of the employer, one represents the interests of the employee, and the chairman selects two impartial members.

The Public Service Arbitration Tribunal is a quasi-judicial body that renders a final and binding award after a hearing. The 1967 Act requires the Tribunal to consider certain factors in rendering an award. It must realize the needs of the public service for qualified employees and examine the conditions of employment in similar occupations outside the public service, including geographic, industrial, or other relevant variations. It must also consider maintenance of appropriate relationships between different grade levels within an occupation and between other occupations in the public service. Furthermore, it must consider the terms and conditions of employment that are fair and reasonable in relation to the qualifications required, the work performed, the responsibility assumed, and the nature of the services. All other factors relevant to the matter in dispute must also be applied. With reference to the utilization of arbitration to resolve contract disputes, Mr. Finkelman stated:

It is a commonly accepted article of faith among trade unionists that collective bargaining and arbitration of negotiation disputes are incompatible; that, once the parties know beforehand that issues in dispute can be resolved by a binding decision made by a third party, the incentive to bargain and make every reasonable effort to make a collective agreement is destroyed. My assessment of the situation is that these fears are not supported by experience under the Public Service Staff Relations Act.[38]

REFERENCES

1. *War Labor Reports*, Vol. 1. Washington, D.C.: The Bureau of National Affairs, pp. XVII, XVIII.
2. Report to Governor Meyner by the Governor's Committee on Legislation Relating to Public Utility Disputes, Table 1, p. 32.
3. Public Laws, New Jersey, 1946, Chapter 38.
4. Public Laws, New Jersey, 1947, Chapter 47.
5. Van Ripper v. Traffic-Telephone Workers' Federation, 2 N.J. 335 (1949).
6. Public Laws, New Jersey, 1949, Chapter 308.
7. Public Laws, New Jersey, 1950, Chapter 14.
8. In the Matter of Amalgamated Association v. Wisconsin Employment Relations Board, 340 U.S. 383 (1951); 71 S. Ct. 359.
9. Wisconsin Employment Relations Board v. Amalgamated Ass'n., 257 Wis. 43, 42 N.W. 2d. 471.
10. In the Matter of the Amalgamated Association v. Wisconsin Employment Relations Board, *op. cit.*
11. Henderson v. State, 65 So. 2d. 22 (1953).
12. Letter to Members of the House, dated March 19, 1951.
13. FMCS report, 1972, Fig. 15, p. 42.
14. Public Employees' Fair Employment Act, Civil Service Law, Sec. 209(2). Chapter 392 of the Laws of 1967, as amended 1969.

15. Postal Service–Employee Agreements, 39 USCA Ch. 12, P.L. 91–375, Aug. 12, 1970.
16. G. Allan Dash, Jr., Presidential address (Thirteenth Annual Meeting of the National Academy of Arbitrators). Washington, D.C.: The Bureau of National Affairs, 1960.
17. John T. Dunlop, "The Settlement of Emergency Disputes" (Proceedings of the IRRA), December 1952.
18. Thomas Kennedy. "The Handling of Emergency Disputes" (Proceedings of the IRRA), December 1949.
19. George W. Taylor, "Is Compulsory Arbitration Inevitable?" (Proceedings of the IRRA), December 1949.
20. ———, *Government Regulation of Industrial Relations.* Englewood Cliffs, N.J.: Prentice-Hall, 1948.
21. Thomas Kennedy, "Freedom to Strike Is in the Public Interest." *Harv. Bus. Rev.* (July–August 1970), p. 45.
22. 66 LRR 317.
23. *The New York Times*, Dec. 17, 1970.
24. *The New York Times*, Dec. 19, 1970.
25. New York Labor Law, Sec. 716 (L 1963, ch. 515, sec. 5, as amended by L 1969, ch. 526, secs. 1–3).
26. *The New York Times*, February 28, 1970.
27. Arvid Anderson, "Compulsory Arbitration Under State Statutes" (Proceedings of New York University Twenty-third Annual Conference on Labor), June 1969.
28. State of Wyoming ex rel Fire Fighters Local v. City of Laramie, 437 P 2d. 295, 304; 68 LRRM 2038, 2044 (1968).
29. Harvey v. Russo, 71 LRRM 2817.
30. City of Warwick v. Warwick Regular Firemen's Association, 71 LRRM 3192, GERR, Aug. 11, 1969, 309, F.1.
31. Mount St. Mary's Hospital of Niagara Falls v. Martin P. Catherwood, as Industrial Commissioner, et al., 26 N.Y. 2d. 493.
32. Michigan Arbitration Statute, GERR, Aug. 25, 1969, 311, F.1.
33. Jack Steibe, "Voluntary Arbitration of Contract Terms" (Proceedings of the Twenty-third Annual Meeting of the National Academy of Arbitrators). Washington, D.C.: The Bureau of National Affairs, 1970, chap. 3.
34. *Ibid.*, Table II, pp. 90–91.
35. Ezra K. Bryan, "Advisory Arbitration of New Contracts—A Case Study" (Proceedings of the Twenty-third Annual Meeting of the National Academy of Arbitrators). Washington, D.C.: The Bureau of National Affairs, 1970.
36. AAA case 75-39-004-72 (1972), GERR (5-8-72).
37. Canadian Public Service Staff Relations Act (1967).
38. J. Finkelman, address to International Conference on Trends in Industrial and Labor Relations, Tel Aviv, Israel, January 1972.

12

PUBLIC SECTOR: COLLECTIVE BARGAINING

While unions in the private sector were successful in improving the wages, hours, and working conditions of its members, public employees were not quite so fortunate.

Historical Background

Wages, hours, and working conditions for public employees have been traditionally set by the unilateral action of the Congress, state legislatures, municipalities, and other governing bodies. When improvements were sought through the political process, employee organizations served as lobbies to influence new legislation that would raise wages and working conditions in the public sector to the level of the private sector. This uphill battle had little success, mostly because legislators did not find it politically expedient to raise taxes.

The recent strike of postal workers, the first in the history of the U.S. Post Office Department, focused attention on the great disparity between wages paid to postal workers and wages paid for comparable work in business and industry, the result of Congress's long delays in passing a legislative remedy. Similar inequity existed in public education. School boards, in an attempt to avoid raising real estate taxes (which comprise the main source of school funds), delayed increasing teachers' salaries. As a result, these salaries were out of line with increases in the cost of living and with salaries paid for comparable work in the private sector. School teachers' grievances were usually subject to the unilateral decisions of principals, superintendents of schools, and school boards, with only limited appeal to state education officials.

The relationship existing between government and its employees was governed by the concept of "sovereign immunity." According to this doctrine, the government or any of its political subdivisions could not divest itself of any authority vested in it by the people. Thus, a government could

172

not submit to a third party, such as an arbitrator, who had the power to make a decision binding on the government.

NEW DIRECTIONS OF PUBLIC SERVICE GRIEVANCES. Although civil service employees have had recourse to appeal procedures for many years, they were increasingly convinced that the decisions rendered were not always impartial, since all appeals were decided by representatives of the government. The widespread adoption in collective bargaining agreements of grievance procedures terminating in arbitration is an indication that neither postal workers, teachers, nor other public employees were satisfied with traditional methods of resolving grievances.

Government, too, found that the appeals system was not working properly, and moved to refine not only the procedures but also the methods of choosing qualified hearing officers. It is significant that Executive Order 11491 (see Appendix III,2), which became effective in January 1970, provides that persons handling appeals through Civil Service procedures must be specially qualified to perform this function.

Development of Grievance Arbitration

A series of landmark cases laid the groundwork for the present system of arbitrating public employees' grievances. Although in earlier cases the courts resorted to "sovereign immunity" as the basis for decisions, this was gradually tempered in later cases. Review of a few cases will show how grievance procedures evolved into a viable system. This is not a chronological development but rather the documentation of precedents established in various places at various times.

In *Mann v. Richardson* (1873)[1] the court held that the highway commissioners, in attempting to resolve a dispute regarding the layout of a road, could not submit the question of damages to binding arbitration. The court found that the commissioners had a personal responsibility placed upon them as public officials, one that could not be relegated to another.

According to Paul Staudohar, "up to the late 1940s, state courts had taken a firm position against binding arbitration in general for public employees, regarding it as an unlawful delegation of authority by the government."[2] This doctrine was not followed by the Supreme Court of Errors in Connecticut in the landmark case of *Norwalk Teachers' Association v. Board of Education* (1951).[3] The court was asked for a declaratory judgment on the following question (among others) regarding relations between an organization of teachers and the Board of Education: Is arbitration a permissible method under Connecticut law to settle or adjust disputes between the plaintiff and defendant?

The court considered various arguments, including the view that arbitration in any form constituted an unlawful delegation of authority. It held:

The power of a town to enter into an agreement of arbitration was originally denied on the ground that it was an unlawful delegation of authority. . . . If it is borne in mind that arbitration is the result of mutual agreement, there is no reason to deny the power of the defendant (the City) to enter voluntarily into a contract to arbitrate a specific dispute. . . . Arbitration as a method of settling disputes is growing in importance and, in a proper case, "deserves the enthusiastic support of the courts. . . ." The best answer we can give is "yes, arbitration may be a permissible method as to certain specific, arbitrable issues." [3]

A Michigan circuit court, deciding in 1967 that the ability to arbitrate disputes did not infringe upon the public employer's policy-making rights, said: "Certainly giving the power to enter into a contract would include the power to settle disputes arising under the terms of such contract. Negotiations as to 'wage, hours and other terms and conditions of employment' can well include the power to arbitrate disputes on these points after the contract is signed." [4]

The Rinelander case (1967),[5] emerging from the Wisconsin courts in 1967, is probably the most definitive court decision dealing with binding arbitration in the public sector. The court found (1) grievance arbitration clauses are binding on the city; (2) such a clause is specifically enforceable in the courts; (3) an employee's discharge is an arbitrable issue under the agreement. "Such a decision, if it is accepted as a national precedent, will make the trend towards binding grievance arbitration in the public sector almost irreversible." [6]

In Cleveland, Ohio, in 1946, the Transit Board set up a grievance procedure and provided for an impartial umpire, who was selected by the Board and the union and paid by both, to "advise" the Board. Also in 1946, a committee appointed by the Mayor of the City of New York recommended advisory arbitration of transit-employee grievances. The committee observed that in its judgment, collective bargaining could function effectively without the right to strike and without binding arbitration if the demand of a large group of employees were coupled with "the persuasion of advisory review, with its impact on public opinion."

In 1950 a fact-finding board in the City of New York recommended advisory arbitration of grievances. Following this recommendation, advisory arbitration was provided for in the agreement between the City Transit Authority and several unions in the early 1960s. The agreement stated that an impartial advisor would give an advisory opinion and make recommendations before final determination of the grievance by members of the Transit Authority.

In early 1954, an agreement between the City of Philadelphia and the American Federation of State, County, and Municipal Employees, District Council No. 33, AFL, provided for the establishment of an advisory board if attempts at settlement between the City's Personnel Director and the union were to fail.

Final and binding arbitration was found in several contracts in the 1940s and 1950s. In 1943 an analysis of 32 agreements negotiated with various cities by the AFL and CIO unions representing state, county, and municipal employees showed that 18 agreements provided for final settlement of grievance by impartial arbitration, either initially or after exhausting the grievance steps. Most of the 18 agreements called for a board of three arbitrators, one designated by the union, one chosen by the highest law-making authority of the city, and a third to be named by these two arbitrators as impartial chairman. Some of the agreements limited the jurisdiction of the board of arbitrators by prohibiting it from infringing on civil service or other state or local laws.[7]

The general public of the City of Detroit voted in 1951 to approve an amendment to the municipal charter which provides for final and binding arbitration of virtually all manner of disputes between fire department employees and the Board of Fire Commissioners, upon request in the form of a petition made by not less than half of the employees in the department.

The Charter of the City of Detroit also provides for arbitration of disputes arising in another area of its employment relationships, that is, the transit system. After providing for municipal ownership and operation of the transit system, and empowering the Board of Street Railway Commissioners to bargain collectively with the employees' representatives, the charter amendment confers authority upon the Board to arbitrate, in the following language: "In case of dispute over wages or conditions of employment, said Board is hereby authorized and directed to arbitrate any question or questions, provided each party shall agree in advance to pay half the expense of such arbitration." [8]

At the federal level, perhaps the most outstanding example of development of binding grievance arbitration is found in the collective bargaining pattern developed by the Tennessee Valley Authority and the unions representing its craftsmen and laborers. This subject is treated at length by Harry Case.[9] The major emphasis of the TVA system is on the day-to-day handling of employee complaints. Arbitration is regarded as a last resort, to be used only after failure of efforts to dispose of grievances at the source and up the line. Final and binding arbitration procedure is provided in agreements covering various classes of employees including (since 1950) white-collar workers.

Collective Bargaining in the Public Sector

During the 1960s the principle of collective bargaining as a method of determining wages, hours, and working conditions was extended to the public sector. The right of federal, state, county, and municipal employees to organize and bargain collectively has now been recognized.

The Right to Strike

In the private sector the right of employees to strike is considered an integral part of the bargaining process. This view was clearly stated in a position paper prepared by the National Association of Manufacturers (NAM) and the U.S. Chamber of Commerce under the leadership of Douglas Soutar, vice-chairman of the Industrial Relations Committee of the NAM. Their position was that collective bargaining as practiced in this country, while it has its imperfections, is infinitely superior to any alternative system, and measures should be taken to preserve and promote free collective bargaining which includes the right to strike.[10]

In the public sector, however, employees are denied the right to strike. Executive Order 11491 [see Appendix III (2)], signed by President Nixon on October 29, 1969, grants federal employees the right to organize, but prohibits strikes. Almost all state statutes also deny public employees the right to strike.

However, those people whose opinions are highly respected in the field of labor–management relations feel that public employees, with the exception of police and fire fighters, should be permitted to strike. Theodore Kheel, a well-known and experienced mediator and arbitrator with considerable experience in the public sector, particularly in New York City, is of the opinion that unless public employees have the right to strike, collective bargaining in the public sector will not function properly.

On the other hand, Arvid Anderson, Chairman of the Office of Collective Bargaining in the City of New York, believes that the right to strike does little to enhance the bargaining power of the bulk of white-collar public employees. He recognizes, however, that it is a powerful weapon in the hands of public employees such as police and fire fighters, who are the protectors of public health and safety.

Impasse Resolution

If public employees are denied the right to strike, procedures must be provided to resolve interest disputes. Mediation is recognized as an effective first step in the resolution of impasses. An effective mediator can help clarify the issues and persuade the parties to submit economic data in support of their respective positions rather than to rely on emotional arguments. A mediator can recognize and try to eliminate personal animosities that are impeding a settlement of the issues. Because of his experience, he can suggest alternative methods of resolving issues and can devise face-saving measures.

Fact finding by a single impartial person or a panel of three impartial persons is also an effective procedure for resolving disputes. It is usually utilized when mediation is not successful. A fact finder conducts a hearing to determine the specific issues, and to gather data and arguments in support of the positions advanced by the parties. His fact-finding report sets forth each issue, the data and arguments submitted by the parties, and his recommended solution. The report presents the reasons why the recommended solution is considered to be equitable and fair. It is based on economic data, logic, and reason, and eliminates those personal elements that frequently make settlements impossible.

In a recent speech, Arvid Anderson said:

It is my view that arbitration, both binding and advisory, and fact finding and impasse panel recommendations, which are first cousins to binding arbitration, can work as effective substitutes and as a bargaining balancer. The extensive experience with fact finding in Michigan, Wisconsin, Connecticut, Massachusetts, New Jersey, New York State, New York City and elsewhere, and the growing volume of arbitration of contract terms for Minnesota and New York hospital workers, policemen and firemen in Michigan, Pennsylvania, Rhode Island, Wyoming, and Maine, have demonstrated that fact finding and arbitration are here to stay as a means of resolving impasses. As important as the new experiments with fact finding and arbitration is the new attitude of the leaders of organized labor to the use of arbitration to resolve disputes. While continuing to condemn compulsory arbitration, George Meany, in supporting the proposed postal reform law, has endorsed the proposal for binding arbitration of contract terms, [stating] that any procedure which preserves workers' rights without strike is fine. Jerry Wurf, President of AFSCME, has endorsed voluntary arbitration of contract terms. The views of these labor leaders appear to be that if labor has an equal voice in selecting arbitrators and a voice in the arbitration procedure, labor will accept the process.[11]

John Lindsay, Mayor of the City of New York, recommended that interest disputes involving public employees should be submitted to fact-finding panels and that unless their recommendations were not modified within 30 days, they should become final and binding on both parties.[12] More than two years later, his recommendation was enacted into law.

Compulsory Arbitration: New York City

On Jan. 12, 1972, Mayor John Lindsay signed a new local law that provides for compulsory arbitration to settle deadlocked labor disputes, in the hope that strikes of public employees could be avoided. Actually, this law amends the New York City Charter as it applies to labor relations between "public" employers, municipal employees, and employee organizations. The new law outlines in detail a procedure for resolution of impasses between city employers and employee organizations, whereby binding arbitration will be invoked if labor negotiations should reach an impasse.

The law provides:

There shall be in the Office of Collective Bargaining a Board of Collective Bargaining, which shall consist of seven members. Two members of the Board shall be City members, two members of the Board shall be labor members, and three members of the Board . . . shall be impartial members. The Mayor shall have the power to appoint the City members of the board to serve at his pleasure, and the labor members of the Board from designations by the Municipal Labor Committee. Each labor and City member shall have an alternate, who shall be appointed and removed in the same manner as the member for whom he is the alternate. The chairman and the other impartial members shall be elected by the unanimous vote of the City and labor members, and shall serve for three year terms.[13]

The law further provides that the Board of Collective Bargaining shall appoint an impasse panel upon the recommendation of the Director of the Office of Collective Bargaining* if he should determine that "negotiations between a public employer and a certified or designated employee organization have been exhausted, and that the conditions are appropriate for the creation of an impasse panel." In addition to such mandatory appointment of a panel, "the Director may also appoint an impasse panel upon request of both parties."

The panel consists of an odd number of persons selected from the Board's register of impasse panel members; preferably, the number of panel members are determined by mutual agreement of the parties and the individuals are selected from a list of seven persons submitted by the director. If the parties cannot agree, the director decides the number and designates the members of the panel.

Pertinent excerpts from the law follow:

(3)(a) An impasse panel shall have the power to mediate, hold hearings, compel the attendance of witnesses and the production of documents, review data, and take whatever action it considers necessary to resolve the impasse. If an impasse panel is unable to resolve an impasse within a reasonable period of time, as determined by the Director, it shall, within such period of time as the Director prescribes, render a written report containing findings of fact, conclusions, and recommendations for terms of settlement.

(b) An impasse panel . . . shall consider wherever relevant the following standards in making its recommendations for terms of settlement:

(1) comparison of the wages, hours, fringe benefits, conditions and characteristics of employment of the public employees involved in the impasse proceeding with the wages, hours, fringe benefits, conditions and characteristics of employment of other employees performing similar work and other employees generally in public or private employment in New York City or comparable communities;

(2) the overall compensation paid to the employees involved in the impasse proceeding, including direct wage compensation, overtime and premium pay, vacations, holidays and other excused time, insurance, pensions, medical and hospitalization benefits, food and apparel furnished, and all other benefits received;

(3) changes in the average consumer prices for goods and services, commonly known as the cost of living;

* The first director of the Office of Collective Bargaining is Arvid Anderson.

(4) the interest and welfare of the public;

(5) such other factors as are normally and customarily considered in the determination of wages, hours, fringe benefits, and other working conditions in collective bargaining or in impasse panel proceedings.

However, action of the impasse panel on salary matters is somewhat limited by the following: "Unless the Mayor agrees otherwise, an impasse panel shall make no report concerning the basic salary and increment structure and pay plan rules of the City's career and salary plan."

The new law further states in paragraph 3 of Section 1173-7.0:

(e) Acceptance or rejection. Within ten days after submission of the panel's report and recommendations, or such additional time not exceeding thirty days as the Director may permit, each party shall notify the other party and the Director, in writing, of its acceptance or rejection of the panel's recommendations. Failure to so notify shall be deemed acceptance of the recommedations.

Review of the impasse panel's recommendations is provided in case either party rejects such recommendations, as follows:

(4)(a) A party who rejects in whole or in part the recommendations of an impasse panel . . . may appeal to the Board of Collective Bargaining for review of the recommendations of the impasse panel by filing a notice of appeal with said Board within ten days of such rejection. The notice of appeal shall also be served upon the other party within said time. Upon failure to appeal within the time provided herein, the recommendations shall be final and binding upon the party failing to so appeal, except that the Board, upon its own initiative, may review recommendations which have been rejected.

(b) The notice of appeal shall specify the grounds upon which the appeal is taken, the alleged errors of the panel, and the modifications requested. The Board shall afford the parties a reasonable opportunity to argue orally before it or to submit briefs, or may permit both argument and briefs. Review of the recommendations shall be based upon the record and evidence made and produced before the impasse panel and the standards set forth in subparagraph (b) of paragraph three of subdivision C of section 1173-7.0. . . .

(c) Upon such review, the Board may affirm or modify the panel recommendations in whole or in part. A modification of the recommendations shall be by the vote of a majority of the Board. . . .

(d) The recommendations of the impasse panel shall be deemed to have been adopted by the Board if the Board fails to issue a final determination within thirty days of the filing of the notice of appeal, or within forty days of a notification of rejection to the director of the Board where the Board, upon its own initiative, reviews the panel's recommendations. . . .

(f) A final determination of the Board pursuant either to subparagraph (c) or (d) of this paragraph four shall be binding upon the parties. Such a final determination shall constitute an award within the meaning of article seventy-five of the civil practice law and rules.

The parties are free to include binding arbitration in their labor agreements if they wish to, as provided in the following paragraph:

(4)(f) Anything in this chapter notwithstanding, public employers and certified or designated employee organizations hereby are empowered to enter into written agreements setting forth procedures to be invoked in the event of an impasse in collective bargaining negotiations, and such agreements may include the undertaking by each party to submit unresolved issues to impartial arbitration. . . .

Victor Gotbaum, leader of District 37 of the State, County, and Municipal Employees, the largest City-employee union, had the following reaction to the law (as reported in *The New York Times*, January 13, 1972): "State law gave us no alternative but to come up with a final and binding procedure." The alternative under the state law provided that deadlocked disputes would have to be settled by the City Council. "That would completely politicalize the bargaining process," said Gotbaum.

Although mediation and fact finding are the most common methods of resolving impasses in the public sector (see Appendix III,3), other methods have been used or recommended. For example, the New York State Taylor law[14] provides for the submission of an impasse to the State Legislature. Section 209 (Resolution of disputes in the course of collective negotiations, Subdivision 3(e)) provides that:

In the event that either the public employer or the employee organization does not accept in whole or part the recommendations of the fact finding board: (i) the chief executive officer of the government involved shall, within ten days after receipt of the findings of fact and recommendations of the fact finding board, submit to the legislative body of the government involved a copy of the findings of fact and recommendation of the fact finding board, together with his recommendations for settling the dispute; (ii) the employee organization may submit to such legislative body its recommendations for settling the dispute; (iii) the legislative body or a duly authorized committee thereof shall forthwith conduct a hearing at which the parties shall be required to explain their positions with respect to the report of the fact finding board; and (iv) thereafter, the legislative body shall take such action as it deems to be in the public interest, including the interest of the public employees involved.[14]

Many labor lawyers feel that the above method of resolving impasses has numerous shortcomings.

The establishment of special labor courts to resolve labor disputes has been suggested. The arguments advanced in favor of this idea are that the judges in such a court would have the expertise to resolve impasses and that they would also have the legal power to enforce their decisions. It is doubtful that persons appointed or elected through our political process would necessarily have the required expertise in labor relations. Moreover, the social philosophy of the judge may reflect that of the appointing agency and his tenure in office would perpetuate this philosophy for many years.

Under this system it would be extremely difficult to remove an unqualified judge. Moreover, as we have seen, when thousands of employees have strong feelings about an issue, the power of the court to force compliance with its orders is limited.

Many practitioners feel our system of arbitration, which is in effect a private court system, could be more effectively used to resolve impasses. The judges in this system are the arbitrators, most of whom have had about 25 years experience, and whose active status during these 25 years is clear proof of their expertise and acceptability by the parties. Since the parties select the arbitrator, his status as an active arbitrator will soon be changed if his general acceptability ceases. This is a guarantee of high professional standards.

If the parties to an impasse voluntarily submit to arbitration, the award is enforceable through the courts. For this reason it is argued that there is no need for labor courts.

Voluntary arbitration, which overcomes some of the objections to compulsory arbitration, is recommended by Arvid Anderson, who believes that "voluntarily selected arbitrators may be more amenable to seeking means of accommodations and of being concerned with the acceptability of their awards than arbitrators appointed unilaterally under a compulsory statute." [15]

Section 209 (2) of the Taylor act provides that public employers may enter into written agreements that set forth precedures to be invoked in a contract dispute and that "such agreements may include the undertaking by each party to submit unresolved issues to impartial arbitration."

Grievance Arbitration

Grievance procedures terminating in final and binding arbitration, universally accepted in the private sector, are now widely used in the public sector.

Within recent years the courts have changed their position and now recognize the validity of agreements entered into between a government agency and a union for final and binding arbitration of grievances. This new concept is recognized in the amended Federal Executive Order 11491 (Appendix III,2), which provides for arbitration of grievances.

REFERENCES

1. Mann v. Richardson, cited by Paul D. Staudohar in "Voluntary Binding Arbitration in Public Employment," *The Arbitration Journal,* Vol. 25, No. 1 (1970), p. 32.
2. Paul D. Staudohar, "Voluntary Binding Arbitration in Public Employment," *The Arbitration Journal,* Vol. 25, No. 1 (1970), p. 32.
3. Norwalk Teachers' Association v. Board of Education, 83 A 2d. 482.

4. International Union of AFSCME Local 953 and AFSCME Council 55 v. School District of Benton Harbor, GERR 216 (E-1) (10-30-67).
5. International Union of AFSCME Local 1226 Rhinelander City Employees v. City of Rhinelander, Wisconson St. Ct. 245 (6-6-67).
6. Steven S. Glickman, "Binding Grievance Arbitration in the Public Sector." (Unpublished manuscript.)
7. "Union Agreements with Municipalities," *Monthly Labor Rev.* (June 1943), p. 1165.
8. Charter of the City of Detroit, Sec. XIX, Title IV, Chapter VIII.
9. Harry L. Case, *Personnel Policy in a Public Agency: The TVA Experience.* New York: Harper & Row, 1955.
10. Douglas Soutar et al., *Emergency Strikes, Union Power and the Public Interest.* Washington, D.C.: Industrial Relations Committee, National Association of Manufacturers, 1969.
11. Arvid Anderson, "The Changing of the Establishment." Address delivered before the United States Conference of Mayors, Denver, Col., June 14, 1970.
12. *The New York Times*, August 2, 1969; GERR 309, 113 (8-11-69).
13. City of New York Administrative Code, Chap. 54, LL 1967, No. 53. Amended January 12, 1972.
14. New York Taylor act, Chapter 392 of the Laws of 1967 as amended 1969.
15. Arvid Anderson, "Compulsory Arbitration Under State Statutes" (Proceeding of New York University Twenty-second Annual Conference on Labor). New York: 1969.

13

PUBLIC SECTOR:
STATE LEGISLATION

During the 1960s the laws relating to the right of public employees to organize and bargain collectively were changed. A large number of states now grant public employees the right to organize and bargain collectively, and require public employers to recognize and bargain with their representatives. Only eight states have no legislation in this area (Arizona, Arkansas, Colorado, Indiana, Iowa, Mississippi, Tennessee, Utah, and West Virginia). Two states (Alabama and Texas) have laws specifically prohibiting collective bargaining.*

Although public employees are in general still prohibited from striking, recent legislation indicates a trend toward granting them the right to strike under limited conditions.

The past decade has also seen a reversal in policy and law regarding agreements by public agencies to arbitrate both rights and interest disputes. Previously it was illegal for a public employer to submit an issue to final and binding arbitration on the grounds that it was an improper delegation of authority to an outside person. Today, compulsory arbitration of interest disputes, particularly involving police and fire fighters, and final and binding arbitration of grievances are commonplace. Arbitration has been added to mediation and fact finding as a procedure for resolving disputes.

An analysis of state statutes reveals considerable variation in philosophy, approach, and procedures. In order to give an overall view, representative state laws dealing with the right of public employees to organize and bargain collectively have been analyzed under the following headings:

1. Coverage.
2. Policy—purpose.
3. Right to organize and bargain collectively.
4. Right to strike.
5. Impasse procedures.

* New laws and modifications of old laws are being enacted almost monthly. Between 1973, when this chapter was written, and the date of this book's publication, some changes in the laws have undoubtedly been made.

6. Guidelines for arbitration.
7. Grievance arbitration.

Coverage

Public employees usually covered by these statutes include state, county, and municipal employees; police, fire fighters, and teachers. Employees of public utilities are sometimes covered, as in the Nebraska and Alaska statutes.

Rhode Island has enacted five separate statutes covering: (1) police, (2) fire fighters, (3) teachers, (4) municipal employees, and (5) state employees.

Massachusetts, on the other hand, has one statute, but it makes a distinction between state and municipal employees.

Michigan has two statutes. One covers police and fire fighters and the other covers all other public employees.

The State of Nebraska has also enacted two statutes: one covers teachers only and the other provides for all other public employees and employees of public utilities.

The State of Maine initially passed a statute to cover fire fighters alone, but later expanded coverage to include all public employees.

In Wisconsin the State Employment Labor Relations Act covers all state employees. A separate law covers municipal employees.

California has three statutes: (1) state and local government employees, (2) teachers, and (3) firemen.

The Alaska statute covers employees of organized boroughs and political subdivisions of the state. However, the local legislative body may reject such coverage. The act divides employees into three classes: (1) police and fire protection, jail, prison and other correctional institution employees, and hospital employees; (2) public utilities, snow removal, sanitation, and public school and other educational institutions employees; and (3) all other employees.

The State of New York has one comprehensive statute covering all public employees.

Several municipalities (such as Los Angeles, California; New York, N.Y.; and Dayton, Ohio) have also passed special legislation covering their own municipal employees.

Policy—Purpose

TEXAS.[1] A Texas statute enacted in 1947 declares public employee bargaining and strikes to be against public policy. The statute provides:

Sec. 1—It is declared to be against public policy of the State of Texas for any official of the State, or County, City, Municipality or other political subdivision of the State, to enter into a collective bargaining contract with a labor organization respecting wages, hours, or conditions of employment of public employees, and any such contracts entered into after the effective date of this Act shall be null and void.

Sec. 2—It is declared to be against the public policy of the State of Texas for any such official or group of officials to recognize a labor organization as the bargaining agent for any group of employees.

Sec. 3—It is declared to be against the public policy of the State of Texas for public employees to engage in strikes. . . .

However, Texas later passed the Fire and Police Employees Relations Act, which became effective on August 27, 1973. This act permits only policemen and fire fighters to organize and bargain collectively with their employers. It should be noted that the law applies only in local jurisdictions where voters petition their municipal governments for a referendum and adopt the law by majority vote.

The law grants exclusive recognition and bargaining rights, prohibits strikes, and permits binding arbitration of bargaining impasses.

ALABAMA. The law enacted in 1953[2] provided that any public employee who continued his union membership 30 days after the effective date of the Act, or who joins a union, forfeits all rights under the state merit system, employment rights, reemployment rights, and other benefits as a result of his public employment. This did not apply to teachers and hospital employees who do not exercise the right to strike.

The Supreme Court of Alabama held in *Operating Engineers v. City of Birmingham* (1964)[3] that public employees cannot bargain with unions without express constitutional or statutory authority to do so.

However, in 1967 when the Fire Fighters Act 229 was passed, fire fighters were permitted to join unions and present proposals, but were prohibited from striking or asserting their right to strike.

WISCONSIN. The Wisconsin State Employment Labor Relations Act[4] is illustrative of modern legislation in this area. In its "Declaration of Policy" it reflects concepts that have become widely accepted.

The public policy of the state as to labor relations and collective bargaining in state employment, in the furtherance of which this subchapter is enacted, is as follows:

(1) It recognizes that there are three major interests involved: that of the public, the state employee, and the state as an employer. These three interests are to a considerable extent interrelated. It is the policy of this state to protect and promote each of these interests with due regard to the situation and to the rights of the others.

(2) Orderly and constructive employment relations for state employees and the efficient administration of state government are promotive of all these interests. They are largely dependent upon the maintenance of fair, friendly and mutually satisfactory employee–management relations in state employment, and the availability of suitable machinery for fair and peaceful adjustment of what-

ever controversies may arise. It is recognized that whatever may be the rights of disputants with respect to each other in any controversy regarding state employment relations, neither party has any right to engage in acts or practices which jeopardize the public safety and interest and interfere with the effective conduct of public business.

(3) Where permitted hereby, negotiations of terms and conditions of state employment should result from voluntary agreement between the state and its agents, as an employer and its employees. For that purpose a state employee may, if he desires, associate with others in organizing and in bargaining collectively through representatives of his own choosing, without intimidation or coercion from any source.

(4) It is the policy of this state, in order to preserve and promote the interests of the public, the state employee and the state as an employer alike, to encourage the practices and procedure of collective bargaining in state employment subject to the requirements of the public service and related laws, rules and policies governing state employment, by establishing standards of fair conduct in state employment relations and by providing a convenient, expeditious and impartial tribunal in which these interests may have their respective rights determined. In the furtherance of this policy the Secretary of Administration shall establish a capability within the Department of Administration. . . . The department shall establish and maintain, wherever practicable, consistent employment relations policies and practices throughout the state service.

NEW JERSEY. The New Jersey Employee Relations Act[5] covers both public and private employees, and its declaration of policy covers both the private and public sectors.

It is hereby declared as the policy of this State that the best interests of the people of the State are served by the prevention or prompt settlement of labor disputes, both in the private and public sectors; that strikes, lockouts, work stoppages and other forms of employer and employee strife, regardless where the merits of the controversy lie, are forces productive ultimately of economic and public waste; that the interests and rights of the consumers and the people of the State, while not direct parties thereto, should always be considered, respected, and protected; and that the voluntary mediation of such public and private employer–employee disputes under the guidance and supervision of a governmental agency will tend to promote permanent, public and private employer–employee peace and the health, welfare, comfort and safety of the people of the state. To carry out such policy, the necessity for the enactment of the provisions of this act is hereby declared as a matter of legislative determination.

RHODE ISLAND. The Rhode Island statute[6] covering teachers states: "It is hereby declared to be the public policy of this state to accord to certified public school teachers the right to organize, to be represented, to negotiate professionally, and to bargain on a collective basis with school committees covering hours, salary, working conditions and other terms of professional employment provided, however, that nothing in this chapter shall be construed to accord to certified public school teachers the right to strike."

MASSACHUSETTS. The Massachusetts statute[7] states: "Employees of the commonwealth or any political subdivision thereof shall have the right to form and join vocational or labor organizations and to present proposals relative to salaries and other conditions of employment through representatives of their own choosing. . . ."

MICHIGAN. The Michigan statute covering police and fire fighters[8] emphasizes conflict resolution. It states: "It is the public policy of this state that in public police and fire departments, where the right of public employees to strike is by law prohibited, it is requisite to the high morale of such employees and the efficient operation of such departments to afford an alternate, expeditious, effective and binding procedure for the resolution of disputes, and to that end the provisions of this act, providing for compulsory arbitration, shall be liberally construed."

MAINE. The Maine statute[9] states: "It is declared to be the public policy of this State and it is the purpose of this chapter to promote the improvement of the relationship between public employers and their employees by providing a uniform basis for recognizing the right of public employees to join labor organizations of their own choosing and to be represented by such organizations in collective bargaining for terms and conditions of employment."

NEBRASKA. The statement of public policy in the State of Nebraska statute[10] emphasizes the right of the people of the State to continuous and uninterrupted governmental services as well as the services of public utilities. To carry out its public policy, the statute creates a "Court of Industrial Relations" composed of five judges appointed by the Governor with the advice and consent of the Legislature. The statute specifies that "Such judges shall be representative of the public. . . ." The statute provides as follows:

(1) The continuous, uninterrupted, and proper functioning and operation of the governmental service including governmental service in a proprietary capacity and of public utilities engaged in the business of furnishing transportation for hire, telephone service, telegraph service, electric light, heat or power service, gas for heating or illuminating, whether natural or artificial, or water service, or any one or more of them, to the people of Nebraska are hereby declared to be essential to their welfare, health, and safety. It is contrary to the public policy of the state to permit any substantial impairment or suspension of the operation of governmental service, including governmental service in a proprietary capacity or any such utility by reason of industrial disputes therein. It is the duty of the State of Nebraska to exercise all available means and every power at its command to prevent the same so as to protect its citizens from any dangers, perils, calamities, or catastrophies which would result therefrom. It is therefore further declared that governmental service including governmental service in a proprietary capacity and the service of such public utilities are clothed with a vital public interest and to protect same it is necessary that the relations between the employers and employees in such industries be regulated by the State of Nebraska to the extent and in the manner herein provided;

(2) No right shall exist in any natural corporate person or group of persons to hinder, delay, limit, or suspend the continuity or efficiency of any governmental service in a proprietary capacity of this state, either by strike, lockout, or other means; and

(3) No right shall exist in any natural or corporate person or group of persons to hinder, delay, limit, or suspend the continuity of efficiency of any public utility service, either by strike, lockout, or other means.

The Nebraska statute covering only teachers provides:

In order to promote the growth and development of education in Nebraska which is essential to the welfare of its people, it is hereby declared to be the policy of the state to promote the improvement of personnel management and relations with certificated employees within the public school districts of the state by providing a uniform basis for recognizing the right of public school certificated employees to join organizations of their own choice in Class III, IV, and V school districts and be represented by such organizations in their professional and employment relations with the school district.

Right to Organize and Bargain Collectively

The Rhode Island fire fighters statute is typical. It provides: "The fire fighters in any city or town shall have the right to bargain collectively with their respective cities or towns and to be represented by a labor organization in such collective bargaining as to wages, rates of pay, hours, working conditions and all other terms and conditions of employment."

The Nebraska statute gives public employees the right to form or join a union as well as the right to refrain from forming or joining a union. Public employees also have "the right to be represented by employee organizations to negotiate collectively with their public employers in the determination of their terms and conditions of employment, and the administration of grievances arising thereunder."

Right to Strike

With few exceptions, strikes by public employees are prohibited. The Michigan statute, which is typical, provides: "No person holding a position by appointment or employment in the government of the State of Michigan, or in the government of any one or more of the political subdivisions thereof, or in the public school service, or in any public or special district, or in the service of any authority, commission, or board, or in any other branch of the public service, hereinafter called a 'public employee' shall strike."

The Maine statute prohibits public employees, public employee organizations, their agents, members, and bargaining agents from engaging in (1) a work stoppage, (2) a slowdown, (3) a strike, and (4) blacklisting of any public employer for the purpose of preventing it from filling employee vacancies.

The State of New York[11] prohibits strikes by public employees and provides remedies for violations of such prohibition.

The New Jersey statute[12] states that strikes and related activities by either private or public employees produce economic waste no matter what the merits of the controversy may be. Although the right to strike is not expressly prohibited, the courts have interpreted the statute to prohibit strikes.

Limited Right to Strike

The Pennsylvania statute[13] grants a limited right to strike except to police, firemen, guards at prisons or mental hospitals, and employees directly involved with and necessary to the functioning of the courts.

Strikes are prohibited by public employees during the pendency of collective bargaining, but are permitted when all procedures to resolve the impasse have been utilized and exhausted, except when such a strike creates a "clear and present danger or threat to the health, safety, or welfare of the public."

Article X, Sec. 1003 of the act provides as follows:

If a strike by public employees occurs after the collective bargaining processes set forth in Sections 801 and 802 of Article VIII of this act have been completely utilized and exhausted, it shall not be prohibited unless or until such a strike creates a clear and present danger or threat to the health, safety or welfare of the public. In such cases the public employer shall initiate, in the Court of Common Pleas of the jurisdiction where such strike occurs, an action for equitable relief including but not limited to appropriate injunctions and shall be entitled to such relief if the court finds that the strike creates a clear and present danger or threat to the health, safety or welfare of the public. . . .

A separate statute covers police and firemen. It provides for compulsory binding arbitration of contract disputes.

The Alaska Public Employment Act[14] gives a limited right to strike to public employees except police, fire, prison, and hospital employees.[15] Alaska has two statutes; one covers teachers and the other all other public employees.

The Hawaii statute[16] grants public employees a limited right to strike. It is *unlawful* for employees to strike

1. When they are not members of a union that has been certified by the Hawaii Public Employment Relations Board.
2. When they are represented by a certified union but disputes are resolved by referral to final and binding arbitration.

It is *lawful* for employees to strike

1. After the procedures relating to the resolution of disputes (fact finding and submission to appropriate legislative body) have been complied with in good faith.

2. After proceedings for the prevention of any prohibited practices have been exhausted.
3. If sixty days have elapsed since the fact-finding board has made public its findings and any recommendations.
4. If the exclusive representative has given a ten-day notice of intent to the board and to the employer.

Montana's statute,[17] effective July 1, 1969, covers nurses employed in public as well as private health care facilities. It allows employees to strike on thirty days written notice as long as there is no strike in effect in another facility within a radius of 150 miles.

Impasse Procedures

When representatives of employees and the public employer fail to agree on all the terms and conditions of employment and an impasse is reached, provision is usually made for mediation, fact finding, and frequently final and binding arbitration, particularly in disputes involving police and fire fighters.

Procedures for handling impasses vary from state to state. Within the last few years, new approaches for the resolution of impasses have been developed. For example, Michigan instituted "last offer" arbitration on January 1, 1972.

ALASKA. Under the Alaska Public Employment Relations Act[18] the second classification of employees discussed above (public utilities, snow removal, sanitation, and public school and other educational institution employees) may be enjoined by a court from striking. If an injunction is issued, the impasse must be submitted to arbitration under the provisions of the Alaska Arbitration Act.

The Alaska Act also provides for the arbitration of impasses involving the final class of employees (police and fire protection employees, jail, prison and other correctional institution employees, and hospital employees).

MICHIGAN. The Michigan statute covering state employees provides for mediation and fact finding but not for arbitration in disputes involving the terms and conditions of a collective bargaining agreement. It is significant that the statute specifically provides that a fact finder may endeavor to mediate a dispute at any time prior to the issuance of his recommendations.

The statute covering municipal employees provides for the compulsory arbitration of contract disputes involving the police. However, there are two alternative forms of arbitration available to law enforcement personnel and fire fighters. In addition to the usual form of binding arbitration, the law provides as follows: "Parties shall submit their final offer in effect at the time that the petition for final and binding arbitration was filed. Either party may amend its final offer within five days of the date of the hearing. The arbitrator shall select the final offer of one of the parties and shall issue an award incorporating that offer without modification."

"Last offer" arbitration is applicable to economic issues that are determined by the panel. Noneconomic issues are not subject to the "last offer" provision.

Effective May 4, 1972, the Police–Fire Fighters Arbitration Act,[19] which was enacted in 1969 with an expiration date of June 30, 1972, was extended to June 30, 1975, and was amended to authorize the chairman of the tripartite arbitration panel to remand the dispute to the parties for further collective bargaining for a period not to exceed three weeks if, in his opinion, it would be useful or beneficial.

MINNESOTA. Under the Minnesota Public Employment Relations Act,[20] which became effective July 1, 1972, either the public employer or an employee organization, or both, may petition the Director of the Bureau of Mediation Services for arbitration, stating that an impasse has been reached. If the Director finds that further mediation efforts would be futile, he will request that each party submit its final position on each of the matters in dispute. The final offer must be submitted at least 75 days prior to the last date the employer is required by law to submit its tax levy (or budget) or to certify the taxes voted to the corporate public agency, or by October 1, whichever is earlier.

The Act further directs that the Bureau maintain a list of arbitrators qualified by experience and training in labor management negotiations and arbitration. A list of seven names is submitted to the parties. Each alternately strikes out two names. The remaining three names constitute the arbitration panel. The parties may agree on one arbitrator.

The arbitration panel submits its order not later than the last day a public employer is required by law to submit its tax levy (or budget) or to certify its taxes voted to the appropriate public agency. The public employer has ten days after submission of the order to reject it. If it is not rejected, the order is binding. The parties may, however, stipulate that the decision of the panel of arbitrators shall be binding. Even though the final offer is submitted, the panel is not required to choose between the final offers.

When the employees involved perform work essential to public health and safety, the public employer and employee organization may request that only the final position of the parties be considered by the panel of arbitrators. In this event, the order is binding on both parties. If no such request is made, the public employer may accept or reject the decision.

NEW MEXICO. Regulations of the New Mexico State Personnel Board[21] became effective May 9, 1972. They provide that when "voluntary arrangements," including the services of the Federal Mediation and Conciliation Service or other third-party mediation, fail to resolve an impasse, either party may request the Personnel Board to consider the matter. The Board either may recommend procedures for resolving the impasse or "may settle the impasse by appropriate action."

It is significant to note that under this statute the parties may use third-party fact finding, with recommendations or arbitration only when authorized and directed by the Board.

NEW HAMPSHIRE. Under the Municipal Police Officers Bargaining Statute,[22] effective May 27, 1972, police officers may meet and confer in good faith with municipal governments with regard to working conditions, salaries, wages, and other benefits, and may enter into a written agreement with the public employer. If the parties are unable to reach an agreement within 40 days after the first meeting, unresolved issues may be submitted to fact finding by either the employee organization or the municipality. The fact-finding panel is tripartite. The neutral member must be selected by the other two members chosen by the parties. If they cannot make a selection, the neutral member is selected in accordance with the rules and procedures of the American Arbitration Association (AAA). The fact-finding report is not binding on the parties, who are required to resume meeting and conferring on the basis of the report.

CITY OF NEW YORK. New impasse procedures became effective on January 12, 1972, as a result of an amendment to the New York City Collective Bargaining Law. They provide that when mediation has failed, an impasse panel is selected. If a party rejects the panel's recommendations he may appeal within ten days of his rejection to the Board of Collective Bargaining. Failure to appeal within the ten-day limitation renders the recommendation final and binding upon the party failing to appeal. The Board may, on its own initiative, also review the recommendations that have been rejected.

The notice of appeal is required to specify the grounds of the appeal and the modifications requested. The Board may affirm, modify, or set aside the recommendations of the panel.

If the Board fails to issue a final determination within 30 days of filing an appeal, the panel's recommendations will be deemed to have been adopted by the Board.

Final determination by the Board is binding on the parties, except that any provision of the Board's determination which requires enactment of law shall not become binding until such law is enacted. Judicial review is limited to questions of due process.

FLORIDA. The Fire Fighters Bargaining Act,[23] effective January 1, 1972, authorizes fire fighters to organize and bargain collectively. Impasses are submitted to advisory arbitration. The arbitration board is composed of three members, one appointed by the fire fighters' organization, one appointed by the public employer, and the third by the other two. If they fail to agree, the third member is selected in accordance with the rules of the American Arbitration Association. The decision must be in writing, with findings of fact, and submitted to the parties for consideration.

RHODE ISLAND. Effective May 8, 1972, the State Employees Labor Relations Act[24] provides that after conciliation and fact finding, unresolved issues between the bargaining agent and the chief executive are to be submitted to binding arbitration. A single arbitrator is selected from a list of certified arbitrators submitted by and in accordance with the rules of the

American Arbitration Association, provided all names submitted are those of Rhode Island residents.

VERMONT. The State Employees Public Employment Relations Act[25] was amended, effective April 3, 1972, to permit the State Employee Relations Board to authorize fact finding. The fact-finding panel consists of three members, one selected from the bargaining unit, one from the employer (State of Vermont), and the third (the chairman) by the other two. In the event the two parties cannot agree on a Chairman, the act provides that he be chosen by the Chief Justice of the State Supreme Court, who must select a resident of the state.

A new Vermont law[26] covering municipal employees became effective July 1, 1973, and will be administered by the State Labor Relations Board. It provides that municipalities employing five or more people are required to bargain with the exclusive employee representative on wages, hours, and conditions of employment. Impasse procedures include mediation, fact finding, voluntary contract arbitration, and a limited right to strike.

STATE OF NEW YORK. The New York Employees' Fair Employment Act,[27] Section 209, also provides procedures for the resolution of impasses.

Public employers are empowered to enter into a collective bargaining agreement, which may include "the undertaking by each party to submit unresolved issues to impartial arbitration."

On request of either party, or on its own motion, the Board may, if it determines that an impasse exists:

1. Appoint a mediator.
2. If the impasse continues, appoint a fact finding board, of not more than three members, each representing the public, from a list of qualified persons maintained by the board who are empowered to make public recommendations for the resolution of the dispute.
3. If the dispute is not resolved at least eighty days prior to the end of the fiscal year of the public employer, or by such other date determined by the board, acting by a majority of its members:
   a. The fact finding board immediately transmits its findings of fact and recommendations for the resolution of the dispute to the chief executive officer of the government and to the employee organization involved.
   b. The fact finding board may assist the parties [in effecting] a voluntary resolution of the dispute.
   c. The fact finding board shall, within five days of such transmission, make public such findings and recommendations.
4. If the impasse continues, the public employment relations board is authorized to take whatever steps it deems appropriate to resolve the dispute, including:
   a. Making its own recommendations after giving consideration to the fact finders finding of fact and recommendations. No further fact finding board shall be appointed.
   b. Upon the request of the parties, assist in providing voluntary arbitration.
5. If the impasse continues:

a. The chief executive shall, within ten days after receipt of the findings of fact and recommendations of the fact finding board, submit to the legislative body of the government involved, a copy of the findings of fact and recommendations of the fact finding board, together with his recommendations for settling the dispute.

b. The employee organization may submit to such legislative body its recommendations for settling the dispute.

c. The legislative body or a duly authorized committee thereof shall forthwith conduct a public hearing at which the parties shall be required to explain their positions with respect to the report of the fact finding board.

d. As the final step, the legislature shall take such action as it deems to be in the public interest.

Guidelines for Arbitrators

Several statutes requiring compulsory arbitration of impasses set forth guidelines for arbitrators. The following provisions are illustrative of factors that arbitrators are expected to consider.

The Michigan statute applicable to police and firemen provides:

(a) The lawful authority of the employer.

(b) Stipulations of the parties.

(c) The interests and welfare of the public and the financial ability of the unit of government to meet those costs.

(d) Comparison of the wages, hours and conditions of employment of the employee involved in the arbitration proceeding with the wages, hours and conditions of employment of other employees performing similar services and with other employees generally: (i) in public employment in comparable communities, (ii) in private employment in comparable communities.

(e) The average consumer prices for goods and services, commonly known as the cost of living.

(f) The overall compensation presently received by the employees, including direct wage compensation, vacations, holidays, and other excused time, insurance and pensions, medical and hospitalization benefits, the continuity and stability of employment, and other benefits received.

(g) Changes in any of the foregoing circumstances during the pendency of the arbitration proceedings.

(h) Such other factors, not confined to the foregoing; which are normally or traditionally taken into consideration in the determination of wages, hours, and conditions of employment through voluntary collective bargaining, mediation, fact finding, arbitration or otherwise between the parties, in the public service or in private employment.

The Firefighters Bargaining Act passed by the State of Florida, effective January 1, 1973,[28] includes the following factors which are to be given weight by arbitrators who are empowered to render an advisory award.

1. Comparison of annual income of employment of the employing authority with the annual income of employment maintained for same or similar work of employees exhibiting like or similar skills under the same or similar working conditions in the local operating area.

2. Comparison of annual income of employment of employer with annual income of employment of employing authorities in municipalities, counties or metropolitan governments or fire districts of comparable size.

3. Interest and welfare of the public.

4. Comparison of peculiarities of employment in regard to other trades or professions, specifically:

(a) Hazard of employment.	(e) Job training and skills.
(b) Physical qualifications.	(f) Retirement plans.
(c) Educational qualifications.	(g) Sick leave.
(d) Mental qualifications.	(h) Job security.

Grievance Arbitration

Prior to 1960 it was illegal for a public employer to agree to submit a grievance to arbitration. When laws were passed granting public employees the right to organize and bargain collectively, the arbitration of grievances became legal by statute. Although at first many contracts provided for advisory arbitration, today the trend is toward final and binding arbitration.

The Hawaii statute specifically gives the public employer "power to enter into a written agreement . . . setting forth a grievance procedure culminating in a final and binding decision. . . ." It also provides that, in the absence of such a procedure, either party may submit the dispute (grievances only) for a final and binding decision.

The Michigan statute also provides that disputes pertaining to the interpretation of a collective bargaining agreement may be submitted to arbitration.

The State of New Mexico authorizes grievance arbitration, but allows either party to file exceptions to the arbitrators award with the State Personnel Board "if the award conflicts with law, or regulations prescribed by the Board."

The New Jersey act provides that the public employer shall

Negotiate written policies setting forth grievance procedures by means of which their employees or representatives of employees may appeal the interpretation, application, or violation of policies, agreements and administrative decisions affecting them provided that such grievance procedures shall be included in any agreement entered into between the public employer and the representative organization. Such grievance procedures may provide for binding arbitration as a means for resolving disputes.

The New York City Collective Bargaining Law provides that:

Executive orders, and collective bargaining agreements between public employee organizations, may contain provisions for grievance procedures, in steps terminating with impartial arbitration of unresolved grievances. Such provisions may provide that the arbitrator's award shall be final and binding and enforceable in any appropriate tribunal in accordance with the applicable law governing arbitration, except that awards as to grievances concerning assignment of employees to duties substantially different from those stated in their job classifications or the use of open competition rather than promotional examinations, shall be final and binding and enforceable only to the extent permitted by law.

REFERENCES

1. (a) Texas, V.A.C.S. Act 5154C.1, 1947, Ch. 135.
   (b) HB 185 L1973; GERR-RF 51:5211.
2. Alabama, Soloman Act, 1953.
3. International Union of Operating Engineers, Local 321, AFL-CIO v. Water Works Board of the City of Birmingham, 276 Ala. 462, 163 So. 2d. 619.
4. Wisconsin, Wisconsin State Employment Labor Relations Act (Ch. III, Sub Chap. V; L1971, Ch. 270, eff. April 30, 1973).
5. New Jersey, N.J.S.A. Title 34, Chap. 13A, L1941 Ch. 100, as amended 1968.
6. Rhode Island, E.L. Sec. 36-11-1-36-11-10; L1958, Ch. 178, as amended.
7. Massachusetts, Chap. 149, Gen. Laws Sec. 178D.
8. Michigan, Michigan Compiled Laws of 1948, Secs. 423.231/423-247; L1969, No. 312, as amended.
9. Maine, M.R.S.A. Title 26, Ch. 9-A, L1969, Ch. 424, as amended.
10. Nebraska, R.S. Neb. Ch. 48; L1947, Ch. 178, as amended.
11. New York, Civil Service Law, Secs. 200-214: L1967, as amended.
12. New Jersey, Bd. of Education v. N.J. Education Assoc., 247 A 2d. 867; N.J. Sup. Ct., 1968.
13. Pennsylvania, Penn. State Annot: Chap. 19; L1970, No. 195.
14. Alaska, Secs. 23.40.070 to 23.40.260; Alaska Statutes, Ch. 113; L1972; GERR-RF 51:1111; SLL 11.211.
15. Alaska, Holland School District v. Holland Education Association, 380 Mich. 314, 157 NW 2d. 206 (1968).
16. Hawaii, Ch. 89, Laws 1970, c 171, as amended.
17. Montana, Ch. 320, L1969; GERR-RF 51:3511.
18. Alaska, Title 23, Ch. 40 L1972, Ch. 94, eff. August 29, 1972.
19. Michigan, C L 423.231 to 423.246; GERR-RF 51:3111; SLL 32.262C.
20. Minnesota, S 134, L.1971 GERR-RF 51:3211; SLL 33:247.
21. New Mexico, GERR-RF 51:4011; SLL 41:207.
22. New Hampshire, N.H. Stat. Ann., Sec. 105-B:1-105-B:14; GERR-RF 51: 3812; SLL 39:205.
23. Florida, Ch. 72-275, L1972; GERR-RF 51:1813; SLL 19:212.
24. Rhode Island, R.I. Gen. LT 36, GERR-RF 51:4811, SLL 50:238.
25. Vermont, VT Stat. Sec. 901-1007, GERR-RF 51:5411; SLL 56:219.
26. Vermont, V.S.A. Ch. 21, as amended by HB 239, L1973.
27. State of New York: The Taylor law (Ch. 392 Laws of 1967, effective September 1, 1967, as amended by L1969, C24, C391, C492, and C494; L1970, C32, C414, and C1020; L1971, C13, C503, and C504; L1972, C26, and C818: Sections 200 to 214.
28. Florida, Ch. 72-275, L1972; GERR-RF 51:1913; SLL 19:212.

14

PUBLIC SECTOR: COURT DECISIONS

Whenever a new statute is passed, it is subject to review by the courts. In the final analysis the courts determine its constitutionality and interpret its provisions. Recent laws regulating employer–employee relations in the public sector have been the subject of many court decisions. These decisions are creating a new body of labor law in the public sector similar to labor law in the private sector. A review of these court decisions is important for an understanding of the rights, powers, and limitations of both the unions representing public employees and representatives of government agencies.

The courts have been called upon to determine the constitutionality of these statutes and to define and interpret their provisions, particularly with regard to the right to organize and bargain, the right to strike, and impasse procedures.

Judicial Review

In reviewing statutes relating to the right of public employees to organize and bargain collectively, the courts look to the legislative purpose and intent for guidance. In *Rankin v. Shanker* (1968),[1] the New York court said: "Our discussion of the statutory question may well begin by noting that a primary command to the judiciary in the interpretation of statutes is to ascertain and effectuate the purpose of the legislation. In finding such purpose one should look to the entire statute, its legislative history and the statutes of which it is made a part."

The validity of an ordinance passed by the City of Dallas, which prohibited municipal employees from organizing as well as bargaining collectively, was questioned in the case of *Beverly v. City of Dallas* (1956).[2] It was argued that the ordinance was inconsistent with a statute passed by the State of Texas, which granted public employees the right to organize but prohibited the right to bargain collectively. The court held: "The Statute restricting collective bargaining and recognition of a union of public employees as a bargaining agent and declaring void contracts between municipalities and any such organizations on that basis, but permitting public employees to present grievances individually or through a representative is not invalid as contradictory." The court also held regarding the right to organize: "We think the trial court was in error in holding that the ordinances of the City of Dallas prohibiting its employees from joining or belonging to labor organizations were valid. Such ordinances as those here involved are in clear conflict with Art. 5154c, one of the General Laws of the State of Texas." [2]

Right to Organize and Bargain Collectively

The legal problems that arise under the heading of the right of public employees to organize and bargain collectively include the duty of the employer to bargain, and the validity and finality of collective negotiations.

The California court, in the case of *California Federation of Teachers v. Oxnard Elementary Schools* (1969),[3] held: "The air is stirring with demands of public employees for recognition and the right to organize in the interests of influencing their employment conditions, and they are entitled to have these demands acknowledged and accorded to them within reasonable statutory bounds and limitations." [3]

In *Porcelli v. Titus* (1969)[4] the New Jersey court held: "There can be no doubt, as plaintiffs (teachers) contend in their brief that the teachers in the Newark school system, as public employees, had the right to organize and, through organizational representation, the right to make proposals which could be effectuated by an enforceable agreement between the school board and its organized employees." [4]

In *Lullo v. International Association of Fire Fighters* (1970),[5] the New Jersey court interpreted the right of public employees to collective negotiations under the statute. They made a distinction between collective bargaining in the private sector and in the public sector. They held:

"We accepted the thesis that the right of collective bargaining in the full sense in which it obtains in the private employment sector is not guaranteed by the paragraph to public employees. With respect to the latter employees, we interpreted the language to impose upon the employer in the public sector only the duty to meet with its employees or their chosen representative and to consider in good faith any grievances or proposals presented on their behalf. . . . It was in this connection that we referred to the continuing power of the lawmakers to enact further statutes as may be compatible with Article 1, par. 19 [of the New Jersey Constitution of 1947] to both substantially and procedurally flesh out the constitutional guarantees.[5]

In the *Oxnard* case,[6] the California court emphasized not only the responsibility of the public employer to bargain in good faith but also the court's responsibility to enforce this responsibility. The court held: "This court has, under the circumstances, the duty and obligation . . . to enjoin

upon appellants (Oxnard Elementary Schools) the responsibility to cooperate and participate in good faith in order to enhance the declared
appropriate legislative objectives." [6]

The courts have also passed on what constitutes a collective bargaining
agreement. In the *DiPrete* case (1968),[7] the union asked the court to direct
the mayor and other city officials to execute a contract including certain
negotiated agreements relating to work conditions. The Rhode Island court
held: ". . . a collective bargaining contract will consist of the parties' mutual
understandings on all of the material issues, whether they were agreed upon
before arbitration, were determined by the decision of the arbitrators, or
were agreed upon at post arbitration negotiations." [7]

The validity and finality of a collective bargaining agreement was upheld
in *Porcelli v. Titus*[8]. The Newark Board of Education suspended the promotional procedure and eligibility lists of teachers and unilaterally instituted a new promotion policy. The union claimed violation of the contract.
The court held: ". . . the instant employment contract must be binding and
enforceable against all parties, including the public employer." The validity
and finality of a collective bargaining agreement was clearly set forth by the
California court in *East Bay Municipal Employees v. County of Alameda*
(1970)[9]. The court held: ". . . when a public employer engages in such
meetings (collective negotiations) with representatives of the public employee organization, any agreement that the public agency is authorized to
make and, in fact, does enter into should be held valid and binding as to
all parties".[9]

A Rhode Island court in the case of *Warren Education Association v.
Richard L. Lapan et al.*[10] held: It is clear from our examination of the
statute and from a review of the facts before us, that contrary to the association's assertions, the State Labor Relations Board may compel the committee to sign a written contract formalizing any prior oral agreement
reached by the parties at the bargaining table".[10]

Right to Strike

Public employee unions have challenged the legal prohibition on the
right of public employees to strike and engage in related concerted activities.

The constitutionality of the Texas statute in this regard was questioned
in 1962 in the case of *South Atlantic and Gulf Coast District of International
Longshoremen's Association, Independent v. Harris County* (1962).[11] The
court held:

We do not think that the provisions of Art. 5154c, V.A.T.S. (Vernons' Ann.
Tex. St.), declaring it to be against the public policy of this State that employees
of The State or a political subdivision thereof shall not have the right to strike,
or our decision that public policy prohibits peaceful picketing for the purpose of

inducing such a strike, violates any constitutional guarantees secured to any of the appellants by either the Constitution of the United States of America or the Constitution of the State of Texas.[11]

In the more recent *City of New York v. De Lury* (1968)[12] case, the court said: "The courts which have dealt with the constitutional question under discussion have concluded that no provision of either the Federal or State Constitution prevents the State from outlawing strikes by public employees".[12]

As was noted previously, the New Jersey statute does not specifically state that public employees do not have the right to strike. Whether by stating that private employees have the right to strike the law intended that public employees have no right to strike was considered in the case of *Board of Education Union Beach v. N.J. Education Association* (1968).[13] The court held: "it has long been the rule in our state that public employees may not strike. . . . The public demand for services which make illegal a strike against government inveighs against any other concerted action designed to deny government the necessary manpower, whether by terminating existing employments in any mode or by obstructing access to the labor market." [13]

A similar conclusion was reached by a California court which reviewed a statute that was silent on the right to strike. In the case of *Los Angeles Metropolitan Transit Authority v. Brotherhood of Railroad Trainmen* (1960)[14] it was held: "In the absence of legislative authorization, public employees in general do not have the right to strike." This view was confirmed in *Almond v. Sacramento County* (1969).[15]

With the enactment of the New York Taylor law to replace the Condon-Wadlin Act, the question of the right of public employees was again answered in the case of *City of New York Board of Education v. Shanker* (1967).[16] The court held: "From time immemorial, it has been a fundamental principle that a government employee may not strike. . . . Although the Condon-Wadlin Act was recently repealed and the Taylor Act . . . substituted in its stead, the prohibition against strikes by public employees was nevertheless carried over into the Taylor Act (sec. 210 sub. 1) with the result that no question therefore exists with regard to the constitutionality of the new Act in so far as it prohibits strikes."

In another New York case[17] the court held:

It is our conclusion that the statutory prohibition against strikes by public employees is reasonably designed to effectuate a valid state policy in an area where it has authority to act and that the provisions of subdivision 1 of section 210 do not offend any due process rights of the defendants. . . . Self interest of individual or organization may not be permitted to endanger the safety, health or public welfare of the state or any of its subdivisions.

In Pennsylvania, a police officer and police chief brought a mandamus action against the Borough Council of East Lansdowne to compel it to enact legislation carrying out an award of the board of arbitrators made in accordance with Public Law No. 1116 (enacted June 24, 1968).[18] The court related the purpose of the arbitration procedure to the policy of the state by declaring: "likewise in this case before us, there is an obvious legislative policy to protect the public from strikes by policemen and firemen, public employees who hold critical positions. . . . To require a more explicit statement of legislative policy in a statute calling for labor arbitration would be sheer folly".[19]

Impasse and Grievance Procedures

Since the right to strike is denied public employees, it is important that procedures be provided for the resolution of impasses. Most statutes provide for mediation and fact finding. Some require arbitration of interest disputes. Grievance procedures terminating in arbitration are also provided for in most statutes. (For example, see Appendix III,3.) The courts have been called on to pass on the legality of some of these procedures.

The Wyoming statute applying to firefighters provides: "In the event that the bargaining agent and the corporate authorities are unable, within thirty (30) days from and including the date of their first meeting, to reach agreement on a contract, any and all unresolved issues shall be submitted to arbitration."

In the case of *State v. City of Laramie* (1968),[20] the court reviewed this provision in a mandamus action by the union to compel the City to comply with the statute and submit to arbitration. It held:

The constitutional prohibition against delegation of power is intended to protect against the exercise of the taxing power and other purely municipal functions by officials not subject to the people's control. . . .

Matters which are administrative only may be delegated without violating the constitutional prohibition against the legislative delegating to a special commissioner power to supervise or interfere with any municipal function. . . . No delegation of power is involved with respect to collective bargaining. . . .

Therefore if the Legislature sees fit to provide for a genuine collective bargaining, an essential adjunct to the bargaining is a provision for unresolved matters to be submitted to arbitration or determined in some other manner. . . .

Even though one of the parties in the arbitration provided for in Ch. 197 is a city, the act of arbitration is no different from the act of arbitration in business and industrial affairs. It is nothing more than the performance of arbitration, and it cannot be said to be the performance of a municipal function.

In *Warwick v. Regular Firemen's Association* (1969)[21] the Rhode Island court was asked to enjoin compulsory binding arbitration by the City of Warwick. In a decision upholding the Union the court said:

We are of the opinion that when the legislature, in an exercise of the lawmaking authority, enacts a statute the purpose of which is to secure to the public some right or benefit, it may delegate to an *appropriate* agency or officer some residuals of its legislative power in order to permit the selected agent to accomplish the ends contemplated in the original legislation. [Italics added.] . . . Each member of boards of arbitration provided for under section 28-9.1-8 is a public officer and . . . collectively these officers constitute an *administrative* or *governmental* agency. [Italics added.]

The legislature in section 28-9.1-10 sets out specifically a number of comprehensive limitations of the actions of a board of arbitration when exercising the power delegated. . . . In our opinion, these standards clearly are sufficient to meet the constitutional requirement that the delegated power be confined by reasonable norms or standards.

The Village of Whitefish Bay, Wisconsin, passed an ordinance relating to local determination of whether conditions for fact finding exist. The Wisconsin Employment Relations Board took the position that the ordinance was invalid. The court held: "The WERB was correct in its conclusions that that part of Ordinance No. 833 which provides local methods to determine whether the conditions for fact finding exist is invalid. This is so because Sec. 111.70 . . . does not in any way authorize municipalities to unilaterally establish procedures to determine whether the conditions for fact finding exist." It also held that the WERB can judge whether or not local ordinances comply with Sec. 111.70 in order to facilitate public policy.

The jurisdiction of the Michigan Labor Mediation Board to hear and determine disputes was upheld in two decisions. In *Labor Mediation Board v. Road Commissioners* (1962),[22] the court said: "The labor mediation board is the administrative tribunal established by the law to hear such disputes, and it is the proper forum for the determination of plaintiffs' grievances."

In *Garden City Schools v. Labor Mediation Board* (1959),[23] a dispute existed between the teachers and the Board of Education concerning "salary and other conditions of employment." When upon petition by the teachers the labor mediation board tried to mediate the dispute, the Board of Education challenged the jurisdiction of the labor mediation board. The court held: "in our opinion, PA 1947, No. 336, plainly gave to the labor mediation board jurisdiction to mediate disputes of the nature of this one."

In another Michigan case,[24] the court found: "Plaintiff's remedy is clearly provided by statute. He is given the right to process his grievances before the labor mediation board, and this affords him as a public employee, protection of his constitutional rights."

In the *Warren* case,[25] a petition was filed to require the school committee to execute a collective bargaining agreement embracing "salaries, working conditions and other incidents of employment." It was held: "In view of the foregoing, therefore, we are of the opinion that the association has in the teachers' arbitration act a very adequate and effective course of relief in this case. The legislature has created therein a remedy for their grievances which significantly enhances their power to bargain with school committees."

In the California *Oxnard* case,[26] the court, in discussing the validity of dispute settlement procedures within school systems as provided in the Winton Act, stated: "The Winton Act may not be declared invalid merely because it establishes a unique or experimental procedure for dealing with employment relations in the public school system."

REFERENCES

1. Rankin v. Shanker, 23 N.Y. 2d. 111; 242 N.E. 2d. 802.
2. Beverly v. City of Dallas, Civ. App. 292 SW 2d. 172.
3. California Federation of Teachers v. Oxnard Elementary Schools, 77 Cal. Rptr. 497.
4. Porcelli v. Titus, 261 A 2d. 364.
5. Lullo v. International Association of Fire Fighters, 262 A 2d. 681.
6. California Federation of Teachers v. Oxnard Elementary Schools, *op. cit.*
7. International Assoc. of Fire Fighters AFL-CIO v. James DiPrete, Jr., Mayor, et al., 239 A 2d. 716.
8. Porcelli v. Titus, *op. cit.*
9. East Bay Municipal Employees Union Local 390 v. County of Alameda, 83 Cal. Rptr. 503.
10 Warren Education Assoc. v. Richard L. Lapan et al., Warren School Committee, 235 A 2d. 866.
11. South Atlantic and Gulf Coast District of International Longshoremans' Association, Independent v. Harris County, Houston Ship Channel Naval District, 358 S.W. 2d. 658.
12. City of New York v. De Lury, 243 N.E. 2d. 128.
13. Board of Education, Borough of Union Beach v. N.J. Education Assoc., 247 A 2d. 867.
14. Los Angeles Metropolitan Transit Authority v. Brotherhood of Railroad Trainmen, 8 Cal. Rptr. 1.
15. Almond v. Sacramento County, 80 Cal. Rptr. 518.
16. City of New York Board of Education v. Shanker, 283 N.Y. Sup. 2d. 432. Affirmed without opinion. 286 N.Y. Sup. 2d. 453, December 14, 1967.
17. City of New York v. De Lury, *op. cit.* 43 P.S., para 217.
18. 43 P.S., para. 217.
19. Harney v. Russo, 71 LRRM 2817 (1969).
20. State of Wyoming ex rel. Fire Fighters Union Local 946 v. City of Laramie, 437 P. 2d. 295.
21. City of Warwick v. Warwick Regular Firemen's Assoc., 71 LRRM 3192.
22. Labor Mediation Board v. Jackson County Road Commissioners, 114 N.W. 2d. 183.
23. School District of Garden City v. Labor Mediation Board, 99 N.W. 2d. 485.
24. Gardnacavice v. Newaygo Board of County Road Commissioners, 341 Mich. 280 (1954).
25. Warren Education Assn. v. Richard L. Lapan et al., *op. cit.*
26. California Federation of Teachers v. Oxnard Elementary Schools, *op. cit.*

15

PUBLIC SECTOR:
FEDERAL EXECUTIVE ORDERS

It has not been generally known that union activity among government employees has existed for a long time. Labor organizations of craftsmen in U.S. Navy installations arose sporadically in the early 1800s. By the late nineteenth century, other unions such as the National Association of Letter Carriers were formed.

Even with the growing interest for unionization among federal employees, there was little legislation concerning employee-management relations. According to Ann Holland:

In the Federal service, unlike private industry, there has been little to guide employee–management relations except the Lloyd–La Follette Act of 1912 permitting employees to join unions, and the regulations of the Civil Service Commission giving employees appeal rights under that Act and the Veterans' Preference Act of 1944. Lloyd–La Follette concerned itself primarily with giving employees the right to organize. The Civil Service Commission was more concerned with adverse actions. For the purpose of employee protection, the C.S.C. requires agencies to develop grievance procedures for handling personnel." [1]

Executive Order 10988

Until President Kennedy took office there had not been even an attempt to formulate a presidential or legislative policy with respect to federal employee–management relations. On June 22, 1961, President Kennedy appointed a special task force to study and recommend actions to be taken to initiate a federal policy. As an interim measure, President Kennedy issued a memorandum to serve as a guideline for federal department and agency heads. It stated:

The right of all employees of the Federal Government to join and participate in the activities of employee organizations, and to seek to improve working conditions and the resolution of grievances should be recognized by management officials at all levels in all departments and agencies. The participation of Federal employees in the formulation and implementation of employee policies and procedures affecting them contributes to the effective conduct of public business. I believe this participation should include consultation by responsible officials with representatives of employees and Federal Employee organizations.[2]

Public hearings were held throughout the United States in order for the task force to obtain the opinions of individuals and groups interested in the many aspects of employee–management relations in the federal sector. At these public hearings the view was expressed that it was desirable for the federal government to establish a positive and comprehensive policy applicable to federal employees. All government departments and agencies were also invited to submit recommendations to the task force.

The findings and recommendations of the task force were presented to the President on November 30, 1961. In making these recommendations, the task force had to keep in mind certain objectives and considerations. These objectives and considerations, including some of the recommendations, were:

1. Preserving public interest as a primary consideration in administration of employee-management relations.
2. Retaining appropriate management responsibilities.
3. Recognizing the right of employees and employee organizations to participate in developing improved personnel policies and working conditions.
4. Federal employees do not have the right to strike.
5. Union shop and closed shop are inappropriate to the Federal Government.
6. Salaries and other conditions of employment fixed by Congress are not subject to negotiation.
7. All agreements must be consistent with merit system principles.
8. Providing arbitration procedures for the handling of individual employee grievances.

On January 17, 1962, President Kennedy signed two Executive Orders: 10987, entitled "Agency Systems for Appeals from Adverse Actions"; and 10988, entitled "Employee–Management Cooperation in the Federal Service."

Executive Order 11491

When Executive Order 10988 was promulgated, it was recognized that it was only the beginning of a new trend that required personnel officials to assume increasingly greater responsibilities in representing management to employees and employee groups. It called upon the agency representative to sit down with the employee and talk with him as an equal on matters of mutual concern. Employees acquired certain concessions as a matter of right, not as a favor, and among these was the right to participate in decisions affecting their welfare.

Questioning of the efficiency and practicability of Executive Order 10988 began as early as 1966, when certain agencies independently studied the problems that arose from the structure and administration of the order. In 1967 President Johnson established a "Review Committee on Federal

Employee–Management Relations." According to W. V. Gill, its recommendations were delayed because of disagreement within the Committee, and therefore its report did not reach President Johnson before he left office.[3] These recommendations were used as source material by a new committee appointed by President Nixon to study federal labor–management relations. This committee investigated the problem and forwarded its report and recommendations to President Nixon in September 1969. On the basis of these recommendations, Executive Order 11491 was formulated.

The complete text of this order, as amended, is reproduced in this book as Appendix III,2. The more significant sections are as follows:

Sec. 1: Establishes employees' rights and privileges.
Sec. 4: Establishes the Federal Labor Relations Council.
Sec. 5: Authorizes the Federal Service Impasses Panel.
Sec. 6: Creates the office of Assistant Secretary of Labor for Labor–Management Relations
Sec. 11: Sets forth procedures to determine negotiability of issues.
Sec. 12: Delineates the basic provisions and requirements of agreements.
Sec. 13: Establishes grievance procedures.
Sec. 15: Describes conditions for approval of agreements.
Sec. 16: Directs the Federal Mediation and Conciliation Service (FMCS) to assist in resolving negotiation disputes.
Sec. 17: Appeal authority is granted to the Federal Service Impasses Panel for settling negotiation disputes arising in FMCS.
Sec. 22: Confers on employees the right to appeal to the Civil Service Commission the adverse decision of administrative officers, in accordance with provisions of the United States Code.

Executive Order 11491 (titled "Labor–Management Relations in the Federal Service") was intended not only to develop policies and procedures to alleviate problems and deficiencies found in Order 10988, but to construct an up-to-date and forward-looking policy for federal labor–management relations in the 1970s. Some of the problems the new order sought to remedy included: (1) lack of central authority to administer the program; (2) inadequate third-party involvement in resolving union–management disputes; (3) weakness, delays, and lack of finality in the negotiation process.

Robert E. Hampton, Chairman of the U.S. Civil Service Commission and the Federal Labor Relations Council in 1970, addressed himself to these inadequacies in Executive Order 10988. Mr. Hampton felt the need for greater third-party involvement and central authority could be summed up in one word, *accountability*. He stated: "The lack of third-party process and final decision making meant in the past that neither party really had to be accountable for its actions. Where there is no accountability, there is little incentive to act responsibly." [4] Mr. Hampton further discussed negotiations and how the new order had achieved some of its objectives to better negotiations through improved "balance": "(1) Third party procedures are available for both parties, and both parties stand equal in their opportunity to prevail on an issue and their responsibility to be bound by the final decision. (2) The obligation to negotiate in good faith is placed equally on both parties." [4]

When President Nixon signed Executive Order 11491 on October 29, 1969, he directed that a review and assessment of operations under the order be made after one year. This review was initiated by the Federal Labor Relations Council in October 1970. Its report, submitted in June 1971, recommended several important changes in E.O. 11491.

With reference to grievance procedures and arbitration (Sec. 13), the Council recommended that the negotiated agreement for an exclusive unit must include a grievance procedure which shall become the exclusive procedure available regarding the interpretation and application of the agreement.

Complaints regarding unfair labor practices were recommended to be within the exclusive jurisdiction of the Assistant Secretary of Labor for Labor–Management Relations and the Federal Labor Relations Council. It was suggested that Section 20 be modified to eliminate the prohibition of employees, when engaged as labor organization representatives, spending official time in negotiations with agency management.

The Council also recommended that Section 21 be revised to eliminate the requirement that the costs of dues deduction must be charged to the labor organization.

Amendment of the Order

As a result of these recommendations, Executive Order 11491 was amended by Executive Order 11616 on August 26, 1971. Sections 20 and 21 were revised as recommended. Of particular interest are the changes made in Section 13, "Grievance and Arbitration Procedures." The new section reads as follows:

(a) An agreement between an agency and a labor organization shall provide a procedure, applicable only to the unit, for the consideration of grievances over the interpretation or application of the agreement. A negotiated grievance procedure may not cover any other matters, including matters for which statutory appeals procedures exist, and shall be the exclusive procedure available to the parties and the employees in the unit for resolving such grievances. However, any employee or group of employees in the unit may present such grievances to the agency and have them adjusted, without the intervention of the exclusive representative, as long as the adjustment is not inconsistent with the terms of the agreement and the exclusive representative has been given opportunity to be present at the adjustment.

(b) A negotiated procedure may provide for the arbitration of grievances over the interpretation or application of the agreement, but not over any other matters. Arbitration may be invoked only by the agency or the exclusive representative. Either party may file exceptions to an arbitrator's award with the Council, under regulations prescribed by the Council.

(c) Grievances initiated by an employee or group of employees in the unit on matters other than the interpretation or application of an existing agreement may be presented under any procedure available for the purpose.

(d) Questions that cannot be resolved by the parties as to whether or not a grievance is on a matter subject to the grievance procedure in an existing agreement, or is subject to arbitration under that agreement, may be referred to the Assistant Secretary for decision.

(e) No agreement may be established, extended or renewed after the effective date of this Order which does not conform to this section. However, this section is not applicable to agreements entered into before the effective date of this Order.

Under the amended Section 4, the Federal Labor Relations Council may consider, subject to its regulations, "exceptions to arbitration awards." A booklet titled "The Arbitration Process," [5] issued by the Department of the Navy, gives the following interpretation of Section 4 as it applies to the finality of the arbitrator's award: "Thus where the parties negotiate a procedure that calls for arbitration, the arbitrator's decision must be accepted by the parties. Challenges to any award should be sustained only on grounds similar to those applied by the courts in private sector labor–management relations, and procedures for the consideration of exceptions on such grounds must be developed by the Federal Labor Relations Council." (Generally, in the private sector, an award can be modified or set aside only if it can be established that there was fraud or misconduct, or that the abritrator clearly exceeded his authority, or that the award is contrary to law or other controlling regulations.)

Section 19 of the amended order deals with unfair labor practices. It specifies practices that are prohibited by an agency management and a labor organization. In general they are the same as those prohibited in the private sector. The procedures in cases involving unfair labor practices are set forth in the accompanying flow chart.

Regarding election practices, the following are the basic principles that the Assistant Secretary of Labor for Labor–Management Relations has adopted for judging pre-election campaigns, election-day activities, and post-election objections under Executive Order 11491:

— Where it wouldn't interfere with production, campaigning by employees on their own time in nonwork areas may not be proscribed.
— No less rigorous standards for conduct of elections should obtain in the Federal sector that in the private sector.
— Mere deviation from the rules, without more, doesn't sustain the burden of proof necessary to set aside the election.
— Nondiscriminatory application of reasonable ground rules doesn't warrant a rerun, either—even though such application may adversely have affected one of the contestants.

Basic Procedures in Cases Involving Unfair Labor Practices Under Executive Order 11491, as Amended.

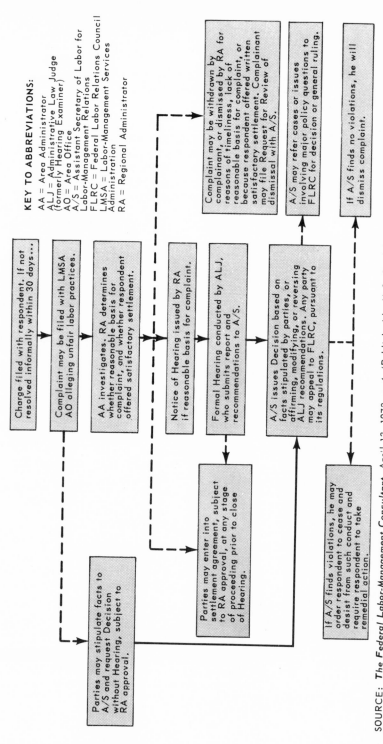

KEY TO ABBREVIATIONS:

AA = Area Administrator
ALJ = Administrative Law Judge
(formerly Hearing Examiner)
AO = Area Office
A/S = Assistant Secretary of Labor for
Labor-Management Relations
FLRC = Federal Labor Relations Council
LMSA = Labor-Management Services
Administration
RA = Regional Administrator

Charge filed with respondent. If not resolved informally within 30 days...

Complaint may be filed with LMSA AO alleging unfair labor practices.

AA investigates, RA determines whether reasonable basis for complaint, and whether respondent offered satisfactory settlement.

Notice of Hearing issued by RA if reasonable basis for complaint.

Formal Hearing conducted by ALJ, who submits report and recommendations to A/S.

A/S issues Decision based on facts stipulated by parties, or affirming, modifying, or reversing ALJ recommendations. Any party may appeal to FLRC, pursuant to its regulations.

Complaint may be withdrawn by complainant, or dismissed by RA for reasons of timeliness, lack of reasonable basis for complaint, or because respondent offered written satisfactory settlement. Complainant may file Request for Review of dismissal with A/S.

A/S may refer major cases or issues involving major policy questions to FLRC for decision or general ruling.

If A/S finds no violations, he will dismiss complaint.

Parties may stipulate facts to A/S and request Decision without Hearing, subject to RA approval.

Parties may enter into settlement agreement, subject to RA approval, at any stage of proceeding prior to close of Hearing.

If A/S finds violations, he may order respondent to cease and desist from such conduct and require respondent to take remedial action.

SOURCE: *The Federal Labor-Management Consultant*, April 13, 1973, p. 4. (Published by U.S. Civil Service Commission, Office of Labor-Management Relations, Washington, D.C.)

— Absent evidence they constitute independent violations of the Order, the Assistant Secretary won't interpret or police side agreements—e.g., on ground rules.*

In order to prepare agency managers to operate under E.O. 11491 as amended, the U.S. Civil Service Commission, the Department of Defense, and other agencies have sponsored conferences on labor–management relations, contract administration, handling grievances, and arbitration. In addition, numerous pamphlets have been published.[6]

Having personally conducted many of these conferences, I am of the opinion that there is a real need for them. It will be some time before agency managers and supervisors can operate effectively under the new policies and procedures.

Looking Ahead

Executive Order 11491 as amended will no doubt be modified. Some feel that future changes should not include private sector practices. Robert E. Hampton said:

I have heard and read a number of comments concerning its similarities to and differences from private sector practices. Some say it has moved too far in the private sector direction and that we have failed to see the significant difference in the public sector; others say it has not moved far enough, that essential elements of collective bargaining such as the right to strike, union security, and full scope of bargaining are missing. The truth is that in our best judgment Federal experience does not warrant an approach identical with that of private industry. The changes from Executive Order 10988 reflect an updating of the program to deal with the special problems and experiences in the Federal system. While many matters dealing with court structure, recognition, and union rights and responsibilities are common to both public and private sectors—and are so reflected in the order—many other matters, particularly in the negotiating process, are not the same and require an approach tailored to Federal needs and experiences.[7]

Differences Between Executive Orders 10988 and 11491

Executive Order 11491 made many changes in and additions to E.O. 10988. By reviewing these changes, the trend of labor–management relations in the federal sector can be clearly discerned.

In the list below, so that there will be no confusion with regard to the resolutions in effect now and those they supersede, reference to sections of

* This summary is from the November 10, 1972, issue of *The Federal Labor-Management Consultant*. This publication, issued biweekly by the U.S. Civil Service Commission, Office of Labor-Management Relations, is an excellent source of information concerning policy, practices, procedures, and arbitration awards relating to Executive Order 11491 as amended.

Executive Order 11491 will be followed by the provisions of Executive Order 10988.

SECTION 1(A): POLICY. This corresponds to the same section of E.O. 10988. The right to join or not to join labor organizations is protected under both E.O. 10988 and E.O. 11491.

SECTION 4: FEDERAL LABOR RELATIONS COUNCIL. This corresponds to Sec. 12 of E.O. 10988. According to Civil Service Commission (CSC) interpretations, Sec. 12 of E.O. 10988 states that "Each agency [is] responsible for observing and enforcing the Order, the Standards and the Code in its own operations, with guidance, technical advice, and training assistance by [the] Civil Service Commission."

The new order ends the decentralized and varying interpretations of the executive order by instituting a Council to administer and interpret the order instead of leaving such authority in the hands of the many agencies. The change, as again noted by the CSC, is that E.O. 11491 "Sets up [a] top-level interagency committee as [a] central authority to oversee [the] program, settle policy issues, and act as [a] final appeals body on labor management disputs except negotiation impasses on substantive issues."

SECTION 5: FEDERAL SERVICE IMPASSES PANEL. This section corresponds to clauses 6(b) and 8(b) of E.O. 10988. Clause 6(b) is concerned with the rights and duties of a labor organization as an exclusive representative, especially with its right to negotiate with management. One of these rights is the authority to help determine "appropriate techniques" to assist in negotiations, including settling impasses. Clause 8(b) limits the extent of these techniques. This section concludes that the settlement procedure or arbitration "shall extend only to the interpretation or application of agreements or agency policy. . . ."

In establishing the Federal Service Impasses Panel, the new order formed a Panel (nonexistent in E.O. 10988) to assist the parties in resolving impasses. The Panel is also given authority expressly denied in E.O. 10988.

SECTION 11: NEGOTIATION OF AGREEMENTS. Clauses 11(a) and (b) of E.O. 11491 roughly correspond to clause 6(b) of E.O. 10988. Clause 11(a) states the rights and duties of a labor organization that has been given exclusive recognition with respect to its members and negotiations. The only difference between clause 11(a) of E.O. 11491 and clause 6(b) of E.O. 10988 is that 11(a) includes the provision that both parties must negotiate in good faith. It also clarifies the framework of law and policy within which negotiation takes place.

Clause 11(b) refers to the items that are not negotiable. There are two minor changes from E.O. 10988. First, clause 11(b) increases the clarification and enumeration of exclusions from the scope of negotiations. The second minor change is the addition of "internal security practices" as an exclusion.

The basic difference between Sec. 11 of E.O. 11491 and clause 6(b) of 10988 is clause 11(c). This clause, as interpreted by the CSC, is a change from E.O. 10988 because it adds rules for settling disputes on negotiability issues and includes the right of appeal to the council on issues involving law, regulations of authorities outside the agency, or the order. Executive Order 10988 is silent on the subject of dispute settlement (and procedures) on negotiability issues.

SECTION 12: BASIC PROVISIONS OF AGREEMENTS. This section is roughly equivalent to Sec. 7 of E.O. 10988. It refers to the requirements placed on federal agencies and labor organizations in making agreements.

Clause 12(a) is similar to Sec. 7 in that agreement provisions are subject to future laws, regulations, and Federal Personnel Manual Rules. The addition in 12(a) not contained in Sec. 7 of E.O. 10988 is that an agreement is subject only to agency policies and regulations "in existence at the time the agreement was approved. . . ." This prevents future problems in interpreting laws concerned with shifts in government policy or new laws (as evidenced with the change from E.O. 10988 to 11491) because it "adds [a] policy to protect an agreement during its term, from [the] effect of change in agency regulations unless the change is required by outside authority."

Clause 12(b), which along with clause 11(b) delineates most managerial prerogatives, did not add or delete anything from Sec. 7 of E.O. 10988.

The most important addition to Sec. 12 is clause 12(c), which introduces a provision not included in E.O. 10988. By preventing the inclusion of clauses requiring an employee to join or remain in a union, or requiring him to pay dues, this clause prohibits agreements from providing for union or agency shops, or for maintenance of membership.

SECTION 13: GRIEVANCE PROCEDURE. This section corresponds to clause 8(a) of E.O. 10988. Both clauses concur on the right of negotiated agreements to contain provisions for consideration of grievances. Both also agree that these provisions shall apply only to employees in the Unit and that they shall conform to standards set by the Civil Service Commission. The basic change is that Sec. 13 of E.O. 11491 "permits elimination of dual 'agency system' and 'negotiated system' for resolving employee grievances." This refers to subclause 8(a)(2) of E.O. 10988, which states that an employee is not limited to the grievance procedure included in the agreement, and that he may utilize any procedure or action that would be open to him in the absence of any such grievance procedure. Section 13 of E.O. 11491 nullifies this policy by making any negotiated procedure the exclusive procedure available to employees.

SECTION 17: NEGOTIATION IMPASSES. This section, which has no counterpart in E.O. 10988, delineates the authority vested in the Panel. This section allows either party to request the services of the Panel in resolving negotiation impasses when voluntary procedures, the services of the Federal Mediation and Conciliation Service, and/or other third-party mediation fails to do so. Under these circumstances, the Panel has two avenues open to it. The Panel can recommend procedures for resolving the dispute or it may settle the impasse by "appropriate action." This action may include arbitration or third-party fact finding with recommendations.

REFERENCES

1. Ann Holland, "Unions Are Here to Stay." *Society for Personnel Administration, Pamphlet No. 17,* February 1962, p. 2.
2. *Ibid,* p. 3.
3. W. V. Gill, "A New Start in Federal Labor Relations." *Civil Service Journal* (January–March 1970).
4. Robert E. Hampton, "The ABC's of E.O. 11491." *Civil Service Journal* (April–June 1970).
5. "The Arbitration Process." Office of Civilian Manpower Management, Department of the Navy, Labor and Employee Relations Division, NAVSOP 3089, October 1969.
6. Typical of these publications is one entitled "The Supervisor's Guide to Labor Relations in the Federal Government," 4th edition. Washington, D.C.: U.S. Civil Service Commission, Bureau of Training, Labor Relations Training Center, February 1972.
7. Robert E. Hampton, *op. cit.*

16

NEW DEVELOPMENTS
IN ARBITRATION

The success of voluntary impartial arbitration as a means of resolving grievances in unionized plants has generated interest in this process as a means of settling a variety of conflict situations. In addition to being utilized to resolve grievances in some non-unionized plants, arbitration is being used to resolve social conflicts such as complaints by inmates of a correctional institution in Boston.

Grievance-arbitration procedures have been adopted by colleges and universities where faculties have been organized, and a small but growing number of non-unionized colleges and universities have taken the first step toward arbitration by establishing grievance procedures.

An important development has been the adoption by the Roman Catholic Church of mediation and arbitration procedures to resolve dispute's involving bishops, priests, and teachers in Catholic schools.

Arbitration in the Roman Catholic Church

In the spirit of the Second Vatican Council and responding to a demand for more democratic procedures in establishing policy and a method of resolving personnel problems, a national conference of Roman Catholic bishops in 1969 adopted the following resolution:

Therefore, BE IT RESOLVED, that the National Conference of Catholic Bishops, properly aware of the urgency of the problem recommends to its members experimentation with procedures such as are outlined in the Agenda Report on what is called Due Process, adapted where necessary to local circumstances, and to the prompt implementation on the diocesan, provincial and regional levels of this and other well-conceived plans which may become advisable for that secure protection of human rights and freedoms which should always be among the goals of the church.[1]

The reasons for this action are contained in the remarks made by Father Robert Kennedy, President of the Canon Law Society of America and former chairman of its Due Process Committee at its 1967 Conference, who said:

We have already indicated our belief that it is in the field of administrative action that conflict is most often spawned today. This is due, we believe, to the immense amount of unstructured and uncontrolled discretionary power exercised by administrative authorities. Where the exercise of discretion is unlimited and unchecked there exist manifold opportunities for widespread supposition on the part of those adversely affected by administrative decisions that the actions were arbitrary and unjust. The greatest promise for minimizing conflicts in the Church and for easing tension lies in eliminating unnecessary discretionary powers where it exists and in limiting and controlling necessary discretionary power which must exist in any kind of governmental system.[1]

The committee recommended that the following steps be taken to eliminate the causes of conflict. (For the complete report on arbitration procedure, see Appendix VI,2.)

1. The power of administrative bodies and administrators should be carefully defined and limited to avoid overlapping. This will tend to avoid "one of the great causes of unrest . . . lack of knowledge as to who made a particular decision. . . . Not only is it difficult, and at times impossible to pin down who made a particular decision, but competence of administrative bodies often is seen to overlap without any clear delineation."

2. Administrative bodies and administrators should publish written policies and standards. "It is crucial to the minimization of disputes that there be known what standards and what criteria will be used by particular administrators or administrative bodies in reaching decisions in individual cases. . . . It permits intelligent review of a particular administrative action."

3. The people who will be affected by policies should be encouraged to participate in the formulation of those policies. "It also would insure greater acceptability of policies by people who would realize that they did have the opportunities to contribute to the formulation of policy."

4. Administrative decisions in individual cases should be accompanied by clearly stated finding of fact and supporting reasons. "Few things, I think, spawn unrest and cater to the human fear of the unknown as much as administrative decisions secretly made, isolated from criticism, unsupported by findings of fact, unexplained by reasoned opinions and free from any requirement that they be related to past precedents."

5. Not only should decision-making procedures on all levels in a diocese be fair, but also they should be recognized as fair. "The People of God need to know that a bishop or a pastor or other diocesan authority hears before he acts, that there has been a fair hearing, a process due the dignity of Christian persons, and that whatever action is taken is consequent upon such a process." In accordance with this principle, then, when any administrative action affects a person adversely, he is notified of the action before it takes place, and the information used in reaching an administrative decision should be made known to the parties concerned.

6. Conciliation, arbitration, and adjudication should be applicable to disputes arising out of the exercise of administrative authority on all levels. The Code itself does not extend its provisions to such disputes. According to the Code, disputes arising out of administrative action are resolved administratively. Recourse for one aggrieved by administrative action is by way of appeal to the next highest echelon of administrative authority. "The experience of the last fifty years has taught us that the largest area of conflict in the Church arises out of the exercise of administrative authority and that merely administrative avenues of recourse for the resolution of such disputes are not effective."

The committee suggested a threefold structure for the resolution of disputes:

(a) The first aspect of the threefold structure is conciliation. It is the heart of conciliation that two disputants agree to engage the service of a third person or persons who will seek to bring them to agreement. The conciliator or mediator makes no decision.

(b) The second aspect of the proposed structure for resolving disputes is arbitration. Arbitration differs from conciliation, . . . in that it entails decision making by the intervening third party or parties. The disputants agree to submit their dispute for decision by an arbitrator or arbitrators and to be bound by the decision so made.

(c) The third aspect of the proposed structure for resolving disputes in the Church is a suggestion that a judicial process be used on rare occasions. This process could develop a . . . body of precedents . . . regarding human and ecclesiastical rights of persons in the Church.

．　　．　　．

The availability of a judicial process would also seem advisable for the resolution of disputes in the Church where one or the other party is unwilling to conciliate or submit to arbitration.

The report of the Canon Law Society to the National Conference of Catholic Bishops on the subject of due process contained specific recommendations regarding structures, processes, and procedures.With regard to the process of conciliation the report states that

. . . the following elements are essential to any process for conciliation:

1. Each participant must have the opportunity of a face-to-face dialogue with the person with whom he is in conflict. To be treated as a human person is to be given not only a hearing, but a response. There is no substitute for the dialogue of persons.

2. Unmediated dialogue may become debate; each participant, therefore, must have the opportunity of stating his side of the conflict to a conciliator who will attempt to lead the participants to be reconciled with one another. The conciliator should be informed of the facts and feelings of each participant so that he may understand what each participant believes to be "the real reason" for the dispute.

3. Dialogue and mediation will fail if either side is convinced that abstract principles such as "the right of conscience" or "the rights of authority" be vindicated at any cost. There are few imperatives of conscience that make only

one course of action mandatory, and few rights or authority which can be asserted in only one specific way.

4. Delay and concealment of relevant information have no place in a process of conciliation. Wounds should be healed quickly. Persons should not be left in suspense about their status for protracted periods. The candor of brothers, not the paternalistic assumption that the truth cannot be borne, must characterize exchange designed to heal.

5. The obligation rests with each person in authority or guided by authority to teach by his example that he belongs to a religion whose essence is love.

The report states that since all controversies cannot be settled by the process of conciliation "there should be established a Process for Arbitration. . . . In referring a matter to arbitration, parties are presumed to have explored every avenue of negotiation and settlement. It is as a last resort that they call upon impartial persons for a definitive decision and agree to abide by the result."

The report emphasizes the importance of observing the time allocation to each step of arbitration so that injustices will not be prolonged or compounded. It also gives guidelines pertaining to the requisites of an arbitrator and of the composition of an arbitration panel: "The principle of impartiality would indicate a panel of arbitrators should be selected on a broader basis than the merely diocesan. A regional panel of arbitrators would be highly desirable."

It is significant that the report recommends that the Bishop establish by law the Office of Arbitration and then "enter into a contract with the priests of the diocese in which he, as well as they, agree to submit to arbitration any controversy that may arise among them in the diocese." The following sample agreement is recommended:

We, the bishops and priests of the diocese of ———, recognizing the value of a process of arbitration commensurate with the needs of our times and the expectation of our people, vote for the establishment of an Office of Arbitration in this diocese, and agree to submit to arbitration, in accordance with the rules and procedures of such Office, any and all controversies arising among all in the diocese.

The report also gives the following sample of a submission agreement for each individual dispute:

We, the undersigned parties, hereby agree to submit to arbitration under the rules of the Office of Arbitration, the following controversy: (cite briefly). We further agree that the above controversy be submitted to (1), (3) arbitrators, selected from the panel of arbitrators submitted by the Office of Arbitration. We further agree that we will faithfully observe this agreement and the rules, and that we will abide by and perform any award rendered by the arbitrators.

The report sets forth in detail the recommended structures and procedures for both conciliation and arbitration. Because they are applicable with little modification to organizations other than the Church, such as colleges and universities, they are quoted in full in Appendix VI.

Grievance and Arbitration Procedures in Non-Union Plants

Almost all collective bargaining agreements provide for grievance procedures terminating in arbitration, but very few non-union companies have such procedures. There appears, however, to be a trend toward providing some type of grievance procedure for non-unionized employees. Unfortunately, no formalized study of this subject has been made. My opinions are based on informal conversations with executives of non-unionized plants.

In order to obtain some information on the subject, I made an informal survey of thirty-four companies who stated that they had grievance procedures. The breakdown was as follows:

— Seven companies had informal open-door policies.
— Four companies included a policy statement in their employee handbooks, which allowed employees to present their individual complaints (to in-line levels of supervision) up to the General Manager.
— Eighteen companies had formalized grievance procedures which went through a number of defined steps prior to being presented to the General Manager for final resolution.
— Five companies had grievance procedures which ended in binding third-party arbitration.

Companies included in this sampling were, among others, TWA, Northrup Corporation, Ohio Power & Light Co., Kodak, General Mills, Perkin Elmer and Harris Intertype.

INFORMAL OPEN-DOOR POLICIES. A typical "open door" policy statement contained in one company handbook states:

All problems should be taken up initially with the employee's immediate supervisor. Most of the problems will be settled at this point to the satisfaction of the employee. There may be times, however, when the nature of the problem is such that the supervisor may not be able to give an immediate answer. In those instances where the immediate supervisor is unable to satisfactorily solve the problem within two (2) working days following the date of presentation by the employee, the employee may review the problem with his departmental manager or superintendent. In situations where, after having discussed his problem with this immediate supervisor and departmental manager or superintendent, an employee still has questions, he may take the problem to the Personnel Manager for disposition.

SEMIFORMAL GRIEVANCE PROCEDURES. A typical simplified grievance procedure might read as follows:

If something goes wrong or if you feel you have been mistreated or if you have a personal problem for which you need help, first talk it over with your supervisor. It is our sincere desire that all employees are treated with respect, consideration, and fairness in their day-to-day work relationship. Therefore, if a problem should occur, it is to everyone's benefit to assure a fair and prompt solution.

If you have a complaint or problem and want help, here are the steps you may take:

1. See your immediate supervisor and talk the matter over with him as soon as possible. It is part of his responsibility to help you and correct situations that are not right. Generally, your problem can be solved by the two of you to your mutual satisfaction.

2. If you and your immediate supervisor do not reach a solution, you may ask for an appointment to see the department head and talk the problem over with him. Your immediate supervisor will arrange this appointment without prejudice to you—this, too, is part of his responsibility.

3. If you still feel that you have not been given a fair and helpful answer and your problem is not resolved by your immediate supervisor or department head, you should ask for an appointment with the Employee Relations Manager.

4. If the Employee Relations Manager is unable to give you an answer that resolves your problem, he will be happy to get you an appointment with the General Manager, who will give a fair and just answer to your problem after reviewing the facts.

If you follow these steps, no one may criticize you, penalize you, or discriminate against you in any way. If you have a very personal problem that you wish to discuss with the Employee Relations Manager or any member of management, just tell your immediate supervisor of this fact and he will get you an appointment.

FORMALIZED GRIEVANCE PROCEDURES. Among the most typical non-unionized grievance procedures is the following example (titled "Action Review for Salaried Employees"):

POLICY

It is our policy to provide a pleasant working environment for all employees. This is achieved by developing and maintaining cooperative working relationships among employees based on mutual respect and understanding. We recognize the need for a procedure which will allow employees to call attention to work-related matters which are troubling them and which they feel need correction. The following procedure may be used for resolving such work-related problems.

PROCEDURE

A grievance is defined as an alleged violation by the company of its established policies and/or practices with respect to wages, hours, or conditions of work, or where an employee claims that the company has shown discrimination among employees in the application of its policies and/or practices.

It is the employee's right to make his grievances known. Any employee, in any position, who feels that he has a just grievance is encouraged to make use of the following procedure with the guarantee that in so doing he will in no way place his standing or job in jeopardy. If the basis of his complaint is found valid, immediate steps will be taken to correct the matter.

The Employee Relations Specialist is available upon request by the employee to assist in preparation and presentation of grievances at any step. The employee should be advised of this service.

Step 1—Immediate Supervisor
A. The employee normally is expected to present his grievance to his imme-

diate supervisor either verbally or in writing, but must do so within three (3) working days of the alleged violation.

B. In unusual cases where the grievance is of a personal nature, the employee may discuss it with the Employee Relations Specialist. The Employee Relations Specialist will then arrange a meeting between the employee and his supervisor which the Employee Relations Specialist will attend if the employee so requests.

C. The immediate supervisor will, within three (3) working days, give the employee an answer (in writing, if the employee so requests).

To retain flexibility and to reduce the number of formal steps in this procedure the immediate supervisor should confer with all appropriate line management below the level of Department Head where it is deemed necessary. The answer given to the employee will then represent the combined opinion of the section head, foreman, assistant foreman, etc.

Step 2—Department Head

A. If the grievance is not solved in Step 1 above, the employee may, within three (3) working days, reduce his grievance to writing. Grievance forms may be obtained from the immediate supervisor or the office of the Employee Relations Specialist.

B. The immediate supervisor will add his answer to the written grievance and immediately submit it to the Department Head.

C. The Department Head will, within three (3) working days, meet with the employee.

All levels of supervision involved in the Step 1 answer shall initial the written grievance before it is sent to the Department Head.

The Employee Relations Specialist shall be notified by the immediate supervisor of any grievance reduced to writing for Step 2 consideration.

The Department Head will discuss the grievance with the immediate supervisor and other appropriate supervision before meeting with the employee and may call the immediate supervisor into the meeting to clear up any conflicting information given by the employee during the meeting.

Step 3—General Management Review

A. If the grievance is not resolved in Step 2 above, it may be referred to the Director of Personnel who will, within five (5) working days, establish a date for a meeting with the General Manager and the employee. The meeting will be arranged at the earliest possible time convenient to all parties concerned.

The Department Head shall refer the grievance to the Director of Personnel in all cases requiring Step 3 consideration. The Director of Personnel shall contact the employee to orient him to his Step 3 session with the General Manager.

The General Manager will discuss the grievance with the immediate supervisor and other appropriate supervision before meeting with the employee and may call the immediate supervisor into the meeting to clear up any conflicting information given by the employee during the meeting.

B. After hearing the facts presented by the parties the General Manager will, within five (5) working days, render his decision in writing.

The General Manager's decision will be presented to the employee through the employee's immediate supervisor.

If an employee wishes to express his opinion concerning policies, practices, or rules concerning wages, hours, or conditions of work, he should be encouraged to do so. Although this expression of opinion is not a grievance as such, the employee has the opportunity to express himself to his supervisor, manager, department head, personnel director, and the General Manager. When an employee expresses a desire to present his opinions to Management, contact the Employee Relations Department who will then make the appropriate arrangements.

FORMALIZED ARBITRATION PROCEDURES. Those companies which included binding arbitration by a third party as the final step had formal, sophisticated grievance procedures generally similar to the procedures stipulated in most union contracts.

According to Harry R. Gudenberg, director of labor relations at ITT, an effective grievance procedure for the non-union work force should contain the following features[2]:

— Three to five steps of appeal, depending upon the size of the organization, should be provided. Three steps usually will be enough.
— A written account of the grievance should be made if it goes past the first level. This facilitates communication and defines the issues.
— Alternate routes of appeal should be open so that the employee can bypass his supervisor if he so desires. (The personnel department may be the most logical alternate route.)
— A time limit should be fixed for each step of the appeal so that the employee has some idea of when to expect an answer.
— The system should have the support of all levels of management.
— The employee must have the right to ask one or two co-workers to accompany him. This "safety in numbers" approach helps to overcome fear of reprisal.
— If the employee has a justified grievance, the condition which brought about the grievance should be corrected. The system must function on the basis of good will, equity, and integrity if it is to gain the respect of employees and supervisors.
— Both management and the employee must have the right to appeal ultimately to a corporate ombudsman, as an impartial neutral within the family circle, or to an outside impartial arbitrator.

Expedited Arbitration in the Steel Industry

The steel industry has long utilized arbitration to resolve grievances. However, because of problems confronting the parties in processing grievances, which resulted in a large backlog of cases, member companies of the Union and Industry Coordinating Committee suggested that a joint study committee be appointed to make an in-depth study of all phases of the grievance–arbitration systems. The Joint Study Committee started its work on January 12, 1971. It surveyed (by means of questionnaires and visitations) steel plants in 13 locations in 18 districts and 7 states. It also had special meetings with the five permanent arbitrators: David Cole, Inland Steel; Louis Crane, Jones & Laughlin Steel; Silvester Garrett, U.S. Steel; Bert Lusken, Republic Steel; and Ralph Seward, Bethlehem Steel. The Committee's report contained many suggestions for improving the grievance–

arbitration machinery. These included delegating responsibility and authority to front-line participants for the investigation, reviews, screening, and resolution of everyday types of grievances; the preferential treatment of discharge cases by filing a grievance directly into Step 3 (General Management Review); and modification of grievance procedures to expedite processing.

According to Lawrence E. Pope, associate professor of law at the University of Akron School of Law, who serves as one of the arbitrators:[2]

Under the system of expedited arbitration, cases which cannot be resolved by negotiation in the lower steps of the grievance machinery will be sent in one of two directions at the option of the parties. If both parties agree, grievances may be sent to "expedited arbitration" instead of the more formal regular arbitration. The main features of the new system are designed to emphasize speed, informality, and lower expense. Legal counsel is not permitted, stenographic transcripts are not taken, and decisions of the arbitrator will not serve as precedent in the industry. Because of the lack of counsel, the arbitrator is charged with the responsibility of insuring that an adequate record is built. Once the hearing has been held, the decision must be rendered within 48 hours. Such decisions will be considered binding on all parties as in any arbitration case.

There are seven panels of arbitrators corresponding to the geographical location of the steel industry in the United States. The new arbitrators are legally trained, but they do not necessarily have previous arbitration experience. Each panel contains approximately thirty members who will be selected at random as cases arise.

It is anticipated that should the new system work, many cases which might otherwise be sent to formal arbitration will be transferred to expedited arbitration. Cases of major importance will continue to be directed to formal arbitration.

The expedited arbitration system is in its infancy, but if it operates satisfactorily, it will enable the steel industry to reduce its backlog of grievances by resolving many small claims short of the more expensive, formal arbitration step.

American Arbitration Association: New Procedures

The American Arbitration Association has been a leader in the development of more effective arbitral procedures. It has recently established the Expedited Labor Arbitration Tribunal, which commenced operations on April 7, 1972. Under these new procedures, cases are scheduled for a hearing no later than approximately two weeks following submission. Hearings are scheduled on Fridays of each week and awards are rendered within one week after completion of the hearing. (See Appendix II,2 for rules.)

The announced procedures are as follows:

1. Cases may be submitted by mutual agreement of the parties in a manner prescribed by the AAA, or in accordance with an arbitration clause in a collective bargaining agreement which provides for the Expedited Labor Arbitration Tribunal.
2. The Arbitrator will be designated and appointed by the Association from a

Standing Panel of Arbitrators whose names and qualifications are attached. Each Panel Member has been carefully screened for ability, impartiality and integrity.

3. The parties will not file briefs or employ a stenographic record.

4. The Arbitrator will render an Award not later than five calendar days from the conclusion of the hearing.

5. Preparation of an Opinion shall be discretionary with the Arbitrator and the Association.

6. Total cost to each party will be $100 for a half-day of hearing, and $200 for a full day, which will include AAA costs and Arbitrator's fees.

7. Eric J. Schmertz, the 1972 occupant of the J. Noble Braden Chair of Labor Arbitration of the American Arbitration Association, will monitor the operation of the Expedited Program. The work of the panelists, which in all instances will be their own, will be subject to continuing review by the Association and Mr. Schmertz.

The American Arbitration Association's National Center for Dispute Settlement, which handles disputes involving community relations in co-operation with the Massachusetts Correctional Administration, has designed a grievance procedure for inmates of correctional institutions. Under this procedure Albert J. Hoban, a labor arbitrator on the AAA national panel, resolved a dispute between inmates of the Massachusetts Correctional Institution at Concord and the administrators of the prison. The issue was whether, in view of thefts of personal property such as radios, TV sets, and stereo equipment (which inmates are allowed to keep), inmates should be issued keys and be permitted to lock their doors while out of the cells.

Inmates had been permitted key privileges until November 1972, when a major disturbance took place. Key privileges were then withdrawn and cells were left open, but thefts greatly increased. As chairman of a tripartite panel which included an inmate representative and the warden of another institution, Hoban held:

It is the decision of the Panel that the institution provide a military-size foot-locker for each room, complete with hasp, and that at least two grades of padlocks be made available for purchase by the residents through the steward's office. If money to purchase the locks becomes a problem we suggest that consideration be given to a loan fund system. . . . If the institution cannot obtain surplus military lockers through the usual channels, it would provide suitable new or used lumber and arrange for the construction of the lockers as a Jaycees project.

In the words of Robert Coulson, president of the American Arbitration Association,[2]

The American Arbitration Association wants to make simplified arbitration more available to those parties that desire it. Expedited procedures are offered throughout the country, based upon a pilot program established in New York City during the early summer of 1972. For the less important cases involving smaller parties, these simplified procedures offer an opportunity to obtain the benefits of arbitration quickly, economically and with less aggravation to the work force. It is important that such alternative methods of arbitration be available for the parties.

There is a clear difference between arbitration cases. Some involve the most vital interests between labor and management. Others concern only a few people within either organization. The arbitration process should reflect the needs of union and management representatives. Arbitration is a participatory process. It reflects the philosophy of the individual union representative and executives involved in working out the bargaining problems of the enterprise.

The best evidence that voluntary labor arbitration is working well in the private sector may be its significant introduction into public employment relationships. In recent years, Government workers have been organized on a monumental scale, first in larger urban areas. City, county and state employees have rapidly been organized into bargaining units for the purpose of collective bargaining. In addition, as a result of Executive Orders and a continuing drive for organization, Federal employees have been organized. Employees of service entities such as the Federal Reserve and the Postal System have participated in a similar movement.

Now, one sees voluntary arbitration being used in the public sector to almost the same degree as in the private sector. The fastest growing unions are clearly those in which the members are government employees. The greatest expansion of arbitration is in this sector.

In response to this growth, the American Arbitration Association now publishes two new publications: *Arbitration in the Schools* and *Labor Arbitration in Government*. These services fill a clear need for educational material, permitting new practitioners in the arbitration field to learn what developments are taking place around them in grievance arbitration.

Arbitration also is being used in the public sector to resolve contract disputes. Here, the private sector may learn from the public sector. We see renewed interest in the use of arbitration to resolve bargaining disputes in the private sector. This may be done by the parties voluntarily, by an agreement that the arbitrator's decision will be accepted for a short period, pending further negotiations. Or the parties may utilize voluntary arbitration to resolve certain residual issues, when all other issues have been settled through collective bargaining. In any case, one can anticipate an increased use of voluntary arbitration for bargaining issues. Many practitioners would welcome such a development: the social cost of strikes has become considerable in recent years.

Almost everybody rejects the concept of compulsory arbitration of collective bargaining impasses, particularly in the private sector. But many management and labor leaders are encouraging the increased use of voluntary arbitration, to obtain a rational resolution of bargaining impasses. The climate may be particularly ripe for this when a governmental wage control policy is in effect, when parties are not in a position to exercise the full range of their power in the bargaining process.

The major use of arbitration will probably continue to be in the resolution of grievances under the collective bargaining agreements in the public sector. In addition, collective bargaining is creeping into other units in society. Professionals, employees of non-profit service organizations and even executives are being organized into bargaining units. Here, arbitration should be particularly useful. It is relatively simple to resolve disputes between individuals and institutions. It also provides an appropriate tribunal for handling the most complicated policy questions that may arise between a bargaining organization and the institution which it confronts. Arbitration makes it possible to resolve disputes on a rational basis, whether those disputes involve the fears and insecurities of individual employees, or whether they involve policy issues going to the very heart of the purpose of the enterprise. By carefully selecting an arbitrator to hear and determine the case, it is possible to obtain a high degree of expertise in almost any field.

Here again, the American Arbitration Association serves as a resource for information on how arbitration can best be used to resolve a variety of disputes. By arbitration, I do not intend to limit consideration to traditional, formal arbitration proceedings. Other forms of impartial dispute settlement are also available, including fact-finding, mediation, advisory arbitration and various forms of election or consensus dispute settlement. Here, the AAA and its National Center for Dispute Settlement are an important national resource, available to all parties for help in designing and administering dispute settlement systems.

Disputes are best resolved by systems in which the parties themselves participate, both in designing the tribunal, presenting the case and selecting the impartial arbitrator who works with them and for them in reaching a decision or resolution of the matter. The flexibility of the process is greatly enhanced by the fact that it is designed and utilized by the parties themselves. An administrative agency such as the American Arbitration Association serves the parties by providing a smorgasbord of arbitration rules and procedures under which they can select an appropriate system for their own use. There is a choice of systems. There is also a wide choice of impartial arbitrators, each one provided with unique experiences and training. In voluntary arbitration, there is great emphasis upon the mutual choice of the individual arbitrator, making it possible for the parties to accommodate their own requirements to a decision maker best qualified to reach an informed, impartial decision on the case.

In conclusion, one can forecast an increased use of arbitration in the public sector, in areas of employment where previously collective bargaining has not been known, and into new substantive issues where representative groups are demanding new rights to participate in the policy-making apparatus of the employer. With this expansion will come new challenges both upon the individual arbitrators and upon the administrative agencies that work with them. But the major challenge will be upon the parties themselves, to design and adopt rational systems of dispute settlement for new kinds of conflict.

REFERENCES

1. *On Due Process.* National Conference of Catholic Bishops, 1969.
2. I wish to thank Harry Gudenberg for his statement on non-union grievance procedures; and Lawrence Pope and Robert Coulson for their respective statements on expedited arbitration procedures.

PART TWO

Issues: Arbitration Cases

INTRODUCTION

The *issue*, the focal point of the arbitral process, presents to the arbitrator specific questions that require specific answers. The *award* made by the arbitrator is his solution to the problem presented by the issue. The analysis by the arbitrator contains the reasons why he arrived at his conclusions. It sets out guideposts by which management and labor can resolve day-to-day problems.

As a result of studying these issues and analyses, collective bargaining agreements are more carefully drawn and contractual obligations are more clearly defined and understood. Collectively, the analyses and awards of arbitrators constitute a new body of industrial jurisprudence out of which are emerging principles of law that are affecting relations between management and labor.

In order to understand labor–management problems in terms of specific situations, not generalities, and to comprehend the manifold factors involved in their solution, it is essential that these opinions be read. Part II of this book has therefore been devoted to some of the more important issues in arbitration and to the opinions of arbitrators on these issues.

In a short introduction to the major issues, the various problems that arise in these disputes between management and labor are pointed out. Pertinent citations to published cases are also included.

Following each introductory statement are significant illustrative cases that will enable the reader to gain a better insight into the entire arbitral process. Although some of these cases are over twenty years old, the principles involved are just as applicable today.

1

DISCIPLINE AND DISCHARGE

Almost all collective bargaining agreements place limitations upon the employer's right to discipline or discharge. This is usually done in a clause that requires that any disciplinary action (including discharge) taken by an employer against an employee must be "for cause," or "for just cause," or "for proper cause."

Federal and state labor relations acts and other laws dealing with discrimination restrict management's right to discipline or discharge. They apply whether or not there is a collective agreement.

If an agreement is silent on the subject—that is, if it does not in any way expressly limit the right to discharge or discipline—does this mean that the company is free to exercise this right, subject only to the provisions of some applicable law? One board of arbitration stated: "If the Company can discharge without cause, it can lay off without cause. It can recall, transfer, or promote in violation of the seniority provisions simply by invoking its claimed right to discharge." The board continued: "To interpret the agreement in this manner would reduce to a nullity the fundamental provision of a labor–management agreement—the security of a worker in his job." [1]

Many contracts contain clauses that specifically indicate the offenses for which an employee may be discharged. The principal grounds for discharge include violation of the contract by an unauthorized strike or slowdown, incompetence of the employee, violation of company rules, unauthorized absences, fighting, insubordination, and intoxication. The fact that some grounds for discharge are spelled out in the contract does not mean that the list is exclusive or that an employee cannot be disciplined for "other cause." [2]

A number of agreements require that various preliminary steps be taken before a discharge is made final, such as notice to the employee and/or the union, and suspension pending hearing or at least further investigation into the facts. Some contracts also give the discharged employee a personal right to appeal, first through the grievance procedure and ultimately through arbitration.

[1] Atwater Mfg. Co., 13 LA 749.
[2] Spokane-Idahoe Mining Co., 9 LA 749.

231

PROGRESSIVE DISCIPLINE

Primarily as a result of arbitration awards, the doctrine of corrective or progressive discipline is now accepted industrial practice. The doctrine is based upon the concept that the purpose of discipline is to correct improper behavior patterns. Except for the more serious offenses, an employer is expected to give an employee (depending upon the nature of the offense) an oral warning, written warning, or disciplinary layoff before he is discharged. An arbitrator will not generally uphold a discharge for the first offense (except when it is serious) if the employee has many years of service and a good work record.

In a recent case a supervisor reported to the plant manager that an employee had refused to do an assigned task and had left the plant at 10.00 A.M. The plant manager called the employee at his home to obtain his side of the story. The employee explained that when his supervisor asked him to report for work in the shipping department he had objected because he had been repeatedly selected—because he was a dependable worker—to do jobs others did not want to do. He also explained that he told the supervisor he would not be able to do the new job beyond 12:00 noon because he was not feeling well, and he then walked in the direction of the new job assignment. However, a few minutes later he thought it over and told his supervisor that he would check out at the present time, which was 10:00 A.M.

The plant manager explained that since the supervisor did not mention illness as a reason for the employee's leaving the plant, he had assumed that the employee had made up this excuse to justify his actions. He thereupon notified the employee on the phone that he was being discharged. At the hearing it was established that the plant manager did not again question the supervisor with regard to the employee's claim of illness. The record also showed that the grievant had been absent only five times in four years, had no prior offenses, and had been a very good worker. It was also admitted that the few words exchanged between the employee and his supervisor were in a low tone and without anger. The arbitrator reinstated the employee.

A large percentage of cases heard by arbitrators involve the issue of discipline and discharge. Unions tend to challenge almost every discharge because it is considered "capital punishment." When a man is discharged, he not only loses his job, but he also loses his job security if he has many years of seniority. In addition, he may have difficulty in locating a new job. In one case a copywriter with a successful past record was employed to prepare a booklet describing complicated mechanical controls. He was unable to do this because he did not have an engineering background, as did the other copywriters. As a result he was discharged for the reason of "not meeting work standards." Prospective employers, not knowing the circumstances, interpreted this as incompetence, and he found it impossible to obtain employment for almost one year. During the course of the hearing the company agreed to find other employment for which he was qualified in another division of the company. He was made editor of the house organ—a job in which he was successful.

There are some cases in which employees have taken advantage of the company's attempts to correct improper work habits. Some employees take the attitude that they cannot be discharged no matter what they do.

In one unpublished case, an employee who had been repeatedly warned and given a disciplinary suspension because of his absence and lateness record was finally discharged. Some of his absences were due to his consistent failure to read posted overtime schedules. It was argued by the employee and the union that the foreman was required to personally request the grievant to work overtime and obtain the grievant's acceptance of the overtime assignment. The arbitrator held that the grievant was obligated to read the overtime schedule, which was posted several days prior to the time scheduled, and if he could not work overtime he had the responsibility of notifying his foreman. The discharge was sustained.

It is essential that companies develop fair and consistently applied personnel policies. They should also make certain that their supervisors are properly trained to deal with disciplinary problems and that investigative procedures are carefully followed so as to ascertain the facts before disciplinary action is taken. Too many decisions are based upon assumptions, a lack of essential information, or misinformation.

CASE: PROGRESSIVE DISCIPLINE
JUVENILE COURT OF CUYAHOGA COUNTY, OHIO,
AND AMERICAN FEDERATION OF STATE, COUNTY AND
MUNICIPAL EMPLOYEES, GREATER CLEVELAND DISTRICT
COUNCIL 78, LOCAL 1746, CCH 71–1, PARA. 8418.
ARBITRATOR: IPAVEC.

Issue. On June 30, 1971, a hearing was held to decide if the action of the Court was for just and proper cause when it subjected Grievant S. to a one-day disciplinary suspension.

Background. The court of Cuyahoga County, Ohio, classifies its probation officers into two categories. A Supervisory Probation Officer is required to file a white form and a green form on the first working day of each month. An Investigative Probation Officer files the white form and a yellow form. One supervisor directs all supervisory cases, and another supervisor is in charge of all investigative cases. If any probation officer has a supervisory load and an investigative case load, he falls under the jurisdiction of two administrative supervisors.

Grievant S. was in such a position. He had been assigned as a Supervisory Probation Officer, and in September 1970 he was reassigned as an Investigative Probation Officer. For this reason he gradually transferred his supervisory case load to Probation Officer P. On October 1, 1970, he filed a white form for his supervisory cases, a yellow form to report his investigative cases, and a green form. On November 3, 1970, he submitted the yellow and green forms to his Investigative Supervisor. He did not submit a white form to J., his supervisor for supervisor cases, but J. verbally requested the October white form, and on November 5, 1970, he issued to S. a written request for the white form. On November 6, 1970, S. received a notice advising him of an anticipated suspension. On November 16, 1970, S. was suspended for one day for failure to submit the October report and for failure to transfer all his cases to P. by October 16, 1970.

Union's Position. The union argued that other employees who had been late in submitting monthly reports in the past had not been disciplined, and that Grievant S. was being discriminated against because of his union membership. The grievant was burdened with a greater case load than non-union employees, and Grievant S. was being harassed for his "activities on behalf of the Union. . . ."

Company's Position. The Cuyahoga County Court contended that the one-day disciplinary suspension of S. was for "just cause" because the grievant failed to complete his report for October 1970, "even after an oral request to do so was followed by a written request the following day. . . ."

In failing to follow the established procedure, the grievant disrupted the administrative duties of Supervisory Officer J. Further, S.'s argument that he did not have any time to complete the forms was countered by the court's contention that the preparation of the white form reports did not require more than one hour.

Arbitrator's Analysis. The arbitrator raised two questions: First, was the grievant afforded due process before being given a penalty, and secondly, did the court, in imposing the penalty, act for just and proper cause? To answer these questions, the arbitrator set up five guidelines:

1. Was the rule sought to be enforced, along with the possible consequences of noncompliance, properly promulgated so that grievant was aware of what was expected and aware that discipline, in all probability, would result from disobedience?
2. Did the employer make a fair and objective investigation into the alleged wrongdoing and all circumstances attendant thereto?
3. Does the penalty withstand the test that it be "even-handed"?
4. Does the evidence support the employer's conclusion that a disciplinary offense was committed?
5. If the evidence does support the employer's conclusion, was the penalty imposed appropriate in the accepted concepts of progressive discipline and justified by the gravity of the offense?

The arbitrator agreed that reports are necessary and vital to the court administration, and that the grievant knew that all three reports were due on the first working day of each month. The grievant testified that he received the oral and written warnings.

The arbitrator concluded that the rule of submitting the white form was sought to be enforced, that S. was aware of the rule, and that "the grievant well understood that he, in all probability, would be subject to discipline if he persisted in ignoring the directive, oral and written, from Supervisor J.

The court administration did investigate the grievant's contention that he had no time in which to complete the form. The court found that he was extremely busy but needed only an hour to fill out the white form.

The arbitrator was of the opinion that "the Court Administration conducted a fair and objective investigation into grievant's reasons for not complying with the directions of supervisor J."

The arbitrator dismissed the union's allegation of an anti-union animosity by saying that whenever the union interposed a defense of discrimination for union activity it must assume the burden of proving such an allegation. No evidence was shown by the union to support the charge of discrimination. The arbitrator concluded that the court's action was even-handed.

There was no dispute over the fact that Grievant S. did not complete his October form, nor had transferred his supervisory load before October 16, 1970. Therefore, "the evidence as hereinabove set forth, does support the Court's conclusion that an offense was committed by Grievant S. for which he could be disciplined."

Before discussing the fifth guideline, the arbitrator elaborated on the concept of progressive discipline:

Within the concept of progressive discipline we find certain notions of procedural fairness. First, an employee should be given adequate notice of his deficiencies, and where such deficiencies are remedial, he should be given an opportunity to correct them. Second, an employee should be given a warning of the consequences in the event that improvement is not forthcoming. It is through the process of progressive discipline that an employee is made aware of the danger he is in. In progressive discipline, penalties are not imposed merely for the sake of punishing the wayward employee, but rather, the penalty, accompanied by a warning for failure to improve, is imposed as a corrective measure with a view to helping the employee "mend his ways."

Supervisor J. issued a written directive on October 1, 1970, and on November 5, 1970; "however, neither of these directives can be construed as reprimands." The notice received by S. on November 6 "was the first time Grievant was aware he was in danger of disciplinary action."

In addition, since no disciplinary action was instituted against S. for failing to transfer his supervisory case load by October 16, 1970, the grievant was lulled into a false sense of security and assumed that no disciplinary action would be taken as a result of his failure to comply with the directives from Supervisor J. When the grievant received notice of an anticipated suspension there was no time lapse between the penalty of reprimand and the penalty of one-day suspension. Thus, S. had no opportunity to rehabilitate himself between the time of the reprimand and the time of the one-day suspension.

The failure of S. to comply with the two directives from J. could not be condoned, but in this case "the Court's action in the written disciplinary matter was contrary to the accepted principle of progressive discipline."

Award. The arbitrator sustained the grievance and reduced the penalty to a written reprimand.

JUST CAUSE

It is one thing to say that an employee may not be discharged except for just cause, but it is quite another to define what is meant by "just cause." This is the function of the arbitrator. He must decide whether, on all the evidence presented, the employee has been discharged for just cause.

Unfortunately, no standards exist for defining "just cause." Arbitrator H. H. Platt, in discussing this problem in one of his early cases,[1] stated: "No standards exist to aid an arbitrator in finding a conclusive answer to such a question and, therefore, perhaps the best he can do is to decide what a reasonable man, mindful of the habits and customs of industrial life and the standards of justice and fair dealing prevalent in the community ought to have done under similar circumstances and in that light to decide whether the conduct of the discharged employee was defensible and the disciplinary penalty just."

Although arbitrators in individual cases apply commonly accepted industrial and community standards, through their decisions they have collectively influenced the concept of what constitutes just cause. The doctrine of corrective or progressive discipline is an illustration of the influence of the arbitral process on that concept.

Most of the cases heard to decide whether an employee has been disciplined or discharged for just cause are not simple or clear-cut. They present complex interpersonal relationships that are affected by individual personalities and attitudes and by cultural patterns, which in turn are influenced by racial, religious, and ethnic factors. These cases are also complicated by the tendency of people to listen and see selectively. This causes them to remember only that which supports their positions or decisions. Moreover, seldom are two cases alike, and each case usually involves many factors, each of which must be considered and evaluated before an arbitrator makes a determination. The following are some of these factors:

1. Degree of severity of the offense.
2. Length of service with the company.
3. Provocation, if any, that may have led to the offense.
4. The number of previous offenses.
5. The nature of the previous offenses.
6. Previous warnings or other disciplinary action for previous offenses.
7. Company rules: Are they clear? Are they reasonable? Have they been communicated by the employee?
8. Have company rules and regulations been consistently applied?
9. Past disciplinary actions for similar offenses by other employees.
10. Employee's pattern of conduct.
11. Supervisory practices.
12. Is the penalty reasonable and appropriate to the offense?

In order to determine whether a given set of circumstances constitutes "just cause" for discharge, each of the factors involved must be carefully evaluated and accorded its proper weight in the total situation. Often the alleged act that management considered "just cause" for discharge is in dispute. The employee simply denies committing the act or acts that—according to management—established the immediate cause of his discharge. The arbitrator must then decide who is telling the truth.

In the final analysis, it is the arbitrator's own sense of justice and fair play, combined with his understanding of human relations in the industrial setting, which will determine what constitutes "just cause" in a particular case.[2]

It must be recognized that many cases arise where reasonable men differ honestly on the meaning of the term "just cause." They will interpret differently the same set of facts; they will apply different value judgments in their analyses and attach different weights to the various factors. Intimate familiarity with human problems in industry, supplemented by a study of cases involving "just cause" issues already arbitrated, is probably the best way for anyone connected with the arbitral process to develop a sense of what is and what is not "just cause."

Even where the contract does not specifically include a "just cause" provision, the arbitrators are inclined to judge the case on that basis, as indicated in the following case.

CASE 1: JUST CAUSE
OAKLAND HILLS COUNTRY CLUB AND HOTEL AND
RESTAURANT EMPLOYEES AND BARTENDERS' INTERNATIONAL
UNION, LOCAL 705, CCH 71–1, PARA. 8080.
ARBITRATORS: KEEFE (CHAIRMAN), KENNY, AND WOLFGANG.

Issue. A hearing was held on December 15, 1970, at which two issues were submitted: (1) Was the grievant discharged for just cause? If not, what shall be the remedy? (2) Did the employer need to show cause for discharge of Grievant J.?

Background. On Saturday, August 8, 1970, Grievant J. was working at the Oakland Hills Country Club. He was dispensing beer and, in addition, was assigned one table on the far side of the dance floor and another table on the other side, near the beer station. Grievant J. was the only waiter assigned a split station. He complained to Head Waiter H., who told him "to do as he wanted." Having H.'s permission, J. then gave his table on the far side of the room to another waiter. When the Assistant Manager learned of the switch he informed J. that "he was going to need another job" as a result. Grievant J.'s services were needed and used the following Sunday, Wednesday, and Thursday; he was discharged after completing his shift on Thursday, August 13, 1970.

Contract Provisions. Section XIII, Section 3, states that "seniority shall terminate if an employee quits, retires, fails to report to work after a leave of absence, or . . . is discharged for violation of posted house rules. . . ."

Union's Position. The union asserted that "the House rules are completely silent on the impropriety of waiters giving up tables to coworkers." Thus, contractually there was no basis for the discharge.

Company's Position. The employer contended that, in giving up his table, Grievant J. committed a serious infraction of the rules. The club maintained that "it is basic, in the absence of written agreement to the contrary, that such an employer–employee relationship can be terminated at the option of either side. The employee may quit, or the employer may sever him, but, in either case, neither has to serve notice nor show good cause." The employer asserted that there is "utter absence" in the collective bargaining agreement of any requirement that the employer show just cause for discharge.

Arbitrators' Analysis. In deciding this case the arbitrators first assessed whether the incident was sufficient cause for discharge. They found, on the basis of the evidence, insufficient cause for the action taken. That the grievant was allowed to work through the following Thursday was inconsistent with any reasonable assessment of discipline for a dischargeable offense. They concluded that the employer had failed to prove that "the grievant gave away his table without permission of the Head Waiter."

Because of insufficient evidence, the arbitrators ruled it inconsequential whether there existed a posted rule prohibiting such table changes, inasmuch as a violation could not be sustained. However, they advised the employer to review and revise its promulgated code of required conduct.

They also rejected the employer's contention that "just cause" need not be demonstrated in disciplinary discharge. If the employer enjoyed an uncurbed right to discharge without cause, he could not only wreak grievous injury on hapless individuals but could also instantly uproot the union's right to representation. The principle of "just cause" is inescapably the foundation on which discharges must be grounded under the contract.

Award. The arbitrators sustained the grievance and ordered that Grievant J. be restored to his job with full seniority and compensated for all losses he suffered because of being denied work at the club.

CASE 2: NO "JUST CAUSE" PROVISION IN THE CONTRACT
CAMERON IRON WORKS, INC. AND INTERNATIONAL
ASSOCIATION OF MACHINISTS, 25 LA 295 (DIGESTED).
ARBITRATORS: BOLES (CHAIRMAN), PENNINGTON, AND HAMPTON.

Issue. The primary question in this case is as follows: If the collective bargaining agreement does not explicitly state that disciplinary action must be based upon "just cause," does this mean that the broad issue of "just cause" cannot be raised under the contract as drafted? A subordinate question is: If the company is late in making a reply when the contract grievance procedure fixes a definite time, does this give an automatic default judgment to the grievant?

Background. The grievant was discharged for insubordination because he used foul and threatening language to his supervisor. The case was further complicated by the union's assertion that an award should be made in the grievant's favor because the company had extended the time limit by one day in making a third-step answer as provided in contract procedure.

Contract Provisions. The agreement includes conventional grievance procedure and arbitration clauses, none of which contain a "just cause" or "proper cause" provision. The only restriction on the right of management to discharge appears in the "management rights" clause, which affirms the company's "right to hire, discipline, suspend, discharge, transfer, relieve employees from duty because of lack of work, or for other legitimate reasons," and then declares that these rights "and all other rights not herein expressly relinquished are vested exclusively in the Company." The restriction is made in the following form: "This authority (i.e., the authority to exercise the rights of management) will not be used for purposes of discrimination."

Union's Position. The union contended that the contract was silent on the specific issue of just cause but was quite specific on the prohibition of management's right to exercise its authority for purposes of discrimination. A secondary argument was the failure of the company to comply with the time limits of the grievance procedure at the third step; such failure constituted affirmation of the union's position by default.

Company's Position. With reference to the union's contention concerning the timing of management's third-step answer, the company argued that nothing in the contract provided "that failure to make timely disposition of a grievance by management at any step . . . shall constitute an automatic default judgment for the grieving employee." If the parties had intended this, they would have spelled it out clearly in the agreement.

Furthermore, said the company, its right to discharge was limited only by the proviso that such right "will not be used for purposes of discrimination," and since the union's evidence did not establish that the grievant's discharge was discriminatory, the arbitrator had no choice but to sustain the company's action. But even if the arbitrator should construe the contract language as permitting the broad issue of "just cause" to be raised, instead of the narrower question of whether the discharge was discriminatory, the union's case must fail because there *was* just cause: The grievant's insubordination justified discharge. The discharge was made only after careful investigation and it was not arbitrary, capricious, or discriminatory. Accordingly, the company concluded, the arbitrator should not substitute his judgment for that of the management.

Arbitrators' Analysis. Examining the effect of the company's delay in answering the grievance, the arbitrator denied the union's motion that an award be rendered reinstating the discharged employee on the grounds that the company was one day late in making its third-step answer. To explain his reasons for rejecting the union's position, the arbitrator said that a diligent search of reported decisions revealed only one award[3] on the point involved and that supported his own ruling.

The arbitrator quoted from two of his previous decisions. "Arbitration parties are not lightly to be deprived of awards on grounds which are too narrowly technical; the issues should be disposed of if a reasonable basis of action can be found. In other words, undue legalism can defeat the basic aims of the parties who drafted the grievance procedure." [4] And again: "The impartial arbitrator sees no evidence of a studied intent to ignore or abuse the grievance procedure time limits. . . ." [5]

Concluding his remarks on this lesser phase of the case, the arbitrator wrote: "Now the fact that in the present matter the Company went past a time limit does not in any way change the basic 'policy' principle that an arbitrator should hear a case on the merits if it is at all possible to find a valid basis on which to assert jurisdiction. In this instance there is such a basis."

Turning now to the major question of "just cause," the arbitrator's written opinion admitted that he was unable to find the words referring to "just cause" in the contract negotiated by the parties. He agreed that an arbitrator has no right to amend a contract and disavowed any intention of doing so in the case before him. Nevertheless, he felt "impelled to deal with this matter on the basis of 'just cause' considerations," and said that even though the contract is silent on the "just cause" test for disciplinary action by the company, the grievance procedure and arbitration clauses "do not expressly preclude processing of disciplinary grievances on the basis of 'just cause.' " The arbitrator quoted one of his previous decisions:

The arbitrator is fully aware that the contract between these parties does not contain the conventional just or proper clause language in connection with disciplinary matters. But certain realities must be recognized. . . . The first reality in the situation is that the arbitrator *must* consider this issue on the same basis he would use if the contract provided for discharge for just cause. Any other approach simply is not realistic in 1954 (when the great bulk of the 100,000 collective bargaining agreements contain just cause or comparable language). If parties today do not intend that arbitrators make just cause appraisals they should so indicate in their writing. . . .[6]

In other words, the arbitrator believed that a "just cause" basis for consideration of disciplinary action is, in the absence of a clear proviso to the contrary, implied in a modern collective bargaining agreement. Thus, the arbitrator rejected two basic contentions, one by the union and the other put forth by the company, both of somewhat legalistic nature. For the arbitrator, the most crucial inquiry was: Did the grievant threaten the foreman's life?

Award. After carefully considering the evidence, particularly the demeanor of the witnesses, the arbitrator found that the grievant did so threaten the foreman, and accordingly he denied the grievance.

CASE 3: NO "JUST CAUSE" PROVISION IN THE CONTRACT
HUBER, HUNT, AND NICHOLS AND INTERNATIONAL
BROTHERHOOD OF CARPENTERS AND JOURNEYMEN OF AMERICA,
LOCAL 1438, CCH 69–2, PARA. 8679. ARBITRATOR: KABAKER.

Issue. Is the discharge of union employees arbitrable when the contract is silent on the subject of discharge?

Background. On May 2, 1969, the Assistant Superintendent of the company discharged three carpenter crew members, T., L., and P. The union filed a grievance alleging that the discharge of the three men was without just cause. The company argued that the grievance was not arbitrable. The issue of arbitrability was submitted to arbitration.

Contract Provisions. The labor agreement contains no clause in relation to the matter of discharge of an employee, although Article 5 refers to discharge of a union representative: "The recognized steward on the job shall not be discharged without just cause."

Union's Position. The union argued that it is fundamental to the employer–union relationship, even though the agreement is silent, that just cause must exist for discharge. It contended that the arbitrator may imply that there can be no discharge except for just cause, since the tenure of the employer–employee relationship goes to the heart of the labor agreement itself; the right to fire for reasons without just cause would defeat the purpose of the labor agreement.

Company's Position. The position of the company was that the arbitrator did not have the right to rule on its decision to discharge the three grievants. It pointed out that the labor agreement was silent in relation to the matter of discharge of an employee, and it therefore asserted that the matter of discharges lay within the sole discretion of management. To support its position, the company pointed out that Article 3 of the agreement excludes all employees except the shop steward and that if the parties did not stipulate this clause as applicable to other employees, it indicated that no such limitation was to be imposed. The company argued that if the arbitrator were to consider whether or not just cause existed for the discharge, he would be exceeding his authority under the labor agreement, since his authority was limited to deciding matters related to the interpretation and application of the provision of the agreement.

Arbitrator's Analysis. The arbitrator found the agreement contained no "management rights" clause and no provision relating to management's right to discharge. He held, however, that basic to the employer–employee relationship is management's right to discharge where cause exists to justify discharge. Although the company has the right to discharge, the question arises whether such company action is subject to challenge by the union through the arbitral process.

The arbitrator noted that Article 6, Paragraph C, of the labor agreement provides a procedure for referring deadlocked issues to a disinterested arbitration board.

In interpreting this provision of the contract, he held: "In the case of discharge of a carpenter the 'question at issue' before the Joint Arbitration Committee is the propriety of the discharge and it is this same question which is later presented to the Board of Arbitration. Certainly the Board is authorized by Paragraph C to hear and decide that question at issue. Thus, although the contract is silent with respect to provisions of just cause for discharge of employees, just cause is considered to be an unwritten obligation."

The arbitrator also held that the fact that the agreement provides only that a "recognized steward on a job shall not be discharged without just cause" is insufficient proof that just cause is not a requirement for the discharge of other employees. A steward "might have more frequent conflicts with Management than an employee. . . . It is only natural that the Parties spell out that the recognized steward . . . shall not be discharged without just cause. . . ."

Award. The arbitrator concluded that by virtue of Article 6, Paragraph C, he was empowered to hear and decide the issue.

REFERENCES

1. Riley Stoker Corp., 7 LA 764.
2. Auto Lite Battery Corp., 3 LA 122; Ford Motor Co., 6 LA 853.
3. John Deere Tractor Co., 3 LA 737.
4. Gulf Oil Corp. v. OWIU Local No. 11 (unpublished).
5. Teamsters v. T&P Motor Transport Co. (unreported).
6. CWA-CIO and Southwestern Bell Telephone Co. (unpublished).

REASONABLENESS OF PENALTY

CASE 1: REASONABLENESS OF PENALTY
RILEY STOKER CORPORATION AND UNITED STEEL
WORKERS OF AMERICA, 7 LA 764 (DIGESTED).
ARBITRATORS: PLATT (CHAIRMAN), LAVEY, AND TREAT.

Issue. Among the basic questions considered in this case are: (1) What is "just cause" for discharge? (2) If there is not just cause for discharge, is there sufficient cause for some lesser penalty?

Background. The company had formulated plant rules and regulations, which were posted on all bulletin boards throughout the plant and incorporated in a booklet distributed to all employees. One of the rules was that three violations of company rules by an employee would "automatically" result in his discharge.

Grievant A., with almost seven years of seniority, was discharged because of a third violation of plant rules. This consisted of his using company time to drill a hole on a fishing rod belonging to another employee and in visiting with an employee in another department. There had been two earlier violations.

Contract Provisions. The union agreement under which this case arose contains a "management rights" clause, which provided in part that "the right of the management to discharge any employee for . . . failure to observe plant rules and regulations or any other justifiable cause, is vested exclusively in the Company, provided that this will not be used for the purpose of discrimination against any member of the Union."

Another clause on "discharge cases" states: "In the event that any member of the Union shall be discharged from his employment . . . and believes that he has been dealt with unjustly, then such discharge shall constitute a cause arising under the method and sequence of adjusting grievances hereinbefore provided." In the event that his grievance is substantiated, the company agrees to reinstate such employee without loss of seniority, and to pay the employee full compensation for the time lost.

Union's Position. The union denied that the grievant was guilty of any serious breaches of duty as an employee. It denied that it ever consented to the plant rules and particularly the one that "three violations will result in automatic discharge." According to the union, this rule was invalid and unenforceable in a case where discharge is not otherwise justified. Under the circumstances of this case, the union believed that a reasonable disciplinary penalty would have been a layoff of five or six days, but that the penalty of discharge was wholly unwarranted.

Company's Position. The company argued (1) that the grievant was well informed in advance of the edict that three violations of any plant rule would result in discharge; (2) that imposition of that penalty becomes automatic upon proof of three violations; (3) that the establishment and enforcement of plant rules are the exclusive prerogatives of management and therefore the arbitrators* were without power to modify the penalty; and finally, (4) that the "management rights" clause vests exclusively in the company the right to discharge as long as this is not used "for the purpose of discrimination against any member of the Union." Since no discrimination against the grievant had been proved, the discharge was just and should therefore stand without modification.

Arbitrators' Analysis. In weighing the facts of the case and reasoning through to a decision, the arbitrators found that the grievant did commit three violations of plant rules in that on three occasions he visited with other employees during working hours. On one occasion he left his work and went to the washroom eight minutes before quitting time; and finally, he used company time to enlarge a hole on a fishing rod.

The evidence did not show too clearly how much time the grievant wasted in his various forbidden activities, but the arbitrators estimated that it did not exceed one full hour. "In these circumstances," the arbitrators asked, "was the penalty of discharge . . . a reasonable one or was it too severe?"

The arbitrators did not think very much of the company's claimed right to discharge automatically any employee guilty of three rule violations. The majority drew a clear distinction between the right of management to promulgate and enforce reasonable rules of conduct necessary to efficient plant operation (they conceded this to be a "management prerogative") on the one hand, and on the other hand, the right to establish *unilaterally* a condition of employment that specified a fixed number of rule violations as an absolute cause for discharge, regardless of the seriousness of the violations or the circumstances under which they were committed.

The true intent of the parties, the arbitrators reasoned, must be determined not from a single word or phrase, but from the contract as a whole. And the meaning of a word or part must be interpreted in connection with the whole, in its relation to all other parts or provisions. Construing the contract in this light, the arbitrators came to the conclusion that what the parties had intended was to qualify the right of the company to discharge employees by requiring "sufficient cause" to exist. The final decision of whether the cause for discharge was sufficient and whether the discharged employee was "dealt with unjustly" should be made through the grievance procedure and, if necessary, arbitration. Finally, the question of fairness of the penalty must be considered in the light of all circumstances in the case and not solely on the grounds that the employee was guilty of three plant rule violations, without giving consideration to the seriousness of the violations or of the employee's past record, his ability and capacity for work, and

---

* In this case there were three arbitrators: the impartial chairman, the employer representative, and the union representative. Since the employer and union representatives can hardly be called neutral, it seems something of a misnomer to designate them as "arbitrators." Would it not be better to name them "employer representative in arbitration" and "union representative in arbitration," respectively?

other factors. Although the promulgation and enforcement of reasonable rules is within the permissible limits of managerial discretion, the company may not unilaterally impose arbitrarily an additional working condition as an absolute cause for discharge. If this prerogative were accorded exclusively to the company, then the grievance procedure would have only a limited usefulness and the right of a discharged employee in such circumstances to resort to the grievance procedure would be meaningless. The arbitrators could not conceive, after a study of the contract and all it contained, that the parties had intended such a result. While the employer might, without consulting the union, establish a practice of giving warning notices to employees or fixing the number of such notices before disciplinary action was taken, under this agreement the employee still had the right to have his case tried on the merits and to contest the severity of the penalty imposed on him. These safeguards would be nullified if the arbitrators sustained the company's argument that a specified number of violations constituted an absolute cause for discharge, especially where the right to impose it was claimed to rest exclusively in management.

Even if the union had specifically agreed to the discharge-for-three-violations rule (which it did not), the arbitrators would not have justified its legitimacy because it would counteract the right to seek redress through the grievance procedure. Such justification would in turn "vest the Union with wholly unwarranted and dictatorial powers over members and would be clearly contrary to public policy."

The arbitrators considered it to be their right and duty to examine the reasonableness of the penalty imposed. On the basis of the facts, which clearly called for disciplinary action, "we cannot in good conscience say that it warranted the extreme penalty of discharge. . . . In industrial relations as well as in social relations, the punishment should fit the crime and we are convinced that under all the facts and circumstances of this case, the penalty of discharge imposed was too severe."

Award. The award ordered that the grievant should be reinstated in his job with full seniority rights, but without back pay. Thus, the arbitrators disagreed with the company that just cause for discharge existed. They agreed that sufficient cause for a lesser penalty was present. The result was a compromise between the five- or six-day disciplinary layoff suggested by the union and the discharge attempted by the company. Reinstatement without back pay in this case meant a disciplinary layoff of about five weeks.

CASE 2: DISCHARGE AS ONLY PENALTY
PORTLAND GAS AND COKE COMPANY (PORTLAND, ORE.)
AND INTERNATIONAL CHEMICAL WORKERS UNION,
23 LA 711. ARBITRATOR: KLEINSORGE.

Issue. Can the company exercise its right to discipline employees short of discharge when the contract specifies only the grounds for immediate discharge?

Contract Provisions. The issue involved an interpretation of Article 7, Sections 1 and 2, of the labor relations agreement entered into by the parties on March 13, 1953. The article, which is entitled "Fair Treatment, Discipline, and Discharges," reads as follows:

SECTION 1. No member of the Union shall be discriminated against by any Foreman, Supervisor, or other representative of the Company for any unjust cause. The Company retains the right to discharge any Employee for incompetence or other just cause; but, upon written request of the Union to the Company within ten (10) days of the Union's receipt of notice of the discharge of an Employee, the Company shall inform the Union of the reason for such discharge. In the absence of just cause of such discharge, the Employee shall be reinstated and shall be paid for the time lost at his regular rate of pay for the work being performed by him at the time of such discharge.

SECTION 2. Any of the following causes shall be recognized as a just ground for immediate discharge, namely:

(a) Insubordination, defined as: Refusal or failure to comply with the Company's posted or published rules or refusal or failure to comply with orders or instructions given by a superior representative of the Company;

(b) Insobriety;

(c) Absence without authority or just cause;

(d) Advocacy of communism, naziism, fascism, or any act or omission for the purpose of sabotage, or giving aid to any enemy of the United States of America;

(e) Dishonesty, consisting of illegal removal of money, material, or the falsification of records;

(f) Physical or mental disability, subject, however, to the provision of Article 18 of this Agreement.

SECTION 3.

(a) In case of discharge for any other cause, the Employee shall be given a written warning by the Company after the first offense; but upon repetition of the offense after such a warning, his employment may be terminated at the discretion of the Company.

(b) Copy of such written warning given to the Employee will not be given to the Union Division Steward, but the latter will be notified in writing by the Company in each instance that the Employee named therein "has received a Warning Notice on this date."

(c) Upon the expiration of six (6) months from the date of issuance of any such warning notice, without termination of employment, such warning notice shall become null and void.

SECTION 4. The provisions of this Article do not preclude the Union from putting into motion the Grievance Procedure provided for by Article 6 of this Agreement.

Union's Position. The union maintained that the language of Article 7, Section 2, required immediate discharge or no penalty at all. It was further stated that inadequacies of past practice, danger of intimidation, and the lack of specific provision permitted degrees of penalties. If penalties short of discharge had been intended, they would have been stated in the agreement and correlated with the seriousness of the offenses.

Company's Position. The company argued it had certain management prerogatives, some of which were limited by Article 7. However, Section 2 provided for some discretion and did not mean that immediate discharge was mandatory for any offense among those listed; the right to exercise judgment was not restricted.

Arbitrator's Analysis. The arbitrator was impressed by the company's argument concerning prerogatives. Many provisions in collective bargaining contracts represent limitations upon rights enjoyed by management prior to the advent of labor organizations. Some provisions may represent limitations upon the activities of unions, but Article 7 in the present agreement was aimed at restricting company action. Therefore, the restrictions limiting powers previously exercised should have been stated definitely. Restrictions were stated in Sections 1 and 3, but Section 2 appeared to be a reaffirmation of company prerogatives with regard to certain offenses. Section 1 limited the right of the company to discharge to cases involving "incompetence or other just cause." Section 2 listed the "just causes" where the company's right to discharge was unrestricted. Section 2 did not limit the powers previously exercised by the company in these areas, and therefore the company still retained these powers.

The first phrase of Section 2 listed grounds for immediate discharge but did not say that any of the causes *shall result* in immediate discharge. If such a restriction in company action had been intended, it should have been stated definitely in the agreement. Section 2 provided for an area of discretion. For a cause to be recognized as a *just ground* for immediate discharge did not mean that immediate discharge was mandatory. The company was not restricted in its rights to use its judgment and to impose a lesser penalty if it wished.

Even the union argument admitted a lesser penalty—no penalty at all. In the arbitrator's opinion, it would not have been wise or in the interests of justice to restrict the company to the extremes. The important conclusion was that the agreement did not provide for such restrictions, and according to the principle that the lesser is included within the greater, the company could impose degrees of penalties if it wished.

Award. On these bases the arbitrator's decision was that the company had the right under the terms of the 1953 agreement to apply disciplinary treatment less than absolute discharge if its employees engaged in misconduct.

SLEEPING ON THE JOB

Sleeping on the job is a frequent cause for disciplinary action. The grievant, however, may deny he was sleeping. In one case an employee was found sitting on two oil drums four feet off the ground with his head down and eyes closed. The union claimed that it was impossible for a person to sleep in this position, and that the grievant was resting his eyes. In another case a grievant denied he was asleep but the evidence showed that cold towels had to be applied before he awoke.

In some cases the grievant may admit he was asleep but not "on the job." Is a man sleeping during his lunch break sleeping "on the job"? In one case a man was discharged after being found asleep in a chair in a room where he was expected to wait when no work was available for him to perform. The arbitrator reduced the penalty.

CASE: SLEEPING ON THE JOB
CHAMBERLAIN CORPORATION OF THE BURLINGTON
ARMY AMMUNITIONS PLANT AND UNITED STEELWORKERS
OF AMERICA, LOCAL 7108, CCH 69–2,
PARA. 8820. ARBITRATOR: TROTTA.

Issue. Was Grievant P. discharged for just cause?

Background. The company rules list "sleeping on the job" as a major offense that may subject an employee to discharge.

Grievant P. worked on the "C" shift (11:00 P.M. to 7:30 A.M.). His lunch break was from 3.00 A.M. to 3:30 A.M. The grievant was discharged for sleeping on the job.

Union's Position. The grievant denied he was asleep. The union argued that even if he were asleep, he had been on his lunch hour and was not sleeping on the job. The union further claimed that the reason the grievant was not at his work station was that at about 2:00 A.M. the foreman had assigned him to another job.

Company's Position. Foreman E. testified that at 1:10 A.M. he had assigned Grievant P. to a job that should have occupied him for the remainder of the shift. However, a short time later he needed the grievant to replace a shear pin that was causing a problem. He looked for the grievant, could not find him, and assigned another man to replace the shear pin.

At about 2:20 A.M. he again looked around the area for the grievant but did not see him. He went to the grievant's work station at about 2:45 A.M. and stayed until 3:00 A.M. He did not see the grievant and saw no evidence of any work performed by him.

Since the employees were breaking for lunch at 3:00 A.M., the foreman went into the cafeteria, but could not find the grievant. At about 3:10 A.M. he found the grievant asleep in a room next to his work station. He then secured another foreman, S., to be a witness. Both foremen testified that they arrived at the room where the grievant was asleep at about 3.17 A.M. and sat at a desk alongside the partition that divided the room. The grievant was sitting on one side of the partition and the two foremen on the other side. The foremen testified that they waited until 3:32 A.M. and then called the guard to have the grievant removed from the plant.

Arbitrator's Analysis. The arbitrator found that the grievant was asleep when he was observed by the foremen but that there was no evidence that he was asleep before 3:00 A.M. The arbitrator held that "on the basis of the evidence it is obvious that the foreman honestly believed that the grievant was asleep between 2:00 A.M. and 3:00 A.M. when he was supposed to be working. He looked for him, could not find him for over an hour, and then found him asleep. It was not unreasonable for the foreman to assume that the grievant must have been asleep since about 2:00 A.M. The arbitrator said, however, that there is a big difference between an assumption and a fact. Merely because E. did not see P. is no proof that P. was asleep on the job. When a man is discharged for sleeping on the job, there must be proof that he was actually asleep on the job. Assumptions, even though honestly made, cannot be the basis for discharge.

There was no question that sleeping on the job may be grounds for discharge. The rule against sleeping on the job was intended to apply to situations where a man is asleep while he is supposed to be working. The rule was not intended to apply to situations when a man is not on the job or when he is on his lunch break. When a man is on his lunch break he is not "on the job" within the meaning of the rule that prohibits sleeping on the job. If a company does not compensate an employee during his lunch break, the control it has over his activities during the lunch break cannot be the same as its control over his activities when he is being paid to work, even though he may still be on company premises. The fact that E. waited until 3:32 A.M. before calling the guard is a clear indication that he recognized this distinction.

Award. The arbitrator found that the grievant was not discharged for just cause.

ABSENTEEISM AND LATENESS

There is little doubt that chronic absenteeism or chronic tardiness constitutes sufficient grounds for disciplinary action. In many cases excessive absenteeism and lateness will result in discharge, since a stable work force is a critical ingredient to the proper functioning of an industrial community.

A study of cases discloses that the factors which determine the arbitrator's decision appear to be: (1) the number of times the grievant was absent or late; (2) the reasons for each absence or tardiness[1]; (3) the treatment by the company of similar offenders; (4) the general conduct of the employee; (5) the length of time the employee was absent; (6) the number of warnings given the employee[2]; and (7) the employer's attempts to solve the problem.[3]

Issues of absenteeism often arise when an employee requests a leave of absence for some reason unconvincing to the company and his request is denied, but the employee absents himself without permission for the projected leave period.[4] A similar issue would arise if an employer refused to adjust a vacation schedule to suit a particular employee's needs and the employee made such adjustments without permission.[5] Arbitrators have often held that when an employee is absent under these circumstances, discharge is justified on the grounds that management's right to schedule the work force has been violated.

When an employee must be absent or late, it is a commonly accepted rule that he must notify the company.[6] If, for instance, illness required an employee to visit the doctor before reporting for work or to remain at home for a few days, he would be expected to notify the company and give a reason for his lateness or absence. Except under unusual circumstances, failure to notify the company justifies disciplinary action by the company.

CASE: UNAUTHORIZED LEAVE OF ABSENCE
THE KROGER COMPANY (MADISON, WIS.) AND RETAIL CLERKS
INTERNATIONAL ASSOCIATION, LOCAL 1401 (AFL), 24
LA 593. ARBITRATORS: SLAVNEY (CHAIRMAN), BEDELL, AND CLARK.

Issue. Prior to the taking of evidence at the hearing, it was determined that the matters to be arbitrated were as follows: Was termination of the employment status of the grievant for cause? If the termination of the grievant's employment status was found to be for cause, was the action of the employer in refusing to reestablish employee status an excessive penalty, and if excessive, what is the equitable penalty to be imposed upon the grievant?

Background. The grievant commenced her employment with the employer in one of its Madison, Wisconsin, stores on January 26, 1953, and continued in said employment as a checker until February 28, 1955, when her employment status was terminated by the employer. The grievant was a member of the union and was within the bargaining unit covered by the collective bargaining agreement. On or about January 25, 1955, she made inquiry of the union's business agent concerning her eligibility for vacation. He told her that she was qualified for a two-week vacation under the terms of the collective bargaining agreement and suggested that she should give the employer 30 days notice before she intended to start it. Shortly thereafter she asked the Store Manager, her immediate supervisor, whether she could take her vacation during the winter months, but did not mention a specific date. The Store Manager said that the vacation could probably be arranged and requested a two-week advance notice.

On February 10, 1955, the grievant told the Store Manager that she wanted to commence her vacation on Monday, February 28, and that she had arranged for another employee to work for her on the preceding Saturday, February 26. He told her the District Manager would have to approve the request. Two days later the Store Manager learned that the employer was planning a store-wide promotional sale at the end of the month and that he would have to hire an additional checker for the sale. Although the business agent was confident this would not interfere with the grievant's vacation, the District Manager would not approve it because the sale started on February 27. The grievant was not aware of this decision when she later spoke with the business agent and told him she had not received her vacation check. Thereupon the business agent called the employer's Personnel Manager, who informed him that the only way the grievant could have a vacation at that time was to quit. In a telephone conversation later, on the same day, with the business agent, the grievant declared that she could not change her plans and would leave on vacation regardless of management's decision.

In the meantime her substitute worker for February 26 had been instructed to report for work on February 26, but when the grievant reminded her of the previous arrangement, she made no mention of the instruction. On February 25, the grievant received her wages for the period and noted that vacation pay was not included. She mentioned this to the Store Manager, but nothing was said about her vacation. She departed on her vacation as planned and did not return to her residence until two weeks later.

The management tried repeatedly to reach the grievant in order to explain the denial of vacation at that time. Finally a letter was sent to her in which she was notified of dismissal. At the beginning of March the union's business agent wrote to the employer's Personnel Manager, setting forth the facts of the case.

When the grievant returned on March 15, she was not permitted to work. The business agent then notified the employer that if reinstatement was not forthcoming, arbitration of the matter would be sought.

Contract Provisions. The union and the employer were parties to a collective bargaining agreement, which by its terms became effective on May 31, 1954, and continued to May 28, 1956. The agreement contains the following pertinent clauses:

ARTICLE 4: MANAGEMENT RIGHTS

The management of the business and the direction of the working forces, including the right to plan, direct, and control retail store operations, hire, suspend or discharge for proper cause, transfer or relieve employees from duty because of lack of work or for other legitimate reasons, the right to study or introduce new or improved production methods or facilities, and the right to establish and maintain rules and regulations covering the operation of the stores, a violation of which shall be among the causes for discharge, are vested in the Employer, provided, however, that this right shall be exercised with due regard for the rights of the employees and provided that it will be used for the purpose of discrimination against any employee.

ARTICLE 5: DISPUTE PROCEDURE

A. Should any differences, disputes or complaints arise over the interpretation or application of the contents of this Agreement, there shall be an earnest effort on the part of both parties to settle such promptly through the following steps:

Step 1. By conference between the aggrieved employee, an official of the Union, or both, and the store manager.

Step 2. By conference between an official or the Union and the District Manager.

Step 3. By conference between an official or officials of the Union and the Branch Manager or a representative of the Company designated by the Branch Manager.

Step 4. In the event that the last step fails to settle the complaint it shall be referred to the Board of Arbitration.

B. The Board of Arbitration shall consist of one person appointed by the representative of the Union and one person appointed by the Employer. Said two persons shall within two days after disagreement request the Wisconsin Employment Relations Board to appoint a third arbitrator and the decision of the majority shall be binding on both parties. The expenses of the third arbitrator shall be paid for jointly. The decision of the Board of Arbitration shall be rendered within twenty (20) days after receipt of the dispute.

C. The Employer may at any time discharge any worker for proper cause. The Union may file a written complaint with the Employer within five (5) days after the discharge, asserting that the discharge was improper. Such complaint must be taken up promptly, and if the Employer and the Union fail to agree within forty-eight (48) hours, it shall be referred within twenty-four (24) hours to the Board of Arbitration. Should the board determine that it was an unfair discharge, the Employer shall reinstate the employee and pay him compensation at his regular rate for the time lost. Such a complaint must be settled within twenty (20) days from its receipt, including the decision of the board of arbitration.

D. No grievances will be discussed unless the outlined procedure has been followed. . . .

H. Grievances must be taken up promptly, and no grievance will be considered or discussed which is presented later than ten calendar days after such has happened.

ARTICLE 10: VACATIONS

For the period from May 31, 1954 through May 28, 1955, all full-time employees shall be entitled to one week's vacation with forty-two and one-half (42½) hours straight time pay after one year of continuous service and to two weeks' vacation with eighty-five (85) hours straight time pay after two years of continuous service.

Union's Position. The union contended that the collective bargaining agreement entitled the grievant to a vacation, that she had the right to plan such vacation, and that the employer should have worked out a reasonable arrangement for taking said vacation. It further contended that the employer inadvertently caused a misunderstanding with regard to the grievant's request inasmuch as the employer delayed its decision and gave the grievant no definite answer with regard to her request, and that therefore the employer was not entitled to its full prerogative under the collective bargaining agreement. The union further argued that, inasmuch as the grievant did not know where she stood, and because her plans could not be changed, she had no other choice but to go on her vacation when she did. The union contended that she should be reinstated.

Company's Position. The employer contended that the collective bargaining agreement granted the employer the prerogative of scheduling vacation for its employees, that the grievant had not been told she could take her vacation, and that the preponderance of the evidence established that she had been told she could *not* have her vacation for the period requested.

Arbitrators' Analysis. The record established the fact that the grievant asked for a vacation for a specific period of time and that her request was refused by the Store Manager and the Branch Manager. This refusal was made known to grievant by these individuals. The fact that she was denied a vacation, in addition to being corroborated by the testimony of her supervisors, was further established in the letter written by the business agent of the union, dated March 1, 1955, to the Personnel Manager, wherein the union representative stated in part, "She asked again in February and received no answer until she was denied a vacation at the start of your sales promotion." The record disclosed that the union's business agent had such knowledge on February 24, when, in a telephone conversation, the Personnel Manager advised the agent that the only way the grievant could take her vacation was for her to quit. Despite this knowledge, the agent nevertheless advised the grievant to take her vacation and that, if any trouble arose, he "would fight it."

It appeared, therefore, that as far back as February 17, the date of the commencement of the promotional sale, the grievant had knowledge of the fact that the employer would not grant her request. Knowing the employer's attitude, she subsequently made further attempts to obtain permission to take her vacation on the dates requested. However, these further requests did not change the employer's decision. Therefore, it was the conclusion of the arbitrators that the grievant took her vacation without permission and contrary to the expressed refusal of the employer. Under Article 4 of the collective bargaining agreement, the employer had "the right to establish and maintain rules and regulations covering the operation of the stores, a violation of which shall be among the causes for discharge." Thus the employer had the right, in the absence of a specific vacation period provided in the agreement, to establish vacation periods for his employees. Therefore, an employee's taking her vacation contrary to the expressed refusal of the employer constituted a violation of the employer's right under the quoted language of Article 4, and consequently such action on the part of the employee constituted cause for discharge. The record established that the grievant took her vacation contrary to the expressed refusal of the employer. Therefore, the termination of her employment was for cause.

Award. The action of the employer in refusing to reinstate the grievant as an employee was not unreasonable nor was it an excessive penalty, and was therefore sustained.

REFERENCES

1. Bell Aircraft Corp., 16 LA 281.
2. Pacific Mills, 8 LA 141; Dayton Steel Foundry Co., 31 LA 865.
3. Pacific Tel. and Tel. Co., 32 LA 178.
4. Union Oil Co., 3 LA 108.
5. Kroger Co., 24 LA 593.
6. Koolvent Metal Awning Co., 21 LA 322; Ultra Chemical Works, Inc., 25 LA 846.

DISHONESTY

When an employee has been discharged on the grounds of dishonesty, his ability to obtain employment elsewhere may be seriously impaired. Because of this possible consequence, arbitrators require proof, almost beyond a reasonable doubt, of the alleged dishonesty.[1] The credibility of the witnesses is carefully weighed, and the rules of evidence used by the courts are often followed. The employee involved is considered innocent of the charges until proven guilty, and the proof, therefore, must be strong and convincing.

There are times when the employee admits the action of which he is accused, but denies it as an act of dishonesty. This compels a determination by the arbitrator of the question of intent. In one case, an employee admitted taking for his personal use a small piece of lumber, which he thought was scrap. The company admitted that the lumber used was scrap, and therefore the arbitrator held that there was no intent to be dishonest.

While dishonest acts committed in the course of employment cause injury to the employer and are grounds for disciplinary action, including discharge, it is not so clear what the employer may do with regard to acts that occur outside the scope of employment and cause no injury to the employer.[2] To illustrate, a man employed as a common laborer was charged by the FBI with participating in the theft of clothing from an army post. He was discharged by his employer but reinstated by an arbitrator on the ground that the indictment against the employee did not constitute proof that he was in fact guilty. At a subsequent court trial, he was acquitted.

The problem is complicated when the employee's duties are such that dishonest acts unrelated to the scope of employment may reflect on his suitability for his job—for example, a bank teller. In such cases, disciplinary action by the company would usually be upheld by an arbitrator.

Where an employee deals dishonestly with patrons of the employer and the injury to the employer is manifest, it is clear that disciplinary action by the company would be justified. Under the common law, an employee owes a duty to his employer and cannot act against the employer's interest.[3] This is true whether the employee's acts are committed during or outside of working hours.

Fraudulent representations on an application for employment will usually justify disciplinary action unless the representation is clearly irrelevant or innocently negligent.[4] Where the facts make it clear that the employer would never have employed the applicant had the truth been known, discharge will be upheld.

CASE: DISHONESTY
THE KROGER COMPANY, GRAND RAPIDS BRANCH, AND
INTERNATIONAL BROTHERHOOD OF TEAMSTERS,
CHAUFFEURS, WAREHOUSEMEN AND HELPERS OF AMERICA,
25 LA 906. ARBITRATOR: SMITH.

Issue. Was the company justified in refusing to reinstate an employee who had been accused of theft of company property after he had been acquitted by a jury trial? If not, what is the remedy?

Background. Grievant was employed by the company at its Grand Rapids warehouse in May 1954, and worked until August 22, 1955. On that day, another warehouse employee was apprehended in the act of stealing merchandise from the warehouse. He implicated grievant and two other employees in earlier thefts. Grievant was brought to police headquarters and, after being interviewed, was placed under arrest on charges of larceny. He entered a plea of "not guilty" upon being arraigned and was bound over to Superior Court for trial. Although he was released on bond, he was not permitted to return to work.

On September 27, 1955, the grievant was tried in Superior Court and acquitted. Thereupon he filed a grievance against the company, stating that he was available for work, that he had been temporarily laid off even though he had been unjustly accused, and that he should be reinstated in his job. The company did not file a written answer at the hearing held subsequent to the presentation of the grievance, but in its post-hearing brief it claimed that the grievant had "knowingly participated in the theft of company property."

Contract Provision. The collective agreement between the parties reserves to the company the right to "discharge any worker for proper cause."

Union's Position. The reasons for the company's original and continuing refusal to permit grievant's return to work were never formally communicated to him in writing. Although he had been indicted by the court for "theft" and "dishonesty," he had been found not guilty. The grievant's acquittal by a jury of larceny charges occurred after the company's original decision to discharge him. If the jury acted responsibly, it must have believed that the State had failed to prove its case beyond reasonable doubt. The union's counsel argued that " a finding by twelve impartial citizens should be persuasive in resolving this factual question" (that is, whether proper cause had been established beyond reasonable doubt).

Company's Position. The company maintained that "proper cause" could not be circumscribed by the rules of evidence prevailing in criminal actions. Counsel stated: "Arbitration is in the nature of a civil suit, where the degree of proof is, of course, the preponderance of evidence" rather than proof beyond a reasonable doubt, as in criminal proceedings. The evidence is that if the grievant was not a participant, he had at least been guilty of collusion.

Arbitrator's Analysis. The principle has become firmly established in arbitration that, on the question of the existence of "cause," or "proper cause," for disciplinary action or discharge, the employer has the burden of proof. The company evidently accepted this proposition. However, the parties differed concerning the extent of this burden. The company claimed that, as in ordinary civil litigation, the "preponderance of the evidence" rule applied, whereas the union contended that, since grievant was accused of committing a "criminal act," his guilt must, as in criminal proceedings, be established "beyond all reasonable doubt."

There is no controlling authority on this question. In general, arbitrators probably have used the "preponderance of the evidence" rule or some similar standard in deciding fact issues before them, including issues presented by ordinary discipline and discharge cases. However, as the union pointed out, it has been held that where the alleged "cause" for disciplinary action or discharge was misconduct of a kind recognized and punished by the criminal law, the employer must meet a higher standard of proof. The arbitrator said that it seems reasonable and proper to hold that alleged misconduct of a kind that carries the stigma of general social disapproval as well as disapproval under accepted canons of plant discipline should be clearly and convincingly established by the evidence. Reasonable doubts raised by the proofs should be resolved in favor of the accused.

The company's case against grievant rested on the testimony of the employee who had been apprehended in an act of theft from the warehouse. When the grievant was questioned by a police officer and the Warehouse Manager, he made certain admissions, although he denied in court that he had ever been involved in thefts of company property. Grievant's testimony obviously was self-serving, and certain incidents in his past raised considerable question concerning his respect for the truth. Nevertheless, the company was obligated to establish by convincing evidence the charges it had made.

Three possible bases for a charge of "dishonesty" against grievant were: (1) he participated in the actual theft (taking property from the warehouse); (2) he participated in the theft of other company property; (3) at the very least, he divided a case of roast beef with the acknowledged perpetrator of the theft (J.B.), knowing that it was company property. Insofar as the testimony of J.B. was concerned (and this was the only testimony, apart from grievant's alleged admissions, directly connecting grievant with any specific act of misconduct and hence, in the criminal law aspect, tending to prove a *corpus delicti*), grievant was involved only in the division of the roast beef, not in taking it or in taking or dividing up any other merchandise. There was no prearrangement or agreement between the two, of any kind, prior to the theft of the roast beef. It is doubtful whether, on this kind of evidence, the conviction of grievant on a charge of larceny, or of conspiracy to commit larceny, would be warranted. Perhaps this explained the verdict of the jury in the criminal proceeding.

The arbitrator was convinced that the evidence was insufficient to sustain a charge of theft or of knowing participation in the theft of company property. If the grievant *was* guilty, the company had not established this by sufficient evidence. Therefore, the arbitrator concluded that, since the grievant had been acquitted of the criminal charge, the company had failed to prove that the grievant was an active party to the theft, either directly or as a member of a conspiracy. However, he did receive half of the contents of the case of roast beef and the circumstances of this division of the fruits of the thievery were such as to indicate that the grievant either knew what had been done, or should have reported the theft or at least should have refused to have anything to do with it. In other words, he demonstrated something considerably less than complete integrity.

A basic problem of this case was that the company, both in instituting the criminal proceedings and in refusing further employment to the grievant, had acted on the assumption that the grievant was guilty of larceny and that this could be proved. This assumption did not materialize. Something less than larceny had been proved. Considering all the circumstances, the arbitrator concluded that the full penalty of discharge could not be upheld and that the grievant should be reinstated, but that a penalty consisting of the denial of back pay was fully warranted.

Award. Grievance is sustained in part and denied in part. Grievant should be reinstated to his former employment with the company, without loss of seniority but without back pay for wages lost since August 22.

REFERENCES

1. Fruehauf Trailer Co., 21 LA 832; General Refractories Co., 24 LA 470; Chrysler Corp., 24 LA 549.
2. Mansfield Tire and Rubber Co., 31 LA 775.
3. Carl Fischer Inc., 24 LA 674; Consolidated Western Steel Corp., 13 LA 721; Branch River Wool Combing Co., 31 LA 547; Four Wheel Drive Auto Co., 20 LA 823.
4. North American Aviation, Inc., 12 LA 225.

INCOMPETENCE AND INEFFICIENCY

Where the employer can show that an employee is either inefficient or incompetent, most arbitrators would deem this just cause for either discharge or some lesser form of discipline.[1] The latter might be demotion or transfer to another type of work for which the employee is better suited.[2]

It has not always been clear what constitutes incompetence, but it is fair to say that submission to the arbitrator of work sheets, production records, and even samples of workmanship are usually the most adequate witnesses to the quality of the employee's skills.[3] No employee can be held to absolute perfection. The mere fact that his work has occasional defects or is marked by occasional lapses is not enough to subject him to discipline. What has evolved is a sort of average-worker test that holds the employee to a rational standard. The employee must, in the usual instance, be given a reasonable opportunity to demonstrate his ability. It is often held that he must be given adequate training to allow him to qualify for the position.[4] The measure of training is what is ordinarily required for others in a similar position.[5]

Other factors considered by arbitrators are (1) the presence of adequate supervision, (2) the availability of proper equipment, (3) the number of warnings issued to bring the employee to task,[6] (4) whether prior lapses have been sanctioned by the foreman, (5) the cause of the incompetence (i.e., physical or otherwise),[7] (6) whether the employee has previously been awarded merit increases, (7) whether the employee's acts are willful or unduly negligent, (8) whether the facts show "hounding" of the employee (i.e., an attempt to catch the employee by incessant badgering), and (9) the nature of the employer's product.

CASE: FAILURE TO MEET INCENTIVE STANDARDS
TEXAS ELECTRIC STEEL CASTING COMPANY,
HOUSTON PLANT, AND UNITED STEEL WORKERS OF AMERICA,
27 LA 55. ARBITRATOR: LEHOCZKY.

Issue. The grievance, dated June 1, 1956, read: "The foreman said I was not coming up to standards. I am asking for my job back with full seniority and pay for all time lost because I was discharged without a just cause."

Background. The grievant had been in the employ of the company since November 9, 1950, and except for several relatively short intervals had been working as a grinder for the entire period of his service. His record indicated no irregularities until about a year (or so) ago, when the company claimed that his output gradually fell off and he soon became "the lowest producer." Shortly thereafter he was transferred from the East End to a vacancy at the

West End, where he and a fellow employee came to the attention of the Supervisor as exceptionally poor producers. Following a series of warnings coupled with a two-week written ultimatum, the grievant's production record showed little improvement and he was discharged. The other employee "changed into a new man" and was not discharged.

Contract Provisions. Section IV/E of the current agreement states: "The present incentive payment plan now in effect will be continued in effect for the term of this contract."

Union's Position. The incentive system affected the grievant in several respects. First, neither he nor some of the other workers knew how it worked because they did not comprehend the mathematics of its operation. Second, a worker's production was evaluated as a percentage of the "normal expectation" and each job was so rated. Production above the normal expectation was rewarded by a bonus. In the grievant's job (grinder), the normal "net" was 80 percent. When production fell below 80 percent, excessive labor costs were incurred because these, too, had been estimated at an expected norm. Third, output was measured in terms of quantity rather than quality and this standard reflected on the grievant's capability because he had an excellent record of good work. Fourth, employees had to keep accurate records (downtime, types of grind, etc.) and use symbols to enter information on the record. The grievant had had difficulty with this process and had not related their significance to the earnings setup. Fifth, some orders from the supervisors affected output adversely; since other employees did not conscientiously follow these orders, but the grievant did, his output suffered and fell below the normal expectation, even though his adherence to the orders probably saved the company money.

The union contended that the incentive system was not the proper criterion by which to measure the worth of an employee. It also claimed that the company agreed not to penalize an employee "for failure to work at an incentive pace."

Company's Position. The company claimed that numerous observations of the grievant showed that he did "slow motion work." He was also accused of a number of time-wasting infractions and the use of production time for servicing equipment. Production records introduced by the company showed that the grievant had produced only half of the output of other bench grinders. Since output statistics are the only common denominator of production jobs, and the grievant's job had been assigned its normal expectancy rating, failure to qualify at this rate warranted his dismissal.

Arbitrator's Analysis. The agreement between the parties did not define what was meant by "failure to work at an incentive pace." The normal understanding of such an expression is "failure to earn a bonus." That the agreement could possibly have meant that no employee would ever be penalized regardless of how little work he performed was not a plausible deduction. The average employee who is not on incentive would be expected to perform below the normal pace expected of an incentive-rated employee. Thus, a normal pace of 80 net for grinders may well fall to perhaps 64 percent net when no incentive intent exists.

However, this particular job was on an incentive basis and therefore incentive effort became part of the job requirement. Any employee who would rather not work on an incentive basis should have transferred to a nonincentive-rated job. Consequently, the alleged agreement was interpreted to mean that no grinder would be penalized if he failed to show an average above 80 net, and not to mean that the company gave away its right to penalize an employee who performs at less than 50 percent of the norm.

The evidence presented by the witness explained in part the grievant's failure to produce, but evidently the major reason for his failure to produce rested in his lack of understanding of what his duties were, of what was expected of him, of how his earnings were computed, and in the hopelessness that must inevitably grow out of such a situation. This deduction was based on observation at the hearing, upon the testimony he gave, and upon his general attitude. In light of the type of industrial relations policy practiced in this plant, the arbitrator ruled that it would be discriminatory not to give the grievant another trial period, this time under proper controls. The trial period should be set up in such a manner that both the company and the union would be satisfied that the grievant understood the symbols, the quality standards, the method of keeping records, the duties he must perform, the duties the service man must perform, downtime, and related matters. His daily production record was to be discussed with him as fast as it was compiled. If at the end of the trial period he could not show an overall average of 80 net, his discharge would become final unless he was able and willing to transfer to a nonincentive-rated job in the interim.

Award. The company's general action of disciplining incentive-rated employees whose overall production average falls below normal (80 percent net in the case of grinders) was upheld. In full consideration of the specific facts in the case, the grievant was to be returned to his job for a one-month trial period. If at the end of the trial period his production average for the entire period was below 80 net, his discharge would become final. If by the end of the trial period his production average (for the period) was 80 net or more, he would be reinstated without loss in seniority, but without pay for the period of his layoff.

REFERENCES

1. Russell Creamery Co., 21 LA 293; Menasco Manufacturing Co., 31 LA 33.
2. Bell Aircraft Corp., 20 LA 551; Dow Chemical Co., 12 LA 1061.
3. North American Aviation, Inc., 17 LA 784; Jonco Aircraft Corp., 22 LA 819; Timm Industries, Inc., 11 LA 308.
4. Texas Electrical Steel Casting Co., 27 LA 55.
5. Friden Calculating Machine Co., 27 LA 496; North American Aviation, Inc., 18 LA 359.

6. Weber Aircraft Corp., 22 LA 23; Kraft Foods Corp., 15 LA 38.
7. General Electric Co., 15 LA 664.

INTOXICATION

Many contracts contain clauses that make the drinking of intoxicating beverages on the job,[1] or being intoxicated on duty,[2] grounds for summary discharge. Whether the intoxication occurs after working hours and whether it is related to the job are additional factors to be considered.[3] In one case an employee stopped off at a local tavern after work on Friday night and had one drink too many. As he searched his pockets for his wallet to pay for his drinks, he remembered that he had left his wallet in his locker. He went back to the plant in an inebriated condition, was seen by his foreman, and was discharged.

The difficult problem in intoxication cases is one of proof.[4] While medical examination will be sufficient to justify the company's action, there may be some question, about relying on the opinion of a nonprofessional company official. Credibility and reliability are important factors in evaluating the testimony of management representatives as to the alleged condition of the employee. A common defense is that the employee was under the influence of ordinary drugs or was suffering from some temporary malady that made him appear to be drunk.

CASE 1: PROOF OF INTOXICATION
SOUTH PENN OIL COMPANY AND OIL, CHEMICAL AND
ATOMIC WORKERS INTERNATIONAL UNION, 29 LA 718
(DIGESTED). ARBITRATOR: DUFF.

Issue. Was the grievant discharged for just cause? If not, what shall be the remedy?

Background. A suspended employee, pending investigation, was notified by letter that his employment with the company was terminated because he had allegedly been so drunk that he could not do his work. The employee filed a complaint in which he denied the charge and asked to be reinstated with full pay. Arbitration resulted when no mutually satisfactory settlement could be reached through the contractual grievance procedure.

Union's Position. The union did not question the rights of the company to discharge an employee for just cause and to strictly enforce the company rule regarding drinking and intoxication. However, inasmuch as the contract did not specify that the mere *use* of intoxicants was a sufficient grounds for discharge, the severity of the penalty was questioned.

Company's Position. The company discharged the employee "for being under the influence of intoxicating liquors to such an extent that he could not properly perform the duties of his job." The company maintained that it had acted within its contractual rights and that the discharge was for "proper cause" because the employee had clearly violated company rules.

Arbitrator's Analysis. Both the company and the union produced witnesses to support their claims. The arbitrator was obviously faced with the difficult task of determining the credibility of the witnesses for both parties. Therefore, he considered each witness from the following points of view: (1) *interest* in the outcome of the case, (2) *perception* of conditions surrounding his initial observation of the employee's behavior, (3) *memory* capability and the accuracy of precise details, and (4) *manner* of testifying and communicating recollection of the occurrence.

Some of the evidence was circumstantial and the arbitrator had the additional responsibility of determining its probative value.

After evaluating all testimony, the arbitrator concluded that the conduct of the employee merited some discipline. Although it had not been proved that the employee was intoxicated, there was sufficient evidence to show that his *inclination* to work had been affected, if not his ability. Under these circumstances the company's desire to discipline the employee seemed justified.

Award. The arbitrator's award upheld the company's right to discipline, although it questioned the propriety of the severity of the penalty (discharge) and modified the penalty to a three-month disciplinary layoff. The reinstatement of the employee was ordered, effective at the expiration of the suspension, without loss of seniority but without back wages for time lost.

CASE 2: DRINKING ON COMPANY PROPERTY
PENNSYLVANIA GREYHOUND BUS COMPANY AND AMALGAMATED
ASSOCIATION OF STREET, ELECTRIC RAILWAY AND MOTOR
COACH EMPLOYEES OF AMERICA, 18 LA 400.
ARBITRATORS: DASH (CHAIRMAN), SYME, AND STRUGGLES.

Issue. The question at issue was whether discharge for infraction of the rules was justified. While some discipline was warranted, was the extreme penalty of discharge in order when the company was in no way subject to any serious potential loss to its business?

Background. A bus driver was discharged by a supervisor for being under the influence of alcohol while on company property. He had completed an extended and exhausting tour of duty, admittedly had drunk some beer, and had gone to bed in the company dormitory. He awoke later and appeared to be in an intoxicated condition.

Contract Provisions. The company and the union were working under a "Manual of Rules for Bus Operators." These rules covered a number of prohibitions, including one on intoxication, which specifically prohibited an employee from being under the influence of intoxicants while on company property, even though the riding public did not frequent the property.

Union's Position. The union contended that the grievant was not intoxicated but exhausted, and that the supervisor misjudged the grievant's condition because he detected the aroma of a low-alcoholic-content beverage. The union claimed that the supervisor's opinion was an unsupported assumption. Further, the grievant was not on duty and could not affect company interests or property while asleep.

Company's Position. The clause of the agreement clearly stated that use of intoxicants on company property, which included the dormitory, was strictly prohibited. The grievant admitted consuming an alcoholic beverage, however weak it may have been. The physical evidences of an intoxicated condition as compared with those of exhaustion are easily recognized by a knowledgeable and experienced supervisor. The admission of the grievant and the observation of the supervisor are conclusive confirmation of the grievant's violation of the rules. Therefore the action of the company was justified.

Arbitrators' Analysis. The arbitrators did not consider that the company rule regarding intoxicants was unreasonable. Its purpose was to protect the company, the employee, and the public. However, when broken, the rule must be applied with reasonableness in individual cases.

While the evidence did not clearly establish that the employee was intoxicated, he was obviously partly under the influence of an intoxicating beverage and had unquestionably violated company rules.

The arbitrators pointed out in their analysis of the facts presented that penalty of discharge should not be applied indiscriminately. Employees respond much more favorably to a rule that is enforced with reasonable recognition of the variety of acts against which the rule is directed than they do to a rule that is enforced with absolute rigidity, regardless of the situation involved.

Award. The arbitrators said that the discharge of the employee for being partially under the influence of an intoxicating beverage was too severe a penalty for infraction of the company rule. They rescinded the discharge and substituted a 60-day disciplinary layoff. In the absence of any prior decision for this type of case during the relationship between the company and the union, back pay was not granted to the employee for the additional loss of pay suffered over and above the 60-day disciplinary layoff.

REFERENCES

1. South Penn Oil Co., 29 LA 718; Altamil Corp., 71-1 CCH, Para. 8198.
2. Fruehauf Trailer Co., 29 LA 362; Brink's Inc., 19 LA 724.
3. Modern Coach Corp., 24 LA 810.
4. Kaiser Steel Corp., 31 LA 832; McCormick & Baxter Creosoting Co., 71-1 CCH, para. 8137.

NEGLIGENCE AND ACCIDENTS

When an employee works in a negligent manner and thereby disregards the safety of himself or others,[1] or his actions constitute a threat to the property of his employer, he is liable to dismissal or other discipline.[2] Some contracts expressly provide that management may discharge employees for violating safety rules.[3]

In industries such as public transportation, where the safety of the public is paramount, arbitrators will require a high degree of care on the part of employees.[4] Inspectors usually will be held to a greater degree of responsibility than will an operator.[5]

While negligent work may appear to be a form of inefficiency or incompetence, it constitutes a separate type of offense. A competent worker may be careless, regardless of his ability to do the job.

When an employee breaches a safety rule and an accident results, the company is usually able to support strong disciplinary action.

CASE 1: DEGREE OF NEGLIGENCE
SOUTHERN PIPE AND CASING COMPANY, A DIVISION OF
U.S. INDUSTRIES, AND INTERNATIONAL ASSOCIATION
OF MACHINISTS, 29 LA 224. ARBITRATOR: LENWARD.

Issue. Was the company justified in imposing a disciplinary layoff of 2½ days without pay on K.W. and J.H. for not having tightened flange bolts properly?

Background. K.W., a maintenance mechanic, and J.H., a maintenance repair man, were suspended from their employment by the company on June 25, 1957 for a period of 20 hours each.

The aggrieved employees were assigned on June 24 to work at a coal-tar spinner, replacing a tube. The assignment required the tightening of bolts through the flanges. They reported to their foreman that the job had been completed and that the bolts were tight. When the pump was turned on the following day, coal tar at a temperature of 450 degrees squirted through the flanges. Their foreman and other company supervisors observed that the bolts were not tight, some were "finger loose," and one was so loose that light passed between the flange and the bolt. The incident was extremely dangerous and could have caused severe injury to nearby employees. The men were promptly suspended for the balance of the week.

Each man testified he had properly tightened the bolts and that they were tight when the job was completed. Each suggested the possibility of other causes for the escape of hot tar, but all the possible reasons were found to be unlikely or impossible because the bolts were retightened and the machine was used again shortly after the accident without further mishap. No explanation for the occurrence, other than loose bolts, seemed plausible.

Contract Provisions. Article XVI provides that in the case of minor, repeated acts of unsatisfactory work or conduct, the employee shall be given a written notice before any disciplinary action is taken. Under Article XVII, "The Company shall have the right to discharge employees without previous warning notice for good and sufficient causes such as gross carelessness."

Union's Position. The union contended that even if loose bolts caused the squirting of hot tar, the deficiency did not give the company the right to discipline these employees under the terms of the collective bargaining agreement. It claimed that at worst the men's omission was carelessness, not gross carelessness, and that only gross carelessness justified this type of discipline without a previous written warning notice. (Neither man had received a warning notice since the inception of the union–management agreement.)

The union presented evidence of previous incidents of inefficient workmanship or negligence involving other employees or supervisors, which did not result in suspension of the employee. It argued that these cases represented the prevailing practice of the company and its interpretation of "carelessness" and "gross carelessness," and that these cases supported the union's view that this incident was at worst "carelessness." It asserted this to be a minor infraction, not a major offense, and governed by the section of the contract requiring a warning notice.

Company's Position. The company argued that the conduct of K.W. and J.H. was gross carelessness, that terrible injury could have been caused, and that the company had in fact acted leniently in merely suspending the employees, since it had the right to dismiss them under the terms of the contract. With respect to the other incidents of inefficiency or carelessness cited by the union, the company argued that no proof was offered that the cause of those accidents was "gross" carelessness. It rejected the union's charge.

Arbitrator's Analysis. The arbitrator was satisfied that the amount of care reasonably required of an employee is greater where his own safety and the safety of others depend upon such care than could be reasonably required in the absence of great danger. Maximum diligence could be reasonably required of an employee in tightening bolts where human life is at stake, and even a little bit less than maximum diligence in such a case might be gross carelessness. Something less than maximum diligence may be acceptable where human life would not otherwise be jeopardized, as for example in bolting an advertising sign to a wall; in that case the employee's failure to tighten the bolt may simply be negligence, but not of a gross kind. In this dispute, there was a good deal less than maximum diligence. Reliable testimony, accepted by the arbitrator, established that many of the bolts were extremely loose. Because of the hazard to persons near the machine, which was known to both aggrieved employees, their carelessness was extreme, or gross.

The arbitrator gave no weight to the union's argument that precedent was established by allegedly similar instances in the past, where no suspension was ordered by the company. Each of these incidents was too uncertain. Further, no evidence was found to support the claim that omissions on the part of the company to impose discipline constituted a binding past practice. Even if the company had failed to impose a suspension or to effect a discharge in previous serious incidents, its failure might reflect its recognition that it had no power to do so without a prior warning notice, or it might indicate leniency toward the employee because of the circumstances known to it. These other cases did not influence the arbitrator's opinion that K.W. and J.H., although otherwise concededly qualified and competent employees, were grossly careless on June 24. It was therefore found that the company did not violate the labor–management agreement by imposing a 2½-day layoff as a disciplinary measure.

Award. The company did not violate the existing agreement when it disciplined K.W. and J.H. for gross carelessness by imposing a 2½-day layoff. Grievance was denied.

CASE 2: PENALTY FOR NEGLIGENCE
GENERAL METALS CORPORATION, ADEL DIVISION
[BURBANK, CALIF.] AND INTERNATIONAL ASSOCIATION OF
MACHINISTS, 25LA 323. ARBITRATOR: GAFFEY.

Issue. Was the company justified in discharging F.A. and F.B. for their negligence in not properly inspecting certain machine parts? If not, what should the penalty have been, if any?

Background. The company manufactures hydraulic equipment for aircraft. The work requires a high degree of skill and precision. In order to be sure that its products meet the specifications of the U.S. Air Force, the company employs many inspectors. The job descriptions of the inspectors involved herein had been approved by the company and the union.

F.A. was employed as an inspector for about two years. He had a good record and was promoted through a series of steps to Set-Up Inspector. He held this position for about nine months. A Set-Up Inspector's principal duties are to determine the acceptability of the "first parts" produced by a manufacturing operation. He is required to inspect five first samples of complex parts for quality of workmanship, dimensional accuracy, and conformance to specifications. When he finds the samples of the part acceptable, he stamps and initials records that authorize the production run of the part. The production run of a part cannot be started until a Set-Up Inspector has accepted the first parts. The Set-Up Inspector prepares and maintains certain required records of his acceptances and rejections.

F.B. was employed here as an inspector for about 3¼ years. He had a good record and was promoted through a series of steps to Floor Inspector. He was in this position for about two years. A Floor Inspector's principal duties are to make periodic random sample inspections of parts in production to determine whether they conform to specifications. The instructions specify that each inspection must consist of a full check of five parts selected at random from the run. Each Floor Inspector accepts or rejects parts on the basis of his inspections and prepares certain required reports, charts, and other quality control records. He is required to inspect frequently enough to determine whether the quality of the product is being maintained in production. When he finds that the parts do not meet specifications, it is his responsibility to call this fact to the attention of the Production Foreman at once. The Floor Inspector's foreman is also notified. When a Floor Inspector deems it necessary, and his foreman concurs, production of a part is held up until the difficulty is corrected.

Despite these procedures and instructions, on August 2, 3, and 4, 1955, 218 defective pieces of a complex aluminium casting were run on turret lathes on three day shifts and two night shifts. The defect was serious and should have been obvious to qualified inspectors. No inspector observed it. An operator finally noticed it on the third day. The parts were scrapped at a loss of several thousand dollars.

F.A. had approved the first parts and F.B. had approved production runs of the defective parts. The company discharged F.A., F.B., and one other employee involved on August 5, 1955.

Contract Provisions. Article XVI, Section 1, specifically permits the company to discharge employees for gross carelessness without previous warning notice.

Union's Position. The number of parts delivered for inspection was so much in excess of normal production volume that neither inspector could allow sufficient time for the customary complete check of part dimensions without creating downtime on the production run line. To cope with the overburden, they inspected what they considered the most important characteristics, depending on specification tolerances allowed for other dimensions.

Company's Position. The company considered that both inspectors were guilty of gross negligence. It was not their function to accommodate inspection time to the possibility of downtime or slowdown on the production line. Nor was it their function to judge or choose part dimensions that could be neglected. Their duties had been clearly defined and arbitrary deviation from the prescribed inspection processes constituted gross negligence, resulting in a financial loss to the company.

Arbitrator's Analysis. The functions of the arbitrator are strictly limited by the agreement between the parties. Though he is empowered to decide the questions submitted to him, he cannot add to or subtract from the provisions of the agreement, but must ascertain the essential facts and circumstances and determine whether the company had violated the agreement by discharging the two men.

The job of both Set-Up Inspector and Floor Inspector is to make careful examinations of a number of sample parts and to subject them to a series of prescribed measurements and tests to determine whether they conform to the applicable planning sheet and blueprint requirements. Both job descriptions specifically stated that the inspector is required to inspect the parts for conformance to blueprint requirements. Both men admitted that they did not do so. They made superficial inspections, which were largely confined to certain minor characteristics of the parts, instead of making the thoroughly complete inspections which their instructions required them to make.

Both men stated that they had more than the usual amount of work to do. F.A. further explained how his attention became focused upon the threads to the exclusion of the other features of the part. Although these circumstances explain how they happened to fail to make the required thorough inspections, they did not excuse either man's omission of essential steps in his inspections.

The large loss to the company was the result of the combination of at least three improper inspections. If F.A. had performed his job properly, F.B.'s superficial inspections might not have mattered. Likewise, if either of F.B.'s inspections had been as thorough as his instructions required them to be, the loss resulting from F.A.'s lapse would have been minimized.

But neither of these facts had any material effect upon either man's offense. F.A.'s responsibility was somewhat greater because his was the first inspection and authorized the start of the run. His job is rated one step higher than F.B.'s, who had a continuing responsibility during the run. F.A. made two superficial, ineffective inspections, which did not find the rather obvious defect in the part.

Considering all extenuating circumstances, the arbitrator concluded that the offenses of both men constituted "gross carelessness" within the meaning of Article XVI, Section 1, of the agreement. Both men failed to perform the essential duties of their jobs on major tasks, and both omissions resulted in a substantial loss to the company. This precluded further consideration of the employees' previous records for purposes of modifying the penalty. The employer might well have taken these records into account in determining the penalty, but the agreement did not require the company to do so.

The arbitrator considered the question of whether the penalties were discriminatory and therefore violated the agreement. The penalties imposed upon the grievants were much more severe than those imposed upon the machine operators involved, but only because inspectors have a higher degree of responsibility. They had failed to perform the fundamental, essential portion of their function. The responsibility and degree of fault of the machine operators were considerably less.

Although at the hearing two other specific situations involving spoiled parts were described, it was brought out that in both cases the plans, or the blueprints themselves, were subject to alternative interpretations. In this case the blueprints were clear. The inspectors merely failed to use them. Although there were general allusions to lesser penalties for other spoiled work, no other specific instances were cited at the hearing. Thus, no other situations involving lesser penalties for comparable errors were brought out at the hearing. The arbitrator therefore concluded that the penalties invoked by management against the grievants should not be barred on grounds of discrimination.

Award. Upon full consideration of all the evidence, arguments, and records presented, it was the decision of the arbitrator that the company did not violate the labor–management agreement of August 26, 1954, by discharging the grievants for gross negligence.

REFERENCES

1. Southern Pipe and Casing Co., 29 LA 224; Active Products Corp., CCH 71-1, para. 8254.
2. Wiley Machine Co., 14 LA 770; Ideal Cement Co., 21 LA 314; Velsicol Chemical Corp., CCH 71-1, para. 8109.
3. National Petro-Chemicals Corp., 25 LA 235.
4. Safe Bus Co., Inc., 21 LA 456.
5. General Metals Corp., 25 LA 118.

STRIKE ACTIVITY AND SLOWDOWNS

Discharge of an employee for violation of a no-strike clause will ordinarily be sustained unless the union can make out a strong showing of anti-union bias and discrimination. To make the discharge "stick," the employer has to show that no such bias determined the judgment. Other factors that the arbitrator will weigh are: (1) the predominance of union members or leaders among the discharged and those offered reinstatement; (2) the degree of union activity of the individual employee; and (3) the posture of the employer with regard to union membership.

In the early arbitration cases much was made of the employer's anti-union statements. The more recent awards, however, turn on the degree of responsibility of the individual employee. A higher standard is imposed on the union representative. He is held strictly to account where he knowingly participates in, or remains passive to, an illegal strike or slowdown.[1] Of course, where he is the instigator he is susceptible to discharge.[2] Employee misconduct during a legal strike has also been a factor in a number of discipline cases. The main concern of the arbitrator appears to be the degree of responsibility of the individuals involved, along with the usual mitigating factors present in all discharge cases.[3]

Slowdowns are difficult to prove, and responsibility for them often eludes precise determination. Arbitrators have accepted production records as material evidence in support of a discharge action.[4] While leading a slowdown is ample cause for disciplinary action, there is little uniformity in the decisions as to how the arbitrator determines its existence, and how responsibility is ascertained in the absence of clear evidence of statements or acts of the leaders.[5]

Where the discharged or disciplined employee is a union representative, it is normal to expect the union to contend in his defense that the reason he was disciplined was because of his union activity. Invariably this defense is interposed no matter what the employer's charge. Plainly, the union representative is immune from discipline for his legitimate union activities or duties. But while performing his duties as an employee, no such immunity attaches. It is here again that the arbitrator must attempt to discern whether a union's allegation of anti-union bias as the motivating force of the discipline has any substance.

CASE 1: INCITING WORK STOPPAGE

GREENVILLE STEEL CAR COMPANY AND GREENVILLE
STEEL CAR BUILDERS ASSOCIATION,
46 LA 120. ARBITRATOR: DUFF.

Issue. The grievant, X, claimed that the company was unjustified in discharging him.

Background. The company manufactures steel railroad cars and operates yards and shops at Greenville, Pennsylvania. Grievant X worked as a welder in the area known as the Morgan Yard, where railroad cars are manufactured on an assembly line.

On August 10, 1965, the union and management were discussing a problem that had arisen in another area of the plant called the G.E. shop. On August 11, while the discussion was still going on, the workers of the G.E. shop stopped working pending the outcome of the dispute. The grievant, employed by the company at Morgan Yard, which had no relation to the G.E. shop, learned of this work stoppage. The grievant, through his actions and allegedly through his words, induced other employees at Morgan Yard to engage in an unauthorized strike. He had been told by the foreman and the president of the union that his actions were in violation of the agreement. He was discharged.

Contract Provisions. Article III, Section 1, asserts the right of the employer to discharge employees for proper cause or for the violation of established rules or provisions of the contract, and that these rights are vested exclusively in the company, provided this right will not be used for purposes of discrimination against any member of the union. Any employee discharged shall have the right to a hearing, to be handled as a grievance under Article V, Section 1. In Section 2 the union pledges that any dispute will be settled in the manner provided in the grievance article of the agreement, and that the union agrees not to oppose the discharge or discipline of anyone who instigates, leads, or induces another employee to take part in an unauthorized strike.

Arbitrator's Analysis. It was held that the company was justified in discharging the grievant, and that his actions were a serious breach of the labor agreement. In support of his decision, the arbitrator quoted from another case[6]: "In essence, a Labor Agreement is a part of a system of industrial self-government. Where the parties have mutually agreed that there shall be no strikes or work stoppages and that no employee shall participate in any such activities, an employee who acts contrary to such contractual provision commits a serious offense."

Award. The grievance was denied, and the discharge of X for a just cause under the contract was confirmed.

CASE 2: WORK STOPPAGE
A. P. MEIRILLAND COMPANY INCORPORATED AND RETAIL
WHOLESALE AND DEPARTMENT STORE UNION, CCH 71–1,
PARA. 8103. ARBITRATOR: WILLIAMS.

Issue. Was the grievant discharged for just cause?

Background. On October 30, 1970, a boiler in the plant broke down. The maintenance crew repaired the boiler in four hours while the employees remained at the plant awaiting resumption of operation. After the four hours, the employees worked eight hours. On November 2, 1970, the Vice President in charge of Operation, M., met with members of the grievance committee (including grievant) and offered to pay the employees two hours' wages for the four hours downtime. The committee demanded four hours pay. On the next day, the grievant, who was a Shop Steward, reported M.'s offer to a group of 55 workers, including the grievant. The employees demanded to see M., and after he appeared, they began walking off their jobs. Vice President M. told the workers that all those who participated in the walk-off would be subject to discharge.

On the next day, November 4, 1970, the grievant and the workers returned to work, whereupon she and ten other employees were discharged. The grievant alleged that she had been discharged without just cause.

Contract Provisions. The provision in the Agreement on Strikes and Lockouts (Article X) acknowledges that union officers and members agree that for the duration of the agreement, there would be no strikes, no stoppages of work, or any acts that would interfere with business or production. For violations of Article X, the agreement provided that "any employee, including Local Union officers or members of the Grievance Committee who take part in . . . any violation of this Agreement shall be subject to immediate discharge by the Company. . . . It is not necessary that the Company discharge all the employees who take part, to preclude any charge of discrimination."

Positions of the Parties. The company attempted to prove that the grievant was one of the leaders in the walkout and that she had incited other employees to leave the plant on November 3, 1970. The union, on the other hand, attempted to show that the grievant had attempted to prevent the strike.

Arbitrator's Analysis. The arbitrator considered the testimony of the grievant, in which she stated that she had "participated in the strike, and did so with full awareness of the Agreement and that she would be subject to discharge for her participation." The grievant, by her testimony, had become an employee who "takes part . . . in any violation of this Agreement" and thus became subject to immediate discharge.

Award. The grievance was denied.

CASE 3: SLOWDOWN
SUFFOLK COUNTY WATER AUTHORITY AND
UTILITY WORKERS OF AMERICA, LOCAL 393,
CCH 71-1, PARA. 8338. ARBITRATOR: TROTTA.

Issue. The Suffolk County Water Authority selected and suspended 23 employees "for substandard performance." The case was submitted to arbitration. The issue was: "Was the one day's suspension of 23 employees on July 21 and July 22, 1970, for just cause? If not, what shall the remedy be?"

Background. Evidence submitted by management showed that "on or about July 14, 1970, it became evident that a number of employees were performing their work in a significantly substandard fashion . . . . Whereas normal and average meter readings were about one hundred per day, on or about July 14, 1970, they averaged half this number." The Assistant General Manager advised the men that if their work did not improve, disciplinary action would be taken. The work did not improve and management decided to suspend the men "over a period of three or four days until all employees who were producing substandard work would be suspended for one day." However, the matter was settled before all were suspended.

Contract Provisions. Article 1, Section 3, of the agreement stipulates that "the exercise of rights and powers [to suspend] shall not be arbitrary or unfair to any employee."

Union's Position. According to the union, the men were selected randomly and only some of those whom the company alleges participated in the slowdown were penalized. It was unfair for the employer to penalize only some of the men.

Employer's Position. The Water Authority supported the position that the selective staggered suspensions were proper by stating that "it is a public benefit corporation . . . which supplies water to approximately 175,000 accounts." Thus, it is "engaged in furnishing an essential public service vital to . . . the population . . . ." As stated in the agreement, the Authority "has a high degree of responsibility to the public in so serving the public without interruption of this essential service, and . . . cannot meet this responsibility unless it has the conscientious cooperation of its employees, and it is therefore essential . . . that disputes arising between the Authority and its employees be adjusted and settled in an orderly manner without interruption of service . . . ."

The Authority contended that the disciplinary action was reasonable and that the selected suspensions were nondiscriminatory because "the persons selected did participate in a slowdown, and except for the request by the Union to meet and settle the matter, all other employees whose performance was substandard would have been suspended for one day."

Arbitrator's Analysis. The arbitrator examined the work records of the men suspended and found "that the twenty-three men [suspended] did not perform up to standard." The crucial question then became whether the method of selecting the 23 men was arbitrary. The arbitrator found that:

The evidence supports the contention of the Authority that it intended to suspend all the men within a period of a few days, and if it had suspended them all at the same time it would not have fulfilled its responsibility to supply essential services to the public.

It was at the request of the Union that the Authority suspended its decision to penalize all the men involved in substandard work. Therefore it was an act of the Union which caused only 23 men to be penalized.

It appears to me that the Authority acted in the only logical way open to it, considering its obligations to the public.

Award. The arbitrator ruled that the suspension of the 23 men for one day was for just cause.

CASE 4: REASONABLENESS OF PENALTY

CHRYSLER CORPORATION, LOS ANGELES PLANT (LOS ANGELES, CALIF.), AND UNITED AUTOMOBILE, AIRCRAFT & AGRICULTURAL IMPLEMENT WORKERS OF AMERICA, 19 LA 818. ARBITRATOR: WOLFF.

Issue. Was management justified in discharging the two grievants for their part in picketing the plant? If not, what penalty, if any, should management have imposed on them?

Background. The grievants, C. and F., were discharged for being the leaders of the respective picket line in which each participated at two plant gates on July 24, 1952. The lines prevented employees from reporting to work at their regular starting time. Insofar as the record shows, no other employee connected with the picket lines received discipline of any kind.

Both grievants, neither being union representatives at the time, had been active in discussions with management on previous days. These discussions had to do with the general dispute that preceded the picketing.

Contract Provisions. Article I, Section 6, of the agreement provides in part that no member of the union would picket any of the corporation's plants or premises until all bargaining procedures as outlined in the agreement had been exhausted. The corporation reserved the right to discipline any employee taking part in any violation of this section of the agreement.

Union's Position. According to union witnesses, small groups of employees had assembled before Grievant C. arrived. Arm bands bearing the word "Picket" had been brought by employees of another company, who placed them on the ground or gave them to the pickets. Grievant C. was in the group of pickets but gave no orders, prevented no one from entering the plant, did not attempt to coerce or influence any employee, and did not vocally or actively resist the attempts of union officials to disperse the groups. The picket line had formed before Grievant F. arrived; the arm bands, provided by strikers from a nearby plant, had been passed out by several known and named employees.

Company's Position. According to company witnesses, Grievant C. was present at one of the plant gates more than an hour before the starting time of the general shift. He talked with three female employees who had been about to report for work but who thereupon did not report. He commenced to walk in front of the gate, whereupon some employees who were standing nearby followed him and formed a picket line. He moved along the picket line and passed out arm bands to some of the people in the line and to some who then joined the line. Other witnesses said that Grievant F. led employees standing outside the gate in starting the picket line. At about 6:27 A.M., while in the line, Grievant F. waved his arms and shouted to a group of employees who were across the street: "Over here is the picket line, let's go." At about 6:32 A.M. he passed out arm bands and conferred with other employees who then joined the picket line.

Arbitrator's Analysis. The arbitrator commented that some company witnesses may have overemphasized and overstated the activities in, and responsibilities for, the picket line attributed to Grievants C. and F., particularly when considered on a comparative basis. On the other hand, careful examination of all the proof left no doubt that both grievants had offered a certain amount of leadership.

Determination of the fact of leadership of a picket line, unauthorized and contrary to the terms of the agreement, supports the propriety of the imposition of substantial penalties, including discharge, for such activities. However, it must be recognized that the reasonableness and justice of the degree of severity of the penalty given in this case depended upon the particular facts and circumstances involved.

Both grievants had excellent prior records. While clearly a contributing factor, such leadership as was shown by them, improper as it was, hardly could by itself have resulted in obtaining the cooperation of fellow employees in starting the lines. Rather than being primarily a response to the leadership of the grievants, the entire affair, including the picketing, seemed to have been in the nature of an activity decided on by the group, either largely spontaneous or as a result of undisclosed instructions of undisclosed principals. Because of these circumstances, and because management imposed no discipline of any kind on any others involved (some of whom were specifically stated to have openly participated in more than routine fashion), the arbitrator's opinion was that, while the imposing of substantial discipline on the grievants was warranted, on a relative basis the penalty of discharge could not be justifiably approved.

Award. It was ordered that the discharge of the grievants be reduced to disciplinary layoffs without back pay, and that they must be offered reemployment immediately.

REFERENCES

1. Jones and Laughlin Steel Corp., 29 LA 644; Green River Steel Corp., 25 LA 774; General Aniline & Film Corp., 30 LA 109.
2. Chrysler Corp., 19 LA 818; Inland Steel Co., 19 LA 601; Gardener-Denver Co., 15 LA 829.
3. Univis Lens Co., 11 LA 211; Glass Container Manufacturers Institute, 27 LA 131; Southern Bell Telephone & Telegraph Co., 25 LA 410.
4. Timken Roller Bearing Co., 14 LA 475; John Deere Harvester Works, 27 LA 744.
5. Standard Steel Spring Co., 17 LA 423; International Nickel Co., Inc., 31 LA 914.
6. A. M. Byers Co., 31 LA 210.

FIGHTING

Employees who engaged in fighting on company property and during working hours are subject to disciplinary action by the company. Frequently, collective bargaining agreements provide that an employee who is guilty of fighting is subject to summary discharge. Even outside of working hours, altercations on company property are disciplinable offenses.[1]

In cases where the issue is fighting, questions frequently arise as to whether the employee involved was the aggressor or merely acted in self-defense.[2] Consideration must also be given to whether the alleged act was part of a course of conduct or an isolated incident committed under extreme provocation by an otherwise good employee.[3]

Mischievous conduct, short of fighting, is also an offense and may lead to discipline, even discharge. But "horseplay" is often not enough to call for more than a suspension or reprimand.[4]

CASE 1: PROVOCATION
DOUGLAS AIRCRAFT COMPANY, INC., AND
INTERNATIONAL ASSOCIATION OF MACHINISTS,
23 LA 645 (DIGESTED). ARBITRATOR: JONES.

Issue. The issue to be decided in this case was whether the company had misapplied the provisions of an existing agreement when it discharged an employee for fighting in the plant.

Background. The grievant had an altercation with a fellow employee in the plant about the use of a certain piece of equipment. When the co-worker engaged in highly abusive language and generally provocative conduct, the grievant struck him. Both men were discharged, the grievant for violating the company's rule against fighting and the other employee for his use of abusive racial epithets.

Contract Provisions. Article II, Section 2, of the collective bargaining agreement made provision for "Guides in the Adjustment of Differences." These guides stipulated that "the management of the plant and the direction of working forces . . . are vested exclusively in the company." This included the right "to discharge, suspend or otherwise discipline employees" for just cause, provided no action taken was prohibited by the agreement. The agreement applied to all employees "without discrimination on account of race, national origin, sex, color or creed."

Union's Position. The union sought reinstatement with pay for the grievant on the grounds that (1) he did not "fight" as the word is commonly understood, (2) if it be concluded that he did "fight," he was justified by extreme provocation, and therefore no just cause existed for his discharge. The union cited two apparently similar instances where the penalty of discharge had not been imposed for fighting.

It asserted that discharge would be discriminating and would violate the agreement, which prohibits discrimination "of any kind." The union deprecated the racial slur, indicating that a decision upholding discharge would encourage racial bigotry. Finally, the union emphasized the grievant's good record with the company and pointed out that the company had been willing to reinstate him without pay for time lost at a pre-arbitration step in grievance procedure.

Company's Position. The company deplored the racial incident and cited its discharge of the employee who provoked it. It argued, however, that it was well known to all employees that fighting automatically means discharge, irrespective of provocation, even if one party involved acts in self-defense. It pointed out that its rigid policy against fighting was not limited to instances of physical contact, but also applied where there was an overt act short of physical contact.

The company, moreover, insisted that the discharge was justified because the safety of employees working at machines had been endangered. The company's potential legal liability for resultant injuries to principals and bystanders was also pointed out. Its good safety record was attributed in part to rigid adherence to a rule whereby employees know they will be discharged if they participate in a fight.

The two isolated instances of nondischarge fights cited by the union were regarded by the company as "neither signifying discrimination, nor nullifying the intendment of the company's policy nor erasing the significance of [the] latter in the minds of its employees." "This is so," the company argued, "whether these two decisions not to discharge were made under special circumstances not here present, as the company believed, or under facts quite similar, as the union asserts. In that latter event they would simply be mistaken deviations from a settled policy."

Arbitrator's Analysis. The arbitrator first pointed out that this case had its genesis in a fundamental sociological problem. Resort to violence in response to a reflection on one's racial background is an understandable human reaction. It may on one occasion command sympathy, but it is not an acceptable form of conduct. People of diverse racial and ethnic origins are committed to the peaceful evolution of equality of opportunity for all citizens in an atmosphere of mutual respect. This can come about only through the peaceful solution of many of our problems of human relationships in the spirit of realistic cooperation under an accepted rule of law.

An important issue facing the arbitrator was whether to find that the agreement denied the company the right to institute a policy that assured an abatement of discrimination. Other considerations further supported the company's position in this discharge. Among industrial relations experts there is substantial agreement that management cannot tolerate fighting among its employees on the job, which is not only hazardous to the safety of its employees but which imposes by rigid state law a liability on the company for injuries sustained by employees.

In the judgment of the arbitrator, the two instances cited by the union of nondischarge for fighting did not alter the case. Even assuming some factual similarity to be relevant, two instances in a period of years do not establish a course of action that would distract the company from reliance on its no-fight rule as a basis for discharge.

The arbitrator did not consider whether a discharge for fighting would be for "just cause" if an employee were to defend himself against an attacker, since the grievant admittedly took the initiative.

Award. The grievance was denied. The arbitrator felt he could not require that the grievant be reemployed, because the principle at stake was so unanimously defined in the agreement. He did recommend, however, that the employee be favorably considered for reemployment.

CASE 2: APPROPRIATENESS OF PENALTY
INTERNATIONAL HARVESTER COMPANY, FORT WAYNE WORKS,
AND UNITED AUTOMOBILE, AIRCRAFT & AGRICULTURAL
IMPLEMENT WORKERS OF AMERICA, 21 LA 32. ARBITRATOR: COLE.

Issue. An employee was discharged for hitting a fellow worker. He filed a grievance in which he charged the company had violated the provision of the contract with the union regarding employee discipline and requested full reinstatement with pay for the time lost. The major question was whether the disciplinary action taken was reasonably necessary or whether it should be modified.

Background. The employee admitted he had struck a fellow worker. No serious question was raised as to whether the company had just cause for exercising "its rights to invoke disciplinary measures."

The testimony of witnesses at the hearing was conflicting, but it seemed to be reasonably well established that undue provocation led to an assault, although this did not excuse the employee for his unwarranted action.

Contract Provisions. The pertinent provisions of the master contract were:

Section 1: The company, in directing the working force, may exercise its right to invoke disciplinary measures for good cause, subject to the terms and conditions of this contract.

Section 2: Disciplinary measures include reprimand, suspension and discharge.

Section 3: Permitted the company to invoke disciplinary measures to "maintain efficiency, safe practices and discipline, and for directing, leading, causing or participating in any interference with or interruption of production. . . ."

Section 6: In the event that there was not "good cause for the disciplinary measure imposed" and the action taken by the company should be set aside or modified, the company agreed to reinstate the employee and "all hours he would otherwise have worked . . . shall be counted as hours worked for vacation purposes." The company further agreed to pay any wages due to the employee as a result of the decision; however, the arbitrator shall rule whether or not any money received by the employee, through other employment since his discharge, should be deducted from the amount the company is required to pay under the provisions of the contract.

Arbitrator's Analysis. The arbitrator recognized the company's right to maintain orderliness and discipline and to prohibit and punish fighting. Although the discharged employee had a clean record with the company, extending over a period of years, he felt some punishment was in order as a deterrent to other employees. Moreover, he believed a severe suspension without pay would serve the purpose, and publication of this opinion would have a marked effect on all other employees. The arbitrator recognized the seriousness of fighting and the importance of the severity on the part of management when it occurs. Had he not been convinced that there was extreme provocation, he would not have disturbed the penalty applied by management.

Award. The arbitrator decided that the disciplinary penalty should be changed from discharge to suspension for one month without pay. He directed reinstatement at the expiration of the suspension period.

REFERENCES

1. Stewart Warner Corp., 21 LA 186; Union Carbide Corp., CCH 71-1, para. 8354.
2. Texas Co., 24 LA 240.
3. International Harvester Co., 21 LA 32; Douglas Aircraft Co., 23 LA 645; Swift and Co., 11 LA 581.
4. Trane Co., 14 LA 1039; Jackson Products Co., CCH 71-1, para. 8099.

MISCONDUCT: OFF-DUTY/ON-DUTY

An employee may commit improper acts which subject him to disciplinary action while he is on duty or off duty. The most common cases involve on-duty misconduct. However, employees are also frequently disciplined or discharged for committing improper acts while off duty. In the latter type of cases, arbitrators have held that to justify disciplinary action, including discharge, there must be some evidence of damage to the company.

In an unpublished case, a 15-year employee with a good record, who worked in the shipping department of a foundry, was discharged upon conviction on a morals charge. He was sentenced to jail for two years, but after 30 days his case was reconsidered. The judge released him, put him on probation, and ordered him to have psychiatric treatment, which he did.

The employee then sought to be reinstated. The company refused reinstatement because it had an unwritten rule that any person convicted of a crime would be automatically discharged. The union challenged the action of the company on the following grounds: (1) The word "crime" was not defined and its interpretation depended upon the subjective values of the personnel manager; (2) the conviction was in no way related to the employee's work, nor did it harm the company in any way; (3) the employee was being punished by society for the same act; and (4) if all persons who have committed offenses against society are prevented from working, the rehabilitation of convicted persons is made impossible. The employee was reinstated.

In another case an employee went to the home of his supervisor and assaulted him. He was then discharged. It was disclosed at an arbitration hearing that the supervisor was having an affair with the employee's wife. The arbitrator upheld the union's argument that this was a private affair and should not be grounds for discharge.

Where, however, the offense committed is related to a man's job and is damaging to the company, discharge may be proper.

CASE 1: OFF-DUTY MISCONDUCT
SEALED POWER CORPORATION AND INTERNATIONAL UNION, UNITED AUTOMOBILE AEROSPACE AND AGRICULTURAL IMPLEMENT WORKERS OF AMERICA LOCAL 637, CCH 71-1, PARA. 8136. ABRITRATOR: CASSELMAN.

Issue. Did the company have just cause to discharge Grievant S. on or about March 13, 1970?

Background. On March 9, 1970, Grievant S. was arrested and taken to Flint, Michigan, to face a court citation for back child-support. S. called his company and informed the operator that he would be out of town for a week on personal business. On March 11, 1970, he was sentenced to a year's imprisonment. On March 12, 1970, the grievant's mother reported to the company that S. had been sentenced for nonsupport of his child and would not be available for work. On March 13, 1970, the company discharged S. because he had been incarcerated. On March 17, S. was able to post bond, was released, and returned home. The next day he filed a grievance against the company.

Contract Provisions. Rule 27 of the agreement states that "conviction or imprisonment arising from a criminal charge" is just cause for disciplinary action, including discharge.

Union's Position. The union contended that the grievant reasonably assumed that he had a leave of absence when he was given an "OK" by the operator. The union asserted that the grievant made every effort to protect his job and that in previous cases employees had been allowed to use earned vacation time to cover a period of incarceration. In three similar cases, arrangements had been made to take earned vacation while in jail. These employees were not disciplined, on the theory that they may use their vacation time as they see fit.

Company's Position. According to the agreement, leave of absence must be formally requested and approved by a designated supervisor. The grievant's message did not conform with this requirement. Furthermore, the company had been advised by a supposedly knowledgeable and authoritative person that the grievant had been incarcerated for a period of time. The company argued that the agreement was clear and did not allow for the probability of suspended incarceration.

Arbitrator's Analysis. It appeared crucial to the arbitrator that the grievant's discharge was effected in his absence and before he could state his case. In three of the previous cases involving violation of Rule 27, employees were allowed to use their accumulated vacation time during their period of confinement. It appeared to the arbitrator that it was incumbent on management to advise the grievant that his job was in jeopardy and that this avenue was available to him.

The arbitrator was satisfied that the grievant made a reasonable effort to protect his job and had informed the company of the reason for his absence. It was the responsibility of the company to inform the grievant of his privilege of using his accumulated vacation time, and at least to listen to him before discharging him. Since the company did not review the facts pertinent to the situation prior to discharge, the discharge could not be for just cause and could not be sustained.

Award. The arbitrator ruled that the grievant should not have been separated by the company without a prior hearing and without advising him of the possibility of substituting accumulated vacation time. The arbitrator sustained the grievance and awarded the grievant his job with back pay, except for one week.

CASE 2: ON-DUTY MISCONDUCT
SOUTH CENTRAL BELL TELEPHONE COMPANY
AND COMMUNICATIONS WORKERS OF AMERICA,
CCH 71-1, PARA. 8297. ARBITRATOR: RAY.

Issue. Was the company justified in discharging the grievant for apparent immoral conduct?

Background. On April 18, 1969, a customer, Miss B., was visited in her newly occupied apartment by a telephone company employee, T., whom she recognized as the installer of her telephone at her previous apartment. The man carried a 25-foot telephone cord and proceeded to show how far it would reach around the room. When she asked its cost, she was told there would be no charge if she would "give him some." She understood that he was proposing sexual intercourse and refused, but he proceeded to install the cord. After repeating his invitation and receiving a negative answer, he left, but a week later he called and again suggested a reward for giving her the cord. Following this call, Miss B. reported T.'s conduct to the telephone business office, and as a result he was discharged after a hearing.

Contract Provisions. The sections of the agreement relating to improper employee conduct are as follows:

5.01 Employees of the Company are often directed to go to the premises of customers for the purpose of installing, maintaining, and repairing telephone equipment and for other business reasons. In some instances they have been accused by the customers or some other person of engaging in immoral acts such as attempted assaults and sexual crimes.

5.03 Where the evidence clearly shows that the employee was not conducting himself in accordance with accepted standards of conduct, disciplinary action including dismissal will be taken.

Union's Position. The union counsel argued that the existence of the conduct must be proved beyond a reasonable doubt before the discharge can be sustained. The grievant had testified at the hearing of his knowledge that Miss B. had been consorting with a male companion at her previous apartment. Under these circumstances he assumed that Miss B. would consider his advances at the later date when he installed a telephone in her new apartment. He contended that she was not offended by his proposition. He admitted calling her again and proposing that they could "make a deal," meaning sexual intercourse.

Counsel argued that T.'s conduct was not immoral because "the circumstances under which the illicit statements were made should be considered." In view of these facts and the fact that T. did not press his advances, discharge was too severe a penalty.

Company's Position, The company contended that prior knowledge of the customer's domestic situation was not license to pursue immoral objectives. The grievant was present on the customer's premises as a representative of the company and thus had violated Rules 5.01 and 5.03 of the personnel policy manual by making immoral propositions.

Arbitrator's Analysis. The arbitrator held that the answer to this question was that Miss B.'s morals were not in issue; the issue was the grievant's conduct. After examining the evidence, the arbitrator said that there had been no doubt in his mind that the grievant was guilty of the conduct charged; that is, he did propose sexual intercourse to Miss B.

Award. The arbitrator felt that since T. had demonstrated his tendency to engage in offensive behavior, there was no basis for any reasonable belief that he would not do it again. The grievance was denied.

INSUBORDINATION AND ABUSIVE CONDUCT

In general, if an employee refuses to obey an order or defies the authority of management, he is guilty of insubordination.[1] This is a serious offense and may justify disciplinary measures, including discharge.

An employee may be charged with insubordination not only if he wilfully disobeys an order, but also if he fails to follow an order. He may also be guilty of insubordination if he refuses or fails to follow company rules and regulations; uses abusive, threatening, or profane language in speaking to management; or assaults a representative of management. In most cases that come before arbitrators, the employee either denies the alleged subordinate act or gives reasons why it was justified.

It is a generally accepted rule that if an employee thinks a supervisor's order violates the contract or is improper or unfair, he should nevertheless obey the order unless compliance would jeopardize his health, life, or limb, and then file a grievance.[2]

CASE 1: WILLFUL REFUSAL TO OBEY—NEW WORK METHODS
CORN PRODUCTS COMPANY, ARGO PLANT
(ARGO, ILLINOIS) AND OIL, CHEMICAL AND
ATOMIC WORKERS INTERNATIONAL UNION
LOCAL 7-507, 42 LA 172. ARBITRATOR: KAMIN.

Issue. Did management have sufficient cause to suspend the grievant for five days without pay for refusing to obey his supervisor's instructions? If not, what should the penalty be?

Background. On April 22, 1963, the grievant was employed in the shipping division of the company. He was assigned to load 100-pound bags of the company product into box cars for shipment. The foreman told the grievant to use the hand truck instead of the roller for loading the bags. After raising an objection, the grievant continued to use the roller. Grievant was suspended for five days for his refusal to use the techniques prescribed by the foreman. He then filed a grievance.

Contract Provisions. Article II, Section 2, of the agreement states that management has the exclusive right and power to manage the plant and direct the work force, including discipline and discharge.

Arbitrator's Analysis. It was the opinion of the arbitrator that insubordination is not a concept of employee misbehavior that is limited to refusals to perform work assignments. An employee may also be insubordinate when he is willing to work but is unwilling to obey supervisory directions concerning the methods or devices to be employed in such work.

Unless a labor agreement otherwise specifies, industrial management, through its supervisors, has the right and responsibility to prescribe the techniques, tools, and equipment by which work in its behalf shall be performed.

Award. Grievance denied.

CASE 2: WILLFUL REFUSAL TO OBEY—OPERATION UNSAFE
HALSTED METAL PRODUCTS, INC. (ZELIENOPLE, PA.)
AND UNITED STEELWORKERS OF AMERICA LOCAL
7032, 49 LA 325. ARBITRATOR: WAGNER.

Issue. Was the management justified in suspending the grievants for five days without pay for refusing to operate a machine because they considered it to be unsafe? If not, what should the remedy be?

Background. In an effort to increase the efficiency of its operations and improve material handling and material flow, the company redesigned one of its machines. After briefly operating the machine, the grievants refused to operate it without a crane because they judged it to be unsafe. The foreman told them to operate the machine "as is" or go home. The grievants chose the latter and were suspended for five days.

Contract Provisions. Article III, Section 1, of the agreement confirms management's rights to determine violations and impose penalties for insubordination, given just cause. Article VIII, Section 1, states that any employee may be discharged for proper cause, but Section 2 dictates that "any permanent employee who may be discharged must be suspended for a period not to exceed five days to allow him to file a grievance. Article XIV on plant rules provides in Section 1 that "failure or refusal to comply with the [plant] rules shall be cause for the disciplinary action indicated," and in Section 2 grants the company the exclusive right to change these rules.

The above conditions are supplemented by the "Plant Rules Booklet (Group III)," which states: "Committing any of the following violations will be sufficient reason for disciplinary action in the form of: (1) discharge for the first offense; (2) suspension."

Union's Position. The grievants, after operating the machine, felt it was unsafe. The unsafe aspects of the machinery, as claimed by the grievants, were actually detected and were corrected the following weekend, proving their point that the machinery was unsafe. At the time of their complaint, they were given the choice of working or going home, and were never warned of possible disciplinary action.

Company's Position. The machine was deemed safe by the Plant Superintendent, Day Foreman, and Safety Supervisor, as well as by the union representative. The machine was used without incident on two shifts before the grievants' shift. The company contended it had the right to make necessary and expedient changes to improve company operations and to take disciplinary action for violation of plant rules.

Arbitrator's Analysis. It was held that the grievants' fear of bodily harm was justified. The arbitrator agreed with the principles set forth in a similar case[3]: "It would be impossible to run an industrial enterprise if the employees were free to refuse the instructions of Management whenever they felt that such instructions were improper or violative of the Agreement. This is true even though the position of the employees may be held to be completely correct in the final determination. It is recognized that there may be exceptions to this rule. An employee may be justified in refusing an assignment which he has good reason to believe would endanger his health or physical safety."

Award. The arbitrator ruled that the suspension was not justified, that the grievants should be fully reimbursed for earnings lost, and that the penalty should be expunged from their employment records.

CASE 3. REFUSAL TO OBEY RULES AND REGULATIONS
VENTURA CORPORATION (ELWOOD, IND.) AND
UNITED STEELWORKERS OF AMERICA LOCAL 5576,
30 LA 132. ARBITRATOR: DAVIS.

Issue. Was management justified in discharging grievant for breaking the company rule that prohibits horseplay? If not, what penalty, if any, should be imposed?

Background. The grievant was discharged for horseplay. The grievant had tapped another employee on the leg with a stick when passing him in the course of his job duties. The employee fell off a platform but was not hurt. Similar incidents had happened before in the plant without being subjected to disciplinary measures.

Contract Provisions. The fifth step in adjustment of grievances (Section 11 of the agreement) provides for arbitration in case the previous four steps have failed. In Section 12 (Discharge, Demotion, and Layoff Cases), "if an employee has been discharged, demoted, or laid off, he can resort to the grievance procedure set up in Section 11."

Union's Position. The grievant was discharged without just cause. The horseplay had gone on before, but management had not followed a consistent disciplinary policy in handling such incidents.

Company's Position. The contract gives the company the right to discharge for just cause. Horseplay is grounds for discipline, and in this case grievous physical harm might have resulted from the grievant's actions.

Arbitrator's Analysis. At the hearing, the grievant in this case admitted he knew horseplay was against company rules. Thus, there was no doubt that he was properly subject to disciplinary action for the act.

Award. The arbitrator ruled that the discharge was too harsh a penalty. He instructed that grievant be reinstated, but without back pay as a disciplinary measure for grievant's offense.

CASE 4: FAILURE TO OBEY
ELBERTA CRATE AND BOX COMPANY (TALLAHASSEE, FLA.)
AND INTERNATIONAL WOODWORKERS OF AMERICA LOCAL
NO. 5–181, 30 LA 502. ARBITRATOR: WILLIAMS.

Issue. Was the grievant fired for just cause when she refused to perform duties other than her own?

Background. The grievant's job was to pick up wood stock as it emerged from the kiln at her position, rejecting unsatisfactory pieces and stocking the others. Five Graders (grievant's title) worked at one time. A Grader was absent one night and the other four, including the grievant, were told to spread out and handle the five positions. The grievant moved to the end position and handled two positions by herself for one hour; then she went back to handling only her own position, at which point she was discharged.

Union's Position. The grievant was discharged without just cause. The grievant was not given clear instructions and did not disobey those instructions as she understood them.

Company's Position. The grievant was discharged for just cause, since she failed to obey a reasonable order.

Arbitrator's Analysis. The instructions could not have been unclear because the grievant's experience was sufficiently extensive so that she knew she had to work the end position. "Management's right to direct its working force in a manner not inconsistent with the Agreement is clear, and this right must be protected. Insubordination and refusal to carry out legitimate orders cannot be tolerated."

Award. Grievance denied.

CASE 5: COUNTERMANDING SUPERVISOR'S ORDERS
FORD MOTOR COMPANY, SPRING AND UPSET BUILDING (RIVER ROUGE, MICH.), AND INTERNATIONAL UNION, UNITED AUTOMOBILE, AIRCRAFT & AGRICULTURAL IMPLEMENT WORKERS OF AMERICA. 3 LA 779. ARBITRATOR: SHULMAN.

Issue. Was the discharge of X, a District Committeeman, justified in view of his having countermanded orders of a supervisor to employees to work out of their normal classifications in order to meet a production schedule?

Background. Because Gates 9 and 10 at the Rouge Plant's aircraft building were blocked by employee action on March 15, 1944, many employees in other buildings were unable to report to work. The Spring & Upset building was undermanned by about 40 percent that day. It was important to keep the supercharger operating in that building to avoid shutting down jobs involving numerous men in other buildings that were dependent on the supercharger. Accordingly, Spring & Upset supervisors assigned men temporarily to work out of their classifications on the supercharger and on other jobs. The company found that X, the District Committeeman in this unit, had instructed employees not to work outside their classifications. As a result of his instructions, certain employees, although otherwise willing to accept the assignments, refused to do so. Consequently, the needed production was not maintained, at least not until top officers of Local 600 came into the building and straightened out the matter. Committeeman X was thereupon suspended pending further investigation, and on March 24 he was discharged. He then filed a grievance.

Contract Provisions. The agreement establishes job classifications and the compensation thereof, and provides that when an employee is transferred to a new classification of work and remains there for three continuous days, his rate is then subject to change as of the original date of transfer, the effective date depending on the part of the pay period in which the original date of transfer falls.

Union's Position. It had been a long-established and mutually accepted policy in the Spring & Upset building that employees may be temporarily assigned to work in a lower classification but not a higher one. The general practice in this building was that when an employee was transferred to a higher classification and remained there for three continuous days, his rate was then subject to change. The union asserted that the purpose of this practice was to determine the employee's qualification for the new classification. It was intended to apply to permanent transfers and not to temporary assignments. To avoid abuse of the practice, the union contended that a policy had been established in the Spring & Upset building prohibiting the temporary working of people in a higher-paying classification than the one they held permanently. Grievant X did not instruct employees not to work out of classification, but rather told them that they were not supposed to work in a higher classification. He did not forbid, but merely *advised* in response to questions. He did not object to temporary assignments to lower-paying jobs. In so doing, X was following the established policy and the instructions given that day by the building Chairman to the building Committeemen, who also acted accordingly.

Company's Position. The company agrees that it is building policy not to have employees work in a higher classification except when the employee is transferred on a definite or permanent basis. It insists, however, that no employee was asked to work on a higher classification, that X prevented employees from working on a lower or equal classification, and that he was the most active Committeeman in that respect. In large part, he was conspicuous because he was concerned with the supercharger job, which was supervision's chief worry. Moreover, the rate for supercharger platers was the subject matter of a grievance then in process. X regarded their rate as properly $1.25; supervision regarded it as $1.20.

Arbitrator's Analysis. The undisputed testimony as to the policy of the building and the disputed testimony as to X's actual instructions were both premised on the assumption that a Committeeman may countermand supervision's orders and instruct employees not to do what supervision requires. That assumption is wrong. No Committeeman or other union officer is entitled to instruct employees to disobey supervision's orders. If he believes that an improper order has been issued, his course is to take up the matter with the supervisor and try to adjust it. If this fails, he may file a grievance.

The employee himself must also normally obey the order even though he thinks it improper. His remedy is prescribed in the grievance procedure. In the absence of justifying factors, an employee may not refuse to obey a supervisory order merely because the order violates his contractural rights, but must resort to the grievance procedure and the grievance procedure alone. The Committeeman must so advise the employee when queried.

Nothing in the contract even suggests the idea that only doubtful violations are subject to the grievance procedure and that clear violations can be resisted through individual self-help. Whether "clear" or "doubtful," all grievances must be handled in the manner described in the contract.

The arbitrator then discussed generally the universality of problems arising from management's responsibility of maintaining an uninterrupted operation of an enterprise and how they related to both inter- and intra-operations of unions and other organizations.

X's conduct in this case was clearly in violation of these rules. He should not have instructed or advised employees to disobey. However, the penalty for X's conduct must be considered in light of the mitigating circumstances. He was following the instructions of his building Chairman, given that morning—instructions that were equally improper. X's conduct was no different from that of the other Committeemen in the building. No other Committeeman was disciplined or investigated. Supervision's recommendation that X be transferred out of the building, not discharged, was admittedly based on a feeling that he was troublesome apart from this incident, since there had been fairly widespread misunderstanding as to the duties of employees and Committeemen with respect to orders they deemed to be in violation of the contract. Taking all the circumstances into account, X's penalty should not exceed a layoff of four days.

Award. The arbitrator reinstated X without loss of seniority and with compensation, in accordance with Paragraph 29 (10) (f) of the parties' agreement for time lost in excess of four days.

Abusive Language

The use of abusive, threatening, or profane language, especially if it is accompanied by displays of violent temper, is regarded as insubordination and therefore as just cause for discharge.[4] However, the arbitrator—in order to determine whether the words spoken were in fact intended to be abusive, threatening, or profane—must take into consideration the atmosphere in which they were spoken, the normal language used by the parties involved, and the nature of the business. Other factors considered by arbitrators in these cases are (1) whether the words or acts were a momentary display of unpleasantness; (2) whether the words or acts were provoked[5]; (3) the behavior pattern of the employee involved[6]; (4) the length of service of the employee involved; and (5) the effect upon department and plant morale.[7]

CASE 6: ABUSIVE LANGUAGE BY UNION STEWARD
THE GLENN L. MARTIN COMPANY AND UNITED
AUTOMOBILE, AIRCRAFT & AGRICULTURAL IMPLEMENT
WORKERS OF AMERICA, 21 LA 53
(DIGESTED). ARBITRATOR: JAFFEE.

Issue. An employee had been reprimanded by the company, and the issue to be decided by the arbitrator was whether the employee had been unjustifiably reprimanded, and also whether the company in so doing had exceeded its scope of authority.

Background. The employee, who was also a union steward and a member of the Executive Board of the Local, had requested and received a pass to leave her job for the purpose of handling a grievance. On the way out, the employee stopped at the desk of the supervisor of her department. The phone rang and the employee answered. The call was from a senior foreman who was endeavoring to locate another employee. When he learned who had answered the telephone, he immediately commented that the steward was not hired to answer the telephone. The ensuing conversation evidently provoked the steward, who told the foreman to "drop dead." This brought about the reprimand, which in turn resulted in the grievance.

Contract Provisions. Three pertinent articles in the collective bargaining agreement relate to the issue:

1. Management's Prerogatives—The right to . . . discipline . . . for cause . . . is vested exclusively in the Company, provided that this will not . . . be used for the purpose of discrimination against any member of the Union as such. . . .

2. Arbitration—Insofar as a grievance shall involve the interpretation and application of the provisions of this agreement and has not been settled, [then it shall be submitted to arbitration as provided]. . . .

3. The arbitrator shall have no authority to add to, subtract from, modify or amend any provisions of this agreement. The arbitrator shall have no authority . . . to consider . . . matters relating to management prerogatives, or any other matter not specifically set forth in this agreement.

Company's Position. At the hearing, the company defended its action on the ground that the contract specifically granted this authority.

Union's Position. The union, on the other hand, maintained that the action was unjustifiable and that the reprimand should be "removed from all records."

Arbitrator's Analysis. The arbitrator weighed the following points in rendering his decision:

1. He did not dispute management's prerogative under the contract, but he had to consider what constituted "cause" and the "interpretation and application" of the provision with respect to arbitrability. He assumed the dispute was arbitrable.

2. The hearing did not show that there had been any discrimination against the employee as a union member or representative. But whether or not she was on union business did not give her license to say what she did in the telephone conversation.

3. As to proper or reasonable cause, the arbitrator reasoned as follows: (a) The employee must have realized from the conversation that a supervisor was at the other end of the line; (b) the remark of the employee was deliberate and not "casual"; (c) the evidence as a whole did not show that there was sufficient provocation for such an intemperate remark; and (d) no employee should manifest disrespect to supervision, and in so doing the grievant gave sufficient cause for the imposition of a fair measure of discipline.

Award. The arbitrator denied the employee's claim and dismissed the grievance. He did not feel the reprimand was an unreasonable measure or that he had a right to disturb it.

CASE 7: REASONABLENESS OF PENALTY
HIGGINS INDUSTRIES, INC., AND SHIP CARPENTERS, CAULKERS & JOINERS, 25 LA 439. ARBITRATOR: HERBERT.

Issues. The issues to be decided by the arbitrator were whether the company had violated the collective bargaining agreement, whether the employee was guilty of insubordination as charged and was deserving of the severe penalty of discharge, whether he should be compensated for back pay, and finally, whether his seniority rights should be affected.

Background. An employee was discharged after a brief altercation with his foreman over an alleged violation of rules affecting a customary rest period. This resulted in objectionable language being used by both "the foreman and the employee, which was the basic reason for discharge." The termination notice gave the reason for discharge as "Insubordination, Cursing Foreman."

Contract Provisions. The provisions in the collective bargaining agreement pertaining to the issues are as follows:

1. The management of the plant and direction of the working forces are vested exclusively with the company. The company has the sole right to hire, discipline, discharge, lay off, assign, promote, and transfer employees, and to determine the starting and quitting time and the number of hours to be worked, subject to the restrictions and regulations governing the exercise of these rights as are expressly provided in the contract.

2. If the employee be *terminated for cause*, all credit toward paid vacation would be immediately canceled.

3. Employees lose all seniority rights if they are discharged for cause.

Union's Position. The union maintained that the provision of the contract meant that the parties had never contemplated that there should be a management right to discharge an employee without "cause." According to their interpretation, discharge cases were not to be excluded from the scope of review provided by the grievance procedure. In support of this point of view, the union stated that a reading of the contract in its entirety demonstrated conclusively that the parties did not intend that the company should have unrestricted or unlimited right of discharge regardless of "cause."

Company's Position. The company contended that the contract imposed no limitation on the company's right to discharge an employee. There was no express clause, as is common in most collective bargaining agreements, providing that discipline or discharge must be "for just cause." The discharge, therefore, should stand as a primary matter of contract interpretation.

Arbitrator's Analysis. The arbitrator concluded that the contract as a whole, considering its purpose and interest, did not permit the discharge of an employee unless there was "cause," meaning that there must be a substantial basis for such action.

He also reasoned that one of the cardinal objectives of collective bargaining agreements was job security for an employee, that there must be a fair and legitimate reason for discharge, that it must not be arbitrary, and that the economic penalty must not be out of proportion to the gravity of the offense.

Award. The arbitrator's opinion was that the discharge was an unreasonably severe penalty and that the discharge could not be sustained. However, the grievant's conduct was unwarranted and some penalty was in order as a warning that dismissal might ensue should his conduct and attitude toward his foreman result in further incidents that constitute a serious breach of plant discipline.

Further, it was the arbitrator's opinion that it would be unreasonable to reinstate the grievant with back pay. Accordingly, he directed that the employee be reinstated with full seniority rights, but without back pay.

CASE 8: PROVOCATION

SUPERMATIC PRODUCTS CORP. AND INTERNATIONAL ASSOCIATION
OF MACHINISTS, 21 LA 512. ARBITRATOR: BERNSTEIN.

Issues. Was the company's discharge of grievant (the union's Chief Steward) justified by the facts presented at the hearing? If not, under what conditions should the grievant be returned to his job, specifically with regard to restoration of job seniority rights, reimbursement of lost wages, and penalty imposed?

Background. An employee suffered two broken toes when a hand truck fell on his foot while at work. On the advice of the compensation doctor, he remained away from work for one week. Yet in spite of these instructions to the employee, the doctor stated in his accident report that the injury would cause no loss of work time and no permanent disability. On the first payday following his return, the employee expected to be compensated for the first seven days of disability in accordance with his understanding of the collective bargaining agreement. When he received pay for only a single day of the week he was absent, he complained to the Chief Steward, who took up the matter with the Factory Manager. The latter said that further discussion would be a waste of time and ordered the steward to return to work, whereupon the steward used extreme language in the presence of other employees. The Factory Manager fired him immediately, but later he telephoned the doctor, who confirmed the employee's version of the disability and admitted an error in the report submitted to the company. The employee was promptly paid for the outstanding 32 hours.

Contract Provisions. The company is obligated under an article of the collective bargaining agreement to pay an employee for 40 hours for the first seven days of disability. It is normal practice to require a doctor's verification.

Union's Position. The union admitted that the grievant's act justified the extreme penalty of discharge, provided there was no provocation by the company. The union argued that the grievant had been provoked and offered several contentions, namely: (1) The Factory Manager had refused to meet with the Chief Steward regarding a legitimate grievance in violation of contract. (2) The company had allowed grievance machinery to deteriorate, thereby frustrating the orderly processing of grievances. (3) The Factory Manager's unwillingness to talk to the steward constituted discrimination for union activity.

Company's Position. Simply stated, the company maintained that the discharge was justified and that there had not been a violation of the collective bargaining agreement.

Arbitrator's Analysis. The arbitrator dismissed the first contention of the union's position as having little substance. The Factory Manager had discussed the matter on both occasions with the steward when the latter had raised it. At no time did he refuse to pay the employee, and the company did eventually pay. The Factory Manager's concern with medical verification was both usual and proper.

The second union argument, concerning the breakdown of the grievance procedure, was not considered by the arbitrator as material to the issues. Granted that the procedure was not functioning properly, it seemed clearly evident that practice was loose on both sides.

The final union argument, discrimination, had not been established. The grievant had not been discharged because he was the union's chief steward, but rather because he swore at the Factory Manager.

Award. The facts as presented to the arbitrator justified the discharge. The grievance was denied.

Assault

An assault by an employee on his supervisor is a serious act of insubordination that may justify discharge. However, if the altercation between the two men is unrelated to their working relationship, is of a purely personal nature, and occurs off company premises, it is usually not considered insubordination.

In one case a foreman reported to the director of personnel that an employee assaulted him the previous night while leaving a bowling alley. The employee was discharged. At the arbitration hearing, the employee claimed that the foreman, who worked in another building and whom he had met previously only once or twice, had struck him first. It was held that the events were of a personal nature and had nothing to do with the employment relationship. The employee was reinstated.

CASE 9: ASSAULT
HOPPER PAPER COMPANY (TAYLORVILLE, ILL.)
AND UNITED PAPERMAKERS AND PAPERWORKERS LOCAL
229, 30 LA 763. ARBITRATOR: FLEMING.

Issue. Was the grievant's conduct in an off-the-job situation properly disciplined by a suspension when the company had made a substantial contribution to the arrangement that encouraged such conduct?

Background. The grievant had been with the company for 33 years before the incident, and had never been in trouble before. On December 15, 1957, the company held its annual Christmas party on company grounds, during which free food and unlimited liquor were served. While at this party, the grievant drank considerably, threw a can of beer at the Industrial Relations Manager, and later slapped him. Grievant was laid off for 30 days.

Union's Position. The company supplied an unlimited quantity of liquor at a party that was a social occasion and at which normal plant rules did not apply. The grievant's act did not take place in the context of an employer–employee relationship.

Company's Position. The grievant was not so drunk that he did not know what he was doing. The company had the right to discipline conduct detrimental to the company.

Arbitrator's Analysis. The arbitrator was inclined to believe that the offense in this case was not really the kind of off-the-job conduct that could be said to be detrimental to the proper functioning of the plant, and therefore properly within the company's system of discipline.

The company furnished free and unlimited liquor at this party. It is common knowledge that in any reasonably large gathering where liquor is available in unlimited quantities, some of the people present will imbibe too much. Thus, to a certain extent, when the company made the decision to provide free and unlimited liquor on such occasions, it ran the risk of predictable consequences.

Award. The layoff was unjustified. The arbitrator ruled that the grievant be fully reimbursed for the time he lost due to improper layoff.

CASE 10: ASSAULT—ALLEGED PROVOCATION
ALLEGHENY LUDLEM STEEL CORPORATION, WATERVLIET
PLANT (WATERVLIET, N.Y.), AND UNITED
STEELWORKERS OF AMERICA LOCAL 2378 CIO,
22 LA 255. ARBITRATOR: SHIPMAN.

Issue. Was the discharge of grievant jusified for the offense of physically assaulting a supervisor?

Background. On December 20, 1953, the shift supervisor questioned the grievant about allegedly hiding some work sheets. The grievant became angry and struck the supervisor. He was subsequently discharged.

Union's Position. The grievant stated he did not hide the work sheets. He said he was "sore" at being questioned and pushed the supervisor, but did not punch him.

Company's Position. The assault was just cause for discharging the grievant, especially since the grievant had been guilty of previous acts of insubordination.

Arbitrator's Analysis. One of the most heinous offenses that an employee can commit is that of physical assault upon a fellow employee. When the employee assaulted is a supervisor, the offense involves not only the problem of employee safety and health, but also one of plant discipline and morale.

Award. Grievance denied.

REFERENCES

1. For a fuller treatment of insubordination, see Maurice S. Trotta, *Insubordination,* Bureau of National Affairs, Washington, D.C. (1967).
2. Gorden Pew Fisheries Co. Inc., 11 LA 15; Oronite Chemical Co., 20 LA 875.
3. In Re Beaunit Corp., AAA 100-14 (1967). Arbitrator: Hill.
4. Reynolds Metals Co., 17 LA 710; Cameron Iron Works Inc., 25 LA 295; International Harvester Co., 13 LA 986.
5. Glenn L. Martin Co., 21 LA 53; Supermatic Products Corp., 21 LA 512.
6. Higgins Industries Inc., 25 LA 439; Crawford Clothes Inc., 19 LA 475; Pursons Casket Hardware Co., 14 LA 247.
7. Jacob Walder Co., 12 LA 903.

2

CONTRACT INTERPRETATION

The cases in the preceding section dealt with an interpretation of the just-cause provisions found in almost every contract. Since a large percentage of cases submitted to arbitration involve these discipline and discharge issues, they have been treated separately. The following cases involve an interpretation of other provisions of the collective bargaining agreement.

ACCUMULATION OF SENIORITY BY SUPERVISORS

Arbitrable issue affecting foremen and supervisors usually concern the seniority and displacement of supervisory personnel. A union will file a grievance if management downgrades a foreman or supervisor and assigns him to a bargaining unit job, which might result in the layoff of a union member.

Most labor contracts are vague and often ambiguous with regard to the seniority rights of foremen and supervisors. A complicating factor is the conflicting attitudes taken by unions. Some feel that when a member accepts a supervisory post he should forfeit all seniority rights. Other unions take the position that a member who advances to a supervisory post not only retains his current seniority, but also continues to accumulate additional seniority. Some contracts make a distinction between seniority acquired under a collective bargaining agreement and seniority acquired outside the agreement by virtue of employment with the company.[1]

It is not uncommon for a collective bargaining agreement to permit a man who was previously with the bargaining unit to retain only the seniority rights that he had acquired as a member of the unit.[2]

When supervisors are not among those promoted from jobs covered by the collective bargaining agreement, the union's position is that they do not have any seniority rights and cannot be permitted to displace an employee who is a union member. If the company wishes to employ a supervisor in a job covered by the collective bargaining agreement, he must be considered as a new employee.[3]

Management's point of view frequently is that the seniority rights of foremen and supervisors should be based upon length of service, and that there should be no distinction between seniority rights acquired under a collective bargaining agreement and rights acquired by virtue of employment with the company. It is often argued that a supervisor who has been in the employ of a company for many years and is highly skilled should be given preference over an employee who has been with the company for a short time. The company also feels a moral obligation to give preferential treatment to employees with long years of service. An ever present complication is the fact that many companies do not follow the principle of seniority for determining the status of supervisory employees.

Arbitrators, therefore, must always be concerned with the following important questions:

1. Can a distinction be drawn between seniority rights acquired under a collective bargaining agreement and rights acquired by virtue of employment?
2. Should a distinction be drawn between the seniority rights of a foreman or supervisor who was previously a member of the bargaining unit and one who was not?
3. When a union member becomes a foreman or supervisor, are his seniority rights lost or retained? [4]
4. Does a foreman or supervisor who was never a member of the bargaining unit acquire any seniority rights that may be used to displace a union member?
5. Are the seniority rights of a foreman or supervisor who voluntarily relinquishes his position different from those of one who is demoted or downgraded because management is obliged to reduced its working force?
6. Is a particular employee a supervisor? [5]

✓Three criteria are used by arbitrators as a guide in determining the seniority rights of foremen and supervisors: namely, the language of the contract,[6] past company practice,[7] and industry practice.

CASE: ACCUMULATION OF SENIORITY BY SUPERVISORS
MCLOUTH STEEL CORPORATION AND UNITED
STEELWORKERS OF AMERICA, 28 LA 315. ARBITRATORS:
HAUGHTON (CHAIRMAN), ABBOTT, AND MENOZZI

Issue. Members of the Blast Furnace Department protested the company's action in placing men from supervision back into the union ranks with full seniority. Although the union was notified that these supervisory jobs were temporary, the union observed that the men were on supervision more months of the year than they were in the union. The union therefore contended that the supervisory jobs were not temporary and that these men should not have been credited with seniority while working as supervisors.

Background. In July 1954 the company began to receive ore for the blast furnace at its ore docks. It decided that four employees from the bargaining unit would be promoted temporarily to serve as foremen on the ore docks for the purpose of supervising the unloading of ore during the 1955 season.

In May 1955 the Assistant Superintendent of the blast furnace interviewed four employees and explained the work to them, inquired whether they would accept the foreman jobs, and told them that the promotions would last only during the shipping season, after which they would be returned to their regular jobs in the bargaining unit.

Company representatives met with the union's grievance committee in the same month and explained that the promotions would be on a temporary basis and that the men would be moved back to their regular jobs at the end of the season when they would no longer be needed as foremen. The chairman of the grievance committee accepted the decision, stating that temporary assignments were a general practice and there would be no difficulty in returning the men to their original jobs.

As a result of the promotion of the four men, vacancies were created in the bargaining unit, and these were filled by the company's posting of notices that such jobs were to be offered on a temporary basis.

The four promoted employees were returned to their bargaining units after the shipping season was over. The company allowed the time spent in the supervisory job to accumulate as seniority. Three of the men returned to jobs they had held prior to promotion, and as a consequence bumped three junior employees. The fourth man returned to another job on which he had bid. All four had continued payment of their regular union dues during the period of their employment as supervisors.

Contract Provisions. The agreement states that an employee promoted from the bargaining unit group, except for a temporary promotion, will have his accumulated seniority frozen as of the date of the promotion. If he subsequently returns to the bargaining group, he is to resume seniority status as of the date of the promotion and will be eligible for any job in the bargaining group for which he qualifies by virtue of seniority.

Union's Position. The union contended that under the provisions of Article VI, Section 7, of the collective bargaining agreement, the seniority of the promoted employees should have been frozen as of the dates of their promotion and should not have accumulated while they were working as foremen.

The union denied that the four men were given "temporary" promotion within the meaning of Section 7. It argued that they were promoted to "seasonal" rather than "temporary" jobs, and spent more time out of the bargaining unit than in it. Accordingly, it argued that if their seniority had been frozen, they would have had insufficient seniority to bump the employees whom they did, but would have been required to bump other junior employees. Therefore, it requested reimbursement for the bumped employees in the amount of the difference between the rates for the job classifications they had held and the rates for the classifications to which they were demoted at the time the four involved employees returned to the bargaining unit.

Company's Position. The company contended that the four employees were promoted out of the bargaining unit to positions of foremen on the ore docks only on a temporary basis. It noted that Article VI, Section 7, was clear in its provision that their seniority was not frozen.

The company argued that the facts were substantiated by the preliminary interview with the four men, by the minutes of the meeting with the grievance committee, and by the content of the notices offering replacement openings.

Finally, the company showed that, under the recently negotiated 1956 agreement, the problem involved in the present case could not recur because revised Section 7 provided that an employee promoted out of the bargaining unit to a temporary promotion could continue to accumulate seniority for a period not to exceed 60 days.

Arbitrators' Analysis. That this case involved a temporary promotion within the meaning of Article VI, Section 7, was evident from the understanding between the four promoted men and the company; the minutes of the grievance-committee meeting of May 27, 1955; the posting of notices of temporary job openings; the payment and acceptance of union dues during the periods of promotion; and the provisions of the new 1956 agreement limiting temporary promotion out of the bargaining unit to 60 days for the purpose of accumulating seniority.

The term "temporary promotion" ordinarily would mean a promotion which is to last only for a limited time. It is the opposite of "permanent promotion," which implies an indefinite period of time. With this in mind, the conclusion must be that the promotions under consideration here were temporary. It was clear that they were limited and definite in point of time. The test was not necessarily the duration of the promotion, but rather the fact that the promotion would definitely terminate after a reasonably limited period of time.

Seasonal employment is, of course, geared to the particular season involved, but contrary to the union's position, it is temporary, since it is of limited duration and will definitely come to an end. There is no inconsistency or conflict in designating seasonal employment as temporary. Therefore, while the union's designation of a "seasonal promotion" was correct, it could not be held that such designation excluded the application of the "temporary promotion" exception contained in Section 7.

In consideration of all these conclusions, the finding was that the seniority of the four protesting employees had not been frozen as of the dates of their temporary promotions out of the bargaining unit, and that they had been properly returned to the bargaining unit with accumulated seniority. *Award.* The grievance was dismissed.

REFERENCES

1. Borg-Warner Corp., 13 LA 107; Libby, McNeill and Libby, 14 LA 482; International Shoe Co., 31 LA 739.
2. Maremount Automatic Products Inc., 12 LA 673; Corning Glass Co., 12 LA 1033; Wright Aeronautical Corp., 14 LA 1012.
3. Chrysler Corp., 32 LA 274.
4. Republic Steel Corp., 17 LA 105.
5. Republic Steel Corp., 11 LA 428; North American Aviation, Inc., 15 LA 598; Linde Air Products, 26 LA 67.
6. Olin Corp., CCH 71-1, para. 8415.
7. Pearl Brewing Co., CCH 71-1, para. 8062.

GRIEVANCE PROCEDURES

A grievance procedure is an essential part of every collective bargaining agreement. It establishes a series of steps through which disputes must be processed before they reach the terminal step of arbitration. The process provides an orderly means for successively higher levels of management and union officials to endeavor to settle disputes.

The initial step in the grievance procedure is the presentation of the grievance by the employee to his immediate supervisor.[1] If the matter in dispute is not settled at the first step, a written grievance is filed and the supervisor replies on the standard grievance form. It is then discussed by the union grievance committee and the personnel manager and, if unsettled at this stage, it is considered by the international representative of the union and the plant manager. Finally, if it is still unsettled, the dispute goes to arbitration.[2]

Arbitrators will usually not assume jurisdiction of a dispute unless the parties have processed the grievance through the various steps in the procedure provided by the collective bargaining agreement.[3] Grievances must be filed within definite time limits, and if this requirement is breached the matter in dispute may not be arbitrable.[4] Arbitrators are frequently asked to find that time limits are not binding when the following conditions are present: (1) Neither party had previously followed the prescribed time limits; (2) the company or the union had failed to raise the issue during the various steps preceding arbitration; and (3) an act by one party prevented the other party from following the time limitation. Some arbitrators do not strictly construe the time limitations in the contract. Their reasoning is that technicalities should not prevent a consideration of the merits of the issue. Other issues that frequently arise include:

1. Does a union have a right to file a grievance on behalf of an employee? [5]
2. Does an employee on leave of absence have the right to serve on a union grievance committee? [6]
3. May a union require that a supervisor appear before a grievance committee? [7]
4. Does an employee have a right to file a grievance even though the union agrees with the company's action? [8]
5. Are the parties obligated to bargain on a grievance before submission to arbitration? [9]
6. May a union file a grievance that does not involve a particular employee? [10]
7. Under what circumstances are union committeemen entitled to receive compensation from the company for time spent on grievances? [11]
8. Are employees who are required to attend grievance meetings entitled to compensation? [12]
9. Under what circumstances are union committeemen entitled to access to a plant to investigate grievances? [13]

CASE: OBLIGATION OF THE PARTIES
TO FOLLOW GRIEVANCE PROCEDURE
BRIDGEPORT BRASS COMPANY (BRIDGEPORT, CONN.) AND
BRASS WORKERS DIRECTLY AFFILIATED LABOR UNION, 30 LA 622.
ARBITRATORS: DONNELLY (CHAIRMAN), MCDONOUGH, CURRY.

Issue. The matter for arbitration is related to Article 9 of the contract, which sets forth the procedures for handling grievances.

Background. The union accused the company of failing to follow the terms of the contract in that its stewards and committeemen were impeded in their efforts to handle grievances. The presentations of the grievance were revised and resubmitted to management in three different forms, each of which is referred to as a "case."

The first case stated: "The Company is in violation of the Contract—specifically to matters relating to Grievance Procedure, Article 9. The Union considers this a policy matter and requests the Negotiating Committee to sit in." This case was submitted to the foreman, who rejected it with: "There is no specific infringement of the Agreement charged. No violation." The union repeated its charge and requested that a hearing be advanced to a third step outlined in the contract, namely, the Negotiating Committee for Management.

However, the company required elucidation of the grievance statement and insisted that the conditions of Step 2 in the grievance procedure be followed. (See section on "Contract Provisions," below.) The company contended that:

1. The submission was unintelligible and fatally defective because it did not recite facts showing that there was any difference between the company and the union concerning the interpretation and application of the labor agreement. After a matter has been discussed with the foreman (Step 1) and an attempt has been made to settle it orally, any written submission (Step 2) should identify: (a) the name, department, and clock number of each of the employees alleged to be aggrieved; (b) the article and section of the labor agreement alleged to have been violated together with a short statement of the reasons for the charge; and (c) any other information needed in order to determine the matter. Unless sufficient data are given, a matter cannot be settled. The attempted "grievance" was so vague and indefinite that it did not present a dispute susceptible of settlement pursuant to Section 9, Step 1.

2. From the foregoing answer it is obvious that no dispute as to the interpretation and application of the labor agreement existed between the parties.

This requirement for a detailed grievance statement was accepted by the union and a new statement of grievance (Case 2) was submitted as follows:

The company violated the contract in that

1. It refused to permit union stewards to investigate grievances.
2. It refused to discuss grievances with union stewards.
3. It refused to accept written grievances from union stewards.
4. It refused to permit union grievance committeemen to investigate grievances.
5. It refused to discuss grievances with union grievance committeemen.
6. It refused to grant releases to union stewards at the request of union grievance committeemen in accordance with the negotiated and agreed-upon detailed procedure for releasing union stewards.
7. It failed to arrange for relief of union stewards and union grievance committeemen for the purpose of adjusting grievances.

The union demanded that the company immediately stop its improper conduct and live up to its obligations under the terms of the contract. The union considered this grievance a policy matter and requested a meeting of the "six-man grievance [committee] covering both plants." Again the union requested proceeding to the third step (consideration by the Negotiating Committee for Management).

The company again rejected the union's statement (Case 2) and stated:

1. None of the vague allegations in items 1 through 7 had been discussed with the foreman of the aggrieved employees (if there were aggrieved employees) prior to being "reduced in writing . . . and presented to the foreman." This oral discussion is a necessary prerequisite before a written grievance may be validly submitted under Section 9-1 of the labor agreement [refers to Step 1 in Article 9].
2. The submission . . . made vague charges in items 1 through 7 but did not identify the date, the time, the department, the aggrieved employee and his foreman, the action protested, and the section of the labor
3. The company knew of no actual incidents in which it had violated the agreement believed to be involved.
   contract "in any of the ways vaguely charged . . . in items 1 through 7."
4. The company and its representatives had complied with the labor agreement. The labor agreement had not been violated.
5. The company, through its representatives, would continue to apply the provisions of the labor agreement to releases for the purposes of adjusting grievances, and would comply with its obligations under that agreement.

In response to this statement by the company, the union prepared a new grievance declaration (Case 3), which was substantially the same as that of Case 2. Since no satisfactory settlement had been made, the matter then entered Step 4 of Article 9 of the contract (was referred to the State Board of Mediation and Arbitration).

Contract Provisions. Article 9 of the contract sets forth steps to be taken in processing grievances:

STEP 1. An employee should discuss his grievance with his foreman with or without his steward.

If the employee desires, the steward may discuss the matter with the foreman without the employee being present. In such cases the foreman may discuss the matter with the employee after notifying the steward and the steward may be present if he so desires. Both parties should discuss the grievance in a friendly manner and reach a satisfactory settlement at this point.

STEP 2. After the grievance has been discussed with the foreman and is not satisfactorily settled, the grievance shall be reduced in writing on forms provided by the Company and presented to the foreman for his written answer. . . .

STEP 3. If it is mutually agreed by the parties that the subject matter of a grievance is of an emergency nature or involves a matter of broad Company policy, the same shall be considered to fall in Step 3 of this Article, and discussion of the same shall commence in the first instance in accordance with the provision of said Step 3. . . .

STEP 4. If all previous steps fail in reaching a satisfactory settlement, the grievance shall be presented to the State Board of Mediation and Arbitration of the State of Connecticut for settlement by mediation. . . .

STEP 5. If a grievance in a case concerning the interpretation or application of this Agreement is not settled at such meetings, it may be referred for arbitration to the State Board of Mediation and Arbitration of the State of Connecticut whose decision shall be final and binding if the case requires arbitration. If there is a dispute between the Company and the Union as to whether a particular grievance is arbitrable, that question shall be submitted to the State Board of Mediation and Arbitration of the State of Connecticut, and this issue shall be first decided by the State Board before it proceeds further with the case. . . .

Union's Position. The union claimed that the grievances had been filed only after repeated violations of the negotiated Release Procedure of the parties. Since the union considered this a policy matter, it had filed identical grievances in all three cases.

The union maintained that the grievances had been properly processed through the grievance procedure, but that at each step of the processing the company in both plants had refused to discuss the merits of the grievance. It contended that the company met with the three-man committee of the union only to submit already prepared answers, none of which admitted the merits of the grievances.

The union denied that it had refused to give any details as to what the grievances covered, and said it had informed the company clearly and forcibly of many of the incidents that precipitated the grievances. Furthermore, it refuted the company's statement that it had asked for details or had permitted the union to present details within the steps of the grievance procedure. The company's claim that the union had refused to provide details except in arbitration was erroneously applied to a remark made by the union's international representative after the grievances had moved to arbitration.

Company's Position. The company made the following statements:

1. The grievances were not arbitrable because they had not been discussed in the grievance procedure and, accordingly, no serious effort had been made to settle the grievances by the procedures provided in the contract.
2. The union had refused to give the company detailed information on the violations claimed, and had repeatedly insisted that the details would be provided only if the company agreed to discuss them with the six-man grievance committee of the union.
3. The union had no right under the agreement to take such a position and to petition for the third step (policy grievance) unless both parties had agreed that the matter was one of policy.
4. The grievances were filed against management in two plants separately.
5. In the absence of information, which the union refused to give, the company had no way of knowing whether or not the matters involved warranted the company's meeting with the six-man grievance committee.

The company stated that it had proceeded through the various steps of the grievance procedure, but that the union at each step had not only refused to discuss the grievance but had also refused to identify the circumstances of the claimed violations. Consequently, the company felt the grievances had been settled at the first step, when the company had assured the union that it would abide by the agreement.

The company stated that the apparent background of the grievances was an insistence on the part of the company that the members of the six-man grievance committee report at their regular jobs and be excused only when necessary to handle grievances. The company claimed that for some years these employees had not worked at their jobs except when overtime was involved. In 1957, having been advised that paying these employees while they were not working was contrary to law, the company discussed the matter with the union and after some time the union agreed that the members of the six-man grievance committee would return to their jobs. The company drafted a new Release Procedure providing that stewards and committeemen should be released for grievance work only as provided in the agreement. Subsequently, the company was threatened with a strike, but the strike was averted by an agreement with the union that it would abide by the terms of the grievance procedure for the release of stewards and committeemen. This agreement, which was not reduced to writing, settled all aspects of this dispute between the parties.

The company maintained that the board of arbitrators lacked jurisdiction in this matter and that the board must find itself without authority in the agreement to proceed. As provided in the grievance procedure, the parties had not made a serious effort to resolve these grievances. The matters had not been properly processed in the steps of the grievance procedure.

Arbitrators' Analysis. The oral testimony offered to the arbitrators by witnesses from both parties was at complete variance, and therefore it was concluded that one of the parties was at least unobjective or at best mistaken in the testimony it offered.

An arbitrator recalled that the late Professor Harry Shulman once referred to the grievance procedure as "the heart of the collective bargaining agreement," because it is the part that has a special relationship to all other parts of the agreement. If the parties dispute their rights under any other section of the agreement, it is the grievance procedure to which they turn to resolve the dispute and to allay any misunderstandings. No dispute should go to arbitration until all possibilities of a settlement at the negotiated stages of the grievance procedure have been exhausted. This is what the parties obviously intended when they wrote into the first paragraph of the grievance procedure that "an earnest effort shall be made to settle such differences promptly."

The evidence submitted in this matter gave no indication of any serious attempt to execute this professional intention. Whereas the greater possibility for this failure lies in violent dispute in the oral testimony, some indication of the failure was detected in the evidence of the events that preceded the board's hearing, and which was set forth in the written statements of the grievance forms.

What was involved was not a question of whether or not the grievance was arbitrable as a claimed violation of the agreement. The principal objection of the company was not based on the claim that no violation of the agreement was involved, but rather that the grievance was not arbitrable because the union had not followed the agreement in its attempt to carry the matter through the grievance procedure.

Thus, the company argued that in Step 1 of the grievance procedure the union had listed very vague charges but had failed to support them with citations of any specific violations. In its reply the company requested that the union cite chapter and verse as to the violations, and it added an assertion that the company would live up to the terms of the agreement. It was at this point that the case of the union began to weaken. It had listed in its grievance seven general charges against the company. The charges listed no individual employees, no departments, no union stewards discriminated against. As listed, none of the charges could be investigated by the company. To evaluate intelligently the charges of the union, the company requested (and rightfully so) more specific information. If the union had contemplated "an earnest effort . . . to settle such differences" as provided in the contract, it would seem that the union would have replied promptly and in detail with the requested information. It did not do this, either informally or by completion of the official grievance form, on which it had every opportunity to list the detailed information requested. On the basis of the written grievance form itself, the arbitrators concluded that the union had completely ignored the request for further information.

The most disputed area of this controversy was whether or not the union had been permitted to discuss the merits of the dispute with the company. The oral testimony was directly at variance. The union's failure to comply with the requests of the company was certainly irrefutable and established a sound presumption of the validity of the company's claim that the union had ignored the orderly provisions of the grievance procedure. The observance of the provisions of the grievance procedure was generally recognized by the arbitrators as a condition precedent to the assumption of jurisdiction and the granting of relief. Under Article IX of the agreement, neither party had the right to ignore the grievance machinery and submit a dispute to arbitration, and equally clearly the parties never intended to give the Board the authority to arbitrate absent any effort to settle a dispute in the grievance procedure.

Article IX provided that the parties would make an earnest effort to settle grievances in the grievance procedure, but no such effort was made. It provided for discussion of the grievance even before a written grievance is prepared, but no such discussion was held. Article IX provided mediation "if all previous steps fail in reaching a satisfactory settlement"; disputes can go to arbitration only after previous steps have been used and have brought no solution.

Since the company in replying to the union in Step 1 protested that it would fulfill its obligations under the agreement, since the company reiterated before the Board that it would entertain any grievance in this matter in which the union cited specific violations of the agreement, and since the written grievance indicated during the grievance procedures the union had made no attempt to inform the company as to the specific violations of the contract involved, the Board found no basis for belief that the union had, as it claimed, made every effort to fulfill its obligations under the grievance procedure, only to be stopped by the company's refusal to discuss the matter in dispute.

Award. On the basis of the evidence outlined above, the Board found no authority under the agreement to arbitrate the grievances submitted by the union.

However, the decision was not unanimous. One member disagreed with the award on the following basis: The background of the grievance should have made it clear to the Board that the seven points recited in the grievance arose out of the company's action in instituting a Release Procedure affecting union stewards and grievance committeemen over the union's protest. There can be no question that the company knew at the time this grievance was filed that it was another sequel to unilateral action with respect to the Release Procedure. The grievance presented a clear statement that the company had violated a specific article of the agreement. It is erroneous to assume that a grievance may not be filed unless there is a specific person involved or a specific incident involved. This grievance was proper and clear in Step 1 of the grievance procedure when it was originally filed. The company should not have been allowed to come before the Board claiming that a grievance which should properly be before the Board under this grievance procedure is not an arbitrable issue, thus creating a condition that would prevent proper functioning of the collective bargaining agreement. The board should have found this case to be an arbitrable issue and ordered the company to settle it or arbitrate it without further delay.

REFERENCES

1. Texas Company, 32 LA 413; E. I. DuPont de Nemours and Co., 29 LA 646; Independent Lock Company, 30 LA 744; Quaker Oats Co., 14 LA 899. See Taft-Hartley Act, Section 9(a), which provides that an employee may present a grievance to his supervisor for adjustment without the intervention of the union. The adjustment must conform to the provisions of the collective bargaining agreement and the representative of the union must be given an opportunity to be present.
2. North American Aviation, Inc., 19 LA 729.
3. Bridgeport Brass Co., 30 LA 622; North American Aviation, Inc., 17 LA 121; Danly Machine Specialities, 15 LA 115; Consolidated Vultee Aircraft Corp., 12 LA 786; Reynolds Metals Co., 13 LA 439; Pacific Mills, 14 LA 387.
4. Creamery Package Manufacturing Co., 31 LA 917; Kaiser Aluminium and Chemical Corp., 32 LA 704.

5. North American Aviation, Inc., 12 LA 657; U.S. Ceramic Tile Co., 28 LA 167.
6. American Potash and Chemical Corp., 17 LA 364.
7. Jonco Aircraft Corp., 20 LA 211.
8. Chrysler Corporation, 12 LA 738.
9. North American Aviation, 19 LA 729.
10. Mercury Engineering Corp., 14 LA 1049.
11. International Harvester Company, 16 LA 240; Standard Oil Co., 16 LA 734; Asbestos Manufacturing Co., 31 LA 155; Bethlehem Steel Co., 17 LA 436.
12. Bethlehem Steel Co., 19 LA 261; Fitzgerald Mills Corp., 13 LA 418.
13. Wheland Co., 32 LA 1004.

HOLIDAYS AND HOLIDAY PAY

Most agreements provide that certain conditions be performed before an employee is eligible to receive holiday pay.[1] This often requires that the employee work the day before and the day after the holiday.[2] This is clearly aimed at discouraging long weekends or vacations, but whether this requires the employee to work the full day before and after the holiday is often the subject of dispute. The problem also obtains with the employee who is sick the day before or after,[3] who has to attend a funeral, or is on vacation.[4]

It is not always clear from the contract whether an employee on vacation is entitled to the holiday pay when the holiday falls in his vacation, during a period of layoff,[5] or on days not included in the workweek.[6] If an employee is on a disciplinary layoff, further problems are created.[7] Other questions arise when there is a conflict between holiday pay provisions and clauses pertaining to overtime,[8] shift differentials, strikes,[9] or part-time employees.[10]

CASE 1: HOLIDAY PAY
PERFLEX INCORPORATED AND UNITED RUBBER, CORK, LINOLEUM AND PLASTIC WORKERS OF AMERICA LOCAL 690, CCH 64–3, PARA. 9147. ARBITRATOR: KALLENBACK.

Issue. Was the company's interpretation of the contract correct in paying for the Memorial Day holiday? If not, what is the remedy?

Background. Following the Memorial Day holiday of Saturday, May 30,

1964, the company, in computing the pay of employees who did not work that day, counted in eight hours on a straight-time basis.

Contract Provisions. The following quotations are from Article XI, "Hours of Work."

Section 1. Regular Workday: Eight (8) consecutive hours in any twenty-four (24) hour period shall constitute a regular workday.

Section 2. Regular Workweek: Five (5) consecutive eight (8) hour days beginning with the starting time of the employee's shift on Monday shall constitute a regular workweek.

Section 3. Overtime Provision: Employees shall receive time and one-half for all work over eight hours in one day or forty (40) hours in one week. If an employee is off due to being sent home by management, overtime pay on Saturday will be paid.

Section 4: Double-Time Provision: Double time shall be paid for all work performed on Sunday.

Section 5. Triple-Time Provision: Triple time shall be paid for New Year's Day, Memorial Day, Fourth of July, Labor Day, Thanksgiving Day, and Christmas if worked.

Section 6. Holiday Pay: All employees on the seniority list will receive eight (8) hours pay at straight-time rate for the following six and one-half holidays if not worked: New Year's Day, Memorial Day, Fourth of July, Labor Day, Thanksgiving Day, Christmas, and one-half New Years Eve Day. . . .

Section 7. Requirement for Holiday: Any employee who fails to work on the workdays immediately prior and subsequent to such holidays within the workweek shall not be entitled to any compensation for that holiday, except in case of illness confirmed by his superior for a valid reason, or a condition beyond the employee's control. . . .

. . .

Section 10. Holiday on Sunday: When a holiday falls on Sunday, Monday shall be considered as the holiday and shall be paid for at the rate of triple time if worked.

Section 11. Holiday on Vacation: When a holiday falls in a period when an employee is on vacation and he is absent from work because of such vacation, the employee shall be paid for such holiday.

Section 12. Overtime-Pay Computation: For the purpose of computing pay, the holiday shall be considered as time worked.

Union's Position. Employees working 40 hours the week before Memorial Day are entitled to time and one-half if they did not work.

Company's Position. Article XI, Section 6, states that Memorial Day holiday pay will be computed on a straight-time basis if not worked.

Arbitrator's Analysis. It was the arbitrator's opinion that despite a clause stating that a holiday, whether scheduled as a workday or not, should be "counted" in determining applicability of the 40-hour-week overtime pay rule, the contract in no wise provided that such an unworked holiday in itself constituted a day of overtime work. In a similar case[11] leading to the same conclusion as that reached here, it was decided that to rule otherwise would have necessitated disregarding another clause that stipulated an employee shall receive straight-time pay for a holiday not worked.

Award. Grievance denied.

CASE 2: WHAT CONSTITUTES A DAY NOT WORKED?
JOHN DEERE PLANTER WORKS OF DEERE & COMPANY AND UNITED AUTOMOBILE, AIRCRAFT & AGRICULTURAL IMPLEMENT WORKERS OF AMERICA, 26 LA 322. ARBITRATOR: DAVEY.

Issue. The issue for determination is whether the Grievant, X, should be held to have been present or absent on the workday preceding the holiday.

Background. Grievant X was denied holiday pay for Thanksgiving Day. It is agreed that X reported for work at the proper time on the workday before the holiday. Approximately one-half hour after the shift began, X was discovered unconscious on the floor. Apparently, in falling he had suffered a blow on the head, which knocked him out. He was taken to the hospital and was absent from work the week following the holiday. Under ordinary circumstances, as stated in the agreement, being absent from work both the workday before and the workday following a holiday, for whatever reason, would disqualify the employee for holiday pay. The dispute over interpretation is on the question of whether X was "absent" on the workday preceding the holiday or whether he should be held to have worked the day before the holiday.

Contract Provisions. The contract provides for seven paid holidays and lays down certain conditions governing eligibility for holiday pay. An employee who is absent the workday preceding the holiday or the workday following the holiday is not eligible for holiday pay, unless his absence on one (but not both) of these days is due to one of the factors specified as an excusable absence. The excusable absences are listed in Article XVI, Section 2, as follows:

1. Formal leave of absence for more than three days, as provided in Section 1 of Article VI, "Leaves of Absence."
2. Leave of absence for union business, as provided in Section 2 and Section 3 of Article VI, "Leaves of Absence."
3. Plant-incurred injury.
4. Jury duty.
5. Confining illness of the employee substantiated by a statement from the attending physician.
6. Death in the employee's immediate family. (Immediate family is defined as grandfather, grandmother, granddaughter, grandson, father, mother, mother-in-law, father-in-law, brother, sister, spouse, son-in-law, daughter-in-law.) If requested to do so the employee will furnish substantiating evidence.
7. A temporary condition of no work available, due to such causes as material

shortages or trouble with machines or equipment, but not including cases of separation from the payroll.
8. An employee reporting for work on one of his regularly scheduled work-days is sent home because no work is available.

Union's Position. The union claimed that the grievant fulfilled the con-tract requirements for holiday pay. He reported for work the day before the holiday and worked until illness or a plant-incurred injury was responsible for his inability to complete the day's work. Had X not become incapac-itated, he would have undoubtedly completed the day's work. That he was unable to work the entire day was due to circumstances over which he had no control. He actually did some work the day before the holiday and thereby fully satisfied the spirit of the holiday-pay clause restrictions. The purpose of these restrictions is to prevent employees from "stretching" a holiday with pay. No such intent was shown or alleged in X's case. There-fore, the union asked for a ruling that X was not absent on the workday preceding the holiday within the meaning of the contract and thus was entitled to pay for Thanksgiving Day.

Company's Position. In the company's view, there was no question that X was absent on the workday preceding the holiday. The exceptions listed applied only to one day, either the day before or after the holiday, and not to both. He was admittedly absent the day after and on the workday preceding the holiday—there could be no argument that he was "more absent than present." At most he was in the plant an hour that day and worked not more than one-half hour. It would be different if the man had worked most of the day and then had to leave the plant early for some good reason. Here, however, it would be absurd to say that the man was present on a day when he was in the plant not more than an hour.

The company stressed that it had no desire to penalize the grievant because of the unfortunate occurrence that necessitated his absence. How-ever, the company felt that it was essential to establish the principle that anyone absent for a major portion of a day, as this man had been, must be held absent. A contrary ruling would encourage abuse by employees who might claim that they were sick the day before a holiday. Therefore, the company urged the arbitrator to rule that X was absent on the workday preceding the Thanksgiving holiday and to deny the grievance.

Arbitrator's Analysis. The parties agreed that the particular factual cir-cumstances involved were not anticipated by them when the list of excus-able absences was worked out during negotiations. The case presented a distinct departure from the usual holiday-pay eligibility issue. Most such cases require a determination as to whether a particular absence was excus-able under the contract. This case involved a determination as to what constitutes presence or absence on a day partially worked.

The company's argument was essentially a quantitative one when it urged that on the day in question, the grievant was "more absent than present."

The company conceded that if a man worked the greater part of a day and then left early for good reason, it would not regard him as having been "absent." However, in this case the company contended that the man had worked at most one-half hour and therefore must be held to have been absent on the workday preceding the holiday. The union's argument suggested that merely reporting for work on a pre-holiday shift was enough to immunize the employee against being defined as "absent" on that day. This was also in a sense a quantitative argument.

After careful consideration of the contract, the arbitrator said that a mathematical or majority-of-time criterion was inappropriate for reaching a sound and equitable determination as to the meaning of the contract language. The manifest purpose of the eligibility restrictions on holiday pay was to prevent stretching a paid holiday at either end by disqualifying the employee if he were absent the workday preceding or the workday following the holiday. Liberalization of this either-or restriction would extend to one day or the other, but not to both if the reason for absence was one specified by the contract. Thus, the contractual emphasis was on avoiding absence the day before or the day after a holiday. The contract stressed and enumerated what were to be regarded as excusable reasons for being absent, but was silent as to what constitutes enough "presence" to avoid a charge of being absent.

The arbitrator was of the opinion that what constituted enough "presence" to avoid being defined as "absent" should be determined on the basis of the intent of the stricture on holiday pay, and did not relate on a mathematical basis to how much of the day the employee worked. The grievant reported for work and began work. His inability to continue that day was clearly due to circumstances over which he had no control. Obviously he had no intent to defeat the strictures of the holiday-pay section against stretching the holiday. Presumably, if he had worked four hours or more that day before experiencing the seizure and fall that led to his hospitalization, the company would have paid him for Thanksgiving Day. The arbitrator could not accept that his eligibility or ineligibility should hinge upon a mathematical calculation as to how much of the day he worked.

The company's apprehension that a ruling to the effect that X was not absent would lead to abuse and malingering by other employees was a possibility that could not be discounted entirely. However, fear of possible abuse is not a proper basis for rejecting a construction of contract that appears to be otherwise sound, equitable, and consistent with the intent and purpose of the holiday-pay provisions. As the union pointed out in its rebuttal, an employee claiming illness had to report to First Aid. If there was any evidence of "goldbricking," the employee would be properly subject to disciplinary action. Such a possibility would be preferable to a ruling that barred a man from holiday pay when admittedly he had no intent to defeat the purposes of the holiday-pay restrictions. From a purely quantitative standpoint the company was undoubtedly correct that X was "more absent than present" on the day in question, but a quantitative standard was inappropriate for a determination of the issue in this case. It was the arbitrator's judgment that a ruling consistent with the intent of the contract must hold that an employee who reports for work the day before a holiday and who begins his day's work but is unable to complete it because of circumstances admittedly beyond his control should not be disqualified for holiday pay on the basis that he was absent on the workday preceding the holiday.

Award. Based on the contract as applied to the agreed circumstances of this particular case, the arbitrator found that the grievant was not absent within the meaning of the contract on the workday preceding Thanksgiving Day, and therefore the grievance was sustained.

REFERENCES

1. Master Engravers Guild, 17 LA 556; McKinney Mfg. Co., 19 LA 73; Brookhaven National Laboratory, 20 LA 547; Bethlehem Steel Co., 25 LA 680.
2. Ford Motor Co., 11 LA 1181; Chesapeake & Potomac Telephone Co., 16 LA 844; Wolverine Shoe & Tanning Corp., 15 LA 195.
3. John Deere Planter Works, 26 LA 322; Bakers Negotiating Committee, 24 LA 694; Eastern Tool & Mfg. Co., 11 LA 923.
4. Olin Mathieson Chemical Corp., 24 LA 116; Geeco, Inc., 29 LA 658.
5. Continental Emsco Co., 31 LA 449; Precision Scientific Co., CCH 71-1, para. 8150.
6. Theatrical Costumers Assn., 12 LA 174; International Harvester Co., 13 LA 983; Central Soya Co., 25 LA 496.
7. McInerney Spring & Wire Co., 11 LA 1195.
8. Houston Newspaper Publishers, 28 LA 818; California Cotton Mills, 16 LA 335; Allegheny Ludlum Steel Corp., 23 LA 504.
9. Continental Can Co., 31 LA 558.
10. Glass Containers Corp., CCH 71-1, para. 8036.
11. Jones & Laughlin Steel Corp., 31 LA 589, 1958.

HOURS OF WORK

Modern collective bargaining agreements make provision for the duration of the workday and workweek. The purpose is to delineate the period of the employee's daily obligation and fix the foundation upon which any claim to overtime or other premium time can stand.[1] Sharp incursions have been evident on what was traditionally considered the prerogative of management to schedule the workforce.

Many contracts provide for the arbitration of disputes that may arise when one party wishes to change the length of the workday or workweek, or the time a shift begins and ends.[2] An arbitrator also may be called upon to decide whether a split shift or a rotating shift is required. In these cases the prevailing practice in the industry is considered to be a significant factor.[3]

Other disputes in this category concern the problem of time spent for washing up and changing clothes.[4] Should this be counted toward the daily work schedule? The question also arises as to meal periods,[5] rest periods, and travel time.

CASE: CHANGE OF WORK SCHEDULE
LUKENS STEEL COMPANY AND UNITED STEELWORKERS
OF AMERICA, 14 LA 890. ARBITRATORS: D'ANDRADE
(CHAIRMAN), ROOT, CURTISS.

Issue. The question raised is whether management changed the grievant's schedule without the proper notification, in direct violation of the contract, and thereby deprived him of overtime to which he would have been entitled if the proper schedule had been posted.

Background. An operating schedule is posted by each department, usually on Thursday or Friday of each week, to cover the operations of the department for the subsequent week, beginning with the day shift on Sunday. Such a schedule was posted by the Flanging Department on Thursday, September 15, 1949, to cover operations for the subsequent week beginning on September 18, 1949. According to this posted schedule, the grievant was assigned work on the 8:00 A.M. to 4:00 P.M. turn, beginning on September 18, 1949. After this schedule was posted, it was discovered by the supervisor of the department that the grievant would be entitled to overtime on the basis of having worked more than eight hours within a 24-hour cycle. Accordingly, the grievant was notified, while he was working on his last turn for the week ending September 17, 1949 (4:00 P.M. to 12:00 midnight), that he was being shifted from the 8:00 A.M. to 4:00 P.M. turn, to the 12:00 midnight to 8:00 A.M. turn starting on September 18, 1949.

Contract Provisions. Article VI, Section 1, Paragraph F, of the labor agreement reads as follows: "Determination of starting times shall be made by the Company from time to time to suit varying conditions of the business; provided, however, that indiscriminate changes shall not be made in such schedules and provided further that changes deemed necessary by the Company shall be made known to the plant representatives of the Union as far in advance of such changes as is possible."

Union's Position. The union claimed that contract language prohibited the company from changing an individual's work schedule without proper notice or, in lieu of notice, payment of a premium. The change in the grievant's schedule did not follow this procedure and as a consequence he had suffered a loss of earnings. Nothing in the agreement permitted the company's arbitrary interpretation of Article VI, Section 1, so as to discriminate against an employee in a premium-pay assignment.

Company's Position. Contract language permitted the company to modify individual work schedules without penalty. The schedules referred to in the agreement applied only to group work schedules, and not to the schedules of individual workers as the union implied.

Arbitrators' Analysis. The board of arbitrators believed that had the parties meant the word "schedule" in Section 1 to apply only to work schedules, the intent could have been clarified by inserting the word "work" in front of the word "schedule." Since this restriction had not been applied, it could be presumed that it was not intended, and the word "schedule" should therefore be considered as being used in the broader sense, covering both the work schedule and the individual schedule. Evidently the schedule of the grievant was changed in order to avoid payment of overtime. Admittedly there was no requirement that the company provide overtime work for its employees. Further, good management requires that overtime should be avoided wherever possible, in order to reduce operational costs.

As interpreted by the arbitrators, the company had the right under Paragraph F to change an individual's schedule in order to suit varying conditions of the business. Clearly, the payment of overtime, or the avoidance of such payment, is not a varying condition of business within the meaning of this paragraph. Therefore, the changing of the grievant's schedule in order to avoid the payment of overtime was contrary to the provisions of the contract, and the grievant was entitled to reimbursement of the wages lost as a result of this change.

Award. The grievance was allowed and the company was directed to pay the grievant for four hours at the rate per hour he was receiving on September 18, 1949.

REFERENCES

1. Western Automatic Machine and Screw Co., 12 LA 38; Co-Operative Farm Chemicals Association, 31 LA 382.
2. Westinghouse Air Brake Co., 12 LA 307; Lukens Steel Co., 14 LA 890; Menasco Manufacturing Co., 30 LA 465; North Carolina Pulp Co., 28 LA 379; C. O. Porter Machinery Co., 16 LA 379; Bethlehem Steel Co., 18 LA 683.
3. Printing Industry of Indiana, Inc., 29 LA 7.
4. Fred W. Baldau Co., 13 LA 140.
5. Merrill Stevens Dry Dock and Repair Co., 17 LA 516; Bakelite Company, 29 LA 555.

LEAVES OF ABSENCE

A leave of absence is construed to mean a period of time off at the employee's request. The conditions governing leaves of absence are often ✓ stated specifically in the contract. If not, they are usually considered to be within the employer's discretion. Problems arise in relation to the effect of a leave on the employee's seniority,[1] vacation, holiday pay,[2] and job rights.

Is the employer obligated to grant the employee's or the union's request for a leave of absence, provided a valid or acceptable reason is given? [3] On what grounds may management deny such a request? [4] Must management, in fact, give any reason at all in denying such a request? Most arbi-✓ trators will not overrule management's decision unless it can be shown that the decision was discriminatory or arbitrary. Some employees resent the insistence of a company that they undergo a physical examination on returning from an extended leave.

Apart from the effect of a leave on the employee's own seniority and job rights, there is the added impact of his return on the status of the employee who has replaced him.[5] The "temporary" status of the latter employee may give rise to complications on the returned employee's arrival. Whether the returning employee can bump back into his old position—or bump any position available during his absence—may present troublesome issues. Should the employee overstay his leave, it is ordinarily treated like any other absence without permission,[6] but a satisfactory excuse usually facilitates his reinstatement.[7]

CASE: REASONABLENESS OF REQUEST
LEWIS MANUFACTURING COMPANY AND UNITED TOBACCO
WORKERS UNION, 12 LA 661. ARBITRATOR: WAITE.

Issue. This grievance resulted from different interpretations of articles in the contract relating to leaves of absence.

Background. It was customary when leave was requested, by agreement of the parties, that the employee make written application on a form (Employee's Request for Leave of Absence) furnished by the company.

Contract Provisions. No clause in the contract states the specific conditions that mandate approval of a request for leave of absence, nor does any clause state the reasons for which leave might be denied. However, the company is obligated to respond to requests within seven days.

Union's Position. The union maintained that the contractual provisions made it mandatory for the company to grant *any* leave of absence, up to two weeks, provided the request was made by formal written request and regardless of the reason for the leave. Further, if the request was made as required, a leave of up to two weeks would be automatic, with longer periods subject to negotiation.

Company's Position. Management maintained that the contract should be interpreted to mean that the company had the right to refuse to grant a leave of absence if it deemed the reason for the leave to be insufficient. The company also maintained that it was improper to interpret the contract to permit an employee to take an extra week following a leave of absence without incurring a penalty .

Arbitrator's Analysis. The arbitrator found that the contract presupposed the company's right to grant or withhold approval of requests for a leave of absence according to the reasonableness of the employee's excuse in support of his request. Granting of leave was mandatory, however, in the case of illness and attendance to union duties, but not under other circumstances.

It was acknowledged by the parties that management, in discharging its responsibilities, must have control over the number and type of employees on duty. It would, therefore, be unreasonable to assume that workers could decide when and to whom leaves were to be granted.

The arbitrator felt that the contract enabled both the company and the employee to negotiate for a leave in excess of two weeks on any reasonable request. In the event that an extended leave was granted without negotiation, no precedent was established for subsequent cases.

If an employee was granted a leave of absence for two weeks and overstayed the leave by not more than one week, and promptly offered a reasonable excuse within seven days, his action could not be made the cause of discharge. On the other hand, if an employee's request for a leave was denied and he deliberately absented himself from work, he was liable to discharge.

Award. The arbitrator decided that the request for a leave of absence for any period up to two weeks should be granted if, in the company's judgment, there was reasonable necessity for the leave and if the absence of an employee did not hamper the work of the organization as a whole.

Requests for longer leave were to be honored by the company at its discretion or made the subject of negotiation with the union. The arbitrator also directed the company to accept a reasonable excuse offered within the first seven days of absence, as stipulated in the contract between the parties.

REFERENCES

1. Gem Electric Manufacturing Co., 11 LA 684.
2. Thermoid Western Co., 29 LA 424; International Harvester Co., 11 LA 1166.
3. C & D Batteries Inc., 32 LA 589; I. Lewis Cigar Manufacturing Co., 12 LA 661.
4. Hayes Manufacturing Corp., 17 LA 412.

5. Colony Furniture Co., 12 LA 89.
6. Celanese Corp. of America, 26 LA 786.
7. Branch River Wool Combing Co., 19 LA 244.

SUBCONTRACTING

Work subcontracted to outside firms to produce goods or render services that could be performed by bargaining unit employees with the company's facilities gives rise to many disputes. The transfer of work from the bargaining unit to non-unit employees or to another plant of the same company is considered subcontracting.

Unions view outside contracting as a threat to job security.[1] But from the company's point of view, the right to subcontract is a prerogative reserved to management and essential for efficient operations.[2] Frequently companies find that it is cheaper to subcontract maintenance work,[3] installation work,[4] cleaning services,[5] and plant cafeteria work.[6] Unions view the loss of jobs that may result as a threat to an employee's security, arguing that if a company has the right to subcontract, it has the power to destroy the union.

An excellent analysis of the subcontracting issue and the factors pertaining to it is contained in a decision handed down by Klein,[7] which is abstracted below.

DISCUSSION

Subcontracting is one of the most fundamental and controversial issues in industrial relations. Although it has been one of the most prolific sources of arbitrations during the past decade and a half, a study of the vast number of decisions and articles dealing with this subject seems to leave the reader in a state of even greater confusion that he was at the inception of his analysis. After making such a study, Arbitrator Sanford H. Kadish stated as follows in his decision in KVP Sutherland Paper Co. 40 LA 737 (1963):

"After examining these studies, and many of the decisions discussed, it is fair to conclude that no one, whatever his initial inclinations or prejudices, will go away from them without finding something he likes. Like the town fair, there is something there for everyone."

Although the verity of the hereinabove set forth comment by Arbitrator Kadish cannot be controverted, a chronological study of the arbitration decisions dealing with this subject indicates that a metamorphosis appears to be taking place. When the question of whether a Company had the right to subcontract was first presented, two extreme positions were taken by Companies and Unions.

One, the Union view, being that even in the absence of an express provision in the Collective Agreement prohibiting subcontracting, the Recognition, Union Security, Job Classification, Seniority, Wage and certain other contractual provisions considered as a whole imposed an implied restriction upon the Company, entitling employees to all work encompassed by the Collective Bargaining Agreement. (This approach is predicated on the proposition that if the Company had the right to subcontract work, it could undermine the very foundation of the Collective Bargaining Agreement and deny the Union the benefits it had achieved at the bargaining table.) The other, the Company view, being that in the absence of an express limitation against subcontracting, the Company possesses the unlimited right to subcontract (the theory being that the Management Prerogative Clause of the Contract retains for the Company all authority not surrendered by the express terms of the Contract). In the early years, the latter of these two views was adopted by a clear majority of the Arbitrators. As time passed, the trend became a little more favorable to the Union—See Griffin Pipe Products Co. [63-2 ARB ¶8647], 40 LA 946 (1963); Elizabeth Arden Sales Corp. 39 LA 1048 (1962); and in the last few years, Arbitrators seem to be striking a medium or middle ground between these two diametrically opposed schools of thought, having generally abandoned the two extreme positions—See Crompton & Knowles Corp. 40 LA 1333 (1963); Station KORD [63-2 ARB ¶8505], 40 LA 638 (1963); KVP Sutherland Paper Co., supra; U.S. Potash Co. 37 LA 442 (1961); Bendix Corp. 41 LA 905 (1963). This "compromise" approach recognizes that neither of the extreme positions is sound. In the opinion of this Arbitrator, it is the most logical and the one adopted by him. It might very well be described as the application of a "rule of reason." This concept is ably stated as follows by Arbitrator Carl A. Warns in Bendix Corp., supra:

". . . So the balance of interests of the parties as reflected in their negotiated agreement (the Management clause as against the Union seniority, recognition and other limitations on the Company) demands that each case of contracting out be examined in the light of its own facts. These interests, viewed separately, are legitimate. The Company has the right to get the job done as efficiently and with as low a cost as possible. The employees as individuals can insist that they receive the 'fruits of the contract' as negotiated. The Union can assume that the contract it negotiates for the bargaining unit will not be bypassed in regard to anticipated benefits unless reasonable men would agree that the larger interests of the company's relationship with the market place at the moment compel the use of other employees in place of its own. But such compelling circumstances must be viewed closely. The Company has no right to unilaterally reduce the negotiated wages of its employees because of the pressure of competition. Similarly, the Company has no right to bring the employees of others on its premises to perform services normally done by its own employees, absent special circumstances to be discussed, solely because the other employees will work at a cheaper rate. There is no difference in principle between holding that the Company cannot reduce wages unilaterally and denying the Company the right to bring outsiders into the plant for customary services solely on the basis of lower costs. Both would be a violation of Williston's implied covenant . . . 'that neither party shall do anything which will have the effect of destroying or injuring the rights of the other party to receive the fruits of the contract.' . . . 3 Williston (Rev. ED., 1936, Section 670).

"It becomes apparent then that I do not agree, as a matter of basic contract interpretation, with the broad general positions of either the Company or the Union, that is, that under the contract before me as written, the Company has the right to contract out because there is no express limitation on that right, or that alternatively the Company cannot under any circumstances assign to non-employees work in the plant customarily performed by the grievants." (Emphasis added.)

A similar rule is stated by Arbitrator Sanford H. Kadish in KVP Sutherland Paper Co., supra as follows:

". . . Of course, the Company may use outside contractors, just as it may on other grounds find reason to increase, decrease or modify jobs within the bargaining unit. But this does not mean that it may abuse that right by so exercising it that the benefits of the bargain are taken from the Union. And it is of course also true that the representation and related clauses do impose an obligation upon the Company not to subcontract in circumstances in which the integrity of the bargain is undermined. But this does [not] mean that the Union may prevent all subcontracting by the employer. Ultimately the question in this case, as in any case, entails weighting the Company's affirmative case for the particular decision to subcontract against the impact that decision has upon the subject matter of the bargain. The integrity of the bargain, protected by the very execution of the contract, the recognition, wage and related clauses, may be said to have been violated where the balance favors the Union; otherwise not."

FACTORS TO CONSIDER

The factors to be considered in determining whether a company's decision to subcontract is "reasonable" under the circumstances is as follows (It is very seldom that all of these factors are applicable to a case—Sometimes one of them standing alone is deemed to be decisive; more frequently, however, several factors are taken into consideration and applied in combination):

1. The discussion or treatment, if any, of the subject of subcontracting during contract negotiations.
2. The "good faith" of the employer in subcontracting the work. (Was the decision to subcontract motivated by anti-Union bias? Was it designed to discriminate against the Union?)
3. Any lay-offs resulting from the subcontracting. (Were regular employees deprived of work?)
4. The effect or impact that subcontracting will have on the Union and/or bargaining unit. (Was the required work part of the main operation of the plant?)
5. Possession by the Company of the proper equipment, tools, or facilities to perform the required work.
6. Was the required work performed on Company premises?
7. Was the required work an experiment into a speciality line?
8. Any compelling business reasons, economic considerations, or unusual circumstances justifying the subcontracting. (Was the work contracted out peformed at a substantial lower cost?)
9. Any special skills, experience, or techniques required to perform the required work.

10. The similarity of the required work to the work regularly performed by bargaining unit employees.
11. Past practice in the plant with respect to subcontracting this type of work.
12. The existence of any emergency condition. (Were properly qualified bargaining unit employees available to complete the work within required time limits?)
13. Was the required work included within the duties specified for a particular job classification?

CASE: SUBCONTRACTING BECAUSE OF FINANCIAL SAVING
FAULTLESS RUBBER COMPANY AND UNITED RUBBER, CORK, LINOLEUM
& PLASTIC WORKERS OF AMERICA LOCAL 196,
CCH 64–1, PARA. 8382. ARBITRATOR: DWORKIN.

Issue. Did the company violate the agreement by subcontracting work that could have been performed by its own employees?

Background. The company subcontracted work involving the production of 120 molds, which could have been produced in the Machine Shop by bargaining unit employees. Management made a trial run, for experimental purposes, of ten molds in its own Machine Shop, and then had outside contractors give quotations. The price given by the latter was lower than in-plant cost by $15.70 per mold.

Contract Provisions. Article 12, Section (b)(2), of the agreement specifically states: "Employees of the Company will be given preference in the performance of work within their respective classifications or for which they are qualified. The Company will explain in full to the Union representative involved before the letting of outside contracts for work that could be done in the maintenance shops were it not for the fact that time, expense, or facilities prevent the maintenance shops from performing the work. Work shall not be contracted out to avoid the payment of overtime."

Union's Position. The production of the 120 molds should have been done by Machine Shop employees, since under the contract they are to be given "preference in the performance of work." The company did not advise the employees of the Machine Shop of the amount of work involved or of the cost estimates.

Company's Position. The sole reason for subcontracting was that the company realized a substantial saving after figuring out the cost per mold of producing it in the Machine Shop. The company did advise the union that it was subcontracting.

Arbitrator's Analysis. The contract provided that a decision to engage an outside contractor is proper where it is established by a preponderance of the available evidence that management's judgment is reasonably supported by factors of time, expense, or the lack of facilities. The evidence reasonably established that the company had notified the union in advance of its decision and had explained that the work was being contracted out because of an estimated cost savings. In the judgment of the arbitrator, a consideration of the respective positions of the parties established by a preponderance of the evidence that the company definitely realized a substantial cost savings due to contracting out the work.

Award. The grievance was denied.

REFERENCES

1. American Cyanamid Co., 13 LA 652.
2. Bethlehem Steel Company, 30 LA 678.
3. Bendix Aviation Corp., 30 LA 827.
4. International Harvester Company, 12 LA 707.
5. Parke, Davis & Co., 15 LA 111.
6. The Linde Company, 30 LA 998.
7. Diebold, Inc., CCH 64-2, para. 8465A.

LAYOFFS

A layoff is a temporary termination of work for economic reasons.* The right to control the size of the active work force is a management prerogative. Collective bargaining agreements, however, frequently limit this right by requiring the company to (a) confer with the union,[1] and (b) reduce the length of the workweek before a layoff is invoked,[2] or give notice of intended layoff.[3] The order in which employees are laid off is usually determined by seniority,[4] which remains unimpaired for a definite period of time. Issues involving vacation pay[5] and holiday pay[6] during the period of layoff are also the subject of arbitration.

Layoffs are a part of the plant employee's life. Most industries, even during periods of prosperity, experience some fluctuation in their employment needs depending on seasonal demands, market changes, supply shortages, retooling requirements, and a host of other causes. The employer feels that it is his prerogative to retain the most productive employees when faced with the need to reduce his work force. The union, on the other hand, believes that the order of layoff should be strictly on the basis of seniority. Most union contracts today require that management observe seniority in layoffs and recalls.[7] However, management usually retains a measure of control over such requirements as ability, skill, or efficiency.[8] Even when the seniority provision governs, the employee must be capable of doing the job.[9]

* A disciplinary layoff is more accurately referred to as a suspension.

CASE 1: WHAT IS A LAYOFF?
PRECISION RUBBER PRODUCTS CORPORATION (DAYTON, OHIO)
AND UNITED RUBBER, CORK, LINOLEUM
& PLASTIC WORKERS OF AMERICA, 31 LA 1066.
ARBITRATOR: MCINTOSH.

Issue. Did the company violate the contract in scheduling off-time of one day for each of the grievants?

Background. Beginning in the early part of 1958, the company's business did not warrant a full-time workweek. In lieu of a layoff, an agreement was made between the union and management to schedule a four-day workweek. About the end of March, after the term of the agreement and a renewal thereof had almost expired, the union notified the company that the adjustment of the workweek would no longer be acceptable. At that time, however, some employees were on layoff, and on about the first of May additional layoffs were made. At the same time, management, with the concurrence of the union, set up vacations over a three-month period in an effort to spread the work over as much manpower as was possible and to avoid extensive layoffs. This, however, did not solve the problem entirely. The company then asked for volunteers to take off a day a week. Many employees did so, but the company found in the weeks of May 5 and May 16 that there still was not enough work to occupy the time of the available work force.

Accordingly, during the week of May 5 the company scheduled certain employees in Department 3, including Grievants E. and R., for four days. During the following week, that of May 16, the company scheduled other employees in another department, including Grievants W. and S., for four days. These four filed grievances, one for E. and R., and one for W. and S.

Contract Provisions. Under Article V, Section G, the contract provides: "All available hours shall be distributed as equally as possible to employees in the same job classification within a department. When hours are equalized, senior employees shall receive first preference to work." However, Article VII, Section D-2, refers to reduction of force due to curtailment of production and states that "employees affected will be permitted to displace any other employee with less seniority within the department or take a layoff until work is available."

Union's Position. The union's position was that these employees had more seniority than others who worked and that this was a layoff and should have been governed by the seniority provision of Article VII, D-2.

Company's Position. The company maintained that this was not an indefinite layoff and that Article VII, D-2, did not apply, but that Article V, Section C, was the proper contract section, since this was an equalization of hours. The company had tried to comply with the literal interpretation of the contract through a practical solution to a production-volume problem.

Arbitrator's Analysis. The dispute between the parties hinged on whether the cessation of work for these four employees was specific or indefinite. It was a layoff without doubt, because any relief from work at the direction of management must be termed a layoff. However, the contract made no provision for any layoff except one of indefinite duration. That the parties admitted this to be true was implicit in the evidence and in the union's argument that the company did not know at the time these persons were scheduled just how long they would be laid off. Further, the union claimed that there had been a layoff several months before, and at the time the present conduct was protested, the company again laid off others. Thus, it had established a pattern of layoff policy incompatible with contract provisions.

The company argued that these employees were off only the one day and worked a full week thereafter. It was undisputed that the company was faced with the problem of distributing a certain amount of work over the greatest number of employees. Since the seniority provisions were applicable only to an indefinite layoff, and this was to be only a one-day layoff, the company had to find some fair means under the contract to solve the problem. It would have been unnecessarily complicated to declare the layoff an indefinite one, knowing that it would be for only one day, and thus have to rearrange the entire work force by seniority bumping and by recalling employees just as soon as they had been laid off, a procedure required under the seniority provisions.

The only other provision that might have offered a solution was the equalization of hours provision, so the company used that, although this provision was somewhat ambiguous as to when it was applicable. However, there was sufficient evidence of the company's past practice in using Section I in this manner, plus the fact that a number of other employees laid off for one day did not file a grievance, which indicated to some extent that the company's procedure had been accepted.

The arbitrator felt compelled to rule on the basis of the evidence and the general rule that management has all powers except those bargained away in the contract. Hence, he believed that the grievances should be disallowed. Since the hours of employees had been equalized so no unfairness or discrimination was evident, he held that the company had not violated the contract.

Award. In both grievances the company had not violated the contract in scheduling these four employees off for one day each during the weeks of May 5 and May 16, 1958.

CASE 2: REDUCING THE WORKWEEK
BADENHOUSEN CORPORATION AND UNITED STEELWORKERS
OF AMERICA LOCAL 2954, CCH 64–2, PARA. 8532.
ARBITRATORS: TROTTA (CHAIRMAN), HOPPOCK, KELLER.

Issue. Did the company violate the contract by scheduling a 32-hour workweek?

Background. Paragraph 97 of Article XI ("Seniority") of the 1954 contract obligated the company when production is reduced "to shorten the length of the workweek before resorting to layoff of employees." During the 1957 negotiations, the union requested and the company agreed to delete this provision. In 1963 the company reduced the workweek from 40 hours to 32 hours.

Contract Provisions. Article VII ("Hours of Work"), Paragraph 21, states: "The normal workweek for all employees is five (5) consecutive eight-hour (8 hr.) days, Monday through Friday. This shall not be construed to be a guarantee of hours work per day or per week. Management shall have the exclusive right to determine work schedules and hours of work, provided this shall not be used for purposes of discrimination."

Seniority provisions are covered by Article XIII, Paragraph 98, and state: "Whenever possible, employees shall be temporarily transferred to other departments rather than be laid off. A temporary transfer shall be defined as a transfer of forty-five (45) working days or less, unless extended by mutual agreement between the Company and the Union." Further, in subparagraph (a) the agreement stipulates that "an employee having been so transferred to another department, where others have seniority above him, shall, before being laid off, be given a change to transfer, if practicable, to his old department, where his original seniority shall prevail."

In Paragraph 100 of Article XIII, the order of layoff with respect to seniority is stated as: "If in the judgment of the Management, it becomes necessary to reduce the work force, those employees of the affected classifications with the least amount of service in the department are to be laid off first and reinstated last. If by following such a procedure a senior employee is laid off and a junior employee is retained within the department, the senior employee may claim the job of the junior employee, providing the senior employee has the necessary skill and ability to do the junior employee's job."

Union's Position. The union argued that since the provision in the contract allowing management to shorten the workweek had been deleted, the scheduling of a 32-hour workweek was improper.

Company's Position. The deletion of Paragraph 21 of Article VII relieved the company of the obligation to reduce the workweek, but it did not prohibit it from doing so.

Arbitrators' Analysis. The arbitrators concluded that merely because the company had agreed to a deletion of the policy adopted in Paragraph 21 in 1954 (shortening the workweek), it was not forbidden, under any and all circumstances, to reduce the workweek.

Award. Grievance denied.

REFERENCES

1. Chesapeake and Potomac Telephone Co. of Maryland, 31 LA 680.
2. Precision Rubber Products Corp., 31 LA 1066.

3. Fruehauf Trailer Co., 13 LA 163; American Iron & Machine Works Co., 18 LA 285.
4. Ohmer Corp., 13 LA 364; Bethlehem Steel Co., 15 LA 761; Chrysler Corp., 12 LA 738; Colonial Bronze Co., 19 LA 294 (superseniority).
5. Wauregan Mills, Inc., 31 LA 522; Fairbanks, Morse, and Co., 32 LA 278.
6. O'Brien Suburban Press, Inc., 18 LA 721.
7. Enterprise Wheel and Car Corp., 32 LA 681; Laher Battery Production Corp., 11 LA 41.
8. Rudiger-Lang Co., 11 LA 567.
9. Westinghouse Electric Corp., 30 LA 988.

VACANCIES

Job vacancies occur when a new job is created or the incumbent is promoted, transferred, or discharged. The right to fill such a vacancy is a management prerogative, but it is usually limited by the collective bargaining agreement.

Contracts sometimes contain such provisions as "Employees outside the bargaining unit will not be transferred, promoted or hired to jobs in the bargaining unit, unless regular employees in the bargaining unit are unable at that time to perform the work available." [1]

Employers are often required to post a notice of a vacancy[2] and fill the job "only from submitted bids, except should no qualified employee submit a bid, or should no bid be received on a job vacancy." [3] The temporary or permanent nature of the job vacancy is an issue in many cases,[4] as well as the obligation of an employee to accept a temporary[5] or permanent vacancy.[6]

A combination of seniority and ability to perform the work is the most frequent criterion for selection. There is considerable variation in collective bargaining provisions that purport to recognize management's responsibility for the efficient operation of the plant and also protect senior employees. The interpretation of these clauses presents some of the most difficult problems in arbitration.[7]

An employee is often allowed a period of time to work on the new job before a final decision is made.[8]

Unions guard their seniority rights carefully and are quick to file a grievance when a junior employee is selected to fill a vacancy. Management, on the other hand, is more concerned with selecting the most efficient worker, particularly when a promotion is involved.[9]

CASE 1: ABILITY TO PERFORM JOB
INTERNATIONAL PAPER COMPANY, SOUTHERN KRAFT
DIVISION [MOSS POINT, MISS.] AND INTERNATIONAL
BROTHERHOOD OF PAPER MAKERS, 19 LA 402. ARBITRATORS:
RALSTON (CHAIRMAN), VANDILLON, HOLST.

Issue. In filling the position of Head Operating Electrician in the Electrical Department, did the company violate the seniority provision of the 1951 labor agreement when it bypassed Grievant R., the senior employee, and promoted E., the junior employee?

Background. In 1951, to accommodate the expanded plant facilities at its Moss Point mill, the company set up four new positions with the job classification of Head Operating Electrician. These jobs were filled by promoting four Journeyman Electricians to Head Operating Electricians. Since these new jobs were covered by the collective bargaining agreement, the promotions were to be made in accordance with the applicable provisions therein.

The two electricians with greatest seniority were promoted. The next seven electricians in order of seniority, including Grievant R., were passed over for one reason or another and the remaining two promotions were given to E. and another electrician with less seniority.

Contract Provisions. The contract provision pertinent to this grievance is Section VI, Paragraph (B)(1), "Seniority": "When promotions are to be made the Management will take into consideration seniority and ability, and when all the factors which constitute ability are relatively equal, then Job Seniority shall determine the promotion. Where Job Seniority is equal, Department Seniority shall determine the promotion. When Job Seniority and Department Seniority are both equal, then Company Seniority shall determine the promotion."

Union's Position. The company passed over Grievant R., a senior employee, for promotion in violation of Section VI of the agreement.

Company's Position. On November 8, 1951, the company advised the grievant by letter of the reasons why men of lesser seniority had been promoted to the job of Head Operating Electrician. The pertinent portion of the letter stated that the grievant had been considered by the Promotion Board but that it was the unanimous decision of the board that presently he did not have the qualifications necessary to perform satisfactorily the duties of Head Operating Electrician. The factors that the board discussed, and which its members found lacking, were initiative, judgment, and the ability to make accurate reports to his superiors. These deductions had been made from observations of job situations in which the grievant's dependence on his superiors evidently had been the result of indecision and poor judgment rather than a question of knowledge and capability. It was also observed that the grievant's inability to make accurate reports was not due to ignorance of the facts but to the stress invoked by requests for information.

Arbitrators' Analysis. It was the contention of the union that the company had violated Section VI(B)(1) of the contract in promoting E. over Grievant R. The ability of R. was relatively equal to that of E., and he therefore should have been promoted. The grievant was admittedly a good employee and he should have been given an opportunity to qualify for the position of Head Operating Electrician, especially because no evidence showed that he was unable to perform the job.

The argument of the company was that management had the right under the contract to judge the abilities of both men. After fair and careful consideration it concluded that all factors that constitute ability were not equal in the case of E. and R., and that E. had greater ability for the job of Head Operating Electrician. Accordingly, the company had acted within its authority under Section VI(B)(1) of the contract in bypassing R., and its action should be sustained.

The arbitrators interpreted Section VI(B)(1) to mean that job seniority determines promotion only "when all the factors which constitute ability are relatively equal." Management had the right under this provision to make the decision of whether the factors that constitute ability were relatively equal. Although this decision was not an unqualified right and was subject to review by the arbitration procedure, the arbitrators could not lightly substitute their judgment for that of management. In order to set aside such a decision, evidence must offer proof that the decision was unreasonable; was not a bona fide exercise of discretion; was the result of bias, favoritism, anti-union prejudice; or was the result of a clear mistake. In this case there had been no evidence to show such abuse of discretion. Rather, the evidence accentuated the Promotion Board's conclusion that E.'s ability, capability, and experience were superior to those of the grievant. The decision to bypass R. for E. was reached in a Promotion Board meeting in accordance with standard company policy.

The principal evidence to refute the company's decision was the fact that the grievant had done a good job in his present position of Journeyman Electrician. However, present job performance was not at issue. It was the relative ability of R. and E. to perform the job of Head Operating Electrician that determined their right to the promotion. Under the facts of the case the arbitrators could not conclude that the Promotion Board had acted unreasonably or improperly.

Award. The award was granted by a majority of the arbitrators. It was concluded that the company did not violate the seniority provisions of the 1951 labor agreement when it bypassed R., the senior employee, and promoted E., the junior employee, in filling the position of Head Operating Electrician.

CASE 2: VACANCIES—JOB BIDDING
VULCAN MOLD & IRON COMPANY AND UNITED AUTO WORKERS
LOCAL 758, CCH 64–3, PARA. 8950. ARBITRATOR: DUFF.

Issue. Did the company violate the contract by promoting a man with less seniority than a man who was available and willing to be promoted?

Background. The company produces and sells ingot molds. On January 28, 1964, a vacancy in job no. 113, Helper Blacksmith, was posted for bid in accordance with the contract. The grievant, who had greatest seniority, applied for the job but was rejected because company officials felt he lacked the aptitude for the job.

Contract Provisions. Article V, Paragraph C, states that when a job is open, it must be advertised so that eligible employees can apply for the vacancy. In such cases, seniority and aptitude for the job are considered in making the selection. An employee who is awarded a job is allowed a 30-day trial. If he fails to perform satisfactorily, he will be returned to his previous classification.

Eligibility is defined by Section 2 of Article VII, entitled "General Working Conditions." Effective with the signing of the agreement, all job advertisements thereafter (as specified in Article V, Paragraph C) for helpers on certain jobs must declare that a successful applicant is to learn the job for which he is a helper so that eventually he may qualify for a higher classification in case a temporary or permanent vacancy occurs. Promoted helpers are allowed a 60-day trial period in which to qualify before they revert to the labor force if unsuccessful.

The status of helper and the particular jobs in the helper category are governed by Article VII, Paragraph 2A, as follows:

> Provisions of this paragraph shall apply to the rotary planer operator helper (assistant) and blacksmith helper. . . . Helper jobs enumerated in this paragraph shall remain helpers until such time as a temporary or permanent vacancy occurs in the job for which he is a helper, at which time the senior employee on the helper job shall fill said vacancy, provided, however, he has completed the required period of training specified in our job evaluation for the job for which he is a helper. Any employee so promoted shall be given a trial period of up to thirty (30) days maximum to prove his abilities and qualifications; failing such he shall revert to the labor force. . . .

Union's Position. The grievant was entitled to the promotion because he had sufficient aptitude for the job and was qualified by seniority.

Company's Position. The grievant lacked sufficient aptitude for the job.

Arbitrator's Analysis. Where the difference in length of service is substantial, in this case 11 years, the company must be prepared to support its choice of the junior employee with clear and reasonably concrete proof that the senior employee lacked aptitude for the job. If the senior employee can perform the job in a good, workmanlike manner after he has been given the training period set forth in the contract, he is entitled to the job.

The evidence supports a finding that the grievant was entitled to the training period provided in the contract.

Award. The company was ordered to place the grievant in the job of Blacksmith Helper, to determine whether or not he could satisfactorily perform the job. If he did succeed, he was to be reimbursed for any financial loss sustained by the company's failure to assign him to the job on February 6, 1964.

REFERENCES

1. Metropolitan Body Company, 15 LA 207.
2. Durham Hosiery Mills, 12 LA 311; Research Corporation, 17 LA 796.
3. General Telephone Company of Kentucky, 31 LA 347.
4. Bethlehem Steel Company, 32 LA 145.
5. Jones and Laughlin Steel Corp., 16 LA 767; Reynolds Metals Co., 16 LA 352.
6. Philips Oil Company, 18 LA 798.
7. Coca-Cola Bottling Company, 18 LA 757; Southwestern Bell Telephone Co., 30 LA 862; Branch River Wool Combing Company, 11 LA 346; Dairyland Power Co-Operative, 11 LA 797; Chrysler Corporation, 32 LA 988.
8. Columbian Carbon Company, 18 LA 242; American Republic Corporation, 16 LA 454.
9. Northwestern Bell Telephone Co., 19 LA 47; Atlas Powder Company, 30 LA 674.

OVERTIME

Overtime pay is provided for in most collective bargaining agreements and also is required by both state and federal statutes. Disputes discussed here arise under the contractual provisions. Contracts usually stipulate that overtime shall be deemed to be time worked in excess of eight hours in any one day[1] or forty hours in a workweek.[2] The rate to be paid is ordinarily fixed in the contract and is usually time and one-half the normal rate for the job.[3] But what appears simple on its face does not prove to be so simple in practice.

It is not always clear how the employees who are asked to work overtime shall be chosen. When only a small portion of the work force is needed, the problem of who shall get the overtime arises. Many contracts require management to spread the work, thus assuring eligible employees an equitable portion of the overtime work,[4] with a proviso accommodating diverse adaptability to the particular task.[5] Disputes arise as to whether the choice of a particular employee was fair,[6] whether a list should be posted to keep a daily check on the status of overtime distribution, whether a particular period is an adequate test to measure the employer's conformity with the requirement for equitable distribution, and whether the distribution was in fact fair.

Another issue commonly disputed is whether or not the employees must work overtime when asked to do so.[7] Employees are prone to argue that in the absence of an express requirement in the contract, they are obligated to work only forty hours and any more is only consensual. On the other hand, management argues that the employees are insubordinate for failing to comply with the request to work overtime unless management is being unreasonable in its demand.[8] Although support for both views may be found in arbitration awards, the preponderance of opinion supports the view that employees are required to work a reasonable amount of overtime if they are given proper advance notice.

Numerous grievances also arise in connection with the effect of an employee's absences on his right to overtime, and also on the right of management to assign overtime work to supervisory personnel. Many grievances are caused by contracts that do not state clearly that "pyramiding" of overtime will not be allowed.[9]

CASE 1: OBLIGATION TO WORK OVERTIME

LEAR, INCORPORATED (GRAND RAPIDS, MICH.), AND UNITED
AUTOMOBILE, AIRCRAFT & AGRICULTURAL IMPLEMENT
WORKERS OF AMERICA, 28 LA 242. ARBITRATOR: BRADLEY.

Issue. Grievant R., after being directed by his foreman to work overtime, refused to do so, and as a result the company took disciplinary action. The question subject to arbitration was whether he had violated the agreement.

Background. Grievant R. was employed in the Precision Machinist Sheet Metal Department from September of 1955 to October 5, 1956. While on his vacation during the first half of June 1956, a new foreman was assigned to his department. During June employees of the department were notified that, until further notice, overtime was to be scheduled at the end of the regular shift. Any employee desiring to be excused from overtime could submit this request and reasons therefor to his foreman during the regular shift preceding the overtime. The posting of overtime schedules and the procedure for being excused therefrom were consistent with prior practice and recognized by the company and the union.

From June until September all six employees of this department, with occasional exceptions, worked the overtime scheduled and the grievant worked every overtime period. During August, management placed a new employee in the department, but in the opinion of the other six employees, the new man did not meet the qualifications for the job. At the end of August the foreman turned over to another department some tooling for sheet metal parts. This action was protested by the original six employees. On September 4, the day after Labor Day, the union steward informed the foreman during the regular shift that to assign the tooling to another department was not permitted. When the foreman replied that this was a matter within his discretion and that he would continue to do so, the steward stated that a grievance would be filed. At the end of that shift, all six of the original employees left work without making any request to be excused from working overtime.

On September 5 the union submitted a formal grievance based upon the placement of the new employee in the department and the assignment to another department of the tooling job mentioned above. This grievance was processed through the grievance procedure under the contract but later was withdrawn by the union. The six employees again left at the end of the regular shift on September 5 and 6 without informing the foreman.

On September 7, the foreman advised the union steward that the company intended to suspend any of these employees who refused to work overtime that day. The union requested that such action be postponed because all of the men were expected to resume working overtime on September 10. Following this conference with union representatives, all employees of the department were notified by the foreman that they were expected to work overtime at the end of the regular shift that day. Four of the employees. including the grievant, refused and were then informed that they had their choice of working overtime or being suspended. After continued refusal to accept overtime assignments, the grievant received a three-day disciplinary suspension, after which he worked for the company until October 5 and then left for employment with another concern.

Separate grievances were filed by the four employees who had received disciplinary suspension, but only the grievant's case was presented at this hearing, in accordance with the union's preference.

Contract Provisions. Article III of the contract between the company and the union sets forth in detail the agreement concerning the standard workday and workweek; overtime pay at time and one-half or double time; distribution of overtime among employees of a department; and restrictions to prohibit unequal allocation of overtime. Section 9(e) of this article provides that employees and union representatives will cooperate in working overtime, and that each employee will decide for himself, at the time he is asked to work overtime, if he can do so; if he cannot, he must ask to be excused. Any deliberate action by any employee (including a union committeeman or steward) which is designed to keep employees from working overtime is a violation of the contract.

During negotiations concerning the provisions of a new contract, the company had requested that subparagraph (f) be included in Section 9 of Article III. This subparagraph stated that any concerted refusal to work overtime on the part of employees would be considered a violation of the no-strike, no-lockout agreement and the matter would be handled appropriately as a violation of the agreement. The contract accepted by the parties on February 1, 1956, did not include subparagraph (f), but on January 27, 1956, the union wrote the company as follows: "This will confirm our understanding that Section 9(e) of Article III of the new contract is understood by the Union to prohibit any concerted refusal by members of Local 330 to work overtime."

Union's Position. The grievant did not refuse to work overtime in violation of Section 9(e) of the contract.

Company's Position. The grievant was given a suspension for arbitrarily refusing overtime in violation of a written commitment from the union dated February 1, 1956.

Arbitrator's Analysis. As contended by the union, no express provision in the contract compelled employees to work overtime. Neither was there any provision in the contract limiting the number of hours the employees were to work. Section 1 of Article III defines the standard workday as eight hours and the standard workweek as forty hours, Monday through Friday inclusive. In defining the standard workday and workweek, the contract recognized by implication that a workday and workweek could be nonstandard. In addition to this implication, the contract specifically recognized a nonstandard workday and workweek in that the subsequent sections of Article III set forth in detail the provisions governing overtime pay and definitely recognized overtime as an obligation under the contract. As a part of this obligation the union and the employees agreed under Section 9(e) to cooperate in working overtime, and established the conditions under which an employee could be exempted. While the union was correct in that nothing in the contract required compulsory overtime, the detailed provisions of the contract itself and the negotiations leading up to the contract clearly indicated that overtime work was one of the primary considerations in the new contract and that employees had committed themselves to work overtime upon proper notice and unless they requested to be excused therefrom.

Where the contract between the company and the union defines the normal workday and workweek, places no limitation on the number of hours an employee may work during any one day or any one week, and provides additional pay for overtime, the company has the right to require its employees to work overtime and the employees are obligated to work overtime unless specifically excused.[10]

Based upon the evidence submitted, it appeared that there was an agreement between the company and the grievant arising out of the conduct of the parties. The company had agreed with the grievant, by scheduling continuous overtime, that it would employ him for overtime work at the end of each and every shift until further notice. Under this arrangement the grievant and the company could look forward to increased mutual benefits. Each acquired certain rights and obligations under this arrangement. By a uniform course of conduct from June 18 to September 4, each party recognized these rights and obligations. The grievant violated his obligation when he failed to work overtime and gave no notice thereof. He further violated it by his action on September 7 when he refused to work overtime but did not ask to be excused. The terms of the agreement under Article III, 9(e), were mandatory and he was obligated to choose one of two alternatives—work overtime or ask to be excused. He did neither. No overtime was worked by him on the four days involved. On the first three days he did not notify the foreman that he would not work overtime. Off-the-record side remarks could not be construed as asking to be excused, especially when considered with his commitment to "cooperate" in working overtime.

From the testimony of the grievant it appeared that his decision to refuse further overtime was based upon two decisions of management: the upgrading of a new employee and the assignment of work to another department. Article XIX of the contract provides adequate procedure for handling grievances by an employee and was invoked on these two matters. This was the proper method of settling the dispute—not by refusal to work. Under Article XXIII, Section 2, of the contract the employees agreed not to take part in any strike or work stoppage. Where the contract between the company and the union establishes a grievance procedure for the settlement of disputes and bans work stoppages, an employee does not have the right to refuse to work in order to compel action on a grievance.[11]

In view of the evidence, the arbitrator did not deem it necessary to decide whether there was concerted action on the part of the grievant and other employees to refuse overtime.

Award. It was the decision of the arbitrator that the grievant violated Article III, Section 9(e) of the contract between the company and the union, and therefore the grievance was denied.

CASE 2: REMEDY FOR CONTRACT VIOLATION
INTERNATIONAL HARVESTER COMPANY, MEMPHIS WORKS,
AND UNITED AUTOMOBILE, AIRCRAFT & AGRICULTURAL
IMPLEMENT WORKERS OF AMERICA, 14 LA 430.
ARBITRATOR: MCCOY.

Issue. Did the company meet its obligation to give preferential treatment to a union steward for Saturday overtime when it passed over him in error and offered to correct the oversight by providing a compensatory opportunity on another Saturday? Did this offer discharge the company's obligation?

Background. Acting upon a bona fide belief that the grievant, a union steward, was not qualified to perform the work involved in a Saturday overtime assignment, the foreman refused him the job. Some days later, a higher supervisor determined that the foreman had made an error. The grievant was thereupon offered the opportunity to work on some other Saturday within the next few weeks to make up for the earlier denial of work. This offer was refused, and the grievant claimed pay that would have been due him if he had received proper assignment of overtime.

Contract Provisions. Article IV, Section 9(a) states that "if more than one employee within the agreed upon area is required to work on such days (off-duty days), the Steward of such area will be offered the opportunity to work . . . provided he can perform one of the jobs scheduled."

Union's Position. The steward was denied work in violation of Article IV, Sec. 9(a), requiring that a steward have the opportunity to work overtime when more than one employee is involved.

Company's Position. The company argued that to award the grievant back pay in view of the offer of make-up work would in effect impose a penalty upon the company because the company would be required to pay for work not performed. Two fallacies are inherent in that solution: first, the award of compensatory damages would be construed as a "penalty," thus confusing compensatory and punitive damages; second, it would alter the sense of the grievance to a claim that the company should pay for work not performed, whereas the award sought is not "for work not performed," but for the loss sustained from a breach of contract.

The company cited two similar cases[12] to support its denial of a breach of contract, and argued that, in concurrence with the provision of Article VI, Section 4, no wage loss had been caused by the company's action and therefore the company was under no obligation to make wage adjustments.

Finally, the company referred to Article XIV, Section 7, which provides for the equal division of overtime work for all employees, and specifies that failure to divide such overtime and premium pay equally obligates the company only to arrange future overtime and premium pay schedules to permit the employees to make it up.

Arbitrator's Analysis. The section of the contract that was violated in this case [Article IV, Section 9(a)] did not provide for equalizing overtime, although it gave the steward the absolute right to overtime work in specified cases. The cases cited by the company were inapplicable here because they did not pertain to a breach of contract but merely to balancing the hours of work. In this case the company admitted a breach of contract [Article IV, Section 9(a)], and the attempt to conciliate that breach by the introduction of Article XIV, Section 7, failed in its purpose because it had no relation to the facts shown. A wage loss *was* caused by the company's failure to assign overtime to the steward, and the offer of redress made later to the grievant, which seemed fair and appropriate, did not alter the fact that a wage loss had been suffered.

The arbitrator held that in the absence of some specific limitation in the contract, the measure of damages for denial of work to an employee is the sum he would have earned if he had been permitted to work, less any sums earned at other employment that he may have found to replace the work refused. The grievant had not had other work available to him.

Award. The grievant was awarded the overtime pay for the day's work that he would have done had he been properly assigned.

REFERENCES

1. Pittsburgh Plate Glass Co., 14 LA 1; Carnegie-Illinois Steel Corp., 15 LA 818.
2. Harrison Walker Refractories Co., 13 LA 22; Volco Brass & Copper Co., 11 LA 1154.
3. Kroger Co., 13 LA 788; International Harvester Co., 12 LA 650.
4. Pittsburgh Plate Glass Co., 32 LA 622.
5. John Deere Ottumwa Works, 20 LA 737.
6. McInerney Spring & Wire Co., 11 LA 679.
7. Great Lakes Spring Corp., 12 LA 779.
8. Flour Mills of America Inc., 20 LA 564.
9. Southern Clays, Inc., 31 LA 784; LA Jewish Community Council, 11 LA 869; Kroger Co., 15 LA 363; California Cotton Mills, 16 LA 335; Coca-Cola Bottling Works Co., 19 LA 432.
10. Carnegie-Illinois Steel Corp., 12 LA 810; Nebraska Consolidated Mills Co., 13 LA 211.
11. United Engineering & Foundry Co., 21 LA 145.
12. Goodyear Tire and Rubber Co., 5 LA 30; B. F. Goodrich Co., 8 LA 883, 887.

SENIORITY

All collective bargaining agreements contain provisions dealing with seniority, which is particularly important to the individual employee. His seniority rights will in many cases determine whether he is to remain on the payroll or be laid off and whether he has the right to transfer to a more desirable job or shift. Seniority may also be considered a factor in promotions or demotions.[1]

Seniority may begin to accrue from the date of employment,[2] from the end of the probationary period,[3] or even from the date the employee joined the union. All such provisions are contained in the contract. Seniority may be companywide or restricted to a plant, department, or particular craft.[4] Some contracts combine company and departmental seniority. In rare instances a master agreement covering an entire industry may provide for industrywide seniority.

An employee has greater job security if seniority is on a broad unit basis. When the unit is restricted, it is possible that an employee working under departmental seniority for a long period of time may be laid off while a fellow employee in a different department might be retained even though he has a much shorter seniority credit.

Breaks in continuity of employment, such as leaves of absence, layoffs, and illness, may affect seniority. Although layoffs do not necessarily stop the accumulation of seniority, definite limits are either expressly provided for or implied. For example, accrual of seniority may cease at the end of one year even though a layoff extends beyond that time.

Collective bargaining agreements usually include "superseniority" rights[5] for certain union officials. This means that they are placed at the head of the seniority list, irrespective of their actual service with the company. The purpose of this provision is to insure the stability of the union during periods of layoff.

CASE 1: PART-TIME EMPLOYEES
JONES & LAUGHLIN STEEL CORPORATION, PITTSBURGH WORKS, AND UNITED STEEL WORKERS OF AMERICA, 16 LA 890.
ARBITRATORS: COHN (CHAIRMAN), DYE, BURKE.

Issue. Does a full-time employee who accepts part-time employment continue to accrue seniority under the 1947 agreement during his employment as a part-time employee?

Background. The grievant returned to work in October 1945 after a military leave of absence, and worked as a full-time day employee until September 5, 1948, at which time he was transferred to night work at his own request so that he could attend school. When he found this arrangement too burdensome, he requested to be put on part-time work. Accordingly, on November 11, 1948, he was terminated as a full-time employee and was immediately rehired as a part-time employee. On that occasion he signed an application for part-time work in which he acknowledged that his status as a part-time employee did not earn job seniority, continuity of service, or other such privileges normally enjoyed by regular employees, and that his vacation rights were only as provided under Paragraph J, Section 12, of the 1947 agreement. He also acknowledged that his part-time employment was subject to cancellation at any time and would continue in that category until such time as he made known to his department superintendent his availability for full-time employment. He agreed that after clearance through the Employment Department, his continuity of service would begin as of the date of his full-time employment.

On December 5, 1948, the grievant was laid off as a result of curtailed operations. He did not return to work for the company until October 5, 1950, when he was rehired as a new employee and at which time he was advised that his continuous service for purposes of seniority would begin as of that date. Thereupon, the union demanded that the grievant be credited with unbroken, continuous service from October 17, 1945.

Contract Provisions. The issue involved is covered by Section XIII of the agreement of April 29, 1947.

Union's Position. The basic issue is whether part-time employees are covered by and are entitled to the seniority benefits of the contract between the parties. The union contended that since the contract covered "all the employees" of the company except those expressly excluded in Section II of the agreement, and since the latter section made no mention of part-time employees, such employees were completely covered by the contract and were entitled to all the benefits presently conferred on full-time employees. These benefits included the right to accrue continuous service for seniority purposes, except insofar as the right to vacations was expressly limited by Section XII, Paragraph J, of the agreement.

Company's Position. The company claimed that part-time employees had never been regarded and had never been treated by either party as coming within the coverage of the contract, and that the contract provision with regard to vacations was the only item in respect to which they had been included in the collective bargaining between the parties. The company claimed, therefore, that part-time employees were not entitled to any seniority rights under the agreement.

Arbitrators' Analysis. The arbitrators had no precedent upon which to establish the rights of part-time employees, and thus they entertained for the first time the question of the rights of such employees under the agreement.

It was the opinion of the arbitrators that, as a matter of contract construction, the company could not escape from the logic of the union's contention that part-time employees, not being specifically excluded from the agreement by the terms of Section II, were covered by the agreement and were entitled to the benefits of its seniority provisions. The preamble to the agreement of April 29, 1947, declared that it was entered into by the union "on behalf of all the employees of the Corporation, except as set forth in Section II hereof." There was not the slightest evidence in the agreement itself of any intention to qualify or limit its coverage in any other respect. Furthermore, the fact that part-time employees had been expressly mentioned in Section XII, Paragraph J, constituted objective evidence that such employees, far from being excluded from consideration in the negotiations, were actually a subject of negotiations.

The arbitrators recognized that until the grievant posed the issue, part-time employees had not been accorded any rights under the agreement, except with respect to vacations, and specifically that they had not received any seniority rights. It was noted, too, that the policy statement issued by the company to its superintendents on February 12, 1948, stated that "employees employed as part-time workers do not have job seniority rights," and that the contents of the application for part-time employment also repeated this assertion. However, neither the failure of the parties to give proper recognition to the status of part-time employees, nor statements contained in unilateral expressions of policy, which were contrary to the provisions of the agreement, could be binding upon the arbitrators in interpreting the contract as written. Therefore, under the 1947 agreement, part-time employees were entitled to receive credit for continuous service for purposes of seniority.

With regard to the question of the proper seniority date for the grievant, the record made it perfectly clear that the severance of the grievant from employment as a full-time employee on November 11, 1948, came about at his own request and for his own convenience. It therefore constituted a voluntary quitting on his part. It was immaterial that he was immediately rehired as a part-time employee, or even that the quitting of employment had been required by the company as a condition of his being given part-time employment. The company was not required to give part-time employment, and was not prohibited by any contractual provision from imposing as a condition of part-time employment that the employee first terminate any other connection he might have with the company. A quitting of employment under such circumstances is a voluntary one on the employee's part, and by so doing he had broken his continuous service within the meaning of Section XIII of the agreement. He began to accrue continuous service again upon being rehired as a part-time employee on November 11, 1948. His subsequent layoff, from December 5, 1948, to October 5, 1950, being less than two years in duration, did not constitute a break in his continuous service in view of the provisions of Section XIII. The fact that the company had chosen to reemploy him as a new employee did not transform his layoff into a voluntary quitting, and no evidence of any kind indicates that the grievant voluntarily quit the service of the company between the date of his layoff and the date when he was rehired.

Award. The arbitrators ruled that the grievant's continuous service for purposes of seniority should therefore be dated from the time of his engagement as a part-time employee.

CASE 2: SUPERSENIORITY
LINDE COMPANY, A DIVISION OF UNION CARBIDE CORPORATION, AND OIL, CHEMICAL, & ATOMIC WORKERS INTERNATIONAL UNION, 32 LA 885.
ARBITRATOR: SHISTER

Issue. Should an employee who has been laid off be recalled to work by the company before the recall of a union representative who has less seniority and whose transfer to a different shift had canceled his status as a shop steward?

Background. During a layoff in February 1958 the grievant, who had greatest seniority in his departmental unit, was unable to bump elsewhere so that he could continue working. However, the shop steward in his department, who had less seniority but who was granted top seniority because of his union office, was retained on the job. Some weeks after the grievant's layoff, the second shift, on which both employees had worked, was eliminated. The steward was assigned to the day shift, thereby losing his stewardship, and was later laid off. When the company began recall, the steward was recalled before the grievant. The grievant then filed his claim that the company had acted improperly and that he was entitled to the wages lost from the time he should have been recalled to the time when he was actually recalled.

Contract Provisions. Several articles of the contract apply to the issue involved, including:

1. Article VIII, Section 20—This states that when it is necessary to reduce the labor force in any job title in any seniority unit, employees will be deposed in the following order: (A) employees without seniority status; (B) employees who are unable to perform satisfactorily the job requirements at the time of reduction in the force; and (C) employees in inverse order of their unit seniority.

2. Article VIII, Section 25—In relation to layoff only, elected union officers, stewards, and members of the grievance committee, as provided for in Article IX of the contract, who have one year or more of company service credit, shall have top priority rating in their respective seniority units during their term of office.

3. Article VIII, Section 26—When the working forces are to be increased, employees covered in item (C) of Section 20, and employees who displaced others and were later displaced themselves, will be the first offered the opportunity to return to such jobs in inverse order of their layoff, demotion, or transfer. Employees who were deposed under Section 20, but who were unable, because of seniority, to depose anyone in the next "best-graded job from which they were formerly promoted," but who did accept and work on a still lower-graded job, will be offered the opportunity of recall to such "next best-graded job" in the order of their seniority as compared with those deposed under item (C) in Section 20.

Union's Position. A steward who is given top seniority by virtue of Article VIII, Section 25, of the agreement retains his top seniority *only during the term of his office.* After losing his stewardship, he no longer comes under the provisions of Section 25. Thus, in recalling him first on the basis of this seniority rather than on company service seniority, the company violated the contract. Once a steward is laid off, he is no longer a steward. Nothing in the contract gives an ex-steward special privileges over seniority. After he loses his status through layoff, recall processes must be effected as stipulated in Article VIII, Section 26.

Company's Position. Although the grievant did have more service seniority than did the steward, the steward was properly recalled in accordance with Article VIII, Section 26. That section supersedes all other contractual provisions insofar as recalls are concerned, for it is the only provision that deals directly and specifically with the subject of recall. Since the section dictates that employees are recalled in the inverse order of their layoff, it means that the steward was properly recalled before the grievant.

Arbitrator's Analysis. Section 26 clearly specified that employees would be recalled "in the inverse order of their layoff," and no other criterion was mentioned. The issue related solely to recall and did not pertain to any contractual violation in layoffs. The evidence was that the Manager of Industrial Relations emphasized to the union during contract negotiations that union officials have "double protection"—superseniority in the event of a layoff, and recall based not on their regular seniority but on the principle of "last out, first back." At that time the union offered no objection to this understanding. Prior to arbitration proceedings, the company and the union had a tentative agreement to amend the current contract so that this formula would be replaced by a seniority clause, but following a disagreement about the extent of the revision, both parties withdrew. Thus, the pertinent clauses of the contract applied currently.

The company maintained that the grievance before the arbitrator was not valid because it had not been filed within 30 days after the steward was recalled to work, a condition required by the contract. The arbitrator ruled that the matter requested for consideration was purely academic and therefore would not be ruled on, since the company had expressed a willingness to consider the principle further, to the exclusion of back pay for the grievant.

Award. The company had not violated the contract. The grievance was denied.

REFERENCES

1. Lukens Steel Co., 17 LA 455; E. I. DuPont de Nemours & Co., 14 LA 494.
2. Plastic Jewel Corp., 14 LA 775.
3. Pee Dee Textile Co., 14 LA 963.
4. Den-Ark Tool & Die Company, 20 LA 300; General Dynamics, CCH 64-3, para. 9171.
5. McCord Corp., 28 LA 904; Standard Steel Spring Co., 17 LA 423.

BUMPING

The term "bumping" describes the right of a senior employee, whose position has been eliminated by layoff, to displace a junior employee who occupies a position that remains necessary to the operation.[1] In exercising his "right" to bump, an employee's ability appears as a determinative factor. The senior employee ordinarily need not be as able as the regular incumbent of the position, but he should possess the ability of any beginner on the job.[2] Some contracts do require more. Where this is the case, arbitrators will insist on a showing of equal capability.[3]

CASE 1: STANDARD OF PERFORMANCE

INTERNATIONAL HARVESTER COMPANY, MCCORMICK TWINE
MILLS, AND UNITED FARM EQUIPMENT & METAL WORKERS
COUNCIL, 15 LA 587. ARBITRATOR: SEWARD.

Issue. Was the grievant given a fair trial in order to qualify for a job that would have saved her from being laid off?

Background. The grievant was employed as an Extra Spinner, but was laid off from her job on January 27, 1950. On January 30, 1950, the union filed a grievance, pointing out that shorter-service employees were then employed as Doffer-Cleaners, and claimed that the grievant should have been given a reasonable three-day break-in to test her ability to perform the doffing job and qualify for displacing one of these employees. As a result, the grievant was given a three-day trial as a Doffer-Cleaner. At the end of this period, management held that she had failed to qualify.

Union's Position. The grievant performed equally to, if not better than, the three other qualified doffers who were working at that time. In her first two days of the test period she completed most, although not all, of her doffs within the required time. On the third day she slowed down somewhat, but made up the production rate within two hours on her fourth day. The union claimed that the test standard was higher than the production rate actually being achieved by the qualified doffers and therefore the test was unfair. As a result, the grievant was laid off and suffered a loss of pay from the time of her disqualification to the time she was recalled to fill another job. She claimed reimbursement for this loss of income.

Company's Position. The purpose of the break-in test is not to determine whether the employee can eventually learn the job and perform it capably, but whether she can learn and perform it within three days. The employee is not attempting to fill a vacancy but is asserting her seniority right to displace another employee, who presumably has qualified to management's satisfaction. The break-in test is intended to make sure that such displacement will not result in substituting an unqualified operator, with a consequent loss in efficiency.

Arbitrator's Analysis. It was the arbitrator's opinion that the three-day break-in period was not a test of potential ability but one of present performance, and was a means of judging capability through observing performance.

In adopting the provision for a three-day break-in period, the parties were clearly endeavoring to get away from subjective estimates of ability; they were saying that the right of a longer-service employee to displace a shorter-service employee should be determined not by what a foreman thinks the longer-service employee can or cannot do, but by what such an employee actually does on the job. Thus, the test of adequate performance is not some ideal or theoretical performance standard, but is the standard actually applied by supervision in day-to-day operation. Management has every right to see that the level of performance that it requires and accepts in actual practice will not be lowered as the result of a seniority displacement. The employees, on the other hand, have every right to insist that the standards by which their break-in performance is judged are not more severe than those management applies in the normal operation of the department.

The question in this and similar cases was not what standards supervision ought to require but what standards it did require. The question here, in other words, was not whether the 22-minute doffing standard was too "tight," but whether or not the doffers were being held to that level of performance for eight hours at a stretch in actual practice.

The arbitrator found that the testimony was in conflict. His judgment of the probable truth was that at the time this break-in test was given, the 22-minute standard was an objective toward which supervision was working. It was not being achieved in practice by the qualified employees on the job. In the arbitrator's judgment, management had acted improperly in requiring of the grievant a degree of perfection that other employees had not yet attained. The evidence had established that on that day she had equaled or exceeded the performance of other operators on the job.

The arbitrator concluded that if the grievant had been allowed to displace one of the incumbent operators, the performance of the department would not have suffered. Under these circumstances, in the arbitrator's opinion, her seniority had entitled her to the job of doffer, and the company had erred in not granting it.

Award. In appealing to arbitration, the grievant had not requested placement in a doffing job. Accordingly, the arbitrator limited the award to back pay for the wages lost from January 30, 1950 (when the original grievance had been first filed) to August 28, 1950, when the grievant was recalled.

CASE 2: DETERMINING ABILITY TO PERFORM
INDIAN SALES CORPORATION (SPRINGFIELD, MASS.) AND
INDIAN INDEPENDENT UNION, 20 LA 394. ARBITRATOR: LOW.

Issue. Did the company violate the letter and spirit of the contract in applying the seniority section to a layoff of the grievant if he was quailfied to fill vacancies in other labor grades?

Background. The grievant was laid off in his classification of Helper Maintenance Man, a new job classified in Labor Grade 10, which he was the first employee to fill. This job required three years of service before he could qualify for Maintenance Man. At the time of the layoff no other jobs in Labor Grade 10 were available nor were there openings in lower grades that he might fill by virtue of seniority. The grievant requested a transfer to the higher-paying, higher-classified Labor Grade 7 on the assembly line or to Labor Grade 9 (Miscellaneous Bench Worker), both of which were filled by probational employees. However, the company disqualified him on the basis of insufficient knowledge and experience, and applied the criterion of seniority in authorizing his layoff at the Labor Grade 10 level. The union claimed that this action of the company violated Article VI, Section A, of the labor contract.

Contract Provisions. Article VI, Section A, states: "It is agreed that in all cases of increases and decreases in the work force, the length of continuous service with the Company shall be the determining factor. Seniority shall be accumulated on a plantwide basis. In all cases of layoff, probationary employees shall be laid off first. If an employee is being laid off in his classification and has the ability to perform the work in any other classification, he shall be entitled to perform the work in any other classification, providing he has sufficient knowledge. Ability includes job knowledge, experience, and efficiency required to perform the job in an average and/or satisfactory manner."

Union's Position. The union's letter to the company concerning "Breakage of Seniority Clause of the Union Contract," February 22, 1953, stated that the grievant had not been given a chance to prove his ability on any other job for which he could claim seniority and which he claimed ability to perform. The union said that because the company failed to give the grievant the "chance to prove his ability," it had also failed to live up to the clause in the labor contract and therefore that the seniority rights of union members were in future danger of being circumvented. Employees in the probationary category, who had been on the payroll for a period of less than 60 days, were filling jobs that the grievant had the ability to do but had had no opportunity to prove he could do. The length of service and ability to do the job were the controlling factors, and the contract did not limit an employee to transfers simply within his own labor grade or to a lower labor grade; he had the right to be considered for "any other classification."

The union claimed that, in combating the company's unwillingness to transfer the grievant, it had contacted a foreman who stated that the acceptance of the grievant into a job in a higher classification would not cause hardship to the company.

Company's Position. The grievant was given his chance to prove that he had the ability to perform the work in other classifications. As had been management's past practice in placements and possible transfers, judgment had been based on the determining factors of length of service, plus a complete review of a grievant's record of job knowledge and the related experience that would allow him to do a satisfactory job in the classification into which he was seeking to be transferred.

As part of the standard practice, the grievant had been questioned regarding his knowledge of transmission work, and was found not to have the knowledge and experience that would allow him to qualify as a Transmission Assembler or as a Miscellaneous Bench Worker.

The company stated that the qualification procedure had been followed even though in management's opinion the transfer of an employee to a job in a higher classification and labor grade, provided he met the specifications, was not a contract obligation, since the company was obligated only by the *content* of the contract. The company contended that the union was reading into the spirit of the contract those agreements contained in another contract that had been effected with the parent union, from which the present union had separated.

Arbitrator's Analysis. The wording of the contract did not prohibit an employee who was being laid off from seeking to replace a probationary worker or an employee whom he outranked in length of service, regardless of the job classification or labor grade. The real issue was whether or not the grievant was given a chance to prove that he had the ability, as determined by the degree of job knowledge, experience, and efficiency, required to perform the job in an average and/or satisfactory manner.

The fact that there were no probationary workers in Labor Grade 10, which was the grievant's grade, and no employees with less length of service, plus the fact that the grievant aspired to a higher labor grade, meant that the contract obligated the company to determine if he had the necessary qualifications that would enable him to be transferred and fill a higher classification satisfactorily.

The arbitrator found that the company had fulfilled its obligation in the manner that had been its past practice in placements, upgrading, and transferring. In the absence of anything in the contract that determined who had the final right to evaluate the ability of the grievant to satisfactorily meet the required specifications of the job in the higher labor grades, the arbitrator based his judgment on the facts presented and ruled that the grievant had been given the customary "chance to prove his ability on any other job which he had seniority on, which he claims he can perform," and that the company had been within its rights when it decided that the grievant did not possess the necessary "ability."

Award. The grievance was denied.

REFERENCES

1. Howard Paper Mills Inc., 32 LA 869.
2. International Harvester Co., 17 LA 93; Indian Sales Corp., 20 LA 394.
3. Allentown Portland Cement Co., 31 LA 476; West Virginia Pulp and Paper Co., 12 LA 391; International Harvester Co., 15 LA 587.

TRANSFERS, PROMOTIONS, AND DEMOTIONS

The right to transfer employees is a basic management prerogative, but like many management rights, it is limited by the collective bargaining agreement. One frequent clause provides that "the company may when necessary to insure continuity of production, make temporary transfers from one job to another. . . . Such transfers shall be without prejudice and shall take into consideration seniority and the wishes of the employee involved."[1]

A distinction must be made between a permanent and a temporary transfer. In most cases an employee who is temporarily transferred receives his own rate or the rate of the job to which he is assigned, whichever is higher.[2] Determining whether the rate to be paid is the minimum or maximum of the rate range is often a problem for the arbitrator. If there is an incentive system, the payment of basic rates or incentive earnings may be an issue.[3] If, as the result of a layoff, an employee accepts a transfer to a lower-rate job, he usually receives the lower rate.[4] The lower rate is also paid when an employee is demoted for lack of ability to perform the work assigned to him.[5]

CASE 1: WHAT IS A TRANSFER?
BETHLEHEM STEEL COMPANY, LACKAWANNA PLANT,
AND UNITED STEELWORKERS OF AMERICA,
30 LA 550. ARBITRATOR: SEWARD.

Issue. Did the company violate the agreement when it assigned lower-seniority employees to a higher-earnings job when higher-seniority employees were available in the same classification?

Background. In the early part of 1957, a new Cincinnati milling machine was put in operation in the machine shop. Supervision selected four employees from the Machinist force and assigned them to the new machine. Pending the establishment of incentive rates for the operation, they were paid position average earnings, amounting to something like 25¢ above the Machinist standard hourly wage rate. Incentive earnings, after the work became incentive-rated, were apparently substantial.

At the time the new milling machine was installed, the grievant was assigned to floor work and was making less substantial incentive earnings. Although he had greater length of service than three of the four employees assigned to the new machine, his ability relative to them did not become an issue. He claimed that his seniority rights under Article X, Section 1, had been violated by his supervisor's refusal to select him in preference to one of the other three Machinists. He asked for a ruling affirming his right to be assigned to the new milling machine, an assignment that offered higher incentive earnings.

Contract Provisions. Article X, Section 1, of the contract does not restrict management in assigning and reassigning employees within their own classification. It contains no "local working condition" clause that might govern the move requested by the grievant.

Union's Position. The union's case rested solely on the contention that a move of the grievant from floor work to the new milling machine would have constituted a promotion within the meaning of Article X, Section 1.

Company's Position. Though the assignment to the new machine was a continuous one and though the grievant, if assigned to the new milling machine, would have earned more than on his present assignment, there nevertheless was no contractual support for granting his request. He was asking to be moved from one assignment to another *within* his own Machinist classification. It had been well established by a long line of arbitration holdings that such reassignments are not governed by the seniority provisions of Article X, Section 1.

Arbitrator's Analysis. The arbitrator referred to a closely related case in which a grievant had claimed a promotional vacancy in his same job class, and for which contractual provisions or practice offered no justification or precedent. He held that the grievant did not have the right to fill the vacancy under Article X, Section 1, because the move he requested did not constitute a promotion within the meaning of that provision. The arbitrator did not define the word "promotion" only in terms of a move from one job to another but held that promotion based on higher incentive earnings must be considered in conjunction with that definition, an established practice customarily applied. No contention had been made in the present case that assignments within the Machinist classification in this machine shop, based on earning potential, had been governed by practice.

Obviously, if a lateral move *between* two separately classified jobs is held not to constitute a promotion within the meaning of Article X, Section 1, the same would be true with at least equal force of a move from one work station to another *within* the same classification.

Award. The arbitrator held that the grievance lacked contractual support, and was therefore denied.

CASE 2: WHAT IS THE PROPER RATE OF PAY?
COURTAULDS, INC. AND COURTAULDS (ALABAMA) INC.
(LE MOYNE, ALA.) AND TEXTILE WORKERS UNION OF
AMERICA, 32 LA 643. ARBITRATOR: MCCOY.

Issue. Three grievances of like nature were involved here. Two employees were temporarily assigned to fill jobs having higher rates of compensation but for which they were paid at the rates of their normal classification. Should they have been compensated at the higher rate while performing the work of their temporary assignments?

Background. Grievant C., a No. 1 Utility Operator, had been on the job for four years, and drew the top rate of the classification, $2.33. On December 11 and 12 he was assigned to fill a two-day vacancy created by the absence of the No. 2 Churn Operator, who was at the top rate of that classification, $2.42. C. was paid his own rate of $2.33 but contended he should have been paid $2.42.

This move required the filling of Grievant C.'s job. Grievant P., a No. 3 Utility Operator who earned the top rate of that classification, $2.23, was assigned to it for those two days. He was paid his own rate, but contended for the top rate of the No. 1 Utility Operator job which he filled, $2.33. Grievant M. in turn filled Grievant P.'s job.

Contract Provisions. Article XI, Section K, of the collective bargaining agreement of November 12, 1958, applies to the issue.

Temporary Assignments. If an Employee shall be assigned temporarily at the direction of the Company from his regular job to another job when work is available to him on his regular job for which the Employee would otherwise have been scheduled, he shall receive *the established rate of pay for the job performed.* In addition, while performing work in such circumstances, such Employee shall receive such special allowances as may be required to equal the earnings that he would otherwise have realized. The above shall not apply when temporary assignments are made to avoid layoffs. [Italics added.]

The rates, and a "Wage Plan," are set forth in Appendix A to the contract, expressly referred to in Article IX, and were adopted as a part of the contract.

Union's Position. The union contended that the established rate for the employee replaced was the proper rate to be paid to the temporary assignee.

Company's Position. The company stated that the phrase "established rate of pay" in relation to a temporary assignment clearly referred to the minimum rate in the scale and could not possibly be interpreted as that rate which the permanent holder of the job may have reached through seniority or other qualification. The minimum rate for a No. 2 Churn Operator was $2.31, so the company had paid Grievant C. his own rate of $2.33. Or, to employ the terminology of Section K, it paid him the minimum rate of the No. 2 Churn Operator plus an allowance to bring him up to his own rate. Similarly, the minimum rate for No. 1 Utility Operator is $2.11 and Grievant P. had been paid his own rate of $2.23.

Arbitrator's Analysis. The arbitrator observed that though worded differently from the ordinary provision of this sort,* the meaning of the contract provision was the same: The employee who is temporarily assigned gets his own rate or the rate of the job to which he is assigned, whichever is higher. The difficulty presented was in the use of the phrase "established rate of pay."

In view of the fact that every classification in the plant had several rates (minimum, maximum, and from one to four specified intermediate steps) spelled out in the contract in dollars and cents, it was surprising that such an ambiguous phrase should have been used in writing Section K. Nothing in the minutes of contract negotiations defined the ambiguous words, which could mean the minimum rate, or the maximum rate, or that intermediate rate that had been "established" on the job by the man temporarily replaced.

---

* The usual wording is: "shall receive his own rate of pay or the rate of pay of the job to which transferred, whichever is higher."

The question then was whether one party had so acted, or used such words, as to reasonably indicate to the other that the intent was identical and mutual. If so, then the intent of the one misled, though innocently, prevails. This is elementary law in the interpretation of contracts.

The arbitrator then reviewed the aspects of this interpretation:

Subsidiary, or corollary, to this rule, is the rule that ambiguous language is to be construed most strictly against the party responsible for the use of that language. The phrase in question was the Company's; it appeared in the proposals of the Company, not in a proposal of the Union. Under this rule, unless other considerations and other rules dictate otherwise, the phrase should be construed to conform to the intent of the Union negotiators. There was no actual testimony as to that intent, but I think it fair to presume that it was to secure the usual benefit of transfer contained in most labor contracts. Indeed that intent is shown by the written proposals of the Union, which adopted the usual language of labor contracts [as quoted in the footnote on page 347]. Such evidence is usually more reliable than would be mere testimony as to intent. Under the usual labor contract, a replacement for an absentee gets either the rate of the absentee or his own rate, whichever is higher.

General principles recognized in industrial relations and in labor contracts are not without importance in judging of intent, or at least of objective intent. When a man is temporarily transferred to a job calling for higher skill, greater responsibility, etc., and carrying a higher rate, he expects to get a higher rate, and generally does, for the justice of that expectation is appreciated by management. To adopt the Company's interpretation here would result, and did in these cases result, in these grievants having to exercise that higher skill, greater responsibility, etc., without receiving any higher rate.

As further supporting the Union's case, it is to be noted that elsewhere in the Contract, when reference is made to the minimum rate, the unambiguous words "minimum rate" are used. It is only in Section K that the words in question are used. Thus in the Appendix, also worded by the Company, the term "minimum rate" is used in Paragraphs 4, 5, and 7 of the General Rules of the Wage Plan, in Paragraphs 1, 2, and 3 of the Departmental Rules relating to the Chemical Laboratory, in Paragraphs 1, 3, and 5 of the Craft Section Rules, in Paragraphs 1 and 2 of the Planning Section Rules, and in similar rules for other sections and departments. For this reason, when the Company's proposals for Section K failed to use the same words, the effect was misleading, though I am sure unintentionally so.

The company relied chiefly on Paragraph 7 of the Wage Plan incorporated into the contract as Appendix A, which provided that employees promoted or transferred would start at the minimum rate for the job to which the transfer was made. It conceded, however, that this general provision of a plan, in effect years before the first contract was negotiated, must yield (if there is conflict) to a more specific provision contained in the contract proper. That there was conflict with Section K seemed quite apparent, unless Paragraph 7 were to be construed as covering only permanent promotions and transfers. None of the grievants were paid as provided in Paragraph 7, but in conflict with it, each received more than the minimum rate. Therefore, the arbitrator construed Paragraph 7 as applying only to permanent promotions and transfers.

The company argued that the contract provision related to the established rate "of the *job*," not "of the *man* replaced." But this argument was not supported by the provisions of the contract, which did not establish *one* rate for each job. For each classification it established several rates, with rules for going from one rate to another on the basis of merit and length of service. The question then was: Which of these several rates could most reasonably be called *the* established rate in the context of Section K? The conclusion could only be that the "established rate of the *man*" was also an "established rate of the *job*." If any of the established rates were entitled to the article "the" in reference to it, it appeared most reasonable to say that it was that one of the established rates which had been actually paid to the absentee.

The argument was advanced by the company that jobs were evaluated and minimum rates rather than the maximum rates were based on those evaluations. Though the rates were originally set by job evaluation methods, they were *established* by the joint action of company and union negotiators. Therefore *all* rates were established by them, not just the minimums.

Finally, the company argued that to adopt the interpretation contended for by the union might result in inequities because a temporary man might receive a higher rate than a permanent man in the same classification working alongside him. However, inequities of a temporary nature are not usually a serious matter. Furthermore, similar inequities would be created even under the company's interpretation, for in paying $2.33, it paid him more than a regular incumbent on the job might be getting if he had not been long on the job. There was no evidence that such possible inequities were in the minds of anyone when the contract language was agreed upon.

Upon careful consideration of all the evidence and arguments, the arbitrator concluded that the words "the established rate of the job" could be interpreted only as "that rate of the job, whether minimum, maximum, or intermediate, established by the man replaced."

Award. The grievances were sustained, and the compensation requested was awarded.

REFERENCES

1. Collective bargaining contract between American Thread Company and Textile Workers Union of America, Local 134 (CIO), para. 7.7 (1953). See 20 LA 56.
2. Courtaulds, Inc., 32 LA 643; Reynolds Metals Company, 19 LA 63; Honolulu Star Bulletin Ltd., 29 LA 391.
3. Bethlehem Steel Co., 30 LA 550.
4. Mergenthaler Linotype Company, 15 LA 707.
5. Dow Chemical Company, 12 LA 1061.

VACATIONS AND VACATION PAY

Most agreements state the requirements for eligibility for vacation, as well as the amount of vacation to which a specified length of service entitles the employee.[1] Ordinarily, vacations vary in length, depending on length of service.[2]

Where the plant cannot be shut down for a set period, scheduling problems arise. While management generally retains the right to schedule vacations,[3] there is frequently a contractual limitation on that right. Some provisions require that the employees who have greatest service seniority will have a choice of available vacation periods.

Arbitrators are called upon to determine employees' eligibility for vacation. When an employee is laid off, the arbitrator has to decide whether his vacation rights are still in force.[4] He may also have to decide whether vacation rights continue to accrue while he is out of work but on layoff status.[5] Another problem may be the effect on various employee rights when a holiday falls within the vacation period.[6] Furthermore, calculation of vacation pay is often troublesome,[7] especially if at the time the vacation becomes due the employee is working at a job paying more or less than his normal rate or if he regularly works overtime.

Some companies are willing to allow employees to forgo their vacations and continue working. When this occurs, the employee is normally entitled to pay in lieu of vacation.[8]

CASE: VACATION RIGHTS—PLANT CLOSED
WAUREGAN MILLS, INC. AND TEXTILE WORKERS UNION OF AMERICA, 31 LA 522. ARBITRATOR: HOBAN.

Issue. Is the matter of vacation pay for the year 1958 arbitrable under the contract? If so, how is the pay to be determined?

Background. During 1957 the business of the company had been declining and the stockholders voted to cease manufacturing at Wauregan, Connecticut. All manufacturing operations at the plant ceased on February 16, 1958. Between June 2, 1957, and April 1, 1958, all but a few employees in the bargaining unit had been given notice that they were laid off. At a meeting with the company on March 18, 1958, the union claimed that employees who worked for the company on and after June 2, 1957, were entitled to receive vacation pay for 1958. The president of the company gave a personal opinion that such employees were not entitled to vacation pay, but said he would attempt to obtain a legal opinion from counsel for the company. When the legal opinion offered by the company was not forthcoming, the union notified the American Arbitration Association of its desire to arbitrate the dispute concerning vacations.

The arbitrator was appointed by the Association in accordance with the terms of the agreement. The company filed an action for a declaratory judgment in the superior court for New London County and moved for a continuance of the arbitration proceedings until a decision could be handed down by the court. The arbitrator heard arguments from both parties on the motion and denied it. When the declaratory judgment petition came before the Supreme Court, the parties agreed to continue arbitration. The judge entered his decision, which in effect permitted the arbitration to go forward. The arbitrator held a hearing at which the company appeared specially and the union generally. The company rested its case on the ground that the arbitrator was without jurisdiction and introduced evidence to support this contention. Briefs were filed by the parties and oral argument presented.

Contract Provisions. The company and the union were parties to a collective bargaining agreement dated April 15, 1957, which by its terms was to continue in full force and effect, subject to the usual 60-day termination provision. The whole agreement is pertinent to the questions before the arbitrators, but the following sections required particular attention:

1. Article VII, No Strikes or Lockouts, Arbitration. Either party may refer to arbitration any dispute, difference, or disagreement concerning wages, hours, or other conditions of employment if the matter has not been settled within 15 days after initiation of conferences between the union and the company.

2. Article IX, Seniority. An employee may be terminated by discharge for cause, by voluntary quitting, or if he fails to return to work at the end of a leave of absence. He may also be terminated if he does not report for work immediately (if available) after recall, but in any event within 72 hours after recall, with the exception that an incapacitating illness substantiated by a physician will be sufficient excuse if notification is given within 48 hours after receipt of recall notice. Other reasons for termination are failure, after layoff due to lack of work, to communicate with the company within seven days after being recalled by a formal notice sent to his address; refusal, in the event his job is discontinued, to accept another job offered by the company within 12 months thereafter; remaining on continuous leave of absence for a period of two years unless his leave is specifically extended by the Company.

3. Article XI, Vacation and Vacation Pay. This article is the key reference to the issue with relation to vacation rights and vacation pay.

A. QUALIFICATION FOR AND EXTENT OF VACATIONS. Each employee in the employ of the Company on June 1st of any contract year, hereinafter called the "eligibility date;" (1) who has been employed by the Company for one (1) year or more but less than three (3) years, immediately prior thereto, shall receive a vacation of one (1) week with vacation pay equal to two percent (2%) of his or her total annual earnings for the full year immediately prior to the eligibility date; (2) who has been employed by the Company for three (3) years but less than five (5) years, immediately prior to the eligibility date shall receive a vacation of one week with vacation pay equal to three percent (3%) of his or her total annual earnings for the full year immediately prior to the eligibility date; (3) who has been employed by the Company for five (5) years or more, immediately prior to the eligibility date shall receive a vacation of one (1) week with vacation pay equal to four percent (4%) of his or her total earnings for the full year immediately prior to the eligibility date; and (4) who has been employed by the Company for three (3) months or more but less than one (1) year immediately prior to the eligibilty date shall receive two percent (2%) of his or her total earnings for the period of employment as vacation pay.

Union's Position. The union asserted that the words "contract year" (Article XI, Paragraph A) did not refer to a June 1st on which the contract must be in effect, but to the yearly term of the contract. The union cited cases in which the arbitrators held that to assume that termination of the agreement automatically cut off accrued vacation rights would put the employer in the position of unilaterally removing his contractual obligation by termination.

Company's Position. In a letter to the AAA the company took the position that there existed no arbitrable controversy between it and the union. The company claimed that even if the claimants were in the employ of the company on June 1, 1958, this was not the June 1st of a *contract year* because the contract had been terminated on the preceding April 15th. The company had given the union the notice required to terminate the agreement.

As each of the claimants was let go, he had been notified that he was being "laid off for lack of work." The union had been told that there was no prospect of a resumption of operations. Before 1958 the practice had been to give vacations to employees who were on a layoff status on June 1. Article IX, "Seniority," contained no express provision for termination of employment by a permanent closing of the plant. A reasonable interpretation of the first sentence of Article XI on vacation privileges would be that the claimants retained their seniority rights in the event the plant reopened and continued "in the employ" of the company after they were laid off and if they were in its employ on June 1, 1958.

Arbitrator's Analysis. After reading the briefs and listening to the arguments of both sides the arbitrator said that, in his opinion, the employees in question had earned 1958 vacation rights by working during the year next preceding June 1, 1958. He said: "The doctrine that vacation pay represents a form of wages, payment of which is deferred, is now accepted everywhere. It was certainly accepted in the textile industry when the parties negotiated this agreement and there is nothing in the language of this agreement to indicate that they were departing from the general understanding."

The company had testified that for each week after June 2, 1957, the company had set aside on its books a percentage of weekly earnings to cover vacations.

The difficult problem was to determine whether the grievants qualified as "each employee in the employ of the Company on June 1st." The evidence established that as a matter of practice outside the contract, the company had taken away the accrued vacation rights of an employee who voluntarily quit or was discharged for cause before he took his vacation. The arbitrator reasoned that the words fixing the qualifications for vacations and vacation pay did not stop with the language "in the employ of the Company on June 1st" because they were followed by "of any contract year." These additional words could not be brushed aside by the arbitrator even in the absence of the customary clause stipulating that the arbitrator may not alter or add to the language of the agreement.

Neither could the termination of the collective bargaining agreement necessarily end the employee status for the purpose of vacation pay. The obligations under a collective bargaining contract survive after its termination date in many respects because it provides for such fringe benefits as pensions, severance pay, and vacation pay. Where something earned today may not be paid until a year or more later, it is not uncommon for the employer to have continuing obligations under a collective bargaining agreement after its termination date. The right of employees to have disputes arising during a contract arbitrated after its termination date cannot be questioned. From these conclusions, the arbitrator ruled that the employment status of the claimants did not end on April 15, 1958, the termination date of the collective bargaining agreement, and therefore they retained their earned vacation rights. He stated:

This is one of those situations in which as a practical man the arbitrator is certain that he is applying contract language to facts which were not in the contemplation of the people who wrote the contract. I do not believe that during negotiations either party to this agreement considered what effects a shutdown of the plant and termination of the collective bargaining agreement would have on accrued vacation rights.

There is no rule of *stare decisis* in labor arbitration and the decisions of other arbitrators are not binding in this case. In all except one of the cases cited by the Union the language of the agreement was not the same as it is here. Nevertheless, the reasoning of other arbitrators is persuasive and I have given it considerable weight.

On the basis of the broad arbitration clause in the agreement, the arbitrator found that the claim for vacation pay made by the union was arbitrable. In deciding this case, he reasoned that the claimants had earned their vacation rights during the weeks from June 2, 1957, to the time the plant closed, and that these rights should not be taken away from them unless the contract expressly or by clear implication showed that they were to lose such rights if the contract were terminated before June 1 of a year in which they had not yet received their vacation.

Award. The company was instructed to issue vacation pay to each employee within the bargaining unit who received wages for work performed after June 1, 1957. The amount of money to which each employee was entitled was to be determined by applying the formula set forth in Article XI of the collective bargaining agreement dated April 15, 1957.

REFERENCES

1. Dunphy Boat Corp., 13 LA 880.
2. Highway Transport Assn., 11 LA 1081; Button Corp. of America, 12 LA 13; International Harvester Co., 15 LA 644.
3. Servel Inc., 20 LA 684; Sinclair Refining Co., 12 LA 183; National Tube Co., 19 LA 330; Wauregan Mills, 31 LA 522 (permanent shutdown).
4. Acro Switch Co., 14 LA 256 (terminated employees); North American Aviation, Inc., 20 LA 686 (leave); Ford Motor Co., 20 LA 121 (retired employees).
5. Button Corp. of America, 12 LA 13; Chrysler Corp., 16 LA 510 (military leave).
6. Continental-Emsco Co., 31 LA 449; Menasco Mfg. Co., 32 LA 406.
7. Bendix Aviation Corp., 12 LA 330 (pro rata pay—plant closing).
8. See Republic Steel Corp., 31 LA 173 (for a variant of this problem).

PERSONAL APPEARANCE

The trend toward wearing long hair, beards, sideburns, and mustaches has created a series of cases regarding failure to conform to plant rules governing personal appearance. In deciding these cases, arbitrators ask three questions. First, does the length of hair on the head or on the face of the employee constitute a health or safety hazard? The company has the burden of proving that the style of hair or beard worn by the grievant is likely to cause an accident. The company must cite evidence, not plant rules; Arbitrator Stutz stated: "In view of the variety of facial adornments the men of America are wearing these days, it would be impossible to lay down any intelligent guidelines [concerning safety factors]. . . . Each mustache and each pair of sideburns will have to be measured against the safety factor and treated accordingly." [1]

Secondly, is or is not the appearance of the employee directly related to the success of the company's business? The company has the burden of proving that (1) the employee comes in contact with potential customers, and (2) if the company permitted the employee to wear a beard, mustache, or long hair, it would lose many of its customers, thus damaging its business.

The extent to which the company must prove the adverse effect of the employee's appearance is not consistent among arbitrators. In the Tradewell Stores case (Case 1), the arbitrator did not require the company to furnish written proof, but merely proof that the danger existed. However, the arbitrators deciding the Greyhound Lines case (Case 2) insisted upon written proof, which in this case was the recorded complaints against the grievant by customers.

If there is no safety factor or danger of adverse public reaction, enforcement of plant rules regarding personal appearance may be an infringement upon an employee's rights. It is impossible for a man to wear a beard when off-duty and be clean-shaven during the day. Overly long hair can be disguised, but wearing a wig may cause physical discomfort.

The company's rule may be detrimental to the employee's outside activities. The union must prove that a grievant's personal appearance is important to his off-duty activities. In the Greyhound case (Case 2), the union contended that the grievant's beard was important to his off-duty activities as a magician. In such a situation, enforcement of company rules infringes upon the employee's personal life.

CASE 1: PERSONAL APPEARANCE
ALLIED EMPLOYERS, INC., REPRESENTING
TRADEWELL STORES, INC., AND RETAIL CLERKS'
INTERNATIONAL ASSOCIATIONS, LOCAL 1105,
CCH 71–1, PARA. 8078. ARBITRATOR: KLEINSORGE.

Issue. The issue comprises two interrelated grievances: (1) Was R. discharged for just cause, and (2) has R. been discriminated against according to the terms of the labor agreement?

Background. Grievant R. was employed as a Stock Clerk in a Tradewell store. In February 1970 he began letting his hair grow, and by August he was warned that if he did not cut his hair and shave his mustache, he would be discharged. He tried wearing a wig, but felt very uncomfortable and complained of headaches. In two days he stopped wearing the wig and was discharged by the company.

Union's Position. The union countered the company's argument by saying that no company rule clearly related to the length of a male employee's hair, and made no distinction between the hair length of males and females. Thus, the union contended that no requirement for male employees to wear their hair short was stipulated in the agreement or the company's employee booklet. Thus, the union contended that the company had presented no evidence to justify the grievant's discharge, neither customers' complaints about hair length or personal grooming nor loss of sales, profit, or the company's image.

Therefore, the company had violated Section 15101 of the agreement, which acknowledges the responsibilities of the union and the company under Title 7 of the Civil Rights Act of 1964 in that the company discriminated against the grievant because of his sex, since it had admitted that "it would not have discharged a female clerk whose hair was as long and neatly kept as R.'s" Therefore, the grievant was discharged solely because he was a male.

Company's Position. The company justified the discharge of Grievant R. on the grounds that he had violated Rule 16 of the personnel manual issued by the company, namely: "Hair should be properly groomed and arranged in such a manner that it will remain securely in place, and not be unduly conspicuous." The company argued that it could devise work rules unilaterally if they were reasonable and were applied without discrimination, and that Rule 16 was reasonably related to the orderly and efficient operation of the business. It said that customers' preference of a supermarket is largely due to their approval of the clerks with whom they come in contact. "Appearance of the clerks means a great deal, and may make a considerable difference in the profitability of a store." The company claimed that customers are critical of males with long hair, and identify them with violence, immorality, and irresponsibility. "The Company fears that it would lose the patronage of many of its customers if it permitted its male clerks (who come into contact with the public) to wear long hair." The adverse reaction of the public is not to be judged as right or wrong; what is important is that this reaction affects the company's business, and therefore the issue is restricted to the company's right to formulate rules concerning the personal appearance of its clerks.

Arbitrator's Analysis. The arbitrator agreed with the company that it had the right to formulate reasonable rules of conduct for its employees when they were on the job. Other supermarkets in the same area also considered the appearance of their clerks as being directly related to the successful conduct of their business, and have reduced to writing the rules concerning the appearance of their clerks. The arbitrator reasoned that:

There appears to be no basis for an objection to his appearance except for the length of his hair and such objection would seem to stem from the prejudice that exists. If it exists (and the arbitrator believes it does) it could affect the Company's business adversely. . . . The arbitrator does not believe that the Company needs to show that complaints were lodged against R., or that certain customers were lost. If the danger is there and if application of the rule will remove the danger, the Company is acting reasonably in attempting to protect itself. . . . In general the rule . . . has been applied when the occasion arose and not in a discriminatory manner. Rule 16 requires that hair not be unduly conspicuous. . . . Long hair on a man might be very conspicuous, while the same length hair on a woman would not be.

The arbitrator discounted the alleged violation of the Civil Rights Act of 1964. He held that "this is not sex discrimination in the same sense that the term is used in the Civil Rights Act of 1964."

Award. The arbitrator found that the discharge of the grievant was based on noncompliance with a reasonable rule and that the grievant was discharged for just cause.

CASE 2: PERSONAL APPEARANCE

GREYHOUND LINES, INC., GREYHOUND LINES–WEST

DIVISION, AND COUNCIL OF WESTERN GREYHOUND

AMALGAMATED DIVISIONS, DIVISION 1225 AMALGAMATED TRANSIT

UNION, 56 LA 458. ARBITRATORS: BURNS, SHEW, KELLET.

Issue. Did Greyhound Lines–West have sufficient cause within the meaning of Section 5 of the agreement to terminate Grievant X? If not, what should be the remedy?

Background. The company had for some time a rule against male beards and goatees; it also placed certain limitations on sideburns, length of hair, and types of mustaches worn by male employees. The rule was repeated in a reissue (January 25, 1970) of an executive bulletin that contained guidelines for acceptable and nonacceptable length of hair and other facial adornment. The union opposed the rule and asked for discussion by the Joint Council, but the company refused to modify the directive.

Grievant X had been employed by the company since October 11, 1950, except for a two-year tour of duty in the military service. He had served as a station employee and Ticket Clerk in three different cities, most recently in Sacramento. His record with the company was good.

When he returned from military service in July 1954, he was wearing a mustache. Later he grew a goatee, which he shaved off several times and then regrew. When he moved to the company's Sacramento office in 1967, he was clean-shaven, but thereafter he regrew his beard. The Terminal Manager did not instruct him to remove it, but told him he must maintain a neat appearance.

The grievant was an amateur magician and gave benefit performances at church and at other functions. The goatee was part of his stage image and he personally preferred his appearance with the goatee.

Grievant X received five different written warnings in April 1970, the first one on April 23, informing him he would not be permitted to work as a Ticket Clerk unless he complied with the bulletin by removing his goatee. He did not remove his goatee, and therefore his employment was terminated by the company on May 1, 1970.

Union's Position. The union's main contention was that the company's requirement interfered with the grievant's constitutional rights, a claim often upheld by the courts. The union pointed out that the company's regulation interfered with the grievants appearance during his off hours because he could not wear a beard in off hours and present a clean-shaven face by day, as would be the case with a uniform. The grievant's goatee was his hallmark as a practicing amateur magician, and the company's rule impaired his off-hours avocation as well as attempted to control his appearance when not on duty. Moreover, changing styles tended toward beards and different hair arrangements and were becoming acceptable to the public. The company had offered no evidence that its patrons and customers did object or would object to a beard of the type worn by the grievant.

Company's Position. The company contended that, as a service organization, it must retain customers' goodwill and give them satisfactory service. Therefore, the company must maintain its long-standing image of being neat and clean. For this reason, rules regarding employees' appearance and dress have been considered important for many years. These rules were reemphasized in 1969 when a merger occurred, and again on January 26, 1970, by executive bulletin—which action was strictly within the prerogatives of management. Since the union's council had agreed in their April 20, 1970, letter that it was in general agreement with the objective of the regulations, the company argued that it apparently objected only to the company's right to unilaterally adopt appearance policies and not to the reasonableness of the rule. The union had not contested the reasonableness of the rule in previous discussions, nor had it elected to appeal to arbitration the company's rejection of its protest.

The company also pointed out that "arbitration decisions uniformly hold that an anti-beard rule is reasonable when the presence of a beard can reasonably threaten the company's relations with its customers."

Arbitrators' Analysis. The arbitrators first considered the union's objection to the rule on the ground that it was established unilaterally by the company, and the company's contention that the union had not followed up its protest by taking this issue to arbitration, thereby, in effect, losing its right to further objection. They held that a rule requiring "adherence to accepted business standards of neat personal appearance" is undoubtedly valid as long as the particular definition or application of "neat personal appearance" is reasonable under the circumstances, is reasonably related to the business of the company, and does not unreasonably interfere with the rights of employees when they are not on duty. It did not follow, however, that all guidelines and details of the company's rule were necessarily reasonable or valid in particular cases or circumstances.

The arbitrators held that the company rule as applied to grievant under the circumstances peculiar to this case did not necessarily protect the company's business, was an unreasonable infringement on his off-duty life, and was therefore invalid in this particular instance.

Award. On the bases of contractual agreements, the evidence, and the stipulations of the parties, the arbitrators ruled that (1) the company did not have sufficient cause within the meaning of Section 5 of the agreement to terminate Grievant X, and (2) Grievant X be reinstated in his former position with seniority rights and other benefits unimpaired and with back pay from the date of his discharge until the date of his reinstatement, less any wages or earnings received by the grievant since the date of his discharge.

REFERENCE

1. City of Waterbury, Conn. and International Assoc. of Firefighters Local 1339, CCH 70-1, No. 8395. January 26, 1970.

RACIAL DISCRIMINATION

Within recent years many issues involving racial discrimination have been submitted to arbitration. The grievances filed have alleged racial discrimination with regard to hiring,[1] apprenticeships, transfers, overtime, promotion, and termination.[2]

CASE: RACIAL DISCRIMINATION
MCCALL CORPORATION AND INTERNATIONAL
PRINTING PRESSMEN AND ASSISTANTS UNION OF
NORTH AMERICA LOCAL 54, CCH 67–2,
PARA. 8498. ARBITRATOR: MCINTOSH.

Issue. Did the company discriminate against the grievant by not selecting him to be an apprentice?

Background. The grievant alleged that another employee with less seniority had been placed in the Apprentice Offset Plate Maker classification and that he had not been selected because he was black. He said that since he had become qualified for the position, 26 other persons had been given the opportunity to become apprentices.

Contract Provisions. Article XVI, Section 6, of the agreement states that "apprentices for the crafts employed in the offset Preparatory Department shall be selected . . . from applicants who have met standards established by the employer for such positions. Preference shall be given to employees occupying beginner jobs in other departments coming under this Agreement and in other divisions coming under the jurisdiction of the Union, but not to the exclusion of worthy and qualified applicants."

Union's Position. The grievant's capability is attested by the fact that he has earned service seniority in his classification. He is entitled to be placed in the Apprentice Offset Plate Maker classification not only because he is a "worthy and qualified applicant," but also because the contract assures his status in that his classification "comes under the jurisdiction of the Union," which recognizes his seniority as an overriding criterion for selection as an Apprentice.

Company's Position. Apprentices are not guaranteed or reserved to any classification coming under the jurisdiction of the union. The agreement also considers that beginners in other departments are eligible for advancement if they have met standards set for the position in question. Regardless of seniority, "worthy and qualified applicants" means the employees who have demonstrated capabilities applicable to the position sought, the standards for which the company is authorized to establish under the terms of the contract.

Arbitrator's Analysis. The selection of apprentices is an exercise in discretion which, when challenged, is generally tested by the rule of reasonableness. If the history of company decisions shows fair, noncapricious, nondiscriminatory judgment, the challenge must be considered as without factual basis. In this case, the record discloses that the company failed to give fair consideration to the grievant's requests and did discriminate, although neither action appeared to be maliciously or personally motivated.

Award. The company was directed to give the grievant an assignment to the Offset Plate Making apprenticeship on or before six months from date of the award, thus sustaining the grievance.

REFERENCES

1. Sands Hotel, CCH 72-1, para. 8291.
2. Peer Food Products, CCH 67-1, para. 8204; Knight Newspapers, CCH 72-1, para. 8014.

SEX DISCRIMINATION

With the passage of the Civil Rights Act and the greater awareness on the part of women of their civil rights, an increasing number of grievances filed by women employees allege discrimination on the basis of sex. Arbitrators take into consideration whether the company made a reasonable effort to compare the qualifications of the grievant with other (male) employees and to determine whether she had the qualifications and capabilities needed to perform the work.

CASE: SEX DISCRIMINATION
SOUTH PITTSBURGH WATER COMPANY AND UTILITY
WORKERS UNION OF AMERICA LOCAL 174, CCH 71–1,
PARA. 8420. ARBITRATOR: ALTRACK.

Issue. The issue before the arbitrator was whether Grievant S. was discriminated against because of her sex on July 15, 1970, when the job of Work Order Clerk was assigned to Employee O.

Background. The company posted a job opening specifying a male Work Order Clerk. The grievant, a female, charged sex discrimination and alleged she was capable of performing the work, but was not given the opportunity to fill the vacancy *only* because she was a female.

Union's Position. During the hearing the union stated that the grievant possessed eight months more seniority than Employee O. and that the union and the company were in agreement that the grievant had the potential ability to perform the duties of Work Order Clerk. However, in considering the grievant's merits for the job, the union contended that the company had not investigated her full qualifications, such as ability to read maps, to operate a two-way radio, and to sketch—all of which were among the important aspects of the job. According to Section II of the agreement, the company's responsibility in cases of promotion is to make a reasonable effort to compare the qualifications of competing employees. Thus, in promoting Employee O. and not considering the grievant, the company violated Section II and Section VI, which prohibit discrimination against employees on the basis of sex.

Company's Position. The company countered the union's arguments by citing evidence of Employee O.'s ability to perform the duties of Work Order Clerk. He had received his promotion because he had nearly 800 hours of contact or training on the Work Order Clerk job while classified as Office Boy. As an Office Boy his duties included acting as relief for a Work Order Clerk, and therefore he had accumulated time on that job. The job descriptions of both jobs provided for lines of progression so as to provide expertise in the area of work-order duties and thus maintain effective performance of them. The company contended that no discrimination had been intended and that it had acted properly in observing the succession requirement stated in the job descriptions.

Arbitrator's Analysis. The arbitrator found that the Office Boy job gave direct access to the Work Order Clerk position. He examined the various job descriptions in the office and judged that the statement of who will fill in for whom, and thereby acquire ability, created two lines of progression, one for women and one for men, with little indication that either had ever crossed lines. He deduced that a female could become a Work Order Clerk only if she had been hired as an Office Girl or if she moved down to Grade I and made a lateral move, a possible but unwieldy route and one that was clearly discriminatory.

The arbitrator did not disagree with the company's policy of creating job duties that build up a person's expertise, but he did object to restricting these duties to "male" jobs.

Award. The arbitrator directed the company and union to do one of three alternatives: (1) arrange to train the grievant by means of fill-in time on the Work Order Clerk job; (2) revamp and modernize the job descriptions; (3) merge the lines of progression to abolish any discrimination because of sex.

WORKING CONDITIONS

Provision for safe and healthful working conditions is found in most collective bargaining agreements. Employees may refuse to work if conditions are unsafe or unhealthy.[1] A typical clause provides that the company and the union will cooperate in the continuing objective to eliminate accidents and health hazards. "The Company shall continue to make reasonable provisions for the safety and health of its employees at the plants during the hours of their employment. . . . Protective devices, wearing apparel, and other equipment necessary properly to protect employees from injury shall be provided by the Company in accordance with practices now prevailing. . . ."[2] Questions involving the obligation of the company to supply work gloves,[3] raincoats,[4] and work clothes[5] have been the subject of arbitration.

Working conditions in effect when the contract is signed are usually considered a contractual obligation of management and not subject to unilateral change. Whether employees are entitled to wash-up time,[6] work breaks,[7] and coffee breaks[8] because of past practice is often in issue.

Related to this problem of working conditions is the physical condition of the employee. Management has the right to require its employees to take a physical examination prior to employment, each year during employment, and after a layoff of more than 30 days.[9]

CASE: CUSTOM AND PRACTICE
FAWICK AIRFLEX COMPANY, INC. AND UNITED
ELECTRICAL, RADIO AND MACHINE WORKERS
OF AMERICA, 11 LA 666. ARBITRATOR: CORNSWEET.

Issue. Did the company violate the contract by not honoring a past practice of providing morning coffee to men who had been asked to work on a weekend?

Background. For several years, starting during World War II, the company had an established practice of providing and serving coffee and doughnuts during a 15-minute coffee break at 9:00 A.M. each morning. During the war, there was an additional afternoon coffee break. On a Saturday and Sunday in August 1948, a number of men came in to work at the company's request and were not served coffee.

Contract Provisions. Article X, Section 2, provides as follows: "The Employer agrees to maintain and improve the conditions of work of its employees."

Union's Position. The union contended that the company violated Article X, Section 2, of the agreement and sought an arbitration award requiring the company to continue to serve coffee on Saturdays and Sundays. The union further contended that the serving of coffee on Saturday and Sunday mornings was a working condition maintained in this plant since its negotiation in April 1943; that the history of its inception and continuance offered clear and convincing proof that it had been regarded as a working condition through the years; that the company had made a formal proposal to eliminate the coffee service and wash-up periods in the May 1948 negotiations and had agreed, after union opposition, to drop the proposal and continue the existing practice; and that as late as June 7, 1948, the company again evidenced its understanding that coffee service was a working condition by affording the union membership an opportunity to vote on the company proposal to discontinue coffee service on overtime days. The union voted to reject the proposal on June 22, but it was nevertheless put in effect.

Company's Position. The company contended that the furnishing of coffee was not negotiated and was a voluntary act instituted under wartime conditions when employees worked long hours and on weekends; that in the 1945 negotiations the company rejected a union proposal for two 15-minute rest periods per shift and for continuance of employee privileges; that in the some negotiations "the Company made it clear that it did not consider the coffee wagon a standard practice which it could not discontinue after return to an eight-hour day"; that, while the company relinquished its proposals in the 1948 wage negotiations, it did not deprive itself of the right to discontinue coffee periods; that, with a return to normal schedules and in the present competitive market, there was no good reason for the coffee period, and the loss of working time involved made it a significant item of labor cost; that only a few men were called upon for Saturday and Sunday work, making it unreasonable to lose the half-hour of the guard's time in preparing coffee; and that the serving of coffee was a privilege like parking facilities or music during work hours, and was not a "working condition" involving "hours of work, health, safety, and similar conditions."

Arbitrator's Analysis. Serving of coffee on weekday mornings had not been discontinued. At the hearing the company stated that it was willing to continue the morning coffee on Saturday and Sunday if a full complement of workers were on the job, but not if only a few men were at work. It was also noted that the men took from a minute or two up to 15 minutes to drink the coffee and eat the doughnuts that go with it. The arbitrator understood that these refreshments were more extensive on weekdays and that the cost of refreshments, including coffee, was always borne by the employees, while the time consumed was working time.

Whether the serving of coffee—or more accurately the permission to prepare and consume refreshment during working hours—was either worthwhile or wasteful, desirable or undesirable, justified or unjustified, could not be a matter of consideration and decision by the arbitrator. The sole question before him, as the briefs of both parties indicated, was whether or not it constituted a "working condition." If it was a working condition, then, under Article X, Section 2, of the agreement, it had to be maintained during the life of the agreement. If it was merely a "voluntary act" on the part of the company, then the company had a right to discontinue it.

How the parties themselves regarded the practice over a period of some years had to be considered in any determination. Whether the practice of workers leaving their machines at 9:00 A.M. and 2:00 P.M. to go to the commissary for refreshments was the result of negotiation back in 1942 could not be ascertained. There was no doubt, however, that in 1943 the union requested and the company agreed that coffee be added to the twice-a-day refreshment. The union considered that it was an accepted suggestion and cited Article X, Section 1, of the agreement then effective, which provided that the employer would receive and consider constructive suggestions for improvements in working conditions.

In 1945 negotiations, the matter arose again. The claims of the parties conflicted, but the least that could be said was that the matter had been discussed in collective bargaining sessions. If it were not a working condition, it is hardly probable that it would have received attention at contract negotiation time.

Again, in 1946, the matter arose when the company requested that afternoon refreshments be discontinued. The union agreed. Thereafter, coffee and refreshments were made available only in the morning. If, as the company contended, it was a "voluntary act" by the company, why was the request made by the company? It is an indication, at least, that the company considered it a working condition.

The arbitrator then considered the wage negotiations of May 1948. The vice-president of the company stated unequivocally that the serving of coffee was a working condition that the company was bound to maintain under the agreement. He proposed its elimination, but the union would not agree and the practice was continued. At the same time, elimination of wash-up periods was also sought by the company, without success. This fact leads to an examination of the question: "What is a working condition and is the coffee period one?" It was established to the arbitrator's satisfaction that *the parties themselves* did consider the coffee period as a working condition. The arbitrator said that there is a fairly clear line of demarcation in labor-management relations between a working condition and a privilege or gratuity. Lunch periods, wash-up time, and rest periods are accepted working conditions, and one factor common to working conditions is *time not worked*. Thus, working conditions are properly the subject of collective bargaining, which cannot be discontinued unilaterally. Privileges and gratuities, on the other hand, are enjoyed only as long as the employer chooses to continue them.

In this case, the coffee was not in dispute. It was the *time taken* in its preparation and consumption—the time not worked during the shift. The arbitrator found that coffee time, like the lunch and the wash-up period, is a condition of work. As such, under the agreement it must be maintained and cannot be unilaterally discontinued. The decision was based on the facts that (1) the coffee period met the accepted criterion for working conditions, and (2) the parties themselves, by past practice clearly shown, so interpreted it.

Award. The arbitrator upheld the grievance and ruled that the working condition of providing coffee during the morning period should be maintained as requested by the union.

REFERENCES

1. United States Potash Company, 30 LA 1039; Jones & Laughlin Steel Corp., 30 LA 395.
2. United States Steel Co., 20 LA 434.
3. *Ibid.*
4. Jones & Laughlin Steel Corp., 20 LA 112.
5. Union Carbide & Carbon Corp., 16 LA 707.
6. Donaldson Company, 20 LA 826.
7. Thor Corporation, 18 LA 693.
8. Fawick Airflex Co., 11 LA 666.
9. Pittsburgh Plate Glass, 19 LA 621; Borg-Warner Corp., 16 LA 446; Mosaic Tile Company, 14 LA 953.

3

ARBITRATION IN
THE PUBLIC SECTOR

During the past several years, the growth of collective bargaining in the public sector, and the adoption of arbitration as the terminal point for grievances as well as interest disputes, have greatly increased the number of issues submitted to arbitration. Summaries of cases in the public sector may be found in two relatively new publications of the American Arbitration Association, *Labor Arbitration in Government* and *Arbitration in the Schools* (both published monthly).

The issues arbitrated in the public sector are very similar to those in the private sector. An analysis of the cases reported in *Labor Arbitration in Government* reveals that a large number of public-sector cases—as in the private sector—involve discipline and discharge. Other cases involve questions such as arbitrability, bumping rights, job bidding, job posting, work assignments, and work rules. With the growth of compulsory arbitration in the public sector, there has been an increase in the number of cases involving wages and other terms and conditions of new contracts.

A review of the case summaries in *Arbitration and the Schools* shows that there are cases involving the interpretation of clauses relating to leaves of absence, seniority and ability, rate of pay, grievance procedures, and so on, such as are found in the private sector. There are also a number of issues peculiar to schools. These include class size, extracurricular assignments, and tenure.

Tenure

Teachers in our public school system and in our colleges and universities who have served satisfactorily for a specified number of years usually receive tenure. This gives the teacher protection from arbitrary discharge. In order to dismiss a tenured teacher, charges must be filed and supported at a formal hearing.

At the university level the principle of tenure was developed to protect academic freedom. One of the traditional functions of the American Association of University Professors (AAUP) has been to investigate cases where it appeared that instructors were dismissed not because of poor teaching or research but because their ideas did not coincide with those of the president or a member of the board of trustees. Within the past two years the AAUP has undertaken to represent college professors who wish to organize and engage in collective negotiations leading to a contract. Several of these contracts provide for grievance arbitration.

Because of the importance of tenure, it is anticipated that this issue will be the subject of many arbitrations. In institutions where academic governance is not a reality, the decision to grant tenure is made by the president or the dean on the basis of recommendations by the department chairman. Experience in the private sector indicates that these types of managerial decisions are frequently based upon assumptions, misunderstandings, personal antagonisms, and misinformation, and often the decision is made without giving the person affected an opportunity to be heard.

CASE: GRANTING OF TENURE
BOARD OF HIGHER EDUCATION OF THE CITY OF
NEW YORK (CITY UNIVERSITY OF NEW YORK)
AND LEGISLATIVE CONFERENCE. AAA CASE
#1339–0706–70, 15–AD–12. ARBITRATOR: ROBERTS.

Issue. Can a school administration properly deny tenure if the processes for evaluating an instructor's qualification have not been carried out?

Background. Miss P., an instructor in the art department at Brooklyn College, was denied reappointment as an instructor with tenure for the academic year 1970–1971. She filed a grievance, alleging violation of procedures for observing her work and evaluating her performance as an instructor.

Contract Provisions. Article XVII of the bylaws of the Board of Higher Education of the City of New York stipulates due process procedures, and the agreement with the teachers' organization prescribes the standards to be applied in evaluating the academic performance of a nontenured teacher.

Union's Position. The grievant alleged that in the three years of her instructorship, her performance was never evaluated by the chairman of her department, nor were the required number of observations made to concur with those necessary for qualification as a tenured instructor. At no time was she advised of weaknesses that might disqualify her. In view of the failure to follow these procedures, it was Miss P.'s contention that the college personnel and budget committee had been biased by the lack of a full and fair appraisal, and therefore her tenure as an instructor should be granted.

Board's Position. The Board rejected the claim that no observations of Miss P.'s performance had been made. It pointed out that such supervisory attendance had been carried out on many occasions between 1969 and 1970, although it could offer no evidence that the departmental chairman had participated.

Arbitrator's Analysis. The arbitrator observed that the bylaws formalized the due process procedures and that it was the responsibility of the department chairman to ensure their propriety in this critical decision-making process. The exposure to reports that do not conform to the standards prescribed in the agreement and the bylaws of the Board in order to safeguard their totality was obviously highly improper, and for the committee to have them surely would violate the employee's substantive rights with respect to appointment and reappointment, with or without tenure. The requirements could not have been satisfied without the committee's having what had been characterized as "cognizable" observations and evaluations.

The arbitrator said the absence of required observations and evaluations, and the use of observations that were not properly processed to the evaluation and corrective stages but were nevertheless considered by the committees that made the recommendations on Miss P.'s reappointment with tenure, had manifested an arbitrary use of the established and required observation and evaluation procedures.

Award. The arbitrator found that the university did not follow the prescribed procedures, and as a result the decision not to reappoint the grievant was improper.

4

ARBITRATION IN THE ROMAN CATHOLIC CHURCH

With the adoption of arbitration as a means of resolving disputes within the Catholic Church (see Appendix VI), there will be a growing number of arbitration cases involving teachers in Catholic schools, priests, and laymen. Many of the cases involve issues common to the private and public sectors.

CASE 1: VACATION PAY
JOHN DOE AND [ANONYMOUS RELIGIOUS
PUBLICATION]. ARBITRATOR: ANONYMOUS.

Issue. Should the employer withhold vacation pay due an employee if he has resigned but is absent for the two weeks preceding the effective resignation date?

Background. Grievant D. had been employed by the company since November 2, 1962. Initially he worked as a salesman, and for the past few years had served as sales manager. He took his first two-week vacation in October 1964 (nearly two years after his hiring date) and took two-week vacations each of the years 1965 through 1969.

On July 15, 1970, he submitted a written notice of resignation, which was to become effective on July 30. He offered to remain working for the additional two weeks through July 30, but requested that he be permitted to be absent during these two weeks in order to enjoy a vacation with his family. Both the Editor and the Auditor assured him he could proceed with his vacation plans, and he did so. He was paid in advance for these two weeks. When his termination became effective, he received only certain commission monies due him, but not the two weeks' salary for vacation pay, to which he believed he was entitled.

In the absence of a contract, the employer had an established vacation policy, as follows:

The Company policy regarding vacations is that an employee is entitled to two weeks' paid vacation after one full year's employment. However, after six months of satisfactory employment, an employee may take one week of paid vacation and be given the option to take a second week, at that time, without pay.

369

However, upon the anniversary date of his employment, the second week's pay is paid. . . . The Company policy, further, has been to compensate an employee upon resignation, for vacation which is due but not taken, in the following manner: If the employee works through the date of termination, then the two weeks of vacation pay are given in cash with the final wage payment.

Grievant's Position. The grievant contended that he had requested a leave of absence only and did not agree to accept the leave in lieu of vacation to which he was entitled.

Company's Position. The grievant had submitted his resignation and requested permission to take the last two weeks on vacation as he had originally planned. The company had granted permission and paid him his vacation pay in advance to July 30. Finally, on July 30, he had been paid all commissions due him. Therefore, the full salary and commissions owed had been paid to the grievant. If he had been at work during the final two weeks of July, he would have been paid the two weeks' salary and given two weeks of vacation pay in cash. Neither the Auditor nor the Editor have admitted that they told the grievant he would receive two weeks of pay in cash on or after July 30 in addition to the two weeks' pay given him before his vacation.

Arbitrator's Analysis. The arbitrator observed that the testimony of the witnesses presented a credibility issue and did not in any way clarify what was said or meant at the time immediately before the grievant took his two weeks' vacation in 1970. However, the arbitrator felt it unnecessary to resolve this apparent credibility question in light of other aspects of the decision. In his opinion the basic issue was the determination of the nature of the vacation rights of the employer's employees generally, and of the grievant in particular. He said that the courts have long held vacations to be actually a deferred form of wages.[1] Based upon this conclusion, numerous courts and arbitrators have found that the employee's right to vacation pay becomes a vested one, once the employee has completed the requisite hours of employment.[2]

The company's policy regarding vacations concurred with the opinions of these legal authorities in that the policy requires some definite period of employment before vacation is earned by the employee. This conclusion was reinforced by the provision of vacation and vacation pay for employees with more than six months' but less than one year's employment. According to the declared policy of the company, the grievant was entitled to seven two-week vacations for the length of his employment from November 1962 through November 1969. However, up until July 1970, he had taken only six two-week vacations, and therefore had a vested right to one two-week vacation plus any additional vacation credits he had earned from November 2, 1969. His two weeks of vacation in July 1970 were those which his employment through November 1969 had earned him. On July 30, 1970, he was therefore entitled to nine months of vacation credit for his work from November 2, 1969, through July 30, 1970. Thus, the grievant had a vested right to $9/12$ (or $3/4$) of his two weeks' vacation.

Award. The grievance was validated and the arbitrator ruled that the company should pay the grievant an amount of money equal to three-fourths of two weeks' pay, based upon his salary as of July 1970.

CASE 2: TENURE/INSUBORDINATION
ABC HIGH SCHOOL V. MR. X. ARBITRATION BOARD:
REV. K. (CHAIRMAN), REV. F., AND MR. B.

Issue. Was it proper for ABC High School to deny grievant tenure and dismiss him for insubordination?

Background. Mr. X had been employed as a teacher at ABC High School for eight or nine years. Some time prior to the issuance of his current contract, he had given to his students an examination in which a question concerned the generally accepted scientific theory of evolution. When the pastor objected to this question, he withdrew it from subsequent examinations. After this incident, the pastor later requested that he distribute to his students a booklet that explained the Catholic teachings with respect to evolution, and suggested that the students be permitted to retain the booklet for one week or longer. Mr. X apparently did not realize the importance attached by the pastor to the time element suggested, for he recalled the booklets three days after their distribution. This incident resulted in a heated dispute between Mr. X and the pastor, in which strong language was used. When Mr. X's current contract expired, the school failed to renew it for the 1970–1971 school year. Mr. X thereupon appealed to the school's Board of Arbitration.

Contract Provisions. The contract form used by the ABC High School did contain references to tenure, but the clauses pertaining to it became operative only when the name of the school had been entered in the space provided, to indicate acceptance. In Mr. X's contract, this space had not been filled in. However, in the final paragraph of the contract, where exclusions of contract clauses were to be listed, tenure was not excluded. Nevertheless, all contracts are officially addended by Appendix A of the booklet *On Due Process* (see Appendix VI), which states that "school boards . . . should have basic policies of hiring and firing teachers."

Grievant's Position. No argument had been presented by the grievant when the pastor had previously objected to an examination question in variance with the theosophical interpretation of evolution, nor was one intended insofar as distribution of the booklet was concerned. No definite time had been allocated to student study of the booklet, and the grievant believed the suggestion of a week's time to be merely approximate. When, after the booklet was withdrawn, an argument ensued between the grievant and the pastor and renewal of Mr. X's contract was subsequently denied, it seemed evident to the grievant that the confrontation was instrumental in effecting his dismissal.

School's Position. The question of Catholic teachings on evolution was not the issue, nor was it in fact that Mr. X's extremely poor eyesight handicapped his performance as a teacher. It was the contention of the administrator that Mr. X's recall of the booklet was a direct violation of a reasonable order and that therefore he was guilty of insubordination.

Arbitrators' Analysis. All three arbitrators hearing this case agreed very closely on the essential points. Summaries of the three opinions follow.

Reverend K.'s opinion was that even though some mention of tenure was made in the contract, the implication had no significance, since the "tenure policy" mentioned in the contract quite obviously did not exist. He believed that the failure of the school to renew Mr. X's contract seemed to be the result of personal feelings, and that ABC High School ought to have had more serious reasons for firing Mr. X. Nothing in his record showed that his performance was not satisfactory, although he might have been handicapped by poor eyesight. However, he had developed a feeling of security over nine years, and to dismiss him summarily for personal reasons of the pastor seemed to be a heavy blow indeed. Mr. X should be given recompense for the time that he had been away from teaching, and his contract should be renewed for the present year.

Mr. B's opinion was that the reference in the teacher contract to "the tenure policy [with] a three-year probationary period" and the statement that "termination of employment for tenure teachers is governed by the tenure policy" were misleading. No evidence had been presented to show that a tenure policy or a termination policy existed. Rather, the administration was obligated to follow the guidelines in Appendix A of the booklet *On Due Process* (see Appendix VI). Therefore, since in the present case no such policies existed, the panel of arbitrators should apply "a principle of justice rather than a specific rule of law," as stated in Appendix X of the *On Due Process* booklet. Mr. B. said:

> Regardless of implicit contractual provisions, both employer and employee have obligations to each other which arise first from their common humanity and secondly from the definite social situation in which their agreement was made. . . . Each side must take into consideration the legitimate interests and expectations of the other. . . . The employer must dismiss only for "just cause," which includes "only factors pertinent to the running of a business." . . . The whim of the employer, his personal political convictions, and the annoying mannerisms of an employee are not just causes. . . . Since length of service changes the relationships, . . . the reason for dismissal must be more serious in the case of a veteran employee than in the case of an apprentice.

The following evidence must be considered . . .: (1) Mr. X had been employed for 8 years at ABC High School; (2) the only reason given for not renewing the contract for the 1970–1971 school year was that Mr. X had distributed a booklet on Catholic teaching on evolution . . . and had the students return it three days later. . . . The Pastor had requested that the students be permitted to keep the book for one week or longer. . . . This incident resulted in the use of strong language. . . .

The . . . public schools and Catholic schools provide tenure after a 3 year probationary period as was stated in the contract form used. . . . Since Mr. X had been employed for 8 years at ABC High School, . . . it appears to me that a much more serious reason would be necessary than that given. . . .

In the absence of just cause for failure to renew the 1970–1971 school year contract, it is my opinion that Mr. X should be paid according to the Archdiocese salary schedule for the period . . . when he was not employed and that a contract be issued to him for the 1970–1971 school year.

Reverend F's opinion reflected the same viewpoints expressed by his two colleagues. He said that the contract was ambiguous in that it mentioned tenure but did not spell out specific tenure rights. The school contended that the failure to write in the school name in the space provided meant that no tenure rights had been intended and, although tenure had not been listed as an exclusion, it was in fact excluded.

Reverend F. noted that the evidence referred to three incidents of the teacher's violation of school policy, only one of which was the subject at issue—insubordination. "Apparently the teacher continued to rely primarily upon the standard text for [the theory of evolution] and distributed the pamphlet to his students for only two or three days. The principal considered this a deliberate disregard of instructions." With regard to tenure, Reverend F. said:

The binding existence of teacher tenure is not shown. It almost seems that the school wanted to create the impression that a tenure policy existed without accepting any of the unpleasant obligations of such a policy. . . . The principal's instructions or suggestions for the content of the course are heavy handed. The teacher's response, though it probably included a degree of displeasure at the principal's intrusion, cannot be considered a serious act of insubordination.

The simple question is whether a school incurs any responsibilities to a teacher simply through the passage of years. My answer is yes. It is this responsibility which underlies . . . tenure policy. ABC High School did not accept such a responsibility, and in so doing it acted unfairly towards the teacher. . . . The plaintiff's request for compensation is justified.

Award. The consensus of the arbitrators was that the refusal of ABC High School to renew Mr. X's contract was not justified. They ruled that ABC High School should remunerate Mr. X for the month during which he was not functioning as a teacher there, according to the salary scale of the Archdiocese, and that he be reinstated as a teacher at ABC High School, with all the rights and privileges he enjoyed before his dismissal.

CASE 3: TENURE/FAILURE TO NOTIFY
IN THE MATTER OF MRS. K. AND XYZ SCHOOL.
ARBITRATOR: ANONYMOUS.

Issue. If tenure has been acquired on the basis of length of service, or presumed to have been acquired, must formal notice of dismissal precede the date on which such tenure acquisition occurs?

Background. Mrs. K, a certified-degree teacher with 35 years' experience as a teacher of kindergarten, Head Start, and adult classes, resigned from the public school system (at reduced pension) in order to teach at XYZ School. In the second year of Mrs. K's service, Mr. B. became principal of the XYZ School. From the beginning of their association, there was conflict between them. At one time the principal told her she was fired, but no formal notice was served, nor did Mrs. K. resign. Despite this incompatibility, Mrs. K. received a salary raise for the 1970–1971 year.

During Mrs. K.'s third year, the conflict became crucial, and Mr. B. told her that one of them must leave because of the personality conflict. Still, after inquiry about the 1971–1972 school-year contracts, she had no reason to believe that her contract would not be renewed. It was not until after the close of the 1970–1971 year in June 1971 that Mr. B. spoke to Mrs. K. and told her she would not be rehired for the 1971–1972 year.

There was no contract. The question of tenure could be resolved only by Archdiocesan School Board Policy, which states: "After three years of satisfactory work in a parochial school of the Archdiocese . . ., a lay teacher will acquire tenure in that school and may not be dismissed except by written notice which sets forth the specific reasons for dismissal. Such notice must be given thirty days before dismissal."

Grievant's Position. None of the incidents between the grievant and the principal had major importance. The principal often made statements that implied termination of her services, but she had received no formal termination notice. She claimed that after the beginning of 1971, conflict situations were more or less isolated and not recurring. She was aware that Mr. B's policy was to begin contract negotiations for the 1971–1972 year shortly after the turn of the calendar year, and when he did not approach her on the subject, she asked the pastor of the parish about it and was told that Mr. B. was in the process of negotiating contracts. The grievant claimed that she was not properly notified of her termination until after the close of the current year and that at that time she had earned tenure.

Employer's Position. On numerous occasions the grievant had disputed the directives of the principal and had displayed other acts of noncooperation. The principal had innovated and introduced into the XYZ School a number of curriculum and procedural changes to which the grievant seemed unable to adapt or seemed willfully determined to resist. Despite repeated warnings about her noncooperative and argumentative attitudes, no perceptible correction had been observed, and in the judgment of the principal the conflict was not resolvable.

Arbitrator's Analysis. If in fact Mrs. K. had acquired tenure under the policy of the school board, she had been dismissed without sufficient cause and should be reinstated. The question, therefore, was whether she had acquired tenure. The arbitrator pointed out that the courts of the state have generally strictly construed tenure statutes, since they are incompatible with the common law. In essence, such contractual agreements establish obligations that would otherwise not exist and thereby create a new liability on the responsibility of school boards. It was the arbitrator's opinion that Archdiocesan School Board Policy should be similarly construed.

Whether a teacher's work is or is not "satisfactory," as defined by the School Board Policy, could be determined only by the administrator of the school. Any other conclusion would confer a degree of tenure to teachers who had completed only one or two years of probationary teaching. In this case Mr. B., as principal of XYZ School, did make the decision that the work of the grievant in her third year at XYZ School was not "satisfactory."

Whether the Archdiocesan School Board Policy required notice of such decision to be communicated to the affected teacher before the end of her third year was another matter. School Board Policy in this case clearly stated that notice must be given to a tenured teacher, must be in writing, must set forth the specific reasons for dismissal, and must be given 30 days before dismissal. No requirements were stated with respect to the termination of a teacher approaching tenure, although equitable considerations would seem to require that these procedures be followed. Section 3 of the contract between XYZ School and Mrs. K. also required the school "wherever possible" to give notice of dissatisfaction with a teacher's work or conduct.

Although Mr. B. did not formally advise the grievant prior to the end of the 1970–1971 school year that she was not to be rehired or that her services were to be terminated, the arbitrator found that in effect he had communicated his decision when he told her that "one of us has to go." Furthermore, Mrs. K.'s testimony acknowledged that she knew or reasonably deduced that Mr. B. was dissatisfied with her work and that her services at XYZ School were to be terminated.

Award. On the basis of the evidence, the arbitrator ruled that the grievant had not acquired tenure and that the termination of her services had not been improper. He emphasized that neither decision reflected on Mrs. K.'s credentials or competence as a teacher. Factually, the grievant had not acquired tenure before notification and was therefore not protected in her job. The compounding difficulty was an unfortunate clash of personalities, which in most cases is a situation where blame must be shared.

The arbitrator recommended that the Archdiocesan School Board personnel office be asked to assist the grievant, at her request, in obtaining a position in another Archdiocesan school, and that, if possible, she be afforded tenure in that position after a one-year or shorter probationary period.

REFERENCES

1. Wil-Low Cafeterias, 111 F. 2d 429.
2. Smith v. Kingsport Press, Inc., 366 F. 2d 416.

PART THREE

Appendixes

Appendix I

CODE OF ETHICS AND LIST OF MODERN ARBITRATION STATUTES

CODE OF ETHICS AND PROCEDURAL STANDARDS FOR LABOR–MANAGEMENT ARBITRATION*

PART I

CODE OF ETHICS FOR ARBITRATORS

1. CHARACTER OF THE OFFICE

The function of an arbitrator is to decide disputes. He should, therefore, adhere to such general standards of adjudicatory bodies as require a full, impartial and orderly consideration of evidence and argument, in accordance with arbitration law and the rules or general understandings or practices of the parties.

The parties in dispute, in referring a matter to arbitration, have indicated their desire not to resort to litigation or to economic conflict. They have delegated to the arbitrator power to settle their differences. It follows that the assumption of the office of arbitrator places upon the incumbent solemn duties and responsibilities. Every person who acts in this capacity should uphold the traditional honor, dignity, integrity and prestige of the office.

2. THE TRI-PARTITE BOARD

Where tri-partite boards serve in labor arbitrations, it is the duty of the parties' nominees to make every reasonable effort to promote fair and objective conduct of the proceedings, to aid the arbitration board in its deliberations and to bring a just and harmonious disposition of the controversy. It is recognized, however, that the parties frequently expect their appointees to serve also as representatives of their respective points of view. In such cases, the rules of ethics in this Code, insofar as they relate to the obligations of strict impartiality, are to be taken as applying only to the third or neutral arbitrator.

Such representatives, however, unless the parties agree otherwise, should refrain from conveying to the parties who appointed them, the discussions which take place in executive session and any information concerning the deliberations of the board. No information concerning the decision should be given in advance of its delivery simultaneously to both parties.

3. QUALIFICATION FOR OFFICE

Any person whom the parties or the appointing agency choose to regard as qualified to determine their dispute is entitled to act as their arbitrator. It is, however, incumbent upon the arbitrator at the time of his selection to disclose to the parties any circumstances, associations or relationships that might reasonably raise any doubt as to his impartiality or his technical qualifications for the particular case.

4. ESSENTIAL CONDUCT

(a) The arbitrator should be conscientious, considerate and patient in the discharge of his functions. There should be no doubt as to his complete impartiality.

* Prepared by the American Arbitration Association and the National Academy of Arbitrators and approved for arbitrations by the Federal Mediation and Conciliation Service. A new code is presently being formulated.

He should be fearless of public clamor and indifferent to private, political or partisan influences.

(b) The arbitrator should not undertake or incur obligations to either party which may interfere with his impartial determination of the issue submitted to him.

5. DUTY TO THE PARTIES

The arbitrator's duty is to determine the matters in dispute, which may involve differences over the interpretation of existing provisions or terms and conditions of a new contract. In either event, the arbitrator shall be governed by the wishes of the parties, which may be expressed in their agreement, arbitration submission or in any other form of understanding. He should not undertake to induce a settlement of the dispute against the wishes of either party. If, however, an atmosphere is created or the issues are so simplified or reduced as to lead to a voluntary settlement by the parties, a function of his office has been fulfilled.

6. ACCEPTANCE, REFUSAL OR WITHDRAWAL FROM OFFICE

The arbitrator, being appointed by voluntary act of the parties, may accept or decline the appointment. When he accepts he should continue in office until the matter submitted to him is finally determined. When there are circumstances which, in his judgment, compel his withdrawal, the parties are entitled to prompt notice and explanation.

7. OATH OF OFFICE

When an oath of office is taken it should serve as the arbitrator's guide. When an oath is not required or is waived by the parties, the arbitrator should nevertheless observe the standards which the oath imposes.

8. PRIVACY OF THE ARBITRATION

(a) An arbitrator should not, without the approval of the parties, disclose to third persons any evidence, argument or discussions pertaining to the arbitration.

(b) There should be no disclosure of the terms of an award by any arbitrator until after it is delivered simultaneously to all of the parties and publication or public disclosure should be only with the parties' consent.

Discussions within an arbitration board should be held in confidence. Dissenting opinions may be filed, however, but they should be based on the arbitrators' views on the evidence and controlling principles, and not on the discussions which took place in the executive sessions of the board.

9. ADVERTISING AND SOLICITATION

Advertising by an arbitrator and soliciting of cases is improper and not in accordance with the dignity of the office. No arbitrator should suggest to any party that future cases be referred to him.

PART II

PROCEDURAL STANDARDS FOR ARBITRATORS

The standards set forth in the following sections are intended only as general guides to arbitrators and to parties in arbitration proceedings. It is not intended that they will be literally adhered to in every particular, nor are they intended to supplant contrary practices which in particular cases have been established or accepted by the parties. These standards are meant to be equally applicable to partisan and neutral members of arbitration boards.

These standards of procedure are not to be deemed mandatory precepts or controlling rules which will furnish a basis for attacking awards or enlarging the grounds prescribed by law for the impeachment of awards.

1. COMPENSATION AND EXPENSES OF THE ARBITRATOR

(a) Arbitrators serving in labor–management disputes generally receive compensation. The position of an arbitrator, whether compensated or not, is an honorary one and is accepted as an opportunity for public service.

(b) Compensation for arbitrators' services should be reasonable and consistent with the nature of the case and the circumstances of the parties. A fee previously fixed by the parties, or by schedule, should not be altered during the proceeding or after the award is delivered.

(c) It is commonly understood that necessary expenses, including travel, communications and maintenance, may be incurred by the abritrator and that such expenses are reimbursable. The arbitrator should be prepared to render a statement of his expenses if the parties desire it.

2. HEARING ARRANGEMENTS

(a) The arbitrator should consult the convenience of the parties in fixing the time and place for the hearing but should not allow one party to delay unduly the fixing of a date for the hearing. Written and timely notice of the date, time and place of the hearing should be given.

(b) Whenever the law permits, the arbitrator in his discretion may issue subpoenas.

3. OATH OF OFFICE

The following is the general form of oath which the law of certain states requires the arbitrator to take:

.... being duly sworn deposes and says that he will faithfully and fairly hear and examine the matter in controversy between the above named Parties, and that he will make a just award according to the best of his understanding.

4. THE HEARING

(a) The arbitrator should be prompt in his attendance at the hearing and should so conduct the proceeding as to reflect the importance and seriousness of the issue before him. The orderly conduct of the proceeding is under his jurisdiction and control, subject to such rules of procedure as the parties may prescribe. He should proceed promptly with the hearing and determination of the dispute. He should countenance no unnecessary delays in the examination of witnesses or in the presentation of evidence. Where the law requires it, witnesses must be sworn unless the parties duly waive this requirement.

(b) The arbitrator may participate in the examination of parties or witnesses in order to classify the issues and bring to light all relevant facts necessary to a fair and informed decision of the issues submitted to him. However, he should bear in mind that undue interference or emphasis upon his own knowledge or view may tend to prevent the proper presentation of the case by a party. Examinations should be fair and courteous and directed toward encouraging a full presentation of the case. The arbitrator should avoid assuming a controversial attitude toward witnesses, parties or other arbitrators. He should avoid expressing a premature opinion.

(c) The informality of the hearings should not be allowed to affect decorum and the orderly presentation of proof. The arbitrator should seek to prevent any argument or conduct at the hearings which would tend to cause bitterness or acrimony.

(d) Unless the parties approve, the arbitrator should not, in the absence of or without notice to one party, hold interviews with, or consider arguments or communications from the other party. If any such communications be received, their contents should be disclosed to all parties and an opportunity afforded to comment thereon.

(e) The arbitrator should allow a fair hearing, with full opportunity to the parties to offer all evidence which they deem reasonably material. He may, however, exclude evidence which is clearly immaterial. He may receive and consider affidavits, giving them such weight as the circumstances warrant, but in so doing, he should afford the other side an opportunity to cross-examine the persons making the affidavits or to take their depositions or otherwise interrogate them.

(f) The arbitrator is expected to exercise his own best judgment. He is not required except by specific agreement of the parties to follow precedent. He should not, however, prevent the parties from presenting the decisions of other arbitrators in support of their positions. When the parties have selected a continuing arbitrator, it is generally recognized that he may establish or follow precedents for the same parties.

5. The Award

(a) The arbitrator should render his award promptly and must render his award within the time prescribed, if any. The award should be definite, certain and final, and should dispose of all matters submitted. It should reserve no future duties to the arbitrator except by agreement of the parties.

(b) The award should be stated separately from the opinion, if an opinion is rendered.

(c) It is discretionary with the arbitrator, upon the request of all parties, to give the terms of their voluntary settlement the status of an award.

(d) The award should be personally signed by the arbitrator and delivered simultaneously to all parties. The arbitrator should exercise extreme care to see that the contractual or legal requirements for making and delivering the award are met.

(e) It is discretionary with the arbitrator to state reasons for his decision or to accompany the award with an opinion. Opinions should not contain gratuitous advice or comments not related or necessary to the determination of the issues. If either party requests the arbitrator to prepare an opinion, such request should be followed.

(f) After the award has been rendered, the arbitrator should not issue any clarification or interpretation thereof, or comments thereon, except at the request of both parties, unless the agreement provides therefor.

6. Privacy of Proceeding and Award

The arbitrator should not publish or publicly comment on the proceedings or the award against the wishes of the parties.

PART III

CONDUCT AND BEHAVIOR OF PARTIES

1. GENERAL

Arbitration is predicated on the voluntary agreement of the parties to submit a dispute to a disinterested third party for final determination. It implies not only the willingness to arbitrate but the willingness to attend a hearing, submit evidence, submit to cross-examination and to abide by the decision of the arbitrator.

2. SCOPE

The power of the arbitrator depends upon the agreement of the parties. Accordingly, the contract or the submission agreement should define his powers. In initiating an arbitration—whether under a clause in a collective bargaining agreement or under a submission agreement or a stipulation—it is the duty of the parties to set forth the nature of the controversy, the claim asserted and the remedy sought. The initiating party has the duty of setting forth its claim and the defending party the right to outline its position.

3. SELECTION OF ARBITRATOR

The parties should select the arbitrator, in accordance with their agreement, to determine the controversy existing between them and his designation should be based on his integrity, knowledge and judgment. A party should not seek to obtain the appointment of an arbitrator in the belief that he will favor that party and thereby give him an advantage over his adversary.

In keeping with the desire for complete impartiality, parties should reject as arbitrators persons who solicit cases.

4. THE TRI-PARTITE BOARD

When parties select members of tri-partite boards, it is recognized that generally each will select a representative rather than an impartial arbitrator, but in making such appointment parties should select persons who will join with the impartial arbitrator in a full and fair discussion and consideration of the merits of the question to be determined.

5. ESSENTIAL CONDUCT

Parties should approach arbitration in a spirit of cooperation with the arbitrator and should seek to aid him in the performance of his duties.

Having selected an arbitrator, the parties are under a duty not to subject him to improper pressures or influences which may tend to prejudice his judgment. They should neither give nor offer favors of any kind to the arbitrator. As a general rule they should not communicate with him privately; and if it becomes necessary to communicate with him, it should be done in writing and a copy thereof should be simultaneously delivered to the other party.

Parties should respect the office of the arbitrator and recognize his essential right to control the conduct of the arbitration and should abide by whatever rulings he may make.

When an arbitrator elects to withdraw from a proceeding and gives the parties his reasons, they should respect his right to do so in the interest of good arbitration.

6. THE HEARING

Parties should not unduly delay the fixing of a date for the hearing nor the completion of the hearing. They should be prepared to proceed expeditiously with the evidence and their witnesses, have their exhibits ready and cooperate with the arbitrator in furnishing whatever additional information he may deem necessary.

They should be prompt in attendance at the hearing.

Parties should be fair and courteous in their examination of witnesses and in their presentation of facts. Concealment of necessary facts or the use of exaggeration is not conducive to a good or sound determination of the differences between the parties. Acrimonious, bitter or ill-mannered conduct is harmful to the cause of good arbitration.

When hearings are concluded, parties should not attempt to communicate any additional information to the arbitrator. If new evidence becomes available, written application for the re-opening of the proceeding with the reasons therefor should be made to the arbitrator and a copy transmitted simultaneously to the other party.

When it has been agreed that briefs will be submitted, they should be filed prompty on the date arranged and no new matter should be included in the briefs. Briefs should be a summarization of the evidence presented at the hearing, together with arguments of the parties and their comments on the evidence.

7. PRIVACY OF THE ARBITRATION

The parties should consider whether the subject matter of the arbitration is of such public interest as to warrant publicity concerning the proceeding and publication of the award and opinion, if any; and should advise the arbitrator accordingly on the record or in writing.

8. ARBITRATOR'S EXECUTIVE MEETINGS

Meetings of the arbitrators and discussions in executive sessions by members of boards of arbitration are private and confidential and parties should not seek to obtain information concerning such meetings either from the third arbitrator or from their nominees. Parties should likewise refrain from attempting to secure in advance from the arbitrator or their nominees information concerning the award but should wait until the award is received in the regular course by both parties.

9. THE AWARD

Parties, having agreed to arbitration, should accept and abide by the award.

After an award has been rendered, neither party should unilaterally request a clarification or interpretation of the award from the arbitrator. If one is necessary, it should be requested jointly by both parties.

10. SETTLEMENTS

If the parties reach a settlement of their dispute but desire nevertheless to have an award made, they should give the arbitrator a full explanation of the reasons therefor in order that he may judge whether he desires to make or join in such an award.

11. COMPENSATION OF THE ARBITRATOR

Parties should agree in advance of the hearing with the arbitrator on his compensation or the basis upon which it will be determined, but such arrangements

should be made only in the presence of both parties. If the parties do not agree
with one another as to the compensation, they should discuss the matter in the
absence of the arbitrator in order that there be no intimidation or suggestion
that one party is willing to pay more compensation than the other and thereby
raise the possibility of a question thereafter as to partiality on the part of the
arbitrator.

Having agreed on the compensation for an arbitrator's services or to the reimbursement of his necessary expenses, parties should remit promptly and under
no circumstances should such payment be withheld because of displeasure over
the award.

LIST OF MODERN ARBITRATION STATUTES IN THE UNITED STATES

United States Arbitration Act. U.S. Code, Title 9, Sections 1-14; 61 Stat. 669, as amended by Sec. 19 of Public Law 779, of September 3, 1954, 68 Stat. 1233.

Alaska Stats. Ann. §09.43.010 to 09.43.180 (1968).

Ariz. Rev. Stats. §§12-1501 to 12-1516 (1962).

Ark. Stats. Ann. §§34-501 to 34-510 (1947).

Cal. Code of Civil Procedure §1280 to 1294 (Supp. 1961).

Conn. Gen. Stats. Ann. §§52-401 to 52-424 (Rev. 1958).

Fla. Stats. Ann. §§682.01 to 682.22 (1969).

Rev. Laws of Hawaii §§188-1 to 188-15 (1955).

Ill. Rev. Stats. §101 (1961, 1962 Cum. Ann. Pocket Part., p. 192).

Ind. Stats. Ann. §§3-201 to 3-220 (1968).

La. Rev. Stats. §§4201 to 4217 (West, 1951).

Me. Rev. Stats. Ann. §881-960 (1964).

Maryland Act. Ch. 231 (eff. June 1, 1965).

Ann. Laws of Mass. §§1 to 10 (Supp. 1961).

Mich. Stats. Ann. §§27.2483 to 27.2505, as amended by Public Act. No. 27 of 1963; Michigan Sup. Ct. Rules, Rule 769 (1963).

Minn. Stats. Ann. §§572.08 to 572.30 (Supp. 1961).

Nev. Rev. Stats. Vol. 2, Chap. 38, §§38.010 to 38.240 (1967).

N.H. Rev. Stats. Ann. §§542:1 to 542:10 (1955).

N.J. Stats. §§2A:24-1 to 2A:24-11.

N.M. Stats, Ann. §22-3-9 to 31 (1971 Supp.).

N.Y. C.P.L.R. §7501, as amended by N.Y. Laws 1962, 308 (eff. 9/1/63).

Ohio Rev. Code Ann. §§2711.01 to 2711.15, as amended 6/30/55 (Laws of Ohio, vol. 126, p. 304 (Page 1954), 1961 Supp., p. 46.)

Ore. Rev. Stats. §§33.210 to 33.340 (1955 Replacement Parts).

Pa. Stats. Ann. §§1 to 181 (Purdon).

Gen. Laws of R.I. §§10-3-1 to 10-3-20 (1956).

S. D. Comp. Laws §21-25A-1 to 38 (1971 Supp.).

Texas Ann. Civ. St. Art. 224-238-6 (Vernon, eff. 1/1/66).

Code of Va. Vol. 2, §§8-503 to 8-507 (1950).

Rev. Code of Wash. §§7.04-010 to 7.04-220.

Wis. Stats. Ann. §§298.01 to 298.18 (West's).

Wyo. Stats. Chapter 37 (1963 Supp.).

Appendix II

AMERICAN ARBITRATION ASSOCIATION RULES

AMERICAN ARBITRATION ASSOCIATION VOLUNTARY LABOR ARBITRATION RULES

1. Agreement of Parties—The parties shall be deemed to have made these Rules a part of their arbitration agreement whenever, in a collective bargaining agreement or submission, they have provided for arbitration by the American Arbitration Association (hereinafter AAA) or under its Rules. These Rules shall apply in the form obtaining at the time the arbitration is initiated.

2. Name of Tribunal—Any Tribunal constituted by the parties under these Rules shall be called the Voluntary Labor Arbitration Tribunal.

3. Administrator—When parties agree to arbitrate under these Rules and an arbitration is instituted thereunder, they thereby authorize the AAA to administer the arbitration. The authority and obligations of the Administrator are as provided in the agreement of the parties and in these Rules.

4. Delegation of Duties—The duties of the AAA may be carried out through such representatives or committees as the AAA may direct.

5. National Panel of Labor Arbitrators—The AAA shall establish and maintain a National Panel of Labor Arbitrators and shall appoint arbitrators therefrom, as hereinafter provided.

6. Office of Tribunal—The general office of the Labor Arbitration Tribunal is the headquarters of the AAA, which may, however, assign the administration of an arbitration to any of its Regional Offices.

7. Initiation Under an Arbitration Clause in a Collective Bargaining Agreement—Arbitration under an arbitration clause in a collective bargaining agreement under these Rules may be initiated by either party in the following manner:

(a) By giving written notice to the other party of intention to arbitrate (Demand), which notice shall contain a statement setting forth the nature of the dispute and the remedy sought, and

(b) By filing at any Regional Office of the AAA three copies of said notice, together with a copy of the collective bargaining agreement, or such parts thereof as relate to the dispute, including the arbitration provisions. After the Arbitrator is appointed, no new or different claim may be submitted to him except with the consent of the Arbitrator and all other parties.

8. Answer—The party upon whom the Demand for Arbitration is made may file an answering statement with the AAA within seven days after notice from the AAA, in which event he shall simultaneously send a copy of his answer to the other party. If no answer is filed within the stated time, it will be assumed that the claim is denied. Failure to file an answer shall not operate to delay the arbitration.

9. Initiation Under a Submission—Parties to any collective bargaining agreement may initiate an arbitration under these Rules by filing at any Regional Office of the AAA two copies of a written agreement to arbitrate under these Rules (Submission), signed by the parties and setting forth the nature of the dispute and the remedy sought.

10. Fixing of Locale—The parties may mutually agree upon the locale where the arbitration is to be held. If the locale is not designated in the collective bargaining agreement or Submission, and if there is a dispute as to the appropriate locale, the AAA shall have the power to determine the locale and its decision shall be binding.

11. Qualifications of Arbitrator—No person shall serve as a neutral Arbitrator in any arbitration in which he has any financial or personal interest in the result of the arbitration, unless the parties, in writing, waive such disqualification.

12. Appointment from Panel—If the parties have not appointed an Arbitrator and have not provided any other method of appointment, the Arbitrator shall be appointed in the following manner: Immediately after the filing of the Demand or Submission, the AAA shall submit simultaneously to each party an identical list of names of persons chosen from the Labor Panel. Each party shall have seven days from the mailing date in which to cross off any names to which he objects, number the remaining names indicating the order of his preference, and return the list to the AAA. If a party does not return the list within the time specified, all persons named therein shall be deemed acceptable. From among the persons who have been approved on both lists, and in accordance with the designated order of mutual preference, the AAA shall invite the acceptance of an Arbitrator to serve. If the parties fail to agree upon any of the persons named or if those named decline or are unable to act, or if for any other reason the appointment cannot be made from the submitted lists, the Administrator shall have power to make the appointment from other members of the Panel without the submission of any additional lists.

13. Direct Appointment by Parties—If the agreement of the parties names an Arbitrator or specifies a method of appointing an Arbitrator, that designation or method shall be followed. The notice of appointment, with the name and address of such Arbitrator, shall be filed with the AAA by the appointing party.

If the agreement specifies a period of time within which an Arbitrator shall be appointed, and any party fails to make such appointment within that period, the AAA may make the appointment.

If no period of time is specified in the agreement, the AAA shall notify the parties to make the appointment and if within seven days thereafter such Arbitrator has not been so appointed, the AAA shall make the appointment.

14. Appointment of Neutral Arbitrator by Party-Appointed Arbitrators—If the parties have appointed their Arbitrators, or if either or both of them have been appointed as provided in Section 13, and have authorized such Arbitrators to appoint a neutral Arbitrator within a specified time and no appointment is made within such time or any agreed extension thereof, the AAA may appoint a neutral Arbitrator, who shall act as Chairman.

If no period of time is specified for appointment of the neutral Arbitrator and the parties do not make the appointment within seven days from the date of the appointment of the last party-appointed Arbitrator, the AAA shall appoint such neutral Arbitrator, who shall act as Chairman.

If the parties have agreed that the Arbitrators shall appoint the neutral Arbitrator from the Panel, the AAA shall furnish to the party-appointed Arbitrators, in the manner prescribed in Section 12, a list selected from the Panel, and the appointment of the neutral Arbitrator shall be made as prescribed in such Section.

15. Number of Arbitrators—If the arbitration agreement does not specify the number of Arbitrators, the dispute shall be heard and determined by one Arbitrator, unless the parties otherwise agree.

16. Notice to Arbitrator of His Appointment—Notice of the appointment of the neutral Arbitrator shall be mailed to the Arbitrator by the AAA and the signed acceptance of the Arbitrator shall be filed with the AAA prior to the opening of the first hearing.

17. Disclosure by Arbitrator of Disqualification—Prior to accepting his appointment, the prospective neutral Arbitrator shall disclose any circumstances likely to create a presumption of bias or which he believes might disqualify him as an impartial Arbitrator. Upon receipt of such information, the AAA shall immediately disclose it to the parties. If either party declines to waive the presumptive disqualification, the vacancy thus created shall be filled in accordance with the applicable provisions of these Rules.

18. Vacancies—If any Arbitrator should resign, die, withdraw, refuse or be unable or disqualified to perform the duties of his office, the AAA shall, on proof satisfactory to it, declare the office vacant. Vacancies shall be filled in the same manner as that governing the making of the original appointment, and the matter shall be reheard by the new Arbitrator.

19. Time and Place of Hearing—The Arbitrator shall fix the time and place for each hearing. At least five days prior thereto the AAA shall mail notice of the time and place of hearing to each party, unless the parties otherwise agree.

20. Representation by Counsel—Any party may be represented at the hearing by counsel or by other authorized representative.

21. Stenographic Record—Any party may request a stenographic record by making arrangements for same through the AAA. If such transcript is agreed by the parties to be, or in appropriate cases determined by the arbitrator to be the official record of the proceeding, it must be made available to the arbitrator, and to the other party for inspection, at a time and place determined by the arbitrator. The total cost of such a record shall be shared equally by those parties that order copies.

22. Attendance at Hearings—Persons having a direct interest in the arbitration are entitled to attend hearings. The Arbitrator shall have the power to require the retirement of any witness or witnesses during the testimony of other witnesses. It shall be discretionary with the Arbitrator to determine the propriety of the attendance of any other persons.

23. Adjournments—The Arbitrator for good cause shown may adjourn the hearing upon the request of a party or upon his own initiative, and shall adjourn when all the parties agree thereto.

24. Oaths—Before proceeding with the first hearing, each Arbitrator may take an Oath of Office, and if required by law, shall do so. The Arbitrator may, in his discretion, require witnesses to testify under oath administered by any duly qualified person, and if required by law or requested by either party, shall do so.

25. Majority Decision—Whenever there is more than one Arbitrator, all decisions of the Arbitrators shall be by majority vote. The award shall also be made by majority vote unless the concurrence of all is expressly required.

26. Order of Proceedings—A hearing shall be opened by the filing of the Oath of the Arbitrator, where required, and by the recording of the place, time and date of hearing, the presence of the Arbitrator and parties, and counsel if any, and the receipt by the Arbitrator of the Demand and answer, if any, or the Submission.

Exhibits, when offered by either party, may be received in evidence by the Arbitrator. The names and addresses of all witnesses and exhibits in order received shall be made a part of the record.

The Arbitrator may, in his discretion, vary the normal procedure under which the initiating party first presents his claim, but in any case shall afford full and equal opportunity to all parties for presentation of relevant proofs.

27. Arbitration in the Absence of a Party—Unless the law provides to the contrary, the arbitration may proceed in the absence of any party, who, after due notice, fails to be present or fails to obtain an adjournment. An award shall not be made solely on the default of a party. The Arbitrator shall require the other party to submit such evidence as he may require for the making of an award.

28. Evidence—The parties may offer such evidence as they desire and shall produce such additional evidence as the Arbitrator may deem necessary to an understanding and determination of the dispute. When the Arbitrator is authorized by law to subpoena witnesses and documents, he may do so upon his own initiative or upon the request of any party. The Arbitrator shall be the judge of the relevancy and materiality of the evidence offered and conformity to legal rules of evidence shall not be necessary. All evidence shall be taken in the presence of all of the Arbitrators and all of the parties except where any of the parties is absent in default or has waived his right to be present.

29. Evidence by Affidavit and Filing of Documents—The Arbitrator may receive and consider the evidence of witnesses by affidavit, but shall give it only such weight as he deems proper after consideration of any objections made to its admission.

All documents not filed with the Arbitrator at the hearing but which are arranged at the hearing or subsequently by agreement of the parties to be submitted, shall be filed with the AAA for transmission to the Arbitrator. All parties shall be afforded opportunity to examine such documents.

30. **Inspection**—Whenever the Arbitrator deems it necessary, he may make an inspection in connection with the subject matter of the dispute after written notice to the parties who may, if they so desire, be present at such inspection.

31. **Closing of Hearings**—The Arbitrator shall inquire of all parties whether they have any further proofs to offer or witnesses to be heard. Upon receiving negative replies, the Arbitrator shall declare the hearings closed and a minute thereof shall be recorded. If briefs or other documents are to be filed, the hearings shall be declared closed as of the final date set by the Arbitrator for filing with the AAA. The time limit within which the Arbitrator is required to make his award shall commence to run, in the absence of other agreement by the parties, upon the closing of the hearings.

32. **Reopening of Hearings**—The hearings may be reopened by the Arbitrator on his own motion, or on the motion of either party, for good cause shown, at any time before the award is made, but if the reopening of the hearing would prevent the making of the award within the specific time agreed upon by the parties in the contract out of which the controversy has arisen, the matter may not be reopened, unless both parties agree upon the extension of such time limit. When no specific date is fixed in the contract, the Arbitrator may reopen the hearings, and the Arbitrator shall have 30 days from the closing of the reopened hearings within which to make an award.

33. **Waiver of Rules**—Any party who proceeds with the arbitration after knowledge that any provision or requirement of these Rules has not been complied with and who fails to state his objection thereto in writing, shall be deemed to have waived his right to object.

34. **Waiver of Oral Hearings**—The parties may provide, by written agreement, for the waiver of oral hearings. If the parties are unable to agree as to the procedure, the AAA shall specify a fair and equitable procedure.

35. **Extensions of Time**—The parties may modify any period of time by mutual agreement. The AAA for good cause may extend any period of time established by these Rules, except the time for making the award. The AAA shall notify the parties of any such extension of time and its reason therefor.

36. **Serving of Notices**—Each party to a Submission or other agreement which provides for arbitration under these Rules shall be deemed to have consented and shall consent that any papers, notices or process necessary or proper for the initiation or continuation of an arbitration under these Rules and for any court action in connection therewith or the entry of judgment on an award made thereunder, may be served upon such party (a) by mail addressed to such party or his attorney at his last known address, or (b) by personal service, within or without the state wherein the arbitration is to be held.

37. **Time of Award**—The award shall be rendered promptly by the Arbitrator and, unless otherwise agreed by the parties, or specified by the law, not later than 30 days from the date of closing the hearings, or if oral hearings have been waived, then from the date of transmitting the final statements and proofs to the Arbitrator.

38. **Form of Award**—The award shall be in writing and shall be signed either by the neutral Arbitrator or by a concurring majority if there be more than one Arbitrator. The parties shall advise the AAA whenever they do not require the Arbitrator to accompany the award with an opinion.

39. **Award Upon Settlement**—If the parties settle their dispute during the course of the arbitration, the Arbitrator, upon their request, may set forth the terms of the agreed settlement in an award.

40. **Delivery of Award to Parties**—Parties shall accept as legal delivery of the award the placing of the award or a true copy thereof in the mail by the AAA, addressed to such party at his last known address or to his attorney, or personal service of the award, or the filing of the award in any manner which may be prescribed by law.

41. **Release of Documents for Judicial Proceedings**—The AAA shall, upon the written request of a party, furnish to such party at his expense certified facsimiles of any papers in the AAA's possession that may be required in judicial proceedings relating to the arbitration.

42. **Judicial Proceedings**—The AAA is not a necessary party in judicial proceedings relating to the arbitration.

43. **Administrative Fee**—As a nonprofit organization, the AAA shall prescribe an administrative fee schedule to compensate it for the cost of providing administrative services. The schedule in effect at the time of filing shall be applicable.

44. **Expenses**—The expenses of witnesses for either side shall be paid by the party producing such witnesses.

Expenses of the arbitration, other than the cost of the stenographic record, including required traveling and other expenses of the Arbitrator and of AAA representatives, and the expenses of any witnesses or the cost of any proofs produced at the direct request of the Arbitrator, shall be borne equally by the parties unless they agree otherwise, or unless the Arbitrator in his award assesses such expenses or any part thereof against any specified party or parties.

45. **Communication with Arbitrator**—There shall be no communication between the parties and a neutral Arbitrator other than at oral hearings. Any other oral or written communications from the parties to the Arbitrator shall be directed to the AAA for transmittal to the Arbitrator.

46. **Interpretation and Application of Rules**—The Arbitrator shall interpret and apply these Rules insofar as they relate to his powers and duties. When there is more than one Arbitrator and a difference arises among them concerning the meaning or application of any such Rules, it shall be decided by majority vote. If that is unobtainable, either Arbitrator or party may refer the question to the AAA for final decision. All other Rules shall be interpreted and applied by the AAA.

EXPEDITED LABOR ARBITRATION

Recently there has been increasing concern over rising costs and delays in grievance arbitration. The Labor-Management Committee of the American Arbitration Association recommended the establishment of an expedited procedure, under which cases could be scheduled promptly and an award rendered within five days of the hearing. Simplified procedures would also reduce the cost.

In return for giving up their right to some of the procedural advantages of traditional labor arbitration, the parties could get a quick decision, at a reduced cost.

These New Expedited Rules provide such a procedure for use in appropriate cases. Many of the leading labor arbitrators have indicated a willingness to offer their services. Now, it is up to the labor-management community to use this system to its maximum benefit.

AMERICAN ARBITRATION ASSOCIATION EXPEDITED LABOR ARBITRATION RULES

1. **Agreement of Parties** - These Rules shall apply whenever the parties have agreed to arbitrate under them, in the form obtaining at the time the arbitration is initiated.
2. **Appointment of Neutral Arbitrator** - The AAA shall appoint a single neutral Arbitrator from its Panel of Labor Arbitrators, who shall hear and determine the case promptly.
3. **Initiation of Expedited Arbitration Proceeding** - Cases may be initiated by joint submission in writing, or in accordance with a collective bargaining agreement.
4. **Qualifications of Neutral Arbitrator** - No person shall serve as a neutral Arbitrator in any arbitration in which that person has any financial or personal interest in the result of the arbitration. Prior to accepting an appointment, the prospective Arbitrator shall disclose any circumstances likely to prevent a prompt hearing or to create a presumption of bias. Upon receipt of such information, the AAA shall immediately replace that Arbitrator or communicate the information to the parties.
5. **Vacancy** - The AAA is authorized to substitute another Arbitrator if a vacancy occurs or if an appointed Arbitrator is unable to serve promptly.
6. **Time and Place of Hearing** - The AAA shall fix a mutually convenient time and place of the hearing, notice of which must be given at least 24 hours in advance. Such notice may be given orally.
7. **Representation by Counsel** - Any party may be represented at the hearing by counsel or other representative.
8. **Attendance at Hearings** - Persons having a direct interest in the arbitration are entitled to attend hearings.

The Arbitrator may require the retirement of any witness during the testimony of other witnesses. The Arbitrator shall determine whether any other person may attend the hearing.

9. **Adjournments** - Hearings shall be adjourned by the Arbitrator only for good cause, and an appropriate fee will be charged by the AAA against the party causing the adjournment.
10. **Oaths** - Before proceeding with the first hearing, the Arbitrator shall take an oath of office. The Arbitrator may require witnesses to testify under oath.
11. **No Stenographic Record** - There shall be no stenographic record of the proceedings.
12. **Proceedings** - The hearing shall be conducted by the Arbitrator in whatever manner will most expeditiously permit full presentation of the evidence and the arguments of the parties. The Arbitrator shall make an appropriate minute of the proceedings. Normally, the hearing shall be completed within one day. In unusual circumstances and for good cause shown, the Arbitrator may schedule an additional hearing, within five days.
13. **Arbitration in the Absence of a Party** - The arbitration may proceed in the absence of any party who, after due notice, fails to be present. An award shall not be made solely on the default of a party. The Arbitrator shall require the attending party to submit supporting evidence.
14. **Evidence** - The Arbitrator shall be the sole judge of the relevancy and materiality of the evidence offered.
15. **Evidence by Affidavit and Filing of Documents** - The Arbitrator may receive and consider evidence in the form of an affidavit, but shall give appropriate weight to any objections made. All documents to be considered by the Arbitrator shall be filed at the hearing. There shall be no post hearing briefs.
16. **Close of Hearings** - The Arbitrator shall ask whether parties have any further proofs to offer or witnesses to be heard. Upon receiving negative replies, the Arbitrator shall declare and note the hearing closed.
17. **Waiver of Rules** - Any party who proceeds with the arbitration after knowledge that any provision or requirement of these Rules has not been complied with and who fails to state his objections thereto in writing shall be deemed to have waived his right to object.
18. **Serving of Notices** - Any papers or process necessary or proper for the initiation or continuation of an arbitration under these Rules and for any court action in connection therewith or for the entry of judgment on an Award made thereunder, may be served upon such party (a) by mail addressed to such party or its attorney at its last known address, or (b) by personal service, or (c) as otherwise provided in these Rules.
19. **Time of Award** - The award shall be rendered promptly by the Arbitrator and, unless otherwise agreed by the parties, not later than five business days from the date of the closing of the hearing.
20. **Form of Award** - The Award shall be in writing and shall be signed by the Arbitrator. If the Arbitrator determines that an opinion is necessary, it shall be in summary form.
21. **Delivery of Award to Parties** - Parties shall accept as legal delivery of the award the placing of the award or a true copy thereof in the mail by the AAA, addressed to such party at its last known address or to its attorney, or personal service of the award, or the filing of the award in any manner which may be prescribed by law.
22. **Expenses** - The expenses of witnesses for either side shall be paid by the party producing such witnesses.
23. **Interpretation and Application of Rules** - The Arbitrater shall interpret and apply these Rules insofar as they relate to his powers and duties. All other Rules shall be interpreted and applied by the AAA, as Adminstrator.

Appendix III

FEDERAL LAWS: EXECUTIVE ORDERS AND RULES

THE UNITED STATES ARBITRATION ACT

Title 9, U.S. Code §§1-14, first enacted February 12, 1925 (43 Stat. 883), codified July 30, 1947 (61 Stat. 669), and amended September 3, 1954 (68 Stat. 1233). Chapter 2 added July 31, 1970 (84 Stat. 692).

ARBITRATION

CHAPTER 1.—GENERAL PROVISIONS

§1. "Maritime Transactions" and "Commerce" Defined; Exceptions to Operation of Title

"Maritime transactions," as herein defined, means charter parties, bills of lading of water carriers, agreements relating to wharfage, supplies furnished vessels or repairs of vessels, collisions, or any other matters in foreign commerce which, if the subject of controversy, would be embraced within admiralty jurisdiction; "commerce," as herein defined, means commerce among the several States or with foreign nations, or in any Territory of the United States or in the District of Columbia, or between any such Territory and another, or between any such Territory and any State or foreign nation, or between the District of Columbia and any State or Territory or foreign nation, but nothing herein contained shall apply to contracts of employment of seamen, railroad employees, or any other class of workers engaged in foreign or interstate commerce.

§2. Validity, Irrevocability, and Enforcement of Agreements to Arbitrate

A written provision in any maritime transaction or a contract evidencing a transaction involving commerce to settle by arbitration a controversy thereafter arising out of such contract or transaction, or the refusal to perform the whole or any part thereof, or an agreement in writing to submit to arbitration an existing controversy arising out of such a contract, transaction, or refusal, shall be valid, irrevocable, and enforceable, save upon such grounds as exist at law or in equity for the revocation of any contract.

§3. Stay of Proceedings Where Issue Therein Referable to Arbitration

If any suit or proceding be brought in any of the courts of the United States upon any issue referable to arbitration under an agreement in writing for such arbitration, the court in which such suit is pending, upon being satisfied that the issue involved in such suit or proceeding is referable to arbitration under such an agreement, shall on application of one of the parties stay the trial of the action until such arbitration has been had in accordance with the terms of the agreement, providing the applicant for the stay is not in default in proceeding with such arbitration.

§4. Failure to Arbitrate Under Agreement; Petition to United States Court Having Jurisdiction for Order to Compel Arbitration; Notice and Service Thereof; Hearing and Determination

A party aggrieved by the alleged failure, neglect, or refusal of another to arbitrate under a written agreement for arbitration may petition any United States district court which, save for such agreement, would have jurisdiction under Title 28, in a civil action or in admiralty of the subject matter of a suit arising out of the controversy between the parties, for an order directing that such arbitration proceed in the manner provided for in such agreement. Five days' notice in writing of such application shall be served upon the party in default. Service thereof shall be made in the manner provided by the Federal Rules of Civil Procedure. The court shall hear the parties, and upon being satisfied that the making of the agreement for arbitration or the failure to comply therewith is not in issue, the court shall make an order directing the parties to proceed to arbitration in accordance with the terms of the agreement. The hearing and proceedings, under such agreement, shall be within the district in which the petition for an order directing such arbitration is filed. If the making of the arbitration agreement or the failure, neglect, or refusal to perform the same be in issue, the court shall proceed summarily to the trial thereof. If no jury trial be demanded by the party alleged to be in default, or if the matter in dispute is within admiralty jurisdiction, the court shall hear and determine such issue. Where such an issue is raised, the party alleged to be in default may, except in cases of admiralty, on or before the return day of the notice of application, demand a jury trial of such issue, and upon such demand the court shall make an order referring the issue or issues to a jury in the manner provided by the Federal Rules of Civil Procedure, or may specially call a jury for that purpose. If the jury find that no agreement in writing for arbitration was made or that there is no default in proceeding thereunder, the proceeding shall be dismissed. If the jury find that an agreement for arbitration was made in writing and that there is a default in proceeding thereunder, the court shall make an order summarily directing the parties to proceed with the arbitration in accordance with the terms thereof.

§5. Appointment of Arbitrators or Umpire

If in the agreement provision be made for a method of naming or appointing an arbitrator or arbitrators or an umpire, such method shall be followed; but if no method be provided therein, or if a method be provided and any party thereto shall fail to avail himself of such method, or if for any other reason there shall be a lapse in the naming of an arbitrator or arbitrators or umpire, or in filling a vacancy, then upon the application of either party to the controversy the court shall designate and appoint an arbitrator or arbitrators or umpire, as the case may require, who shall act under the said agreement with the same force and effect as if he or they had been specifically named therein; and unless otherwise provided in the agreement the arbitration shall be by a single arbitrator.

§6. Application Heard as Motion

Any application to the court hereunder shall be made and heard in the manner provided by law for the making and hearing of motions, except as otherwise herein expressly provided.

§7. Witnesses Before Arbitrators; Fees; Compelling Attendance

The arbitrators selected either as prescribed in this title or otherwise, or a majority of them, may summon in writing any person to attend before them or any of them as a witness and in a proper case to bring with him or them any book, record, document, or paper which may be deemed material as evidence in the case. The fees for such attendance shall be the same as the fees of witnesses before masters of the United States courts. Said summons shall issue in the name of the arbitrator or arbitrators, or a majority of them, and shall be signed by the arbitrators, or a majority of them, and shall be directed to the said person and shall be served in the same manner as subpoenas to appear and testify before the court; if any person or persons so summoned to testify shall refuse or neglect to obey said summons, upon petition the United States court in and for the district in which such arbitrators, or a majority of them, are sitting may compel the attendance of such person or persons before said arbitrator or arbitrators, or punish said person or persons for contempt in the same manner provided on February 12, 1925, for securing the attendance of witnesses or their punishment for neglect or refusal to attend in the courts of the United States.

§8. Proceedings Begun by Libel in Admiralty and Seizure of Vessel or Property

If the basis of jurisdiction be a cause of action otherwise justiciable in admiralty, then, notwithstanding anything herein to the contrary the party claiming to be aggrieved may begin his proceeding hereunder by libel and seizure of the vessel or other property of the other party according to the usual course of admiralty proceedings, and the court shall then have jurisdiction to direct the parties to proceed with the arbitration and shall retain jurisdiction to enter its decree upon the award.

§9. Award of Arbitrators; Confirmation; Jurisdiction; Procedure

If the parties in their agreement have agreed that a judgment of the court shall be entered upon the award made pursuant to the arbitration, and shall specify the court, then at any time within one year after the award is made any party to the arbitration may apply to the court so specified for an order confirming the award, and thereupon the court must grant such an order unless the award is vacated, modified, or corrected as prescribed in sections 10 and 11 of this title. If no court is specified in the agreement of the parties, then such application may be made to the United States court in and for the district within which such award was made. Notice of the application shall be served upon the adverse par-

ty, and thereupon the court shall have jurisdiction of such party as though he had appeared generally in the proceeding. If the adverse party is a resident of the district within which the award was made, such service shall be made upon the adverse party or his attorney as prescribed by law for service of notice of motion in an action in the same court. If the adverse party shall be a nonresident, then the notice of the application shall be served by the marshal of any district within which the adverse party may be found in like manner as other process of the court.

§10. Same; Vacation; Grounds; Rehearing

In either of the following cases the United States court in and for the district wherein the award was made may make an order vacating the award upon the application of any party to the arbitration—

(a) Where the award was procured by corruption, fraud, or undue means.

(b) Where there was evident partiality or corruption in the arbitrators, or either of them.

(c) Where the arbitrators were guilty of misconduct in refusing to postpone the hearing, upon sufficient cause shown, or in refusing to hear evidence pertinent and material to the controversy; or of any other misbehavior by which the rights of any party have been prejudiced.

(d) Where the arbitrators exceeded their powers, or so imperfectly executed them that a mutual, final, and definite award upon the subject matter submitted was not made.

(e) Where an award is vacated and the time within which the agreement required the award to be made has not expired the court may, in its discretion, direct a rehearing by the arbitrators.

§11. Same; Modification or Correction; Grounds; Order

In either of the following cases the United States court in and for the district wherein the award was made may make an order modifying or correcting the award upon the application of any party to the arbitration—

(a) Where there was an evident material miscalculation of figures or an evident material mistake in the description of any person, thing, or property referred to in the award.

(b) Where the arbitrators have awarded upon a matter not submitted to them, unless it is a matter not affecting the merits of the decision upon the matter submitted.

(c) Where the award is imperfect in matter of form not affecting the merits of the controversy.

The order may modify and correct the award, so as to effect the intent thereof and promote justice between the parties.

§12. Notice of Motions to Vacate or Modify; Service; Stay of Proceedings

Notice of a motion to vacate, modify, or correct an award must be served upon the adverse party or his attorney within three months after the award is filed or delivered. If the adverse party is a resident of the district within which the award was made, such service shall be made upon the adverse party or his attorney as prescribed by law for service of notice of motion in an action in the same court. If the adverse party shall be a nonresident then the notice of the application shall be served by the marshal of any district within which the adverse party may be found in like manner as other process of the court. For the purposes of the motion any judge who might make an order to stay the proceedings in an action brought in the same court may make an order, to be served with the notice of motion, staying the proceedings of the adverse party to enforce the award.

§13. Papers Filed with Order on Motions; Judgment; Docketing; Force and Effect; Enforcement

The party moving for an order confirming, modifying, or correcting an award shall, at the time such order is filed with the clerk for the entry of judgment thereon, also file the following papers with the clerk:

(a) The agreement; the selection or appointment, if any, of an additional arbitrator or um-

pire; and each written extension of the time, if any, within which to make the award.

(b) The award.

(c) Each notice, affidavit, or other paper used upon an application to confirm, modify, or correct the award, and a copy of each order of the court upon such an application.

The judgment shall be docketed as if it was rendered in an action.

The judgment so entered shall have the same force and effect, in all respects, as, and be subject to all the provisions of law relating to, a judgment in an action; and it may be enforced as if it had been rendered in an action in the court in which it is entered.

§14. Contracts Not Affected

This title shall not apply to contracts made prior to January 1, 1926.

CHAPTER 2.—CONVENTION ON THE RECOGNITION AND ENFORCEMENT OF FOREIGN ARBITRAL AWARDS

§201. Enforcement of Convention

The Convention on the Recognition and Enforcement of Foreign Arbitral Awards of June 10, 1958, shall be enforced in United States courts in accordance with this chapter.

§202. Agreement or Award Falling Under the Convention

An arbitration agreement or arbitral award arising out of a legal relationship, whether contractual or not, which is considered as commercial, including a transaction, contract, or agreement described in section 2 of this title, falls under the Convention. An agreement or award arising out of such a relationship which is entirely between citizens of the United States shall be deemed not to fall under the Convention unless that relationship involves property located abroad, envisages performance or enforcement abroad, or has some other reasonable relation with one or more foreign states. For the purpose of this section a corporation is a citizen of the United States if it is incorporated or has its principal place of business in the United States.

§203. Jurisdiction; Amount in Controversy

An action or proceeding falling under the Convention shall be deemed to arise under the laws and treaties of the United States. The district courts of the United States (including the courts enumerated in section 460 of title 28) shall have original jurisdiction over such an action or proceeding, regardless of the amount in controversy.

§204. Venue

An action or proceeding over which the district courts have jurisdiction pursuant to section 203 of this title may be brought in any such court in which save for the arbitration agreement an action or proceeding with respect to the controversy between the parties could be brought, or in such court for the district and division which embraces the place designated in the agreement as the place of arbitration if such place is within the United States.

§205. Removal of Cases from State Courts

Where the subject matter of an action or proceeding pending in a State court relates to an arbitration agreement or award falling under the Convention, the defendant or the defendants may, at any time before the trial thereof, remove such action or proceeding to the district court of the United States for the district and division embracing the place where the action or proceeding is pending. The procedure for removal of causes otherwise provided by law shall apply, except that the ground for removal provided in this section need not appear on the face of the complaint but may be shown in the petition for removal. For the purposes of Chapter 1 of this title any action or proceeding removed under this section shall be deemed to have been brought in the district court to which it is removed.

§206. Order to Compel Arbitration;
         Appointment of Arbitrators

A court having jurisdiction under this chapter may direct that arbitration be held in accordance with the agreement at any place therein provided for, whether that place is within or without the United States. Such court may also appoint arbitrators in accordance with the provisions of the agreement.

§207. Award of Arbitrators; Confirmation;
         Jurisdiction; Proceeding

Within three years after an arbitral award falling under the Convention is made, any party to the arbitration may apply to any court having jurisdiction under this chapter for an order confirming the award as against any other party to the arbitration. The court shall confirm the award unless it finds one of the grounds for refusal or deferral of recognition or enforcement of the award specified in the said Convention.

§208. Chapter 1; Residual Application

Chapter 1 applies to actions and proceedings brought under this chapter to the extent that chapter is not in conflict with this chapter or the Convention as ratified by the United States.

EXECUTIVE ORDER 11491
AS AMENDED *

LABOR-MANAGEMENT RELATIONS
IN THE FEDERAL SERVICE

WHEREAS the public interest requires high standards of employee performance and the continual development and implementation of modern and progressive work practices to facilitate improved employee performance and efficiency; and

WHEREAS the well-being of employees and efficient administration of the Government are benefited by providing employees an opportunity to participate in the formulation and implementation of personnel policies and practices affecting the conditions of their employment; and

WHEREAS the participation of employees should be improved through the maintenance of constructive and cooperative relationships between labor organizations and management officials; and

WHEREAS subject to law and the paramount requirements of public service, effective labor-management relations within the Federal service require a clear statement of the respective rights and obligations of labor organizations and agency management:

NOW, THEREFORE, by virtue of the authority vested in me by the Constitution and statutes of the United States, including sections 3301 and 7301 of title 5 of the United States Code, and as President of the United States, I hereby direct that the following policies shall govern officers and agencies of the executive branch of the Government in all dealings with Federal employees and organizations representing such employees.

GENERAL PROVISIONS

Section 1. *Policy.* (a) Each employee of the executive branch of the Federal Government has the right, freely and without fear of penalty or reprisal, to form, join, and assist a labor organization or to refrain from any such activity, and each employee shall be protected in the exercise of this right. Except as otherwise expressly provided in this Order, the right to assist a labor organization extends to participation in the management of the organization and acting for the organization in the capacity of an organization representative, including presentation of its views to officials of the executive branch, the Congress, or other appropriate authority. The head of each agency shall take the action required to assure that employees in the agency are apprised of their rights under this section, and that no interference, restraint, coercion, or discrimination is practiced within his agency to encourage or discourage membership in a labor organization.

(b) Paragraph (a) of this section does not authorize participation in the management of a labor organization or acting as a representative of such an organization by a supervisor, except as provided in section 24 of this Order, or by an employee when the participation or activity would result in a conflict or apparent conflict of interest or otherwise be incompatible with law or with the official duties of the employee.

Sec. 2. *Definitions.* When used in this Order, the term—

(a) "Agency" means an executive department, a Government corporation, and an independent establishment as defined in section 104 of title 5, United States Code, except the General Accounting Office;

---

* Additions made by Executive Order 11616 of August 26, 1971, are shown in boldface type.

(b) "Employee" means an employee of an agency and an employee of a nonappropriated fund instrumentality of the United States but does not include, for the purpose of exclusive recognition or national consultation rights, a supervisor, except as provided in section 24 of this Order;

(c) "Supervisor" means an employee having authority, in the interest of an agency, to hire, transfer, suspend, lay off, recall, promote, discharge, assign, reward, or discipline other employees, or responsibly to direct them, or to evaluate their performance, or to adjust their grievances, or effectively to recommend such action, if in connection with the foregoing the exercise of authority is not of a merely routine or clerical nature, but requires the use of independent judgment;

(d) "Guard" means an employee assigned to enforce against employees and other persons rules to protect agency property or the safety of persons on agency premises, or to maintain law and order in areas or facilities under Government control;

(e) "Labor organization" means a lawful organization of any kind in which employees participate and which exists for the purpose, in whole or in part, of dealing with agencies concerning grievances, personnel policies and practices, or other matters affecting the working conditions of their employees; but does not include an organization which—

(1) consists of management officials or supervisors, except as provided in section 24 of this Order;

(2) assists or participates in a strike against the Government of the United States or any agency thereof or imposes a duty or obligation to conduct, assist, or participate in such a strike;

(3) advocates the overthrow of the constitutional form of government in the United States; or

(4) discriminates with regard to the terms or conditions of membership because of race, color, creed, sex, age, or national origin;

(f) "Agency management" means the agency head and all management officials, supervisors, and other representatives of management having authority to act for the agency on any matters relating to the implementation of the agency labor-management relations program established under this Order;

(g) "Council" means the Federal Labor Relations Council established by this Order;

(h) "Panel" means the Federal Service Impasses Panel established by this Order; and

(i) "Assistant Secretary" means the Assistant Secretary of Labor for Labor-Management Relations.

Sec. 3. *Application.* (a) This Order applies to all employees and agencies in the executive branch, except as provided in paragraphs (b), (c) and (d) of this section.

(b) This Order (except section 22) does not apply to—

(1) the Federal Bureau of Investigation;

(2) the Central Intelligence Agency;

(3) any other agency, or office, bureau, or entity within an agency, which has as a primary function intelligence, investigative, or security work, when the head of the agency determines, in his sole judgment, that the Order cannot be applied in a manner consistent with national security requirements and considerations; or

(4) any office, bureau or entity within an agency which has as a primary function investigation or audit of the conduct or work of officials or employees of the agency for the purpose of ensuring honesty and integrity in the discharge of their official duties, when the head of the agency determines, in his sole judgment, that the Order cannot be applied in a manner consistent with the internal security of the agency.

(c) The head of an agency may, in his sole judgment, suspend any provision of this Order (except section 22) with respect to any agency installation or activity located outside the United States, when he determines that this is necessary in the national interest, subject to the conditions he prescribes.

(d) Employees engaged in administering a labor-management relations law or this Order shall not be represented by a labor organization which also represents other groups of employees under the law or this Order, or which is affiliated directly or indirectly with an organization which represents such a group of employees.

ADMINISTRATION

Sec. 4. *Federal Labor Relations Council.* (a) There is hereby established the Federal Labor Relations Council, which consists of the Chairman of the Civil Service Commission, who shall be chairman of the Council, the Secretary of Labor, the Director of the Office of Management and Budget, and such other officials of the executive branch as the President may designate from time to time. The Civil Service Commission shall provide administrative support and services to the Council to the extent authorized by law.

(b) The Council shall administer and interpret this Order, decide major policy issues, prescribe regulations, and from time to time, report and make recommendations to the President.

(c) The Council may consider, subject to its regulations—

(1) appeals from decisions of the Assistant Secretary issued pursuant to section 6 of this Order;

(2) appeals on negotiability issues as provided in section 11(c) of this Order;

(3) exceptions to arbitration awards; and

(4) other matters it deems appropriate to assure the effectuation of the purposes of this Order.

Sec. 5. *Federal Service Impasses Panel.* (a) There is hereby established the Federal Service Impasses Panel as an agency within the Council. The Panel consists of at least three members appointed by the President, one of whom he designates as chairman. The Council shall provide the services and staff assistance needed by the Panel.

(b) The Panel may consider negotiation impasses as provided in section 17 of this Order and may take any action it considers necessary to settle an impasse.

(c) The Panel shall prescribe regulations needed to administer its function under this Order.

Sec. 6. *Assistant Secretary of Labor for Labor-Management Relations.* (a) The Assistant Secretary shall—

(1) decide questions as to the appropriate unit for the purpose of exclusive recognition and related issues submitted for his consideration;

(2) supervise elections to determine whether a labor organization is the choice of a majority of the employees in an appropriate unit as their exclusive representative, and certify the results;

(3) decide questions as to the eligibility of labor organizations for national consultation rights under criteria prescribed by the Council;

(4) decide unfair labor practice complaints and alleged violations of the standards of conduct for labor organizations; and

(5) decide questions as to whether a grievance is subject to a negotiated grievance procedure or subject to arbitration under an agreement.

(b) In any matters arising under paragraph (a) of this section, the Assistant Secretary may require an agency or a labor organization to cease and desist from violations of this Order and require it to take such affirmative action as he considers appropriate to effectuate the policies of this Order.

(c) In performing the duties imposed on him by this section, the Assistant Secretary may request and use the services and assistance of employees of other agencies in accordance with section 1 of the Act of March 4, 1915, (38 Stat. 1084, as amended; 31 U.S.C. § 686).

(d) The Assistant Secretary shall prescribe regulations needed to administer his functions under this Order.

(e) If any matters arising under paragraph (a) of this section involve the Department of Labor, the duties of the Assistant Secretary described in paragraphs (a) and (b) of this section shall be performed by a member of the Civil Service Commission designated by the Chairman of the Commission.

RECOGNITION

Sec. 7. *Recognition in general.* (a) An agency shall accord exclusive recognition or national consultation rights at the request of a labor organization which meets the requirements for the recognition or consultation rights under this Order.

(b) A labor organization seeking recognition shall submit to the agency. a roster of its officers and representatives, a copy of its constitution and by-laws, and a statement of its objectives.

(c) When recognition of a labor organization has been accorded, the recognition continues as long as the organization continues to meet the requirements of this Order applicable to that recognition, except that this section does not require an election to determine whether an organization should become, or continue to be recognized as, exclusive representative of the employees in any unit or subdivision thereof within 12 months after a prior valid election with respect to such unit.

(d) Recognition of a labor organization does not—

(1) preclude an employee, regardless of whether he is in a unit of exclusive recognition from exercising grievance or appellate rights established by law or regulations; or from choosing his own representative in a grievance or appellate action, except when presenting a grievance under a negotiated procedure as provided in section 13;

(2) preclude or restrict consultations and dealings between an agency and a veterans organization with respect to matters of particular interest to employees with veterans preference; or

(3) preclude an agency from consulting or dealing with a religious, social, fraternal, professional or other lawful association, not qualified as a labor organization, with respect to matters or policies which involve individual members of the association or are of particular applicability to it or its members. Consultations and dealings under subparagraph (3) of this paragraph shall be so limited that they do not assume the character of formal consultation on matters of general employee-management policy, except as provided in paragraph (e) of this section, or extend to areas where recognition of the interests of one employee group may result in discrimination against or injury to the interests of other employees.

(e) An agency shall establish a system for intra-management communication and consultation with its supervisors or associations of supervisors. These communications and consultations shall have as their purposes the improvement of agency operations, the improvement of working conditions of supervisors, the exchange of information, the improvement of managerial effectiveness, and the establishment of policies that best serve the public interest in accomplishing the mission of the agency.

(f) Informal recognition **or formal recognition** shall not be accorded.

Sec. 8. [Revoked.]

Sec. 9. *National consultation rights.* (a) An agency shall accord national consultation rights to a labor organization which qualifies under criteria established by the Federal Labor Relations Council as the representative of a substantial number of employees of the agency. National consultation rights shall not be accorded for any unit where a labor organization already holds exclusive recognition at the national level for that unit. The granting of national consultation rights does not preclude an agency from appropriate dealings at the national level with other organizations on matters affecting their members. An agency shall terminate national consultation rights when the labor organization ceases to qualify under the established criteria.

(b) When a labor organization has been accorded national consultation rights, the agency, through appropriate officials, shall notify representatives of the organization of proposed substantive changes in personnel policies that affect employees it represents and provide an opportunity for the organization to comment on the proposed changes. The labor organization may suggest changes in the agency's personnel policies and have its views carefully considered. It may confer in person at reasonable times, on request, with appropriate officials on personnel policy matters, and at all times present its views thereon in writing. An agency is not required to consult with a labor organization on any matter on which it would not be required to meet and confer if the organization were entitled to exclusive recognition.

(c) Questions as to the eligibility of labor organizations for national consultation rights may be referred to the Assistant Secretary for decision.

Sec. 10. *Exclusive recognition.* (a) An agency shall accord exclusive recognition to a labor organization when the organization has been selected, in a secret ballot election, by a majority of the employees in an appropriate unit as their representative.

(b) A unit may be established on a plant or installation, craft, functional, or other basis which will ensure a clear and identifiable community of interest among the employees concerned and will promote effective dealings and efficiency of agency operations. A unit shall not be established solely on the basis of the extent to which employees in the proposed unit have organized, nor shall a unit be established if it includes—

(1) any management official or supervisor, except as provided in section 24;
(2) an employee engaged in Federal personnel work in other than a purely clerical capacity;
(3) any guard together with other employees; or
(4) both professional and nonprofessional employees, unless a majority of the professional employees vote for inclusion in the unit.
Questions as to the appropriate unit and related issues may be referred to the Assistant Secretary for decision.

(c) An agency shall not accord exclusive recognition to a labor organization as the representative of employees in a unit of guards if the organization admits to membership, or is affiliated directly or indirectly with an organization which admits to membership, employees other than guards.

(d) All elections shall be conducted under the supervision of the Assistant Secretary, or persons designated by him, and shall be by secret ballot. Each employee eligible to vote shall be provided the opportunity to choose the labor organization he wishes to represent him, from among those on the ballot, or "no union." Elections may be held to determine whether—

(1) a labor organization should be recognized as the exclusive representative of employees in a unit;

(2) a labor organization should replace another labor organization as the exclusive representative; or

(3) a labor organization should cease to be the exclusive representative.

(e) When a labor organization has been accorded exclusive recognition, it is the exclusive representative of employees in the unit and is entitled to act for and to negotiate agreements covering all employees in the unit. It is responsible for representing the interests of all employees in the unit without discrimination and without regard to labor organization membership. The labor organization shall be given the opportunity to be represented at formal discussions between management and employees or employee representatives concerning grievances, personnel policies and practices, or other matters affecting general working conditions of employees in the unit.

AGREEMENTS

Sec. 11. *Negotiation of agreements.* (a) An agency and a labor organization that has been accorded exclusive recognition, through appropriate representatives, shall meet at reasonable times and confer in good faith with respect to personnel policies and practices and matters affecting working conditions, so far as may be appropriate under applicable laws and regulations, including policies set forth in the Federal Personnel Manual, published agency policies and regulations, a national or other controlling agreement at a higher level in the agency, and this Order. They may negotiate an agreement, or any question arising thereunder; determine appropriate techniques, consistent with section 17 of this Order, to assist in such negotiation; and execute a written agreement or memorandum of understanding.

(b) In prescribing regulations relating to personnel policies and practices and working conditions, an agency shall have due regard for the obligation imposed by paragraph (a) of this section. However, the obligation to meet and confer does not include matters with respect to the mission of an agency; its budget; its organization; the number of employees; and the numbers, types, and grades of positions or employees assigned to an organizational unit, work project or tour of duty; the technology of performing its work; or its internal security practices. This does not preclude the parties from negotiating agreements providing appropriate arrangements for employees adversely affected by the impact of realignment of work forces or technological change.

(c) If, in connection with negotiations, an issue develops as to whether a proposal is contrary to law, regulation, controlling agreement, or this Order and therefore not negotiable, it shall be resolved as follows:

(1) An issue which involves interpretation of a controlling agreement at a higher agency level is resolved under the procedures of the controlling agreement, or, if none, under agency regulations;

(2) An issue other than as described in subparagraph (1) of this paragraph which arises at a local level may be referred by either party to the head of the agency for determination;

(3) An agency head's determination as to the interpretation of the agency's regulations with respect to a proposal is final;

(4) A labor organization may appeal to the Council for a decision when—

(i) it disagrees with an agency head's determination that a proposal would violate applicable law, regulation of appropriate authority outside the agency, or this Order, or

(ii) it believes that an agency's regulations, as interpreted by the agency head, violate applicable law, regulation of appropriate authority outside the agency, or this Order.

Sec. 12. *Basic provisions of agreements.* Each agreement between an agency and a labor organization is subject to the following requirements—

(a) in the administration of all matters covered by the agreement, officials and employees are governed by existing or future laws and the regulations of appropriate authorities, including policies set forth in the Federal Personnel Manual; by published agency policies and regulations in existence at the time the agreement was approved; and by subsequently published agency policies and regulations required by law or by the regulations of appropriate authorities, or authorized by the terms of a controlling agreement at a higher agency level;

(b) management officials of the agency retain the right, in accordance with applicable laws and regulations—

(1) to direct employees of the agency;

(2) to hire, promote, transfer, assign, and retain employees in positions within the agency, and to suspend, demote, discharge, or take other disciplinary action against employees;

(3) to relieve employees from duties because of lack of work or for other legitimate reasons;

(4) to maintain the efficiency of the Government operations entrusted to them;

(5) to determine the methods, means, and personnel by which such operations are to be conducted; and

(6) to take whatever actions may be necessary to carry out the mission of the agency in situations of emergency; and

(c) nothing in the agreement shall require an employee to become or to remain a member of a labor organization, or to pay money to the organization except pursuant to a voluntary, written authorization by a member for the payment of dues through payroll deductions.

The requirements of this section shall be expressly stated in the initial or basic agreement and apply to all supplemental, implementing, subsidiary, or informal agreements between the agency and the organization.

Sec. 13. *Grievance and arbitration procedures.* (a) An agreement between an agency and a labor organization shall provide a procedure, applicable only to the unit, for the consideration of grievances over the interpretation or application of the agreement. A negotiated grievance procedure may not cover any other matters, including matters for which statutory appeals procedures exist, and shall be the exclusive procedure available to the parties and the employees in the unit for resolving such grievances. However, any employee or group of employees in the unit may present such grievances to the agency and have them adjusted, without the intervention of the exclusive representative, as long as the adjustment is not inconsistent with the terms of the agreement and the exclusive representative has been given opportunity to be present at the adjustment.

(b) A negotiated procedure may provide for the arbitration of grievances over the interpretation or application of the agreement, but not over any other matters. Arbitration may be invoked only by the agency or the exclusive representative. Either party may file exceptions to an arbitrator's award with the Council, under regulations prescribed by the Council.

(c) Grievances initiated by an employee or group of employees in the unit on matters other than the interpretation or application of an existing agreement may be presented under any procedure available for the purpose.

(d) Questions that cannot be resolved by the parties as to whether or not a grievance is in a matter subject to the grievance procedure in an existing agreement, or is subject to arbitration under that agreement, may be referred to the Assistant Secretary for decision.

(e) No agreement may be established, extended or renewed after the effective date of this Order which does not conform to this section. However, this section is not applicable to agreements entered into before the effective date of this Order.

Sec. 14. [Revoked.]

Sec. 15. *Approval of agreements.* An agreement with a labor organization as the exclusive representative of employees in a unit is subject to the approval of the head of the agency or an official designated by him. An agreement shall be approved if it conforms to applicable laws, existing published agency policies and regulations (unless the agency has granted an exception to a policy or regulation) and regulations of other appropriate authorities. A local agreement subject to a national or other controlling agreement at a higher level shall be approved under the procedures of the controlling agreement, or, if none, under agency regulations.

NEGOTIATION DISPUTES AND IMPASSES

Sec. 16. *Negotiation disputes.* The Federal Mediation and Conciliation Service shall provide services and assistance to Federal agencies and labor organizations in the resolution of negotiation disputes. The Service shall determine under what circumstances and in what manner it shall proffer its services.

Sec. 17. *Negotiation impasses.* When voluntary arrangements, including the services of the Federal Mediation and Conciliation Service or other third-party mediation, fail to resolve a negotiation impasse, either party may request the Federal Service Impasses Panel to consider the matter. The Panel, in its discretion and under the regulations it prescribes, may consider the matter and may recommend procedures to the parties for the resolution of the impasse or may settle the impasse by appropriate action. Arbitration or third-party fact finding with recommendation to assist in the resolution of an impasse may be used by the parties only when authorized or directed by the Panel.

CONDUCT OF LABOR ORGANIZATIONS AND MANAGEMENT

Sec. 18. *Standards of conduct for labor organizations.* (a) An agency shall accord recognition only to a labor organization that is free from corrupt influences and influences opposed to basic democratic principles. Except as provided in paragraph (b) of this section, an organization is not required to prove that it has the required freedom when it is subject to governing requirements adopted by the organization or by a national or international labor organization or federation of labor organizations with which it is affiliated or in which it participates, containing explicit and detailed provisions to which it subscribes calling for—

(1) the maintenance of democratic procedures and practices, including provisions for periodic elections to be conducted subject to recognized safeguards and provisions defining and securing the right of individual members to participation in the affairs of the organization, to fair and equal treatment under the governing rules of the organization, and to fair process in disciplinary proceedings;

(2) the exclusion from office in the organization of persons affiliated with Communist or other totalitarian movements and persons identified with corrupt influences;

(3) the prohibition of business or financial interests on the part of organization officers and agents which conflict with their duty to the organization and its members; and

(4) the maintenance of fiscal integrity in the conduct of the affairs of the organization including provision for accounting and financial controls and regular financial reports or summaries to be made available to members.

(b) Notwithstanding the fact that a labor organization has adopted or subscribed standards of conduct as provided in paragraph (a) of this section, the organization is required to furnish evidence of its freedom from corrupt influences or influences opposed to basic democratic principles when there is reasonable cause to believe that—

(1) the organization has been suspended or expelled from or is subject to other sanctions by a parent labor organization or federation of organizations with which it had been affiliated because it has demonstrated an unwillingness or inability to comply with governing requirements comparable in purpose to those required by paragraph (a) of this section; or

(2) the organization is in fact subject to influences that would preclude recognition under this Order.

(c) A labor organization which has or seeks recognition as a representative of employees under this Order shall file financial and other reports, provide for bonding of officials and employees of the organization, and comply with trusteeship and election standards.

(d) The Assistant Secretary shall prescribe the regulations needed to effectuate this section. These regulations shall conform generally to the principles applied to unions in the private sector. Complaints of violations of this section shall be filed with the Assistant Secretary.

Sec. 19. *Unfair labor practices.* (a) Agency management shall not —

(1) interfere with, restrain, or coerce an employee in the exercise of the rights assured by this Order;

(2) encourage or discourage membership in a labor organization by discrimination in regard to hiring, tenure, promotion, or other conditions of employment;

(3) sponsor, control, or otherwise assist a labor organization, except that an agency may furnish customary and routine services and facilities under section 23 of this Order when consistent with the best interests of the agency, its employees, and the organization, and when the services and facilities are furnished, if requested, on an impartial basis to organizations having equivalent status;

(4) discipline or otherwise discriminate against an employee because he has filed a complaint or given testimony under this Order;

(5) refuse to accord appropriate recognition to a labor organization qualified for such recognition; or

(6) refuse to consult, confer, or negotiate with a labor organization as required by this Order.

(b) A labor organization shall not—

(1) interfere with, restrain, or coerce an employee in the exercise of his rights assured by this Order;

(2) attempt to induce agency management to coerce an employee in the exercise of his rights under this Order;

(3) coerce, attempt to coerce, or discipline, fine, or take other economic sanction against a member of the organization as punishment or reprisal for, or for the purpose of hindering or impeding his work performance, his productivity, or the discharge of his duties owed as an officer or employee of the United States;

(4) call or engage in a strike, work stoppage, or slowdown; picket an agency in a labor-management dispute; or condone any such activity by failing to take affirmative action to prevent or stop it;

(5) discriminate against an employee with regard to the terms or conditions of membership because of race, color, creed, sex, age, or national origin; or

(6) refuse to consult, confer, or negotiate with an agency as required by this Order.

(c) A labor organization which is accorded exclusive recognition shall not deny membership to any employee in the appropriate unit except for failure to meet reasonable occupational standards uniformly required for admission, or for failure to tender initiation fees and dues uniformly required as a condition of acquiring and retaining membership. This paragraph does not preclude a labor organization from enforcing discipline in accordance with procedures under its constitution or by-laws which conform to the requirements of this Order.

(d) Issues which can properly be raised under an appeals procedure may not be raised under this section. Issues which can be raised under a grievance procedure may, in the discretion of the aggrieved party, be raised under that procedure or the complaint procedure under this section, but not under both procedures. Appeals or grievance decisions shall not be con-

strued as unfair labor practice decisions under this Order nor as precedent for such decisions
All complaints under this section that cannot be resolved by the parties shall be filed with
the Assistant Secretary.

MISCELLANEOUS PROVISIONS

Sec. 20. *Use of official time.* Solicitation of membership or dues, and other internal busi
ness of a labor organization, shall be conducted during the non-duty hours of the employee
concerned. Employees who represent a recognized labor organization shall not be on offici:
time when negotiating an agreement with agency management, except to the extent that th
negotiating parties agree to other arrangements which may provide that the agency will eithe
authorize official time for up to 40 hours or authorize up to one-half the time spent in ne
gotiations during regular working hours, for a reasonable number of employees, which number
normally shall not exceed the number of management representatives.

Sec. 21. *Allotment of dues.* (a) When a labor organization holds exclusive recognition
and the agency and the organization agree in writing to this course of action, an agency may
deduct the regular and periodic dues of the organization from the pay of members of the or
ganization in the unit of recognition who make a voluntary allotment for that purpose. Such
an allotment is subject to the regulations of the Civil Service Commission, which shall includ
provision for the employee to revoke his authorization at stated six-month intervals. Such a
allotment terminates when—

(1) the dues withholding agreement between the agency and the labor organization is te:
minated or ceases to be applicable to the employee; or

(2) the employee has been suspended or expelled from the labor organization.

(b) An agency may deduct the regular and periodic dues of an association of manage
ment officials or supervisors from the pay of members of the association who make a volun
tary allotment for that purpose, when the agency and the association agree in writing to th
course of action. Such an allotment is subject to the regulations of the Civil Service Commi
sion.

Sec. 22. *Adverse action appeals.* The head of each agency, in accordance with the prov
sions of this Order and regulations prescribed by the Civil Service Commission, shall exter
to all employees in the competitive civil service rights identical in adverse action cases to tho
provided preference eligibles under sections 7511-7512 of title 5 of the United States Cod
Each employee in the competitive service shall have the right to appeal to the Civil Servi
Commission from an adverse decision of the administrative officer so acting, such appeal to l
processed in an identical manner to that provided for appeals under section 7701 of title
of the United States Code. Any recommendation by the Civil Service Commission submitte
to the head of an agency on the basis of an appeal by an employee in the competitive servi
shall be complied with by the head of the agency.

Sec. 23. *Agency implementation.* No later than April 1, 1970, each agency shall issue a
propriate policies and regulations consistent with this Order for its implementation. This i
cludes but is not limited to a clear statement of the rights of its employees under this Orde
procedures with respect to recognition of labor organizations, determination of appropria
units, consultation and negotiation with labor organizations, approval of agreements, medi
tion, and impasse resolution; policies with respect to the use of agency facilities by lab
organizations; and policies and practices regarding consultation with other organizations ai
associations and individual employees. Insofar as practicable, agencies shall consult with repr
sentatives of labor organizations in the formulation of these policies and regulations, oth
than those for the implementation of section 7(e) of this Order.

Sec. 24. *Savings clauses.* This Order does not preclude—

(1) the renewal or continuation of a lawful agreement between an agency and a representative of its employees entered into before the effective date of Executive Order No. 10988 (January 17, 1962) ; or

(2) the renewal, continuation, or initial according of recognition for units of management officials or supervisors represented by labor organizations which historically or traditionally represent the management officials or supervisors in private industry and which hold exclusive recognition for units of such officials or supervisors in any agency on the date of this Order.

Sec. 25. *Guidance, training, review and information.* (a) The Civil Service Commission, in conjunction with the Office of Management and Budget, shall establish and maintain a program for the policy guidance of agencies on labor-management relations in the Federal service and periodically review the implementation of these policies. The Civil Service Commission shall continuously review the operation of the Federal labor-management relations program to assist in assuring adherence to its provisions and merit system requirements; implement technical advice and information programs for the agencies; assist in the development of programs for training agency personnel and management officials in labor-management relations; and, from time to time, report to the Council on the state of the program with any recommendations for its improvement.

(b) The Department of Labor and the Civil Service Commission shall develop programs for the collection and dissemination of information appropriate to the needs of agencies, organizations and the public.

Sec. 26. *Effective date.* This Order is effective on January 1, 1970, except sections 7(f) and 8 which are effective immediately. Effective January 1, 1970, Executive Order No. 10988 and the President's Memorandum of May 21, 1963, entitled Standards of Conduct for Employee Organizations and Code of Fair Labor Practices are revoked.

RICHARD NIXON

THE WHITE HOUSE
October 29, 1969

FEDERAL SERVICE IMPASSES PANEL

5 CFR Parts 2470 and 2471

GENERAL; PROCEDURES OF THE PANEL

Notice of Proposed Rule Making

Notice is hereby given that the Federal Service Impasses Panel, pursuant to Section 5 of Executive Order 11491 of October 29, 1969, is considering the adoption of rules governing the organization and responsibilities of the Panel. A draft of these rules is set out below as Parts 2470 and 2471, Subchapter C, Chapter XIV of Title 5 of the Code of Federal Regulations. Interested persons may submit their views and suggestions in writing to the Executive Secretary, Federal Service Impasses Panel, 1900 E Street, N.W., Washington, D.C. 20415. All communications received within 20 days after publication of this notice in the Federal Register will be considered before the Panel takes final action on the proposed rules.

CHAPTER XIV, SUBCHAPTER C, FEDERAL SERVICE IMPASSES PANEL

PART 2470 GENERAL

Authority: The provisions of Part 2470 issued under 5 U.S.C. 3301, 7301; E. O. 11491, 34 F.R. 17605, 3 CFR 191, 1969 Comp.

SUBPART A - PURPOSE

Sec. 2470.1 Purpose.

The regulations contained in this subchapter are intended to implement the provisions of Sections 5 and 17 of Executive Order 11491 of October 29, 1969, entitled "Labor-Management Relations in the Federal Service." They prescribe procedures and methods which the Federal Service Impasses Panel may utilize in the resolution of negotiation impasses when the parties negotiating a labor agreement have failed to reach a full settlement by voluntary arrangements.

SUBPART B - DEFINITIONS

Sec. 2470.2 Definitions.

The following definitions are used in this subchapter:

Executive Secretary means the Executive Secretary of the Panel.

Factfinder(s) means members or staff of the Panel, individuals designated by the Panel, or other persons selected jointly by the parties when so authorized or directed by the Panel.

Impasse means that point in negotiations at which the parties are unable to reach full agreement; provided, however, that they have made earnest efforts to reach agreement by direct negotiations and have used without success voluntary arrangements for settlement.

Panel means the Federal Service Impasses Panel or a quorum thereof.

Party means the Federal agency, establishment or activity or the labor organization, as defined in Sections 2(a) and (e) of the Order, participating in the negotiation of a labor-management agreement.

Voluntary arrangements means those methods adopted by the parties for the purpose of assisting them in their negotiation of a labor agreement, which may include (a) joint fact-finding committees without recommendations; (b) referral to a higher authority within the agency and/or the labor organization; (c) utilization of the services of the Federal Mediation and Conciliation Service or other third-party mediation assistance; or (d) any other method which the parties deem appropriate except third-party factfinding with recommendations, or arbitration unless these methods are expressly authorized or directed by the Panel.

PART 2471 PROCEDURES OF THE PANEL

Authority: The provisions of Part 2471 issued under 5 U.S.C. 3301, 7301; E. O. 11491, 34 F.R. 17605, 3 CFR 191, 1969 Comp.

Sec. 2471.1 Who may initiate.

(a) When an impasse occurs during the course of labor negotiations, either party, or the parties jointly, may request the Panel to consider the matter, by filing a request as hereinafter provided.

(b) The Panel may, upon the referral of the Executive Secretary, undertake the consideration of any matter where voluntary arrangements have failed and neither party has requested the Panel's consideration.

Sec. 2471.2   What to file.

A request to the Panel for consideration of an impasse must be in writing and include the following essential information:

(a) Identification of the parties and person(s) authorized to initiate the request;

(b) Statement that an impasse has been reached;

(c) Statement of unresolved issues and the present position(s) of the initiating party or parties with respect to those issues; and

(d) The nature and extent of all voluntary arrangements utilized.

Sec. 2471.3 Request form.

FSIP Form 1 has been prepared for use by the parties in filing a request to the Panel for consideration of a negotiation impasse. [1] Copies are available upon request to the Office of the Executive Secretary.

Sec. 2471.4 Where to file.

Requests to the Panel provided for in this part, and inquiries or correspondence on the status of impasses or other related matters, should be directed to the Executive Secretary, Federal Service Impasses Panel, 1900 E Street, N.W., Washington, D.C. 20415.

Sec. 2471.5 Copies and service.

Concurrently with the submission of a request for Panel consideration, or when the Panel acts on its own motion, a copy of such request or Panel action shall be served by the party initiating the request or by the Panel on the party(ies) to the dispute and on any third party, if utilized.

Sec. 2471.6 Initial procedures of the Panel.

(a) Upon receipt of a request for consideration of an impasse, the Panel will review the request and determine whether:

(1) Negotiations should be resumed;

(2) Other voluntary arrangements should be utilized by the parties to help resolve the impasse; or

---

[1] Filed as a part of the original document.

(3) The Panel will proceed under its authority as prescribed in
Sections 2471.7 - 2471.14.

(b) The Panel will not process requests whenever it determines
that the impasse is based solely on the negotiability of an issue or
issues. In such cases, the filing party will be directed to avail itself
of the remedies provided for in Section 11(c) of the Order. However,
when any of the several subjects of the impasse is based on the negotiability of an issue, then such subject(s) shall be referred for handling
under Section 11(c) and the balance of the dispute will be considered by
the Panel.

(c) The parties will be promptly advised in writing of the Panel's
decision.

Sec. 2471.7 Use of voluntary factfinding with recommendations, or
             arbitration.

The parties may resort to voluntary factfinding with recommendations, or arbitration, to resolve an impasse, only when authorized or
directed by the Panel, and provided they have:

(a) Made a joint request to the Panel in writing for such
authority;

(b) Agreed on the method of selecting the thrid party;

(c) Agreed to share the cost of the proceedings; and

(d) Used without success any other voluntary arrangement for
settlement.

Sec. 2471.8 Definition of issue(s); appointment of factfinder(s).

When the Panel determines that resolution of an impasse requires
factfinding, it will:

(a) Specify the issue(s) to be resolved; and

(b) Appoint a factfinder(s) to conduct the hearing.

Sec. 2471.9 Notice of hearing.

The notice of hearing will provide at least ten (10) days notice
and shall be served on the parties to the impasse and will include:

(a) The names of the parties to the dispute;

(b) The time, place and nature of the hearing;

(c) The issues to be resolved; and

(d) The name(s) of the factfinder(s) appointed.

Sec. 2471.10 Authority of factfinder(s).

Factfinders are authorized to:

(a) Administer oaths or affirmations;

(b) Take testimony by deposition;

(c) Require a verbatim report of the proceedings;

(d) Conduct the hearing in open or closed sessions; and

(e) Permit briefs to be filed after the close of a hearing.

Sec. 2471.11 Availability of hearing transcript.

When a verbatim report of any proceeding is authorized, the parties
will make their own arrangements with the reporter for the purchase of
copies. A copy will be available for inspection by either party to the
proceeding at the Office of the Executive Secretary.

Sec. 2471.12 Report of the factfinder(s) and action by the Panel.

(a) The factfinder(s) shall submit a report to the Panel within
a reasonable time, normally not to exceed 30 days, after the close of
the hearing. The parties will be advised when the report has been transmitted to the Panel. The report will include findings on:

(1) The history of the current negotiations, including the initial
positions of the parties, and a report of items agreed to in whole or
part;

(2) The unresolved issues and the efforts made by the parties to
reach agreement thereon;

(3) The context within which the negotiations have taken place; and

(4) Any other matters relevant to the impasse.

(b) After receipt of the report of the factfinder(s), the Panel
will evaluate the impasse and issue its recommendations to the parties
for settlement.

Sec. 2471.13 Duty of each party.

(a) Within a period not to exceed thirty (30) days following receipt of the Panel's recommendations for settlement, each party must eithe

(1) Accept the Panel's recommendations and so notify the Executive Secretary; or

(2) Reach with the other party a settlement of all unresolved issues, and so notify the Executive Secretary; or

(3) Submit a written statement to the Panel setting forth its reasons for not accepting the Panel's recommendations and reaching a settlement of all unresolved issues.

(b) A reasonable extension of the 30-day period may be authorized by the Executive Secretary for good cause shown when requested in writing by either party prior to the expiration of the 30-day period.

Sec. 2471.14 Settlement action by the Panel.

In the event that there remains any unresolved issues thirty (30) days following issuance of the Panel's recommendations, or any extension thereof, the Panel, after due consideration of the reports of the parties, will take whatever action it deems necessary to bring the dispute to settlement.

David T. Roadley
Executive Secretary

FEDERAL MEDIATION AND CONCILIATION SERVICE: ARBITRATION POLICIES, FUNCTIONS, AND PROCEDURES

CHAPTER XII—FEDERAL MEDIATION AND CONCILIATION SERVICE

PART 1404—ARBITRATION

On June 21, 1968, notice of proposed rule changes was published in the *Federal Register* (68 F.R. 7358). There were set out therein the proposed revisions of Chapter XII, Title 29, of the Code of Federal Regulations, relating to the Service's arbitration policies and procedures. Comments which were received concerning the proposed regulations have been considered. The amendatory regulations as set forth below are hereby adopted to be effective October 21, 1968, and shall as of that date supersede the present regulations which are set forth in 29 CFR Part 1404.

Authority: The provisions of this Part 1404 issued under sec. 202, 61 Stat. 153, as amended; 29 U.S.C. 172. Interpret or apply sec. 3, 80 Stat. 250, sec. 203, 61 Stat. 153; 5 U.S.C. 552, 29 U.S.C. 173.

§ 1404.1 ARBITRATION

The labor policy of the U.S. Government is designed to foster and promote free collective bargaining. Voluntary arbitration is encouraged by public policy and is in fact almost universally utilized by the parties to resolve disputes involving the interpretation or application of collective bargaining agreements. Also, in appropriate cases, voluntary arbitration or factfinding are tools of free collective bargaining and may be desirable alternatives to economic strife in determining terms of a collective bargaining agreement. The parties assume broad responsibilities for the success of the private juridical system they have chosen. The Service will assist the parties in their selection of arbitrators.

§ 1404.2 COMPOSITION OF ROSTER MAINTAINED BY THE SERVICE

(a) It is the policy of the Service to maintain on its roster only those arbitrators who are qualified and acceptable, and who adhere to ethical standards.

(b) Applicants for inclusion on its roster must not only be well-grounded in the field of labor-management relations, but, also, usually possess experience in the labor arbitration field or its equivalent. After a careful screening and evaluation of the applicant's experience, the Service contacts representatives of both labor and management since arbitrators must be generally acceptable to those who utilize its arbitration facilities. The responses to such inquiries are carefully weighed before an otherwise qualified arbitrator is included on the Service's roster. Persons employed full time as representatives of management, labor, or the Federal Government are not included on the Service's roster.

(c) The arbitrators on the roster are expected to keep the Service informed of changes in address, occupation or availability, and of any business connections with or of concern to labor or management. The Service reserves the right to remove names from the active roster or to take other appropriate action where there is good reason to believe that an arbitrator is not adhering to these regulations and related policy.

§ 1404.3 SECURITY STATUS

The arbitrators on the Service's roster are not employees of the Federal Government, and, because of this status, the Service does not investigate their security status. Moreover, when an arbitrator is selected by the parties, he is retained by them and, accordingly, they must assume complete responsibility for the arbitrator's security status.

§ 1404.4 PROCEDURES; HOW TO REQUEST ARBITRATION SERVICES

The Service prefers to act upon a joint request which should be addressed to the Director of the Federal Mediation and Conciliation Service, Washington, D.C. 20427. In the event that the request is made by only one party, the Service may act if the parties have agreed that either of them may seek a panel of arbitrators, either by specific ad hoc agreement or by specific language in the applicable collective bargaining agreement. A brief statement of the nature of the issues in dispute should accompany the request, to enable the Service to submit the names of arbitrators qualified for the issues involved. The request should also include a copy of the collective bargaining agreement or stipulation. In the event that the entire agreement is not available, a verbatim copy of the provisions relating to arbitration should accompany the request.

§ 1404.5 ARBITRABILITY

Where either party claims that a dispute is not subject to arbitration, the Service will not decide the merits of such claim. The submission of a panel should not be construed as anything more than compliance with a request.

§ 1404.6 NOMINATIONS OF ARBITRATORS

(a) When the parties have been unable to agree on an arbitrator, the Service will submit to the parties the names of seven arbitrators unless the applicable collective bargaining agreement provides for a different number, or unless the parties themselves request a different number. Together with the submission of a panel of suggested arbitrators, the Service furnishes a short statement of the background, qualifications, experience and per diem fee of each of the nominees.

(b) In selecting names for inclusion on a panel, the Service considers many factors, but the desires of the parties are, of course, the foremost consideration. If at any time both the company and the union suggest that a name or names be omitted from a panel, such name or names will be omitted. If one party only (a company or a union) suggests that a name or names be omitted from a panel, such name or names will generally be omitted, subject to the following qualifications: (1) If the suggested omissions are excessive in number or otherwise appear to lack careful consideration, they will not be considered; (2) all such suggested omissions should be reviewed after the passage of a reasonable period of time. The Service will not place names on a panel at the request of one party unless the other party has knowledge of such request and has no objection thereto, or unless both parties join in such request. If the issue described in the request appears to require special technical experience or qualifications, arbitrators who possess such qualifications will, where possible, be included in the list submitted to the parties. Where the parties expressly request that the list be composed entirely of technicians, or that it be all-local or nonlocal, such request will be honored, if qualified arbitrators are available.

(c) Two possible methods of selection from a panel are—(1) at a joint meeting, alternately striking names from the submitted panel until one remains, and (2) each party separately advising the Service of its order of preferences by numbering each name of the panel. In almost all cases, an arbitrator is chosen from one panel of names. However, if a request for another panel is made, the Service will comply with the request, providing that additional panels are permissible under the terms of the agreement or the parties so stipulate.

(d) Subsequent adjustment of disputes is not precluded by the submission of a panel or an appointment. A substantial number of issues are being settled by the parties themselves after the initial request for a panel and after selection of the arbitrator. Notice of such settlement should be sent promptly to the arbitrator and to the Service.

(e) The arbitrator is entitled to be compensated whenever he receives insufficient notice of settlement to enable him to rearrange his schedule of arbitration hearings or working hours. In other situations, when an arbitrator spends an unusually large amount of time in arranging or rearranging hearing dates, it may be appropriate for him to make an administraitve charge to the parties in the event the case is settled before hearing.

§ 1404.7 APPOINTMENT OF ARBITRATORS

(a) After the parties notify the Service of their selection, the arbitrator is appointed by the Director. If any party fails to notify the Service within 15 days after the date of mailing the panel, all persons named therein may be deemed acceptable to such party. The service will make a direct appointment of an arbitrator based upon a joint request, or upon a unilateral request when the applicable collective bargaining agreement so authorizes.

(b) The arbitrator, upon appointment notification, is requested to communicate with the parties immediately to arrange for preliminary matters such as date and place of hearing.

§ 1404.8 STATUS OF ARBITRATORS AFTER APPOINTMENT

After appointment, the legal relationship of arbitrators is with the parties rather than the Service, though the Service does have a continuing interest in the proceedings. Industrial peace and good labor relations are enhanced by arbitrators who function justly, expeditiously and impartially so as to obtain and retain the respect, esteem and confidence of all participants in the arbitration proceedings. The conduct of the arbitration proceeding is under the arbitrator's jurisdiction and control, subject to such rules of procedure as the parties may jointly prescribe. He is to make his own decisions based on the record in the proceedings. The arbitrator may, unless prohibited by law, proceed in the absence of any party who, after due notice, fails to be present or to obtain a postponement. The award, however, must be supported by evidence.

§ 1404.9 PROMPT DECISION

(a) Early hearing and decision of industrial disputes is desirable in the interest of good labor relations. The parties should inform the Service whenever a decision is unduly delayed. The Service expects to be notified by the arbitrator if and when (1) he cannot schedule, hear and determine issues promptly, and (2) he is advised that a dispute has been settled by the parties prior to arbitration.

(b) The award shall be made not later than 30 days from the date of the closing of the hearing, or the receipt of a transcript and any post-hearing briefs, or if oral hearings have been waived, then from the date of receipt of the final statements and proof by the arbitrator, unless otherwise agreed upon by the parties or specified by law. However, a failure to make such an award within 30 days shall not invalidate an award.

§ 1404.10 ARBITRATOR'S AWARD AND REPORT

(a) At the conclusion of the hearing and after the award has been submitted to the parties, each arbitrator is required to file a copy with the Service. The arbitrator is further required to submit a report showing a breakdown of his fees and expense charges so that the Service may be in a position to check conformance with its fee policies. Cooperation in filing both award and report within 15 days after handing down the award is expected of all arbitrators.

(b) It is the policy of the Service not to release arbitration decisions for publication without the consent of both parties. Furthermore, the Service expects the arbitrators it has nominated or appointed not to give publicity to awards they may issue, except in a manner agreeable to both parties.

§ 1404.11 FEES OF ARBITRATORS

(a) No administrative or filing fee is charged by the Service. The current policy of the Service permits each of its nominees or appointees to charge a per diem fee for his services, the amount of which is certified in advance by him to the Service. Each arbitrator's maximum per diem fee is set forth on his biographical sketch which is sent to the parties at such time as his name is submitted to them for consideration. The arbitrator shall not change his per diem fee without giving at least 90 days advance notice to the Service of his intention to do so.

(b) in those rare instances where arbitrators fix wages or other important terms of a new contract, the maximum fee noted above may be exceeded by the arbitrator after agreement by the parties. Conversely, an arbitrator may give due consideration to the financial condition of the parties and charge less than his usual fee in appropriate cases.

§ 1404.12 CONDUCT OF HEARINGS

The Service does not prescribe detailed or specific rules of procedure for the conduct of an arbitration proceeding because it favors flexibility in labor relations. Questions such as hearing rooms, submission of prehearing or posthearing briefs, and recording of testimony, are left to the discretion of the individual arbitrator and to the parties. The Service does, however, expect its arbitrators and the parties to conform to applicable laws, and to be guided by ethical and procedural standards as codified by appropriate professional organizations and generally accepted by the industrial community and experienced arbitrators.

In cities where the Service maintains offices, the parties are welcome upon request to the Service to use its conference rooms when they are available.

Appendix IV

TYPICAL STATE
ARBITRATION STATUTES

NEW YORK STATE ARBITRATION LAW,

ARTICLE 75

§ 7501. **Effect of arbitration agreement.**

A written agreement to submit any controversy thereafter arising or any existing controversy to arbitration is enforceable without regard to the justiciable character of the controversy and confers jurisdiction on the courts of the state to enforce it and to enter judgment on an award.

§ 7502. **Applications to the court; venue; statutes of limitation.**

(a) **Applications to the court; venue.** A special proceeding shall be used to bring before a court the first application arising out of an arbitrable controversy which is not made by motion in a pending action. The proceeding shall be brought in the court and county specified in the agreement; or, if none be specified, in a court in the county in which one of the parties resides or is doing business, or, if there is no such county, in a court in any county; or in a court in the county in which the arbitration was held. All subsequent applications shall be made by motion in the pending action or the special proceeding.

(b) **Limitation of time.** If, at the time that a demand for arbitration was made or a notice of intention to arbitrate was served, the claim sought to be arbitrated would have been barred by limitation of time had it been asserted in a court of the state, a party may assert the limitation as a bar to the arbitration on an application to the court as provided in section 7503 or subdivision (b) of section 7511. The failure to assert such bar by such application shall not preclude its assertion before the arbitrators, who may, in their sole discretion, apply or not apply the bar. Except as provided in subdivision (b) of section 7511, such exercise of discretion by the arbitrators shall not be subject to review by a court on an application to confirm, vacate or modify the award.

§ 7503.   **Application to compel or stay arbitration; stay of action; notice of intention to arbitrate.**

(a) **Application to compel arbitration; stay of action.** A party aggrieved by the failure of another to arbitrate may apply for an order compelling arbitration. Where there is no substantial question whether a valid agreement was made or complied with, and the claim sought to be arbitrated is not barred by limitation under subdivision (b) of section 7502, the court shall direct the parties to arbitrate. Where any such question is raised, it shall be tried forthwith in said court. If an issue claimed to be arbitrable is involved in an action pending in a court having jurisdiction to hear a motion to compel arbitration, the application shall be made by motion in that action. If the application is granted, the order shall operate to stay a pending or subsequent action, or so much of it as is referable to arbitration.

(b) **Application to stay arbitration.** Subject to the provisions of subdivision (c), a party who has not participated in the arbitration and who has not made or been served with an application to compel arbitration, may apply to stay arbitration on the ground that a valid agreement was not made or has not been complied with or that the claim sought to be, arbitrated is barred by limitation under subdivision (b) of section 7502.

(c) **Notice of intention to arbitrate.** A party may serve upon another party a notice of intention to arbitrate, specifying the agreement pursuant to which arbitration is sought and the name and address of the party serving the notice, or of an officer or agent thereof if such party is an association or corporation, and stating that unless the party served applies to stay the arbitration within ten days after such service he shall thereafter be precluded from objecting that a valid agreement was not made or has not been complied with and from asserting in court the bar of a limitation of time. Such notice shall be served in the same manner as a summons or by registered or certified mail, return receipt requested. An application to stay arbitration must be made by the party served within ten days after service upon him of the notice or he shall be so precluded. Notice of such application shall be served in the same manner as a summons or by registered or certified mail, return receipt requested.

§ 7504.   **Court appointment of arbitrator.**

If the arbitration agreement does not provide for a method of appointment of an arbitrator, or if the agreed method fails or for any reason is not followed, or if an arbitrator fails to act and his successor has not been appointed, the court, on application of a party, shall appoint an arbitrator.

§ 7505. Powers of arbitrator.

An arbitrator and any attorney of record in the arbitration proceeding has the power to issue subpoenas. An arbitrator has the power to administer oaths.

§ 7506. Hearing.

(a) **Oath of arbitrator.** Before hearing any testimony, an arbitrator shall be sworn to hear and decide the controversy faithfully and fairly by an officer authorized to administer an oath.

(b) **Time and place.** The arbitrator shall appoint a time and place for the hearing and notify the parties in writing personally or by registered or certified mail not less than eight days before the hearing. The arbitrator may adjourn or postpone the hearing. The court, upon application of any party, may direct the arbitrator to proceed promptly with the hearing and determination of the controversy.

(c) **Evidence.** The parties are entitled to be heard, to present evidence and to cross-examine witnesses. Notwithstanding the failure of a party duly notified to appear, the arbitrator may hear and determine the controversy upon the evidence produced.

(d) **Representation by attorney.** A party has the right to be represented by an attorney and may claim such right at any time as to any part of the arbitration or hearings which have not taken place. This right may not be waived. If a party is represented by an attorney, papers to be served on the party shall be served upon his attorney.

(e) **Determination by majority.** The hearing shall be conducted by all the arbitrators, but a majority may determine any question and render an award.

(f) **Waiver.** Except as provided in subdivision (d), a requirement of this section may be waived by written consent of the parties and it is waived if the parties continue with the arbitration without objection.

§ 7507. Award; form; time; delivery.

Except as provided in section 7508, the award shall be in writing, signed and acknowledged by the arbitrator making it within the time fixed by the agreement, or, if the time is not fixed, within such time as the court orders. The parties may in writing extend the time either before or after its expiration. A party waives the objection that an award was not made within the time required unless he notifies the arbitrator in writing of his objection prior to the delivery of the award to him. The arbitrator shall deliver a copy of the award to each party in the manner provided in the agreement, or, if no provision is so made, personally or by registered or certified mail, return receipt requested.

§ 7508. **Award by confession.**

(a) **When available.** An award by confession may be made for money due or to become due at any time before an award is otherwise made. The award shall be based upon a statement, verified by each party, containing an authorization to make the award, the sum of the award or the method of ascertaining it, and the facts constituting the liability.

(b) **Time of award.** The award may be made at any time within three months after the statement is verified.

(c) **Person or agency making award.** The award may be made by an arbitrator or by the agency or person named by the parties to designate the arbitrator.

§ 7509. **Modification of award by arbitrator.**

On written application of a party to the arbitrators within twenty days after delivery of the award to the applicant, the arbitrators may modify the award upon the grounds stated in subdivision (c) of section 7511. Written notice of the application shall be given to other parties to the arbitration. Written objection to modification must be served on the arbitrators and other parties to the arbitration within ten days of receipt of the notice. The arbitrators shall dispose of any application made under this section in writing, signed and acknowledged by them, within thirty days after either written objection to modification has been served on them or the time for serving said objection has expired, whichever is earlier. The parties may in writing extend the time for such disposition either before or after its expiration.

§ 7510. **Confirmation of award.**

The court shall confirm an award upon application of a party made within one year after its delivery to him, unless the award is vacated or modified upon a ground specified in section 7511.

§ 7511. **Vacating or modifying award.**

(a) **When application made.** An application to vacate or modify an award may be made by a party within ninety days after its delivery to him.

(b) **Grounds for vacating.**

1. The award shall be vacated on the application of a party who either participated in the arbitration or was served with a notice of intention to arbitrate if the court finds that the rights of that party were prejudiced by:

(i) corruption, fraud or misconduct in procuring the award; or

(ii) partiality of an arbitrator appointed as a neutral, except where the award was by confession; or

(iii) an arbitrator, or agency or person making the award exceeded his power or so imperfectly executed it that a final and definite award upon the subject matter submitted was not made; or

(iv) failure to follow the procedure of this article, unless the party applying to vacate the award continued with the arbitration with notice of the defect and without objection.

2. The award shall be vacated on the application of a party who neither participated in the arbitration nor was served with a notice of intention to arbitrate if the court finds that:

(i) the rights of that party were prejudiced by one of the grounds specified in paragraph one; or

(ii) a valid agreement to arbitrate was not made; or

(iii) the agreement to arbitrate had not been complied with; or

(iv) the arbitrated claim was barred by limitation under subdivision (b) of section 7502.

(c) **Grounds for modifying.** The court shall modify the award if:

1. there was a miscalculation of figures or a mistake in the description of any person, thing or property referred to in the award; or

2. the arbitrators have awarded upon a matter not submitted to them and the award may be corrected without affecting the merits of the decision upon the issues submitted; or

3. the award is imperfect in a matter of form, not affecting the merits of the controversy.

(d) **Rehearing.** Upon vacating an award, the court may order a rehearing and determination of all or any of the issues either before the same arbitrator or before a new arbitrator appointed in accordance with this article. Time in any provision limiting the time for a hearing or award shall be measured from the date of such order or rehearing, whichever is appropriate, or a time may be specified by the court.

(e) **Confirmation.** Upon the granting of a motion to modify, the court shall confirm the award as modified; upon the denial of a motion to vacate or modify, it shall confirm the award.

§ 7512.   Death or incompetency of a party.

Where a party dies after making a written agreement to submit a controversy to arbitration, the proceedings may be begun or continued upon the application of, or upon notice to, his executor or administrator or, where it relates to real property, his distributee or devisee who has succeeded to his interest in the real property. Where a committee of the property or of the person of a party to such an agreement is appointed, the proceedings may be continued upon the application of, or notice to, the committee. Upon the death or incompetency of a party, the court may extend the time within which an application to confirm, vacate or modify the award or to stay arbitration must be made. Where a party has died since an award was delivered, the proceedings thereupon are the same as where a party dies after a verdict.

§ 7513.   Fees and expenses.

Unless otherwise provided in the agreement to arbitrate, the arbitrators' expenses and fees, together with other expenses, not including attorney's fees, incurred in the conduct of the arbitration, shall be paid as provided in the award. The court, on application, may reduce or disallow any fee or expense it finds excessive or allocate it as justice requires.

§ 7514.   Judgment on an award.

(a) **Entry.** A judgment shall be entered upon the confirmation of an award.

(b) **Judgment-roll.** The judgment-roll consists of the original or a copy of the agreement and each written extention[1] of time within which to make an award; the statement required by section seventy-five hundred eight where the award was by confession; the award; each paper submitted to the court and each order of the court upon an application under sections 7510 and 7511; and a copy of the judgment.

---
[1] So in original. Probably should read "extension."

NEW JERSEY ARBITRATION LAW

Chapter 24
ARBITRATION AND AWARD

2A:24-1. Arbitration provisions; validity and effect. A provision in a written contract to settle by arbitration a controversy that may arise therefrom or a refusal to perform the whole or a part thereof or a written agreement to submit, pursuant to section 2A:24-2 of this title, any existing controversy to arbitration, whether the controversy arise out of contract or otherwise, shall be valid, enforceable and irrevocable, except upon such gounds as exist at law or in equity for the revocation of a contract.

Source. R. S. 2:40-10.

2A:24-2. Who may submit to arbitration; agreement for judgment upon award by specified court. 2 or more persons by their agreement in writing may submit to arbitration a controversy existing between them at the time of the agreement, whether the controversy arises out of a contract or the refusal to perform the whole or a part thereof or out of any other matter. They may also agree in writing that a judgment of a court of record, chosen by them shall be rendered upon the award made pursuant to the submission. If the county court or county district court is so chosen, they may also choose said court of any county in which to enter the judgment, or if no county is chosen, judgment may be entered in said court of any county.

Source. R. S. 2:40-11.

2A:24-3. Nonperformance of agreement; action for order of arbitration. Where a party is aggrieved by the failure, neglect or refusal of another to perform under a written agreement providing for arbitration the superior court, or the county court of the county where either party resides, may in a summary action direct that the arbitration proceed in the manner provided for in the agreement. The party alleged to be in default may demand a jury trial as to the issue that there has been no agreement in writing for an arbitration or that there has been no failure to comply therewith.

Source. R. S. 2:40-12.

2A:24-4. Stay of action or proceeding subject to arbitration. In an action brought in any court upon an issue arising out of an agreement providing for the arbitration thereof, the court, upon being satisfied that the issue involved is referable to arbitration, shall stay the action, if the applicant for the stay is not in default in proceeding with the arbitration, until an arbitration has been had in accordance with the terms of the agreement.

Source. R. S. 2:40-14.

2A:24-5. Naming arbitrators or umpire. If a method is provided in the agreement for naming or appointing an arbitrator or an umpire, it shall be followed; but if not so provided, or if one is provided and a party thereto shall fail to avail himself thereof, or for other reasons there shall be a lapse or failure in the naming of an arbitrator or an umpire or in filing a vacancy, the superior court, or the county court of the county where either party resides, may in the summary action provided for in section 2A:24-3 of this title or in another action, designate and appoint an arbitrator or an umpire, as the case may require, who shall act thereunder with the same force and effect as if specifically named therein. The arbitration shall be by a single arbitrator unless otherwise provided.

Source. R. S. 2:40-15.

2A:24-6. Hearing by arbitrators; witnesses; fees; subpoena. When more than 1 arbitrator is agreed upon, all the arbitrators shall sit at the hearing of the case, unless by written consent, all parties agree to a less number.

The arbitrator so sitting may require the attendance of any person as a witness and, in a proper case, to bring with him any book or written instrument. The fees for the attendance shall be those allowed witnesses in a civil action in a court of record.

Subpoena shall issue in the name of and be signed by the arbitrators, or a majority of them and shall be directed to the person therein named and served in the same manner as a subpoena to testify before a court of record. If any person so subpoenaed to testify shall refuse or neglect to obey such subpoena, the court aforesaid, upon motion, may compel his attendance before the arbitrator or punish him for contempt in the manner provided for the attendance of witnesses or their punishment in the courts.

Source. R. S. 2:40-17.

2A:24-7. Application for confirmation, vacation or modification of award. The award must be in writing and acknowledged or proved in like manner as a deed for the conveyance of real estate and delivered to one of the parties or his attorney.

A party to the arbitration may, within 3 months after the award is delivered to him, unless the parties shall extend the time in writing, commence a summary action in the court aforesaid for the confirmation of the award or for its vacation, modification or correction. Such confirmation shall be granted unless the award is vacated, modified or corrected.

Source. R. S. 2:40-18.

2A:24-8. Vacation of award; rehearing. The court shall vacate the award in any of the following cases:

a. Where the award was procured by corruption, fraud or undue means;

b. Where there was either evident partiality or corruption in the arbitrators, or any thereof;

c. Where the arbitrators were guilty of misconduct in refusing to postpone the hearing, upon sufficient cause being shown therefor, or in refusing to hear evidence, pertinent and material to the controversy, or of any other misbehaviors prejudicial to the rights of any party;

d. Where the arbitrators exceeded or so imperfectly executed their powers that a mutual, final and definite award upon the subject matter submitted was not made.

When an award is vacated and the time within which the agreement required the award to be made has not expired, the court may, in its discretion, direct a rehearing by the arbitrators.

Source. R. S. 2:40-19.

2A:24-9. Modification or correction of award; order. The court shall modify or correct the award in any of the following cases:

a. Where there was an evident miscalculation of figures or an evident mistake in the description of a person, thing or property referred to therein;

b. Where the arbitrators awarded upon a matter not submitted to them unless it affects the merit of the decision upon the matter submitted; and

c. Where the award is imperfect in a matter of form not affecting the merits of the controversy.

The court shall modify and correct the award, to effect the intent thereof and promote justice between the parties.

Source. R. S. 2:40-20.

2A:24-10. Force and effect of judgment. The judgment confirming, modifying or correcting an award or a judgment in any action under this chapter shall have the same effect, in all respects, as, and is subject to all the provisions of law relating to, a judgment in any other action and may be enforced as if rendered in any other action in the court in which it is entered.

Source: R. S. 2:40-24.

2A:24-11. Contracts made before July 4, 1923, unaffected. This article shall not apply to contracts made prior to July 4, 1923; nor shall it apply to acts heretofore performed.

Source. R. S. 2:40-26.

PROPOSED UNIFORM ARBITRATION ACT

Introduction

The text of the Uniform Arbitration Law (Adopted by the National Conference of the Commissioners on Uniform State Laws in 1955 and amended in 1956, and approved by the House of Delegates of the American Bar Association on August 26, 1955 and August 30, 1956) has been reprinted by the American Arbitration Association in convenient form for the assistance of legislators, lawyers, and businessmen who wish to improve the arbitration legislation in their own states.

Many agreements to arbitrate are specifically enforceable under the Federation Arbitration Act and under modern arbitration laws similar in content to the Uniform Act. In thirty states, the general advantages of such modern laws are that they make possible the use of future dispute arbitration clauses in a wide variety of contracts. At the same time, they include minimum standards of procedure and rules for confirming awards in court and invalidating awards for procedural defects. They establish procedures by which court actions in violation of agreements to arbitrate may be stayed. The effect of modern arbitration statutes is to endow agreements to arbitrate with the same legal protections that other legitimate private agreements have. This makes it possible for the lawyer to use arbitration as one of the effective tools in his profession.

• • •

ACT RELATING TO ARBITRATION AND TO MAKE UNIFORM THE LAW WITH REFERENCE THERETO

SECTION 1. (*Validity of Arbitration Agreement.*) A written agreement to submit any existing controversy to arbitration or a provision in a written contract to submit to arbitration any controversy thereafter arising between the parties is valid, enforceable and irrevocable, save upon such grounds as exist at law or in equity for the revocation of any contract. This act also applies to arbitration agreements between employers and employees or between their respective representatives (unless otherwise provided in the agreement.)

SECTION 2. (*Proceedings to Compel or Stay Arbitration.*)

(a) On application of a party showing an agreement described in Section 1, and the opposing party's refusal to arbitrate, the Court shall order the parties to proceed with arbitration, but if the opposing party denies the existence of the agreement to arbitrate, the Court shall proceed summarily to the determination of the issue so raised and shall order arbitration if found for the moving party, otherwise, the application shall be denied.

(b) On application, the court may stay an arbitration proceeding commenced or threatened on a showing that there is no agreement to arbitrate. Such an issue, when in substantial and bona fide dispute, shall be forthwith and summarily tried and the stay ordered if found for the moving party. If found for the opposing party, the court shall order the parties to proceed to arbitration.

(c) If an issue referable to arbitration under the alleged agreement is involved in action or proceeding pending in a court having jurisdiction to hear applications under subdivision (a) of this Section, the application shall be made therein. Otherwise and subject to Section 18, the application may be made in any court of competent jurisdiction.

(d) Any action or proceeding involving an issue subject to arbitration shall be stayed if an order for arbitration or an application therefor has been made under this section or, if the issue is severable, the stay may be with respect thereto only. When the application is made in such action or proceeding, the order for arbitration shall include such stay.

(e) An order for arbitration shall not be refused on the ground that the claim in issue lacks merit or bona fides or because any fault or grounds for the claim sought to be arbitrated have not been shown.

SECTION 3. (*Appointment of Arbitrators by Court.*) If the arbitration agreement provides a method of appointment of arbitrators, this method shall be followed. In the absence thereof, or if the agreed method fails or for any reason cannot be followed, or when an arbitrator appointed fails or is unable to act and his successor has not been duly appointed, the court on application of a party shall appoint one or more arbitrators. An arbitrator so appointed has all the powers of one specifically named in the agreement.

SECTION 4. (*Majority Action by Arbitrators.*) The powers of the arbitrators may be exercised by a majority unless otherwise provided by the agreement or by this act.

SECTION 5. (*Hearing.*) Unless otherwise provided by the agreement:

(a) The arbitrators shall appoint a time and place for the hearing and cause notification to the parties to be served personally or by registered mail not less than five days before the hearing. Appearance at the hearing waives such notice. The arbitrators may adjourn the hearing from time to time as necessary and, on request of a party and for good cause, or upon their own motion may postpone the hearing to a time not later than the date fixed by the agreement for making the award unless the parties consent to a later date. The arbitrators may hear and determine the controversy upon the evidence produced notwithstanding the failure of a party duly notified to appear. The court on application may direct the arbitrators to proceed promptly with the hearing and determination of the controversy.

(b) The parties are entitled to be heard, to present evidence material to the controversy and to cross-examine witnesses appearing at the hearing.

(c) The hearing shall be conducted by all the arbitrators but a majority may determine any question and render a final award. If, during the course of the hearing, an arbitrator for any reason ceases to act, the remaining arbitrator or arbitrators appointed to act as neutrals may continue with the hearing and determination of the controversy.

SECTION 6. (*Representation by Attorney.*) A party has the right to be represented by an attorney at any proceeding or hearing under this act. A waiver thereof prior to the proceeding or hearing is ineffective.

SECTION 7. (*Witnesses, Subpoenas, Depositions.*)

(a) The arbitrators may issue (cause to be issued) subpoenas for the attendance of witnesses and for the production of books, records, documents and other evidence, and shall have the power to administer oaths. Subpoenas so issued shall be served, and upon application to the Court by a party or the arbitrators, enforced, in the manner provided by law for the service and enforcement of subpoenas in a civil action.

(b) On application of a party and for use as evidence, the arbitrators may permit a deposition to be taken, in the manner and upon the terms designated by the arbitrators, of a witness who cannot be subpoenaed or is unable to attend the hearing.

(c) All provisions of law compelling a person under subpoena to testify are applicable.

(d) Fees for attendance as a witness shall be the same as for a witness in the .... Court.

SECTION 8. (*Award.*)

(a) The award shall be in writing and signed by the arbitrators joining in the award. The arbitrators shall deliver a copy to each party personally or by registered mail, or as provided in the agreement.

(b) An award shall be made within the time fixed therefor by the agreement or, if not so fixed, within such time as the court orders on application of a party. The parties may extend the time in writing either before or after the expiration thereof. A party waives the objection that an award was not made within the time required unless he notifies the arbitrators of his objection prior to the delivery of the award to him.

SECTION 9. (*Change of Award by Arbitrators.*) On application of a party or, if an application to the court is pending under Sections 11, 12 or 13, on submission to the arbitrators by the court under such conditions as the court may order, the arbitrators may modify or correct the award upon the grounds stated in paragraphs (1) and (3) of subdivision (a) of Section 13, or for the purpose of clarifying the award. The application shall be made within twenty days after delivery of the award to the applicant. Written notice thereof shall be given forthwith to the opposing party, stating he must serve his objections thereto, if any, within ten days from the notice. The award so modified or corrected is subject to the provisions of Sections 11, 12 and 13.

SECTION 10. (*Fees and Expenses of Arbitration.*) Unless otherwise provided in the agreement to arbitrate, the arbitrators' expenses and fees, together with other expenses, not including counsel fees, incurred in the conduct of the arbitration, shall be paid as provided in the award.

SECTION 11. (*Confirmation of an Award.*) Upon application of a party, the Court shall confirm an award, unless within the time limits hereinafter imposed grounds are urged for vacating or modifying or correcting the award, in which case the court shall proceed as provided in Sections 12 and 13.

SECTION 12. (*Vacating an Award.*)

(a) Upon application of a party, the court shall vacate an award where:

(1) The award was procured by corruption, fraud or other undue means;

(2) There was evident partiality by an arbitrator appointed as a neutral or corruption in any of the arbitrators or misconduct prejudicing the rights of any party;

(3) The arbitrators exceeded their powers;

(4) The arbitrators refused to postpone the hearing upon sufficient cause being shown therefor or refused to hear evidence material to the controversy or otherwise so conducted the hearing, contrary to the provisions of Section 5, as to prejudice substantially the rights of a party; or

(5) There was no arbitration agreement and the issue was not adversely determined in proceedings under Section 2 and the party did not participate in the arbitration hearing without raising the objection;

But the fact that the relief was such that it could not or would not be granted by a court of law or equity is not ground for vacating or refusing to confirm the award.

(b) An application under this Section shall be made within ninety days after delivery of a copy of the award to the applicant, except that, if predicated upon corruption, fraud or other undue means, it shall be made within ninety days after such grounds are known or should have been known.

(c) In vacating the award on grounds other than stated in clause (5) of Subsection (a) the court may order a rehearing before new arbitrators chosen as provided in the agreement, or in the absence thereof, by the court in accordance with Section 3, or, if the award is vacated on grounds set forth in clauses (3), and (4) of Subsection (a) the court may order a rehearing before the arbitrators who made the award or their successors appointed in accordance with

Section 3. The time within which the agreement requires the award to be made is applicable to the rehearing and commences from the date of the order.

(d) If the application to vacate is denied and no motion to modify or correct the award is pending, the court shall confirm the award.

SECTION 13. (*Modification or Correction of Award.*)

(a) Upon application made within ninety days after delivery of a copy of the award to the applicant, the court shall modify or correct the award where:

(1) There was an evident miscalculation of figures or an evident mistake in the description of any person, thing or property referred to in the award;

(2) The arbitrators have awarded upon a matter not submitted to them and the award may be corrected without affecting the merits of the decision upon the issues submitted; or

(3) The award is imperfect in a matter of form, not affecting the merits of the controversy.

(b) If the application is granted, the court shall modify and correct the award so as to effect its intent and shall confirm the award as so modified and corrected. Otherwise, the court shall confirm the award as made.

(c) An application to modify or correct an award may be joined in the alternative with an application to vacate the award.

SECTION 14. (*Judgment or Decree on Award.*) Upon the granting of an order confirming, modifying or correcting an award, judgment or decree shall be entered in conformity therewith and be enforced as any other judgment or decree. Costs of the application and of the proceedings subsequent thereto, and disbursements may be awarded by the court.

* [SECTION 15. (*Judgment Roll, Docketing.*)

(a) On entry of judgment or decree, the clerk

---

* *Brackets and parenthesis enclose language which the Commissioners suggest may be used by those States desiring to do so.*

shall prepare the judgment roll consisting, to the extent filed, of the following:

(1) The agreement and each written extension of the time within which to make the award;

(2) The award;

(3) A copy of the order confirming, modifying or correcting the award; and

(4) A copy of the judgment or decree.

(b) The judgment or decree may be docketed as if rendered in an action.]

SECTION 16. (*Applications to Court.*) Except as otherwise provided, an application to the court under this act shall be by motion and shall be heard in the manner and upon the notice provided by law or rule of court for the making and hearing of motions. Unless the parties have agreed otherwise, notice of an initial application for an order shall be served in the manner provided by law for the service of a summons in an action.

SECTION 17. (*Court, Jurisdiction.*) The term "court" means any court of competent jurisdiction of this State. The making of an agreement described in Section 1 providing for arbitration in this State confers jurisdiction on the court to enforce the agreement under this Act and to enter judgment on an award thereunder.

SECTION 18. (*Venue.*) An initial application shall be made to the court of the (county) in which the agreement provides the arbitration hearing shall be held or, if the hearing has been held, in the county in which it was held. Otherwise the application shall be made in the (county) where the adverse party resides or has a place of business or, if he has no residence or place of business in this State, to the court of any (county). All subsequent applications shall be made to the court hearing the initial application unless the court otherwise directs.

SECTION 19. (*Appeals.*)

(a) An appeal may be taken from:

(1) An order denying an application to compel arbitration made under Section 2;

(2) An order granting an application to stay arbitration made under Section 2(b);

(3) An order confirming or denying confirmation of an award;

(4) An order modifying or correcting an award;

(5) An order vacating an award without directing a rehearing; or

(6) A judgment or decree entered pursuant to the provisions of this act.

(b) The appeal shall be taken in the manner and to the same extent as from orders or judgments in a civil action.

SECTION 20. (*Act Not Retroactive.*) This act applies only to agreements made subsequent to the taking effect of this act.

SECTION 21. (*Uniformity of Interpretation.*) This act shall be so construed as to effectuate its general purpose to make uniform the law of those states which enact it.

SECTION 22. (*Constitutionality.*) If any provision of this act or the application thereof to any person or circumstance is held invalid, the invalidity shall not affect other provisions or applications of the act which can be given without the invalid provision or application, and to this end the provisions of this act are severable.

SECTION 23. (*Short Title.*) This act may be cited as the Uniform Arbitration Act.

SECTION 24. (*Repeal.*) All acts or parts of acts which are inconsistent with the provisions of this act are hereby repealed.

SECTION 25. (*Time of Taking Effect.*) This act shall take effect ....

Appendix V

SELECTED FORMS

Form 1: American Arbitration Association
DEMAND FOR ARBITRATION

VOLUNTARY LABOR ARBITRATION RULES

DEMAND FOR ARBITRATION

DATE:

TO: (Name) _____
    (of party upon whom the Demand is made)

(Address) _____

(City and State) _____

The undersigned, a Party to an Arbitration Agreement contained in a written contract,

dated _____ , which agreement provides as follows:
                    (Quote Arbitration Clause)

hereby demands arbitration thereunder.

NATURE OF DISPUTE:

REMEDY SOUGHT:

You are hereby notified that copies of our Arbitration Agreement and of this Demand are being filed with the American Arbitration Association at its_____Regional Office, with the request that it commence the administration of the arbitration.

Signed_____

Title_____

Address_____

City and State_____

Telephone_____

To institute proceedings, please send three copies of this Demand and the Arbitration Agreement, with the administrative fee, as provided in Section 43 of the Rules.

CASE NO._____

Form 2: American Arbitration Association
SELECTION OF ARBITRATOR

Case Number: Date List Submitted:

LIST FOR SELECTION OF ARBITRATOR

You may
indicate your
preference by
number.
Otherwise,
we will try to
appoint an
arbitrator who
can hear your
case promptly.
Leave as many
names as
possible.

_____

_____

_____

_____

_____

_____

_____

_____

_____

_____

_____

Party_____

By_____ Title_____

NOTE: Biographical information about the above-listed arbitrators is attached. Unless your list is received by the Association within seven days, all names submitted may be deemed acceptable. If an appointment cannot be made from this list, and the parties do not both request a further list, the Association may appoint an arbitrator.

Form 3: American Arbitration Association
NOTICE OF APPOINTMENT AND OATH OF ABRITRATOR

Voluntary Labor Arbitration Tribunal

In the Matter of the Arbitration between

Notice of Appointment
and
Oath of Arbitrator

Case Number:

TO:

PLEASE TAKE NOTICE that, pursuant to the Voluntary Labor Arbitration Rules, you have been appointed to serve as Arbitrator in the above-entitled Arbitration. Please execute the following oath and return one copy to this office.

DATED: ....
American Arbitration Association, Administrator

STATE OF

} S.S.:

COUNTY OF

being duly sworn, deposes and says that he is aware of the requirements for impartiality contained in Sections 11 and 17 of the Voluntary Labor Arbitration Rules and accepts this appointment and will faithfully and fairly hear and examine the matters in controversy between the above-named Parties, in accordance with the Arbitration Agreement dated the   day of   , 19   , and that he will make a just Award according to the best of his understanding.

Date .... Signed ....
Arbitrator

Sworn to before me

this   day of   19

Form 4: American Arbitration Association
NOTICE OF HEARING

In the Matter of the Arbitration between

CASE NUMBER: _____

NOTICE OF HEARING

TO:

PLEASE TAKE NOTICE that a Hearing in the above-entitled Arbitration will be held at the Arbitration Tribunal of the American Arbitration Association,

At _____

Date _____

Hour _____

Before _____

_____

_____ Arbitrator(s)

Please attend promptly with your witnesses and be prepared to present your proofs.

DATED: _____

Tribunal Administrator

NOTICE: The Arbitrator(s) have arranged their schedule and reserved the above date to meet the convenience of the Parties. Therefore, every effort should be made to appear on the date scheduled. In the event that unforeseen circumstances make it impossible to attend the hearing as scheduled, the Parties are to request a postponement no less than 48 hours before the time and date set for hearing. All requests for postponements must be communicated to the Tribunal Administrator (not the Arbitrator). There should be no communication between parties and the Arbitrator other than at oral hearings. Any party desiring to have a stenographic record of the testimony taken should make arrangements with the Tribunal Administrator in advance of the hearing.

cc: arbitrator(s)

Form 5: American Arbitration Association
SUBMISSION TO ARBITRATION

SUBMISSION TO ARBITRATION

Date:

The named Parties hereby submit the following dispute to arbitration under the VOLUNTARY LABOR ARBITRATION RULES of the American Arbitration Association:

We agree that we will abide by and perform any Award rendered hereunder and that a judgment may be entered upon the Award.

Employer ....

Signed by .... Title ....

Address ....

Union .... Local ....

Signed by .... Title ....

Address ....

PLEASE FILE TWO COPIES

Form 6: American Arbitration Association
STIPULATION

Voluntary Labor Arbitration Tribunal

In the Matter of the Arbitration between

Stipulation

Case Number:

IT IS HEREBY STIPULATED AND AGREED between the Parties to the above entitled Arbitration, which arises under an arbitration provision in a collective bargaining agreement dated ...., that said arbitration shall be conducted under the Voluntary Labor Arbitration Rules of the American Arbitration Association.

Signed ....
(Name of Party)
Title ....

Signed ....
(Name of Party)
Title ....

Form 7: American Arbitration Association
SUBPOENA DUCES TECUM (DEMAND FOR DOCUMENTS)

**ARBITRATION TRIBUNALS of the
AMERICAN ARBITRATION ASSOCIATION**

In the Matter of the Arbitration between

}

Subpoena Duces Tecum
(Documents)

THE PEOPLE OF THE STATE OF

To:

GREETING:

WE COMMAND YOU, that all business and excuses being laid aside, you and each of you appear and attend before

, Arbitrator(s)

acting under the Arbitration Law of this State, at the American Arbitration Association,

....
(address)

on the   day of   , 19   , at   o'clock
to testify and give evidence in a certain Arbitration, then and there to be held between the above entitled parties, and that you bring with you and produce certain

now in your custody.

Requested by: ....

Signed: ....

Signed: ....

....
Name of Attorney

Arbitrator(s)

....
Address

....
Telephone

Dated: ....

Form 8: American Arbitration Association
AWARD OF ARBITRATOR

VOLUNTARY LABOR ARBITRATION TRIBUNAL

In the Matter of the Arbitration between

CASE NUMBER:

AWARD OF ARBITRATOR

THE UNDERSIGNED ARBITRATOR(S), having been designated in accordance with the Arbitration Agreement entered into by the above-named Parties, and dated and having been duly sworn and having duly heard the proofs and allegations of the Parties, AWARDS as follows:

DATED:
STATE OF   } SS.:
COUNTY OF

      On this   day of   , 19   , before me personally came and appeared

to me known and known to me to be the individual(s) described in and who executed the foregoing instrument and   he   acknowledged to me that   he   executed the same.

Form 9: New York State Board of Mediation
REQUEST FOR DESIGNATION OF ARBITRATOR

STATE OF NEW YORK
STATE MEDIATION BOARD

REQUEST FOR DESIGNATION OF ARBITRATOR

(Send one copy to State Mediation Board and one to other party)

(Please fill in form completely to avoid delay in scheduling)

The undersigned hereby requests the State Mediation Board to designate an arbitrator under the terms of an agreement between the parties.

EMPLOYER: _____
                   (Name)   (Address)   (Tel.)

ATTORNEY: _____
                   (Name)   (Address)   (Tel.)

UNION: _____
                   (Name)   (Address)   (Tel.)

ATTORNEY: _____
                   (Name)   (Address)   (Tel.)

ISSUES TO BE ARBITRATED (State all issues and include names of individuals where appropriate. Use additional sheets if necessary.)

Number of Employees in Firm: _____ Number involved in dispute _____

I hereby certify that the agreement between the parties empowers the State Mediation Board to designate an arbitrator. (Attach copy of contract, if available, or give text of contract clause or agreement providing for arbitration.)

COPY OF THIS REQUEST HAS
BEEN SENT TO (COMPANY)   _____
(UNION)   (Signature)
ON _____
          (Date)
                                                                      _____
                                                                            (Title)

                                          Representing above named (Company) (Union)

                                          Date of Request: _____

Form 10a: New York State Board of Mediation
SUBMISSION OF NAMES OF ARBITRATORS

STATE OF NEW YORK

STATE MEDIATION BOARD

VINCENT D. McDONNELL
JOHN F. HANS
MEYER DRUCKER, DIRECTOR

UPSTATE OFFICES

ALBANY
BUFFALO
SYRACUSE

TWO WORLD TRADE CENTER
NEW YORK, N.Y. 10047
TELEPHONE: AREA CODE 212
488-3735

This Board has been advised that the above parties have entered into a contract which requires the Board to designate an arbitrator in the event of a dispute. We have now been requested to make such designation. Listed below is a panel of five (5) persons selected from our Panel of Arbitrators:

Please make your selection or choice of arbitrator on the enclosed form in compliance with the instructions stated on the form. Upon receipt of the selection from both sides, the arbitrator will be designated. If we do not receive your properly executed list within five (5) days (exclusive of Saturday and Sunday) from the date of this letter, we will have no alternative but to designate the arbitrator from the selection of the other party.

Please note that it is customary for panel arbitrators to receive a fee for their services and for such fee to be shared equally by the parties. Copies of biographical sketches of panel members are enclosed for your convenience.

If you have any questions, please call the Calendar Clerk, at 212-488-6631.

Very truly yours,

Vincent D. McDonnell
Chairman

Enc:

Form 10b: New York State Board of Mediation
SELECTION OF ARBITRATOR

NEW YORK
STATE MEDIATION BOARD
Thirty-Fourth Floor
Two World Trade Center, New York, N.Y. 10047

SELECTION FROM LIST OF PANEL ARBITRATORS

TO: New York State Mediation Board

There is listed below, our selection from the list of panel arbitrators submitted by you in compliance with the request for the appointment of an arbitrator to hear and determine a labor dispute. We have stricken out the names of two arbitrators on the list whom we do not desire to hear this dispute and have numbered the remaining three by order of choice as 1, 2, and 3.

NOTE: *Failure to number three choices shall be considered a complete rejection of the list. Each party is entitled to one rejection of an entire panel.*

☐ FOR THE UNION: Date _____   ☐ FOR THE COMPANY: Date _____

By_____   By_____

Title _____   Title _____

Local_____   Company _____

APPOINTMENT: In view of the authority vested in me, by contract and statute, and because of the selection made by the parties, I hereby designate   as arbitrator in this dispute.

By: _____
( ) CHAIRMAN
( ) EXECUTIVE SECRETARY

Form 11a: New York State Board of Mediation
NOTICE TO ARBITRATOR OF APPOINTMENT

STATE OF NEW YORK

STATE MEDIATION BOARD

VINCENT D. McDONNELL, CHAIRMAN

JOHN F. HANS
GERALD J. RYAN

MEYER DRUCKER
EXECUTIVE SECRETARY

270 BROADWAY
NEW YORK, N. Y. 10007
TELEPHONE: AREA CODE 212
488-3735

UPSTATE OFFICES

ALBANY
BUFFALO
SYRACUSE

The parties listed below have requested this Board to appoint an arbitrator in the above dispute. In compliance with the procedures of the Board, you have been selected as arbitrator. Please communicate with the parties to arrange a date, time and place for the hearing.

When you have completed the arbitration, please quickly fill in the enclosed record sheets, in duplicate, and return them together with your copy of the award. Please see that all items in the form are completed.

Notify this office in the event any litigation involving this case comes to your attention.

If you have any questions on this appointment, please call the Calendar Clerk, at 212-488-6631.

Very truly yours,

Vincent D. McDonnell
Chairman

Enc.

RE: Employer:
    Address:
    Telephone:
    Representative:
    Address:
    Telephone:

    Union:
    Address:
    Telephone:
    Representative:
    Address:
    Telephone:

Form 11b: New York State Board of Mediation
NOTICE TO PARTIES OF APPOINTMENT

STATE OF NEW YORK

STATE MEDIATION BOARD

VINCENT D. McDONNELL
JOHN F. HANS
MEYER DRUCKER, DIRECTOR

UPSTATE OFFICES

ALBANY
BUFFALO
SYRACUSE

270 BROADWAY
NEW YORK, N. Y. 10007
TELEPHONE: AREA CODE 212
488-3735

This has reference to our previous letter on the appointment of an arbitrator. In compliance with the procedures of this Board, the arbitrator for this case is

The arbitrator will communicate with you to set a date, time and place for the hearing.

It is customary for panel arbitrators to receive a fee for their services (such fee to be shared equally by the parties). The fee may be established on a per diem or case basis. Among the factors generally taken into consideration are the complexity and importance of the issues, the time spent in the hearing and in the preparation of the award and the ability of the parties to pay.

If you have any questions, please call the Calendar Clerk, at 212-488-6631.

Very truly yours,

Vincent D. McDonnell

Vincent D. McDonnell
Chairman

Form 12: New York State Board of Mediation
OATH OF ARBITRATOR

STATE OF NEW YORK
STATE MEDIATION BOARD

In the Matter of the Arbitration

Between

And

} OATH OF ARBITRATOR

Case No._____

STATE OF NEW YORK } SS
COUNTY OF

being duly sworn deposes and says that he will faithfully and fairly hear
and examine the matters in controversy between the above-named parties, in
accordance with the Agreement dated the   day of   19 ,
and that he will make a just Award according to the best of his understanding.

Sworn to before me

this   day of   19   _____

Form 13: New York State Board of Mediation
REPORT OF PANEL ARBITRATOR

☐ ALBANY ☐ NEW YORK
☐ BUFFALO ☐ SYRACUSE

CASE NO. _____

NEW YORK
STATE MEDIATION BOARD

REPORT OF PANEL ARBITRATOR

*Please complete this report in duplicate and send to the designating officer.
If an award was written, panel members should attach TWO copies.*

ARBITRATOR _____ DATE RECEIVED _____

LOCATION
OF HEARING _____

DATE OF AWARD
OR CLOSING DATE _____

A. EMPLOYER - Name	B. UNION - Name
Address & City	Local No.
	☐ AFL-CIO ☐ Ind.
Attorney	Attorney
Address & City	Address & City
Phone	Employer's Business	Phone

C. NO. EMPLOYERS
IN DISPUTE

D. NO. ESTABLISHMENTS
IN DISPUTE

E. TOTAL NO.
EMPLOYEES

F. NO. EMPLOYEES
DIRECTLY INVOLVED

G. TYPE OF DISPUTE

1. ☐ Initial Contract
2. ☐ Renewal Contract
3. ☐ Contract Reopening
4. ☐ Dispute Under Contract
5. ☐ Other (specify)

H. INTERVENTION REQUESTED

1. ☐ By Union
2. ☐ By Employer
3. ☐ Jointly
4. ☐ As Result of Mediation
   If yes, Case No.

I. DISPOSITION

1. ☐ By Award
2. ☐ Withdrawn or Settled Before Hearing
3. ☐ Voluntary Settlement During or After Hearing

J. ISSUES DETERMINED BY AWARD

K. STATISTICAL SUMMARY

1. No. of Hearings _____
2. No. of Study Days _____
3. Total Time _____
4. Hearing Dates _____

L. FEES (TOTAL FROM BOTH PARTIES)

1. Per Diem Fee $ _____
2. Total Fee $ _____

Form 14: New Jersey State Board of Mediation
SUBMISSION OF NAMES OF ARBITRATORS

NEW JERSEY STATE BOARD OF MEDIATION
1100 Raymond Boulevard - Room 306
Newark, New Jersey 07102

FORM A

      CASE NO._____   DATE_____

At the request of the   for arbitration of a dispute over

we are submitting the names of the following seven Arbitrators on our Arbitration
Panel in order that you may participate in the selection of the Arbitrator who
will hear and decide the matter in dispute:

      ARBITRATOR   PER DIEM FEE

In accordance with Section IV 2 (a) of our Rules and Regulations for
Arbitration the parties are requested to strike out the names of those whom
they deem unsatisfactory and return this form to the Board within 10 working
days from this date so that we may designate an Arbitrator who is acceptable to
both sides. When either party or both parties fail to return the list
within the specified ten days, any person named therein shall be deemed
acceptable, and the Board shall be empowered to designate any arbitrator named
on that list. Such designation will be made in accordance with the order of
an available listing, if any.

If we do not hear from you within 10 working days, we will proceed under our
Rules and Regulations to designate the Arbitrator and schedule a hearing.

PLEASE FILL IN:

      Name of Company or Union Representative returning list.

DATE_____   _____

            TITLE_____

Form 15: New Jersey State Board of Mediation
NOTICE TO ARBITRATOR OF APPOINTMENT

NEW JERSEY STATE BOARD OF MEDIATION
1100 Raymond Boulevard - Rm. 306
Newark, New Jersey 07102
(201) 648-2860

RE: Case No.

Dear

You have been designated as Arbitrator in the above matter.

Please contact the representatives whose names appear on the attached
Arbitrator's Report Form and make such arrangements as are mutually
satisfactory for a hearing. If it is desired to use a conference room
at the Mediation Board for such hearing, please advise us of the time
and date and then please be sure to notify us of any changes in the
date of hearing so we can make appropriate changes in our lists of room
reservations.

Following the conclusion of the case, we ask that you submit your award
and statement of fee directly to the parties and that you complete the
Arbitrator's Report Form and return it to this office together with a
copy of your award.

Thank you very much for your cooperation.

Very truly yours,

Executive Director

Form 16: New Jersey State Board of Mediation
OATH OF ARBITRATOR

NEW JERSEY STATE BOARD OF MEDIATION
1100 Raymond Boulevard
Newark, New Jersey   07102

CASE NO.

In the Matter of the Arbitration	)
Between	)
	)
	)
	)
Employer	)
	) OATH OF ARBITRATOR
and	)
	)
	)
Employee or Union Representative	)

Being duly sworn according to Law, on his
oath deposes and says that he will faithfully and impartially hear and
examine the grievance and dispute in question, and discharge his duties
as such Arbitrator according to the best of his skill and understanding.

ARBITRATOR

Sworn to and subscribed before me this

day of   A.D., 19

Form 17: New Jersey State Board of Mediation
NOTICE TO PARTIES OF APPOINTMENT

NEW JERSEY STATE BOARD OF MEDIATION
1100 Raymond Boulevard - Room 306
Newark, New Jersey 07102
(201) 648-2860

RE: **Case No.**

Dear Sir:

Please be advised that   has been
designated as Arbitrator to hear and decide the matter in dispute
in the above-captioned case. The Arbitrator will contact you
respecting date, time and place of hearing.

Very truly yours,

Executive Director

Form 18: New Jersey State Board of Mediation
SUBMISSION AGREEMENT

NEW JERSEY STATE BOARD OF MEDIATION
1100 Raymond Boulevard-Room 306
Newark, New Jersey 07102

CASE NO:

In the matter of Arbitration
Between

Employer
-and-   SUBMISSION

Employee or Union Representative

We, the undersigned, hereby agree to submit the following controversy to Arbitration: (No. Persons involved   )

A collective bargaining contract exists between

and

a copy of which is annexed hereto.

We hereby agree to submit such controversy for decision to:

We further agree that we will faithfully abide by and perform any award made pursuant to this agreement and that such award shall be binding and conclusive upon us.

_____
(For Employer)

_____
(For Union)

WITNESS:

_____

DATED:

_____

Form 19: New Jersey State Board of Mediation
ARBITRATOR'S REPORT

NEW JERSEY STATE BOARD OF MEDIATION

ARBITRATOR'S REPORT

Case No._____

Arbitrator_____   Date Received_____

Location of Hearing: Date of Award
                                   or Closing Date_____
_____

_____

Employer - Name	: Union - Name
Address & City	: Address & City
Representatives Tel. No.	: Representatives Tel. No.
1._____	: 1. _____
2._____	: 2. _____
No. of Employees Directly involved:	:

Issue (s) in Arbitration:

_____
Disposition: (Summary of Award or other disposition)

1. No. of Hearings	: 1. Per Diem Fee $
2. No. of Study Days	: 2. Total Fee $
3. Total Time	:
4. Date (s) of Hearing	:

Form 20: New York State Public Employment Relations Board
SUBMISSION OF NAMES OF ARBITRATORS

STATE OF NEW YORK
PUBLIC EMPLOYMENT RELATIONS BOARD
50 WOLF ROAD
ALBANY, NEW YORK 12205

Re: Case No.

Dear

    We have been notified that pursuant to the collective
negotiations contract currently in effect between the above-
captioned parties there is a requirement that in the event
of a dispute between the parties the Public Employment Relations Board shall designate an arbitrator to resolve such
dispute.

    Pursuant to our procedures we are submitting a list of
five persons selected from our arbitration panel. The parties
shall, independently, strike two names from the list and then
rank the remaining three names in order of their preference,
numbering them 1, 2 and 3. The duplicate copy shall then be
signed by an authorized representative of each party and returned to the Director of Conciliation. Upon receipt of the
selections from both sides the arbitrator will be designated.

    Unless your reply is received within seven days from date
of this letter, the designation of the arbitrator will be made
from the list submitted by the other party. It is understood
that the cost of such arbitration shall be borne by the respective parties. Following is the list with attached resumes:

1.   4.
2.   5.
3.

Sincerely,

Encs.   Director of Conciliation

Form 21: New York State Public Employment Relations Board
NOTICE TO ARBITRATOR OF APPOINTMENT

STATE OF NEW YORK
PUBLIC EMPLOYMENT RELATIONS BOARD
50 WOLF ROAD
ALBANY, NEW YORK 12205

Re: Case No.

Dear

    The parties listed below have requested the Director of
Conciliation to designate an arbitrator in the above-captioned
dispute.   Pursuant to the procedures of the Public Employment
Relations Board, you have been selected as arbitrator.   Please
contact the parties to arrange a date, time and place for the
arbitration hearing.

    Upon completion of your assignment, please complete the
enclosed statistical report form and return it, together with
a copy of your award, to the Director of Conciliation.   Arrangements for payment of your fee should be made through the
parties.

    In the event of any litigation involving this case, please
notify this office.   Should you have any questions regarding
this appointment, please feel free to contact this office.

Sincerely,

Director of Conciliation

Enc.

Employer:

Employee Organization:

Form 22: New York State Public Employment Relations Board
NOTICE TO PARTIES OF APPOINTMENT

STATE OF NEW YORK
PUBLIC EMPLOYMENT RELATIONS BOARD
50 WOLF ROAD
ALBANY, NEW YORK 12205

Case No.

Dear

Your attention is directed to our previous letter regarding the appointment of an arbitrator. Pursuant to the procedures of the Public Employment Relations Board, the arbitrator in the above captioned case shall be:

The arbitrator has been instructed to contact you to arrange the date, time and place for the arbitration hearing.

If you have any questions regarding this appointment, please feel free to contact us.

Sincerely,

Director of Conciliation

Form 23: New York State Public Employment Relations Board
ARBITRATOR'S REPORT

N.Y.S. PUBLIC EMPLOYMENT RELATIONS BOARD

ARBITRATION REPORT FORM

CASE #_____   ISSUE_____
                                                     _____
                                                     _____

Upon completion of assignment please complete and return this form and a copy of your
award if issued to the Director of Conciliation.

ARBITRATOR_____   DATE REC'D_____

LOCATION OF   DATE OF AWARD
HEARING_____   OR CLOSING DATE_____

1. EMPLOYER: 2. EMPLOYEE ORGANIZATION:

   ADDRESS: ADDRESS:

   PHONE: PHONE:

   REPRESENTATIVE (NAME & TITLE)   REPRESENTATIVE (NAME & TITLE)

   ADDRESS: ADDRESS:

   PHONE: PHONE:

3. TOTAL NO. EMPLOYEES_____   NO. DIRECTLY INVOLVED_____

4. TYPE OF DISPUTE   5. DISPOSITION
   A. ____ Initial Contract   A. ____ By Award
   B. ____ Contract Renewal   B. ____ Withdrawn from Hearing
   C. ____ Contract Reopening   C. ____ Voluntary Settlement
   D. ____ Grievance   before or after hearing
   E. ____ Other (Specify)   D. ____ Mediation

6. INTERVENTION REQUESTED   7. STATISTICAL SUMMARY
   A. ____ By Emp. Org.   A. ____ No. of Hearing
   B. ____ By Employer   B. ____ Dates of Hearings
   C. ____ Jointly   C. ____ No. of Study Days
   D. ____ As a result of Mediation   D. ____ Total Time
           If so, Case No.

8. FEES CHARGED
   A. _____ Per Diem Fee
   B. _____ Total Fee

COMMENTS: (Use reverse side if more space is required)

Appendix VI

ARBITRATION IN THE ROMAN CATHOLIC CHURCH

Materials in this Appendix are quoted in full from the booklet ON DUE PROCESS, *which is a summary of actions taken by the National Conference of Catholic Bishops in 1969.*

PROCESS FOR CONCILIATION AND ARBITRATION

PROCESS FOR CONCILIATION

ARTICLE I. ESTABLISHMENT

1. Each diocese accepting this proposal shall set up a Council of Conciliation, composed as follows:
— Two persons appointed by the Ordinary of the diocese;
— Two persons elected by the Priests' Senate of the Diocese, or, if there is no senate, by all the clergy of the diocese;
— One person by the faculty of the Catholic college of the diocese. If there is more than one Catholic college, the colleges, in alphabetical order, shall rotate the election. If there is no Catholic college, then the Priests' Senate shall elect three persons, or if there is no senate, all the clergy of the diocese shall elect three persons.

2. The term of office shall be three years.

3. These exceptions shall apply to the initial members of the Council:
— The first appointee of the Ordinary shall have a term of three years.
— The person receiving the largest vote from the Priests' Senate or clergy shall have a term of two years.
— The second appointee of the Ordinary shall have a term of one year.
— The person receiving the second largest vote from the Priests' Senate or clergy shall have a term of one year.

4. The Council shall elect its Chairman, Secretary and Treasurer.

5. The diocese shall reimburse the Council for its expenses upon presentation of a statement signed by the Chairman and Treasurer.

6. The establishment of the Council, its purposes, the biographies of its members, and its rules of operation shall be announced by a letter from the Ordinary to the clergy and faithful of the diocese and by appropriate publicity in the diocesan and secular press.

ARTICLE II. STARTING THE PROCESS

1. Any person in conflict with the Ordinary of the diocese, an appointee of the Ordinary, a priest in the diocese, a Catholic college, hospital, or other charitable or educational institution in the diocese, a parish or a diocesan council, a parish or diocesan school board, a Catholic cemetery organization or burial association, or any other person, group or institution exercising administrative authority in the diocese, may have recourse to the Council.

2. A person having recourse to the Council shall be styled the "initating participant," and the person, group or institution with whom he is in conflict shall be styled the "convoked participant." Recourse to the Council shall be styled the "initiative," and the acceptance of a process for reconciliation by the convoked participant shall be styled "an affirmative response." The conflict shall be designated as "the problem."

3. An initiating participant may take the initiative by sending to any Member of the Council a statement that he has a problem involving one or more of the persons, groups or institutions described in paragraph one, and setting forth the gist of the problem.

4. The Member receiving this statement shall contact the convoked participant both in writing and by telephone, shall apprise him of the problem stated by the initiating participant, and shall inquire if he will accept conciliation. The convoked participant shall be given a description of the purposes of the Council of Conciliation, the biographies of its Members, and a copy of its rules of procedure. He shall be asked if he would accept as a conciliator the Member addressed by the initiating participant or if he would prefer that the Chairman designate a different Member or Members. He shall be advised that the Council is supposed to proceed with dispatch and that his affirmative response to the initiative is expected within two weeks of the notice to him.

5. If the convoked participant fails to give an affirmative response, the Member shall refer the matter to the Chairman who shall endeavor to persuade the convoked participant to give such response.

6. If, four weeks from the date of the initiative, no affirmative response has been made by the convoked participant, the Member shall refer the matter to the Ordinary who shall endeavor to persuade the convoked participant to give such response.

7. In the event that the convoked participant is the Ordinary of the diocese himself, the provisions of paragraph six shall not apply, and if, four weeks from the date of the initiative, there is no affirmative response, the Member shall refer the matter to the Chairman of the Bishops' Committee on Arbitration and Mediation, who, by telephone and letter and, if possible, by personal conference, shall endeavor to persuade the Ordinary to give such response.

8. In the event that the Member fails to discharge any of his responsibilities for referring the matter to the Ordinary or the Chairman of the Bishops' Committee, as the case may be, the initiating participant may ask the Chairman of the Council of Conciliation to make the referral; should the Chairman fail to do so, the initiating participant may make the referral himself.

ARTICLE III. THE PROCESS

1. The Member addressed by the initiating participant and agreed to by the convoked participant shall act as conciliator in the process. In the event there is no agreement, the Chairman shall designate a Member or Members to act as conciliator or conciliators in the process.

2. Within three weeks of the affirmative response, the conciliating Member shall meet alone with each participant for oral discussion of the problem.

3. Within one week of the second of these conferences, the Member shall meet with both participants together and endeavor to guide them to a peaceful resolution of their problem. The Member shall schedule as many of these joint meetings as seem to him to be necessary in order to progress to conciliation.

4. The Member shall endeavor to assure that each participant answers the questions which the other participant believes are essential if he is to understand the actions of the other. While the Member should exercise his discretion, he should act in the knowledge that paternalistic concealment of facts is no longer an acceptable mode of behavior to many persons, and he should, therefore, encourage a trust in candor on both sides.

5. The first joint meeting of the participants and the Member shall be restricted to these persons. Thereafter, in the discretion of the Member, each participant may have with him one or two advisers—theologians, lawyers, friends, or whomever he chooses. In the event that one participant desires to have such advisers, and the Member agrees, the Member shall notify the other participant that he may come with an equal number of advisers. In the discretion of the Member and with the agreement of the participants other Members of the Council of Conciliation or other persons may join the meeting from time to time.

6. If the problem is resolved by agreement, the Member shall prepare a summary statement of the problem and its resolution, and shall submit it for the approval and signature of the participants. If the problem is unresolved after the meetings arranged by the Member have been held, and in any event if the problem is unresolved six months from the initiative, the Member shall ask the participants if they are willing to continue discussions of the problem with him, with another Member of the Council, with a person designated by the Ordinary, or, in a case where the Ordinary is participant, with a person designated by the Chairman of the Bishops' Committee on Arbitration and Mediation. If the participants agree in their response, the Member shall arrange the desired continuation. If one or more participants decline to engage in further discussion, the Member shall file a report with the Council and, where the Ordinary is participant, with the Chairman of the Bishops' Committee on Arbitration and Mediation. This report shall contain the names of the participants, a summary of the problem and the discussions taken to resolve it, and certification by the Member that, despite the good faith of the participants, no resolution could be reached.

7. The Member shall have no power to force the participants to adopt a solution. He shall have power, however, to determine that any participant is not cooperating in good faith. Prima facie evidence of lack of good faith will be failure to attend three scheduled meetings, failure to respond to a substantial number of questions which the Member believes appropriate, or failure to suggest any way of accommodating the interests of the other participant. In the event that for these or other reasons the Member believes that a participant is not cooperating in good faith, he shall apprise him of this belief orally and, failing cooperation, shall apprise him again in writing. If there is no cooperation after the written communication, the Member shall at once notify the Ordinary of the diocese, or, if the Ordinary is a participant, the Chairman of the Bishops' Committee on Arbitration and Mediation. The Ordinary or the Chairman shall endeavor to persuade the participant to cooperate.

8. Meetings shall be private without publicity. All communications made to a Member or between participants shall be treated as confidential by all who share in them. If the problem is resolved by agreement, and the parties agree to publicizing the solution, announcement of it shall be made. If there is no agreement on a solution or on publicizing it, no announcement shall be made.

PROCESS FOR ARBITRATION

ARTICLE I. ESTABLISHMENT

1. Each diocese accepting this proposal shall set up an "Office of Arbitration." The Office shall consist of five persons, two of whom shall be appointed by the Ordinary, and three shall be selected by the Priests' Senate, or, if there is no senate, by all the clergy of the diocese.

2. The members of the Office of Arbitration shall serve for a term of three years. No member shall have more than two consecutive terms in office.

For the purposes of continuity, the terms of the initial members shall be staggered in the following manner:

— The first appointee of the Ordinary shall have a term of three years.

— The second appointee of the Ordinary shall have a term of two years.

— The first person chosen by the Priests' Senate, or clergy of the diocese, shall have a term of three years.

— The second person chosen by the Priests' Senate, or clergy of the diocese, shall have a term of two years.

— The third person chosen by the Priests' Senate, or clergy of the diocese, shall have a term of one year.

3. The Office of Arbitration shall select from its own members a chairman and a secretary-treasurer, each of whom shall serve for a term of one year in that respective capacity.

4. It shall be the responsibility of the Office of Arbitration:

a. to select a sufficient number of qualified persons to be arbitrators;

b. to accept all complaints made to it in writing by any member of the diocese and to determine whether or not the case falls within the competence of the Office as set forth in Article IV;

c. to assist the parties in the selection of an arbitrator;

d. to supervise and administer the over-all program and to interpret rules of procedure to be followed in arbitration when questions are referred to it by either the arbitrators or the parties themselves.

ARTICLE II. SELECTION OF ARBITRATORS

1. Arbitrators should be selected for their impartiality and competence.

a. Impartiality. The arbitrator must receive no direct benefit from the outcome of the decision he makes. The following, therefore, are disqualified to serve as arbitrators:

i. Anyone related by consanguinity or affinity to one or another of the parties, or who is a guardian of one of the parties.

ii. Anyone involved with one or another of the parties in such a way as to have a particular interest in the outcome of the dispute.

iii. Anyone who can be shown to be inimical to one of the parties.

b. Competence. The arbitrator should have some understanding of how a hearing should be conducted. Expertise in the area under discussion is helpful, but not absolutely necessary. If the arbitrator is not himself an expert, he should feel free to call in experts during the hearing.

2. Method of Selection in General.

a. It is the responsibility of the Office of Arbitration in each diocese to select a panel of arbitrators from among the laity, religious, and clergy. It is not necessary that a person be a member of the diocese in order to be included on the panel of arbitrators. It is recommended that there be an exchange of panels between neighboring dioceses where possible.

b. The Office of Arbitration has the responsibility of screening candidates for the panel of arbitrators. The Office shall solicit nominations from any organized group in the diocese, or in any other way to be determined by the Office itself.

c. There shall be maintained a minimum panel of ten arbitrators in order to insure an adequate choice of selection for the parties.

3. Method of Selection for a Specific Case.

a. If the arbitration agreement applicable to a particular case provides a method of appointment of arbitrators, this method shall be followed. In the absence thereof, or if the agreed method fails, or for any reason cannot be followed, or when an arbitrator appointed fails or is unable to act, and no provision has been made for the appointment of his successor, the Office of Arbitration on application of a party shall appoint one or more arbitrators. An arbitrator so appointed has all the powers of one specifically named in the agreement.

b. In the event the arbitration agreement does not provide a method of appointment of arbitrators, the Chairman of the Office of Arbitration shall appoint arbitrators according to the following procedure:

i. The Chairman of the Office of Arbitration shall submit to each party a list of arbitrators, large enough to assure adequate choice.

ii. The parties shall strike out those names not acceptable to themselves and list the others in the order of their preference.

iii. The Chairman of the Office of Arbitration shall then appoint three arbitrators, following as closely as possible the selection of the parties.

iv. The Office of Arbitration shall draft and enforce its own rules with regard to time limits for making the selection, and the consequence of not observing the time limits.

ARTICLE III. PROCEDURE

1. *Initiation of Arbitration.* The parties shall submit to the Chairman of the Office of Arbitration a written statement setting forth the nature of the dispute and the remedies sought.

2. *Time and Place of Hearing.* The arbitrators shall appoint a time and place for hearings and notify the parties not less than five days before each hearing.

3. *Representation by Counsel.* Parties to the dispute may be represented at hearings by counsel or other authorized representative.

4. *Attendance at Hearings.* Persons having a direct interest in the arbitration are entitled to attend hearings. It shall be in the discretion of the arbitrators to determine the propriety of the attendance of any other person.

5. *Adjournments.* For good cause the arbitrators may adjourn the hearing upon the request of a party or upon their own initiative, and shall adjourn when all the parties agree thereto.

6. *Arbitration in the Absence of a Party.* Arbitration may proceed in the absence of any party who, after due notice, fails to be present or fails to obtain an adjournment.

7. *Evidence.* The arbitrators shall hear and determine the controversy upon the evidence produced. Parties may offer such evidence as they desire and shall produce such additional evidence as the arbitrators may deem necessary to an understanding and determination of the dispute. The arbitrators shall judge the relevancy and materiality of the evidence offered, and conformity to legal rules of evidence shall not be necessary. All evidence shall be taken in the presence of all of the arbitrators and all of the parties except where any of the parties is absent in default or has waived his right to be present. The arbitrators may require the parties to submit books, records, documents, and other evidence.

8. *Evidence by Affidavit.* The arbitrators shall have the power to administer oaths and to take evidence from witnesses by deposition whenever witnesses cannot attend the hearing.

9. *Order of Proceedings.* A hearing shall be opened by the recording of the place, time, and date of hearing, the presence of the arbitrators and parties, the presence of counsel, if any, and the receipt by arbitrators of initial statements setting forth the nature of the dispute and the remedies sought. The arbitrator may, in his discretion, vary the normal procedure under which the initiating party first presents his claim, but in any case shall afford full and equal opportunity to all parties for presentation of relevant proofs. The names and addresses of all witnesses, and exhibits offered in evidence, shall be made a part of the record.

10. *Majority Decision.* In the course of the hearing, all decisions of the arbitrators shall be by a majority vote. The award shall also be made by majority vote unless the concurrence of all is expressly required by the terms of a particular arbitration agreement.

11. *Closing of Hearings.* The arbitrators shall inquire of all parties whether they have any further proofs to offer or witnesses to be heard. Upon receiving negative replies, the arbitrators shall declare the hearings closed. The hearings may be reopened by the arbitrators on their own motion, or on the motion of either party, for good cause shown, at any time before the award is made.

12. *Time of Award.* The award shall be rendered promptly by the arbitrators and, unless otherwise agreed by the parties, not later than thirty days from the date of closing the hearings, or if oral hearings have been waived, then from the date of transmitting the final statements and proofs to the arbitrators.

13. *Form of Award.* The award shall be in writing and shall be signed by the arbitrators.

14. *Stenographic Record.* Provision for recording the entire proceedings may be made at the request of either party, or at the discretion of the arbitrators. The total cost of such a record shall be shared equally among the parties ordering copies, unless the parties agree otherwise.

15. *Interpretation and Application of Rules.* Questions concerning the interpretation of these rules shall be referred to the Office of Arbitration for final decision.

ARTICLE IV. COMPETENCE

1. The Process for Arbitration shall extend:

a. To all disputes between individual members of the Church, or groups within the Church, where the controversy concerns an ecclesiastical matter;

b. To all disputes between a person and a diocesan administrator or administrative body, where it is contended that an act or decision (including administrative sanctions and disciplinary actions) has violated Church law or natural equity;

c. To all disputes between administrative bodies of the diocese when the dispute involves conflict of competency.

2. The following, however, shall not be subject to settlement by arbitration:

a. Criminal cases in the strict sense (not administrative sanctions and disciplinary actions);

b. Non-criminal cases where there is question of dissolving a marriage;

c. Matters pertaining to benefices when there is litigation about the title itself to a benefice unless the legitimate authorities sanction arbitration;

d. Spiritual matters whenever the award requires payment by means of temporal goods.

3. Disputes involving temporal ecclesiastical goods or those things which, though annexed to the spiritual, can be dealt with apart from their spiritual aspect, may be settled through arbitration, but the formalities of law for the alienation of ecclesiastical property must be observed if the matter is of sufficient importance.

ARTICLE V. EXPENSES

1. All members of the Office of Arbitration, as well as all arbitrators, shall serve gratis. The parties involved in the arbitration, however, shall be assessed a fee in an amount to be determined by the Office of Arbitration to cover office expenses.

2. The expenses of witnesses shall be paid by the respective parties producing witnesses. Traveling and other expenses of the arbitrators, and the expenses of any witnesses or the cost of any proofs produced at the direct request of the arbitrators, shall be borne equally by the parties unless they agree otherwise, or unless the arbitrator in his award assesses such expenses or any part thereof against any specified party of parties.

ARTICLE VI. COURT OF ARBITRATION

1. There shall be established in each diocese a Court of Arbitration. This Court will function as a board of review. It will not review the merits of the case as such, but rather its purpose will be to hear and render decisions on complaints of nullity or requests for corrections or modifications of the award.

If a tribunal already exists in a particular diocese, this tribunal will perform the function of the Court of Arbitration. A special turnus of judges shall be assigned to handle matters of this nature.

2. The Court of Arbitration shall be competent to review an arbitration award where it is alleged that:

   a. The award was procured by corruption, fraud, or other undue means;

   b. There was evident partiality on the part of an arbitrator;

   c. The arbitrators exceeded their powers;

   d. The arbitrators refused to postpone a hearing notwithstanding the showing of sufficient cause for such postponement, or refused to hear evidence material to the controversy, or otherwise conducted the hearing so as prejudicially to affect a substantial right of one of the parties;

   e. The method of selection of arbitrators, agreed upon by the parties beforehand, was not followed;

   f. The decision was based on documents which are spurious:

   g. New evidence has been discovered of a character which demands a contrary decision;

   h. Principles of fundamental procedural fairness were violated.

3. Where the Court of Arbitration decides in favor of the nullity of an arbitration award, the Court can order a re-hearing either before the arbitrators who made the award or before entirely new arbitrators chosen in the same manner as the original arbitrators. Where an application to vacate an award or nullify a decision is denied, the Court of Arbitration shall confirm the award.

4. Correction or Modification of the Award. Where it is alleged that there was a material error in transcribing the award, in relating the petitions of the parties or the facts, in describing any person, thing, or property referred to in the award, in making calculations or in matters of form not affecting the merits of the controversy, corrections may be made by the arbitrators themselves upon petition of the party, unless the other party opposes such corrections. In the latter event the matter shall be referred to the Court of Arbitration for decision and, where appropriate, for correction or modification of the Award.

A MODEL GRIEVANCE PROCEDURE

*The following model of a grievance procedure culminating in arbitration
is one adopted by an Archdiocese of the Catholic Church.*

PREAMBLE

In implementation of the spirit of the Second Vatican Council and the explicit
legislation of the Code of Canon Law (c.c. 1925–1933), the National Conference of Catholic Bishops in November, 1969, approved a plan for Due Process
prepared by the Canon Law Society of America.

"Due Process" is a long established instrument of our Common (Civil) and
Church law traditions. It is purposed and constructed to a less formal and more
expeditious resolution of disputes than that provided by strictly judicial procedures. Due Process places more emphasis on the contending human persons
than it does on the contentious assertion of rights. It strives for amicable acceptance of settlement or compromise rather than forced submission to judicial
sentence.

Shortly after the 1969 N.C.C. Bishops' meeting, [the Cardinal] appointed a
committee to adapt the approved plan to the needs and the resources of the Archdiocese. . . . This document is the product of its deliberations.

SECTION I.   THE OFFICE OF CONCILIATION AND ARBITRATION

1. The Archdiocese . . . shall establish an Office of Conciliation and Arbitration.
2. The Office of Conciliation and Arbitration shall consist of eleven members.
A. Diocesan priests shall elect two representatives from their number.
B. Religious men, priests and brothers, shall elect two representatives from
their number.
C. Religious women shall elect two representatives from their number.
D. The Archbishop shall appoint one member.
E. Until such time as there is appropriate machinery for the election of lay
members, the Archbishop shall appoint two lay women and two lay men from
a list of six women and six men, selected by a nominating committee composed
of five lay women and five lay men chosen by the governing bodies of the
Archdiocesan Council of Catholic Women, and the Archdiocesan Council of
Catholic Men. This committee is empowered to accept nominations from all
interested groups and individuals in the Archdiocese.
3. If the qualifications of a member are brought into question, the decision concerning his continued service shall be made by the Arbitration Board of Review.
4. The term of office shall be for two years.
A. For the purpose of continuity, five of the original members shall serve
three years. The choice and manner of their choosing shall be determined by
the eleven members of the Office.

B. Replacements shall be made in the original manner and from the original category of members.

C. The Office in Conciliation and Arbitration, in case of an unexpired term of more than six months, shall initiate procedures to fulfill the vacancy.

5. The Office of Conciliation and Arbitration shall elect from its own members its chairman, secretary and treasurer.

6. It shall be the responsibility of the Office of Conciliation and Arbitration:

A. To supervise and administer the program and to interpret rules of procedures to be followed in conciliation and arbitration when questions are referred to it either from conciliators and arbitrators or the parties themselves.

B. To select panels of conciliators and arbitrators from among the laity, religious women and men, and clergy. It is not necessary that a person be a member of the Archdiocese . . . to be included on the panels of conciliators or arbitrators. It is recomended that there be an exchange of lists of panels among neighboring dioceses where possible.

    a. The Office of Conciliation and Arbitration shall solicit and receive nominations for conciliators and arbitrators from any individual or organized group in the diocese.

    b. The Office of Conciliation and Arbitration shall maintain a minimum of twenty-five conciliators and thirty-six arbitrators on the panels to insure an adequate choice of selection for the parties.

C. To assist parties in the selection of conciliators and arbitrators.

7. The Archdiocese shall reimburse the Office of Conciliation and Arbitration for its expenses upon presentation of a statement signed by its chairman and treasurer.

SECTION II.   AREAS OF CONCERN OF THE OFFICE OF
CONCILIATION AND ARBITRATION

1. The process of conciliation and arbitration shall be offered to:

A. Reconcile disputants or arbitrate disputes between individual members of the Archdiocese, or groups within the Archdiocese, in which the controversy concerns an ecclesciastical matter.

B. Reconcile disputants or arbitrate disputes between a person and a diocesan administrator or administrative body when it is contended that an act or decision, including administrative sanctions and disciplinary actions, has violated Church law, formal policy, or natural equity.

C. Reconcile disputants or arbitrate disputes between administrative bodies of the Archdiocese . . . when disputes involve conflict of competency.

2. The process of conciliation and arbitration shall not extend to:

A. Cases involving the validity of marriage.

B. Cases involving labor union contracts.

C. Cases involving religious in their strictly internal affairs, or in those matters adequately covered by the conciliation and arbitration process established by the Conferences of Major Religious Superiors.

D. Cases involving the infliction of penalties by judicial sentence and those requiring a special process according to Part 3 of Book 4 of the Code of Canon Law. However, prior to such processes it is highly recommended that the establishment of fact in such cases be assigned to the Office of Conciliation and Arbitration; and, if the facts so warrant, the award is to be an indication to the Ordinary whether or not he is to initiate required canonical procedures.

E. Cases involving doctrinal matters of faith and morals. The establishment of fact in such cases, however, is within the competence of the Office of Conciliation and Arbitration.

F. Cases involving the academic and internal affairs of Universities, Colleges and Seminaries.

G. Cases in which proper authorities have rendered a decision prior to date of promulgation of this document unless new and weighty evidence warrants a hearing.

SECTION III.   PRIOR AGREEMENT ON PROCEDURE

The provisions of this document do not in any way prejudice the right to submit the problem to the diocesan tribunal in those matters provided for in the Code of Canon Law. If the parties, however, decide to submit the problem to the Office of Conciliation and Arbitration, they thereby agree to forego a formal trial.

SECTION IV.   INITIATING THE PROCESS OF CONCILIATION

1. A person having recourse to the Office of Conciliation and Arbitration shall be styled the "initiator" and the person, group, or institution called to conciliation shall be styled the "respondent." Recourse to the Office shall be styled the "initiative," and the acceptance of the process by the respondent shall be styled "an affirmative response." The difficulty shall be called the "problem."

2. An initiator may take the initiative by sending to the chairman of the Office of Conciliation and Arbitration a statement that he has a problem involving one or more persons, groups, or institutions described in Section II, Paragraph 1, stating the nature of the problem. The chairman of the Office of Conciliation and Arbitration in accordance with procedural rules of the Office determines its competence.

A. A rotating committee of three members of the Office may agree to accept or reject a problem by majority vote of the three members.

B. If the panel decides the problem is frivolous, trivial, or without merit, it shall be within the power of the panel to dismiss the problem immediately, setting forth in writing its reason for dismissal. An appeal of a negative decision may be made to a panel of three other members of the Office.

3. The chairman shall contact by letter the respondent and shall apprise him of the problem stated by the initiator and shall inquire if he will accept conciliation. He shall be asked if he would accept as a conciliator(s) the person(s) acceptable to the initiator or if he would prefer a different person(s).

4. In the event the parties cannot agree on a conciliator(s) and still accept conciliation, the chairman of the Office of Conciliation and Arbitration shall appoint the conciliator(s).

5. If the respondent fails to give an affirmative response, the chairman shall refer the matter immediately to the Ordinary or his delegate who shall endeavor to persuade the respondent to give consent to conciliation.

6. In the event that the respondent is the Ordinary of the diocese himself and there is no affirmative response the chairman shall immediately refer the matter to the chairman of the Bishops' Committee on Arbitration and Mediation who, by letter, shall endeavor to persuade the Ordinary to give such response.

7. In the event that the chairman fails to discharge any of his responsibilities for referring the matter to the Ordinary or the chairman of the Bishop's Committee as the case may be, the initiator may make the referral himself.

SECTION V.   PROCEDURE FOR CONCILIATION

1. Within three weeks of the affirmative response, the Conciliator(s) shall discuss the problem with each of the participants.

2. Within one week of the second of these conferences, the Conciliator(s) shall meet with both participants together and endeavor to guide them to a peaceful resolution of their problem. The Conciliator(s) shall schedule as many of these joint meetings as seem to him necessary in order to progress to a solution.

3. The first joint meeting of the participants and Conciliator(s) shall be restricted to these persons. Thereafter, in the discretion of the Counciliator(s) each participant may have with him advisers. In the event that one participant desires to have advisers, and the Conciliator agrees, the Conciliator shall notify the other participant that he also may come with advisers. At the discretion of the Conciliator and the agreement of the participants, members of the Office of Conciliation and Arbitration or other persons may join the meetings from time to time.

4. The Conciliator shall have no power to force the participants to adopt a solution. He shall have the power, however, to determine that any participant is not cooperating in good faith. Prima facie evidence of lack of good faith will be failure to attend three scheduled meetings, failure to respond to a substantial number of questions which the Conciliator believes appropriate or failure to suggest any way of accommodating the reasonable interests of the other participant. In the event that for these or other reasons the Conciliator believes that a participant is not cooperating in good faith, he shall apprise him of this belief orally, and failing cooperation, shall apprise him of this again in writing. If there is no cooperation after the written communication, the chairman of the Office of Conciliation and Arbitration shall at once notify the Ordinary of the diocese, or, if the Ordinary is a participant, the chairman of the Bishops' Committee on Arbitration and Mediation. The Ordinary or the Chairman shall endeavor to persuade the participant to cooperate.

5. If the problem is resolved by agreement, the Conciliator shall prepare a summary statement of the problem and its resolution, and shall submit it for the approval and signature of the participants.

If the problem is unresolved after three months from the initiative, the matter should be referred to the Office of Conciliation and Arbitration for a determination as to whether further meetings would appear fruitful. If one or more participants decline further discussion, or in the event the Office of Conciliation and Arbitration decided that further discussion would be fruitless, the Conciliator shall file a report with the Office of Conciliation and Arbitration. Where the Ordinary is a participant, the Office shall in turn file a report with the chairman of the Bishops' Committee on Arbitration and Meditation.

This report should contain the names of the participants, a summary of the problems, and the efforts taken to resolve them, and certification by the Conciliator(s) that despite the good faith of the participants, no resolution could be reached.

6. All communications made to the Office of Conciliation and Arbitration or to a Conciliator or between participants shall be treated as confidential by all who share in them. If the problem is resolved by agreement, announcement of the agreement should be worked out by the parties and the Office of Conciliation and Arbitration.

7. If the conciliation fails, and the initiator does not wish to withdraw his complaint, then the problem must be referred by the Office of Conciliation and Arbitration to an arbitrator(s) for resolution of the dispute.

SECTION VI. THE PROCESS OF ARBITRATION

1. When a dispute is submitted for arbitration, the parties shall sign beforehand a specific agreement covering such matters as the nature of the problem and the remedies sought, the number of arbitrators, the manner of their selection, and the commitment of the parties to accept the decision of the arbitrator(s) as final and binding.

2. The arbitrators for a specific case shall be selected in the following manner:

A. If the arbitration agreement applicable to a particular case provides a method of appointment of arbitrators, this method shall be followed. In the absence thereof, or if the agreed method fails or for any reason cannot be followed, or when an arbitrator appointed fails or is unable to act, and no provision has been made for the appointment of his successor, the chairman of the Office of Conciliation and Arbitration shall appoint one or more arbitrators acceptable to both parties according to the method of "B" below. An arbitrator so appointed has all the powers of one specifically named in a prior agreement.

B. In the event the arbitration agreement or the statement at the conclusion of the unsuccessful conciliation does not provide a method of appointment of arbitrators, the chairman of the Office of Conciliation and Arbitration shall appoint arbitrators according to the following procedure:

a. The chairman shall submit to each party a list of arbitrators large enough to assure a choice acceptable to both parties.

b. The parties shall strike out those names not acceptable to themselves.

c. The Chairman of the Office of Conciliation and Arbitration shall then appoint the agreed upon number of arbitrators.

d. The Office of Conciliation and Arbitration shall draft its own rules and procedures with regard to time limits for making the selection and the consequences of not observing time limits.

SECTION VII. PROCEDURE FOR ARBITRATION

1. The Arbitrator(s) shall appoint a time and place for hearings and notify the parties not less than five days before each hearing.

2. Parties to the problem may be represented at hearings by counsel or other authorized representative.

3. Persons having direct interest in the arbitration are entitled to attend hearings. It shall be in the discretion of the Arbitrator(s) to determine the propriety of the attendance of these or any other persons.

4. For good cause, the Arbitrators may adjourn the hearing upon the request of a party or upon their own initiative.

5. Arbitration may proceed in the absence of any party who, after due notice, fails to be present or fails to obtain an adjournment.

6. The Arbitrator(s) shall hear and determine the controversy upon the evidence as they desire and shall produce additional evidence as the Arbitrators may deem necessary to an understanding and determination of the dispute. The Arbitrators shall judge the relevancy and materiality of the evidence offered and conformity to the legal rules of evidence shall not be necessary. All evidence shall be taken in the presence of all the Arbitrators and all of the parties except where any of the parties is absent in default or has waived his right to be present. The Arbitrators may require the parties to submit available books, records, documents, and other evidence.

7. The Arbitrators shall have the power to administer oaths and take evidence by deposition whenever witnesses cannot be present at a hearing, providing that the taking of depositions is done with notification to the disputants who would then have the right to be present.

8. A hearing shall be opened by the recording of the place, time, and date of hearing, the presence of Arbitrators and parties, the presence of counsel, if any, and the receipt by the Arbitrators of initial statements setting forth the nature of the dispute and the remedies sought.

The Arbitrator may, in his discretion, vary the normal procedure under which the initiating party first presents his claim, but in any case shall afford full and equal opportunity to all parties for presentation of relevant proofs.

The names and addresses of all witnesses and exhibits offered in evidence shall be made a part of the record.

9. When more than one Arbitrator is involved, their decisions shall be by a majority vote. The award shall also be made by majority vote unless the concurrence of all is expressly required by the term of a particular agreement.

10. The Arbitrators shall ask all parties whether or not they have further proofs to offer or witnesses to be heard. Upon receiving negative replies, the Arbitrator(s) shall declare the hearings closed. The hearings may be re-opened by the Arbitrators on their own motion, or on the motion of either party, for good cause shown, at any time before the award is made.

11. The award shall be rendered promptly by the Arbitrator(s) and, unless otherwise agreed by the parties, not later than thirty days from the date of closing of the hearings, or if oral hearings have been waived, then from the date of transmitting the final statements and proofs to the Arbitrator.

12. The award shall be in writing and shall be signed by the Arbitrator(s).

13. The recordings of the proceedings in whole or in part will be at the discretion of the Arbitrators. The publication of such recordings will be at the discretion of the Office of Conciliation and Arbitration.

Section VIII. Expenses of Processes of Conciliation and Arbitration

1. All members of the Office of Conciliation and Arbitration, as well as conciliators and arbitrators, shall serve without fee. The initiator in the conciliation–arbitration process, however, shall be assessed a nominal fee, not to exceed $10.00, for the preliminary expenses of the case.

2. The expenses of witnesses shall be paid by the respective parties producing witnesses. Traveling and other expenses of conciliators and arbitrators, or of any witnesses, or the cost of any proof produced directly at the request of the arbitrators, shall be borne equally by the parties unless they agree otherwise, or unless the arbitrator in his award assesses such expenses or any part thereof against any specified party or parties. Expenses may be waived in whole or in part for those unable to pay at the discretion of the arbitrator.

Section IX. Arbitration Board of Review

1. There shall also be established an Arbitration Board of Review. This Board will not review the merits of the case as such, but rather its purpose will be to hear and render decisions on complaints of nullity or requests for corrections of material errors in the award.

2. The Board of Review for a specific case will be constituted by the Office of Conciliation and Arbitration and will consist of not less than three members taken from the panel of arbitrators, excluding those who have had anything to do with the case previously.

3. The Arbitration Board of Review shall be competent to review an arbitration award where it is alleged that:

A. The award was procured by corruption, fraud, or other undue means.

B. There was evident partiality on the part of an arbitrator.

C. The arbitrators exceeded their powers.

D. The arbitrators refused to postpone a hearing notwithstanding the showing of sufficient cause for such postponement, or refused to hear evidence material to the controversy, or otherwise conducted the hearing so as prejudicially to affect a substantial right of one of the parties.

E. The method of selection of arbitrators, agreed upon beforehand by the parties, was not followed.

F. The decision was based on documents which are spurious.

G. New evidence has been discovered of a character which demands a contrary decision.

H. Principles of fundamental procedural fairness were violated.

4. When the Arbitration Board of Review decides in favor of the nullity of an arbitration award, the Arbitration Board of Review through the Office of Conciliation and Arbitration can order a re-hearing before the arbitrators who made the award or before entirely new arbitators chosen in the same manner as the original arbitrators.

5. Where an application to vacate an award or nullify a decision is denied, the Office of Conciliation and Arbitration shall confirm the award.

Appendix A. On Administrative Discretion

Successful implementation of a due process procedure depends in large measure on an equally important prior process. Procedures, policies and standards should be clearly established within administrative bodies, Administrators should also be aware of the need for clearly established policies. These policies, procedures, and standards become the criteria by which fair and acceptable conciliation and just arbitration may be achieved. In addition, the publication of policies will prevent the escalation of many difficulties into major problems to be conciliated and arbitrated. The delineation of competence, standards, and procedural norms may result from legislation, episcopal decree, or the experience and practice of an ecclesiastical body. When the limits of competence, the existence of policies, and the establishing of standards are unknown or not understood, mistrust, a lack of confidence, and conflict may arise.

Administrators and administrative bodies should use standards and procedures which guide decisions in individual cases. For example, school boards, whether local or diocesan, should have basic policies of hiring and firing of teachers; pastors, together with school administrator or school board, should make clear the standards by which students are admitted to the parochial school; diocesan commissions should publicize their norms and guidelines for activities within their competence.

Detailed and precise policy assures consistency in reaching decisions by eliminating ad hoc determination of policy. With prior knowledge of an administrator's position, knowledgeable efforts for intelligent review are possible. Clear policy facilitates the efforts of conciliators and arbitrators in reviewing alleged unfair or arbitrary decisions in individual cases.

Policy-making requires an open policy-making procedure. Interested persons should receive information about policy problems under consideration, the reasons for policy consideration, and the matter being discussed. Those affected by policy should be invited to offer suggestions and criticisms during the policy-making process. Such a procedure of prior process would make additional information and ideas available for discussion. At the same time, it would minimize subsequent tensions arising when individuals lacked knowledge of policy-making.

APPENDIX B.

The Notion of Due Process

The adequate protection of human rights and freedoms is a matter of concern to all men of good will; the adequate protection of specifically ecclesiastical rights and freedoms has increasingly concerned all members of the Church. Rights and freedoms may be protected by education, by a moral consciousness, by development of character, and also by law. Rights without safeguards which precede the establishment of law and provide for recourse under the law are meaningless. In all governmental procedures, respect must be given to the rights of the persons involved.

The protection of ecclesial rights and the resolution of disputes which may arise in any human situation are assured by procedures of prior process and due process.

The concrete expression of the protection of rights in the Church is conditioned by an Anglo-American common law tradition. Substantively, this tradition requires that rights and freedoms cannot be abridged without justification and that protection of rights of those who share in or are guided by authority be protected in administrative and judicial procedures. Among procedural protections are the rights to be informed of proposed actions affecting a person's rights, the right to be heard in defense of one's own rights, the right to be judged by someone other than the accuser, and the right to confront one's own accusers. Procedural protection would also imply a means of reconciling disputes when the need arises.

The process is a principle of justice rather than a specific rule of law. Because circumstances differ from place to place, the implementation of any plan may vary according to needs and conditions of a specific diocese. Due process procedures enhance respect for authority rather than detract from it, nor do they detract from the teaching office in which the bishops share, At the same time, administrators and administrative bodies are more easily held accountable for decisions and actions when they are made. The pastoral concern for resolution of problems can be achieved through a process of conciliation and arbitration.

The Process of Conciliation

There are many scriptural passages which emphasize the need for reconciliation. Saint Paul applies the teaching of Christ on love of enemies, peacemaking, and forgiveness to formal litigation.

In secular situations, litigation is a last resort. Few controversies capable of judicial resolution are judicially resolved. Conflicts are normally settled through negotiated agreements and settlement as well as compromise. The Code of Canon Law discourages litigation and enjoins a process of conciliation.

Conciliation implies that the parties themselves are led to reach a mutually satisfactory agreement assisted by a disinterested third party. Conciliation presupposes the opportunity of a face-to-face dialogue among persons in controversy. To be treated as a human person requires not only a hearing but also a response. A conciliator, informed of the facts and able to sense the real nature of the dispute, can help resolve conflicts. Dialogue and mediation fail if abstract principles of the right of conscience and the right of authority must be vindicated at any cost. There are few imperatives of conscience that make only one course of action mandatory and few rights of authority which can be exercised in only one specific way. The conciliator will try to heal wounds quickly and eliminate suspense for protracted periods since delay and concealment of information have no place in a process of conciliation. Since those in authority or those guided by it realize their comembership in a religion of love, the initial attempt to resolve controversies should be one of conciliation.

The Process of Arbitration

Hopefully, the vast majority of controversies will be settled through a process of conciliation. If, however, . . . the exploration of all avenues of negotiation and settlement [has] been exhausted, impartial persons should be called to render definitive decisions and the parties in controversy should make prior agreement to abide by the results of a decision. When conciliation fails, the process of arbitration is then initiated. This process is defined as the voluntary agreement of parties to refer disputes to an impartial person or persons to determine on the basis of evidence and argument the matter under discussion.

Arbitration is by its very nature a more formal procedure than conciliation. Arbitrators are persons with a judicial temperament, are able to listen well and ask pertinent questions, and understand all points of view. Acting so as not to delay justice, they will render their decisions promptly and accurately to the parties involved.

Neither the process for conciliation nor the process for arbitration represent a radical innovation in the governmental life of the Church, since the Code of Canon Law also makes provisions for conciliation and arbitration.

INDEX

481

G